2019-20
EDITION

Indian Economy

Performance and Policies

Also by the same author :

30th Edition: 2019-20 (Revised)
INDIAN ECONOMY SINCE INDEPENDENCE.

Revised year after year, now into its 30th Edition, this unique book is widely accepted as the core text for graduate/post-graduate courses in Indian economy, in various universities across India. The book is essentially, a collection of select articles by some of India's topmost economists and experts. These highly recommended original readings are well-supported by editorial notes and excerpts from Plan documents, and other official documents that together present a comprehensive and critical analysis of Indian economy since independence: 1947-2019.

2018-19
INDIAN ECONOMY:
ECONOMIC DEVELOPMENT AND POLICY—I
Specially designed to serve as a text book for Indian economy (Course 05) for B.A. Programme, University of Delhi; B.A. (Hons.) Economics (CBCS) Indian Economy—I

2019 Edition
INDIAN ECONOMY—II:
Macroeconomic Policies, Sectoral Developments and Performance
Reference Text for B.A. (Hons.) Paper 13; University of Delhi.

DEMONETISATION: THE ECONOMISTS SPEAK
Uma Kapila (ed.), 2017.

INDIA'S ECONOMY: PRE-LIBERALISATION TO GST
Uma Kapila (ed.), 2017.

UMA KAPILA, author/editor of several other books, has taught Indian Economy to undergraduate students for forty-two years. She retired as Reader from the Department of Economics, Miranda House, University of Delhi. Presently, she is Editorial Director, Academic Foundation.

An Honours Graduate from Miranda House, University of Delhi and M.A. and Ph.D. from Delhi School of Economics, Dr. Uma Kapila has also served on the Planning Commission Study Group on "Agricultural Strategies in the Eastern Region of India for the Seventh Five Year Plan" (Perspective Planning Division).

Dr. (Mrs.) Uma Kapila is the author of the book *Oilseeds Economy of India* (1982) published by the Institute of Economic Growth, Delhi. She is also the author/editor of two other textbooks on Indian economy, one meant for B.A. (Hons.) Economics and the other for B.A. (Programme) (DSE & GE). She has edited and co-edited with Raj Kapila, a number of books on India's economy, banking and finance. Detailed information on these publications is readily available at the publisher's website: *www.academicfoundation.com*

20th Edition

2019-20

Indian Economy

PERFORMANCE AND POLICIES

Uma Kapila

- Recommended text in several universities across India.
- Based on the latest recommended readings and guidelines
- Widely used by students preparing for IAS and other competitive examinations.

ACADEMIC FOUNDATION
NEW DELHI

www.academicfoundation.com

ACADEMIC FOUNDATION

Twentieth Edition, 2019-20

AF PRESS

No. 35, Sector 7,
IMT Manesar,
Gurgaon - 122050.
Phones : +91-124-4215070 / 71.

E-mail : booksaf@gmail.com
www.academicfoundation.org

Kapila, Uma, author.
Indian economy : performance and policies / Uma Kapila. --
20th edition, 2019-20.
pages cm
"Recommended text in several universities across India;
Based on the latest recommended readings and guidelines;
Widely used by students preparing for IAS and other
competitive examinations."
Includes bibliographical references.
ISBN 9789332705180

1. India--Economic conditions--1947- --Textbooks. 2. India–Economic policy--1947- --Textbooks. 3. Economic development--India--Textbooks. I. Title.

LCC HC435.K37 2019 | DDC 330.954 23

Printed and bound in India by PrintShoot, Manesar, Gurugram.
www.printshoot.com

Contents

Section-II

Growth and Distribution

SECTION-III

Current Perspectives in Agriculture

Section-IV

Current Perspectives in Industry and Services

SECTION-V

Financial Sector and External Sector

FINANCIAL SECTOR

EXTERNAL SECTOR

Preface

THIS 20th edition of the text book on Indian economy for undergraduate courses aims to provide a comprehensive coverage of the Indian economy under six sections based on the new guidelines incorporating the latest readings recommended for various courses on Indian economy by the Department of Economics, University of Delhi.

Section I begins with the basic concepts and issues in economic development, underdevelopment as well as human development and sustainable development followed by an analysis of economic development in post-independent India—the institutional framework and the policy regimes.

Section II looks into the growth and distributional issues relating to poverty, inequality and employment.

Sections III and IV are devoted to sectoral development issues. While section III dwells on current perspectives in Indian agriculture: growth, productivity, constraints and pricing, section IV covers industry and services sectors.

The study of Indian economy cannot be complete without looking into the financial sector and the external sector which have become particularly important in this age of globalisation. Therefore, section V briefly looks into the developments in India's financial sector and external sector.

The concluding section (VI) provides a glimpse of Indian economy today: an overview and comparative perspective.

The analyses and discussion covering these six sections in the various chapters of this book are based on the latest revised readings recommended for the various courses. However, where required, I have supplemented from other sources, reference to which is given in the footnotes of the respective chapters.

A more comprehensive coverage of Indian economy is available in my edited book *Indian Economy Since Independence* (running into 30th edition) which in addition to exhaustive editorial notes on various subjects also includes the writings of distinguished economists, experts and policymakers.

I owe my debt of gratitude to Shankar Acharya, Montek S. Ahluwalia, T.C.A. Anant, Pulapre Balakrishnan, Abhijit Banerjee, Kaushik Basu, Jagdish Bhagwati, K.C. Chakraborty, Rupa Chanda, Nitin Desai, S. Mahendra Dev, Biswajit Dhar, Jean Drèze, Tim Dyson, Maitreesh Ghatak, Gita Gopinath, Jim Gordon, Ashok Gulati, Poonam Gupta, P.D. Jeromi, Shikha Jha, Vijay L. Kelkar, A. Kotwal, K.L. Krishna, K.P. Krishnan, Nagesh Kumar, Raghuram Rajan, Prachi Mishra, Rakesh Mohan, Deepak Mohanty, R. Nagaraj, K. Navaneetham, Pulin Nayak, D.M. Nachane, Deepak Nayyar, Arvind Panagariya, Manoj Panda, T.S. Papola, R. Radhakrishna, C. Rangarajan, C.H. Hanumantha Rao, S.K. Ray, Alakh N. Sharma, Mihir S. Sharma, Amartya Sen, Rohini Somanathan, T.N. Srinivasan, Arvind Subramanian, M.H. Bala Subrahmanya, S.D. Tendulkar (late), M. Todaro, A. Vaidyanathan, Pravin Visaria (late) and V.S. Vyas (late)—distinguished economists, experts and policy makers—from whose writings I have been able to draw for the benefit of students.

In addition to the writings of the authors listed above, I have also drawn liberally from the reports/documents of government and non-government organisations/institutions such as Reserve Bank of India, World Bank, IMF, Planning Commission and presently NITI Aayog. I am grateful to all of them.

I would also like to make a special mention of my colleagues teaching in various colleges for making useful suggestions from time-to-time.

I hope this thoroughly revised book on Indian economy will prove handy and useful to students and teachers.

July 2019 — *Uma Kapila*

Section - I

Economic Development in Post-Independent India

Basic Issues in Economic Development:

1. Economic Development and Underdevelopment
2. Human Development
3. India's Economy at Independence

Growth, Institutional Framework and Policy Regime:

4. Economic Planning: Evolution and Strategy
5. Economic Reforms and Liberalisation
6. Demography and Development
7. Land Reforms
8. Growth and Structural Changes since 1951

Section - II

Growth and Distribution

9. Poverty in India
10. Unemployment and Employment Perspective
11. Economic Inequality in India

1

Economic Development and Underdevelopment

Introduction

The world today presents a picture of sharp contrasts between developed/advanced and backward/underdeveloped/developing countries. At one extreme, there are countries like Norway with per capita GNI (gross national income) of $102700 (2013) and on the other extreme are countries like Malawi with per capita GNI of $270.[1]

According to *World Development Report* (2015), around 18 per cent of world population lives in countries which are classified as high income developed countries (like USA, Canada, Australia, countries of Western Europe, New Zealand and some of the Asian countries such as Japan, Singapore, Hong Kong), 82 per cent of the population lives in countries which are in the category of low income and middle income developing economies.

The Growth Report 2008[2] states that growth has accelerated in the global economy and in an even wider set of developing countries. Further, the report projects that the world population is projected to increase by 3 billion people by 2050. Unfortunately, 2 billion of this extra population will live in countries that are currently enjoying little or no growth. Thus, if these trends persist, the proportion of the world population living in low-growth environments might increase.

---

1. World Bank (2015). *World Development Report,* 2015.
2. Commission on Growth and Development (2008). *The Growth Report, Strategies for Sustained Growth and Inclusive Development.*

What Does Development Mean

The term *development* may mean different things to different people. In strictly economic terms, development has traditionally meant a sustained annual increase in gross national product (GNP) [or GDP (gross domestic product)] at rates varying from 5 per cent to 7 per cent or more.[3]

A common alternative economic index of development has been the rates of growth of per capita GNP i.e., the ability of a nation to expand its output at a rate faster than the growth of population. Thus, per capita GNP is equal to GNP divided by population. However, it is the real per capita GNP which measures the overall economic well-being of a population i.e., monetary growth of GNP per capita minus the rate of inflation. If the rate of growth of GNP per capita is, let us say, 4 per cent and the rate of inflation is say 5 or 6 per cent, there cannot be any improvement in the economic well-being of a population.

Economic Growth and Economic Development

Till the 1960s, the term 'economic development' was often used as a synonym of economic growth, the measure for the latter being the rise in per capita GNP in real terms. According to Kindleberger,[4] "Whereas economic growth merely refers to a rise in output, economic development implies changes in technological and institutional organisation of production as well as distributive pattern of income." *Thus, economic development is a broader concept than economic growth.* Compared to the objective of development, economic growth may be easy to realise. By larger mobilisation of resources and raising their productivity, output levels can be raised. The process of development is far more extensive. Apart from the rise in output, it involves changes in the composition of output as well as a shift in the allocation of productive resources to ensure social justice.

In some of the underdeveloped countries, the process of economic growth has been accompanied by economic development. But this may not be the case always. *While there can be growth without development, development without growth is unconceivable.* A substantial rise in a country's GNP is required before it can hope to expand its industries and the services sectors. Nowhere in the world has the occupational distribution of population changed in the absence of growth.

3. Todaro, Michael (2004). *Economic Development in the Third World* (8th ed.), ch.1. Delhi: Pearson Education (Singapore) Pvt. Ltd.
4. Kindleberger, C.P. (1965). *Economic Development* (2nd ed.), ch. 1.

The New View of Economic Development

During the 1950s and 1960s, while many of the Third World nations did realise the economic growth targets, the respective levels of living of the masses remained unchanged. This resulted in the rejection of the narrow definition of economic development by an increasing number of economists who now clamoured for the 'dethronement of GNP' and advocated direct attack on widespread absolute poverty, increasingly inequitable income distribution and rising unemployment. Thus, in the 1970s economic development came to be redefined within the context of a growing economy. 'Redistribution from growth' became a common slogan. In this context, Kindleberger argued that,

> Economic development is generally defined to include improvements in material welfare, especially for persons with the lowest incomes, the eradication of mass poverty with its corelates of illiteracy, diseases and early death, changes in the composition of inputs and outputs that generally include shifts in the underlying structure of production away from agricultural growth towards industrial activities, the organisation of the economy in such a way that productive employment is general among the working age population rather than the situation of a privileged minority and the correspondingly greater participation of broadly based groups in making decisions about the directions, economic and otherwise, in which they should move to improve their welfare.[5]

Seers[6] posed three basic questions about the meaning of development:

What has been happening to poverty?

What has been happening to unemployment?

What has been happening to inequality?

If all three of these have declined from high levels, then beyond doubt this has been a period of development for the country concerned. If one or two of these central problems have been growing worse, especially if all three have, it would be strange to call the result 'development' even if per capita income doubled.[7]

This assertion was a hard reality for a number of developing countries which experienced relatively high rates of growth of per

5. Ibid.
6. Seers, Dudley (1969). "The Meaning of Development", paper presented at the *Eleventh World Conference of the Society for International Development*, New Delhi.
7. Todaro (2004). *op.cit.*

capita income during the 1960s and 1970s but showed little or no improvement or even an actual decline in employment, equality and the real income of the bottom 40 per cent of their population. By the earlier definition of 'growth,' these countries were developing, but by the new criteria of poverty, equality and employment, they were not. The situation in the 1980s worsened further as GNP growth rates turned negative for many less developed countries and the governments, faced with mounting foreign debt problems, were forced to cut back on their already limited social and economic programmes.

While during the 1980s, the World Bank championed 'economic growth' as the goal of development, its *World Development Report of 1991* asserted that,

> The challenge of development ... is to improve the quality of life. For the world's poor countries, a better quality of life generally calls for higher income ... and it involves much more. It encompasses, as ends in themselves, better education, higher standards of health and nutrition, less poverty, a cleaner environment, more equality of opportunity, greater individual freedom, and a richer cultural life.

Development as a Multi-dimensional Process

According to Todaro,

> Development must, therefore, be conceived of as a multi-dimensional process involving major changes in social structures, popular attitudes and national institutions, as well as the acceleration of economic growth, the reduction of inequality and the eradication of absolute poverty.

According to Goulet,[8] at least three basic components as core values should serve as a conceptual basis and practical guidelines for understanding the 'inner' meaning of development. These core values—sustenance, self-esteem and freedom—represent common goals sought by all individuals and societies. They relate to fundamental human needs that find their expression in almost all societies and cultures at all times.

Three Core Values of Development

Sustenance: The life-sustaining basic human needs include food, shelter, health and protection. When any one of these is absent or in critically short supply, a condition of absolute 'underdevelopment' exists.

---

8. Goulet, Denis (1971). *The Cruel Choice: A New Concept in the Theory of Development.* New York: Atheneum. pp.87-94.

Self-esteem: A second universal component of good life is self-esteem—a sense of worth and self-respect—of not being used as a tool by others for their own ends. Due to the significance attached to material values in developed nations, worthiness and esteem are now-a-days increasingly conferred only on countries that possess economic wealth and technological power—those that have developed.

Now-a-days the Third World seeks development in order to gain the esteem which is denied to societies living in a state of disgraceful 'underdevelopment.' Development is legitimised as a goal because it is an important, perhaps even an indispensable, way of gaining esteem.[9]

Freedom from Servitude—To be Able to Choose: Lewis[10] stressed the relationship between economic growth and freedom from servitude when he concluded that "the advantage of economic growth is not that wealth increases happiness, but that it increases the range of human choice." Wealth can enable a person to gain greater control over nature and his physical environment than they would have if they remained poor. It also gives them the freedom to choose greater leisure. The concept of human freedom should encompass various components of political freedom, freedom of expression, political participation and equality of opportunity.

Development, Freedom and Opportunities

According to Drèze and Sen,

> In recent years, development economics has been also taking a much more inclusive view of the nature of economic development. One way of seeing development is in terms of the expansion of the real freedoms that the citizens enjoy to pursue the objectives they have reason to value, and in this sense the expansion of human capability can be, broadly, seen as the central feature of the process of development.[11]

The basic objective of development as the expansion of human capabilities was never completely overlooked in the modern development literature, but the focus has been mainly on the generation of economic growth, in the sense of expanding gross national product

9. Ibid.
10. Lewis, Arthur W. (1963). "Is Economic Growth Desirable?" in Allen and Unwin (eds.), *Theory of Economic Growth*. London. p.420.
11. Drèze, Jean and Amartya Sen (2005). *India Development and Participation* (ch.2). Delhi: Oxford University Press.

and related variables.[12] The expansion of human capabilities can clearly be enhanced by economic growth (even in the limited sense of growth of real income per head), but: (i) there are many influences other than economic growth that work in that direction and (ii) the impact of economic growth on human capabilities can be extremely variable, depending on the nature of that growth (e.g., how equitable and employment-intensive it is, and whether the economic gains from growth are used to address the deprivations of the most needy).

The Three Objectives of Development

According to Todaro, development is both a physical reality and a state of mind in which society has, through some combination of social, economic, and institutional processes, secured the means for obtaining a better life. Whatever the specific components of this better life are, development in all societies must have at least the following three objectives:

1. To increase the availability and widen the distribution of basic life-sustaining goods such as food, shelter, health and protection.
2. To raise levels of living, including, in addition to higher incomes, the provision of more jobs, better education, and greater attention to cultural and human values, all of which will serve not only to enhance material well-being but also to generate greater individual and national self-esteem.
3. To expand the range of economic and social choices available to individuals and nations by freeing them from servitude and dependence not only in relation to other people and nation-states but also to the forces of ignorance and human misery.

The Millennium Development Goals

In September 2000, the 189 member countries of the United Nations at that time adopted eight Millennium Development Goals (MDGs), committing themselves to making substantial progress toward the eradication of poverty and achieving other human development goals by 2015.

12. Arthur Lewis one of the pioneers of development economics, emphasised that the appropriate objective of development is increasing 'the range of human choice,' but nevertheless he decided to concentrate specially on 'the growth of output per head,' since that 'gives man greater control over his environment and thereby increases his freedom' (Lewis, 1955: pp.9-10, 420-1).

The MDGs were developed in consultation with the developing countries, to ensure that they addressed their most pressing problems. In addition, key international agencies, including the United Nations, the World Bank, the International Monetary Fund (IMF), the Organisation for Economic Co-operation and Development (OECD) and the World Trade Organisation (WTO), helped develop the Millennium Declaration and so have a collective policy commitment to attacking poverty directly. The MDGs assign specific responsibilities to rich countries, including increased aid, removal of trade and investment barriers, and eliminating unsustainable debts of the poorest nations (see Appendix Table A-1.1).

Developed and Underdeveloped Countries

Over 75 per cent of world population lives in the poor underdeveloped countries, while just about 25 per cent people inhabit advanced and developed countries. The developed economies have high per capita income that gives their people high standards of living. The USA, the UK, France, Germany, Japan, etc., are among the developed economies. These countries have well-developed and diversified economic structure and high rates of saving and investment that make their growth process self-sustained.

The underdeveloped countries on the other hand have low levels of per capita income and low living standard of their masses. The underdeveloped countries today are also known as developing economies because they are capable of and indeed making efforts towards economic progress through better utilisation of their actual and potential resources. The underdeveloped countries are also known as the Third World countries.

Defining the Developing World

The most common way to define the developing world is by per capita income. Several international agencies, including the OECD and the United Nations, offer classifications of countries by their economic status, but the best-known system is that of the International Bank for Reconstruction and Development (IBRD), more commonly known as the World Bank. In the World Bank's classification system, 208 economies with a population of at least 30,000 are ranked by their levels of gross national income (GNI) per capita. These economies are then classified as low-income countries (LICs), lower-middle-income countries (LMCs), upper-middle-income countries (UMCs), high-income OECD countries and other high-income countries.

Generally speaking, the developing countries are those with low, lower-middle, or upper-middle incomes.

Sometimes a special distinction is made among upper-middle-income or newly high-income economies, designating some that have achieved relatively advanced manufacturing sectors as newly industrialising countries (NICs). Finally, the United Nations Development Program (UNDP) classifies countries according to their level of human development, including health and education attainments.

The World Bank in its *World Development Report 2015* classified the various countries on the basis of per capita GNI.

1. Low income countries with GNI per capita $728 or less (PPP GNI per capita $1,959 or less).
2. Middle income with per capita GNI of more than $4,754 or less than $12,616 (PPP GNI per capita $9,558) (2013). Within middle income, there are lower-middle-income and upper-middle- income countries.

   Lower-middle income countries with per capita GNI of more than $2,074 but less than $7,604 (PPP per capita $5,966) (2013).

   Upper middle income countries with GNI per capita $7,604 (PPP per capita $13,405) (2013).
3. High income countries with per capita GNI of $39,812 or more (PPP per capita $40,788 (2013) or more).

According to data given in the *World Development Report 2015*, in 2013, low-income countries accounted for about 11.91 per cent of the world population but contributed only 1.62 per cent to total world PPP GNI. The middle-income countries constituted 69.75 per cent of world population but accounted for about 46.48 per cent of world PPP GNI. These two groups, popularly described as developing economies or underdeveloped economies, comprise around 82 per cent of the world population but account for around 48 per cent of world PPP GNI. Most countries of Asia, Africa, Latin America and some countries of Europe are included in them.[13]

The high income economies, comprising around 18.3 per cent of world population, contribute around 52 per cent to world PPP GNI.

---

13. *op.cit.* no. 1.

TABLE – 1.1

Distribution of World Population and World GNI among Various Groups of Countries

	Population 2013 Million	*GNI 2013 (Billion $) PPP*	*GNI 2013 (per capita) $ PPP*	*Average Annual Growth of Population (2010-2012)*
World	7125	102,197.6	14343	1.2
Low-income Countries	848.7	1662.6	1959	2.2
Middle-income Countries	4970	47504.0	9558	1.2
Low- and Middle-income Combined	5818.75	49134.9	13405	1.3
High-income Countries	1306	53285.0	40788	0.6
India	**1252.1**	**6700**	**5350**	**1.4**

Source: World Development Report, 2015.

One may make the following observation with regard to this UN classifications of developed and underdeveloped/developing countries on the basis of per capita income. There is gross inequality of income between the rich and the poor countries and this gap is widening over the years. All high-income countries are not necessarily developed countries as Joan Robinson remarked,

> For several of the Arab States, GNP per capita suddenly jumped to levels which exceeded that of the richest western states yet in these countries are found some of the poorest and least developed communities in the world.

According to Todaro (2013), the simple division of the world into developed and developing countries is often useful for analytical and policy purposes. However, the wide income range of the latter serves as an early warning for us not to overgeneralise. Indeed, the economic differences between low-income countries in sub-Saharan Africa and South Asia and between upper-middle-income countries in East Asia and Latin America can be every bit as profound as those between high-income OECD and upper-middle-income developing countries.

As modern development economics defined development as a process involving elimination of poverty, income inequality and unemployment, underdevelopment in this framework would be a situation characterised by the worst kind of deprivation.

Todaro while defining underdevelopment in terms of poverty, states that, "Underdevelopment is a real fact of life for over three billion people in the world."[14]

A different approach to underdevelopment is provided by Jacob Viner. According to Viner, development potential of a country is a much better criterion to judge the extent of its underdevelopment. He defined an underdeveloped country as the one "which has good potential for using more capital or more labour or more available natural resources or all of these, to support its population on a higher level of living." The definition of an underdeveloped country given by the Indian Planning Commission in its Five Year Plan is similar to the one given by Jacob Viner,

> An underdeveloped country's economy is characterised by the existence, in greater or lesser degree, of unutilised or underutilised manpower on the one hand and of unexploited natural resources on the other. This state of affairs may be due to stagnancy of techniques or to certain inhibiting socio-economic factors which prevent the more dynamic forces in an economy from asserting themselves.[15]

Characteristics of the Developing World: Diversity within Commonality

The underdeveloped countries, also known as developing countries or Third World Countries, have some common characteristics. Todaro classifies these common characteristics into 10 broad categories.[16]

There are important historical and economic commonalities among developing countries that have led to their economic development problems being studied within a common analytical framework in development economics. At the same time, however, there is a great deal of diversity across the developing world, even within these areas of broad commonality. Different development problems call for different specific policy responses and general development strategies.

Lower Levels of Living and Productivity

In developing nations, general levels of living tend to be low for the vast majority of people. These low levels of living are manifested in the form of low incomes (poverty), inadequate housing, poor health, limited or low education, high infant mortality and low life expectancy.

---

14. Todaro, P. Michael (2013). *Economic Development* (10th edition). New Delhi: Pearson.
15. Government of India, Planning Commission (1952). *The First Five Year Plan*, Ch. 1, p.7, New Delhi.
16. *op cit.* no. 14.

The GNP per capita is often used as a summary index of the relative economic well-being of people in different nations. On account of low per capita income, population suffers from poor health, low education, high infant mortality and low life expectancy.

Indeed, some star performers among now nearly developed economies such as South Korea and Taiwan were once among the poorest in the world. Some middle-income countries are also relatively stagnant, but others are growing rapidly—China most spectacularly. Indeed, income growth rates have varied greatly in different developing regions and countries, with rapid growth in East Asia, stagnant growth in sub-Saharan Africa, and intermediate levels of growth in other regions.

At very low income levels, in fact, a vicious cycle may set in, whereby low income leads to low investment in education and health as well as plant and equipment and infrastructure, which in turn leads to low productivity and economic stagnation. This is the well-known vicious cycle referred to variously as the poverty trap or by Nobel laureate Gunnar Mydral as "circular and cumulative causation."

In India, at the time of Independence, the life expectancy at birth was 32 and literacy was only 18 per cent. Poverty ratio i.e., percentage of population below poverty line was above 50 per cent. As a result of planned economic development during the last six decades, expectation of life has improved to 66.1 in (2006-2010). Since 2011 literacy rate has marginally improved to 71 per cent in rural India and 86 per cent in urban India while the average for middle income countries is 67. Literacy rate has improved to 74.04 per cent against the average of 83 in lower-middle-income countries and 94 in upper-middle-income countries and 61 in low-income countries. Poverty ratio has also declined considerably from more than 50 per cent to around 20 per cent but the total number of poor is still very high 21.9 per cent (2012). Inspite of significant improvement in various human development indicators, India's rank is still low in several of these indicators.

Throughout the developing world, levels of labour productivity are extremely low compared with those in developed countries. Low level of living and low productivity are self-reinforcing social and economic phenomenon in the Third World countries and as such, are the principal manifestation of, and contributors to, their development. Myrdal's well-known theory of "circular and cumulative causation" in under-developed countries is based on the interaction between low living levels and low productivity.

Low productivity is due to low level of technology. The sharp differences in productivity between developed and underdeveloped nations can be traced to the level of technology in these countries. Productivity level in Indian economy has been low on account of backward or poor technology and this applies to all sectors of the economy—whether it is agriculture, industry or the tertiary sector.

A comparison of productivity levels in Indian agriculture with the levels in other countries shows how low the productivity in Indian agriculture is. Productivity of wheat in India is about 35 per cent of the productivity in France. It is 66 per cent (i.e., less than two-third) of the productivity in comparison to another developing country—China. As far as rice is concerned, productivity in India is 46 per cent of the productivity in China and Japan (i.e., less than half). The productivity of cotton in India is one-third of the productivity in China. Even in comparison to Pakistan, productivity of cotton in India is just 61 per cent. As far as groundnut is concerned, productivity in India is 34 per cent of the productivity in USA, 40 per cent of the productivity in China and 51 per cent of the productivity in Argentina. Similar conclusions hold for most of the other crops.[17] The low levels of productivity in Indian agriculture point to the possibilities of increasing productivity by adopting appropriate strategies and policies.

International comparisons reveal a wide gulf in India's performance between achievements in output and productivity. While India compares favourably in terms of total output, it compares poorly in terms of yield per hectare.

Since around 80 per cent of world population lives in under-developed/developing countries which have around 40 per cent share in world income, it is obvious that a vast majority of people in these countries must be living under conditions of poverty, malnutrition, disease, squalor, illiteracy, etc. Even basic necessities of subsistence such as minimum food, clothing and shelter are not easily accessible to the poor masses. The reasons for this mass poverty and low living standards in these countries are to be found in their stagnating or slow growing economies and rapidly growing population.

Lower Levels of Human Capital

Human capital—health, education and skills—is vital to economic growth and human development. Compared with developed countries,

17. Tata Services (1998-99). *Statistical Outline of India*.

much of the developing world has lagged in its average levels of nutrition, health (as measured by life expectancy) and education (measured by literacy), as seen in Table 1.3. The under-5 mortality is still 15 times higher in low-income countries than in high-income countries.

The well-performing developing countries are much closer to the developed world in health and education standards than they are to the lowest-income countries. While health conditions in East Asia are relatively good, sub-Saharan Africa continues to be plagued by problems of malnourishment, malaria, TB, AIDS and parasitic infections. Despite progress, South Asia continues to have high levels of illiteracy, low schooling attainment and undernourishment. Still, in fields such as primary school completion, low-income countries are also making great progress, for example, enrolments in India are up from 68 per cent in the early 1990s to 89 per cent by 2005. Some development economists contend that a country's level and distribution of education is the most fundamental determinant of future development prospects.

High Rate of Population Growth and Dependency Burden

Population dynamics is another area of wide variation among developing countries. Populations of some developing countries, particularly in Africa, continue to grow rapidly. From 1990 to 2005, population in the low-income countries grew at 2 per cent per year, compared to 1.1 per cent in the middle-income countries, the high-income countries grew at 0.7 per cent per year, reflecting both births and immigration.

Middle-income developing countries show greater variance, with some having achieved lower birth rates closer to those prevailing in rich countries. As seen in Table 1.2, the birth rate is almost three times higher in the low-incoming countries than in the high-income countries.

Developing countries also have higher death rates in each age bracket. However, given their youthful populations, overall death rates are now lower in developing countries (8 per 1,000 population) than in the developed countries (10 per 1,000). As of 2005, the average rate of population growth was about 1.5 per cent in the developing countries (1.8% excluding China).

A major implication of high birth rates in least development country (LDC) is that children under age 15 make up almost 32 per cent of the total population in these countries (35% excluding China) as opposed

TABLE – 1.2

Commonality and Diversity: Some Basic Indicators

Country or Group	*2013 Income Per Capita (US $)*	*2013 PPP (US $)*	*Life Expectancy (Years)*	*Prevalence of Under-nourishment (%)*	*Under 5 Mortality per 1,000 Live Births*	*Crude Birth Rate*	*Adult Literacy 2013*	
							Male	*Female*
Income Group								
Low	728	1,959	59	24	114	29	71	50
Lower middle	2,074	5,966	70	11	39	16	93	85
Upper middle	7,604	13,405	71	4	27	16	96	93
High	39,812	40,788	79	3	7	10	99	98
Country								
Dem. Rep. Congo (LIC)	430	740	44	74	205	50	81	54
India (LIC)	1,570	5,350	67.5 (2009-13)	20	42 (2011)	13.3 (Under 4 2012)	88 (2011)	74
Egypt (LMC)	3,140	10,790	71	4	33	26	83	59
Brazil (UMC)	11,690	14,750	71	7	33	20	88	89
Malaysia (UMC)	10,430	22,530	74	3	12	21	92	85
United States (high-income)	53,470	53,750	78	<2.5	7	14	99[a]	99[a]

Note: a UNDP estimates.

Source: Data from World Bank (2015). *World Development Report 2015*, various tables. Washington, D.C.

to 17 per cent of the total population in the developed countries. Thus in most developing countries, the active labour force has to support proportionally almost twice as many children as it does in richer countries. By contrast, the proportion of people over the age of 65 is much greater in the developed nations. Both older people and children are often referred to as an economic dependency burden in the sense that they are non-productive members of society and therefore must be supported financially by the country's labour force (usually defined as citizens between the ages of 15 and 64). The overall dependency burden (i.e., both young and old) represents only about one-third of the populations of developed countries but almost 40 per cent of the populations of the less developed nations.

Fast growing population in the Third World is both a cause and effect of underdevelopment. These countries have effectively brought down the mortality rates but birth rates continue to be high due to wide spread poverty, ignorance, and social and religious factors. Due to high birth rate, the dependency burden is about half of the population as against one-fourth in developed countries. The active labour force has to support almost twice as many children as it does in richer countries. Population has been growing in the Third World countries in the range of 2 to 3.5 per cent per annum as compared to less than 1 per cent in developed countries. In India, for instance, the rate of growth of population increased from 1.25 per cent per annum in 1951 to 2.5 per cent in 1981. It started declining only thereafter and 1991 census recorded a growth rate of 2 per cent with children under the age 15 forming 38 per cent of the total population. Average annual growth rate during 2000-2012 has been estimated at 1.4 per cent as compared to 0.6 per cent for high-income countries, 1.2 per cent for middle-income, 1.3 per cent in low- and middle-income and 2.2 per cent for low-income countries (*World Development Report, 2012*).

We may conclude, therefore, that not only are developing countries characterised by higher rates of population growth, but they must also contend with greater dependency burdens than rich nations.

Higher Levels of Inequality and Absolute Poverty

The magnitude and extent of poverty in any country depend on two factors: the average level of national income and the degree of inequality in its distribution. Clearly, for any given level of national per capita income, the more unequal the distribution, the greater the incidence of poverty. Similarly, for any given distribution, the lower the average income level, the greater the incidence of poverty.

Development economists use the concept of absolute poverty to represent a specific minimum level of income needed to satisfy the basic physical needs of food, clothing and shelter in order to ensure continued survival. A problem, however, arises when one recognises that these minimum subsistence levels will vary from country to country and region to region, reflecting different physiological as well as social and economic requirements. Economists have therefore tended to make conservative estimates of world poverty in order to avoid unintended exaggeration of the problem.

The incidence of extreme poverty varies widely around the developing world. The World Bank estimates that the share of the population living on less than $1.25 in 2011 per day is 7.9 (forecaste 4.1 in 2015) per cent in East Asia and the Pacific, 4.6 per cent in Latin America and the Caribbean, 1.7 per cent in the Middle East and North Africa (forecaste 2.0 in 2015), 24.5 (forecaste 18.1 in 2015) per cent in South Asia, and 46.8 (forecaste 40.9 in 2015) per cent in sub-Saharan Africa. The share of world population living in extreme poverty has fallen encouragingly an estimated 14.5 per cent in 2011 and is estimated to fall to 11.5 per cent in 2015. As a result, the global incidence of extreme poverty has been increasingly centred in South Asia and sub-Saharan Africa.

Development economists have increasingly focused on ways in which poverty and inequality can lead to slower growth. That is, not only do poverty and inequality result from distorted growth, but they can also be a cause of it.

Greater Social Fractionalisation

Low-income countries more often have ethnic, linguistic and other forms of social divisions, sometimes known as fractionalisation. This is sometimes associated with civil strife and even violent conflict, which can lead developing societies to divert considerable energies to working for political accommodations if not national consolidation. It is one of a variety of governance challenges many developing nations face.

Today, more than 40 per cent of the world's nations have more than five significant ethnic populations. In most cases, one or more of these groups face serious problems of discrimination. Over half of the world's LDCs have recently experienced some form of interethnic conflict. Just in the 1990s, ethnic and religious conflicts leading to widespread death and destruction took place in Afghanistan, Rwanda, Mozambique, Sri Lanka, Iraq, India, Somalia, Ethiopia, Liberia, Angola, Myanmar, Sudan, Yugoslavia, Haiti, Indonesia, and the Democratic Republic of Congo.

Ethnic and religious diversity need not necessarily lead to inequality, turmoil or instability, and unqualified statements about its impact cannot be made. There have been numerous instances of successful economic and social integration of minority or indigenous ethnic populations in countries as diverse as Malaysia and Mauritius. And in the USA, diversity is often cited as source of creativity and innovation. The broader point is that the ethnic and religious composition of a developing nation and whether or not that diversity leads to conflict or cooperation can be important determinants of the success or failure of development efforts.

Larger Rural Populations but Rapid Rural-to-Urban Migration

One of the hallmarks of economic development is a shift from agriculture to manufacturing and services. In developing countries, a much higher share of the population lives in rural areas. Although modernising in many regions, rural areas are poorer and tend to suffer from missing markets, limited information and social stratification. A massive population shift is also under way as hundreds of millions of people are moving from rural to urban areas, fueling rapid urbanisation, with its own attendant problems.

Substantial Dependence on Agricultural Production and Lower Levels of Industrialisation and Manufactured Exports

The vast majority of people in the Third World nations live and work in rural area. Almost 80 per cent are rurally based compared with less than 35 per cent in economically developed countries. The proportion of labour force engaged in agriculture in less developed countries is 66 per cent compared with 21 per cent for developed nations. Moreover, agriculture contributes about 32 per cent to the GNP of the former, while it accounts for only 8 per cent of GNP of the latter.

The basic reason for the concentration of people and production in agricultural and other primary production activities in developing countries is the simple fact that for the low income levels, the first priority is for food, clothing and shelter. Agricultural productivity is low not only because of the large number of people in relation to available land but also because in *lower development countries,* agriculture is often characterised by primitive technologies, poor organisation, and limited physical and human capital inputs.

In India, the predominance of the primary sector is reflected in the contribution of this sector to GDP and employment in the economy. In 1951, the contribution of primary sector to India's GDP was 57 per cent and to employment 73 per cent. Even today, primary sector provides employment to about 60 per cent of the workforce, and its contribution to GDP is around 15 per cent as compared with 3 per cent of workforce engaged in primary sector in the UK and 4 per cent in the USA contributing about 2 per cent to their GDP. Indian economy has moved from underdevelopment to a developing economy.

One of the most widely used terminologies for the Group of Seven (G-7) countries and other advanced economies such as smaller European countries and Australia is the 'industrial countries.' Industrialisation is associated with high productivity and incomes, and has been a hallmark of modernisation and national economic power. It is no accident that most developing-country governments have made industrialisation a high national priority.

Along with lower industrialisation, developing nations have tended to have a higher dependence on primary exports. Most developing countries have diversified away from agricultural and mineral exports to some degree. The middle-income countries are rapidly catching up with the developed world in the share of manufactured goods in their exports, even if these goods are typically much less advanced in their skill and technology content. However, the low-income countries, particularly those in Africa, remain highly dependent on a relatively small number of agricultural and mineral exports.

Underdeveloped Financial and Other Markets

There is a greater prevalence of imperfect markets and incomplete information in developing countries, so that domestic markets, particularly financial markets, have worked less efficiently.

In many LDCs, legal and institutional foundations are either absent or extremely weak. LDCs often lack a legal system that enforces contracts and validates property rights; a stable and trustworthy currency; an infrastructure of roads and utilities that results in low transport and communication costs so as to facilitate interregional trade; a well-developed system of banking and insurance; formal credit markets that select projects and allocate loanable funds on the basis of relative economic profitability and enforce rules of repayment; substantial market information for consumers and producers about prices, quantities, and qualities of products and resources as well as the creditworthiness of potential borrowers; and norms of behaviour that facilitate successful long-term business relationships.

Lingering Colonial Impacts

Most developing countries were once colonies of Europe or otherwise dominated by European powers, and institutions created during the colonial period often had adverse effects on development that in many cases have persisted to the present day. Both domestically and internationally, developing countries have more often lacked institutions and formal organisations of the type that have benefited the developed world: domestically, on average, property rights have been less secure and a smaller segment of society has been able to gain access to and take advantage of economic opportunities.

Decolonisation was one of the most important historical and geopolitical events of the post-World War II era. More than 80 former European colonies have joined the United Nations. But the effects of the colonial era linger for many developing nations, particularly the least developed ones.

External Dependence

Developing countries have also been less well organised and influential in international relations, with sometimes adverse consequences for development. For example, agreements within the World Trade Organization (WTO) and its predecessors concerning matters such as agricultural subsidies in rich countries that harm developing-country farmers and one-sided regulation of intellectual property rights (IPRs) have often been relatively unfavourable to the developing world. More generally, developing nations have weaker bargaining positions than developed nations in international economic relations. Developing nations often also voice great concern over various forms of cultural dependence, from news and entertainment to business practices, lifestyles, and social values. The potential importance of these concerns should not be underestimated, either in their directs effects on development in its broader meanings, or indirect impacts on the speed or character of national development.

In contrast, China and India, with over 40 per cent of the developing world's population and recently enjoying high average income growth and expanding international corporate presence, are gaining considerable autonomy in many respects.

Developing nations are also dependent on the developed world for environmental preservation, on which hopes for sustainable development depend. Of greatest concern, although global warming is projected to harm developing regions more than developed ones, both accumulated and even current greenhouse gas emissions still predominately originate from the high-income countries. Thus the developing world endures what may be called environmental dependence, in which it must rely on the developed world to cease aggravating the problem and to develop solutions.

The net effect of all these factors is to create a situation of 'vulnerability' among the Third World nations in which forces largely outside their control can have decisive and dominating influences on their overall economic and social well-being.

According to Michael Todaro,

> the phenomenon of under-development needs to be viewed in a national and an international context. Economic and social forces, both internal and external, are responsible for the poverty, inequality and low productivity that commonly characterise most Third World nations.[18] The successful pursuit of economic and social development will require not only the formulation of appropriate strategies within the Third World but also a modification of the present international economic order to make it more responsive to the development needs of poor nations.

Nature of Indian Economy

Indian economy certainly had all the characteristics of an underdeveloped economy at the time of Independence but the planned economic development since 1951 has definitely brought Indian economy in the category of developing economies, coming closer to middle-income category countries. Indeed, in terms of growth, India performed much better than the industrialised countries which experienced a slowdown in growth, the transition economies which did badly, and much of the developing world. And it was only east Asia, particularly China, which performed better.

---

18. "The 157 developing African, Asian, and Latin American member countries of the United Nations often collectively refer to themselves as the Third World. They do this primarily to distinguish themselves from the economically advanced capitalist (First World) and the formerly socialist (Second World) countries of eastern Europe and the Soviet Union—some of which could now justifiably be considered part of the Third World. It is unfortunate that the terms first, second, and third may sometimes be taken to connote superiority or inferiority when in fact they merely reflect the historical sequence of industrialisation" Todaro (2013 *op.cit.* no. 14).

India has been widely heralded as a success story for globalisation. Over the past two decades, the country has moved into the premier league of world economic growth; high-technology exports are booming and India's emerging middle-class consumers have become a magnet for foreign investors.

Why has accelerated income growth not moved India onto a faster poverty reduction path? Extreme poverty is concentrated in rural areas of the northern poverty-belt states, including Bihar, Madhya Pradesh, Uttar Pradesh and West Bengal, while income growth has been most dynamic in other states, urban areas and the service sectors.

The deeper problem facing India is its human development legacy. In particular, pervasive gender inequalities, rural poverty and inequalities between states are undermining the potential for converting growth into human development.

The central point to appreciate here, is that while economic growth is an important tool for enhancing living conditions, its reach and impact depend greatly on what is done with the fruits of growth. The relation between economic growth and the advancement of living standards depends on many factors, including economic and social inequality in general, and no less importantly, on what the government does with the public revenue that is generated by economic growth. The importance of economic growth can be adequately understood only in this broader context. It is necessary to recognise the role of growth in facilitating development in the form of enhancing human lives and freedoms, but it is also necessary in this context to appreciate how the growth possibilities of a country depend in turn on the advancement of human capabilities (through education, health care and other facilities), in which the state can play a very constructive part.[19]

So where does India stand now after all this? The economic growth rate is, of course, agreeably high (even at its current lower level, after having hovered above 8 per cent during 2003 to 2012, but the sharing of its benefits is still remarkably unequal. Poverty rates have come down, but not close to what could have been achieved had the distributional side (including the provision of essential services) got more attention. Some failures are huge, like widespread undernourishment in general and child undernutrition in particular—India is among the world's worst performers in this respect (even

19. Dreze, Jean & Amartya Sen (2013). *An Uncertain Glory India and its Contradictions*, Penguin Books.

compared with many countries that are considerably poorer in terms of real GDP per head). Another big failure remains the provision of public health care to the bulk of the population. And there is also the continuing scandal of a quarter of the population (including nearly half the women) remaining effectively illiterate in a country with such high-tech achievements in education based on excellent specialised training and practice. A democratic country can hardly want to become part California and part sub-Saharan Africa.[20]

Looking ahead, two major problems facing the Indian economy can be summed up as follows: (i) removing the sharp disparities that divide the country into the privileged and the rest, while continuing to encourage overall economic growth and expansion, and (ii) bringing more accountability to the running of the economy, particularly in the delivery of public services and the operation of the public sector.[21]

20. Ibid.
21. Ibid.

APPENDIX TABLE – A-1.1

Millennium Development Goals, Targets and Achievements for 2015

Goals	*Targets*	*Achievements*
1. Eradicate extreme poverty and hunger	• Reduce by half the proportion of people living on less than \$1 a day • Reduce by half the proportion of people who suffer from hunger	Developing countries as a whole met the Millennium Development Goal target of halving extreme poverty rates five years ahead of the 2015 deadline. Forecasts indicate that the extreme poverty rate will fall to 13.4 per cent by 2015, a drop of more than two-thirds from the 1990 estimate of 43.6 per cent. East Asia and Pacific has had the most astounding record of poverty alleviation; despite improvements, Sub-Saharan Africa still lags behind and is not forecast to meet the target by 2015.
2. Achieve universal primary	• Ensure that all boys and girls complete education a full course of primary schooling	The primary school completion rate for developing countries reached 91 per cent in 2012 but appears to fall short of the MDG 2 target.
3. Promote gender equality and empower women	• Eliminate gender disparity in primary and secondary education, preferably by 2005, and at all levels by 2015	Developing countries have made substantial gains in closing gender gaps in education and will likely reach gender parity in primary and secondary education. In particular, the ratio of girls' to boys' primary and secondary gross enrollment rate in South Asia was the lowest of all regions in 1990, at 68 percent, but improved dramatically to reach gender parity in 2012, surpassing other regions that were making slower progress.
4. Reduce child mortality mortality rate	• Reduce by two-third among children under 5	The under-five mortality rate in developing countries declined by half, from 99

contd...

...contd...

		deaths per 1,000 live births in 1990 to 50 in 2013. Despite this tremendous progress, developing countries as a whole are likely to fall short of the MDG 4 target of reducing under-five mortality rate by two-thirds between 1990 and 2015. However, East Asia and Pacific and Latin America and the Caribbean have already achieved the target.
5. Improve maternal health	• Reduce by three-quarters the maternal mortality ratio	The maternal mortality ratio has steadily decreased in developing countries as a whole, from 430 in 1990 to 230 in 2013. While substantial, the decline is not enough to achieve the MDG 5 target of reducing the maternal mortality ratio by 75 per cent between 1990 and 2015, though no region is likely to achieve the target on time. Despite considerable drops, the maternal mortality ratio in Sub-Saharan Africa and South Asia remains high.
6. Combat HIV/AIDS, malaria, and other diseases	• Halt and begin to reverse the spread of HIV/AIDS • Halt and begin to reverse the incidence of malaria and other major diseases	The prevalence of HIV is highest in Sub-Saharan Africa. The spread of HIV AIDS there has slowed, and the proportion of adults living with HIV has begun to fall while the survival rate of those with access to antiretroviral drugs has increased. Global prevalence has remained flat since 2000. Tuberculosis prevalence, incidence, and death rates have fallen since 1990. Globally, the target of halting and reversing tuberculosis incidence by 2015 has been achieved.

contd...

...contd...

7.	Ensure environmental sustainability	• Integrate the principles of sustainable development into country policies and programmes; reverse loss of environmental resources • Reduce by half the proportion of people without sustainable access to safe drinking water • Achieve significant improvement in lives of at least 100 million slum dwellers by 2020	In developing countries the proportion of people with access to an improved water source rose from 70 per cent in 1990 to 87 per cent in 2012, achieving the target. The proportion with access to improved sanitation facilities rose from 35 per cent to 57 per cent, but 2.5 billion people still lack access. The large urban-rural disparity, especially in South Asia and Sub-Saharan Africa, is the principal reason the sanitation target is unlikely to be met on time.
8.	Develop a global partnership for development	• Develop further an open, rule-based, predictable, non-discriminatory trading and financial system; include a commitment to good governance, development and poverty reduction—both nationally and internationally • Address the special needs of the least developed countries; include tariff and quota free access for least developed countries' exports; enhanced programme of debt relief for heavily indebted poor countries (HIPCs) and	In 2000 Internet use was rapidly increasing in high-income economies but barely under way in developing countries. Now developing countries are catching up. Internet users per 100 people have grown 27 per cent a year since 2000. The debt service–to-export ratio averaged 11 per cent in 2013 for developing countries, half its 2000 level but with wide disparity across regions. It will likely rise, considering the 33 per cent increase in their combined external debt stock since 2010.

contd...

...contd...

	cancellation of official bilateral debt; and more generous official development assistance (ODA) for countries committed to poverty reduction • Address the special needs of landlocked countries and small island developing states • Deal comprehensively with the debt problems of developing countries through national and international measures in order to make debt sustainable in the long term • In cooperation with developing countries, develop and implement strategies for decent and productive work for youth • In cooperation with pharmaceutical companies, provide access to affordable essential drugs in developing countries • In cooperation with the private sector, make available the benefits of new technologies, especially information and communications	

Source: United Nations Development Program (2007). *Millennium Development Goals. http://www.undp.org/mdg/goallist.shtml*, 16 August.

World Bank (2015). *World Development Report 2015.*

2

Human Development

Human Development

Human development is about human freedoms. It is about building human capabilities—not just for a few, not even for most, but for everyone.[1] In 1990 UNDP published the first Human Development Report (HDR) which focused on the new paradigm of development that puts people at the centre of development. The concept, developed by Mahbub ul Haq and Amartya Sen, is defined as 'the process of enlarging people's choices,' emphasising the freedom to be healthy, to be educated and to enjoy a decent standard of living. But it also stressed that human development and well-being went far beyond these dimensions to encompass a much broader range of capabilities, including political freedoms and human rights.[2] Economic growth is considered only a means of capability expansion and not as an end in itself.

Such a paradigm of development enables all individuals to enlarge their human capabilities to the full and to put these capabilities to their best use in all fields—economic, social, cultural and political. It also protects the options of the unborn generations. It does not run-down the natural resource base needed for sustaining development in the future.

Disadvantaged people are a central focus of human development. This includes people in the future who will suffer the most severe consequences of the risks arising from our activities today.[3]

---

1. UNDP (2018). *Human Development Report 2018.* Statistical Update.
2. UNDP (2010). *Human Development Report 2010.* p.2.
3. UNDP (2011). "Overview", *Human Development Report 2011.* p.1.

Human Development Index

The greatest innovations of the HDRs have been new measurement tools—notably the Human Development Index (HDI), launched in the first HDR (Box 2.1). The underlying principle of the HDI, considered pathbreaking in 1990, was elegantly simple: National development should be measured not only by income per capita, as had long been the practice, but also by health and education achievements. Ranking countries by their HDI value transformed the development discourse and dethroned income per capita as the sole indicator of development progress.

BOX – 2.1

Measuring Human Development

The Human Development Index (HDI) is a composite index focusing on three basic dimensions of human development: the ability to lead a long and healthy life, measured by life expectancy at birth; the ability to acquire knowledge, measured by mean years of schooling and expected years of schooling; and the ability to achieve a decent standard of living, measured by gross national income per capita.

To measure human development more comprehensively, the Human Development Report presents four other composite indices. The Inequality-adjusted HDI discounts the HDI according to the extent of inequality. The Gender Development Index compares female and male HDI values. The Gender Inequality Index highlights women's empowerment. And the Multidimensional Poverty Index measures nonincome dimensions of poverty.

Source: Human Development Report 2018.

The HDI value indicates how far a country has gone to attain certain defined goals: an average life span of 85 years, access to education for all and a decent standard of living. The maximum and minimum values for each variable, which are fixed, are reduced to scale between 0 and 1.

It is 28 years since the launch of the first HDR, and new challenges to human development, especially inequality and sustainability, require concerted measurement and analytical attention. Data availability is expanding with new opportunities for measurement innovation and disaggregation and possibilities for new partnerships growing out of the 2030 Agenda for Sustainable Development (HDR 2018).

Countries are classified into four groups:

1. Very High human development countries: countries with HDI values of 0.800 and above.
2. High human developments countries with HDI values between of 0.700 to 0.800.
3. Medium human development countries: countries with HDI values of 0.556 to 0.699.
4. Low human development countries: countries with HDI values below 0.500.

Inherent in the human development tradition is that the approach be dynamic, not calcified. Human development is an evolving idea—not a fixed, static set of precepts—and as the world changes, analytical tools and concepts evolve.

Are there Limits to Human Development[4]?

Most people around the world have seen major improvements in their lives over the last 40 years. But there are major constraints in our capacity to sustain these trends. If we deal decisively with these challenges, we could be on the cusp of an era of historic opportunities for expanded choices and freedoms. But if we fail to act, future generations may remember the early 21st century as the time when the doors to a better future closed for most of the world's people.

We care about environmental sustainability because of the fundamental injustice of one generation living at the expense of others. Poeple born today should not have a greater claim on Earth's resources than those born a hundred or a thousand years from now. We can do much to ensure that our use of the world's resources does not damage future opportunities. Amartya Sen notes that "a fouled environment in which future generations are denied the presence of fresh air ... will remain foul even if future generations are so very rich." The fundamental uncertainty about what people will value in the future means that we need to ensure equal freedom of choice, the lynchpin of the capability approach, in part by protecting the availability and diversity of natural resources. Such resources are critical in allowing us to lead lives that we value and have reason to value.

The early HDRs recognised the centrality of the environment. The first report warned of the continuing increase in environmental hazards, including health risks from Earth's warming, damage to the ozone layer,

---

4. Ibid.

industrial pollution and environmental disasters. The 1994 HDR asserted "there is no tension between human development and sustainable development. Both are based in the universalism of life claims."

Sustainable development gained prominence with the 1987 publication of Our Common Future, the report of the UN World Commission on Environment and Development, headed by former Norwegian Prime Minister Gro Harlem Brundtland. The report produced what became the standard definition of sustainable development: "development that meets the needs of the present without compromising the ability of future generations to meet their own needs."

Many problems of resource depletion and environmental stress arise from disparities in economic and political power. An industry may get away with unacceptable levels of water pollution because the people who bear the brunt of it are poor and unable to complain effectively. A forest may be destroyed by excessive felling because the people living there have no alternatives or because timber contractors generally have more influence than forest dwellers. Globally, wealthier nations are better placed financially and technologically to cope with the effects of climatic change. Hence, our inability to promote the common interest in sustainable development is often a product of the relative neglect of economic and social justice within and amongst nations.

Sustainable human development addresses both inter-generational and intra-generational equity—enabling all generations, present and future, to make the best use of their potential capabilities. In the final analysis, sustainable human development is *pro-people, pro-jobs and pro-nature*. It gives the highest priority to poverty reduction, productive employment, social integration and environmental regeneration. It accelerates economic growth and translates it into improvements in human lives, without destroying the natural capital needed to protect the opportunities of future generations.

The strongest argument for protecting the environment is the ethical need to guarantee the future generations opportunities similar to the ones previous generations have enjoyed. This guarantee is the foundation of 'sustainable development.'

Sustainability, Equity and Human Development[5]

The human development approach recognises that people have rights that are not affected by the arbitrariness of when they were born.

5. UNDP (2011). *Human Development Report 2011,* ch.1. p.17.

Further, the rights in question refer not only to the capacity to sustain the same living standards but also to access the same opportunities. This limits the substitution that can occur across dimensions of well-being. Today's generation cannot ask future generations to breathe polluted air in exchange for a greater capacity to produce goods and services. That would restrict the freedom of future generations to choose clean air over more goods and services.

A central concern of the human development approach is protecting the most disadvantaged groups. The most disadvantaged are not just the generations that are worse off on average. They are also those who would suffer most from the realisations of the adverse risks they face as a result of our activity. Thus, we are concerned not only with what happens on average or in the most likely scenario but also with what happens in less likely but still possible scenarios, particularly those that entail catastrophic risks.

Promoting human development entails addressing local, national and global sustainability; this can—and should—be equitable and empowering.

Sustainable Development[6]

In recent decades, all over the world, it is hard to think of a subject that generates as much concern today among reflective people everywhere as the serious vulnerability of the environment in which we live. People are deeply worried about how human lives can continue to prosper, even perhaps continue at all in the form that we know them, if the depletion of our environment continues as fast as it is right now.

In India, we have huge reasons to be worried about our treatment of the environment and its implications for the lives people can lead in this increasingly polluted and environmentally devastated country. Indeed, the acceleration of economic growth in recent decades has coincided with unprecedented environmental plunder. Groundwater has been extracted with abandon, leading to a sharp fall in water tables in many areas. Majestic rivers have been reduced to a trickle, or to sewage drains. Mining activities (often illegal) have spread with few safeguards, destroying forests and displacing communities. Air pollution has risen so far that India is now rated as the most polluted among 132 countries for which comparable data are available. India's

6. Dreze, Jean and Amartya Sen (2013). *An Uncertain Glory: India and its Contradiction,* ch.2 excerpts from p.41-44.

'natural wealth' is estimated to have shrunk by about 6 per cent in value terms (more than 30% on a per capita basis) between 1990 and 2008. And all this might be no more than just a harbinger of things to come: many types of environmental damage are likely to accelerate in the near future, with, for instance, hundreds of dams being planned on the Ganges river and its tributaries alone.

The basic challenge of environmental sustainability has been sidelined in the single-minded concentration on the current growth rate of the GDP, which seems to get the lion's share of attention in the media and even in policy discussions about how India should pursue growth and development.

It is important to understand that caring about the environment need not undermine the commitment to development and the removal of poverty and deprivation. In the broader perspective of seeing development in terms of promoting substantive human freedom, fighting poverty and being responsible about the environment cannot but be closely linked. Development is, ultimately, the progress of human freedom and capability to lead the kind of lives that people have reasons to value.

If development is about the expansion of freedom, it has to embrace the removal of poverty as well as paying attention to ecology as integral parts of a unified concern, aimed ultimately at the security and advancement of human freedom. Indeed, important components of human freedoms—and crucial ingredients of our quality of life—are thoroughly dependent on the integrity of the environment, involving the air we breathe, the water we drink, and the epidemiological surroundings in which we live. The opportunity to live the kind of lives that people value—and have reason to value—depends among other things on the nature and robustness of the environment. In this sense, development has to be environment-inclusive, and the belief that development and environment are on a collision course cannot sit comfortably with the recognition of the manifest interdependence and complementarity between the two.

What Makes Development Unsustainable?

When increase in GNP is brought about through depletion of resources under unhealthy environmental conditions by the present generation, the future generations will be left with much depleted resource to produce output under polluted environmental conditions adversely affecting their health and efficiency. Under such circumstances, the rate of economic development in future is bound to fall. Thus, when we are producing more at the cost of future generations the present level of development is not sustainable i.e., we will not be able to maintain it in future.[7]

Even when countries progress in the HDI, they do not necessarily excel in the broader dimensions. It is possible to have a high HDI and be unsustainable, undemocratic and unequal just as it is possible to have a low HDI and be relatively sustainable, democratic and equal. These patterns pose important challenges for how we think about human development, its measurement and the policies to improve outcomes and processes over time.

There is no straightforward pattern relating the HDI to other dimensions of human development such as sustainability and empowerment. An exception is inequality, which is negatively related to the value of the HDI, but even that relationship shows wide variation. The lack of correlation can be seen in the large number of countries that have high HDI values but perform poorly on the other variables: about a quarter of countries have a high HDI but low sustainability; we can see a similar though less marked picture for political freedoms.[8]

But perhaps the greatest challenge to maintaining progress in human development comes from the unsustainability of production and consumption patterns. For human development to become truly sustainable, the close link between economic growth and greenhouse gas emissions needs to be severed. Some developed countries have begun to alleviate the worst effects through recycling and investment in public transport and infrastructure. But most developing countries are hampered by the high costs and low availability of clean energy.

Climate change will be one of the defining forces shaping prospects for human development during the 21st century. Through its impact on ecology, rainfall, temperature and weather systems, global warming will directly affect all countries. Nobody will be immune to its consequences. However, some countries and people are more vulnerable than others. In the long term, the whole of humanity faces risks, but more immediately, the risks and vulnerabilities are skewed towards the world's poorest people (*HDR 2008*).

---

7. OECD (2010). *Sustainable Development: Linking Economy, Society Environment* by Tracey Strange and Anne Bayley. New Delhi: Academic Foundation.
8. UNDP (2010). *Human Development Report 2010,* ch.1.

Concentrated in fragile ecological areas, drought-prone arid lands, flood-prone coastal areas and precarious urban slums, the poor are highly exposed to climate change risks—and they lack the resources to manage those risks.

The Current State of Human Development[9]

Every HDR has monitored human progress, notably through the HDI, a composite measure that includes indicators along three dimensions: life expectancy, educational attainment and command over the resources needed for a decent living. Other indices have delved into inequality, poverty and gender deficits.

Over the past decades, countries across the world have been converging towards higher levels of human development. The pace of progress on the HDI has been fastest in countries in the low and medium human development categories. This is good news. Yet progress requires more than average improvement in HDI value. It will be neither desirable nor sustainable if increases in HDI value are accompanied by rising inequality in income, unsustainable patterns of consumption, high military spending and low social cohesion.

Human Development: International Comparison

The 2018 Update[10] presents HDI values for 189 countries and territories with the most recent data for 2017. Of these countries, 59 are in the very high human development group, 53 in the high, 39 in the medium and only 38 in the low. In 2010, 49 countries were in the low human development group.

The top five countries in the global HDI ranking are Norway (0.953), Switzerland (0.944), Australia (0.939), Ireland (0.938) and Germany (0.936). The bottom five are Burundi (0.417), Chad (0.404), South Sudan (0.388), the Central African Republic (0.367) and Niger (0.354). The largest increases in HDI rank between 2012 and 2017 were for Ireland, which moved up 13 places, and for Botswana, the Dominican Republic and Turkey, which each moved up 8. The largest declines were for the Syrian Arab Republic (down 27), Libya (26) and Yemen (20).[11]

---

9. UNDP (2013). *Human Development Report 2013.*
10. UNDP (2018). *Human Development Indices Indicators 2018.* Statistical Update (Table 1).
11. Ibid.

TABLE – 2.1

India's Position in the Global HDI 2017

Country	*HDI 2017*		*Change in Rank*	*GNI per Capita ($)*	*Life Expectancy at Birth (Years)*	*Expected Years of Schooling (Years)*	*Mean Years of Schooling (Years)*	*Gender Inequality Index 2017*	
	Value	*Rank*	*2012-17*	*2017*	*2017*	*2017a*	*2017a*	*Value*	*Rank*
1	*2*	*3*	*4*	*5*	*6*	*7*	*8*	*9*	*10*
Norway	0.953	1	0	68012	82.3	17.9	12.6	0.048	5
Germany	0.936	4	-1	46136	81.2	17.0	14.1	0.072	14
USA	0.924	12	-5	54941	79.5	16.5	13.4	0.189	41
U K	0.922	14	5	39116	81.7	17.4	12.9	0.116	25
Russian Fed.	0.816	49	3	24233	71.2	15.5	12.0	0.257	53
Malaysia	0.802	57	1	26107	75.5	13.7	10.2	0.287	62
Sri Lanka	0.770	76	-3	11326	75.5	13.9	10.9	0.354	80
Brazil	0.759	79	7	13755	75.7	15.4	7.8	0.407	94
China	0.752	86	7	15270	76.4	13.8	7.8	0.152	36
Egypt	0.696	113	0	10355	71.7	13.1	7.2	0.449	101
Indonesia	0.694	115	-1	10846	69.4	12.8	8.0	0.453	104
South Africa	0.699	111	6	11923	63.4	13.3	10.1	0.389	90
India	**0.640**	**129**	**2**	**6353**	**68.8**	**12.3**	**6.4**	**0.524**	**127**
Bangladesh	0.608	113	7	3677	66.6	11.4f	5.8f	0.524	134
Pakistan	0.562	149	1	5311	66.2	8.6	5.2	0.541	133

Contd...

.contd...

1	2	3	4	5	6	7	8	9	10
Human Development Groups									
Very High Human Development	0.894	-	-	40041	79.5	14.4	12.2	0.170	-
High Human Development	0.757	-	-	14999	76.0	14.1	8.2	0.289	-
Medium Human Developmentt	0.645	-	-	6849	69.1	12.0	6.7	0.489	-
Low Human Development	0.504	-	-	2521	60.8	9.4	4.7	-0.586	-
Developing Countries	0.681	-	-	10055	70.7	12.2	7.3	0.468	-
Regions									
Arab States	0.699	-	-	15837	71.5	11.9	7.0	0.531	-
East Asia and the Pacific	0.733	-	-	13688	74.7	13.3	7.9	0.312	
Europe and Central Asia	0.771	-	-	15331	73.4	14.1	10.3	0.270	-
Latin America and the Caribbean	0.758	-	-	13671	75.7	14.4	8.5	0.386	-
South Asia	0.638	-	-	6473	69.3	11.9	6.4	0.515	-
Sub-Saharan Africa	0.537	-	-	3399	60.7	10.1	5.6	0.569	-
Least developed countries	0.524	-	-	2506	64.8	9.8	4.7	0.559	-
Small island developing states	0.722	-	-	15113	72.3	12.1	8.6	0.447	-
Organisation for Economic Co.operation and Development	0.895	-	-	39595	80.6	16.2	12.0	0.186	-
World	**0.728**	-	-	**15295**	**72.2**	**12.7**	**8.4**	**0.441**	-

Notes: a Data refers to 2017 or the most recent year available; $: Gross National Income (GNI) per capita is based on 2011 dollar purchasing power parity (PPP).

Source: UNDP (2018). Human Development Indices and Indicators 2018 Statistical Update.

Looking back over almost three decades, all regions and human development groups have made substantial progress. The global HDI value in 2017 was 0.728, up about 21.7 per cent from 0.598 in 1990. Across the world, people are living longer, are more educated and have greater livelihood opportunities. The average lifespan is seven years longer than it was in 1990, and more than 130 countries have universal enrolment in primary education.

Although HDI values have been rising across all regions and human development groups, the rates vary significantly.[12] South Asia was the fastest growing region over 1990–2017, at 45.3 per cent, followed by East Asia and the Pacific at 41.8 per cent and Sub- Saharan Africa at 34.9 percent (figure 2.1). The Organisation for Economic Co-operation and Development (OECD) countries, by contrast, grew 14.0 per cent. The trends hold promise for reducing gaps in human development across regions.

FIGURE – 2.1

Human Development Index Values, by Country Grouping, 1990-2017

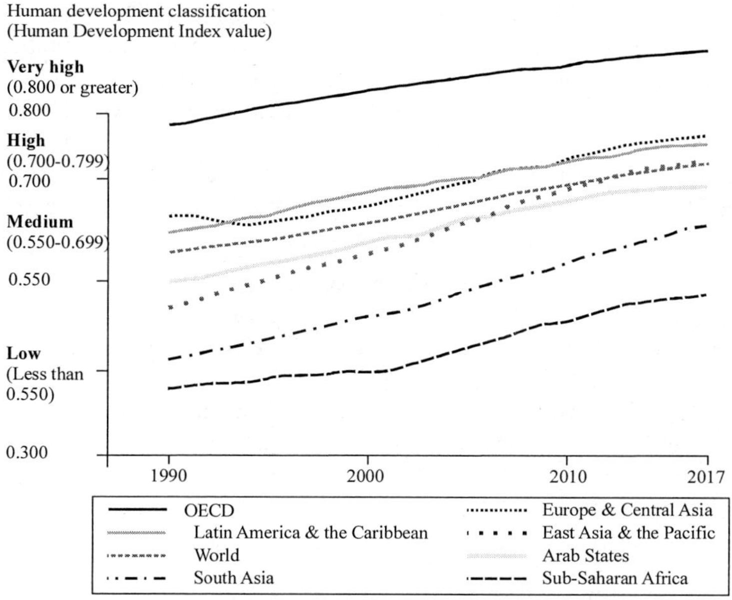

Source: Human Development Report Office.

12. UNDP (2018). *Human Development Indices Indicators 2018.* Statistical Update (Table 2).

But HDI growth has also slowed in all regions, particularly in the last decade. Part of the reason lies in the 2008–2009 global food, financial and economic crises. But part is simply that as human progress advances, slower HDI growth is inevitable, given the growth ceilings of different components of the HDI—as seen with OECD countries. There is a biological limit to life expectancy, and years of schooling and rates of enrolment cannot grow indefinitely. Income is the only component of the HDI that could continue to grow; but even income growth slows as economies mature. As more countries reach the upper limits of HDI dimensions, measures of the quality of human development become more central.

To sum up, there have been significant advances in human development over the past few decades, especially in low human development countries, up 46.6 percent on the HDI since 1990. But some countries have suffered serious setbacks—sometimes erasing in a few years the gains of several decades. And the gaps in human development across countries, while narrowing, remain huge.

Along with HDI, HDR 2018 also gives the Gender Development Index (GDI) for all the 189 countries. The HDI value for gender inequality index in India is 0.524 in 2017, which remains unchanged in comparison to that in 2014. As can be seen in Table 2.1, except Pakistan, all the other four South Asian countries have reported higher HDI values for females in comparison to India. The mean years of schooling for girls in India at 4.8 years is substantially lower than the figure for males (8.2) and shows the extent of educational deprivation of girl children in India's cultural context.

Apart from the cultural and social factors which prevent women from engaging in economically productive activities outside the household, the lack of education and skills restricts them from participating in economic activity, which leads to their further impoverishment and subjugation of women in India. Therefore, in the present cultural context, and with a large proportion of women in the growing population of India, it is necessary to address the gender inequality that is pervasive in education, health and other socio-economic spheres in India.

Gender Issues

Gender discrimination in India, which is embedded in the social fabric, continues in most spheres such as access to education, to social and economic opportunities. The reliance on a legal system to offer gender equality and justice, has not built in a time dimension in the dispensation of justice. Further, dependence on schemes and programmes with inadequate coverage, outlays, inefficiencies and leakages in the delivery mechanism, the social, economic and legal condition of women shows inadequate improvement in terms of several indicators. Gender discrimination in India starts from the womb with sex determination tests and abortion of the female foetuses, discrimination in terms of nutrition offered to the girl child, the length and type of schooling the girl child avails of *vis-à-vis* her male siblings, inadequate or lack of access to higher education, discrimination in opportunities of employment and wages paid and unequal share in inheritance.

Society and the Government has relied on the legal route to address each of these discriminations, without matching changes in the social fabric or role model set by leaders in society from all spheres. The legal route suffers from several shortcomings, especially in terms of time taken for dispensation of justice. For each of the above discrimination, there is a law so all acts of discrimination are illegal, however, compliance requires a lot more to be done.

State of Human Development in India[13]

Over the years, India has made substantial progress in human development. Sustained and high economic growth in the post-reform period reduced the poverty ratio significantly. There was also noteworthy improvement in the literacy rates over time leading to a decline in the absolute number of illiterates.

India's HDI (Human Development Index) has improved significantly over the years between 1990 and 2017. The country's HDI value increased from 0.427 to 0.640, but its position is still lowest among its peer countries (Asian and developing economies). As per the UNDP Human Development Index (HDI), India is ranked 130 among 189 countries in 2017. Moreover, India also reflects inter-State disparities in regional and human development which are reflected by State level HDIs.[14]

The 2017 HDI scores indicate that the States like Kerala, Goa, Himachal Pradesh and Punjab occupy the top four positions while the States like Bihar, UP and MP are at the bottom of the rankings. The States which were the worst-performing ones in HDI during 1990s are

13. Government of India (2016). *Economic Survey 2015-16.*
14. Government of India (2019). *Economic Survey 2018-19.*

presently doing well in the social parameters. The region-wise trend of HDI scores suggests that most Southern and Norther States have performed much better as compared to their Eastern counterparts who have registered poor performance in SHDIs.

India's HDI of 0.640 is little below the average of countries in the medium human development group (0.645) but marginally higher than the HDI average of South Asian countries (0.638). As compared to other BRICS nations, India reports the least mean years of schooling, an LEB that is lower than that of Brazil, China and Russia, but higher. than that of South Africa. The indices of education for India as reflected by the HDI show that the progress made in the education sector needs to be faster, with greater coverage and focus.[15]

However, India has a long way to go as it is still in the medium human development category with countries like China, Egypt, Indonesia, South Africa and even Vietnam having better overall HDI ranking within the same category and Sri Lanka moving to the high human development category from medium in the 2012 HDI ranking despite years of internal conflicts. The existing gap in health and education indicators in India as compared to developed countries and also many of the developing countries highlights the need for much faster and wider spread of basic health and education. Though lower in HDI ranking, in terms of average annual HDI growth rate for 2000-2013, India is well ahead of many countries with high and very high human development. With 1.49 per cent average annual HDI growth it is ahead of China (1.42), Brazil (0.67), Egypt (0.72) and Pakistan (1.30). While China and Egypt performed very well in terms of HDI growth in the 1980s and 1990s, there was a deceleration in the 2000s. On the other hand, India, which seems to have faltered in the 1990s, has picked up again during 2000-2012 (Table 2.2). India is close to China (1.52).

Sustainable Development Goals (SDGs)

On 1 January 2016, the 17 Sustainable Development Goals (SDGs) of the 2030 Agenda for Sustainable Development—adopted by world leaders on 25 September 2015 at an historic UN Summit—officially came into force.[16] The SDGs, also known as Global Goals, build on the success of the Millennium Development Goals (MDGs) aim to go

15. UNDP (2018). *Human Development Report.*

16. *https://www.un.org/sustainabledevelopment/development-agenda/*

TABLE – 2.2

Trends in the Human Development Index (HDI) 1980-2013

HDI Rank	*Country*	*1980*	*1990*	*2000*	*2011*	*Avg. Annual HDI Growth Rate (%)*		
						1980- 1990	*1990-* 2000	*2000-* 2013
1	Norway	0.796	0.844	0.913	0.943	0.59	0.80	0.28
2	Australia	0.850	0.873	0.906	0.929	0.29	0.37	0.29
38	Poland	-	-	0.770	0.813	0.38	0.94	0.48
61	Malaysia	0.559	0.631	0.705	0.761	1.05	1.12	0.58
67	Russian Fed.	-	-	0.691	0.755	....	-0.17	0.64
79	Brazil	0.549	0.600	0.665	0.718	1.16	1.10	0.67
92	Turkey	0.463	0.558	0.634	0.699	1.50	1.27	0.16
91	China	0.404	0.490	0.588	0.687	1.72	1.66	1.52
73	Sri Lanka	0.539	0.583	0.633	0.691	0.87	0.91	0.77
103	Thailand	0.486	0.566	0.626	0.682	1.28	1.27	0.83
112	Philippines	0.550	0.571	0.602	0.644	0.45	0.46	0.49
112	Egypt	0.406	0.497	0.585	0.644	1.91	1.30	0.72
112	Indonesia	0.423	0.481	0.543	0.617	1.16	1.44	0.90
118	South Africa	0.564	0.615	0.616	0.619	0.86	0.14	0.36
123	Vietnam	-	0.435	0.528	0.593	0.28	1.70	0.96
135	**India**	**0.344**	**0.410**	**0.461**	**0.547**	**1.58**	**1.15**	**1.49**
146	Pakistan	0.359	0.399	0.436	0.504	1.22	1.21	1.30
143	Kenya	0.420	0.456	0.443	0.509	0.55	–0.34	1.25
142	Bangladesh	0.303	0.352	0.422	0.500	1.29	1.71	1.62
	World	0.558	0.594	0.634	0.682	0.66	0.67	0.73

Source: UNDP (2014). *Human Development Report 2014*.

TABLE – 2.3

India's Position in the Global HDI 2014

Country	*HDI 2015*		*Change in Rank*	*GNI per Capita ($)*	*LEB (Years)*	*Expected Years of Schooling (Years)*	*Mean Years of Schooling (Years)*	*Income Inequality*		*Gender Inequality Index 2014*	
								Quintile Income Ratio	*Income Gini-Coefficient*		
	Value	*Rank*	*2009-14*	*2014*	*2014*	*2014a*	*2014a*	*2005-13*		*Value*	*Rank*
Norway	0.949	1	0	64992	81.6	17.5	12.6	4.0	26.8	0.067	9
Germany	0.926	4	3	43919	80.9	16.5	13.1	4.7	30.6	0.041	3
USA	0.920	10	-3	52947	79.1	16.5	12.9	9.8	41.1	0.280	55
U K	0.909	16	-2	39267	80.7	16.2	13.1	7.6	38.0	0.177	39
Russian Fed.	0.804	49	8	22352	70.1	14.7	12.0	7.3	39.7	0.276	54
Malaysia	0.789	59	1	22762	74.7	12.7	10.0	11.3	46.2	0.209	42
Sri Lanka	0.766	73	5	9779	74.9	13.7	10.8	5.8	36.4	0.370	72
Brazil	0.754	79	3	15175	74.5	15.2	7.7	16.9	52.7	0.457	97
China	0.738	90	13	12547	75.8	13.1	7.5	10.1	37.0	0.191	40
Egypt	0.691	111	-3	10512	71.1	13.5	6.6	4.4	30.8	0.573	131
Indonesia	0.689	113	3	9788	68.9	13.0	7.6	5.7	38.1	0.494	110
South Africa	0.666	119	4	12122	57.4	13.6	9.9	28.5	65.0	0.407	83
India	**0.624**	**131**	**6**	**5497**	**68.0**	**11.7**	**5.4**	**5.0**	**33.6**	**0.563**	**130**
Bangladesh	0.579	139	0	3191	71.6	10.0	5.1	4.7	32.1	0.503	111
Pakistan	0.550	147	0	4866	66.2	7.8	4.7	4.1	29.6	0.536	121
World	0.717	-		14301	71.5	12.2	7.9			0.449	

Notes: a Data refers to 2014 or the most recent year available; $: Gross National Income (GNI) per capita is based on 2011 dollar purchasing power parity (PPP). LEB is Life Expectancy at Birth.

Source: Human Development Report 2015, 2016.

further to end all forms of poverty. The new goals are unique in that they call for action by all countries, poor, rich and middle-income to promote prosperity while protecting the planet. They recognize that ending poverty must go hand-in-hand with strategies that build economic growth and addresses a range of social needs including education, health, social protection, and job opportunities, while tackling climate change and environmental protection.

While the SDGs are not legally binding, governments are expected to take ownership and establish national frameworks for the achievement of the 17 Goals. Countries have the primary responsibility for follow-up and review of the progress made in implementing the Goals, which will require quality, accessible and timely data collection. Regional follow-up and review will be based on national-level analyses and contribute to follow-up and review at the global level.

How are SDGs different from the MDGs

The 17 Sustainable Development Goals (SDGs) with 169 targets to be achieved by 2030, aimed at addressing global challenges are broader in scope and go further than the MDGs by addressing the root causes of poverty and the universal need for development that works for all people. The goals cover the three dimensions of sustainable development: economic growth, social inclusion and environmental protection.

It is recognised that ending poverty and other deprivations must go hand-in-hand with strategies that improve health and education, reduce inequality and spur economic growth in a sustainable manner. India is home to the world's youngest population as half of its populaiton is below the age of 25. It has also been estimated that demographic advantage in India is available for five decades from 2005-06 to 2055-56, longer than any other country in the world (UNFPA, 2018). This demographic advantage can be reaped only if education, skilling and employment opportunities are provided to the young population.

The achievement of these goals is an imperative for, not just, any particular country but the global community as a whole. The need for global cooperation in helping the developing countries in achieving the climate targets cannot be overstated. India's development agenda has for long been based on principles that are closely rlated to those that have been propounded in the 2030 Development Agenda. Climate change requires concerted global efforts and India has been preserving to address the climate challenges along with other developmental imperatives. The country has been making substantial additions to its installation of renewable power capacity. Increasing growth rate and rapid urbanisation in India have spurred the demand for natural resources, exerting pressures on the environment and raising sustainability concerns. Resource efficiency can be a major tool to meet the resource needs of the country at the least possible cost to the environment. Air pollution has emerged as a serious issue in India. National Clean Air Program (NCAP) has been launched by the Government as a pan-India, time bound, national level initiative to address the country-wide issues of air pollution in a comprehensive manner.

Interlinked Nature of the Sustainable Development Goals

Three years after the adoption of the 2030 Agenda, countries are taking bold actions to achieve the ambitious vision of this transformative plan. As they do so, they face daunting problems: a changing climate, conflict, inequality, persistent pockets of poverty and hunger, rapid urbanization and environmental degradation. Policymakers in every country need to reflect on how societies can be made more resilient while confronting these challenges. A good place to start is by establishing robust water and sanitation infrastructure, ensuring access to clean and affordable energy, building safe and ecologically friendly cities, protecting ecosystems, and instituting sustainable consumption and production patterns.

APPENDIX TABLE – A-2.1

Selected Indicators of Human Development for Major States

Sl. No.	*State*	*Life Expectancy[a] at Birth (2006-2010)*			*Infant Mortality Rate (per 1000 Live Births) (2011)*			*Birth Rate (per 1000) (2011)*	*Death Rate (per 1000) (2011)*
		Male	*Female*	*Total*	*Male*	*Female*	*Total*		
1	*2*	*3*	*4*	*5*	*6*	*7*	*8*	*9*	*10*
1.	Andhra Pradesh	63.5	68.2	65.8	40	46	43	17.5	7.5
2.	Assam	61.0	63.2	61.9	55	56	55	22.8	8.0
3.	Bihar	65.5	66.2	65.8	44	45	44	27.7	6.7
4.	Gujarat	64.9	69.0	66.8	39	42	41	21.3	6.7
5.	Haryana	67.0	69.5	67.0	41	48	44	21.8	6.5
6.	Karnataka	64.9	69.7	67.2	34	35	35	18.8	7.1
7.	Kerala	71.5	76.9	74.2	11	13	12	15.2	7.0
8.	Madhya Pradesh	61.1	63.8	62.4	57	62	59	26.9	8.2
9.	Maharashtra	67.9	71.9	69.9	24	25	25	16.7	6.3
10.	Odisha	62.2	63.9	63.0	55	58	57	20.1	8.5
11.	Punjab	67.4	71.6	69.3	28	33	30	16.2	6.8
12.	Rajasthan	64.7	68.3	66.5	50	53	52	26.2	6.7
13.	Tamil Nadu	67.1	70.9	68.9	21	23	22	15.9	7.4
14.	Uttar Pradesh	61.8	63.7	62.7	55	59	57	27.8	7.9
15.	West Bengal	67.4	71.0	69.0	30	34	32	16.3	6.2
	India	64.6	67.7	66.1	43	46	44	21.8	7.1

Note: Bihar, Madhya Pradesh and Uttar Pradesh excludes Jharkhand, Chhattisgarh and Uttarakhand respectivrly.

Source: Sample Registration System, Office of the Registrar General, India, Ministry of Home Affairs; *Economic Survey 2012-13*. Government of India.

APPENDIX TABLE – A-2.2

The Sustainable Development Goals, Targets and Achievements for 2018

Goals	Targets	Achievements
1. Poverty	End Poverty in all its forms everywhere	While extreme poverty has eased considerably since 1990, pockets of the worst forms of poverty persist. Ending poverty requires universal social protection systems aimed at safeguarding all individuals throughout the life cycle. It also requires targeted measures to reduce vulnerability to disasters and to address specific underserved geographic areas within each country. Only 45 per cent of the world's population are covered by at least one social protection cash benefit Economic losses attributed to disasters were over $300 billion in 2017
2. Hunger and food security	End hunger, achieve food security and improved nutrition and promote sustainable agriculture	After a prolonged decline, world hunger appears to be on the rise again. Conflict, drought and disasters linked to climate change are among the key factors causing this reversal in progress. The proportion of undernourished people worldwide increased from 10.6 per cent in 2015 to 11.0 per cent in 2016. World hunger is on the rise again: 815 million people were undernourished in 2016, up from 777 million in 2015
3. Health	Ensure healthy lives and promote well-being for all at all ages	Many more people today are living healthier lives than in the past decade. Nevertheless, people are still suffering needlessly from preventable diseases, and too many are dying prematurely. Overcoming disease and ill health will require concerted and sustained

contd...

...contd...

			efforts, focusing on population groups and regions that have been neglected. Births attended by skilled health personnel increased globally 62 per cent from 2000-2205 and 80 per cent from 2012-2017.
4.	Education	Ensure inclusive and equitable quality education and promote lifelong learning opportunities for all	More than half of children and adolescents worldwide are not meeting minimum proficiency standards in reading and mathematics. Refocused efforts are needed to improve the quality of education. Disparities in education along the lines of gender, urban-rural location and other dimensions still run deep, and more investments in education infrastructure are required, particularly in LDCs. At the global level, the participation rate in early childhood and primary education was 70 per cent in 2016, up from 63 per cent in 2010. The lowest rates are found in sub-Saharan Africa (41%) and Northern Africa and Western Asia (52%).
5.	Gender equality and women's empowerment	Achieve gender equality and empower all women and girls Women spend about three times as many hours in unpaid domestic and care work as men	While some forms of discrimination against women and girls are diminishing, gender inequality continues to hold women back and deprives them of basic rights and opportunities. Empowering women requires addressing structural issues such as unfair social norms and attitudes as well as developing progressive legal frameworks that promote equality between women and men. Child marriage in Southern Asia decreased by over 40 per cent between 2000 and 2017
6.	Water and Sanitation	Ensure availability and sustainable management of water and sanitation for all	Too many people still lack access to safely managed water supplies and sanitation facilities. Water scarcity, flooding and lack of proper wastewater management also hinder

contd...

...contd...

			social and economic development. Increasing water efficiency and improving water management are critical to balancing the competing and growing water demands from various sectors and users. 3 in 10 people lack access to safely managed drinking water services 6 in 10 people lack access to safely managed sanitation facilitiesData from 79 countries show 59 per cent of all wastewater is safely treated
7.	Energy	Ensure access to affordable, reliable, sustainable and modern energy for all	From 2000 to 2016, the proportion of the global population with access to electricity increased from 78 per cent to 87 per cent, with the absolute number of people living without electricity dipping to just below 1 billion. However, national priorities and policy ambitions still need to be strengthened to put the world on track to meet the energy targets for 2030. 55 per cent of renewable energy was derived from modern forms in 20154 in 10 people still lack access to clean cooking fuels and technologies
8.	Economic Growth	Promote sustained, inclusive and sustainable economic growth, full and productive employment and decent work for all	Globally, labour productivity has increased and the unemployment rate has decreased. However, more progress is needed to increase employment opportunities, especially for young people, reduce informal employment and labour market inequality (particularly in terms of the gender pay gap), promote safe and secure working environments, and improve access to financial services to ensure sustained and inclusive economic growth. Earning inequalities are still pervasive: men earned 12.5 per cent more than women in 40 out of 45 countries with data

contd...

...contd...

		Youth were three times more likely to be unemployed than adults in 2017
9. Infrastructure, industria-lization	Build resilient infrastructure, promote inclusive and sustainable industrialization and foster innovation	Steady progress has been made in the manufacturing industry. To achieve inclusive and sustainable industrialization, competitive economic forces need to be unleashed to generate employment and income, facilitate international trade and enable the efficient use of resources. Global carbon intensity decreased by 19 per cent between 2000 and 2015 Proportion of population covered by a 3G mobile broadband network was lower in the LDCs in 2016
10. Inequality	Reduce inequality within and among countries	Efforts have been made in some countries to reduce income inequality, increase zero-tariff access for exports from LDCs and developing countries, and provide additional assistance to LDCs and small island developing States (SIDS). However, progress will need to accelerate to reduce growing disparities within and among countries. Between 2010 and 2016, in 60 out of 94 countries with data, the incomes of the poorest 40 per cent of the population grew faster than those of the entire population. Products exported by SIDS facing zero tarrifs increased by 20 per cent between 2010 and 2016Remittances to low- and middle-income countries represented over 75 per cent of total global remittances in 2017
11. Cities	Make cities and human settlements inclusive, safe, resilient and sustainable	Between 2000 and 2014, the proportion of the global urban population living in slums dropped from 28.4 per cent to 22.8 per cent. However, the actual number of people living in slums increased from 807 million to 883 million.

contd...

...contd...

		In 2016, 91 per cent of the urban population worldwide were breathing air that did not meet the World Health Organization air quality guidelines value for particulate matter (PM 2.5); more than half were exposed to air pollution levels at least 2.5 times higher than that safety standard. In 2016, an estimated 4.2 million people died as a result of high levels of ambient air pollution. From 1990 to 2013, almost 90 per cent of deaths attributed to internationally reported disasters occurred in low- and middle-income countries. Reported damage to housing attributed to disasters shows a statistically significant rise from 1990 onwards.
12. Sustainable consumption and production	Ensure sustainable consumption and production patterns	Decoupling economic growth from resource use is one of the most critical and complex challenges facing humanity today. Doing so effectively will require policies that create a conducive environment for such change, social and physical infrastructure and markets, and a profound transformation of business practices along global value chains. By 2018, a total of 108 countries had national policies and initiatives relevant to sustainable consumption and production. Globally by 2018, 108 countries had national policies on sustainable consumption and production 93 per cent of the world's 250 largest companies are now reporting on sustainability
13. Climate Change	Take urgent action to combat climate change and its impacts	The year 2017 was one of the three warmest on record and was 1.1 degrees Celsius above the pre-industrial period. An analysis by the World Meteorological Organization shows that the five-year average

contd...

...contd...

		global temperature from 2013 to 2017 was also the highest on record. The world continues to experience rising sea levels, extreme weather conditions and increasing concentrations of greenhouse gases. This calls for urgent and accelerated action by countries as they implement their commitments to the Paris Agreement on Climate Change. Developed country Parties continue to make progress towards the goal of jointly mobilizing $100 billion annually by 2020 to address the needs of developing countries in the context of meaningful mitigation actions. 2017 was the most costly North Atlantic hurricane season on record The majority of countries have ratified the Paris Agreement and provided nationally determined contributions (NDCs)
14. Oceans	Conserve and sustainably use the oceans, seas and marine resources for sustainable development	The global share of marine fish stocks that are within biologically sustainable levels declined from 90 per cent in 1974 to 69 per cent in 2013. Global trends point to continued deterioration of coastal waters due to pollution and eutrophication. Without concerted efforts, coastal eutrophication is expected to increase in 20 per cent of large marine ecosystems by 2050. Mean coverage of marine KBAs increased between 2000 and 2018 Open ocean sites show current levels of acidity have increased by 26 per cent since the start of the Industrial Revolution
15. Biodiversity, forests, desertification	Protect, restore and promote sustainable use of terrestrial ecosystems, sustainably manage forests, combat desertification,	The Earth's forest areas continue to shrink, down from 4.1 billion hectares in 2000 (or 31.2 per cent of total land area) to about 4 billion hectares (30.7 per cent of total land area) in

contd...

...contd...

	and halt and reverse land degradation and halt biodiversity loss	2015. However, the rate of forest loss has been cut by 25 per cent since 2000–2005. About one fifth of the Earth's land surface covered by vegetation showed persistent and declining trends in productivity from 1999 to 2013, threatening the livelihoods of over one billion people. Up to 24 million square kilometres of land were affected, including 19 per cent of cropland, 16 per cent of forest land, 19 per cent of grassland and 28 per cent of rangeland. Land degradation threatens the security and development of all countries The Red List Index shows alarming trend in biodiversity decline for mammals, birds, amphibians, corals and cycads
16. Peace, justice and strong institutions	Promote peaceful and inclusive societies for sustainable development, provide access to justice for all and build effective, accountable and inclusive institutions at all levels	Many regions of the world continue to suffer untold horrors as a result of armed conflict or other forms of violence that occur within societies and at the domestic level. Advances in promoting the rule of law and access to justice are uneven. However, progress is being made in regulations to promote public access to information, albeit slowly, and in strengthening institutions upholding human rights at the national level. Nearly 8 in 10 children aged 1 to 14 years were subjected to some form of psychological aggression and/or physical punishment on a regular basis at home in 81 countries (primarily developing), according to available data from 2005 to 2017. In all but seven of these countries, more than half of children experienced violent forms of discipline. In 2014, the majority of detected trafficking victims were women and

contd...

...contd...

		girls (71%), and about 28 per cent were children (20%t girls and 8% boys). Over 90 per cent of victims detected were trafficked for sexual exploitation or forced labour. Almost one in five firms worldwide report receiving at least one bribery payment request when engaged in regulatory or utility transactions. At least 1,019 human rights defenders, journalists and trade unionists have been killed in 61 countries since 2015. This is equivalent to one person killed every day while working to inform the public and build a world free from fear and want.
17. Partnerships	Strengthen the means of implementation and revitalize the Global Partnership for Sustainable Development	Goal 17 seeks to strengthen global partnerships to support and achieve the ambitious targets of the 2030 Agenda, bringing together national governments, the international community, civil society, the private sector and other actors. Despite advances in certain areas, more needs to be done to accelerate progress. All stakeholders will have to refocus and intensify their efforts on areas where progress has been slow. ODA for capacity building and national planning was $20.4 billion in 2016, which has been stable since 2010 LDCs' share of world merchandise exports fell between 2013 and 2016, after a long period of increase In 2015, developing countries received only 0.3 per cent of total ODA to support all areas of statistics

Source: United Nations Development Program (2018). The Sustainable Development Goals Report 2018. *https://www.un.org/sustainabledevelopment/sustainable-development-goals/* 01 January 2016.

3

India's Economy at Independence

Introduction

The pre-Independence period was a period of near stagnation for the Indian economy. At the time of Independence, Indian economy was caught up in a *vicious circle of poverty* characterised by one of the lowest per capita consumption and income levels among the countries of the world. Low income levels resulted in low levels of saving and capital formation and therefore, low productivity and low level of income and this vicious circle perpetuated poverty in the country. Further, the size of the market being limited because of low incomes, entrepreneurs had little incentive for making investments in diversified fields, and therefore, the productivity in the economy continued to be low thereby perpetuating low incomes and mass poverty.

Judged in terms of per capita incomes and standard of well-being, the Indian economy remained more or less stagnant during the colonial regime. Quoting from the First Five Year Plan document:

> This is primarily because the basic conditions under which an economy can continuously expand have been lacking. The impact of modern industrialism in the latter half of the 19th century was felt in this country initially through imports of machine-made goods from abroad which reacted adversely on the traditional pattern of economic life, but did not create the impulse for development along new lines. The transition that followed was characterised not by expansion of industry and a diversification of the economic structure but by a decay of India's traditional arts, crafts and industries and by an increasing pressure of population on land. This retrogression led to a decline in productivity per person engaged in agriculture, the adverse effects of which were perhaps softened to some extent by the shock absorbing

> capacity of the old institution of the joint family. The result was a continuous increase in under-employment. In such an environment there could be little economic or social progress. Whatever surpluses might have been available in the system under these conditions were directed to the purchase of imports, partly of better finished products from abroad and partly of equipment for the new transportation system designed primarily in the interests of foreign commerce. The responsibility for promoting modern commerce and industry came to be concentrated in the hands of certain classes in the urban areas, and up to the end of the nineteenth century the only major large-scale industries which had taken root in the country were textiles. Little attention was paid to improvement of agriculture or to the needs of the rural areas. (First Five Year Plan, p.28)

Indian economy at the time of Independence was overwhelmingly rural and agricultural in character with nearly 85 per cent of the population living in villages and deriving their livelihood from agricultural and related pursuits using traditional, low productivity techniques. The backwardness of Indian economy is reflected in its unbalanced occupational structure with 70 per cent of working population engaged in agriculture. Even with this large proportion of population engaged in agriculture, the country was not self-sufficient in food and raw materials for industry. The average availability of food was not only deficient in quantity and quality but also precarious as exhibited in recurrent famines. Illiteracy was as high as 84 per cent; majority of children (60%) in the 6-11 age group did not attend school. Mass communicable diseases were widespread, and in the absence of a good public health service, mortality rates were very high (27 per thousand). Thus, the economy was faced with the problems of mass poverty, ignorance and diseases which were aggravated by the unequal distribution of resources between groups and regions.

The India of 1947, under British rule, showed all the signs of what is today called an underdeveloped country.

The Relative Importance of Various Industrial Activities

Composition of National Income

The low degree of economic development can be judged from how income is distributed according to each type of industry.

As can be seen, agricultural activities contributed nearly 50 per cent to India's national income. Mines, factories and small craftsmen's work contributed only one-sixth, even lower than the figure for trade, transport and communications, and hardly greater than that for other services.

TABLE – 3.1

Distribution of National Income Per Sector

(As Percentage of Total Income) in the Year 1948-49

Agriculture, Forestry and Fisheries (Total)	49.1
Mines, Manufacturing Industries, Small Enterprises (Total)	17.1
Trade, Transport and Communications (Total)	18.5
Professions, Administration, Domestic Services and Other Services (Total)	15.7
Net national product at factor cost	100.12
Transfers abroad	0.2
National income	100.0

Source : Bettleheim (1968: 2).

The Working Force

The relative importance of the various industrial activities can also be seen from statistics showing the distribution of labour.

Seventy-two per cent of the total working force was occupied in agriculture, whereas the organised industries employed only about 2 per cent, a figure lower than the number of administrative workers (2.7%). Less than 11 per cent of the working force was employed in all forms of industry, less than 8 per cent in trade and transports, and less than 10 per cent in other services. These statistics speak for low level of industrialisation.

TABLE – 3.2

Occupational Structure

Distribution of Labour 1950-51

		(%)
1.	Agriculture (Total)	72.3
2.	Industry (Total)	10.7
3.	Trade and Transport (Total)	7.7
4.	Services (Total)	9.3
	Grand Total	**100.0**

Source : Bettleheim (1968: 4).

The high percentage of agricultural workers is obviously not the result of a modern capitalist agricultural system, but is simply evidence of agricultural overpopulation. A large proportion of the Indian peasantry did not own land (or owned practically none) and could not always manage to find employment.

Little industrialisation, low agricultural output, a low figure of national income *per capita*, very sluggish economic progress, considerable unemployment and under-employment were some of the main characteristics of India's social and economic situation just after Independence.

The Agrarian Scene

Stagnating Agriculture

Colonialism became a fetter on India's agricultural and industrial development. Agriculture stagnated and even deteriorated over the years, especially during the first half of the 20th century when the full impact of colonialism began to be felt. Per capita agricultural production declined at a rate of 0.72 per cent per year during 1911-1941 (Blyn, 1966). The situation was worse insofar as per capita food grain output was concerned: during the same period, it declined by 29 per cent, i.e., at a rate of 1.14 per cent per year. Even though the per capita non-food grain output grew by 14 per cent, it failed to make up for the decline in foodgrain output (Blyn, 1966).[1]

Whatever the absolute growth in agricultural output, it occurred mainly because of the increase in crop acreage. The rate of increase in all-crop yield per acre was near-zero during 1911-1941. While all-crop and food grain yields declined by 0.02 and 0.44 per cent per year, non-food grain yield went up by 1.15 per cent per year (Blyn, 1966). The increase in yield of non-food grains was basically at the cost of food grain yields, as cultivators shifted better and irrigated land and capital resources to commercial crops in order to earn cash.

Causes

(i) Regressive Agrarian Structure

The stagnation in agriculture is basically explained by the fact that colonialism transformed the agrarian structure in India and made it extremely regressive. As is well-known, the *zamindars* in *zamindari*

---

1. Blyn, G. (1966). *Agricultural Trends in India, 1891-1947*. Philadelphia: Pennsylvania University Press.

areas failed to invest in land and relied on rack-renting, while the peasant proprietors fell into the clutches of the moneylenders and lost control over their lands. Sub-infeudation, tenancy and sharecropping increasingly dominated both the *zamindari* and *ryotwari* areas.[2]

(ii) Internal Drain of Capital

Agricultural surpluses were siphoned from agriculture without any *quid pro quo*, thereby subjecting it to an internal drain of capital. Throughout the 18th and 19th centuries, high land revenue demand ate into the peasant's surplus and even his subsistence. But the government spent very little on improving agriculture as was done, for instance, in Japan. The landlords, old or new, took no interest in agriculture beyond collecting rent. They found rack-rent and usury far more profitable than making productive investment in land. The moneylenders and merchants used their increasing share of agricultural surplus to intensify usury or to take possession of land to become landlords.

(iii) Poor Technology

Another reason for the stagnation of productivity in agriculture was the near absence of change in its technological basis or its productive technique and inputs. As Blyn points out, the type of equipment used changed very little till 1941. Modern machinery was conspicuous by its absence. Improved seeds covered about 1.9 per cent of all crop acreage in 1922-23 and 11.1 per cent in 1938-39, these being largely confined to non-food cash crops.

It is also to be noted that commercialisation did not change the unit or organisation of productive activity (e.g., capitalist farming) or lead to improved technology—only better soil and available water and other resources were diverted from food crops to commercial crops.

India's Industrial Production and its Structure

Another aspect of India's economic backwardness was the state of its industry in spite of her vast industrial resources.

---

2. By 1947, nearly 70 per cent of the total cultivated land in British India was owned by *zamindars* and landlords. According to Nanavati ("Minute of Dissent", in the Famine Inquiry Commission—Final Report, Government of India, Calcutta, 1945), in *ryotwari* areas between 30 to 50 per cent of the land was in the hands of the landlords and most of the rest was heavily under debt. In 1951, 27.8 per cent of rural agricultural families consisted of peasant proprietors while tenants, sharecroppers and labourers made up the remaining families. (Chandra, Bipan (1979). *Nationalism and Colonialism in Modern India*. Delhi: Orient Longman).

India's Industrial Resources[3]

India's iron ore deposits estimated at 21 thousand million are a quarter of the total world deposits, manganese deposits are the third largest in the world. India also possesses deposits of chromium, gold, bauxite and various non-ferrous metals, which are important raw materials for atomic industries. Finally, gypsum also exists, as does mica, the latter deposit being one of the largest in the world. India is equally rich in her energy potential. India's resources as a whole would give her a leading position in world industry, in particular the steel and engineering industries and the chemical industries based on coal.

Given this potential, we may now examine the state of India's industrial development immediately after Independence.

The Decline of Traditional Industry and the Development of Modern Industry

India's industrial situation in 1948 was the result of a long period of change in which modern industry replaced the traditional crafts.

Foreign trade statistics best show the effects of 'deindustrialisation.' India, still an exporter of manufactured products at the end of the 18th century, becomes an importer. From 1815 to 1832, India's cotton exports dropped by 92 per cent. In 1850, India was buying one quarter of Britain's cotton exports. All industrial products shared this fate.

The ruin of the traditional trades and crafts was the result of the British commercial policy. Restrictions were imposed upon Indians exporting to the West, while favours were granted to British exporters, who flooded the Indian markets.[4]

Modern industries began to develop during the second half of the 19th century but their progress was exceedingly slow and stunted. Up to the very end of the colonial period, the level of industry and technology remained low. During the 19th century, industrial development was confined to cotton and jute textiles. The iron and steel industry developed after 1907 while the sugar, cement and paper industries and a few engineering firms came up in the 1930s.

Still, as late as 1946, cotton and jute textiles accounted for nearly 30 per cent of all workers employed in factories.[5]

---

3. Bettleheim, Charles (1968). *India Independent*. London: Macgibbon & Kee. Ch. 3. pp.46-47.
4. Ibid.
5. Kumar, Dharma (ed.) (1984). *Cambridge Economic History of India* (CEHI). Vol. 2, Indian Reprint. Delhi: Orient Longman.

According to the Census of Manufacturing in 1951, which covered the larger enterprises, of the total value added in manufacturing, 56.8 per cent originated in cotton and jute textiles, 6.6 in sugar, 8.4 in engineering, 7.6 in steel, 4.1 in chemicals and 2.1 in cement.[6]

Consequently, even though modern industry developed quite fast after 1918—its rate of growth being 3.8 per cent per annum—it had little impact on the overall economic situation for its share in the national income at the end of British rule at 7.5 per cent was quite insignificant. In 1913, it was 3.8 per cent (Kumar, 1984). Modern industry perhaps barely compensated for the displacement of traditional handicrafts.[7]

In 1951, only about 2.3 per cent of the labour force was employed in modern industries. According to the Planning Commission, the number of persons engaged in processing and manufacturing (including artisanal industries) fell from 10.3 million in 1901 to 8.8 million in 1951, even though the population increased by nearly 40 per cent. Moreover, in 1951, of the total industrial output, at least 60 per cent was by the unorganised, small enterprises.[8]

A very important feature of India's industrial structure was the virtual absence of capital or producer's goods industry. Indian industries had to rely almost wholly on imported machinery and machine tools. In 1950, India met nearly 90 per cent of its need for machine tools through imports.

Similarly, modern banking and insurance were grossly underdeveloped. In 1946, class A and B banks had 4,644 offices or one office for 90,000 inhabitants. Underdeveloped banking and insurance meant that the Indian entrepreneurs could not mobilise the available capital. Also, British-controlled banks starved Indian industry of funds and favoured British-owned and controlled enterprises.

The growth of foreign trade and the rapid construction of railways which could have been the positive factors, unfortunately became instruments for the underdevelopment of the Indian economy. Under conditions of free trade, imports displaced indigenous handicrafts and artisanal industries and prevented the rise of new industries. In the absence of a simultaneous industrial revolution, railways had only

6. Chaudhuri, P. (1979). *The Indian Economy: Poverty and Development*. Delhi: Vikas Publishing House.
7. Jalan, Bimal (1992). *The Indian Economy: Problems and Prospects*. New Delhi: Viking. p.8.
8. Ibid: 10.

introduced a commercial revolution and further colonialised the Indian economy. The layout of railway lines and the railway freight rates policy promoted the export of raw materials and distribution of imported goods for they encouraged traffic with ports as against traffic between inland centres. The railways also did not have any forward or backward linkages. They had encouraged the steel and machine industry, not in India but in Britain. They had served as a social overhead not for Indian but British industry and their external economies were exported back to Britain.

Till the late 1930s, foreign capital dominated the industrial and financial fields and controlled the foreign trade network as also part of the internal trade that fed into exports.

It is important to keep in view, in this respect, that foreign investment rarely marked a transfer of capital to India from abroad. It was far less than the unilateral transfer of capital or the 'drain' from India. Three other characteristics of foreign investment were important:

1. It contributed to 'the guided underdevelopment' of India by concentrating on the production and export of raw materials and foodstuff.
2. It went into sectors which catered to foreign markets and not to India's home market.
3. "The multiplier effects in terms of income, employment, capital, technical knowledge, and growth of external economies of these investments were largely exported back to the developed countries."[9]

We may sum up India's economic profile at the time of Independence as: stagnating per capita national income, abysmal standard of living, stunted industrial development and the bulk of the population dependent on stagnating, low-productivity semi-feudal agriculture.[10]

The end result of colonial underdevelopment was the pauperisation of the people especially the peasantry and the small artisan. Extreme poverty, disease, hunger and starvation were the lot of the ordinary people. The frequent famines in some part or the other in the country was the order of the day. The last major famine in 1943 carried away nearly 3 million people in Bengal.

---

9. Ibid.
10. Ibid.

Some Positive Features

However, during the 1930s and 1940s, some major developments occurred in the Indian economy, which imparted it a certain strength and provided a base for post-Independence economic development. These positive features related to the development of a small but independent (Indian owned and controlled) industrial base and the rise of a substantial indigenous industrial capitalist class with an independent economic and financial base.

During and after the First World War, several consumer industries, such as textiles, sugar, soap, matches and paper, underwent a process of rapid import substitution, so that, by 1939, India was more or less self-sufficient in her major consumer goods requirements. There also occurred a certain diversification and sophistication in industrial production. Some intermediate capital goods industries such as iron and steel, cement, basic chemicals, metallurgy, and engineering also began to develop. In the 1930s, there was also a significant shift of capital from usury, trade and landlordism to industry. In other words, surplus was increasingly getting into the hands of those who would invest it.

By 1947, India also possessed a core of scientific and technical manpower. Unlike the 19th or early 20th century situation, when managerial as well as technical personnel were mostly foreign even in Indian-owned industries, now, most of them are Indian, exceptions being provided by a small number of highly specialised experts. India also had a small but quite well-developed skilled labour force both in consumer goods industries such as textiles and sugar and in the more sophisticated steel, metallurgical and engineering sectors.

Thus, at Indepedence, there was available, an indigenous entrepreneurial class which could be a major agency for carrying out the developmental plan perspective of the newly independent state unlike several African countries which at Independence although adopted grand plan schemes, often borrowing from the Indian blueprint, but lacked an indigenous agency to carry it through.

4

Economic Planning

Evolution and Strategy

Evolution of Planning

Just after the attainment of Independence, the Government of India set up the Planning Commission in 1950 to make an assessment of the material, capital and human resources of the country and to formulate a plan for its most effective and balanced utilisation of the country's resources.

The launching of the First Five Year Plan in April 1951 initiated a process of development aimed not merely at raising the standards of living of the people but also opening out to them new opportunities for a richer and more varied life. This was sought to be achieved by planning for growth and social justice.

The First Five Year Plan contains one of the clearest early formulations of the need for planning and of the State's role in it. Planning, it pointed out, involves "acceptance of a clearly defined set of objectives in terms of which to frame overall policies..., formulation of a strategy for promoting the realisation of the ends defined..., and working out a rational solution to problems—an attempt to coordinate means and ends."

At Independence, India was a predominantly agricultural economy, with more than 70 per cent of the population deriving its livelihood from agriculture, and just under 50 per cent of gross domestic product (GDP) originating in agriculture. The Nehruvian view—derived predominantly from Fabian socialism—endorsed the need for rapid development led by state economic activity and planning. The first few years after Independence were naturally focused predominantly on establishing institutions.[1]

Interestingly, the early planning documents regarded the chief barrier to accelerated growth as the then-low savings rate, and set out a 25-year perspective. The Planning Commission documents stated that a major challenge was to raise the savings rate to 20 per cent and concluded that, if that could be attained, India could achieve a satisfactory growth rate of 5 per cent annually.

Role of the State as Visualised in the 1950s[2]

At this time in the early 1950s, it was believed that the State could play a significant role both in raising the domestic rate of savings and in putting it to more productive use. Pre-industrial economies are predominantly rural and agricultural in character. They have land tenure systems in which a substantial part of the surplus over subsistence needs of cultivators and farm labourers gets appropriated by a small class of non-cultivating land owners and intermediaries (especially under the *zamindari* system and other feudal forms of tenure) and used for non-essential consumption. Abolition of such exploitative and socially wasteful land tenure systems could release surplus for productive investment. Land reforms combined with taxation of agriculture (either directly or indirectly by influencing prices of agricultural commodities relative to that of manufactures) are means of exploiting this potential. Both require strong State intervention.

Apart from its role in maintaining law and order, defining and protecting property rights, enforcement of contracts and the like, the State has to take the primary responsibility for providing elementary education, basic health care, safe drinking water and other facilities which are in the nature of basic needs in any civilised society and which, in addition, have beneficial effects on the general level of productivity. The latter effects—which are referred to as external economies—raise questions as to whether the market mechanism can secure the appropriate sharing of costs and benefits. Where externalities (beneficial or otherwise) happen to be significant, direct State intervention is necessary and justified.

Projects (e.g., road networks, major irrigation, steel plants, railways) which call for investments on a scale far beyond the capacity

---

1. Krueger, Anne O. (ed.) (2002). *Economic Policy Reforms and the Indian Economy*, ch.1. pp.10-11.
2. Kapila, Uma (ed.) (2019). *Indian Economy Since Independence.* 30rd edition, ch.2. New Delhi: Academic Foundation.

of individual investors and/or are in the nature of natural monopolies (e.g., public utilities) form another category where direct involvement of the State is deemed justifiable. In most cases even if the private sector is allowed to operate, the need for effective mechanisms to define and enforce standards, norms of efficiency, "fair" rate of return on investment and the like is universally accepted. All of this calls for State regulation, though not necessarily direct ownership and operation. During the early phases of Indian planning, given that indigenous industrial entrepreneurs were few in number and had relatively limited resources, the industrialists themselves favoured a large, direct role for the State in many of these activities.

The government can also help development by creating conditions which induce people to save more. Low rates of savings are of course partly a reflection of low levels of income. But those who have relatively large incomes may prefer to spend on current consumption rather than save when there are relatively limited opportunities for investments that offer attractive returns. A relatively stagnant, slow growing economy implies that profitable opportunities for investment are limited. State intervention can help expand such opportunities in several ways.

Public mobilisation of idle labour for creating productive assets especially roads, irrigation, land improvement, schools, rural hospitals, etc., increase the potential productivity of private resources and thereby create profitable private investment opportunities. Under certain conditions, increased public expenditure can enlarge the scope for profitable investment by creating additional demand for goods and services. Both these effects are likely to be considerably strengthened if there is a coordinated programme of investments for 'balanced development' ensuring that supplies of key inputs and services grow in step with the demand for them. This aspect is particularly important in the case of activities which are closely inter-related. With a coordinated programme, the risks of shortages or excesses of particular goods or services are substantially reduced. Reduced risks induce business to invest more.

Finally, strong State intervention is a logical corollary of the goals of social justice and preventing concentration of power which have been explicitly incorporated among the Directive Principles of State Policy in the Constitution. In addition, the Directive Principles lay emphasis on:

1. Securing to all citizens the right to an adequate means of livelihood;

2. Ensuring that distribution of ownership and control of material resources is regulated in a manner which best serves the common good;
3. Preventing the concentration of wealth and means of production; and
4. Protecting children from being forced to work or being exploited on account of economic necessity.

Though these provisions lacked legal sanction, they do reflect the importance attached to 'social justice' and have shaped the scope and nature of State intervention.

In his monumental work, *The Discovery of India* (1946), Nehru offers the following fascinating account of the thinking behind the committee's decision in favour of a growth-centred strategy. The ideas developed by the planning committee eventually influenced the design of India's development plans. Growth remained the central (though not exclusive, since redistribution was regarded as a subsidiary) element in the strategy, with poverty alleviation and equity prominently figuring as the true goals. For example, the First Five-Year Plan, spanning 1951-52 to 1955-56, stated at the outset: 'The urge for economic and social change under present conditions comes from the fact of poverty and of inequalities in income, wealth and opportunity. The elimination of poverty cannot, obviously, be achieved merely by redistributing existing wealth. Nor can a programme aiming only at raising production remove existing inequalities. The two have to be considered together; only a simultaneous advance along both these lines can create the conditions in which the community can put forth its best efforts for promoting development' (Bhagwati and Panagariya, 2012).[3]

Altogether, as the First Plan puts it, whether one thinks of the problem of capital formation or of the introduction of new techniques or of the extension of social services or of the overall realignment of the productive forces and class relationships in society, one inevitably comes to the conclusion that a rapid expansion of the economic and social responsibilities of the State will alone be capable of satisfying the legitimate expectations of the people. This need not involve complete nationalisation of the means of production or elimination of private agencies in agriculture or business and industry. It does

---

3. Bhagwati, Jagdish and Arvind Panagariya (2012). *India's Tryst with Destiny: Debunking Myths that Undermine Progress and Addressing New Challenges*. New Delhi: Collins Business.

however mean a progressive widening of the public sector and a reorientation of the private sector to the needs of a planned economy (First Five Year Plan).

Early Experience with Five Year Plans

The First Five Year Plan (1951-52 to 1955-56) was little more than a collection of ongoing public investment projects, most of which were taken from the post-War reconstruction programme evolved before Independence. The Plan aimed at a general increase in the standard of living and also emphasised wider objectives such as full employment and removal of inequalities, but there was no specific analytically directed strategy for development.[4]

The successful completion of the modest first Plan was followed by a very ambitious Second Five Year Plan. The Plan's author, P.C. Mahalanobis, provided an analytical foundation for it with a closed-economy growth model with two sectors, one of which produced consumer goods and the other investment goods, with sector-specific capital as the only factor of production.

The fundamental insight of this model was that the greater the proportion of investment devoted to increasing the capacity of the investment-goods sector, the faster the long-run growth in consumption and investment. In the strategy based on this model, rapid long-run growth was to be achieved without much sacrifice of short-run consumption by concentrating scarce investment in expanding capital goods-producing (and intermediate goods-producing) heavy industry. Current consumption demand was to be met by employing abundant labour resources to manufacture consumer goods using labour-intensive methods that required little capital (Srinivasan and Tendulkar, 2003).

The Second Plan underlined the political constraints on any radical solutions to redressing inequalities and re-emphasised rapid growth and diversification of economic activity through industrialisation as essential for achieving and maintaining full employment at a rising level of productivity. It went on to define a coherent overall strategy whose central elements included stepping up the rate of investment (but at a more moderate pace than envisaged in the first plan) and a conscious policy of developing an indigenous heavy industry base (comprising metallurgical, chemical and machine building industries) to lay the

4. Ahluwalia, Montek Singh (2012). "Planning", in Kaushik Basu and Annemie Maertens (ed.), *The New Oxford Companion to Economics in India*, Vol.II. Delhi: OUP.

foundation for accelerated self-reliant growth, with a leading role for the public sector. Accordingly, the 1956 Industrial Policy Resolution emphasised that the state must play a progressive role in the development of industries and as the Resolution puts it, "the adoption of socialist pattern of society as the national objective, as well as the need for planned and rapid development, require that all industries of basic and strategic importance, or in the nature of public utility services, should be in the public sector. Other industries which are essential and require investment on a scale which only the State, in present circumstances, could provide, have also to be in the public sector. The State has, therefore, to assume direct responsibility for the future development of industries over a wider area." The encouragement of labour-intensive forms of producing mass consumer goods was seen to be a potentially important way of reconciling the conflict between emphasis on heavy industry (which would generate faster growth of income and employment in the long run) and the need to generate adequate jobs for the currently unemployed and underemployed in the transitional period.

The dominant growth oriented Mahalanobis import substitution based industrialisation strategy of the Second Plan was continued in the Third Plan. However, the relatively greater emphasis on the long-term growth in an import-substitution oriented strategy required a modification in the industrialisation process. This consisted of a strong accent on the creation of domestic capacity in the direction of producing capital goods to produce more capital goods. In this strategy, the public sector was expected to play a dual role of: (a) promoting the growth of infrastructural facilities and the creation of capacity in the basic and heavy industries, and (b) reducing the concentration of economic power through the expansion of public ownership of means of production.

An attempt was made with a reasonable success in implementing the long-term growth maximising Mahalanobis strategy during the Second and the Third Five Year Plans. There was, as a result, a considerable acceleration in public sector investment in infrastructure (roads, railways, major and medium irrigation) and indirectly productive investments in universal intermediates like steel, coal, power and heavy electrical machinery. Although the encouragement to the cottage, village and small scale industries as a means of providing employment as well as expanding the supplies of consumer goods were conceived as part of this strategy, very little was achieved in this regard. Similar was the fate in regard to the policies towards the reduction of inequalities.

Planning methodology in the 1960s was dominated by two considerations (Ahluwalia, 2012).[5] The first was the perception that certain sectors were of strategic importance and investment resources must be consciously directed towards expanding capacity in these sectors instead of responding to market forces, which were more likely to draw investment into 'non priority sectors' such as consumer goods. The second consideration dominating Indian planning methodology was the perceived need to deal with scarcity of foreign exchange. Export pessimism led to unwillingness to deal with foreign exchange scarcity by depreciating the exchange rate. Instead, a two-fold approach was adopted of mobilising external assistance to meet foreign exchange needs and rationing scarce foreign exchange by restricting import demand through import licensing. Since import licences were not given if domestic production capacity had been set up, it gave tailer-made protection to domestic industry not surprisingly the industrial structure that emerged was high cost and highly inefficient.

As rightly pointed out by Kaushik Basu, "The actual policy regime that India followed in its early days of independence was a mixture of the two competing (and almost contradictory) visions. A Soviet-style planning system was developed, but without the state having a monopoly of control over the resources. Capitalism was allowed to flourish, but a large bureaucracy was nurtured. Huge investments were made in basic industries, but at the same time several sectors were protected as belonging to the small-scale sector. Capitalism was criticised but it was also relied upon. Socialism was never practiced, but the rhetoric of socialism was the norm. A burgeoning bureaucracy became the surrogate for socialism."[6]

While India's planning strategy in the 1960s clearly emphasised rapid growth, it did not succeed in generating growth at the level targeted. It can also be argued that it did not pay sufficient attention to examining why growth targets were not being achieved and whether changes in economic policies were needed to achieve the stated objectives. There was constant focus on the need for higher levels of investment, especially in the public sector, but not enough attention was paid to factors affecting the efficiency of investment (Ahluwalia, 2012).

Thus, the first phase spanning roughly over the first three Five Year Plan periods was characterised by fairly sustained growth in per capita

5. Ibid
6. Basu, Kaushik (ed.) (2004). "The Indian Economy: Up to 1991 and Since", in *India's Emerging Economy: Performance and Prospects in the 1990s and Beyond.* ch.1. Oxford University Press.

incomes, distinct acceleration in public sector investment and in the growth of industrial output. This phase was dominated by the growth-oriented development strategy.

TABLE – 4.1

Growth Targets and Achievements

(% per year)

		Target	*Actual*
1.	First Plan (1951-1956)	2.1	3.6
2.	Second Plan ((1956-1961)	4.5	4.2
3.	Third Plan (1961-1966)	5.6	2.7
4.	Fourth Plan (1969-1974)	5.7	2.1
5.	Fifth Plan (1974-1979)	4.4	4.8
6.	Sixth Plan (1980-1985)	5.2	5.5
7.	Seventh Plan (1985-1990)	5.0	6.0
8.	Eighth Plan (1992-1997)	5.6	6.7
9.	Ninth Plan (1997-2002)	6.5	5.7
10.	Tenth Plan (2002-2007)	8.0	7.1

Note: The growth targets for the first three plans were set with respect to national income. In the Fourth Plan it was net domestic product. In all Plans thereafter it has been gross domestic product at factor cost.

Source: Ahluwalia, Montek Singh (2012). "Planning", in Kaushik Basu and Annemie Maertens (ed.), *The New Oxford Companion to Economics in India*, Vol.II. Delhi: OUP.

Changing Perceptions

This atmosphere changed dramatically after the drought and the foreign exchange crisis of the mid-sixties. The sudden increase in defence expenditure consequent to the armed conflicts with China and Pakistan and the levelling-off of foreign aid, all in the short span of three years (1962-1965), put the economy under severe strain. A crisis occurred when two consecutive droughts hit the country in 1966 and 1967 and real GDP declined in absolute terms.

The sharp deterioration of the economic situation and the security environment highlighted two main weaknesses of the existing strategy, namely, the relative neglect of agriculture and a critical dependence on foreign aid.

The two-year period 1965 and 1966 witnessed the worst drought in recent memory and consequent famines in large parts of north India. At the same time, all aid was cut off to India by the donor countries on account of the Indo-Pakistan War of 1965, including food aid. The consequence was a virtual collapse of the economy, and recourse had to be taken to extraordinary financing from the International Monetary Fund (IMF) and the World Bank, which were accompanied by stiff conditionalities.

This traumatic experience brought food security into the forefront of our policy imperatives, which was further buttressed by the observation that sustained industrialisation was not possible without adequate provision of wage-goods. The Fourth Plan, conceived after three years of Plan holiday, therefore, had to have food security as its centrepiece.

The Fifth Plan recognised that growth and industrialisation would not necessarily improve the living conditions of the people, particularly the poor. The concepts of "minimum needs" and directed anti-poverty programmes were innovations of this Plan, whatever may have been the success achieved in implementing them effectively. The Fifth Plan also marks the beginning of a period of steady increase in the growth rate of the economy, which continued right through to the Eighth Plan.

The Sixth Plan for the first time recognised that the success of the Mahalanobis heavy industrialisation strategy in raising the savings rate of the country had created a situation where excess capacities were becoming evident in certain industries. A shift in the pattern of industrialisation, with lower emphasis on heavy industries and more on infrastructure, begins here. The Seventh Plan represents the culmination of this shift. In perspective, it may justifiably be termed as the infrastructure plan. It was also during this period that a reappraisal of the import-substitution strategy begins, and a gradual liberalisation of the Indian economy is initiated.

The Eighth Plan was overtaken by the crisis of 1991, and the economic reforms that came in its wake. The dramatic events and policy initiatives of the two-year plan holiday period between 1990 and 1992 demanded a full reappraisal of the planning methodology, and the Eighth Plan represents the first efforts at planning for a market-oriented economy.

Jean Drèze and Amartya Sen (1995)[7] pointed out, "Four decades of allegedly 'interventionist' planning did little to make the country literate, provide a wide-based health service, achieve comprehensive land reforms, or end the rampant social inequalities that blight the material prospects of the underprivileged."

Thus, the Eighth Five Year Plan documents states that, "in the background of our experience of planning for development over the last forty years and under the strong imperatives for change as they have emerged now, a question is generally asked: what will be the role of planning in future?"

Role of Planning in a Market Economy

Can there be a role for centralised planning in a market economy such as India's after liberalisation? The question was debated at some length in the wake of the reforms launched in the nineties to liberate the economy from licensing and controls. It was realised that after liberalisation, planning in the way it was practised in the first four decades after Independence was no longer tenable. In due recognition of this reality, the Eighth Plan (1992-1997), the first to come out after the initiation of the reforms, stated in its preface: "The Plan is indicative in nature". That planning now has to be primarily indicative and the state can at best be a facilitator for private enterprise was reiterated in the two plans that followed, the Ninth and the Tenth.

Following liberalisation, the role of the public sector in the Indian economy has considerably shrunk and is shrinking further. Three-fourths of investments in the economy are now flowing from the private sector. Financial constraints emanating from the fiscal responsibility and budget management law coupled with inefficiency and waste in service deliveries have led to demand for the state to vacate even areas hitherto regarded as the responsibility of the government, like education and health. "Public-private partnership" or PPP is now emerging as the preferred vehicle for initiatives in development, wherever possible. Given this background can or should there be any role for planning? (Bagchi, 2007).[8]

That planning can be helpful in a market economy by providing "indication, coordination and prescription" has been acknowledged

---

7. Drèze, Jean and Amartya Sen (1995). *India's Economic Development and Social Opportunity*. Oxford: Clarendon Press.
8. Bagchi, Amaresh (2007). "Role of Planning Commission in the New Indian Economy: Case for a Review", *Economic and Political Weekly*, November 3-9.

even in countries avowedly market-oriented, like Korea and France (Kuznets, 1990). However there can be no gain-saying that planning in a largely market-driven economy cannot proceed on the same footing as in an economy that is heavily controlled by the state. In the Indian context, this implies that there has to be a clear shift in the focus of planning now as compared to the past.

Redefining the Role of State

The Approach Paper to the Tenth Five Year Plan stated that an important aspect of the redefinition of strategy that is needed relates to the role of Government. It is now generally recognised that Government in the past tended to take on too many responsibilities, imposing severe strains on its limited financial and administrative capabilities and also stifling individual initiative. An all pervasive government role may have appeared necessary at a stage where private sector capabilities were undeveloped, but the situation has changed dramatically in this respect. India now has a strong and vibrant private sector. The public sector is much less dominant than it used to be in many critical sectors and its relative position is likely to decline further as government ownership in many existing public sector organisations is expected to decline to a minority. It is clear that industrial growth in future will depend largely upon the performance of the private sector and our policies must therefore, provide an environment which is conducive to such growth.

This is not to say that Government has no role to play or only a minimalist role, in promoting development. On the contrary, government has a very important role but a different one from that envisaged in the past. There are many areas, e.g., the social sectors, where its role will clearly have to increase. There are other areas, e.g., infrastructure development, where gaps are large and private sector cannot be expected to step in significantly. In these areas, the role of government may have to be restructured. It will have to increase in some areas of infrastructure development which are unlikely to attract private investment e.g., rural infrastructure and road development. In others e.g., telecommunications, power, ports, etc., the private sector can play a much larger role, provided an appropriate policy framework is in place. Here, the role of the Government needs to change to facilitate such investment as much as possible while still remaining a public sector service provider for quite some time. In all these areas, the role of government as a regulatory ensuring a fair deal for consumers, transparency and accountability, and a level playing field is also extremely important.

Economic planning, according to Ahluwalia (2012), must also pay much greater attention in future to the role of the government in the social sector—health and education—especially in rural areas. India lags behind other developing countries in this respect and corrective steps are urgently needed in this area. Since these are areas where the agencies responsible for delivering services are those of state governments, much of the planning for service delivery must necessarily shift to states and local governments.

According to Kaushik Basu, "There is need now for India to move more strongly forward with the reforms, allow private firms to enter sectors earlier kept reserved for state-owned enterprises (this is more important than privatisation), open the economy further, and, in particular, allow Indian companies to go for larger acquisitions abroad. But one must be aware that there are no panaceas in economic policy. One has to be prepared for flexibility, to experiment with policy but be ready to adjust, alter, and on occasion even do a U-turn, depending on the evidence coming in. To stick with one policy, unbendingly, is to make the same mistake of policy stubbornness that led India to its present predicament."[9]

In the Foreword to the Planning Commission's Macro-Modelling for the Eleventh Five Year Plan (2009), Montek Ahluwalia remarks, "The transition of the Indian economy from a 'planned' economy to a more 'market-based economy', and one more integrated with the rest of the world, has seen the role of planning undergoing a change both in terms of priorities as well as instruments. With the growth of a fairly sophisticated private sector with demonstrable entrepreneurial capacity it is felt that government need not try to produce products that can be produced just as well by the market, instead it should devote its scarce resources to providing public goods including especially educational and health services and programmes for social inclusion. Infrastructure development is another priority area since lack of infrastructure is a crucial constraint on the growth of the economy. The role of the government in infrastructure development is obviously critical. The shift to a more open market economy has also created the need to expand modelling capacity to reflect the features of openness including the macroeconomic implications of openness. For all these reasons, the

9. Basu (2004). *op.cit. no. 6.*

modelling framework needed to undergo a change from being more deterministic and disaggregated to being more aggregative and indicative."[10]

Relevance of Planning Commission

According to Rangarajan,

> There is a need to evaluate and restructure every organisation as circumstances change and the Planning Commission is no exception. Restructuring an organisation can be of two types. One approach takes the functions of the organisation as a given and proceeds to restructure it to make it more effective to fulfil those functions. The second approach is more fundamental. It questions the very basis of the organisation and focusses on the relevance of the basic functions it has been performing.

Times have changed. In the post-liberalisation period, the concept of planning itself has undergone a change. We have moved, at best, to an era of indicative planning. The blend of public and private investment has tilted in favour of the private sector. While planning of the type we had in the first five decades after Independence has no relevance, an organisation to look at the basic issues confronting the economy, and preparing a broad framework on how long-term issues can be resolved, is still a necessity.

While the state may play a diminishing role, it still plays a critical role in the economy. In the infrastructure sector, it still has a dominant role. If the centre and states agree on a broad framework through discussions, it would facilitate the adoption of better policies. Such an organisation will be something more than a think tank. Through a broad range of discussions, it should prepare a road map which will be acceptable to both the centre and the states. Thus, the task of preparing a blueprint for the country over a certain period is essential and should continue to be performed. Also, there are issues which cut across ministries, such as energy, transport, water or environment. In terms of policy formulation, this commission can take a holistic view and offer advice.

As we move ahead, there are critical problems facing the economy. Ensuring a faster rate of economic growth with equity is not an easy

---

10. Planning Commission (2009). *Macro-Modelling for the Eleventh Five Year Plan of India*, edited by Kirit S. Parikh. Foreword by Montek Singh Ahluwalia. New Delhi: Academic Foundation.

task. Environmental considerations have emerged as a serious concern. Therefore, an integrated look at the problems faced by the country is very much required. Thus, the need for an organisation for formulating ideas on how to shape the economy over a certain time frame will be helpful. This task, the newly formed NITI Aayog is expected to do.

NITI Aayog: Role and Functions[11]

Quoting from the Three Year Action Agenda 2017-18 to 2019-20:

> On 1st January 2015, the NITI Aayog came into existence as the government's premier thinktank. Subsequently, PMO advised the NITI Aayog to prepare a Fifteen Year Vision, Seven Year Strategy and Three Year Action Agenda documents. Accordingly, the present document is being published to recommend policy changes and programmes for action during the years 2017-18 to 2019-20, the last three years of the Fourteenth Finance Commission. A second document containing the Fifteen Year Vision and Seven Year Strategy is currently under preparation at the NITI Aayog.
>
> The vision, strategy and action agenda exercise represents a departure from the Five Year Plan process, followed with a handful of discontinuities until the fiscal year 2016-17. The 12th Five Year Plan was the last of these plans. It has been felt that with an increasingly open and liberalised economy, we needed to rethink the tools and approaches to conceptualising the development process. It is hoped that the proposed shift represents an important step in this direction. The Vision, Strategy and Action Agenda framework will allow us to better align the development strategy with the changed reality of India.

The Three Year Action Agenda according to NITI Aayog offers ambitious proposals for policy changes within a relatively short period. It is understood that while some may be fully implemented during the three-year period, implementation of others would continue into the subsequent years. Where relevant, we have included possible actions by the states to complement the efforts of the Centre.

The cabinet resolution lists 13 different tasks to NITI Aayog which may be grouped under four major heads, namely: (i) fostering cooperative federalism by providing structured support to states on a continuous basis; (ii) formulation of a strategic vision and long-term policies and programme framework both for the macroeconomy and for

11. Government of India, NITI Aayog (2017). Three Year Action Agenda 2017-18 to 2019-20 (April).

different sectors; (iii) acting as a knowledge and innovation hub and providing research inputs by undertaking and accessing globally available research; and (iv) providing a platform for interdepartmental coordination.

Thus, the effectiveness of NITI will depend on how it charts out a course for itself. Despite the claims of a marked departure from the past, the institution has to function in the prevailing milieu and deal with the burden of legacy. The important question is whether the Aayog will have influence when it does not have the power to give grants and when it does not have the powers to make plan allocations to different ministries and departments.

The legacy issues do not end merely with the abolition of the Planning Commission. There are parallel institutions in the states and it is important to transform them to meet the new requirements. Similarly, the Constitution requires the establishment of district planning committees and metropolitan planning committees. Their role in the new environment needs to be specified. Although the cabinet resolution states that NITI Aayog will facilitate grass roots planning, how exactly this will be carried forward needs to be seen.[12]

The success of the institution in achieving interministerial, interdepartmental coordination will depend on the trust and cooperation it receives from them and the harmony with which the Aayog and various ministries work. There could be tensions between the technocrats in the Aayog and various ministers on the one hand, and between the technocrats and bureaucrats on the other. There is also the danger of bureaucratisation of the Aayog. Similarly, success in fostering cooperative federalism will depend on the trust of and cooperation from the states. In particular, the Aayog will have a tremendous task of shaping the character and charting a course to make it an important institution in Indian federal polity to transform India.[13]

---

12. Rao, M. Govinda (2015). "Role and Functions of NITI Aayog", *Economic and Political Weekly* (4), January 24.
13. Ibid

5

Economic Reforms and Liberalisation

Debate on Liberalisation

The most common connotation of the term liberalisation when used in the context of economic policy is that of reducing government regulation of economic activity and the space for state intervention (except in the all-important matter of guaranteeing private property rights) and allowing for the unfettered operation of market forces in determining economic processes.

According to Deepak Nayyar,

> Economic liberalisation is about bringing market prices closer to efficiency prices and allowing individuals, households or firms more freedom to make economic decisions. This means a reduced role for the State. But co-ordinating the market through rules that govern may in turn imply a need for more state intervention somewhere and different forms of State intervention elsewhere in the pursuit of development objectives. The belief that markets know best is associated with an unstated presumption that State intervention is not needed or is counterproductive in the process of industrialisation. Experience from the second half of the twentieth century suggests that the guiding and the supportive role of the State has been at the foundation of successful development among late industrialisers. Even among the East Asian countries, which are often cited as success stories that depict the magic of the market place, the visible hand of the State is much more in evidence than the invisible hand of the market. In the earlier stages of industrialisation, State intervention creates the conditions for the development of industrial capitalism by establishing a physical infrastructure through government investment, developing human resources through education or facilitating

> institutional change through agrarian reform. In the later stages of industrialisation, State intervention is functional or strategic rather than conducive but remains crucial.[1]

The recent focus on economic liberalisation, in India as well as in other developing and formerly socialist countries, has created the widespread impression that this is a qualitatively new approach. Indeed, the arguments in favour of the market-determination of economic processes and resource allocation, and the counter-arguments based on notions of market failure or inadequacy of markets in meeting social goals, are almost as old as the discipline of economics.[2]

ECONOMIC REFORMS

The Background

After pursuing an inward-looking development strategy with the state assuming an important role for more than four decades, India decided to take a historic step of changing tracks in 1991. It embarked on a comprehensive reform of the economy to widen and deepen its integration with the world economy as a part of structural adjustment. There seems to be a general consensus on the desirability of reforms to dismantle the bureaucratic regulatory apparatus evolved over the years that may have outlived its utility. However, there has been considerable debate on the contents of the reform package, their sequencing and the pace, their implementation and their impact. The initial hesitant steps in the direction of liberalisation were taken in the 1980s but the reform story really begins with the balance of payments (BoP) crisis of 1991.

This crisis was a combined effect of a number of events coinciding. These included collapse of the Soviet Union that had emerged as India's major trading partner. The Gulf War that erupted in January 1991 worsened the BoP crisis, not only with rising oil prices but also by causing a virtual stoppage of remittances from Indian workers in the Gulf. These events coupled with political uncertainty prevailing in the country led international credit rating agencies to lower India's rating both for short- and long-term borrowings. The erosion of international confidence in the Indian economy not only made borrowings in

---

1. Nayyar, Deepak (1996). "Economic Liberalisation in India: Analytics, Experience and Lessons", *R.C. Dutt Lectures on Political Economy*, 1993. New Delhi: Orient Longman.
2. Ghosh, Jayati (1998). "Liberalisation Debates", in Terence J. Byers (ed.), *The Indian Economy: Major Debates since Independence*. Delhi: Oxford University Press.

international markets difficult but also led to outflow of deposits of non-resident Indians with Indian banks. These developments together brought the country to the verge of default with respect to external payments liability which could be averted by resorting to borrowings from the IMF under the standby arrangements and Foreign Currency Assets (FCA) and by mortgaging gold to the Bank of England. This was complemented by emergency measures to restrict imports.

The Macroeconomic Crisis

The macroeconomic crisis was precipitated mainly by the growth of the public spending through the 1980s that increased the budget deficit as a proportion of our gross national product (GNP), although external shocks played a contributory role.

The state of our public finances had indeed reached crisis proportions by the end of the 1980s. The public debt-to-GNP ratio increased through the 1980s, going up to almost 60 per cent at the end of the decade, implying a doubling of the ratio at the end of the previous decade. As is now well-known, the proximate reasons for this situation were the failure of the public sector to generate investible resources and the explosive growth of governmental current spending that saw the budget deficit as a proportion of gross domestic product (GDP) rising from 6.4 to 9 per cent during the 1980s.

According to Bhagwati and Srinivasan (1993),[3] the question must be addressed: Did the microeconomic inefficiencies have anything to do with this, or was 'profligacy' the true, final and sole cause of the macroeconomic crisis? To them, it was the former.

The failure of the public sector enterprises to generate profits (and hence their contribution to the macro crisis) is a microeconomic efficiency failure. Because these enterprises have dominated the provision of infrastructure and critical intermediates, their inefficiency has led to downstream inefficiencies in a multiplier fashion. Then again, the restrictive trade and industrial licensing framework, for instance, led to serious loss of efficiency by reducing the scale of output, eliminating effective competition and creating bottlenecks. The result was to reduce the returns from our investments and our growth rate. In turn, surely the revenues raised from the economy, for any given tax rates, were adversely affected, the political ability to raise tax rates in

---

3. Bhagwati, Jagdish and T.N. Srinivasan (1993). *India's Economic Reforms*. Ministry of Finance, Government of India, New Delhi.

a situation of slowly growing incomes was impaired, and the necessity to undertake budgetary expenditures to support the creation of public sector jobs and for consumption was also increased—all factors contributing to the budget deficit crisis.

The rise in foreign borrowing was a major component of the fiscal crisis, reflecting in turn the excess of domestic expenditure over income. Thus, as evident from the external public sector debt (and not just the domestic public sector debt) increased greatly as a proportion of GNP during the 1980s, rising to 21 per cent by 1987-88. This increase in external indebtedness meant that debt service as a proportion of exports increased more than threefold to 32 per cent in 1996-97 from 1980-81.

The macro imbalance, fueled by the budget deficit and financed by the external borrowings and the decumulation of reserves, was accompanied by accelerated inflation to double-digit levels.

Given the magnitude of the fiscal and BoP problems, there can be no question about the need for structural adjustment. But there were questions about its context as well as viewing it primarily as a means of liberalisation and opening of the economy.

Rationale for the Reforms

As is now well understood, India faced a macroeconomic crisis that required immediate attention when Prime Minister Rao took office. This crisis had to be attended to forthwith. But, as in many South American countries in the 1980s, the macroeconomic crisis became also the occasion for undertaking substantial microeconomic (or what are sometimes called 'structural') reforms that had been long overdue.

In fact, these structural reforms were necessary because we had evidently failed to generate adequate rates of growth of income and of per capita income. Not merely did India's weak performance in this regard fall below her own expectations as defined in the earlier plans, it also put India behind many other developing countries, and way behind the super performers in the Far East. In fact, India had become marginalised in the world economy. Many of our economic policies were also seen as wittingly foolish, senseless bureaucratic controls on production and investment. Perhaps the most compelling reason for reforms was then to clean the house and to restore India eventually to the position of respect in the world economy and polity that she enjoyed during the years of Prime Minister Nehru's stewardship (Bhagwati and Srinivasan, 1993).

Macroeconomic Reforms

The reform package outlined by Manmohan Singh in 1991 had three distinct components:

1. Fiscal stabilisation to check the growing fiscal deficit and contain it at a much lower level in such a manner that public investments in basic social and economic infrastructure could be substantially stepped up without generating inflationary pressures.
2. Internal liberalisation to increase competitive pressures, leaving enterprises free to make their production and investment decisions in the light of market conditions and enlarging the scope and freedom for private enterprise.
3. Integration with the global economy by removing controls on foreign trade and exchange rates, lowering tariffs and rationalising their structure and substantially relaxing regulations regarding external capital flows and a proactive policy for attracting foreign direct investment (FDI). This package, it was claimed, would release powerful growth impulses and lift the economy to a high growth trajectory comparable to that of east Asia. This view prevailed and has come to be accepted by successive governments since.[4]

The policy changes brought into force since July 1991 fall broadly into two categories. The first set of measures is part of what is normally known as stabilisation policy. The second set of measures come under the category of structural reform policies. As Rangarajan[5] rightly points out, while the stabilisation policies were intended to correct the lapses and put the house in order in the short term, the structural reform policies were intended to accelerate economic growth over the medium term. Structural reform policies cannot succeed unless a degree of stabilisation has been brought about. But stabilisation by itself will not be adequate unless structural reforms are undertaken to avoid the recurrence of the problems faced in the recent period.

Structural Reforms

Structural reforms were broadly in the area of industrial licencing and regulation, foreign trade and investment, and the financial sector.

---

4. Vaidyanathan, A. (2003). *India's Economic Reforms and Development.* New Delhi: Academic Foundation. pp.17-18.
5. Rangarajan, C. (2002). "The New Economic Policy and the Role of the State", in Uma Kapila (ed.), *Indian Economy Since Independence* (2002-03 edition). New Delhi: Academic Foundation.

Industrial Policy Reforms

Although some liberalisation and streamlining of the industrial policy had been effected in the mid-1980s, the New Industrial Policy (NIP) announced on 24 July 1991 and subsequent amendments brought far-reaching changes in the policy regime governing industrial investments. The NIP dismantled the industrial licensing (or approval) system that regulated the industrial investments in the country by abolishing the requirement of obtaining an industrial licence from the government in all except five specified industries. These specified industries need to be regulated in view of environmental hazards, national security or social well-being considerations.

NIP has thrown open new industries and services to private including foreign private sector by pruning the list of 'Industries Reserved for the Public Sector.' Only two industries are now reserved for exclusive development by public sector; these are atomic energy and railway transport considered sensitive from national security point of view. Thus, a large number of industries and services including infrastructure such as telecommunication, roads, ports, power generation, petroleum refining have become accessible to the private sector. Considering a large requirements of funds for infrastructure, 100 per cent FDI has been allowed in all infrastructure sectors. The emphasis has been on public-private partnership (PPP) as one of the preferred modes for infrastructure project implementation.

In order to instil healthy competition amongst producers, the list of items reserved for the small-scale sector is reviewed from time to time. The definition of small-scale industry (SSI) has been changed to facilitate modernisation and now only 20 items are reserved for the small-scale sector (2014). FDI up to 100 per cent is allowed under the automatic route in most sectors, with a few exceptions. Manufacturers other than small-scale ones may also manufacture these items provided they undertake an export obligation of 50 per cent of the annual production. NIP accords a much more liberal attitude to FDIs than ever in post-Independence India. A more favourable treatment is also accorded to non-resident Indian (NRI) investors who are allowed up to 100 per cent ownership priority industries.

In the area of foreign investment, the policy statement abolished the threshold of 40 per cent on foreign equity investment. The concept of automatic approval was introduced whereby the Reserve Bank of India was empowered to approve equity investment up to 51 per cent in the 34 'priority' industries traditionally called 'appendix I' industries and now listed in annex III of the new policy. In subsequent years, this policy was considerably liberalised, with automatic approval made available to almost all industries except those subject to public sector monopoly and industrial licensing. Within the context of the NIP, successive governments have steadily opened the Indian economy to foreign investors. Currently, the system operates on a negative list approach such that unless the official DFI policy explicitly spells out specific restrictions, no restriction applies. The current regime prohibits DFI in only four sectors: retail trading (except single-brand product retailing), atomic energy, the lottery business, and betting and other forms of gambling.[6]

In the budget speech 2014-15, the Finance Minister Arun Jaitley clarifying the FDI policy states, the policy of the NDA Government is to promote FDI selectively in sectors where it helps the larger interest of the Indian Economy. FDI in several sectors is an additionality of resource which helps in promoting domestic manufacture and job creation. India today needs a boost for job creation. Our manufacturing sector in particular needs a push for job creation.

Currently FDI in defence manufacturing is permitted up to 26 per cent. The 2014-15 budget raised it to 49 per cent with full Indian management and control through the Foreign Investment Promotion Board (FIPB) route. Similarly the composite cap in the Insurance sector is proposed to be increased up to 49 per cent from the current level of 26 per cent, with full Indian management and control, through the FIPB route.

FDI in the manufacturing sector is today on the automatic route. The manufacturing units will be allowed to sell its products through retail including E-commerce platforms without any additional approval.

A phased programme of disinvestment of public ownership in public sector corporations has been launched. A Disinvestment Commission followed by Department of Disinvestment was set up to make recommendations on the phasing of the disinvestments.

The outward investments by Indian enterprises were also liberalised and proposals fulfilling certain norms could now be granted automatic approval.

Trade Policy Reforms

A major reform of trade policy regime has been effected since 1991. The import licensing system has been dismantled. All non-tariff barriers

6. Panagariya, Arvind (2008). *India: The Emerging Giant*. New Delhi: Oxford University Press. p.104.

(NTBs) have been phased out from all tradables except consumer goods. In spite of stiff resistance from rich industrialists on cutting tariffs, all finance ministers starting from Manmohan Singh in 1991, P. Chidambaram, Yashwant Sinha, Jaswant Singh and again P. Chidambaram forcefully fought on the subject of tariff, and the tariffs have indeed been substantially done away with. Besides, India has also undertaken a major commitment to liberalise its trade regime under WTO Agreement.

Tariffs

Tariffs have come down from a peak rate of 150 per cent in 1990 to a peak non-agricultural rate of 5.8 per cent in 2009-10. Agricultural tariffs remained high till 2007-08 at 19.3 per cent but have fallen drastically in 2008-09 to 4.2 per cent in (MTA 2007-12) and 2.5 per cent in 2009-10. The reduction in tariffs on non-agricultural products has played an important role in the convergence of India's inflation rate to global inflation rates and needs to continue.

As the manufacturing sector is under stress due to a variety of reasons, in the budget 2015-16, the basic customs duties have been reduced from 10 per cent to 2.5 per cent and in some cases, from 5 per cent to nil of specified inputs from manufacturing sector.

Removal of Quantitative Restrictions (QRs)

The process of removal of import restrictions, which began in 1991, has been completed in a phased manner.

Indian Customs Single Window Project: 2014-15

It is also proposed in the Budget 2014-15 to implement the project to facilitate trade. Required permissions, if any, from other regulatory agencies would be obtained online without the trader having to approach these agencies. This would reduce interface with governmental agencies, dwell time and the cost of doing business.

To expedite the process of disposal of appeals, amendments have been proposed in the Customs and Central Excise Acts with a view to freeing appellate authorities from hearing stay applications and to take up regular appeals for final disposal.

Exchange Rate Reforms

The rupee was devalued twice in July 1991 leading to a 20 per cent depreciation in its value. The partial convertibility of rupee on the trade account was announced in the 1992-1993 budget that was subsequently broadened to full convertibility on current account by August 1994.

With respect to capital account liberalisation, India embarked on a gradual and well-sequenced opening up of the capital account. The capital account is virtually free for non-residents and resident corporates with some restrictions on financial institutions and higher restrictions on resident individuals.

Financial Sector Reforms

In January 1993, a package of financial sector reforms was announced that included permission to new private sector banks including foreign joint ventures. The government has also established a policy regime for functioning of private non-banking finance companies (NBFCs) and agencies for rating their credit worthiness.

In the financial sector, the objective was to provide operational flexibility and functional autonomy to banks and other financial institutions so that they could allocate resources more efficiently. Some of the important initiatives in the financial sector were: reduction in statutory pre-emptions so as to release greater funds for commercial lending, interest rate deregulation to enable price discovery, allowing new private sector banks to create a more competitive environment, dilution of government holding in public sector banks (PSBs) and institution of prudential norms such as capital adequacy, income recognition, asset classification, provisioning and exposure norms to strengthen the health of the banking system besides improving transparency and disclosure standards.

Capital Market

The Capital Issues Control Act was repealed and the Securities and Exchange Board of India (SEBI) was set up as a watchdog for regulating the functioning of the capital market. SEBI has focused on regulatory reform of the capital market as well as on market modernisation. Online trading and dematerialised trading have been introduced. Companies have been allowed to buy back their own shares subject to the regulations laid down by SEBI.

In September 1992, the government announced guidelines for investments by foreign institutional investors (FIIs) in the Indian capital market. FIIs were now welcome to invest in all types of securities traded on the primary and secondary market with full repatriation benefits and without restrictions on either volume of trading or lock-in-period.

Fiscal Adjustment and Stabilisation

A key aspect of the structural adjustment programmes is to restrict the fiscal deficits of the governments. Table 5.1 summarises the trends in budget deficit of the central government in the late 1980s and 1990s and beyond. In the second half of 1980s, the fiscal imbalance worsened with average fiscal deficit rising to 8.2 per cent of GDP compared to 6.3 per cent in the early 1980s (*Economic Survey, 1992-93*). Compared to this, the average fiscal deficit in the post-reform period has been around 5 per cent of GDP. This suggests that the government has succeeded in managing the fiscal situation quite well.

Stabilisation of Inflation: An important focus of the stabilisation programme is to bring the rate of inflation under check. Considerable success was also achieved in the post-reform decades in stabilising inflation as well as inflationary expectations. The rate of change in wholesale and consumer prices suggests that the overall trend in prices has been on decline since 1992. One striking trend noticeable from Table 5.6 is the growing divergence between the rate of inflation based on wholesale prices and that for consumer price index (CPI) since 1993-94. Until 1993-94, the two rates generally converged. Since 1995-96, the CPI based rate of inflation has exceeded that of one based on wholesale prices by a wide margin. The diverging trend in the wholesale and consumer prices has been explained in terms of the change in the weighting scheme for the two indices. The CPI has a 57.0 per cent weight of the food group compared to just 27.5 per cent in WPI. The divergence between the two indices, therefore, reflects substantial increases in food prices in the 1990s. Besides, a spurt in prices of housing, medical care and personal care have also contributed to the rise in CPI. The rise in food prices and other goods of mass consumption at a faster rate than prices of other goods also indicates that sharing of burden of adjustment by different sections of society has been uneven and weaker sections may have been affected more.

Economic Progress Post-1991[7]

The initiation of economic reforms in the 1990s saw India gradually breaking free of the low growth trap which was euphemistically called the 'Hindu growth rate' of 3.5 per cent per annum. Real GDP growth averaged 5.7 per cent per annum in the 1990s, which accelerated further to 7.3 per cent per annum in 2000s. A feature of the growth acceleration

7. Kapila, Uma (ed.) (2012). *Two Decades of Economic Reforms: Towards Faster, Sustainable and More Inclusive Growth*, Ch.2. New Delhi: Academic Foundation.

TABLE – 5.1

Trends in Central Government Deficit as Percentage of GDP

Year	*Revenue Deficit*	*Fiscal Deficit*
Average		
1985-1991	2.6	8.2
1992-1999	2.9	5.7
2000-01	4.1	5.7
2001-02	4.4	6.2
2002-03	4.3	5.7
2003-04	3.5	4.3
2004-05	2.4	3.9
2005-06	2.5	4.0
2006-07	1.9	3.3
2007-08	1.1	2.5
2008-09	4.5	6.0
2009-10	5.2	6.5
2010-11	3.2	4.8
2011-12	4.4	5.7
2012-13	3.6	4.8
2013-14	3.57	5.03
2014-15	3.66	5.11
2015-16	3.43	5.33
2016-17	3.16	5.36
2017-18	4.44	5.91
2018-19 (BE)	4.16	6.24

Note: BE - budget estimate

Source: *Economic Survey* various issues including *2018-19*.

during the period was that while the growth rate of industry and services increased, that of agriculture fell. This was because there was no notable technological breakthrough after the 'Green Revolution' of the mid-1960s which saw sharp increase in yields of cereal production particularly in northern part of India. By the 1990s, the momentum of 'Green Revolution' had died down. Consequently, the yield increases in the 2000s were much lower than those experienced even in the 1990s.

Notably, the decade of the 2000s encompassed the inflexion point in the growth trajectory with an annual average GDP growth of about 9 per cent for the five-year period: 2004-2008. Growth in all the sub-sectors of the economy, including agriculture, accelerated during this period. However, this growth process was interrupted by the global financial crisis. Subsequently, the average growth slowed down to 7.8 per cent during 2009-2011 with a noticeable slowdown in both agriculture and industry.

According to Pulin Nayak a key reason for the high growth rate was the high rate of savings and gross fixed capital formation that India had begun to record by the late 1990s. Around 2006-07 the savings rate was around 36 per cent and the gross fixed capital formation was around 37 per cent. With a capital output ratio of around 4, the crude Harrod-Domar formulation would suggest that an overall growth rate of around 9 per cent was perfectly feasible. Behind this high growth rate was the rapid growth of the service sector, driven by a boom in information technology. The share of agriculture in GDP continued to decline, and from a figure of around 55 per cent in 1950 it had declined to around 13.7 per cent by 2013. This was matched by a steady rise in the share of income originating in services. A key feature in all this has been that the share of manufacturing in GDP has remained constant at around 15 per cent to 16 per cent over a long span. It should be noted that manufacturing is recognised to be the most dynamic of all sectors, and one that has the highest potential of generating jobs and therefore absorbing labour. The share of income originating in manufacturing as a fraction of GDP in China is double, at around 32 per cent. The relative constancy in the income originating in manufacturing in India has meant that employment has remained stagnant, and possibly declined, in the organised sector, giving rise to the phenomenon of "jobless growth."[8]

The growth dynamics altered the structure of the Indian economy with a decline in the share of agriculture from 28.4 per cent in the 1990s to about 15 per cent in 2009-2011 (Table 5.2). There was corresponding gain in the share of services, including construction, from 52 per cent to 65 per cent during the same period. What is, however, of concern is that the share of industry has remained unchanged at around 20 per cent of GDP. This suggests that India's growth acceleration during the last two decades has been dominated by the services sector. The pace of average annual industrial growth had nevertheless picked up from 5.7 per cent during the 1990s to 9 per cent during 2004-2008 before being interrupted by the global financial crisis (Mohanty, 2012).[9]

8. Nayak, Pulin (2016). "Revisiting India's Growth", *Economic and Political Weekly*, August 20.
9. Mohanty, Deepak (2012). "Indian Economy: Progress and Prospects", in Uma Kapila (ed.), *Two Decades of Economic Reforms: Towards Faster, Sustainable and More Inclusive Growth.* New Delhi: Academic Foundation.

TABLE – 5.2

Real Economy

Item	*1991-2000*	*2001-2010*	*2004-2008*	*2009-2011*	*2013-14 (2R)*	*2014-15 (1R)*	*2015-16 (AE)*
1	*2*	*3*	*4*	*5*	*6*	*7*	*8*
(Percentage change)							
1. Overall real GDP	5.7	7.3	8.9	7.8	6.6	7.2	7.6
1.1 Agriculture	3.2	2.4	5.0	2.3	4.2	-0.2	1.1
1.2 Industry	5.7	7.3	9.0	6.7	5.0	5.9	7.3
1.2.1 Manufacturing	5.6	8.0	10.0	7.1	5.6	5.5	9.5
1.3 Services	7.1	9.0	10.1	9.5	7.8	10.3	9.2
2. Demand-side aggregates							
2.1 Private final consumption expenditure	4.8	6.4	7.4	7.9	6.8	6.2	7.6
2.2 Government final consumption expenditure	6.3	5.8	5.6	10.6	0.4	12.8	3.3
2.3 Gross fixed capital formation	7.2	10.2	15.7	5.8	3.4	4.9	5.3
(Per cent)							
3. Share in GDP							
3.1 Agriculture	28.4	19.4	18.9	14.9	13.9		
3.2 Industry	20.1	20.0	20.1	20.1	26.1		
3.3 Services	51.5	60.6	61.1	65.0	59.9		

Note: CSO data

Source: *Economic Survey 2012-13, 2013-14, 2014-15.*

While the share of industry in GDP remained stagnant, there was noteworthy structural transformation in manufacturing over the period. As a process of restructuring, while the gross value added in organised manufacturing increased by 8 per cent per annum at current prices, employment fell by 1.5 per cent per annum during 1995-2003. Subsequently, during 2004-2009, gross value added growth accelerated to 20 per cent per annum at current prices, but significantly, employment also increased by 7.5 per cent per annum.

The structure of Indian economy also underwent a change during this period in terms of openness. The stereotypical view that India is a closed economy has not been borne out by the openness of Indian economy which was increasing rapidly. Exports and imports of goods and services have more than doubled from 23 per cent of GDP in the 1990s to 50 per cent in the recent period of 2009-2011. If the trade flows are considered alongside capital flows, the rise in openness (measured as current receipts and payments plus capital receipts and payments) was more dramatic from 42 per cent of GDP in the 1990s to 107 per cent in the recent period (Table 5.3) Empirical evidence suggests that with increasing openness of the Indian economy, the trade and industrial cycles were getting more synchronised with the global business cycle (Mohanty, 2012).

TABLE – 5.3

Openness Indicators

(As per cent to GDP)

Item	*1991-2000*	*2001-2010*	*2004-2008*	*2009-2011*
1. Exports plus imports of goods & services	22.9	39.2	40.8	49.8
2. Current receipts & payments plus capital receipts & payments	41.9	78.7	83.5	106.5

The high growth phase of 2004-2008 was accompanied by sharp increase in exports and imports as well as capital inflows. Net capital inflows as percentage of GDP more than doubled from 2.2 per cent in the 1990s to 4.6 per cent of GDP during 2004-2008. Subsequently, growth rates in both trade and capital inflows moderated following the global financial crisis. The openness of the Indian economy has been accompanied by improvement in India's external position as the debt to GDP ratio fell from about 29 per cent in the 1990s to 19 per cent in the recent period. The debt service ratio has also declined from 25 per cent to under 5 per cent during the period (Mohanty, 2012).

The openness in the capital account has resulted in two-way movement in capital with a sharp pickup in India's outward FDI since the mid-2000s (Table 5.4). Uptrend in outward FDI mainly reflected the large overseas acquisition deals of Indian corporates to gain market share and reap economies of scale amidst progressive liberalisation of the external payments regime.

TABLE – 5.4

Foreign Direct Investment

(US$ billion)

Year	*Inward*	*Outward*	*Net FDI to India*	*Outward/ Inward (%)*
2000-01	4.0	0.8	3.3	18.8
2001-02	6.1	1.4	4.7	22.7
2002-03	5.0	1.8	3.2	36.1
2003-04	4.3	1.9	2.4	44.7
2004-05	6.0	2.3	3.7	38.0
2005-06	8.9	5.9	3.0	65.9
2006-07	22.7	15.0	7.7	66.2
2007-08	34.7	18.8	15.9	54.2
2008-09	37.7	17.9	19.8	47.4
2009-10	33.1	14.4	18.8	43.3
2010-11	23.4	16.2	7.1	69.4

Source: Reserve Bank of India.

Gradual improvements were also observed in the fiscal position with fiscal deficit moderating sharply during the high growth phase of 2004-2008, which also coincided with a period of switch-over to a rule-based fiscal consolidation process. In fact, the high growth phase of 2004-2008 saw a primary surplus for the centre enhancing debt sustainability. The deficit indicators, however, have deteriorated in the recent period following crisis-induced fiscal expansion (Table 5.5).

The average saving rate also showed a substantial increase from 23 per cent of GDP in the 1990s to about 31 per cent in the 2000s with a peak saving rate of over 33 per cent achieved during the high growth phase of 2004-2008. Fiscal consolidation helped in lifting the overall saving rate as public sector saving rose significantly. The efficiency of capital utilisation also improved as the incremental capital output ratio (ICOR) declined to 3.7 during the high growth phase of 2004-2008 from 5 in the 1990s. Subsequently, however, capital efficiency has declined in the post-crisis period (Table 5.6).

TABLE – 5.5

Government Finances

(As per cent to GDP)

Item	*1991-2000*	*2001-2010*	*2004-2008*	*2009-2011*
1. Central government finances				
1.1 Tax revenue	6.8	7.2	7.6	7.4
1.2 Revenue deficit	3.0	3.4	2.3	4.4
1.3 Fiscal deficit	5.9	4.8	3.6	5.8
1.4 Primary deficit	1.6	0.8	-0.2	2.6
2. State finances				
2.1 Gross fiscal deficit	3.1	3.1	2.7	2.6
2.2 Outstanding liabilities	22.3	29.3	30.1	24.8
3. Combined government finances				
3.1 Revenue deficit	4.2	4.4	2.7	4.5
3.2 Fiscal deficit	7.7	7.8	6.3	8.5
3.3 Primary deficit	2.7	2.2	0.7	3.7
3.4 Outstanding liabilities	63.2	75.1	76.5	68.5

TABLE – 5.6

Saving and Investment

Item	*1991-2000*	*2001-2010*	*2004-2008*	*2009-2011*
(As a ratio to GDP at current market prices)				
1. Gross domestic savings	23.0	30.7	33.4	33.0
1.1 Household saving	17.7	23.1	23.4	23.6
1.1.1 Financial assets	9.9	11.0	11.3	11.3
1.1.2 Physical assets	7.8	12.1	12.1	12.4
1.2. Private corporate sector	3.8	6.3	7.2	8.0
1.3. Public sector	1.5	1.3	2.9	1.3
2. Gross domestic capital formation	24.4	31.2	34.3	35.5
3. ICOR*	5.0	4.4	3.7	4.9

Note: * Ratio of real investment rate and real GDP growth.

Source: Mohanty, 2012.

TABLE – 5.7

Inflation

Item	1991-2000	2001-2010	2004-2008	2009-2011
1	2	3	4	5
(Annual average percentage change)				
1. Wholesale price index	8.1	5.4	5.5	7.1
1.1 Food articles	10.2	5.8	5.2	13.3
1.2 Fuel group	10.6	8.9	7.3	7.2
1.3 Non-food manufactured products	6.8	4.0	5.0	4.0
2. CPI: industrial workers	9.5	5.9	5.0	10.6
2.1 CPI: industrial workers food	9.8	6.2	5.5	12.5

Source: Mohanty, 2012.

The high growth was achieved in an environment of price stability as headline wholesale price index (WPI) inflation dropped to an annual average of 5.5 per cent in the 2000s from 8.1 per cent in the 1990s. There was also similar drop in consumer price inflation. Subsequently, however, in the post-crisis period the inflation trend has reversed with the headline WPI inflation averaging over 7 per cent and the consumer price inflation crossing double digits during 2009-2011. The uptick in food price inflation was particularly sharp during 2009-2011 (Table 5.7).

Impact of Economic Reforms on the Vulnerable Sections

Regarding impact of economic reforms on the vulnerable sections, according to Rangarajan, we need to address two sets of issues. One is whether the economic reform measures affect in any way the specific policy measures that we normally undertake in order to improve the conditions of the poor. Second, is there anything in the new economic reform measures which *per se* has an anti-poor bias? It may be emphasised here that the economic reform introduced since 1991 is not the total economic policy of the government. There are many other elements which continue to remain as an integral part of the overall economic policy. Among these are the measures which can be broadly termed as anti-poverty programmes. In the total economic policy, there are four elements which can be identified as being meant specifically for poverty alleviation:

First, since agriculture is the mainstay of the majority of the population, growth in agriculture and, therefore, resources allocated for agriculture are an important part of the attack on poverty. This is not an acceptance of the trickle-down theory. It is common knowledge that in states in which agriculture has made spectacular progress, poverty levels have come down. Therefore, allocation of resources for agriculture is an important indicator.

Second, we have evolved over time a reasonably satisfactory food security system. An integral part of this is the public distribution system. With all its shortcomings, the public distribution system has played a notable role in avoiding acute conditions of scarcity and met to a certain extent the minimum requirements.

Third, there has been a substantial expansion in programmes which are intended to provide additional employment. The various employment guarantee schemes as well as the credit-related integrated rural development programmes are examples of such programmes.

Fourth, expenditure on education and health also has an important bearing on reducing poverty levels.

Conclusions

Judged by many of the externally visible signs, the Indian reforms story has been a remarkable success (Nachane, 2011). After a long period of stagnation in the years following independence, growth rates shifted into high gear sometime during the 1980s and in the last decade accelerated sharply, reaching undreamt heights. This growth resurgence has enabled India to move up in the world per capita (PPP-corrected) GDP rankings from 93 (out of a total of 109 countries) in the mid-1970s to 58 by 2004 (Basu and Maertens, 2007). On several other macroeconomic indicators, the country has been doing equally well. Investment as a proportion of GDP, for example, rose from about 10 per cent in the 1950s to about 23 per cent in the early 1980s and close to 36 per cent (Rangarajan 2012).[10] Similarly, India today qualifies as an 'open economy' with exports (as a percentage of GDP) amounting to nearly 20 per cent, as compared to less than 5 per cent in the mid-1960s. And finally on the forex front, we have transited from a perennially shortage situation

10. Rangarajan, C. (2012). "The Indian Economy: Current Concerns and Future Prospects", in Uma Kapila (ed.), *Two Decades of Economic Reforms,* ch.3. New Delhi: Academic Foundation.

to one of a bundance (Nachane, 2011).[11] Inflation, always a serious concern in the Indian context, was sharply reined in, in the late 1990s, though it has once again shown signs of strong revival.

However, Basu believes, "Ultimately an economy has to be evaluated in terms of what happens to the poorest and the dispossessed. Everything else, such as a nation's income growth rate, is of instrumental value.[12] Not all economists concur with this view. To many, efficiency, growth, and *aggregate* welfare are the ends that they wish to pursue. Amartya Sen has consistently taken a normative stand where these are merely of instrumental value. While Jagdish Bhagwati has argued vigorously for free trade and raising growth, but at the same time he has been categorical:

> As regards the *objective* of development, I should emphasise, as I always have, that growth was seen by me..., from the early 1960s, as simply an instrumental variable, as a means to an end, and the end was clearly the elimination of poverty.[13]

India, unfortunately, still has miles to go, on matters of basic needs and development of the most disadvantaged. Over the last few decades, inequality has been rising, regional disparities have been growing, and poverty and illiteracy continue to be high.

Making an overall assessment of reforms one can say that on the growth front, reforms have indeed delivered beyond expectations, while simultaneously macroeconomic stability has been more or less successfully maintained. But the resultant growth and stability have had a fairly limited impact on poverty and seem to have aggravated both interpersonal and inter-regional inequality. The growth has also had an extremely low employment potential (Nachane, 2011).

Improved economic performance dramatically altered global perceptions of India's potential. An early recognition of this was a Goldman Sachs report of November 2002, which included India, with Brazil, Russia and China, in a new BRIC group of emerging market countries which was predicted to overtake the G-8 in terms of total GDP by 2035. "Continued strong performance in the decade of the 2000s and resilience in the face of a global slowdown, has reinforced this

---

11. Nachane, D.M. (2011). "Overview—Two Decades of Structural Reforms in India: A Balance Sheet", in *India Development Report 2011 (Ch.1)*. Indira Gandhi Institute of Development Research, Mumbai, Oxford, New Delhi.
12. Basu, Kaushik (ed.) (2004). *India's Emerging Economy: Performance and Prospects in the 1990s and Beyond*. Oxford University Press.
13. Bhagwati, Jagdish (1985). *Essays in Development Economics*. Oxford University Press.

positive assessment."[14] However, the recent deceleration in India's real GDP growth has raised questions about the potential growth rate of the economy and the size of the output gap.

Assessing economic reforms on their 25th anniversary, Pulapre Balakrishnan (2016)[15] concludes, "First, it must be acknowledged that India's BoP constraint has been eased. A payments crisis had triggered the reforms of 1991, and to have strengthened India's external position is a substantial achievement. Next, growth and poverty have continued to accelerate and decline respectively. In this way, the reforms have maintained a trend while providing macroeconomic stability. But, 25 years since, India continues to have an unacceptable level of poverty even as it is measured according to a low international standard. The progress made on this front is disappointing given the claim that the reforms mark a sea change in India. Finally, the spread of opportunity has been uneven going by the fact that the sector containing the largest number of workers has been the one growing the slowest. I have emphasised the importance of far greater dynamism in the agricultural sector if we are to move towards an equalisation of opportunities across the economy. Needless to mention, this would also take the economy closer to the dreamt-of double-digit growth. The importance of agriculture for both poverty reduction and growth is evident to us from both the history of East Asia (Hayami and Godo 2005) and the experience of India's economy during the phase of high growth during 2003-2008."

What can we expect with respect to the spread of opportunity from the economic reforms as practised in more or less similar fashion by the two coalitions that have governed India over the past two decades? Not much, if the present situation is any guide. The analysis in this paper shows us why this must be so. First, there is perhaps excessive focus on the interface of India with the rest of the world, when outward orientation is not going to provide the solution to the most pressing of India's problems today. Historically, countries have solved their problems of agricultural supply shortfall and large-scale physical infrastructure provision on their own. China is perhaps the best example. Second, there is excessive focus on higher education compared to schooling. Finally, the approach to the macroeconomic policy is dogmatic, emphasising fiscal consolidation over capital

---

14. Ahluwalia, Montek S. (2015). "Prospects and Policy Challenges in the Twelfth Plan", in Uma Kapila (ed.), *Indian Economy Since Independence* (26th edition).
15. Balakrishnan, P. (2017). "Markets, Growth and Social Opportunity", *Economic and Political Weekly*, January 14, 2017.

formation, making it difficult for the state to make a difference via the provision of infrastructure on a significant scale.

Actually, 'Make in India', a flagship programme of the present government, reflects a failure of the reforms to make a serious dent in the very area in which it focused the most, that is, manufacturing. The failure has also to do with the failure to recognise the importance of demand. Much of the focus, it appears, is on the 'ease of doing business.' While this is hardly irrelevant as a consideration, the dramatic decline in manufacturing growth after close to double-digit growth over 2003-2008 suggests that the supply side is unlikely to be the issue (ibid).

In many ways the coming decade will be crucial for India, remarks Rangarajan[16], If India grows at 8 to 9 per cent per annum, it is estimated that per capita GDP will increase from the current level of US$1,600 to US$8,000 by 2030. Then India will transit from being a low income to a truly middle income country. We need to overcome the low growth phase as quickly as possible, as growth is the answer to many of our socioeconomic problems. In the recent period, we have launched a number of schemes aimed at broadening the base of growth. These include the employment guarantee scheme, universalisation of education, expansion of rural health, and providing food security. All these programmes have made a substantial demand on public expenditure. It has been possible to fund these programmes only because of the strong growth that we have seen in recent years. Growth has facilitated raising more resources by the Government.

Development has many dimensions. It has to be inclusive, it must be poverty reducing, and it must be environment-friendly. We need to incorporate all these elements in the growth process. A strong and balanced growth will enable the economy to achieve multiple goals including reducing poverty. India has to follow a two-fold path of accelerating growth and addressing directly through various schemes for the vulnerable and poor group.[17]

Reforms are not ends in themselves. Even growth is not an end in itself. Ultimately, growth triggered by reforms must benefit all segments of society. Equity and efficiency should not be posed as opposing considerations. They must be weaved together to provide an acceptable pattern of development.[18]

---

16. Rangarajan, C. (2017). "The Journey of India's Economic Reforms", *in Uma Kapila (ed.) (2017), India's Economy: Pre-Liberalisation to GST—Essays in Honour of Raj Kapila.* New Delhi: Academic Foundation.
17. Ibid.
18. Ibid.

To quote Vijay Joshi (2017), "To become a prosperous, high-income country in the next two decades, India will have to achieve, over that time-span, economic growth that is super-fast and inclusive. By 'super-fast growth', I mean a growth rate of 8 per cent a year or more; by 'inclusive growth', I mean growth that is widely shared. The magnitude of the task can be understood by contemplating the sobering fact that fewer than half-a-dozen of the 200-odd countries in the world have achieved super-fast and inclusive growth for two or more decades on the run, and almost all of them were autocracies during their rapid sprints. Can a democratic India do a China or a South Korea? That is the overwhelming question. However, the current context is that far from speeding up, India's growth has shown signs of slowing down. While some temporary and special factors are involved, it is also the case that the 'partial reform model' that has been in operation since 1991 has been running into diminishing returns. India urgently needs another round of radical reforms to keep the engine of productivity growth firing on all cylinders.[19]

The list of desirable reforms according to Joshi is long, but in his opinion they should have a common thread or theme, which is to put right the balance between the state, the market, and the private sector. To quote again "despite some liberalisation, India has not fully recovered from a bad case of old-fashioned socialism, with its fond belief in the benefits of state ownership of the means of production, and its marked propensity for arbitrary state intervention in the operation of the markets. We have yet to complete the move to becoming a modern social democracy. This implies retaining the socialist emphasis on shared prosperity, and the liberal-democratic emphasis on individual freedom and rights, while moving towards greater reliance on private ownership and the market mechanism, with the state performing competently its essential core functions. These core functions include provision of macroeconomic stability, smart regulation, correction of market failures, efficient income redistribution, and effective supply of public services."[20]

After short listing five areas in which radical reforms are required to achieve super-fast and inclusive growth for an extended period: state ownership; employment creation; deep fiscal adjustment; quality of

19. Joshi, Vijay (2017). "India's Economic Reforms: Reflections on the Unfinished Agenda", Eighteenth L.K. Jha Memorial Lecture, December 11, 2017 (RBI Bulletin February 2018) *in Uma Kapila (ed.) (2018), Indian Economy Since Independence (*29th edition, ch. 4). New Delhi: Academic Foundation.

20. Ibid.

education; and state capacity and detailed decision on the above, Joshi concludes with one final remark about desirable reform in India viz., "India needs both less of the state and more of the state. It needs 'less of the state' because the state has become over-extended in areas outside its comparative advantage. But it also needs 'more of the state' because the state does not perform competently the core functions that lie squarely in its domain. How to combine 'less of the state' with 'more of the state' will be the central challenge of India's economic reforms."[21]

Appendix Table A-5.1 →→→

21. Ibid.

APPENDIX TABLE – A-5.1

Annual Growth Rates of Real Gross Value Added at Basic Prices by Industry of Origin (%)

	At Constant Prices					
Year	*Agriculture, forestry & fishing, mining and quarrying*	*Manufacturing, construction, electricity, gas and water supply*	*Trade, hotels, transport & communication*	*Financing, insurance, real estate and business services*	*Community social & personal services*	*Gross value added at basic prices*
(1)	*(2)*	*(3)*	*(4)*	*(5)*	*(6)*	*(7)*
			2011-12 Series			
2012-13	1.4	3.6	9.8	9.7	4.3	5.4
2013-14	4.8	4.2	6.5	11.2	3.8	6.1
2014-15	1.2	6.7	9.4	11.0	8.3	7.2
2015-16	2.1	9.5	10.2	10.7	6.1	8.0
2016-17 (2nd RE)	6.8	7.5	7.7	8.7	9.2	7.9
2017-18 (1st RE)	5.0	6.0	7.8	6.2	11.9	6.9
2018-19 (PE)	2.7	7.5	6.9	7.4	8.6	6.6

Source: *Economic Survey 2018-19 Vol. 2*, Statistical Appendix A13.

Notes: PE : Provisional Estimates, RE: Revised Estimates

6

Demography and Development

IN recent years, there has been an increasing focus on the relationship between population growth and economic development. The most difficult problem for such an analysis is to be able to separate cause from effect. Does economic development accelerate or retard population growth or does population growth contribute to or retard economic development? What are the linkages and how strong they are and in what direction do they operate?

Economic Development and Population Growth

The Theory of Demographic Transition

The theory of demographic transition attempts to explain why all contemporary developed nations have more or less passed through the same three stages of population growth. Before their economic modernisation, these countries, for centuries, had stable or very slow growing population as a result of a combination of high birth rate and almost equally high death rate. With economic development resulting in higher incomes, improved public health facilities, there was a marked decline in mortality that gradually raised life expectancy from under 40 years to over 60 years. However, the decline in death rate was not immediately accompanied by a decline in fertility. With declining death rate but birth rate not falling correspondingly, these countries passed through stage two, marking the beginning of demographic transition i.e., transition from stable or slow growing population to rapidly increasing number. Finally, stage three is reached when the forces and influences of modernisation and economic development cause fertility to decline so that eventually falling birth rate converge with lower death rate leaving little or no population growth.[1] Thus, how does economic development affect population growth can be explained through the theory of demographic transition.

The Microeconomic Theory of Fertility

In recent years, economists have begun to look more closely at the microeconomic determinants of family fertility. They have utilised the principles of economy and optimisation to explain family size decisions. In deciding whether or not to have additional children, parents are assumed to weigh economic benefits against costs. The principle of benefits are the expected income from child labour usually on the farm and their family support for elderly parents. Balance against these benefits are the two principle elements of costs. (i) The opportunity cost of mother's time, the income she could earn if she were not at home caring for her children. (ii) The cost of educating children that is the trade-off between having fewer 'high quality' high cost, educated children with high income earning potentials *versus* more 'low quality,' low cost, uneducated children with much lower earning prospects.

Statistical studies have shown that birth rates among the poor are likely to fall where there is:

1. An increase in the education of women and consequent change in their role and status.
2. An increase in female non-agricultural wage employment opportunities which raises the price or cost of their traditional child bearing activities.
3. A rise in family income through increase in direct employment and earning of husband and wife and or redistribution of income and assets from rich to poor.
4. A reduction in infant mortality through expanded public health programme and better nutritional status for both parent and child.
5. The development of old age and social security systems to bridge the economic dependence of parents on their offsprings.

Thus, efforts to make jobs, education and health more broadly available to poverty groups in the Third World countries will not only contribute to their income and physical well-being but it can also

1. Todaro, Michael (2008). *Economic Development in the Third World* (8th edition). Delhi: Pearson Education (Singapore) Pte. Ltd.

contribute substantially to their motivation for smaller families which is vital to reducing growth rates.

How does Population Growth Affect Economic Development?

So far we have tried to analyse the effect of economic development on population growth, now let us examine how does population growth affect economic development. We may begin by asking the question how does population growth affect the net national product.

Until recently, the literature of economic demography drew attention to two main relationships through which population growth affect the economy, what we may call: (i) the 'saving effect' and (ii) 'composition of investment effect'.[2] The former of these argues that savings are reduced by population growth because of the so-called burden of dependency. With high fertility and declining mortality in younger and older age groups, the population acquires an increasing proportion of people in the non-working age groups relative to those of working age. Since all must consume, in the absence of increasing output per worker, saving per head must fall. Even if productivity is increasing, savings are less than they would be with a smaller number of dependents per worker.

The investment argument is like this: with increasing population, a share of investible resources has to be devoted to reproducing for additional people facilities, duplication of social services which would be unnecessary if population were not growing. A number of studies, starting with Coale and Hoover, have shown through comparison of high and low fertility paths that there has been greater growth of GNP with the lesser rate of population growth. Robert Cassen has raised doubts on the validity of the above saving and investments effect. He argues, if bulk of savings in poor countries come from small wealthy class whose fertility is low and if cost of additional children is met out of consumption rather than saving, the saving cost of additional children would be quite inconsiderable.

The composition of investment argument according to Cassen is really quite general. Wherever population growth requires increase in production, which in turn require investment, a lesser rate of population growth would release investible funds for use elsewhere.

---

2. Cassen, R.H. (1978). *India, Population, Economy and Society*, ch.4. p.221.

One fails to understand why past models have concentrated on welfare investment. Food production is in fact the least postponable of all forms of population-related output needs, and if agriculture enters a phase of fundamental alteration in production function or in other words changing resource requirements for additional output, this can be a major burden of population growth. India reached this stage since mid-1960s when increases in agricultural output had to be brought out by yield improving technology which is capital-intensive instead of increasing acreage.

According to K. Sundaram, the implications of growing demographic pressures in India for the process of development in general and the progress towards poverty eradication become clearer once we focus on the labour force consequences of population growth.[3] The labour force expansion also puts direct pressure on the single most important natural resource in a predominantly agrarian economy, namely, land. Admittedly, the effective supply of land can be augmented by the use of reproducible capital. Irrigation is the most obvious example making it possible to increase the gross cropped area. The inadequate expansion of gross cropped area and of the irrigated area reflects the fact that the irrigation system has not expanded even up to the limits of currently known irrigation potential. This again is a manifestation of the inadequacy of capital resources.

India's Demographic Transition

Table 6.1 suggests that the country's demographic transition really began, rather hesitatingly, with a reduction in the average death rate during the 1920s and 1930s. These decades saw a decline in the frequency and scale of major famines and epidemics, which previously had made people's lives so incredibly precarious. As a result, there was a modest increase in life expectancy. And, with a prevailing crude birth rate of about 45 per thousand, these small gains in mortality were sufficient to raise the average annual rate of population growth to over one per cent per year during the 1920s, the 1930s and the 1940s.

At the time of its independence in 1947, India's population was about 345 million. Life expectancy was around 33 years and the total fertility rate (TFR) was close to six births. The decades following the 1940s have seen great changes.

---

3. Sundaram, K. (1999-2000). "Demography and Development", in Uma Kapila (ed.), *Indian Economy since Independence*. New Delhi: Academic Foundation.

TABLE – 6.1

Key Population Statistics of India, 1901-2011

Census Year	*Total Population (million)*	*Average Annual Growth Rate (per cent)*	*Birth Rate*	*Death Rate*	*Sex Ratio (males per 1000 females)*	*Per Cent of Urban Population*
1901	238.3	0.3	49.2	42.6	1029	10.8
1911	252.0	0.6	48.1	47.2	1038	10.3
1921	251.2	N	46.2	36.3	1047	11.2
1931	278.9	1.1	45.2	31.2	1053	12.0
1941	318.5	1.3	39.9	27.4	1058	13.9
1951	361.0	1.3	40.9	22.8	1057	17.3
1961	439.1	2.0	40.0	17.8	1063	18.0
1971	548.2	2.2[b]	37.8	15.4	1075	19.9
1981	683.3	2.2[b]	33.8	12.3	1071	23.3[a]
1991	846.3	2.1	30.6	10.3	1067	25.7
2001	1027	1.9	25.8	8.5	1072	27.8
2011	121.0	1.7	21.6	7.0	1064	31.2

Notes: a Includes only an estimate for Assam.

b Growth rate for 1961-1971 and 1971-1981 take account of the fact that the reference date of the 1971 Census was 1 April, whereas that of the 1981 Census (like the 1951 and 1961 Census) was 1 March.

N: Negligible.

Source: Visaria, Pravin (2008-09). "Demographic Aspects of Development: The Indian Experience", in Uma Kapila (ed.), *Indian Economy since Independence*. New Delhi: Academic Foundation.

Registrar General & Census Commissioner, India (2011). *Census of India 2011* (Provisional Population Tables).

The most important change relates to mortality. Immediately after Independence, the Government of India (GoI) placed great stress upon improving the health of its people. As a result, death rates have fallen almost everywhere, more or less continuously. At the start of the 21st century, life expectancy is almost double that of 1947 (about 68 years for females and 65 years for males (2006-2010).

The reduction in the death rate after 1947 resulted in a significant rise in the rate of population growth, which reached almost 2 per cent during 1951-1961. In the following three decades, it remained fairly constant at around 2.2 per cent. The birth rate was more resistant to change than the death rate. It was only during the 1991-2001 intercensal decade that the birth rate fell faster than the death rate—so bringing about a significant decline in the rate of population growth.

Although the 'TFR' (the average number of births per couple) for India as a whole is still well above the 'replacement level' (around 2.1), fertility in India has fallen quite sharply in recent decades, from around 6 in 1961 to 3 in 2001 and 2.4 in 2012.

According to Drèze and Sen (2002), in order to interpret these contrasting trends (continuing rapid population growth on the one hand and declining fertility rates on the other), population growth has to be placed in the context of the 'demographic transition' from high to low fertility and mortality rates. In the initial phases of this transition, death rates typically fall faster than birth rates so that the rate of population growth increases: in India, for instance, it increased from virtually zero at the beginning of the 20th century to 2.2 per cent per year in the 1960s and 1970s. As the transition progresses, the rate of decline of birth rates gradually overtakes that of death rates, leading to a decline in the growth rate of population, as began to happen in India about 20 years ago. In some individual states, it happened much earlier.

The decline of population growth, though relatively recent, can be expected to accelerate in the relatively near future, not only due to steadily falling fertility rates but also because of ongoing changes in the age structure of the population. Viewed in the context of this demograpic transition, current patterns of population growth appear less alarming. Indeed, India is now well into the last phase of its demographic transition, involving falling populaton growth and sustained progresss towards 'population stabilisation' (which is expected to occur around the middle of this century), and there is certainly no evidence that a 'population bomb' is ticking away. This does not, of course, detract from the need for concern about rapid population growth at this time, or from the possibility of accelerating the demographic transition through supportive public policy (Drèze and Sen, 2002).

Causes of High Birth Rate

Social Factors

Social factors like universality of marriage and marriage at young age, joint family system, preference for a son result in high birth rate.

Economic Factors

Economic factors such as widespread poverty, high infant mortality and children as an insurance have also contributed to high birth rate.

Poverty

Among poverty groups not much money is spent on the upbringing of the children and hence, they are not much of a liability. Rather they start earning at an early age by doing some work on farms or take up some odd jobs in urban industrial areas. Hence, they add to family income and prove an asset to the family. Among poor families, additional children do not add to any burden, rather they provide helping hands for the family.

Lack of Social Security

Further, low survival rate among infants also encourages high birth rate. As social security like old age pension is not available to the poor masses in India, they expect their children to look after them in their old age. But since infant mortality rate (death rate among infants or very small children) is very high, people like to raise larger families so that some of them survive to look after parents in the old age. Thus, absence of social security combined with high infant mortality contribute to high birth rate. Because of lack of savings due to poverty, a large number of children act like insurance for their parents.

Illiteracy, Ignorance and Belief in Fate

Illiteracy is widespread in India. Illiterate and ignorant people thus accept every child as a will of God and would never think of interfering with His will. This increases the birth rate in India. Moreover, illiterate population does not realise the problems caused by increasing population or the means to keep family size in reasonable limits.

Ineffective Family Planning

Thus, high birth rate in India is the result of a whole lot of social, economic, religious and cultural factors. Unless a change is brought about in our attitude through social and cultural changes by spread of education and enlightenment or through economic and political pressure, not much decline can be expected in the prevailing high birth rate.

Fertility Rate

Fertility rate is a more scientific explanation of population growth rate than the birth rate. The birth rate, which measures the number of live births per thousand of population, is only a crude measure and thus called crude birth rate. It is crude because it associates the total number of live births with total population, whether young or old, male or female or whether they belong to reproductive age group or not.

TFR, on the other hand, measures the average number of children born to a woman up to the end of reproductive period. TFR, which was around 6 during 1951-52 declined to 5.3 during 1970-1972, 4.5 during 1980-1982, and below 4 in 1990-1992 and 2.4 in 2012. Thus, though there has been some decline in TFR, it has not been large enough to much reduce natural growth rate of population in the face of continued decline in mortality rate. TFR in turn depends upon proportion of the married population, age at marriage and the number of children born per married women in course of her reproductive period.

Fertility rates vary radically across the country—between regions, between states and between districts. For example, for the state of Kerala as a whole—consisting of 14 districts—the average fertility rate is now around 1.8, which is lower than the rates for China and the USA, and comparable with those of some West European countries such as Britain and France. In fact, all the four South India states Andhra Pradesh, Tamil Nadu, Kerala and Karnataka as well as Goa, Punjab, Himachal Pradesh, Jammu & Kashmir, Maharashtra, West Bengal, Sikkim, Tripura and the Union Territories of Delhi, Lakshdweep,l Daman and Diu, Andaman and Nicobar and Chandigarh registered a low fertility rate below the crucial 2.1. These states accounted for 50.4 per cent of India's population in 2011. It is expected by 2020, India will reach the replacement level of fertility (*Hindu*, December 14, 2014).

In general, however, the seriousness of the population issue must not be dismissed. Given the density of pupulation that India already has, the environmental and social implications of further significant expansion can indeed be potentially grave.

Causes of Decline in Death Rate

In the early years of 20th century, death rate was very high. It was 42.6 per thousand during 1901-1910 and further increased to 47.2 per thousand during 1911-1920, but came down slowly to 36.3 per thousand in 1921-1930 and remained above 31 per thousand during 1931-1940. However, since the planned economic development of the country, there is a sharp decline in death rate from about 27 per thousand in 1941-1950 to 8.5 per thousand during 1991-2000 and 7.0 in 2011. This decline in death rate was slow and gradual in the earlier decades but became progressively sharper after 1951.

Control of Epidemics

In the earlier years of the 20th century, epidemics like plague, smallpox, malaria, etc., took a heavy toll of life. But with increasing availability of effective medicines and improvement in health care facilities, these epidemics have been controlled. This has contributed to a substantial reduction in the death rate.

Control of Famines

Famines which occurred in India frequently and with marked regularity took a heavy toll of life. The Bengal Famine of 1943, for example, caused thousands of starvation deaths while millions of people fled to other parts of the country in search of food. With the improvement in the means of transport and communications, spread of famines has been effectively checked. Of course, sometimes famine-like conditions do occur in some parts of the country, as had happened during the year 2000 AD in parts of Gujarat and Rajasthan, yet effective measures to make supply of food available in these areas prevented any starvation deaths. Control of famines has been an important factor in the decline of death rate.

Improved Medical Facilities

With the increased investment in health and medical care facilities, many new hospitals have come up and a large number of dispensaries have been opened even in far flung rural areas. Thus, an increasingly greater proportion of population is now being provided medical facilities. This has improved health and prevented deaths due to timely availability of medical aid.

Spread of Maternity Homes

With spread of maternity homes where trained staff looks after child birth, deaths at the time of delivery have been largely prevented.

Impact of Economic Development

Under the impact of development, incomes and living standards of people have improved. This has improved their health and nutritional levels and made them less prone to disease and early death. Improvement in personal hygiene and sanitary conditions which go with better living standard has prevented the spread of communicable diseases. Education has made them aware of preventive measures that ensure disease-free life. Thus, the impact of overall development has been to promote better health and longer life. The life expentancy at birth (number of years a new born child is expected to live) has gone up from 32 years in 1950-51 to nearly 64.6 years for males and 67.7 years for females in 2006-10. This shows that now on an average people live longer. Special programmes aimed at improving income and living standards of the poorer sections of society, provision of basic needs such as pure drinking water, health care facilities, houses for the homeless, etc., have all contributed to better life and lower death rate.

Measures to Reduce Birth Rate

Here, we may just list some of the measures which can help to reduce birth rate and thereby check the growth rate of population.

1. **Spread of education** particularly female education as we have before us the experience of Kerala and Tamil Nadu.

2. **Increase in female wage employment:** Female education and their gainful employment will raise the status of women which will have positive effect on achieving small family norm.

3. **Provision of old age pension and social security** which will reduce the dependence of parents on their children.

4. **Reduction in infant mortality** i.e., death rate of infants and small children through expanded public health programmes and better nutritional standards by ensuring longevity of life for new born children will help in reducing birth rate.

5. **Family planning:** Family planning means planned parenthood where the parents decide to keep their family small by giving birth to one or two children at proper intervals. The

idea is to have a baby by choice and not by chance. Young married couples make use of various birth control devices to limit size of their families. Acceptance of family planning and one or two child norm by a large section of our population in the reproductive age group can help reduce birth rate substantially.

6. **Incentives for small families:** Such incentives as preference in government jobs, housing and other loans at low interest rates, preference in allotment of accommodation to people with small families can have a great impact on cutting down the birth rate. A scheme of disincentive to people with large families can also be devised so that the policy of carrot and stick can yield the desired fall in population growth rate.

Concerns about Population Growth

Although we need not worry about Malthusian fears that population growth in India is outstripping—or will soon outstrip—the growth of food supply, one cannot deny the fact of the widespread prevalence of hunger in India.

The incidence of nutritional deprivation in India is among the highest in the world. General undernourishment—what is sometimes called 'protein-energy malnutrition'—is nearly twice as high in India as in sub-Saharan Africa on the average. Judged in terms of the usual standards of retardation in weight for age, the proportion of undernourished children in Africa is 20-40 per cent, whereas the percentage of undernourished Indian children is very high 40-60 per cent. The proportion of 'severely undernourished' children in India is above 20 per cent in the larger north Indian states (based on the weight-for-age criterion).

As Indians acquire greater purchasing power, and as the biases against particular groups (such as young girls) diminish, the size and composition of food consumption per head will have to change. The challenges of food production and food availability in India have to be seen in that light, rather than in terms of the old Malthusian comparison between the growth of total population and that of aggregate food production (Drèze and Sen, 2002).

Second, the pressure on environmental resources is no less serious than perspective of food production and consumption. We have sufficient evidence of rapid deterioration of the local environment across the country (in addition to India's contribution to global environmental degradation), with a wide range of adversities, varying from overcrowding of habitat and increases in man-made pollution to the denuding of forests and vegetation.

Third, rapid population growth leads to excessive pressure not only on the environment but also on the social infrastructure, including sewage systems, hospital facilities, railway networks, power grids, garbage-processing plants, and many other components of the 'stock' of public amenities. When public authorities are constantly racing to bring this stock in line with a larger population, there is much less room for qualitative improvements in public facilities. This phenomenon is clearly visible in some urban agglomerations, the rapid growth of which has gone hand in hand with a qualitative deterioration of the social infrastructure.

> To summarise, concern about population growth must not be simply dismissed as groundless. The size of the Indian population is already large, and its continued rapid expansion can certainly be a source of anxiety for the environment, in addition to the problems it raises for improving the living standard and economic and social well-being of the people. And yet the population situation is not as terrifying as it is sometimes made to look, based on the citation of selectively chosen statistics (or non-statistics). First, food supply has not been falling behind population—quite firmly to the contrary. The possibility of accommodating considerable increases in food consumption per head—both quantitative and qualitative—is still quite favourable. Second, the fertility rate is falling quite rapidly, and may decline faster still with sensible policies, especially related to child health and women's empowerment. Third, the fertility rate varies widely between different regions in India, and there is much to learn from those that have already achieved low fertility rates, and also much evidence that these achievements are indeed spreading to other regions as well (Drèze and Sen, 2002).

Gender Equity and the Demographic Transition

There is much evidence now, based on inter-country comparisons as well as inter-regional contrasts within India, that women's empowerment (through employment, education, property rights, etc.) can have a very strong effect in reducing fertility rates. Speedy fertility declines in the states of Kerala, Tamil Nadu or Himachal Pradesh in India can be firmly linked to the rapid enhancement of female education and other sources of empowerment of young women. In fact, the principal variables that seem to account for inter-district variations in fertility rates in India are directly linked to women's empowerment, in particular female literacy and women's participation in gainful employment.

Female literacy not only has a strong impact in reducing child mortality rates, which in itself is a great result, it additionally also contributes to reducing fertility. Similarly, the promotion of women's employment opportunities and related sources of empowerment contribute to their security in old age, and offer some protection from the adversities of widowhood. These, again, are important achievements in themselves, and also make a further contribution to fertility decline, insofar as the fear of old-age insecurity often slows down the adoption of small family norms.

Population Policy since 1947

The debate about population growth and family planning received impetus in the late 1940s not only due to the publication of the Bhore Committee Report, but also because of the occurrence of several poor harvests which necessitated the importation of food. Moreover, the 1951 Census revealed significant demographic growth. It was against this background that Nehru announced that India would initiate a national family planning programme. The final document of the First Five Year Plan, presented in the Parliament in 1952, referred specifically to a programme for 'family limitation and population control.' Thus, India became the first country in the world to adopt an official national population policy in support of family planning (Caldwell, 1998; Visaria and Jain, 1976).

During the 1950s, the government allocated modest sums of money to the population programme. At that time, many people had reservations about the promotion of modern contraception. Also as India was a *pioneer*, there was little previous experience on which to draw. However, there were other significant developments in the 1950s. There was increasing achievement in promoting contraception in the larger towns. The government of Madras state began endorsing vasectomy with success, and it was soon followed by Kerala, Mysore and Maharashtra. Madras also began making compensation payments to poor people who were sterilised. By the time of the Third Five Year Plan (1961-1966) the 'objective of stabilising the growth of population (within) a reasonable period' was put 'at the very centre of India's planned development.' The Third Plan document also noted the important role that voluntary sterilisation might make towards achieving this. The budgetary outlay was significantly increased. Sterilisation camps began to be used to promote vasectomy. There was also a shift in the emphasis of family planning delivery, from a clinic-based approach to a wider community extension strategy. The late 1960s also saw the increasing adoption of timebound—and often unrealistic—demographic 'targets.' In 1968, a goal was set to reduce the birth rate from 41 to 23 per 1,000 within 10 years. But at the start of the 21st century, the birth rate was still about 25 (Dyson *et al.*, 2004).

The period of the Fourth Five Year Plan (1969-1974) saw increased concern over the rate of demographic growth. The 1971 Census showed a decadal increment of 109 million. Consequently, there was an increased emphasis upon targets, compensation payments and male sterilisation. This continued into the Fifth Plan, and culminated in the atmosphere of urgency which characterised Indira Gandhi's declaration of Emergency in 1975-1977. The language of the 1976 National Population Policy as quoted in Cassen (1978: 182) is revealing of the time:

> The wait for education and economic development to bring about a drop in fertility is not a practical solution. The very increase in population makes economic development slow and more difficult of achievement. The time factor is so pressing, and the population growth so formidable, that we have to get out of this vicious circle through a direct assault upon this problem as a national commitment.

The Emergency saw a massive increase in vasectomies. But there was later a backlash against the programme, particularly in the northern states, which lasted into the 1980s. Subsequently, although the government family welfare programme has continued to emphasise sterilisation, it has been mainly tubectomy which has been provided.

The rhetoric of population control largely disappeared with the Sixth Plan (1980-1985). Since the Seventh Plan in particular (1986-1990), there has been increasing recognition of the requirements: to tailor the family welfare programme to the conditions prevailing in individual states; to adopt a multi-sectoral approach which recognises the linkages between birth control and programmes in other areas (such as education); and to involve the private sector more in contraceptive delivery. Incentive payments and targets have largely been eliminated. Furthermore, following the 1994 Cairo Population Conference, emphasis has now greater shifted to the reproductive health needs of women.

National Population Policy, 2000

Objectives

The National Population Policy (NPP), 2000, aims at achieving net replacement levels of total fertility rate by 2010 through vigorous implementation of inter-sectoral operational strategies. The long-term objective is to achieve population stabilisation by 2045, at a level consistent with the requirements of sustainable economic growth, social development and environment protection. Crude birth rate has come down, but needs to come down faster in view of the declining crude death rate (Table 6.2).

TABLE – 6.2

India: Selected Health Indicators

Sl. No.	Parameter	1951	1981	1991	2001	Current Level
1.	Crude birth rate (per 1,000 population)	40.8	33.9	29.5	25.4	21.6 (2012*)
2.	Crude death rate (per 1,000 population)	25.1	12.5	9.8	8.4	7.1 (2012*)
3.	Total fertility rate (per woman)	6.0	4.5	3.6	3.1	2.4 (2012*)
4.	Maternal mortality ratio (per 100,000 live births)	NA	NA	NA	301 (1992-93)	178 (2007-2009*)
5.	Infant mortality rate (per 1,000 live births)	146 (1951-1961)	110	80	66 (2011)	42 (2011*)
	5.1 Male				NA	46
	5.2 Female				NA	28
6.	Child (0-4) mortality rate (per 1,000 children)	57.3 (1972)	41.2	26.5	19.3	13.3 (2010*)
7.	Life expectancy at birth:			(1981-85)	(1989-93)	(2006-10)**
	Total		55.5	59.4	63.4	66.1
	7.1 Male	37.2	55.4	59.0	62.3	64.6
	7.2 Female	36.2	55.7	59.7	64.6	67.7

Note: The dates in the brackets indicate years for which latest information is available.
* National Family Health Survey.
** Abridged Life Table 2003-2007 to 2006-2010, RGI India.
NA: Not Available.

Source: Ministry of Health & Family Welfare and Office of the Registrar General, India; *Economic Survey 2009-10, 2010-11, 2011-12, 2012-13, 2013-14.*

According to the Technical Group on Population Projections constituted by the National Commission on Population, May 2006, annual population growth is expected to gradually decelerate from 1.6 per cent in the five years ending in 2006 to 0.9 per cent in the five years ending in 2026 (Table 6.3). India's population, which is estimated to have gone up from the Census 2001 figure of 1,029 million to 1,112 million in 2006, is projected to increase to 1400 million by 2026.

India is passing through a phase of unprecedented demographic changes. These demographic changes are likely to contribute to a substantially increased labour force in the country.

TABLE – 6.3

India: Population Projections

(in millions)

Year	*2001*	*2006*	*2011*	*2016*	*2021*	*2026*
Total	1,029	1,112	1,193	1,269	1,340	1,400
Below 15 years	365*(364)	357	347	340	337	327
15-64 years	619*(613)	699	780	851	908	957
Above 65 years	45*(49)	56	66	78	95	116

Notes:* Figures are as per smoothing of age-groups for working out population projections.

Figures in parenthesis are as per Census of India 2001. These figures will not tally with the total since 'age not stated' is excluded.

2001 figures exclude the population of Paomata, Mao-Maram and Purul sub-divisions of Senapati district of Manipur.

Source: Population Projections for India and States 2001-2026—Census of India 2001: Report of the Technical Group on Population Projections constituted by the National Commission on Population, May 2006.

As per Sample Registration System (SRS) (2013) data, there has been a gradual decline in the share of population in the age group 0-14 from 41.2 to 38.1 per cent during 1971 to 1981 and from 36.3 to 28.4 per cent during 1991 to 2013. On the other hand, the proportion of economically active population (15-59 years) or, India's 'demographic dividend', has increased from 53.4 to 56.3 per cent during 1971 to 1981 and from 57.7 to 63.3 per cent during 1991 to 2013. On account of better education, health facilities, and increase in life expectancy, the percentage of elderly (60+) has gone up from 5.3 to 5.7 per cent and 6.0 to 8.3 per cent respectively in the same two periods (*Economic Survey 2014-15*).

The growth rate of the labour force will continue to be higher than that of the population until 2021. As quoted in the Economic Survey 2014-15, "300 million youth will enter the labour force by 2025, and 25 per cent of the world's workers in the next three years will be Indians. Population projections indicate that in 2020 the average age of India's population will be the lowest in the world—around 29 years compared to 37 years in China and the United States of America, 45 years in West Europe, and 48 years in Japan. Consequently, while the global economy is expected to witness a shortage of young population of around 56 million by 2020, India will be the only country with a youth surplus of 47 million (Labour Bureau, 2014)".

The main issue to address then is not just providing employment but increasing the employability of the labour force in India.

Employability is contingent upon knowledge and skills developed through quality education and training. Thus any solution to the problem lies in a well-designed education and training regime that sets out to meet these objectives. The problem of low employability levels owing to poor quality of education is accentuated by the fact that fewer students opt for higher education.

Every fast-growing Asian economy in recent years has accelerated as it underwent a demographic transition. In India itself, Aiyar and Mody (2011) document that the high growth states (Tamil Nadu, Karnataka and Gujarat) in the period 1991-2001 had a dependency ratio which was 8.7 percentage points lower than that of the low growth states [Bihar, Madhya Pradesh (MP) and Uttar Pradesh (UP)] and an average annual growth rate that was 4.3 percentage points higher. Looking ahead, they argue, the low growth states will benefit more from the demographic dividend, as higher incomes and lower fertility alter demographics. Indeed, over the period 2001-2011, the hitherto laggard states have grown at an average of around 5 per cent annually. The difference between their growth and the growth of the leaders in the period 2001-2011 is just 1.5 percentage points. So demographic transition seems to be correlated with growth, with some reasons to believe that causality flows both ways: lower dependency ratios increase growth and higher growth reduces fertility and consequently dependency ratios.

Growth optimists point to another reason for cheer. Cross-country evidence suggests that productivity is an increasing function of age, with the age group 40-49 being the most productive because of work experience (Feyrer 2007). Nearly half the additions to the Indian labour force over the period 2011-2030 will be in the age group 30-49, even while the share of this group in China, Korea and the US will be declining. That India will be expanding its most productive cohorts even while most developed countries and some developing countries like China will be contracting theirs in the coming decades can be another source of advantage (Economic Survey 2012-13).

Recent economic history is replete with examples of economies that were supposed to have great potential but ultimately did not achieve rapid economic growth and improvements in standards of living. At the same time, we have instances of economies classified as basket cases that achieved rapid turnarounds. India's achievement in the post-reform period and South Korea's rapid transformation surely fall in this latter category. But India's continuing on a rapid growth path is not preordained. Besides favourable circumstances, it requires deft policy making and a broad vision of the future, possible risks, and opportunities. We stand at a crossroads where we need to develop a clear strategy for continued inclusive growth.

Socioeconomic progress—in particular, rises in levels of education and average incomes, and improvements in infrastructure—should also contribute to a continuing reduction in mortality from certain types of infectious disease, such as some forms of diarrhoea and respiratory infection. Fertility decline too should bring benefits to the conditions influencing maternal and child death rates.

The annual Sample Registration System (SRS) survey done by the government's Census Office for the year 1998 and 2008 (October 2012) has come out with some astonishing figures showing dramatic changes taking place in the population indicators of some states that are not reflected in the country-level data. Crude birth rate—the number of live births per 1,000 population—dipped from 26.4 to 22.8 for the whole country between 1998 and 2008. That's a 14 per cent decline. In 2012, it has been reported as 22.1. But in eight major states, the decline was much more. In Punjab, the birth rate fell by a whopping 23 per cent, followed by Kerala and Maharashtra (both 20%) and West Bengal (18%).

Countrywide, the crude death rate, or the number of deaths per 1,000 population, came down by 18 per cent in a decade. Again, there were surprises in the toppers' list. Both MP and Rajasthan saw a 23 per cent dip in death rates, closely followed by Bihar (22%) and UP (20%). The natural growth rate of the population for India declined by 11 per cent, but in Kerala and Punjab, the rate of population growth slowed down by as much as 32 per cent. In Maharashtra, it was down by 23 per cent and in Andhra Pradesh, Tamil Nadu and West Bengal by about 18 per cent.

There has been a significant decline in the infant mortality rate from 72 in 1998 to 53 in 2008 and to 44 in 2012. Many states are way ahead in the fight to bring down baby deaths. Tamil Nadu has slashed infant mortality by an incredible 42 per cent, West Bengal by 34 per cent, Maharashtra by 33 per cent and Odisha by 30 per cent. A few smaller states have actually shown an increase in infant mortality rates. These include Delhi, Jammu & Kashmir (J&K) and Meghalaya.

While all these are comparative rates, the absolute numbers are also important. As of 2012, Kerala had the lowest birth rate of 15 per thousand, followed by Tamil Nady (15.9), Punjab (16.2) and West Bengal (16.3). Death rates are lowest in West Bengal (6.2 per thousand) followed by Kerala, Maharashtra, Rajasthan, Gujarat and Haryana (all around 7). Natural growth rate was lowest in Kerala (8 per thousand) closely followed by Tamil Nadu (8.5).

India is passing through a demographic transition to a society where population will grow slowly, and people will live longer, hopefully leading a healthier life.

However, there will be health problems related to urbanisation, changes in lifestyles and, especially over the longer run, population ageing.

Comparing India to China

Figure 6.1 offers another perspective on economic growth in India by comparing it with that of China. India had 66 per cent higher income per capita than China in 1980, but by the early 1990s, China overtook India. In 2008, the situation was decisively reversed, with income per capita in China double that of India.[4]

FIGURE – 6.1

Real Income per capita in China and India

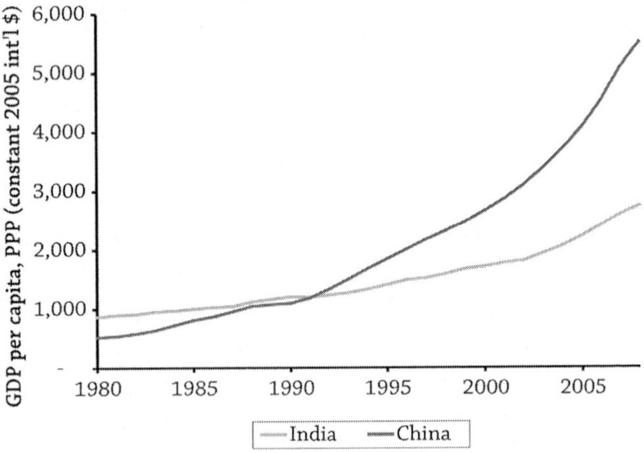

Source: World Bank World Development Indicators, 2009. (Bloom 2012).

4. Bloom, David E. (nd). "Population Dynamics in India and Implications for Economic Growth", edited by Chetan Ghate (2012). Reprinted in Uma Kapila (ed.) (2018), *Indian Economy since Independence* (28th edition). New Delhi: Academic Foundation.

India and China are credited with establishing the world’s earliest national family planning programmes, in 1952 and 1956, respectively. In strictly demographic terms, China’s campaign of ‘later, longer, fewer’[5] and its one-child policy (beginning in 1979) led to a precipitous decline in fertility and a sharp rise in the working-age share of the population (Attane, 2002; Robinson and Ross, 2007). Meanwhile, India’s family planning programme led to political backlash that ultimately setback its family planning efforts and pushed India’s demographic trajectory out of phase with China’s. Demographics are one powerful driver of economic performance, and India and China’s economic trajectories began to diverge (Bloom 2012).

The difference between India’s and China’s economic trajectories may begin to narrow as India’s working-age share continues to rise, positioning India to recoup some of the income per capita ground it had lost relative to China in the past two decades. The very rapid rise in the ratio of China’s working-age to non-working-age population contributed significantly to its extremely fast economic growth since 1980. The corresponding population ratio in India has grown more slowly, which fits well with the slower increase in India’s rate of economic growth. If India follows the UN’s low-fertility projections in the coming decades, its ratio will reach roughly the same level that China has in 2010, with, potentially, a concomitant boost in its income per capita and rate of economic growth. This fertility scenario for India seems, however, implausibly extreme remarks Bloom.

Numerous researchers have explored the China-India comparison in great detail, spurred by China having emerged as a major economic power while India has experienced a much slower economic transformation. Bloom et al., (2010) track key features of economic growth in China and India since 1980, and find that higher rates of economic growth in both countries are attributable to rises in longevity, increased trade or openness of the economy, and a higher share of the working-age population. Notably, the authors predict that moving forward, economic growth in China will be slowed by flattening increases in life expectancy and a rising dependency rate due to a rapidly aging population. In contrast, the authors predict that the effects of a fertility decline and rising longevity in India will create a rise in the working-age share of the total population in that country, allowing for higher growth rates in India over the next 30 years.

Similarly, DaVanzo et al. (2010) compare demographic conditions and their implications in China and India, finding that in the short run,

China holds more of the prerequisites needed to take full advantage of its demographic dividend:

> "more flexible labor markets; higher rates of female labor force participation, more highly educated women, and more open attitudes about women working; less illiteracy in general (and especially for women); better infrastructure; more internal migration...and a higher degree of urbanisation, more openness to foreign trade, and slightly higher rates of coverage by public pensions."

However, in the long run, the authors find that in comparison to India, China's prospects for sustained economic growth might be curtailed by shifting demographics. A rapidly aging population will create new demands and strains, resulting in wealth transfers from working-age populations to the elderly. In this respect, India will have a demographic and economic advantage over China in the decades to come.

Bloom et al. (2010) study economic growth in China and India between 1965-70 and 1995-2000 and find that increases in the working age population share during that period boosted the rate of economic growth in India by an annual average of 0.7 percentage points. According to this study, if India adopts policies that allow the working-age population to be productively employed, India may receive a demographic dividend of roughly 1 percentage point growth in GDP per capita, compounded year by year.

Examining projected changes in the size of the labour force in China, India provides a straightforward way of considering the interaction of population growth, changing age structure, and the supply of labour. India will add roughly 9 million people each year to its labour force over the next decade, while China will add virtually none. With growing competition for young, skilled workers, China will see rising wages. This is beneficial for Chinese workers, but may hinder the growth of China's exports. India's new workers are not as well educated as China's, and if they are employed, their wages are likely to remain low. Although this will aid in the growth of labour-intensive manufacturing, sooner rather than later, India will need to significantly raise the educational level of its workforce if its industries are to produce higher-value goods more efficiently. On a separate note, China's population is aging more rapidly than India's, with consequences for the relative level of resources that will need to be directed toward care of the elderly.

In summary, India's demographic evolution over the coming decades will provide a potential boost to its rate of economic growth—

at a time when China will be losing the demographic impetus that has helped spur its economy. But the process is not automatic. Policy choices in the areas of governance, macroeconomic management, trade, and human capital formation can have a significant effect on realisation of the demographic dividend. Central to capturing, the dividend is providing an economic environment in which working-age people are productively employed. Failure in this endeavour could result in a demographic disaster rather than a demographic dividend.

The Experience of Kerala and Tamil Nadu

The two southern states of Kerala and Tamil Nadu with a population of about 105million (around 10 per cent of the total) in 2011 illustrate the alternative ways of reaching a replacement level of fertility.

In Kerala, with its very low infant and child mortality rate, the adoption of a two-child norm has led to a total fertility rate of 2.0; allowing for mortality, its fertility rate is below (87.8) the replacement level.

An almost universal female literacy and a low level of infant and child mortality, and the high status of women, all intrinsically desirable goals, are considered crucial in the decline in fertility in Kerala. However, other important contributory factors include the very high pressure of population density on land and an associated low proportion of rural male workers engaged in agriculture (the lowest, 54%, among the major states according to the 1987-88 survey of the NSS), a very low proportion of the self-employed and relatively very high rates of open unemployment (the highest in the country). The persistent high level of unemployment has been accompanied by the demonstration by the emigrants to the Middle East of the feasibility of getting out of the vicious circle of poverty. Such a combination of forces favourable to fertility decline through both delayed marriage and control of marital fertility is not easy to find elsewhere in the country.

Tamil Nadu has achieved the largest proportionate reduction in child mortality among all major Indian states other than Kerala. Today, Tamil Nadu has the third-lowest child mortality rate among major Indian states and the second-lowest maternal mortality rate. Over the same period, Tamil Nadu also achieved the largest porportionate reduction in total fertility rate (about 50%). These achievements are all the more remarkable in view of the fact that Tamil Nadu has no less income poverty than the Indian average. In fact, the headcount index of poverty is a little higher in Tamil Nadu than in India as a whole.

The decline in fertility in Tamil Nadu has been attributed to the political support for both an increase in the age at marriage and an imaginative programme of information, education and communication (IEC).

Enabling Factors

Recent studies point to a number of enabling factors that have facilitated Tamil Nadu's rapid demographic transition. Commonly cited factors include a good infrastructure, a rich history of social reform movements, high literacy rates in the younger age groups, wide popular exposure to mass media and strong 'political will.' Less widely discussed is the relatively liberated status of women in contemporary Tamil society. Tamil Nadu has a high female-male ratio, little gender bias in school attendance and high levels of female labour force participation. Also, interesting is some recent information from the second round of the National Family Health Survey (NFHS) (1998-99) relating to different aspects of 'female autonomy'. Whether we look at the proportion of adult women who work outside the household (43%), or who have independent access to money (79%), or who are able to go to the market 'without permission' from other family members (79% again), Tamil Nadu is ahead of all other major states (with one exception—Himachal Pradesh—in the case of 'independent access to money'). Bearing in mind the role of women's agency in the demographic transition, this feature of gender relations is crucial to our understanding of what has happened in Tamil Nadu.

Extensive state initiatives in the fields of child nutrition, health care and social security have also made an important contributon to mortality and fertility decline in Tamil Nadu.

India's Demographic Dividend

Over the past four decades, India has undergone rapid demographic changes. The onset and speed of demographic transition—a process of change whereby societies move from a situation of high mortality and fertility to one of low mortality and fertility—differs from region to region within India. As already discussed while the level of fertility in southern Indian states has reached below replacement, it is still high in many states in north India because, though declining, the decline is at a slower pace. There are two important consequences of demographic transition. The first is population explosion due to a rapid decline in mortality rates amidst the maintenance of a high birth rate. This sudden and sustained increase in population size during the initial phase of demographic transition directly impacts the economy.

Another consequence of demographic transition is a shift in the age structure of the population resulting in broader and long-term age structural transition. In the first phase of the demographic transition, the number of children increases both in relative and absolute size due to high fertility levels and a rapid fall in mortality. After some time lag as fertility rate starts declining, it contributes to a decline in the relative share of the young population. As children born during different phases of demographic transition move from youth to adulthood, and to old age, the age structure of the population undergoes major changes. During this process, there will be a period of 'window of opportunity' where child dependency ratio (ratio of child population to working age population) declines due to decline in fertility as well as increase in the working age population, as children born during the high fertility regime move into working ages. If this window of opportunity is properly exploited, there is greater potential for demographic dividend through increased savings and investment for economic growth (Navaneetham, 2012).[5]

The period of 'window of opportunity' according to Navaneetham can be exploited in three ways to give demographic dividends:

1. By productive employment of the available labour force, which would raise total gross domestic product (GDP).
2. By directing accumulated wealth and savings into productive investments. Households tend to save less when there are more children since a substantial part of the family income is spent on raising them. When fertility declines, the demand on household resources for raising children reduces, allowing households to save more of their income.
3. Fertility decline has immediate and direct impact on the school-going population and provides an opportunity to invest more on their education and health contributing to better-quality human capital in the future. Women with fewer children are more able and often more willing to participate in remunerative work, and are more likely to invest additional income in the health and education of their children.

This would be a one-time only opportunity and its length would be determined by the speed of demographic transition. If appropriate

5. Navaneetham, K. (2012). "Demographic Dividend", in Kaushik Basu and Annemie Maertens (ed.), *The Oxford Companion to Economics in India* (Vol. I). New Delhi: Oxford University Press.

interventions are not made during this period, it would have negative implications for the economy and society. Demographic dividend could explain as much as one-third of the per capita GDP growth rate of the East Asian economies during the period of their economic miracle.

'Window of Opportunity' for India

In India the share of the working-age population (15-64) has been increasing since 1980 and is expected to reach its peak by 2025. Generating new employment opportunities to meet the growing working-age population is a major challenge for India. If it is productively employed it will boost the economy. Among the working-age population, the share of the youth segment (15-24) will decrease from now on, while that of the mature labour force will be increasing. There is also rapid decline in the ratio of youth (15-24) to working-age population (25-64) from 2010. This indicates that there will be less pressure on the economy to generate new employment opportunities and that can lead to a possible reduction in unemployment, which can be described as another window of opportunity for India. Further, this would increase the saving ratio as well as tax revenues, which may augment the capacity for investment and funding of social programmes. It is also likely that the increase in the share of middle working-age population (50-64) would contribute to higher saving rates as it tends to have a greater capacity to save due to higher income and reduced consumption. This opportunity would continue even after 2030 and this can be exploited for economic growth (Navaneetham, 2012).

The size and share of the old-age population will continue to increase during the age structural transition. However, the increase would be greater after 2025. The old dependency ratio would also increase rapidly after 2025. Meeting the healthcare and social security needs of the elderly would be a major challenge for India particularly after 2025.

Estimated Demographic Bonus for India

Bhat (2001) estimated that the demographic bonus was negative during the decades 1951-1971, as the growth rate of total population was higher than that of working-age population. After 1971, the growth rate of working age population was higher than that of total population, resulting in a positive demographic bonus. He also showed that the demographic bonus would be highest during the decade 2001-2011—a contribution of 0.6 per cent GDP growth rate in the total per capita GDP growth rate. The demographic bonus is likely to continue till 2031 and would be negative thereafter.

It may be structural transition would be different in different states. However, the demographic bonus will vary from state to state as the nature of demographic transition is different due to their socioeconomic and cultural differences. The bonus would be positive till 2011 among the demographically advanced states such as Kerala, Tamil Nadu and Punjab, and would be negative thereafter. On the other hand, the BIMARU (Bihar, Madhya Pradesh, Rajasthan and Uttar Pradesh) states where the process of demographic transition began later than in other states started getting greater dividend from 2001 and would be likely to continue to do so till 2031. As there are regional differences in age structural transition, internal migration could be of critical importance in the future as young workers move from underdeveloped to developed regions. The regional differences in age structural transition may also play an important role in terms of convergence in economic growth among the states in India, provided efforts are made to invest in human capital among the BIMARU states as a large share of labour supply in the future would come from them (Navaneetham, 2012).

The demographic dividend is also likely to accrue from the expected increase in labour-force participation of women due to the shortening of the duration of child-bearing years. The total bonus derived from the labour supply during the period 2001-2051 is estimated to be 1 per cent, out of which labour supply effect would be 0.2 per cent and the effect of the expected increase in labour-force participation of women would be 0.8 per cent, keeping labour productivity constant (Bhat, 2001). The savings ratio would increase from 23 per cent in 2001 to 32 per cent in 2031 due to the expected decline in dependency burden, which would contribute to an increase in economic growth rate. It was estimated that the demographic transition would contribute 40 per cent of the per capita GDP growth rate during the period 2001-2051. About 13 per cent of this increase would be due to the increase in labour supply, assuming output per worker remained constant, and the remaining 27 per cent would be due to an increase in the savings ratios, assuming per capita consumption did not change (Navaneetham, 2012).

India's Response to 'Window of Opportunity'

The experience of India so far shows that the 'window of opportunity' has not been exploited though, it has become available since the 1980s (Mitra and Nagarajan, 2005; Chandresekhar *et al.*, 2006). It has been argued that the employment growth rate was low during the 1990s, particularly in the rural areas, and consequently the unemployment rate was high (Chandresekhar *et al.*, 2006). This was the period during which the growth of the youth population was also greater. As new employment opportunities did not grow at the same pace as the numbers of youth, the unemployment rate among the youth increased. But it is encouraging to see that the employment growth rate has increased significantly in both rural and urban areas. It is also likely that the increase in the share of middle working-age population (50-64) would contribute to higher saving rates as it tends to have greater capacity to save due to higher income and reduced consumption. This is likely to continue into the future when the relative share of youth population is expected to decline.

The relative share of childhood population will decline in the future. This provides an opportunity to improve the human capital through public policy measures with respect to nutrition, education and health care. The relatively rapid growth of the labour force would benefit India, if employment opportunities increased with sufficient speed to match the growth in labour supply, maintained growth in labour productivity and invested in infrastructure. However, the size and share of the elderly population would increase rapidly after 2031, and this will pose several policy and programme challenges. To meet these challenges effectively, there will be need for concerted efforts to devise appropriate public and social policies directed at the provision of social security and healthcare, and encouraging the development of social networks. In order to meet the challenges in the future and to prepare for them, it is important for India to exploit the window of opportunity available for a short period, a one-time gift from the demographic transition, with appropriate economic and social policies (Navaneetham, 2012).

Demographic Dividend and Related Policy Interventions

According to UNFPA report, since 2018, India's working-age population (people between 15 and 64 years of age) has grown larger than the dependant population—children aged 14 or below as well as people above 65 years of age. This bulge in the working-age population is going to last till 2055, or 37 years from its beginning.

Many Asian economies—Japan, China, South Korea — were able to use this 'demographic dividend', defined by the UNFPA (United Nations Population Fund) as the growth potential that results from shifts in a population's age structure. This transition happens largely because of a decrease in the total fertility rate (TFR, which is the number of births per woman) after the increase in life expectancy gets stabilised. Japan was among the first major economies to experience rapid growth because of changing population structure. The country's demographic-dividend phase lasted from 1964 to 2004 i.e., 40 years.

China entered this stage in 1994—16 years after Deng Xiaoping's economic reforms started in December 1978. Although its growth accelerated immediately after the reforms, the years of demographic dividend helped sustain this rate for a very long period. In the 16 years between 1978 and 1994 (post-reform, pre-dividend) China saw eight years of double-digit growth (Thakur, 2019).[6]

It is, however, important to note that this change in population structure alone cannot push growth. There are many other factors. In the late 20th century, demographic dividend in Asia resulted in a seven-fold increase in the GDP of many countries. In Latin America the growth was only two-fold. Countries can only harness the economic potential of the youth bulge if they are able to provide good health, quality education and decent employment to its entire population (ibid).

India’s future demographic evolution will have significant implications for the economy, education and the environment. Economic growth may be enhanced by the ‘demographic bonus’ deriving from the projected diminishing age dependency ratio. Benefits will arise if there are consequential increases in savings and investment. But such increases cannot be taken for granted. As Mari Bhat argued, there is nothing automatic about such potentially positive relationships (Bhat, 2001).

Also, as Robert Cassen has remarked, a great challenge for India’s future rests in limiting divergence. The experience of recent decades suggests strongly that the poor states are mostly growing slowly economically and fast demographically, and, conversely, the country’s better-off states are mostly growing fast economically and slowly demographically. In both cases, processes of cumulative causality apply. That is, faster demographic change would bring about faster economic change, and vice versa.

Another study involving the Population Foundation of India and the Population Reference Bureau rightly raises the question as to whether India will be the one and only country ever to contain two

6. Atul Thakur, *Times of India*, July 22, 2019.

billion people (Nanda and Haub, 2007). Such a concern cannot be taken lightly.

Many people, would probably agree with a statement by Montek Singh Ahluwalia (2008) that China's population policy was too drastic (much too drastic). And in any case, such a drastic policy would have been impossible in a democratic society, one where there is attention to due process, such as applies in India. It is inevitable that in such an open society, policies evolve more slowly and therefore, fertility change is slower as a result.

Anyone who neglects the role of India's family planning programme today are closing their eyes to an important instrument of past—and future—change. Clearly, it is far from immaterial whether the country ends up with an eventual population of 1.5 or 2.0 billion. And both of these outcomes are possible. The occurrence of rapid economic growth at present should not distract from this fact. Continuing attention to the provision of high quality family planning and reproductive health care services will benefit the poor—and especially women; there is a massive amount of good demographic evidence to this effect (e.g., see Merrick, 2001). Faster, rather than slower, fertility decline will make it easier to bring education of better quality to all people. It will reduce urban population increase, and growth of the labour force—making it easier to provide better living conditions in the urban sector and better employment prospects. It will reduce pressure on environmental resources, and it may also enhance economic growth. Since the large northern states are where fertility is highest, women are most disadvantaged and services are still weak, it is in there, but not only there, that improved services are required.

To reap the much hyped demographic dividend advantage of India, better educated and healthy population is a must. This calls for more reforms in the education system and health sector. While the National Skill Development Mission is a step in the right direction, much more is needed both in terms of achievements and speed. The Right to Education (RTE) Act must face no implementation deficit for it to work towards realising the demographic dividend. Similar reforms are needed in university and higher education and the demand-supply mismatch in the job market needs to be corrected. Mobilisation of funds for higher education is indeed a challenge for the government. The gap in available resources could possibly be met by a tailor-made PPP mode of funding without diluting the regulatory oversight of the government.

Unleashing the potential of the demographic dividend is the biggest challenge India has to face, particularly now, as it is a time-bound advantage. Therefore, timely action for equipping the young population with high expectations with health, education, adequate skills and security is of paramount importance. For this, massive efforts are needed in the form of investment in social infrastructure, skill development and empowerment of women.

The final challenge is the delivery mechanism. The outlays for different schemes have not often translated fully into outcomes owing to the poor delivery mechanism. The success of programmes and policies of the government lies in the institutional arrangement and attitudinal mindset in the public delivery system.

With women accounting for nearly 48 per cent of India's population (Census 2011), there is need to ensure and safeguard their place in the socio-economic milieu. Since this requires a change in the patriarchal mindset of the larger population, government has to continue to be a proactive facilitator of this change through consistent policies.

Another phenomenon which a population policy must address is the skewed female and child sex ratio which is spreading from urban to rural areas. Discriminatory social barriers like the absence of women's ownership rights over land and property are responsible for the continuing son preference. India's sex ratio at birth (SRB)—the number of female babies born for every 1,000 male babies—fell to an all-time low of 896 in 2015-2017. This would translate into approximately 11.7 lakh girls missing in the country in a span of three years. Five large states, Uttar Pradesh, Rajasthan, Bihar, Maharashtra and Gujarat, with poor sex ratios at birth account for about two thirds of these missing girls.

While the sex ratio continues to decline despite government efforts, India's total fertility rate—the number of kids likely to be born to a woman—which was stuck at 2.3 from 2013 onwards, fell to 2.2 in 2017, close to the replacement level fertility of 2.1.

Replacement fertility is the level at which a population can replace itself from one generation to the next without growing or declining and it is estimated at 2.1 children per woman. Below this level, the population starts shrinking. Nine states, including some of the least developed, have fertility levels higher than 2.1, though two of these, Gujarat and Haryana, are at 2.2. Only in Uttar Pradesh and Bihar are women on average likely to have three or more children.

Of 13 states with below replacement level fertility, Delhi has the lowest at 1.5. Barring Rajasthan, Bihar and Uttar Pradesh, urban population of all states have less than replacement level fertility. In rural areas, MP, UP and Bihar have a fertility rate of three or more. India';s total fertility rate has fallen steadily from 3.2 in 1998 with the most dramatic improvement in the southern states where it fell from about 4 in the 1970s to the current level of 1.6 or 1.7.

The pressure to have smaller families in a society that prefers boys, along with access to sex determination methods and methods of getting rid of female babies could be leading to an alarmingly skewed sex ratio.

Moreover, many states that had earlier recorded high SRBs such as Kerala and Odisha have withnessed a steep decline. Kerala had an SRB of 948, second only to Chhattisgarh, but this has plummeted 26 points from 974 in 2012-2014. In Odisha, the fall from 956 in 2011-2013 to 929 by 2015-2017 is an even sharper 27 points.

These developments need to be confronted as part of a new population policy. It is too serious a matter to be left to political persuasion and occasional nabbing of guilty doctors.

Also, there is the ageing factor. In the next 10 years, the elders will account for 12 per cent of the country's population while India is the envy of the world because of youthful population, but several related factors are pulling back great achievements. A new population policy is needed to protect our demographic assets while preparing for difficult challenges that lie ahead and also protect the future generations from catastrophic consequences.

Human Resource Development

Human resource development plays an important role in economic developments. Third world countries, it is said, have remained under-developed on account of underdevelopment of human resources. The general masses are illiterate or their education level is low, they are unskilled and untrained, and their general health is poor. Therefore, large-scale investment in human resources is required. Investment in education and public health contributes to human resource development. Such investment helps increasing a more productive labour force, empowering it with increased knowledge and skill. Similarly, investment on health is important which takes the form of investment in medical knowledge in disease prevention and in treatment and rehabilitation.

In India, the expenditure on education is not considered an investment. It is treated as a social service and is meant only to improve the quality of man's life. The public outlay on education as percentage of GDP (gross domestic product) had stagnated for three decades since early 1980s. It was only around the mid-1980s that the proportion of public expenditure to GDP started increasing. However, in the 1990s the ratio of public expenditure to GDP has actually declined from a peak of 4.4 per cent in 1981 to 3.6 per cent or so towards the end of the decades as against the goal of 6.0 per cent of GDP.

Public Expenditure and Education Policy

Public expenditure on education is an important policy instrument for realising the education goals and for the development of education. Recognising the contribution of education to economic development, and keeping in line with the human investment revolution in economic thought, the GoI for the first time accepted the concept of 'investment' in education in its 1968 Policy and quantitatively fixed a target of 6 per cent of national income to be invested on education from the public exchequer by 1986. The proportion of GNP invested in education by the government was 3.5 per cent in 2004-05, compared to the very low level of 0.6 per cent in 1951-52. This marks a very significant progress. But it needs to be underlined that the current proportion is less than: (i) the requirements of the education system to provide reasonable levels of quality education to all the students enrolled presently, (ii) the requirements of the system to provide universal elementary education of eight years for every child of the age group 6-14, as universalisation of elementary education, in a comprehensive sense, includes universal provision of resources, universal enrolment and universal retention, and consequent growth in secondary and higher education. The goal of allocating 6 per cent of national income to education has been repeatedly postponed. But provision of appropriate education to all might require resources of a higher order—above 8 per cent of GNP.

According to Jean Drèze and Amartya Sen:

> Ultimately, the expansion on basic education in India depends a great deal on the political factors. There is no question that, even in a country as poor as India, means can be found to ensure universal attainment of literacy and other basic educational achievements. There are important strategic questions to consider in implementing the social commitment, but the primary challenge is to make it a more compelling political issue.

India had no doubt made significant achievements in the development of education. The education system at all levels was thrown open to all—rich, poor and middle-income classes, men and women, rural and urban populations, and backward and non-backward segments of the population. Secondly, as a consequence, there has been a veritable explosion in numbers—student numbers, institutions and teachers. Thirdly, institutions of excellence have been developed, producing highly specialised human capital. Lastly, it could produce the second largest (next only to China) educated and skilled manpower in the world, and the third largest scientific and technical manpower.

While the achievements of six-and-a-half decades of development planning are impressive, the failures are also shocking. Important failures pertain to universalisation of elementary education, a goal set by the Constitution for accomplishment by 1960, transformation of the country from a predominantly illiterate society into a literate one, vocationalisation of secondary education and development of higher education for excellence. Even after nearly seven decades of Independence, the number of children in the compulsory age group (6-14 years) outside the schools system is large. Vocationalisation of secondary education did not take off at all, and higher education is confined to less than 10 per cent of the relevant age group population. Also, despite significant improvements, inequalities—gender, regional and religious/caste—are still high both in the education system and correspondingly in the labour market, though they might have decreased over time. Lastly, the quality of education at all levels is depressingly low.

Education needs to be transformed into a powerful instrument of social change and national development. Unfortunately, neither are the total resources available to education adequate, nor are they spent efficiently on various levels. The costs of underinvestment in education and of the misallocation of resources within education are quite high.

Trends in Social Sector Expenditure

Public expenditure on health in India has hovered around 1 per cent of the country's GDP for most of the last twenty years—very few countries spend less than that on health care, as a ratio of GDP. When the United Progressive Alliance (UPA) government came to office in 2004, one of the core commitments of the coalition government's National Common Minimum Programme was to raise public health expenditure to 'at least 2-3 per cent of the GDP over the next five years'. But the ratio actually declined, to 0.9 per cent of GDP in 2005, before rising very slowly again, partly due (in recent years) to salaryincreases in the public sector. At 1.2 per cent of GDP, public expenditure on health in India today is still exceptionally low in comparative perspective: only nine countries in the world have a lower ratio of public expenditure on health to GDP. India's 1.2 per cent compares with 2.7 per cent in China, 3.8 per cent in Latin America, and a world average of 6.5 per cent (including countries with a national health insurance, such as those in the European Union, where the average ratio of public health expenditure to GDP is around 8 per cent). In absolute terms, this translates (in terms of purchasing-power-parity 2005 international dollars) to $39 per person per year in India, compared with $66 in Sri Lanka, $203 in China and $483 in Brazil.

A related symptom of India's lack of governmental commitment to health care is that public expenditure on health accounts for less than one third of total health expenditure. Only a few countries (such as Afghanistan, Haiti and Sierra Leone) have a lower ratio of public health expenditure to total health expenditure. To put this in perspective, public expenditure accounts for 70 to 85 per cent of total health expenditure in most countries of the European Union and North America, with an average of 77 per cent in the European Union, and one notable outlier—the United States (just below 50%), which remains a bit of a 'developing country' as far as public health care is concerned. Even the US ratio, however, is much higher than India's. The world average is 63 per cent, and even the averages for sub-Saharan Africa (45%) and for the 'least developed countries' in the world (46%) are also much higher than India's 29 per cent (see Table 6.4). These are some indications, among others, that India has one of the most commercialized health care systems in the world.

Even when health facilities are available, their utilization leaves such to be desired. According to a study, absenteeism rates among health workers ranged between 35 and 58 per cent in different Indian states in 2002-03. A similar picture emerges from another study of health services in Udaipur district (Rajasthan): more than half of the health sub-centres were found to be closed during regular opening hours, and even in the PHCs and Community Health Centres, 36 per cent of the personnel were absent on average.

TABLE – 6.4

Public Expenditure on Health, 2010

	As a share of GDP (%)	*As a share of total health expenditure (%)*	*In absolute terms (2005 PPP international dollars)*[a]
India	1.2	29	39
South Asia	1.2	30	36
Sub-Saharan Africab	2.9	45	66
East Asia & Pacificb	2.5	53	167
Middle East & North Africab	2.9	50	199
Latin America & Caribbeanb	3.8	50	424
Europe & Central Asiab	3.8	65	585
World Average	6.5	63	641
European Union	8.1	77	2,499

Note: a Calculated from per capita expenditure on health and share of public health expenditure in total health expenditure.

b 'Developing countries' only.

Source: World Development Indicators (online, 1 January 2013)

Drèze and Sen (2013).

The problem is, naturally, most intense for the poorer Indians, but the bias towards private facilities affects even the relatively well-off, who too often have rather limited access to decent and affordable health care.Fraud, over-medication, exploitative pricing and unnecessary surgery seem to be quite common in the private health sector. The need for reform applies not just to public services, or to the services available to poor households, but to the health sector as a whole.

Public investment in social infrastructure like education and health is critical in the development of an economy. However, the expenditure on social services by the Centre and States as a proportion of GDP has remained in the range of 6 per cent during 2012-13 to 2014-15. There has been a marginal decline to 5.8 per cent in 2015-16 which has further moved up to 6.6 per cent in 2017-18 (BE) (Table 6.5).

As a proportion of the GDP, expenditure on education has been hovering around 2.5 per cent. Similarly, there has not been any significant change in the expenditure on health as a proportion of GDP. India's expenditure on health as a per cent of GDP is very low compared to many other emerging and developed countries. Unlike most

TABLE – 6.5

Trends in Social Services Expenditure by Government (Central and State)

(₹ crore)

Items	*2008-09*	*2011-12*	*2012-13*	*2013-14*	*2014-15*	*2015-16*	*2016-17 RE*	*2017-18 BE*
1	*2*	*5*	*6*	*7*	*8*	*9*	*10*	*11*
As Per Cent of GDP								
Total Expenditure	28.4	27.4	27.1	26.7	26.4	24.7	26.7	26.4
Expenditure on Social Services	6.8	6.6	6.6	6.6	6.2	5.8	6.5	6.6
i) Education	2.9	3.1	3.1	3.1	2.8	2.4	2.6	2.7
ii) Health	1.3	1.2	1.3	1.2	1.2	1.1	1.5	1.4
iii) Others	2.6	2.2	2.2	2.3	2.1	2.2	2.4	2.6
As Percentage to Total Expenditure								
Expenditure on Social Services	23.8	24.0	24.4	24.9	23.4	23.4	24.2	24.9
i) Education	10.1	11.4	11.6	11.6	10.8	9.8	9.7	10.0
ii) Health	4.6	4.6	4.7	4.6	4.5	4.5	5.6	5.1
iii) Others	9.0	8.0	8.2	8.6	8.1	9.1	8.9	9.7
As Percentage to Social Services								
i) Education	42.6	47.7	47.5	46.7	46.1	41.9	40.2	40.3
ii) Health	19.5	19.0	19.1	18.7	19.4	19.2	22.9	20.6
iii) Others	37.9	33.3	33.4	34.7	34.6	38.9	36.9	39.1

Notes: 1. Social services include, education, sports, art and culture; medical and public health, family welfare water supply and sanitation; housing; urban development; welfare of SCs, STs and OBCs, labour and labour welfare; social security and welfare, nutrition, relief on account of natural Calamities etc.

2. Expenditure on 'Education' pertains to expenditure on 'Education, Sports, Arts and Culture'.
3. Expenditure on 'Health' includes expenditure on 'Medical and Public Health', 'Family Welfare' and 'Water Supply and Sanitation'.
4. GDP data from 2011-12 are as per the new base year 2011-12. GDP for 2016-17 and 2017-18 are provisional estimates and advance estimates respectively.
5. Data pertains to Union Government and 26 states.

Source: Budget Documents of Union and State Governments, Reserve Bank of India.
Economic Survey 2017-18.

countries, in India private-sector expenditure on health as a percentage of GDP is higher than public expenditure and was more than double in 2010. Despite this, the total expenditure on health as a percentage of GDP is much lower 1.1 per cent in 2015-16 than in many other developed and emerging countries and the lowest among BRICS (Brazil, Russia, India, China and South Africa) countries (Table 6.6).

TABLE – 6.6

Expenditure on Health in Developed and Emerging Economies

(as percentage of GDP)

Country	*Expenditure on Health (2010 or Latest Available Year)*		
	Public	*Private*	*Total*
Australia	6.2	2.9	9.1
Norway	8.1	1.4	9.4
United Kingdom	8.0	1.6	9.6
United States	8.5	9.1	17.6
Mexico	2.9	3.3	6.2
Indonesia	1.3	1.3	2.6
Brazil	4.2	4.8	9.0
Russian Federation	3.2	1.9	5.1
India	1.2	2.9	4.1
China	2.7	2.4	5.1
South Africa	3.9	5.0	8.9

Source: OECD Factbook 2013: Economic, Environmental and Social Statistics. *Economic Survey 2012-13.*

The Future

According to Dyson[7], during the next few decades, India's population will continue to grow, although at a slowing rate; it will continue to urbanise; and it will start to age (though gradually at first). All demographic growth in the period to 2026 will occur at ages above 15 years. There will be little change in the number of children aged less than 15 in 2026, and possibly a modest decline. By mid-century,

7. Dyson, Tim (2008). "India's Demographic Transition and its Consequences for Development", in Uma Kapila (ed.) (2019), *Indian Economy since Independence* (30th ed.). New Delhi: Academic Foundation.

the country's population will have surpassed that of China—it may do this around the year 2030—and it may well be approaching 1.6 billion. More than half of the demographic growth during 2001-2026 will occur in the main northern states i.e., Bihar, MP, Rajasthan and UP. The populations of these four states will increase by around 45-55 per cent over this period, but those of most of the other states will grow by only about 20-30 per cent.

According to National Population Stabilisation Fund (NPSF an autonomous body under the Union health ministry) on 11th July 2015, the World Population Day, at 5 p.m., India recorded a population of 127,42,39,769 constituting 17.25 per cent of world population and growing at 1.6 per cent per annum could make the country as the most populous in the world by 2050. If current growth rates continue, India will have 1.63 billion people by 2050 and will surpass China. India's population was growing faster than China which is now the World's most populous country at around 1.39 billion. It is expected that India will surpass China by 2025/2030 in population growth which is projected to be 1.65 billion.

Turning to fertility and mortality, it seems reasonable to consider that by 2026, the TFR for the country as a whole will be approximately two births per woman. It also seems plausible to suggest that women will continue to move towards a family building pattern in which they marry young, have two births in quick succession and then get sterilised while still at a relatively young age. The average life expectation for both sexes combined in 2026 may well be about 69 years (perhaps with a 3-year advantage in favour of females). There is considerable scope for future mortality gains—e.g., through higher levels of immunisation, and better control and treatment of diarrhoeal and respiratory infections.

While India is the envy of the world because of youthful population, but several related factors are pulling back great achievements. A new population policy is needed to protect our demographic assets while preparing for difficult challenges that lie ahead and also protect the future generations from catastrophic consequences.[8]

Quoting Economic Survey 2018-19, "as India is a developing economy with resource constraints, we have to prioritize and optimize the expenditure on social infrastructure to promote sustainable and

8. Ibid.

inclusive growth. It is critical at this juncture to focus on public investments in human capital and strengthen the delivery mechanisms of government interventions to ensure transparency and accountability. With India having the demographic advantage, improving educational standards, skilling the youth, enhancing job opportunities, reducing disease burden and empowering women will help in realizing the potential of a buoyant economy in the future." India is home to the world's youngest population as half of its population is below the age of 25. It has also been estimated that demographic advantage in India is available for five decades from 2005-06 to 2055-56, longer than any other country in the world (UNFPA, 2018). This demographic advantage can be reaped only if education, skilling and employment opportunities are provided to the young population.[9]

9. *Economic Survey 2018-19, Vol. 2.*

7

Land Reforms

AT the time of Independence, India inherited a semi-feudal agrarian structure with onerous tenure arrangements over substantial areas. The ownership and control of land was highly concentrated in a relatively few landlords and intermediaries. The principal interest of this controlling group in agriculture was to extract maximum rental from tenants, either in cash or in kind. Often tenants of land under intermediary and landlord control sublet their lands in smaller plots to working cultivators, thus smaller holdings increased. Under this arrangement, economic motivation to develop farm land for increased production or to improve the economic conditions of cultivators was lacking. At the same time, working cultivators after paying high rent had no surplus to invest in farm improvement. They had neither resources nor knowledge for increasing agricultural production. Thus, the agricultural land resource of India, along with its operators, was gradually impoverished because economic motivation tended toward exploitation rather than toward investment and improvement.

With increasing pressure on land, the operating land base of many working cultivators was further reduced. Land occupancy rights became increasingly insecure. Often cultivators were continuously shifted from one plot to another according to the whims of superior holders. Land was divided into small fragments, each owned or leased by cultivators whose objective was subsistence. Over time, a large number of farms became disincentive-ridden due to size disability. A substantial portion of such cultivators sought to supplement their farm income by working as hired labourers competitive with even poorer landless workers. Independent India thus emerged with serious imbalances in man-land relationship among the three principal groups in the agricultural sector, *viz*., proprietors, working cultivators and labourers.

Following Independence, land reform as well as the abolition of intermediaries was considered an essential prerequisite for increasing agricultural production and for establishing an egalitarian society.

In an agrarian economy like India with great scarcity and unequal distribution of land, coupled with a large mass of below poverty-line rural population, there are compelling economic and political arguments for land reform. Not surprisingly, it received top priority on the policy agenda at the time of Independence. In the decades following Independence, India passed several land reform legislations. The Constitution of 1949 left the adoption and implementation of land and tenancy reforms to state governments. This resulted in a lot of variation in the implementation of these reforms across states and over time.[1]

Objectives of Land Reforms

The basic objectives of land reform measures were:

1. to remove such impediments to increase in agricultural production as arise from the agrarian structure inherited from the past and
2. to eliminate all forms of exploitation and social injustice within the agrarian system, to provide security for the tiller of soil and assure equality of status and opportunity to all sections of the rural population.

Land reform measures consisted of the following:

1. Abolition of Intermediaries who were rent collectors under the pre-independence land revenue system.
2. Tenancy reforms which included three measures: (i) Regulation of Rent (ii) Security of Tenure and (iii) Conferment of ownership rights on tenants.
3. Reorganisation of Agriculture which involved (i) Ceiling on Land Holdings and Redistribution of Land and (ii) Consolidation of Holdings.

Among all the land reform measures, abolition of intermediaries is one reform which has been relatively successful. The record in terms of other components is mixed and varies across states. Landowners

---

1. Ghatak, Maitreesh (2012). "Land Reforms", in Kaushik Basu and Annemie Maertens (eds.), *The New Oxford Companion to Economics in India* (Vol.II). New Delhi: Oxford University Press.

generally resisted the implementation of these reforms and used various methods of evasion and coercion. To evade ceiling on land holdings, they transferred land in different names of their relatives. They shuffled tenants on different plots so that they do not acquire occupancy rights which gave their security of tenure. Commenting on the performance of land reforms, S.K. Ray remarked, On balance, there seems to be some reasons to conclude that agrarian reorganisation in India has failed to make any considerable impact on the socio-economic conditions of the working cultivators. Indeed, the record so far is so depressing and frustrating that even an able administrator like Appu, who championed and spent a considerable part of his career in administering land reform programmes noted:

> Thus the programmes of land reform implemented since Independence did not lead to any significant re-distribution of land, or, the removal of all the obstacles to increasing agricultural production. Of the three programmes considered in this study, the laws for the abolition of intermediary interests were implemented fairly well. But in the case of tenancy reform and ceilings on holdings, the policies adopted were ambivalent and there were large gaps between policy and legislation and between legislation and implementation. We have seen that as result of the implementation of the tenancy laws, tenants became owners of or acquired rights in only about 4 per cent of the operated area. The enforcement of ceilings led to the redistribution of less than 2 per cent of the operated area. Thus these two measures taken together led to the redistribution of only about 6 per cent of the operated area (Appu, 1995: 217).

Effects of Land Reforms on Productivity and Poverty[2]

According to a study by Besley and Burgess (2000) abolition of intermediaries had a negative effect on poverty but no effect on productivity, and ceiling on land holding does not seem to have had much effect on either poverty or productivity, while land consolidation of holding had a positive effect on productivity without having any effect on poverty. Infact how effective a legislation is in terms of achieving its objective depends on how effectively it has been implemented. "A poorly implemented tenancy reform may have a net negative effect on productivity by freezing up the land lease market even though it might improve the productivity as well as the income of some tenants" (Ghatak). A study by Banerjee *et al.* (2002) for West

2. Besley and Burgess (2000) have used state-level data for the 16 major states of India for the period 1958-1962.

Bengal where tenancy reforms were very well implemented give totally different conclusions. In West Bengal, tenancy reforms improved agricultural productivity as a result of Operation Barga, a programme to implement and enforce tenancy laws that regulated rents and provided security to tenants of sharecroppers.

The broad conclusion is that political factor had a significant effect in the implementation of land reform legislation especially tenancy reforms. It has also been found that the likelihood of reforms increases where land inequality is high and where peasants have greater political power. Thus land reform seems to be driven by political factors. To quote Appu,

> ...If the political will in favour of meaningful land reform was weak at independence and weaker still later on, it is non-existent today. Land reform has practically disappeared from the agenda of most political parties. This, in my view, is the inevitable consequence of the great changes that have taken place in the social and economic fields. With the abolition of intermediary interests the erstwhile superior tenants belonging mostly to upper and middle castes acquired a higher social status. Rise in agricultural productivity, rising land values and higher incomes from cultivation have added to their economic strength. Substantial landowners who wield great authority in rural India are bitterly opposed to ceilings on agricultural holdings. They are able to have their way because no serious efforts have been made to organise the landless and the land poor and enlist their support in favour of reforms. As for tenancy reform is concerned, there is a certain commonality of interest between all landowners - large, medium, small and even marginal. They are all passionately attached to their land and all of them are opposed to conferring benefits on insecure tenants. In the first round of land reform only the intermediaries were adversely affected. They were few in number and were weak politically. They had also made themselves obnoxious by aligning themselves with the colonial power. So it was easy enough to abolish intermediary interests. And it was done without hurting them much. But injuring the interests of the present class of landowners is an entirely different proposition. No political party that wishes to win elections and come to power can afford to do that. At the time of independence this class of landowners did not wield much political and economic power, and with a modicum of political will the reforms could have been implemented. But now it has become almost impossible to carry out the reforms (Appu, 1995: 232-3).

It thus appears that the present policy environment is unlikely to permit drastic changes in the existing land reform legislations. Several measures need to be taken before considering such changes. An appropriate first step in this direction would be the imposition of agricultural income tax and agricultural holding tax. These measures fit well in the newly advocated philosophy for market friendly approach. They can also help to mobilise the much needed resources for employing the unemployed in the creation of social and physical infrastructure for agricultural development. Moreover, a progressive agricultural holding tax may act as a deterrent against formation of large holdings in the future—while at the same time, it may encourage greater efficiency of farmers who insist on retaining their large holdings.

8

Growth and Structural Changes since 1951

IN this chapter,[1] we analyse the performance of Indian economy since Independence with reference to the experience of growth, development and structural change in different phases of growth and policy regimes across sectors and regions.

The structure of discussion is as follows: Section I outlines the growth experience, the turning points in growth rates of national income, the sectoral contributions and comparison with other countries. In Section II, the discussion is on growth performance of different states, the regional contrasts in terms of growth rates and structural changes. Section III draws some conclusions.

I

Periodisation of Indian Growth Experience[2]

In order to learn lessons from performance, it is useful to try a different type of periodisation based on when the policy regime changed substantially. Looked at this way, the Indian growth experience can be broken up into the periods indicated in Table 8.1.

The first three plan periods up to the drought and war crisis of 1965-66 were the foundational years in which the institutional infrastructure and the policy regimes for development were put in place.

---

1. This chapter is drawn extensively from Kapila, Uma (2019). *Indian Economy since Independence* (30th edition). New Delhi: Academic Foundation.
2. Desai, Nitin (2010). "Sustaining High Growth", in Sameer Kochhar (ed.), *India on the Growth Turnpike (Essays in Honour of Vijay L. Kelkar)*. New Delhi: Academic Foundation.

These were the years when the government launched community development and rural credit cooperatives, industrial and import licensing and industrial development banks, Indian Institutes of Technology (IITs) and many research establishments, and many other institutional and policy initiatives.

TABLE – 8.1

Periodisation of Indian Growth Experience

Period	*Characterisation*	*GDP Growth (Annual Average)*	*GFCF Percentage (Annual Average)*	*ICOR (Column 4 Divided by Column 3)*
(1)	*(2)*	*(3)*	*(4)*	*(5)*
1951-52 to 1964-65	The foundational years	4.1	11.6	2.8
1965-66 to 1969-70	The crisis years	3.0	14.2	4.7
1970-71 to 1979-80	The turbulent years	2.9	15.7	5.4
1980-81 to 1990-91	The transitional years	5.6	20.4	3.6
1991-92 to 2002-03	The reform years	5.5	22.9	4.1
2003-04 to 2007-08	The high growth years— The best phase in growth	8.8	30.2	3.4

Source: Based on data from tables 1.4 and 1.6 of the *Economic Survey 2008-09*, Ministry of Finance.
Desai, Nitin (2010).

An import substituting heavy industry-oriented strategy was put in place with the Second Plan and large investments were made in public sector projects for steel and machine building, major power and river valley developments, and the transport infrastructure. The public sector grew with fresh investment rather than nationalisation. The private sector had ample room to grow and the government was proactive providing technical advice and political support. The growth performance of the economy in this first phase is good in comparision with India's pre-Independence record.

The twin droughts of 1965 and 1966 were a major shock for which the economy was ill-prepared. Food aid prevented large-scale distress but the ambitious development strategy of the foundational years was more or less abandoned. The focus was on agricultural development with substantial results in the form of the Green Revolution. There was also some liberalisation of licensing for agriculture-related industries.

But the overhang of the earlier strategy led to a continued investment in heavy industries, now including fertilisers. This was also the period which saw the real beginnings of the subsidy burden with the growth of the food and fertiliser subsidies.

In terms of policy regimes, 1970-71 is an important break point. By 1970-71, the Green Revolution had stabilised and India was past the worst when it came to food security. The Congress split was over and Mrs Gandhi was firmly in the saddle, *garibi hatao* had become the slogan of the day, poverty eradication rather than growth became the dominating consideration in public policy and a public-sector-oriented strategy was in place. The Monopolies and Restrictive Trade Practices (MRTP) Act was tightened, state trading was actively promoted and for a brief period, the food grain trade was nationalised. The banking system, which was nationalised in 1969, was put under direct bureaucratic control and directed credit with differential interest rates was instituted.

The upheavals of the oil crisis of 1973-74 and the emergency intervened in mid-decade followed by the Janata Party government, which, though more business friendly, continued to pursue an anti-poverty strategy in the guise of employment orientation. These were the years of turbulence when the state was in charge but the governments in charge of the state were buffeted by political currents that made it difficult for them to steer the economy with any sense of long-term purpose.

These middle years between 1965-66 and 1979-80 were the ones when Indian development performance was at its worst. This can be seen in the low growth rates despite relatively high levels of investment. The public investment programme was poorly managed with delays and cost overruns, inefficiencies imposed by multiple lines of tied credits being used for a single plant and input bottlenecks which could not be relieved through trade because of foreign exchange shortages.

The return of the Congress Party to power in 1980 marks a shift in policy relative to the earlier years. Although the rhetoric of *garibi hatao* continued, there were some changes in policy in Mrs Indira Gandhi's second administration that signaled a changed attitude to the private sector. A series of high-level committees under leading figures like L.K. Jha, Vadilal Dagli, Abid Hussain and M. Narasimham laid out an agenda for a more pro-private sector and pro-market policy. But the changes made in the 1980s are nowhere near as deep and far-reaching as the bonfire of controls in 1991.

Many of the more important substantive changes came later in mid-decade in Mr Rajiv Gandhi's administration and Mr V.P. Singh's budgets. The tax reductions that started with the 1985-86 budget conveyed a positive signal to capital markets and may even have led to improved collections as the tax-GDP ratio rose. But public expenditure rose even more rapidly and the combined deficit of the central and state governments rose from 7.5 per cent in 1980-81 to 9.9 per cent in 1986-1987 and fell only slightly to 9.4 per cent by 1990-91.

India's Growth Turnaround

The shift to a higher growth path during the course of the 1980s is referred to as the Indian growth turnaround. Fast growth in India since the early 1980s has placed it amongst the top nine rapidly growing economies in the world (Ahmed and Varshney, 2009).

The upward shift in India's growth path during the 1980s is significant for two reasons: the turnaround happened well before the balance of payments (BoP) crisis of 1991 and the large-scale macroeconomic reforms that ensued.

The second puzzling aspect about India's growth turnaround is that is was not driven by manufactured exports and, therefore, has little in common with the East Asian economic miracle. In particular, there was no industrial policy targeted towards developing specific industries. It was the service sector that led the increase in the overall growth rate in the early 1980s. Since many components of services are income related (such as financial services, business services, and hotels and restaurants) and begin to increase only after a certain stage in development, the fact that India's service sector created the impulse for the growth turnaround is puzzling.

The key issue on which all studies agree is that, at some point during the 1980s, there was an increase in growth, which, from the 1990s, was not only of statistical but also of massive economic significance. What has puzzled many contributors to the literature is that analysis of aggregate data suggests a pickup in growth during the early 1980s, before most of the major policy changes.

While there is a reasonable degree of consensus amongst economists on the timing of India's growth turnaround, there is less agreement about its causes. What is indisputable is that something happened during the 1980s that opened the door to a rise in growth. The challenge facing growth economists is to weave a logically consistent story on the timing and causes of India's growth turnaround (Ghate *et al.*, 2012).[3]

According to Subramanian (2012),[4] a number of plausible explanations can easily be ruled out. External liberalisation could not have been a factor because the Indian trade regime actually became more restrictive during the 1980s, and the full impact of trade reforms implemented in the 1990s was only felt at the end of the 1990s. Very little internal reform, of product and labour markets, was witnessed in the 1980s, and the only serious effort in this areas—the delicensing of Indian manufacturing—started late in the 1980s and was fairly limited in scope; in other words, it was 'too little, too late' to explain the turnaround in performance.

An alternative explanation comprises three elements. First, there was an attitudinal change on the part of the government in the 1980s, signalling a shift in favour of the private sector, with this shift validated in a very haphazard and gradual manner through actual policy changes. Second, this shift and the limited policy changes were pro-business rather than pro-competition, aimed primarily at benefiting incumbents in the formal industrial and commercial sectors. Third, these small shifts elicited a large productivity response because India was far away from its income possibility frontier (Subramanian, 2006).

There were few significant policy changes in the early 1980s, and the changes later on (beginning in 1985) were restricted largely to some internal liberalisation relating to the relaxation of industrial licensing. The limited nature of these changes, as well as the form that they took, is best understood by appreciating the political logic of Indira Gandhi's (and later Rajiv Gandhi's) efforts. These were aimed to gather support from the business establishment rather than to alienate it. Hence there was more action where business support existed—for example in reducing taxes, easing access to imported capital inputs, or liberalising capacity restrictions—than where it did not—for example in external liberalisation.

We may draw distinction here between a pro-market and pro-business orientation. The former focuses on removing impediments to markets and aims to achieve this through economic liberalisation. It favours entrants and consumers. A pro-business orientation, on the other

---

3. Ghate, Chetan *et al.* (2012). "India's Growth Turnaround", in Kaushik Basu and Annemie Maertens (eds.) (2012), *The Concise Oxford Companion to Economics in India*. New Delhi: Oxford University Press.
4. Subramanian, Arvind (2012). "Growth Experience" in Kaushik Basu and Annemie Maertens (eds.) (2012), *op.cit.*

hand, is one that focuses on raising the profitability of the established industrial and commercial establishments. It tends to favour incumbents and producers. Nevertheless, this shift towards a pro-business orientation was the essential trigger that set off the boom of the 1980s.

Another strand of opinion (Ahluwalia, 2000; Srinivasan and Tendulkar, 2003) downplays what happened in the 1980s, arguing that 'the fiscal expansionism of the 1980s, accompanied by some liberalisation of controls on economic activity, generated real GDP growth of more than 5.8 per cent a year. This expansionism, however, was not sustainable and led to the macroeconomic crisis of 1991 (Srinivasan and Tendulkar, 2003-2009).

According to Deepak Nayyar, a convincing explanation must recognise that the acceleration in economic growth, since 1980, was attributable to several factors.

First, expansionary macroeconomic policies which led to an increase in aggregate demand did stimulate an increase in the rate of growth of output.

Second, starting in the late 1970s, there was also a significant increase in public investment which was sustained through the 1980s. Obviously, this contributed to the increase in aggregate demand. However, insofar as such public investment created new infrastructure or improved existing infrastructure, it could have stimulated growth in output by alleviating supply constraints.

Third, trade liberalisation beginning in the late 1970s, combined with some deregulation in industrial policies introduced in the early 1980, also probably contributed to productivity increase and economic growth. In particular, liberalisation of the regime for the import of capital goods and broad-banding which reduced industrial licencing could have played a contributory role.

The cumulative impact of economic policies or public actions over the preceding 30 years possibly played an important role in the turnaround. Institutional capacities were created. The social institutions and the legal framework for a market economy were put in place. A system of higher education was developed. Entrepreneurial talents and managerial capabilities were fostered. Science and technology was accorded a priority. The capital goods sector was established. Much of this did not exist in colonial India. But it was in place by 1980. All this provided the essential foundation (Nayyar, 2006).

According to Drèze and Sen (2005), the fact that the reasonable growth rates of the 1980s have been sustained and surpassed in the 1990s is a noteworthy achievement. This is all the more so in international perspective, considering that the 1990s have been a period of relatively slow economic growth in many other countries. In the international comparative league, India has recently been among the 'fast growers'.

The important point to recognise is not so much the acceleration of economic growth in the 1990s, compared with the 1980s (that acceleration is quite marginal), but the respectable rates of growth of the Indian economy, by international standards, in *both decades combined*. Indeed, few countries have such a good record of sustained rapid growth over that combined period.

Looking at the average annual growth of per-capita GDP in the 1980s and 1990s together, India ranks among the 10 fastest-growing countries in the world, along with China, Vietnam, South Korea, Malaysia, Thailand and Singapore, among others. This achievement is primarily a reflection of the fundamental growth potential of the Indian economy. The economic reforms undertaken so far have helped to enhance that potential in some sectors, but they have not—at least not yet—radically altered it.

Despite a good growth performance, why did the Indian economy hit a crisis in 1991? Basically India had not built up a viable relationship with the international economy. Industry remained highly protected and was not subject to competitive pressures, though some licensing and MRTP constraints were eased after 1985. Exports had not taken off despite a substantial devaluation of the rupee in the latter half of the decade. Perhaps the large increases in oil production from Bombay High had reduced the sense of urgency. The more immediate reasons for the foreign exchange crisis of 1990-91 were the increase in free foreign exchange needed to replace rupee trade imports lost with the collapse of the Soviet Union, the oil price hike and the inability to go to the International Monetary Fund (IMF) before the crisis because of the political upheavals following the break between Rajiv Gandhi and V.P. Singh.

The big change in the policy regime came after the deep foreign exchange crisis of 1991 when the newly elected Congress government, with Dr Manmohan Singh as Finance Minister reversed four decades of state control on the private sector and high levels of protection with massive changes in the license-permit system and sharp reductions in tariff rates.

Along with this, there was a major change in the policy on foreign investment. The policy regime in India now looked more like the regimes in the export-oriented economies of East and South-East Asia. In the financial sector, Securities and Exchange Board of India (SEBI) was established and the National Stock Exchange (NSE) started leading to a sharp shift away from a bureaucratically directed capital market.

2003-2008: The Best Phase in Growth

The best phase in growth was witnessed during 2003-2008 when the annual average growth stood at about 8.5 per cent. India has been among the fastest-growing economies in the world during the last decade. According to Nagaraj (2013), "from 2003, the Indian economy enjoyed a boom in growth for five years. The economy grew at a rate close to 9 per cent per year until it was punched by the financial crisis of 2008." Output expansion according to Nagaraj was underpinned by a sharp rise in the investment rate, largely domestically financed, boosted by an unprecedented influx of foreign private capital under benign macroeconomic conditions. What triggered the boom? According to Nagaraj, from the demand side, a sharp upturn in world trade since 2002, and the technological change in communications (a "revolution", in Alan Blinder's reckoning), combined with the deregulation of the financial sector in the USA gave birth to the outsourcing industry, boosting India's services exports. It was a surely an episode of export-led growth, with the export-to-GDP ratio going up by 9 percentage points in five years. The expansion of bank credit, topped by a flood of foreign private capital, enabled the expansion of aggregate supply. The financial crisis and the world economy slump took away the favourable conditions after 2008. However, growth after the crisis was mostly restored, by loosening the monetary policy and stepping up public expenditure, before it turned distinctively adverse by 2012-13 (Nagaraj, 2013).[5]

The boom has two faces: the real sector and its financial counter part. *Prima facie*, it was an exceptional phase of growth in the industrial and services sectors for five years. However, on a closer look, according to Nagaraj, the expansion had many dark spots:

1. A narrow base, with most of the incremental output coming from a few capital-intensive industries like automobiles and a few services like outsourcing and telecoms.

5. Nagaraj, R. (2013). "India's Dream Run, 2003-2008: Understanding the Boom and its Aftermath", *Economic and Political Weekly* XLVIII(20), May 18.

2. Incremental investment was skewed in favour of capital and skill-intensive registered manufacturing (especially, the automotive industry), with a marginal rise in infrastructure's share, despite a sharp rise in domestic credit and abundant access to foreign capital.

3. The growth in power generation capacity improved during the boom, yet it was not adequate to reverse the long-term decline. Modernisation of the national highway network seems satisfactory, but the record of rural road construction (which is also part of Bharat Nirman) was abysmal during the boom, but improved somewhat afterwards.

4. By type of assets, share of construction in fixed investment declined, and its composition changed in some notable ways. Residential construction's share in the total declined (despite a sharp rise in housing mortgages), at the expense of non-residential construction.

5. The financial crisis hit employment in labour-intensive manufacturing. Between 2004-05 and 2009-10, there was no employment growth, but a distinct decline in female labour force participation rates was discernible. However, wages went up across the board, though at rates lower than the rise in per capita income.

Despite a sharp rise in the domestic savings rate, it was a debt-led growth, financed by burgeoning bank credit to the private corporate sector, and boosted by a surge in foreign private capital in three principal streams, namely, FDI, FPI (foreign portfolio investment) and FCCBs (foreign currency convertible bonds). FDI rose from 0.6 per cent of GDP in 2003-04 to 2.8 per cent of GDP in 2007-08; and, the total capital inflow (sum of FDI, FPI and FCCBs) reached to 10 per cent of GDP just before the financial crisis struck in 2008. While the aggregate FDI inflow was enormous, only about 40 per cent of it went into avenues that could, in principle, augment potential output. PE/VC/HF (the sources with shorter time horizons), and the round-tripped Indian capital that took advantage of tax-free returns, together constituted nearly 60 per cent of the FDI inflows, contributing little by way of technology, or to the economy's long-term growth potential (Nagaraj, 2013).

Disproportionately faster growth of credit and capital inflows, compared to the rate of fixed investment growth, especially in infrastructure, raised corporate leverage. The newer forms of FDI, with shorter time horizons, were invested heavily in newer, and often unlisted, enterprises, which sought to leverage such funds to make it to the big league quickly.

It is hypothesised that such funds have also found their way into asset markets, stoking the prices of stocks, land and property, which have remained stubbornly high, despite the economic slowdown and decline in corporate profitability after the financial crisis. With the decline in external markets, contraction of investment demand and adverse macroeconomic conditions, the corporate debt burden has turned onerous, swelling, in turn, the banking sector's non-performing assets (NPAs), denting its profitability and restricting its lending potential.

According to Nagaraj (2013), if the foregoing reasoning and evidence are credible and weighty, then one perhaps needs to be cautious in signifying the boom as a new phase of growth acceleration. It was a debt-led boom leading to "rapid monetary expansion, inflationary pressures, real exchange rate appreciation and widening current account deficits," as Calvo *et al.* (1996: 124) cautioned against the perils of capital inflows. The boom appears episodic, which is now gradually deflating, unless, of course, domestic output or export markets turn around dramatically.

According to Ahluwalia (2014), the most striking break from the past is the phenomenal growth in corporate savings from around 4 per cent of GDP at the end of the 1990s to 8.8 per cent of GDP in 2007-08. This fuelled a big increase in private sector investment from around 16.5 per cent of GDP at the end of the 1990s to 28.1 per cent of GDP by 2007-08. Since then the global crisis has intervened and the growth rates of GDP in 2008-09 fell to 6.8 per cent. However, the contra-cyclical stimulus measures helped the economy to recover to growth rate of 8.0 per cent and 8.6 per cent in 2009-10 and 2010-11 respectively. Even so, the average for the Eleventh Plan would be 8.2 per cent, a remarkable performance considering that this period saw the greatest economic crisis the world has faced since the great depression.[6]

Recent Deceleration since 2011

After achieving unprecedented growth of over 9 per cent for three successive years between 2005-06 and 2007-08 and recovering swiftly

6. Ahluwalia, Montek S. (2014). "India's Growth Performance and Prospects: An Update", in Uma Kapila (ed.) (2014), *Indian Economy since Independence* (25th edition). New Delhi: Academic Foundation.

from the global financial crisis of 2008-09, the Indian economy has been going through challenging times that culminated in lower than 5 per cent growth of GDP at factor cost at constant prices for two consecutive years, i.e., 2012-13 and 2013-14. Sub-5 per cent GDP growth for two years in succession was last witnessed a quarter of a century ago in 1986-87 and 1987-88. Persistent uncertainty in the global outlook, caused by the crisis in the Euro area and general slowdown in the global economy, compounded by domestic structural constraints and inflationary pressures, resulted in a protracted slowdown. The slowdown is broadly in sync with trends in other emerging economies, but relatively deeper. India's growth declined from an average of 8.3 per cent per annum during 2004-05 to 2011-12 to an average of 4.6 per cent in 2012-13 and 2013-14. Average growth in the emerging markets and developing economies including China declined from 6.8 per cent to 4.9 per cent in this period (calendar-year basis). What is particularly worrisome is the slowdown in manufacturing growth that averaged 0.2 per cent per annum in 2012-13 and 2013-14.

FIGURE – 8.1

Growth in Real GDP (%)

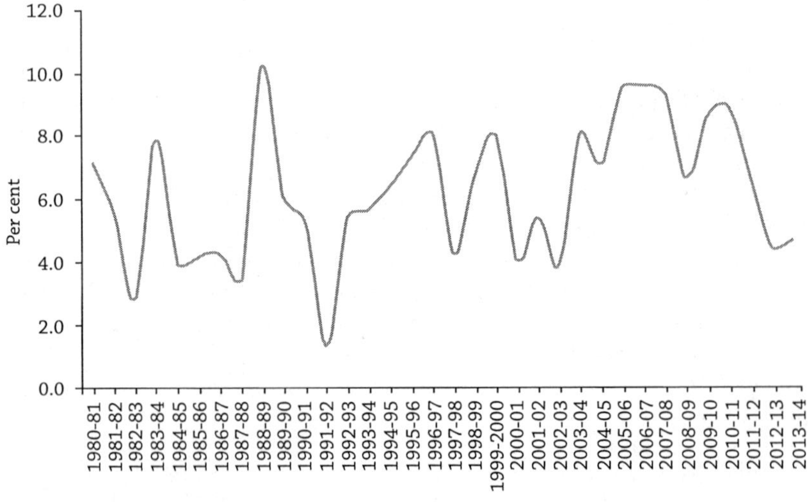

Source: Mishra (2013).

The recent deceleration in India's real GDP growth has raised questions about the potential growth rate of the economy and the size of the output gap. Based on data from the Central Statistical Office (CSO), India's annual growth rate of real GDP (measured at market prices) has fallen to 7.0 per cent in the calendar year 2011 from 10.5 per cent in 2010: a sharp decline of 3-5 percentage points within one year. The first quarter of 2012 was further marked by a decline in growth to 5.6 per cent. This decline in growth has been accompanied by a slowdown in investment (both gross fixed capital formation [GFCF] and infrastructure investment). In addition, India's ranking in the overall global competitiveness index by the World Economic Forum slipped five positions in 2011-12. In April 2012, Standard and Poor's revised India's credit outlook to negative from stable with a one-third chance of a sovereign downgrade, which would result in India dropping off the list of countries with an investment-grade rating. The scope for reducing interest rates by the Reserve Bank of India (RBI) to boost investment is limited due to high and persistent inflationary pressures, way beyond RBI's comfort zone of 3.5-4 per cent. These developments have created pessimism in the policy circles including the government and the RBI (Mishra, 2013).[7]

After reaching a low of 4.4 per cent during the last two quarters (Q3 and Q4) of 2012-13, growth inched up to 4.7 per cent in Q1 of 2013-14 and further to 5.2 per cent in Q2 of 2013-14, only to decline to 4.6 per cent in the next two quarters. The fact that this happened despite a gradual recovery in the global economy indicates the importance of addressing the domestic structural constraints that have engendered an undulating and gradual recovery (Box 8.1).

BOX – 8.1

What are Structural Constraints?

The impact of domestic structural factors on the current economic slowdown in India is often explained in terms of the irreconcilability of rate of fixed investment of around 30 per cent of GDP and sub-5 per cent growth, given India's demand conditions and long-term incremental capital-output ratio. Application of time series techniques that attempt to decompose the slowdown into structural and cyclical components, have acknowledged the presence of both, though the assignment of proportions differs (Chinoy and Aziz [2013]; IMF, WEO [2014]; Mishra [2013], among others). The accentuation of structural

contd. ...

7. Mishra, Prachi (2013). "Has India's Growth Story Withered?", *Economic and Political Weekly* XLVIII(15), April 13.

...contd. ...

constraints has been one of the factors contributing to sub-5 per cent growth without a commensurate large decline in investment rate.

What are these structural factors? Salient among them as indicated by some studies are the following:

- Difficulties in taking quick decisions on project proposals have affected the ease of doing business. This has resulted in considerable project delays and insufficient complementary investments.
- Ill-targeted subsidies cramp the fiscal space for public investment and distort allocation of resources.
- Low manufacturing base, especially of capital goods, and low value addition in manufacturing. Manufacturing growth and exports could be facilitated with simplified procedures, easy credit, and reduced transaction cost.
- Presence of a large informal sector and inadequate labour absorption in the formal sector. Absence of required skills is considered an important reason.
- Sustaining high economic growth is difficult without robust agricultural growth. Low agricultural productivity is hampering this.
- Structural factors engendering continued high food inflation need to be tackled. Issues related to significant presence of intermediaries in the different tiers of marketing, shortage of storage and processing infrastructure, inter-state movement of agricultural produce, etc. need to be addressed.

References

1. Chinoy, Sajjid Z. and Jahangir Aziz (2013). "Why is India's Growth at a 10-year Low?", available at *www.jpmorganmarkets.com.*
2. Mishra, Prachi (2013). "Has India's Growth Story Withered?", *Economic and Political Weekly,* vol. XLVIII (15).
3. International Monetary Fund (IMF) (2014), *World Economic Outlook* (WEO), April.

Source: *Economic Survey 2013-14.*

TABLE – 8.2A

Growth in GDP and Other Key Indicators

Data Categories	*Unit*	*2009-10*	*2010-11*	*2011-12*	*2012-13*	*2013-14*
1. GDP and Related Indicators GDP (current market prices)	₹ crore	6477827	7784115	9009722[2R]	10113281[1R]	11355073[PE]
Growth Rate	%	15.1	20.2	15.7	12.2	12.3
GDP (factor cost 2004-05 prices)	₹ crore	4516071	4918533	5247530[2R]	5482111[1R]	5741791[PE]
Growth Rate	%	8.6	8.9	6.7	4.5	4.7
Savings Rate	% of GDP	33.7	33.7	31.3	30.1	na
Capital Formation Rate	% of GDP	36.5	36.5	35.5	34.8	na
Per Capita Net National Income (factor cost at current prices)	₹	46249	54021	61855	67839	74380

Notes: na: not available. 1R: 1st revised estimates, 2R: 2nd revised estimates, PE: provisional estimates.

Source: CSO.

Govt. of India (2015). *Economic Survey 2014-15*.

Recent Growth Record

Central Statistics Office (CSO) has recently revised the national accounts aggregates by shifting to the new base of 2011-12 from the earlier base of 2004-05.

The new series of national accounts with a revised base year of 2011–12, released by the Central Statistics Office (CSO) on 30 January 2015 is the product of substantial revisions in the methodology of compilation of data, its classifications including the presentation of data for the first time for institutional categories, and choice of new and more sources. The base year of the national accounts is revised from time to time, but this time the CSO has also revised the methodo logy of calculating these statistics in line with requirements of the System of National Accounts (SNA), an inter nationally accepted standard.

This has meant that there have been substantial changes in the overall growth rates of the Indian economy for the past three years. According to the previous, 2004–05, series of national accounts, real growth of gross value added (GVA) at factor cost was 4.7 per cent, and 5.0 per cent for gross domestic product (GDP) at market prices for the year 2013–14. While these growth rates according to the 2011–12 series in the same year went up to 6.6 per cent and 6.9 per cent, respectively. The numbers for 2012–13 in the new series, however, improved only marginally from the old one. GVA at factor cost went from 4.5 per cent to 4.9 per cent, and GDP at market prices went from 4.7 per cent to 5.1 per cent for 2012–13. Why has this been so? Did the economy really surge ahead in 2013–14?

The economic scenario presented by the new series (with 2011-12 as base year) reveals that there was perceptible improvement in some of the macro-aggregates of the economy in 2013-14, which got strengthened in 2014-15. Economic growth, measured by growth in gross domestic product (GDP) at constant market prices, estimated at 5.1 per cent and 6.9 per cent respectively during 2012-13 and 2013-14, was higher than the corresponding figures of 4.7 per cent and 5.0 per cent released under the 2004-05 series in May 2014. That this high growth occurred in a year when the both the savings and investment to GDP ratios were lower than the average of a number of years and when the level of imports (that are generally positively associated with GDP) actually declined by 8.4 per cent in real terms, is somewhat puzzling. One of the reasons why the real GDP growth rate for 2013-14 appears to be strong is the lower GDP level in 2011-12 and 2012-13 along with lower GDP deflators than were thought hitherto *(Economic Survey 2014-15)*.

TABLE – 8.2B

Growth in GDP and Other Key Indicators

Data categories	*Unit*	*2011-12*	*2012-13*	*2013-14*	*2014-15*
1. GDP and Related Indicators					
GDP (constant market prices)	₹ Crore	8832012[NS]	9280803[NS]	9921106[NS]	10656925[AE]
Growth Rate	%	—	5.1	6.9	7.4
GVA at Basic prices (2011-12 prices)	₹ Crore	8195546[NS]	8599224[NS]	9169787[NS]	9857672[AE]
Growth Rate	%	—	4.9	6.6	7.5
Saving Rate	% of GDP	33.9	31.8	30.6	na
Capital Formation (rate)	% of GDP	38.2	36.6	32.3	na
Per Capita Net National Income current market prices)	₹	64316[NS]	71593[NS]	80388[NS]	(A t 88533[AE]

Note: na: Not Available, NS : New Series Estimates. AE : Advance Estimate.
Source: CSO; Economic Survey 2014-15.

The Table 8.3 captures these effects separately based on the new and old series of the GVA at factor cost. The level of GVA was lower in 2011-12 and 2012-13 in the new series vis-àvis the old series, with the degree of change tapering off in successive years. [This cannot be verified for the Advance Estimates (AE) for 2014-15, for which only the data from new series is available]. A greater decline in the level of GDP in 2011-12 and 2012-13, has given an upward push to the growth rate in the 2013-14. On the other hand, the upward revision of inflation in 2012-13, measured by the GDP deflator, gave a downward push to growth, but not to the extent of nullifying the positive effect of relative revisions in absolute levels. In 2013-14, the downward revision in the deflator pushed up real growth in the new series.

The estimates at disaggregated level (Table 8.4) indicate that agriculture and allied sectors—including crops, livestock, forestry and logging, and fishing—picked up growth in 2013-14. This was not unexpected as 2013-14 happened to be an exceptionally good year from the point of view of rainfall.

TABLE – 8.3

Comparison of Old Series and New Series

Item	*Year*	*Difference between new series and old series in percentage points*
Growth in GVA at	2012-13	0.4
factor cost	2013-14	1.9
Growth in	2012-13	0.5
deflator	2013-14	-0.3
Level of GVA at	2011-12	-2.2
factor cost at	2012-13	-1.3
current prices	2013-14	0.2

Source: CSO.

TABLE – 8.4

Growth in GVA at Constant (2011-12) Basic Prices

(%)

	2012-13	*2013-14*	*2014-15*
Agriculture, forestry & fishing	**1.2**	**3.7**	**1.1**
Industry	**2.3**	**4.5**	**5.9**
Mining & quarrying	-0.2	5.4	2.3
Manufacturing	6.2	5.3	6.8
Electricity, gas, water supply, & other utility services	4.0	4.8	9.6
Construction	-4.3	2.5	4.5
Services	**8.0**	**9.1**	**10.6**
Trade, hotels & restaurants, transport & communication	9.6	11.1	8.4
Financing, insurance, real estate & business services	8.8	7.9	13.7
Community, social,& personal services	4.7	7.9	9.0
GVA at basic prices	**4.9**	**6.6**	**7.5**
GDP (at market prices)	**5.1**	**6.9**	**7.4**

Source: Based on the CSO's Press Notes dated 30 January 2015 and 9 February 2015.

Aggregate Demand

Aggregate demand of the economy comprises final consumption and investment along with net exports (exports minus imports) of merchandise and non-factor services. In national accounting identity, the current account balance maps the difference between domestic savings and domestic investment, which conveys the extent of this gap that needs to be bridged by foreign savings.

The recent growth revival in India is predominantly consumption-driven (Box 8.2). To make this clear, the following sections examine the expenditure components of GDP (aggregate demand) in detail.

From the expenditure side, GDP at current market prices can be seen as the sum of (a) consumption—both private and public, (b) investment, also known as Gross Capital Formation (GCF) which comprises fixed capital formation, change in stock and valuables, and, (c) net exports which represent the difference between exports and imports of goods and non-factor services. Gross fixed capital formation or fixed investment mainly refers to the value of new machinery and equipment plus the value of new construction activity undertaken during the year. Net acquisition of valuables covers precious articles, gems and stones, silver, gold, platinum, and gold and silver ornaments.

BOX – 8.2

Global Growth Drivers and the Indian Contrast

Overall, final consumption was the major component of global growth, accounting for nearly 72 per cent of the growth between 1991 and 2013. About one-fourth was accounted for by investment. The average shares of consumption (private and public) and investment in global output during the period were 76.1 per cent and 23.2 per cent respectively. There were, however, substantial variations across periods, countries and continents.

The period 2001-2007 was marked by an increase in the growth of investment globally, with a gradual increase in the share of investment in global output and a pick-up in the rate of growth of the global economy. Given the sheer size of the high-income economies, the global picture closely tracked their patterns. The pick-up in investment growth was the sharpest among the lower middle income countries; and even among them, India stood as a positive outlier. Such movements in investment growth got reflected in the investment share in GDP. The growth surge in India during 2000-2007 could be largely attributed to

contd...

...contd...

a significant increase in investment from about US$146 billion (at constant 2005 US$) in 2000 to US$388 billion in 2007.

The high-income countries generally enjoyed an export surplus, which was compensated by the deficits of the lower income countries. China has also enjoyed an export surplus since the mid-1990s; notably though, China's export surplus has been generally declining since 2007. China, being an upper-middle income (UMI) country with a share of 45 to 50 per cent in the total output of UMI countries, largely influenced the patterns and trends shown by UMI countries as a group (not shown in the figures above). The first half of the 2000s witnessed a general improvement in the net export position of lower-middle income countries and their deficits came down, before worsening steeply. India exhibited these movements in an amplified manner. Corresponding opposite movements can be traced in the net export position of high-income countries.

The high-income countries have a relatively higher share of consumption, which has been sticky downwards, and lower share of investment in GDP, as compared to the middle-income countries. None of the countries/country groups have exhibited a consistently declining propensity to consume with China largely remaining an exception. China's consumption share, always below its upper-middle income peers, trended steeply downwards till 2010 to reach an exceptionally low level of around 49 per cent of GDP. India, as opposed to its lower-middle income peers, started with as high a consumption share in GDP as the high-income countries, and then went through a period of decline in consumption share by about 10 percentage points of GDP from 1993 to 2007, while the other lower-middle income countries generally stayed put. The space vacated by consumption, as noted above, was occupied by investment, engendering a period of investment-led growth for India in the last decade till 2007.

However, the story changed remarkably after 2007-08, the year that marked the global financial crisis. The share of consumption remained more or less the same for the high-income economies, but for a one-off spike in 2009 (which was not because of any growth in consumption, but on account of a significant decline in investment in the year). However, their investment share came down in a couple of years from 2007 and has remained at the reduced level, with a counterbalancing increase in the share of export surpluses. China's investment rate has plateaued at 48 per cent in recent years. India's

contd...

...contd...

has been an exceptional case where economic growth in the post crisis period was propelled by strengthening of consumption growth, thus defying the secular trends of declining share of consumption. The investment share in India declined much more than the average decline in the lower middle income countries. Perhaps with the strengthening of the gradual improvement in corporate investment growth, evidenced by the national accounts for 2014-15, India can get back on an investment-led path.

Source: Economic Survey 2015-16.

Three visible changes are taking place in aggregate demand. First, with improving growth in private consumption, its contribution to GDP growth is getting aligned to its GDP share. Private consumption has strengthened in the current year (Table 8.5). There was a significant increase in the growth of government consumption expenditure in 2014-

TABLE – 8.5

Contribution of Components to Real GDP Growth

Final expenditures	*Share in GDP*		*Growth (in %)*			*Contribution to GDP Growth (in %)*		
	2011-12	*2015-16*	*2013-14*	*2014-15*	*2015-16 (AE)*	*2013-14*	*2014-15*	*2015-16 (AE)*
Private final consumption	56.2	59.8	6.8	6.2	7.6	57.1	48.3	55.9
Government final consumption	11.1	10.7	0.4	12.8	3.3	0.7	17.6	4.5
Fixed capital formation	34.3	29.4	3.4	4.9	5.3	17.5	22.1	22.4
Change in stock	2.4	1.7	-18.6	20.3	5.5	-6.0	4.6	1.4
Valuables	2.9	1.5	-42.2	15.4	13.3	-17.9	3.2	2.9
Net exports	-6.5	-2.6	70.0	11.7	6.1	67.4	2.9	1.2
GDP at constant market prices	100.0	100.0	6.6	7.2	7.6	100.0	100.0	100.0

Note: AE: Advance Estimates. Shares/contributions may not add up to 100 due to errors and omissions.

Source: Central Statistics Office (CSO).
Economic Survey 2015-16.

15, which got corrected in the current year. Second, aided by the growth in capital goods, the growth of fixed capital formation (also known as fixed investment and which reflects addition to the productive capacity in the economy) has picked up. A robust growth in valuables has been recorded during the current year. Third, the substantial erosion of global demand for Indian output, manifest in loss of Indian exports, acts as a drag on domestic growth. It is from this angle that the India's achievement of being able to sustain its growth at a fairly high level, primarily on the strength of her domestic absorption, becomes noteworthy.

As per the four-year data from the new series, the share of private final consumption expenditure in GDP at current market prices increased from 56.2 per cent in 2011-12 to 59.8 per cent in 2015-16. This also supports the argument of the consumptionled growth revival. A decline of household investment in construction activities, and a more pronounced reduction in household acquisition of machinery and equipment, indicates a realignment of household expenditures in favour of consumption. Partly this could be on account of higher inflation in items in the consumption basket than in the investment, as reflected in a higher deflator for private final consumption expenditure than for gross fixed capital formation of the household sector.

Among India's external transactions, exports create demand for Indian output and hence contribute positively to GDP growth, while imports account for India's demand from the rest of the world. Since 1950-51, India has had only seven years of marginal net export (exports minus imports of goods and nonfactor services) surpluses; and never since 1993-94. Thus, India has generally been a net importer. However, the growth contribution of net exports was positive in many years—substantially positive in some—when its negativity declined from the immediately preceding year. For example; in 2013-14, when GCF declined at constant prices, *vis-à-vis* 2012-13, net exports contributed twothirds of the GDP growth. In the current year, the rupee values of exports and imports (of goods and non-factor services) are both projected to decline; the former on account of the sluggish global demand and the latter due to steep decline in international crude oil prices and other commodity prices. Such a dual decline would be the first since 1965-66; nonetheless, the net exports are estimated to make a positive contribution to growth—though marginal—because of the expected decline in the wedge between exports and imports.

Growth in Gross Value Added

The Gross Value Added (GVA), which broadly reflects the supply or production side of the economy, registered an increase in the growth rate from 5.4 per cent in 2012-13 to 7.1 per cent in 2014-15. In the current year, the growth in GVA is likely to increase to 7.3 per cent, as per the Advance Estimates (AE) released by the Central Statistics Office (CSO), affirming the positive trends in the economy indicated by GDP growth.

Growth in the agriculture sector in 2015-16 has continued to be lower than the average of last decade, mainly on account of it being the second successive year of lowerthan- normal monsoon rains. Growth in the services sector moderated slightly, but still remains robust; while the acceleration in manufacturing growth compensated for it (Table 8.6).

TABLE – 8.6

Growth in GDP and Major Sectors

(in %)

Sector	*2013-14 (2R)*	*2014-15 (1R)*	*2015-16 (AE)*
Agriculture, forestry and fishing	4.2	-0.2	1.1
Industry	5.0	5.9	7.3
Mining and quarrying	3.0	10.8	6.9
Manufacturing	5.6	5.5	9.5
Electricity, gas, water supply, etc.	4.7	8.0	5.9
Construction	4.6	4.4	3.7
Services	7.8	10.3	9.2
Trade, hotels, transport and communication	7.8	9.8	9.5
Financing, real estate, professional services, etc.	10.1	10.6	10.3
Public administration, defence and other services	4.5	10.7	6.9
GVA at constant basic prices	6.3	7.1	7.3
GDP at constant market prices	6.6	7.2	7.6

Source: Based on data from CSO; *Economic Survey 2015-16*.

The farm sector has experienced two years of low growth on account of two consecutive years of deficient south-west monsoon

(June-September) rainfall, the only fourth such occurrence during the last 115 years (source; National Council of Applied Economic Research). The post monsoon (October-December) rains also turned out to be below normal. Among the agriculture and allied sectors, crops including fruits and vegetables account for about 61.0 per cent of the GVA; the rest by the allied sectors consisting of livestock products, forestry and fisheries. As per the information of the Department of Agriculture, Cooperation and Farmers Welfare for 2015-16, the production of foodgrains and oil- seeds is estimated to decline by 0.5 per cent and 4.1 per cent respectively; while the production of fruits and vegetables is likely to increase marginally. As per the AE, a brighter picture is expected to emerge from the allied sectors, with a growth exceeding 5.0 per cent in 2015-16, which would have provided some impetus to rural incomes during the year (*Economic Survey 2015-16*).

Growth in industry is estimated to have accelerated during the current year on the strength of improving manufacturing activity (Table 8.6). The private corporate sector, with an around 69 per cent share of the manufacturing sector, is estimated, from available data of listed companies, to grow by 9.9 per cent at current prices in April-December 2015-16. The Index of Industrial Production (IIP) showed that manufacturing production grew by 3.1 per cent during April- December 2015-16, vis-à-vis a growth of 1.8 per cent in the corresponding period of the previous year. The ongoing manufacturing recovery in the current year is aided by robust growth in petroleum refining, automobiles, wearing apparels, chemicals, electrical machinery and wood products and furniture. Apart from manufacturing, the other three segments of the industry sector, i.e. electricity, gas, water supply and related utilities, mining and quarrying and construction activities, are witnessing a deceleration in growth.

The importance of sustaining the revival can be seen from the fact that manufacturing activity contributed only 17.4 per cent (at 2011-12 prices) to the total value addition in the economy; but accounted for more than a third of the production of output. The difference between the output and GVA contributions has not been so stark in any other sector. This indicates that manufacturing provides the demand base for the products of many other growing sectors of the economy, thereby creating substantial backward linkages.

More than half of the Indian economy is the services sector. Being the main driver of the economy, the sector contributed about 69 per cent of the total growth during 2011-12 to 2015-16; in the process expanding its share in the economy by 4 percentage points from 49 to 53 per cent.

Revised Estimates—January 2016

With the revision of the data on annual National Accounts from the Provisional Estimates (PE) of May 2015 to the Revised Estimates (RE) of January 2016, the growth narrative of the Indian economy in the recent past has changed to an extent in certain respects. Such modifications used to occur in the earlier revisions too. This owes to the fact that on certain components of GVA, more comprehensive information becomes available with a lag, like manufacturing growth based on the Annual Survey of Industries and MCA database being different from the results indicated by the IIP. Major changes include the following (*Economic Survey 2015-16*):

(i) The levels of GDP have been revised right from the base year, 2011-2012. Growth rate of GDP at market prices for the years 2012-13, 2013-14 and 2014-15 is currently estimated to be 5.6 per cent, 6.6 per cent and 7.2 per cent respectively. Earlier, these were estimated to be 5.1 per cent, 6.9 per cent and 7.3 per cent respectively. Similarly, growth rate of GVA at basic prices for the years 2012- 13, 2013-14 and 2014-15 is now estimated to be 5.4 per cent, 6.3 per cent and 7.1 per cent respectively as against earlier levels of 4.9 per cent, 6.6 per cent and 7.2 per cent respectively. The growth of sectors, namely agriculture, industry and services, has been also revised.

(ii) A more balanced picture of the ongoing growth recovery emerges from the revision in accounts on the demand side, with the growth rate in fixed investment having been revised upwards. The pre-revised data had indicated a much more consumption-led growth process. The contribution of consumption to overall GDP growth during the period 2012-13 to 2014-15 has been revised downwards from 63.1 per cent to 59.9 per cent, while the corresponding contribution of fixed investment has been revised upwards from 12.2 per cent to 22.6 per cent.

Quarterly Estimates of GVA at Basic Prices 2016-17

With the release of the PE of annual national income, 2016-17 and quarterly estimates of GDP for the fourth quarter (Q4) of 2016-17, it is very clear that the economy has lost momentum over the past year. The data released show not only slow down at the yearly level, but even within a year (Table 8.7).

TABLE – 8.7

Quarterly Estimates of GVA at Basic Prices for 2016-17

(at 2011-12 prices)

		Percentage Change over Previous Year							
		2015-16				*2016-17*			
	Industry	*Q1*	*Q2*	*Q3*	*Q4*	*Q1*	*Q2*	*Q3*	*Q4*
1.	Agriculture, Foresty and Fishing	2.4	2.3	-2.1	1.5	2.5	4.1	6.9	5.2
2.	Mining and Quarrying	8.3	12.2	11.7	10.5	-0.9	-1.3	1.9	6.4
3.	Manufacturing	8.2	9.3	13.2	12.7	10.7	7.7	8.2	5.3
4.	Electricity, Gas, Water Supply and Other Utility Services	2.8	5.7	4.0	7.6	10.3	5.1	7.4	6.1
5.	Construction	6.2	1.6	6.0	6.0	3.1	4.3	3.4	-3.7
6.	Trade, Hotels, Transport & Communication and Services related to Broadcasting	10.3	8.3	10.1	12.8	8.9	7.7	8.3	6.5
7.	Financial, Real Est. and Professional Services	10.1	13.0	10.5	9.0	9.4	7.0	3.3	2.2
8.	Public Administration, Defence and other Services	6.2	7.2	7.5	6.7	8.6	9.5	10.3	17.0
	GVA at Basic Price	7.6	8.2	7.3	8.7	7.6	6.8	6.7	5.6

Source: CSO May 31, 2017.

Here are the relevant quarterly figures for growth (in GVA at basic prices, adjusted for base year 2011-12). Growth in the fourth quarter of 2015-16, i.e. January to March 2016 was 8.7 per cent. In the first quarter of 2016-17, i.e. April to June 2016 it was 7.6 per cent. For July to September 2016 it was 6.8 per cent and for October to December 2016 it was 6.7 per cent. And finally, for the first quarter of this calendar year it was as low of 5.6 per cent. A fairly straight-forward decline from 8.7 per cent quarterly growth to 5.6 per cent quarterly growth—and that too in a year with an excellent monsoon and a reviving world economy.

The subject has been discussed and debated among economists and it is generally believed that apart from the adverse effects of demonetisation on consumptions, investment in India is in a crisis. In

TABLE – 8.8

Quarterly Estimates of GVA at Basic Prices for 2018-19 (at 2011-12 prices)

Industry	*2016-17*				*2017-18*				*2018-19*			
	Q1	*Q2*	*Q3*	*Q4*	*Q1*	*Q2*	*Q3*	*Q4*	*Q1*	*Q2*	*Q3*	*Q4*
1. Agriculture, Forestyand Fishing	2.5	4.1	6.9	5.2	4.2	4.5	4.6	6.5	5.1	4.2	2.7	-0.1
2. Mining and Quarrying	-0.9	-1.3	1.9	6.4	2.9	10.8	4.5	3.8	0.4	-2.1	1.3	4.2
3. Manufacturing	10.7	7.7	8.2	5.3	-1.7	7.1	8.6	9.5	12.4	6.9	6.7	3.1
4. Electricity, Gas, Water Supply and Other Utility Services	10.3	5.1	7.4	6.1	8.6	9.2	7.5	9.2	6.7	8.7	8.2	4.3
5. Construction	3.1	4.3	3.4	-3.7	3.3	4.8	8.0	6.4	9.6	8.5	9.6	7.1
6. Trade, Hotels, Transport & Communication and Services related to Broadcasting	8.9	7.7	8.3	6.5	8.3	8.3	8.3	6.4	7.8	6.9	6.9	6.0
7. Financial, Real Est. and Professional Services	9.4	7.0	3.3	2.2	7.8	4.8	6.8	5.5	6.6	7.2	7.3	9.5
8. Public Administration,Defence and other Services	8.6	9.5	10.3	17.0	14.8	8.8	9.2	15.2	7.6	8.7	7.6	1.7
GVA at Basic Price	7.6	6.8	6.7	5.6	5.9	6.6	7.3	7.9	7.8	6.8	6.3	5.7

Source: CSO May 31, 2017, and May 31, 2019.

2016-17, GFCF, was 29.5 per cent of GDP, as compared to 30.9 per cent of GDP in 2015-16. In the fourth quarter of 2016-17, GFCF was even lower, at 28.5 per cent of GDP. There is no question that private investment is struggling. The government's chosen strategy to deal with this has been to ignore it. It has instead focused on public investment—which is too small to make up for the decline in private investment—and hoping that an infrastructure buildout will incentivise further private investment (Sharma, 2017).[8]

There are several studies which indicate a fall in corporate investment. Every year the Reserve Bank of India (RBI) publishes a forecast of corporate investment. It uses the data made available by banks and other financial institutions on the phasing of capital expenditures of projects sanctioned by them. An article in the March 2019 issue of the RBI Bulletin says that in 2017-18, the capital expenditures of the corporate sector were estimated at Rs. 1,487 billion. There has been a steady decline from Rs. 2,050 billion in 2014-15. The industry-wise distribution of projects sanctioned by banks and other institutions in 2017-18 shows that the power sector accounted for 38.2 per cent of the total expenditure. Pure manufacturing had only a small share.

Demonetisation and GDP Growth

The second quarter estimate of GDP released by the chief statistical adviser confirms the adverse impact of demonetisation on economic activity. The GDP growth during the quarter, at 5.7 per cent, was much lower than 7.9 per cent during the first quarter of last year. In the previous quarter it was 6.1 per cent. The growth in Gross Value Added, which is the real measure of economic activity, at 5.6 per cent, was the same as the previous quarter, but much lower than 7.6 per cent recorded in the first quarter of last year. Indeed, the growth rate of the economy has been decelerating right from the second quarter of last year on the back of decelerating investments largely due to the twin balance sheet crisis. But, during the last quarter of the previous year, when demonetisation was effected, virtually every sector of the economy decelerated except agriculture and public administration—the latter actually grew at 17 per cent. The deceleration in agricultural incomes is stated to be due mainly to animal husbandry. Perhaps, we have been scoring self-goals by putting curbs on the buffalo meat industry remarks Govinda Rao. The sharp deceleration in the manufacturing sector

8. Sharma, Mihir (2017). *Business Standard* XXIV(34), 5 June. New Delhi.

growth during the last quarter has been ascribed to wholesale price index moving from the negative to positive territory and de-stocking by businesses due to GST. This, however, can not entirely explain the sharp reduction in the growth rate, to just 1.2 from 5.3 per cent in the last quarter. Even this is an underestimate as the estimates are based on the formal sector data, and the effect of demonetisation will be clearer only when the revised estimates come in when the informal sector's impact is captured better.

According to Govinda Rao, "the only thing that can be said at present is that there has been substantial disruption on account of demonetisation. Indeed, the government continues to claim that it has scored a goal without admitting that it is a self-goal. After all, it is the player, judge and the jury and neither the ruling party nor the opposition, but the people are the sufferers in these games."[9]

Performance on Inclusiveness

It is more difficult to assess performance on inclusiveness than on growth for three reasons. First, inclusiveness is a multidimensional concept and progress, therefore needs to be assessed in many different dimensions. Second, the data relating to various aspects of inclusiveness become available only after a considerable lag. Third, most policies aimed at inclusiveness have an impact only over a relatively long term, and this means that even when policies are moving in the right direction, the results may only be evident much later. For example, steps taken to improve education for the poor will improve their earning ability in future, but this impact will only be reflected in actual income earning much later (Ahluwalia, 2014).

Multidimensionality of Inclusion

The multidimensional nature of inclusiveness is best illustrated by listing some of the many dimensions that are relevant. The extent of reduction in the percentage of the population below the poverty line is clearly a very important indicator of progress. However, many families that are above the poverty line in terms of per capita consumption may lack access to basic services such as education, health, clean drinking water and sanitation. Inclusiveness must obviously include progress in delivery of these essential services. Inclusiveness must also extend to addressing concerns about inequality. It is sometimes argued that

9. Rao, Govinda M. (2017). *Financial Express*. 5 September. New Delhi.

inequality should not matter as long as the poor are getting better off and it is probably true that a rapid rate of improvement in incomes for the poor may make them willing to accept some increase in inequality. However, large increases in inequality, accompanying only modest improvements in the levels of living of the poor, are unlikely to be acceptable. Inequality in this context relates not only to the distribution of income or consumption across individuals, but also inequality across states, and in some cases, even across regions within states. Inclusiveness in the Indian context also requires a special focus on particular social groups such as the scheduled castes (SC) and scheduled tribes (ST), and also the minorities. Since these groups are concentrated in the lower ranges of the income distribution, it may be thought that an effective strategy for reducing poverty or inequality addresses the concerns of these groups. However, if inclusiveness is defined as bringing these groups at par with the rest of the population, it has to address the issue of achieving a fair representation for these groups along the entire income distribution. This is conceptually very different from reduction in overall poverty or inequality, in the sense that it can be achieved leaving the incidence of poverty and the level of inequality unchanged.

The Eleventh Plan explicitly recognised the multidimensional nature of inclusiveness by enumerating 27 monitorable targets of which GDP growth was only one. The others focused on different aspects of inclusion such as growth in agriculture, reduction in poverty, growth of employment opportunities, etc. One consequence of multidimensionality is that the extent of progress in different dimensions will vary. For example, it is perfectly possible for poverty to decline while inequality increases. Similarly, inequality among households in the country as a whole may decrease, or remain unchanged, while inequality across states increases. Any overall assessment of progress on inclusiveness will have to be based on a composite view of all these developments (Ahluwalia, 2014).

The Need for Faster Growth

Planners are sometimes criticised for focusing too much on GDP growth, when the real objective should be to achieve an improved quality of life of the people across both economic and non-economic dimensions. The Twelfth Plan fully recognises that the objective of development is broad-based improvement in the economic and social conditions of our people. However, rapid growth of GDP is an essential requirement for achieving this objective.

There are two reasons why GDP growth is important for the inclusiveness objective. First, rapid growth of GDP produces a larger expansion in total income and production which, if the growth process is sufficiently inclusive, will directly raise living standards of a large section of our people by providing them with employment and other income enhancing activities. Our focus should not be just on GDP growth itself, but on achieving a growth process that is as inclusive as possible. For example, rapid growth which involves faster growth in agriculture, and especially in rainfed areas where most of the poor live, will be much more inclusive than a GDP growth that is driven entirely by mining or extraction of minerals for exports. Similarly, rapid growth which is based on faster growth for the manufacturing sector as a whole, including MSME, will generate a much broader spread of employment and income earning opportunities and is therefore more inclusive than a growth which is largely driven by extractive industries.

The second reason why rapid growth is important for inclusiveness is that it generates higher revenues, which help to finance critical programmes of inclusiveness. There are many such programmes which either deliver benefits directly to the poor and the excluded groups, or increase their ability to access employment and income opportunities generated by the growth process. Examples of such programmes are the Mahatma Gandhi National Rural Employment Guarantee Act (MGNREGA), Sarva Siksha Abhiyan (SSA), Mid-day Meals (MDMs), Pradhan Mantri Gram Sadak Yojana (PMGSY), Integrated Child Development Services (ICDS), National Rural Health Mission (NRHM), and so on. This is also relevant for the sustainability objective since programmes aimed at making development more sustainable also involve additional costs.

International Comparisons

An interesting insight is provided by a comparison of growth rates in the South Asian region grouped by policy regimes that is presented in Table 8.8 drawn from the analysis presented by Parikh (2006).[10]

The analysis presented in Table 8.8 suggests that GDP growth was correlated with the orientation of policy on two broad fronts—the stance towards the external economy and towards the domestic private sector. A shift towards export orientation and/or a reduction in controls on the domestic private sector pushed the growth rate.

10. Parikh, Kirit S. (2006). *Explaining Growth in South Asia*. New Delhi: Oxford University Press.

High growth in East Asia and in South-East Asia was associated with an outward-oriented trade strategy with a strong export bias, based on undervalued exchange rates or export subsidisation. The degree of openness to foreign investment varied. Japan and Korea followed a very restrictive policy on foreign investment while Singapore and Hong Kong based their strategy on attracting foreign investment. Foreign aid may have helped Korea and Taiwan when they were making their transition to outward-oriented growth but not much after that. China and South-East Asia, who came later to the high growth game, are more open, but even there the bulk of the investment has been domestic rather than foreign.

TABLE – 8.9

Policy Regimes and Growth Rates of GDP in South Asia

Policy Regimes	*India*	*Pakistan*	*Bangladesh*	*Sri Lanka*	*Nepal*
Free market economy; Passive government				1947-1956 3.67%	
Import-substitution; Controlled economy	1950-1967 3.4%	1950-1957 3.1%	1971-1981 2.7%	1956-1965 3.4%	1966-1980 2.3%
Import-substitution Rigid controls; Nationalisation	1967-1980 3.8%	1971-1977 4.7%		1970-1977 2.9%	
Export promotion regulated		1958-1970 6.6%	1981-1989 3.9%		
Deregulation; Import restriction	1980-1990 5.6%	1978-1988 6.1%			1981-1990 4.9%
Liberalisation	1992-1996 6.7% 1997-2000 5.4%	1988-1999 4.4%	1989-1992 6.7% 1992-2000 5.3%	1977-2000 5.0%	1991-2000 5.1%

Source: Parikh (2006) *op. cit.* no. 10.

Growth and Structural Change

Consistent with the trend observed in other countries, India's growth experience has been characterised by a decline in the share of agriculture in GDP and an increase in the shares of industry and services. Between 1951 and 2000, the share of agriculture in GDP fell from 53 per cent to 22 per cent, while the share of industry and the share of services increased from 16 to 27 per cent, and from 30 to 50 per cent, respectively. Between 2000-01 and 2011-12 while the share of agriculture has declined from 22 per cent to 13.9 per cent and services share increased from 50 per cent to 59 per cent, the share of industrial sector remained stagnant at 27 per cent.

The structure of the economy has also undergone significant changes over time. Between 1950-51 and 1980-81, the industrial sector registered a higher growth rate than the services sector. The converse has been the case since then. This resulted in the share of the industry sector in GDP increasing by around 9 percentage points from 16.6 per cent to 25.9 per cent during the period from 1950-51 to 1980-81. The share of the services sector increased from 30.3 per cent in 1950-51 to 38 per cent in 1980-81. It started growing rapidly thereafter and this phenomenon became more pronounced in the 1990s. Consequently, since 1980-81, the share of the industry sector has remained in the range of 26-28 per cent of GDP, while the entire decline in share of agriculture has been balanced by an increase in share of the services sector. Thus, the resilience of the economy to shocks owe to the services sector which has the largest share and most consistent growth performance. The changes in relative shares of these sectors in GDP are shown in the Table 8.10.

TABLE – 8.10

Sectoral Composition of GDP

Year	*Agriculture*	*Industry*	*Services*
1950-51	53.1	16.6	30.3
1960-61	48.7	20.5	30.8
1970-71	42.3	24.0	33.8
1980-81	36.1	25.9	38.0
1990-91	29.6	27.7	42.7
1999-2000	23.2	26.8	50.0
2007-08	10.8	28.7	54.4
2012-13	13.9	27.3	58.8
2013-14(P)	13.9	26.1	59.9

Source: Calculated from CSO data and *Economic Survey 2012-13* and *2013-14*.

TABLE – 8.11

Growth in Real GDP

(% per annum)

Period	*Agriculture*	*Industry*	*Services*	*GDP*
1950s	2.7	5.6	3.9	.36
1960s	2.5	6.3	4.8	4.0
1970s	1.3	3.6	4.4	2.9
1980s	4.4	5.9	6.5	5.6
1990s	3.2	5.7	7.3	5.8
2000s	2.5	7.7	8.6	7.2
2011-12 (2R)	5.0	-	-	6.7
2012-13 (1R)	1.4	27.3	-	4.5
2013-14 (PE)	4.7	26.1	-	4.7

Source: CSO and *Economic Survey 2013-14*.

Sectoral Growth Trends

The disaggregated sectoral trends may be better understood in terms of movement in sectoral shares in GDP, as seen from Table 8.12. The share of the agriculture and allied sectors in GDP has been consistently declining. During the eight years between 1999-2000 and 2007-08, the share of agriculture and allied sectors in GDP declined by 6.4 percentage points, while that of industry and services increased by 1.9 and 4.4 percentage points respectively.

The mining and quarrying sector witnessed continuous decline in GDP share for several years, indicating its inability to cater to requirements of high growth, in the absence of comprehensive reforms.

In the case of manufacturing, most of the gain in share occurred during 2004-05 to 2007-08, when the sector was growing at an annual average rate exceeding 10 per cent, along with robust growth in corporate profits, savings, and investment. Activity was buoyant in registered manufacturing, while the share of unregistered manufacturing remained unchanged during the four years ending 2007-08. During 2008-09 to 2012-13, the share of manufacturing remained roughly constant despite an increase in share of the registered segment, as unregistered manufacturing recorded an average annual growth of only 3.4 per cent.

The share of services has been consistently rising, more so since 2004-05. However, the pace of expansion was not balanced. The biggest drivers of the service sector expansion since 2004-05 were communications and banking and insurance. Robust growth in these sectors primarily drove the expansion of the services sector even after 2010-11. Real estate and business services also gained share. The services that witnessed stagnation/decline in share after 2010-11 include domestic trade, hotels and storage. The inability of some of these employment-intensive sectors to attain sustained momentum is one of the reasons for the less-than commensurate growth in employment in services.

TABLE – 8.12

Sectoral Share in GDP

(Per cent)

Sector	*1999-2000*	*2007-08*	*2012-13*	*2013-14(P)*
Agriculture & allied	23.2	16.8	13.9	13.9
Industry	26.8	28.7	27.3	26.1
Mining & quarrying	3.0	2.5	2.0	1.9
Manufacturing	15.0	16.1	15.8	14.9
Registered manufacturing	9.2	10.7	11.2	NA
Unregistered manufacturing	5.8	5.4	4.5	NA
Services	50.0	54.4	58.8	59.9
Trade, hotels, transport and communication	21.2	25.9	26.9	26.4
Financing, insurance, real estate and business services	14.5	16.1	19.1	20.6
Community, social and personal services	14.4	12.4	12.8	12.9

Note: Industry includes electricity, gas and water supply, and construction sectors that are not indicated in the table.

P: provisional. NA: not available.

Source: Calculated from NAS, CSO and *Economic Survey 2013-14*.

In the absence of sufficiently high growth in agriculture and industry, services would be seriously constrained to sustain growth acceleration on auto-pilot mode since many of the services are dependent on buoyancy in the commodity-producing sectors, especially industry (Box 8.4).

BOX – 8.4

Input Flows in the Economy

One of the ways to study inter-sectoral linkages is by examining the inter-industry input flow matrix. The table below has been constructed from the latest available input-output tables (2007-08) released by the CSO. The information, though slightly dated, could be indicative of the state of inter-sectoral linkages.

Inter-industry Input Flows in the Economy (in per cent)

	Agriculture and allied sector input	*Industrial sector input*	*Service sector input*
Agriculture & allied	55.3	7.7	7.5
Industry	21.4	68.2	45.1
Services	23.3	24.1	47.5

Contribution to Total Inputs in the Economy (in per cent)

Agriculture & allied	11.8
Industry	59.6
Services	28.6

Source: Internal calculations based on the CSO's input-output tables.

The upper panel of the table implies that out of the total input requirement of the agriculture and allied sector, 55.3 per cent was contributed by the sector itself, while industry and services accounted for 21.4 per cent and 23.3 per cent respectively. More than two-thirds of the total inputs required by industry came from industry itself, while nearly one-fourth were from the services sector. Over half the inputs for the services sector came from the industrial and agricultural sectors. The table highlights the importance of the industrial sector in sustaining economic activity in the services sector. As is evident from the lower panel of the table, the agricultural sector accounted for 11.8 per cent of the total inputs employed in the economy, while the industrial and services sectors accounted for 59.6 per cent and 28.6 per cent respectively. Hence a sustained recovery in the industrial sector is at the heart of a sustained growth recovery.

Source: Economic Survey 2013-14.

Growth and Sectoral Shares, Cross-Country Evidence and Indian Experience

The evolution of sectoral shares in output, consumption and employment as economies grow has been studied by economists for well over 50 years. During the 1950s and 1960s, research by Kuznets and Chenery suggested that development would be associated with a sharp decline in the proportion of GDP generated by the primary sector, counterbalanced by a significant increase in industry, and by a more modest increase in the service sector. Sectoral shares in employment were predicted to follow a similar pattern.

With the benefit of more data on development than was available to Kuznets and Chenery, recent literature has tended to emphasise the growing importance of service sector activity (Inman, 1985; Kongsamut, Rebelo and Xie, 2001). For example, Kongsamut *et al.* (2001) analysed a sample of 123 countries for 1970-1989 and showed that rising per capita GDP is associated with an increase in services and a decline in agriculture both in terms of share in GDP and employment. In other words, the sectoral share given up by agriculture as the economy matures goes more to the services sector and less to industry than the Kuznets-Chenery work had suggested. The modern view is that as an economy matures, the share of services (in output, consumption and employment) grows along with a decline in agriculture. By contrast, the share of industry first increases modestly, and then stabilises or declines. (Gordon and Gupta, 2003)

Such a pattern of growth is visible in the cross-country data on shares in GDP (Table 8.13). These data suggest two stages of development. In the first, both industry and services shares increase as countries move from low income to lower middle income status, while in the second, the share of industry declines and that of services increases as the economy moves to upper middle and higher income levels.

How does the Indian experience fit in with this pattern? In the four decade period, 1950-1990, agriculture's share in GDP declined by about 25 percentage points, while industry and services gained equally. The share of industry has stabilised since 1990, and the entire subsequent decline in the share of agriculture has been picked up by the services sector. Thus, while over the four decades, 1950-1990, the services sector gained a 13 per cent share, the gain in the 1990s alone was 8 percentage points. Consequently, at current levels, India's services share of GDP is higher than the average for other low income countries.

TABLE – 8.13

Sectoral Shares in GDP in 2001, Global Averages

(% of GDP)

	Agriculture	*Industry*	*Services*	
Low income	24	32	45	Stage I
Lower middle income	12	40	48	
Upper middle income	7	33	60	Stage II
High income	2	29	70	

Note: Definition: low income: per capita GDP<$745; lower middle: $746-2975; upper middle: $2976-9205; and high: >$9206.

Source: World Bank's *WDI*, 2003, table 4.2.

II

Inter-Regional Disparities in Growth and Development

Prior to 1980, the growth rate of the Indian states was mediocre but relatively uniform. After 1980, however, the fortunes of the states diverged considerably.

A study by Montek Ahluwalia[11] on economic performance of the states in the post-reform period brings out that there is considerable variation in the performance of individual states, with some states growing faster than the average and others slower. What is important is that the degree of dispersion in growth rates of SDP (state domestic product) across states increased significantly in the 1990s. The range of variation in the growth rate of SDP in the 1980s was from a low of 3.6 per cent per year in Kerala to a high of 6.6 per cent in Rajasthan. In the 1990s, the variation was much larger, from a low of 2.7 per cent per year for Bihar to a high of 9.6 per cent for Gujarat.

The differences in performance across states become even more marked when we allow for the differences in the rates of growth of population and evaluate the performance in terms of growth rates of per capita SDP (Table 8.14). The variation in growth rates in the 1980s ranged from a low of 2.1 per cent for Madhya Pradesh to a high of 4.0 for Rajasthan, a factor of 1:2. In the 1990s, it ranged from a low of 1.1

11. Ahluwalia, Montek S. (2002). "State Level Performance under Economic Reforms in India", in A. Krueger (ed.) (2002), *Economic Policy Reforms and the Indian Economy*. New Delhi: Oxford University Press.

per cent per year in Bihar and 1.2 per cent in Uttar Pradesh (UP), to a high of 7.6 per cent per year in Gujarat, with Maharashtra coming next at 6.1 per cent. The ratio between the lowest (Bihar) and the highest (Gujarat) is as much as 1:7.

The increased variation in growth performance across states in the 1990s reflects the fact that whereas growth accelerated for the economy as a whole, it actually decelerated sharply in Bihar, UP and Odisha, all of which had relatively low rates of growth to begin with and were also the poorest states. There was also a deceleration in Haryana and Punjab, but the deceleration was from relatively higher levels of growth in the 1980s, and these states were also the richest.

Six states showed acceleration in growth of SDP in the 1990s. The acceleration was particularly marked in Maharashtra and Gujarat, both of which were among the richer states, but there was also acceleration in West Bengal, Kerala, Tamil Nadu and Madhya Pradesh all belonging to the middle group of states in terms of per capita SDP.

TABLE – 8.14

Annual Rates of Growth of Gross State Domestic Product (GSDP)

(%)

		1980-81 to 1990-91	*1991-92 to 1997-98*
1.	Bihar	2.45	1.12
2.	Rajasthan	3.96	3.96
3.	Uttar Pradesh	2.60	1.24
4.	Odisha	2.38	1.64
5.	Madhya Pradesh	2.08	3.87
6.	Andhra Pradesh	3.34	3.45
7.	Tamil Nadu	3.87	4.95
8.	Kerala	2.19	4.52
9.	Karnataka	3.28	3.45
10.	West Bengal	2.39	5.04
11.	Gujarat	3.08	7.57
12.	Haryana	3.86	2.66
13.	Maharashtra	3.58	6.13
14.	Punjab	3.33	2.80
	Combined SDP of 14 States	**3.03**	**4.02**

Source : SDP and population data obtained from the CSO.

It is important to note that the high growth performers in the 1990s were not concentrated in one part of the country. The six states with growth rates of SDP in the 1990s above 6.0 per cent per year are fairly well distributed regionally i.e., Gujarat (9.6%) and Maharashtra (8.0%) in the west, West Bengal (6.9%) in the east, Tamil Nadu (6.2%) in the south and Madhya Pradesh (6.2%) and Rajasthan (6.5%) in the north.

The performance of Kerala deserves special attention. Kerala has justly celebrated for its achievements in human development but it has also been criticised for under performance in economic growth. It is important to note that its performance in the 1990s showed a marked improvement compared with the 1980s. From an SDP growth rate much below the 14 states average in the 1980s, it accelerated to a growth rate only marginally below the average in the 1990s. However, because of the low population growth, its performance in per capita SDP growth in the 1990s was actually much better than the average.

The fact that Gujarat and Maharashtra grew at rates normally associated with 'miracle growth' economies also deserves special mention. It should be emphasised that if these states have benefited the most in the post-reform period, their superior performance was not the result of any conscious policy of limiting the benefits of liberalisation to these states, as was the case for example in China, where liberalisation was deliberately limited to designated coastal zones. The superior performance of Gujarat and Maharashtra must therefore be attributed to the fact that the states were able to provide an environment most conducive to benefiting from the new policies.

A recent study on Growth Experience of States by Arvind Panagariya (2010)[12] brings out that for every single state in the table, growth rate during 2003-2009 exceeded that in every preceding period, however defined. Growth momentum has now penetrated all large states, which account for 93 per cent of the total population as per 2001 census. Second and related, with the exception of Jammu & Kashmir (J&K) and Assam, both of which have been subject to insurgencies, every single large state and Delhi have grown 6 per cent or faster during the last six financial years. Even J&K and Assam are not far behind, respectively growing 5.7 and 5.5 per cent annually during this period. In comparison, only one state (Delhi) during 1981-1988 and nine states during 1988-2003 grew at rates of 6 per cent or higher. Third, some of the poorest states have shown some of the highest growth rates during 2003-2009. Rajasthan, Orissa and Bihar, all

12. Panagariya (2010) *op. cit.* Table 8.18..

of them among bottom six states (respectively ranking 13th, 15th and 18th), grew at annual rates of 9.4, 9.4 and 8.4 per cent, respectively. Growth rates in Orissa and Rajasthan exceed those in all states except Delhi, Gujarat and Haryana. Finally, the bottom six states, which account for 41.8 per cent of the population as per 2001 census, have together grown at the annual average rate of 7.1 per cent during 2003-2009. This rate is in contrast to 3.8 per cent during 1981-1988 and 4.0 per cent during 1988-2003. A major breakthrough for the bottom two-fifths of India seems clearly to be in the making.

TABLE – 8.15

Annual Average Growth Rates of NSDP at Factor Cost with States Listed in the Descending Order of Per Capita NSDP at Factor Cost in 2005-06

Year	*1981-1988*	*1988-2003*	*2003-2009*	*1981-1992*	*1992-2003*	*1981-2009*
Delhi	7.7	7.8	11.2*	7.9	7.6	8.4
Haryana	4.6	6.6	10.0	5.9	6.1	6.8
Maharashtra	4.2	6.7	8.9*	6.3	5.4	6.5
Punjab	5.5	4.2	6.1	5.3	3.8	4.9
Himachal Pradesh	3.3	6.5	7.5*	4.6	6.6	5.9
Kerala	1.3	6.1	9.4*	3.5	5.8	5.5
Tamil Nadu	4.8	5.5	8.6	5.4	5.1	6.0
Gujarat	2.8	7.8	10.3#	7.0	5.3	6.8
Karnataka	5.1	6.0	7.7	5.5	6.0	6.1
Andhra Pradesh	5.2	6.2	8.6*	5.7	6.0	6.4
West Bengal	4.2	5.9	6.9*	4.4	6.5	5.7
Jammu & Kashmir	0.9	4.7	5.7*	2.9	4.3	3.9
Rajasthan	4.1	6.7	9.4	7.6	3.8	6.6
Assam	4.1	3.0	5.5	3.9	2.6	3.8
Orissa	2.7	3.9	9.4	3.4	3.7	4.8
Madhya Pradesh	3.6	4.3	6.0*	4.1	4.1	4.5
Uttar Pradesh	4.1	3.7	6.1	4.3	3.2	4.3
Bihar	4.3	4.2	8.4	3.3	5.4	5.1

Note: * This growth rate is based on the average of growth rates from 2003-04 to 2007-08 since the NSDP for this state for 2008-09 is still not reported.

This growth rate is based on the average of growth rates from 2003-04 to 2006-07 since the NSDP for this state for 2007-08 and 2008-09 is still not reported.

Source: Author's calculations using state-level data in RBI (2009).

Panagariya, Arvind (2010). *India on the Growth Turnpike: No State Left Behind.* Columbia Program on Indian Economic Policies, Working Paper No. 2010-1.

According to Subramanian (2012)[13], after 1980, some clearer patterns become evident. It appears that two sets of factors played a role. First, different states had different pre-existing capabilities. But these remained latent and could not find expression until the economic environment changed. The trigger—the second set—was the liberalisation begun in 1980, and especially the decentralisation of economic power that was forced by the changing political landscape after 1980. Thus, it was the interaction between pre-existing capabilities and the twin triggers of liberalisation and decentralisation that explains how the different states fared.

What was this pre-existing capability? It turns out that this capability was something more than a state's level of development or educational level or geography. It is best captured by how diversified a state's manufacturing base was. This diversified base is probably a proxy for some generalised capability—human capital, entrepreneurial spirit, organisational capital—that could exploit a favourable economic environment.

Let us now consider the triggers of liberalisation and decentralisation. While the formal reforms at the centre received tremendous publicity, perhaps less noticed was the growing decentralisation of policy.

Greater economic decentralisation meant states could differentiate themselves, not least in their ability to attract private-sector investment. This was, of course, facilitated by the gradual dismantling of the industrial licencing system that used regional equity as one of the primary criteria guiding industrial investments. Further contributing to differentiation over this period was the rising trend in private investment, as well as the falling trend in public investment, with private investment likely to be more sensitive to differences in policies across states.

After all, if the pre-1980s era was about the centre deciding, for example, where and how much electricity capacity to instal, there is little that the states could have done to affect economic performance within their borders. This is exactly what the evidence shows. For example, when state-level growth is related to state-level policies and institutions, the latter are found to have no role in explaining growth prior to 1980 but a robust role in explaining post-1980s, especially post-1990s, growth.[14]

---

13. Subramanian, Arvind (2012). "Growth Experience" in Kaushik Basu and Annemie Maertens (eds.) (2012), *The Concise Oxford Companion to Economics in India*. New Delhi: Oxford University Press.

14. Ibid.

III

The Way Ahead

It is now well established that the inter-state disparities in the growth of gross state domestic product (GSDP) have increased in the post-economic reform period beginning from the early 1990s when compared to the 1980s. In general, the richer states have grown faster than the poorer states (Ahluwalia, 2000; Dev and Ravi, 2003; Bhattacharya and Sakthivel, 2004). The regional disparities in per capita GSDP growth are even greater because the poorer states in general have experienced a faster growth in population. The exercise on Regional Equality presented by the Planning Commission in the 12th Plan confirms this position, despite the recent acceleration in the GSDP growth rates of some poorer states, including especially Bihar, and rise in the ratio of their average growth rates to the all-India average growth rate (Planning Commission, 2012).

Although these disparities have accentuated in the post-reform period, they have been building up in the pre-reform period itself. For example, according to Central Statistical Organisation (CSO) data, in the early 1960s, the per capita GSDP of the richer states like Punjab, Maharashtra and Gujarat was, on an average, about 80 per cent higher than the average per capita GSDP of the bottom four states viz., Bihar, Uttar Pradesh, Orissa and Madhya Pradesh. This disparity increased to 125 per cent by the early 1970s (Rao, 2005) and was contained at a little over 100 per cent during the eighties, but escalated steeply to 156 per cent towards the mid-1990s (1993-96), and further to 176 per cent during 2007-2010.

States whose per capita GSDP is below the national average together account for over 60 per cent of the country's population and as high as 75 per cent of the country's population below the poverty line. Further, these states account for nearly 60 per cent of the population belonging to the socioeconomically disadvantaged sections like scheduled castes (SCs) and scheduled tribes (STs). There is thus a large potential for growth which needs to be exploited for sustaining development in the country over a long period. This is necessary for improving regional and social equity and for strengthening national integration.

It is clear from the foregoing discussion that for reducing regional disparities in development, improving social and economic infrastructure in the backward regions through greater public investment needs to be given the highest priority in the development strategy. The other two areas of priority action for these regions are: speeding up social transformation through the empowerment of the common people and measures for good governance.

While the differences across states have long been a cause of concern, increasingly there is recognition of the problem of severe imbalances within states. Backward districts of otherwise well-performing states, present a dismal picture of intra-state imbalance and neglect. The centre and the states together must deal with this problem on a priority basis. We cannot let large parts of the country be trapped in a prison of discontent, injustice and frustration that will only breed extremism. The spread of Naxalism in more than 100 districts in the country is a warning sign. Pockets of despair where communalism has left scars are also festering with anger. In all areas, despair is the result of visible failures of the state apparatus to ensure good governance and create an environment where the bulk of the people experience the benefit of development.

Special efforts must be made to remove the discontent, instill a sense of fairness among the people and give them dignity and hope. Otherwise, not only will the growth momentum in the rest of the country be disrupted, but we will not attain the dignity and pride of a good society.

Growth Prospect: An Assessment

The Indian economy has undisputedly moved to a higher growth path during the last three decades. The break point from the earlier 'Hindu rate' could be placed in the late 1970s to the early 1990s depending on whether one takes a purely statistical approach or looks for policy changes underlying the process to explain the break. Limited reforms and an expansionary fiscal policy helped the economy to achieve an average growth rate of 5.5 per cent in the 1980s, but its sustainability was doubtful. Lack of resilience was evident when a macroeconomic crisis occurred in the wake of the Gulf War and the oil price rise in 1990s and 1991. The policies of the 1980s were associated with high levels of domestic and foreign debt leading to fiscal and BoP crisis.

Economic reforms initiated in 1991 were wide-ranging, involving abolition of the industrial licensing systems, liberalising trade and unfreezing the exchange rate among others. The resilience of the economy as it developed in the post-reform period gets reflected in successfully meeting several challenges such as the East Asian crisis in the late-1990s, the Gulf War in early 2000 and severe drought in 2002. As discussed earlier, in the wake of the global economic crisis, economic growth in India slowed down considerably in 2009-09 and recovered partly in the next two years. World trade, which fell by about a quarter in 2009, has not yet recovered to the pre-crisis level of $16 trillion. With new signs of a deepening Euro zone crisis, the global economic scenario does not seem promising at present. Yet, India continues to perform reasonably well in comparison to most other nations.

Attaining above 8 per cent growth consecutively for five years between 2003 and 2007 by the Indian economy attracted world-wide attention and many observers believed that India, like China, was riding on the high road of growth. The post-reform experience shows that India's growth path, unlike that of China, is going to be considerably uneven. Some analysts believe that the high growth story has come to an end and an average growth rate of 5-6 per cent might be more of a rule and see this as the 'new Hindu rate' of growth. Many others, however, are more optimistic and argue that conditions are ripe to maintain an average growth rate of 7-8 per cent as experienced in the last decade.

In the absence of the revival of the manufacturing sector, a higher GDP growth rate cannot be achieved. Given that the nature of the Indian manufacturing sector has been 'idiosyncratic' (Kochhar et at., 2006), it is necessary to create an enabling environment for private investors to cope with business and financial risks in an unprotected environment and meet challenges of global competitiveness. Panagariya (2008) makes a persuasive case that large private firms will not enter into labour-intensive manufacturing without labour market reforms leading to a flexible exit policy. Policy initiatives must also be strengthened to close both physical and human infrastructure gaps, particularly in the backward regions.

A number of structural factors have contributed to a higher growth rate in the last decade. The rise in the gross capital formation rate from 25 per cent of GDP to 38 per cent during 2002-2008 played an important role in rasing GDP growth during this period. As discussed earlier, it dropped by about 3 percentage points after the global crisis, mirroring a similar fall in domestic savings rate which was primarily due to a fall in government savings. Raising government savings will be a critical element in restoring savings and investment levels in the economy. This in turn will depend on: (i) rationalisation and restructuring of government current expenditure and (ii) raising the volume of tax revenue. Non-merit goods subsidies such as those on oil or power once introduced are difficult to reduce or remove in a democratic set-up. Yet, the need for a broad agreement among the major political parties on prioritising the subsidies and limiting them to essentials such as food, drinking water, health and education cannot be overemphasised for maintaining macroeconomic stability. Proper monitoring of the several welfare programmes, particularly the centrally sponsored schemes, is another area that can raise efficiency of the programmes and reduce expenditure.

Another factor that may contribute in pushing the long-term growth rate upwards is the so-called demographic dividend. The current age structure of the population is such that the proportion of the working age population to the total population is expected to increase in the coming decades. If the available labour force can be engaged in productive activities without a decline in productivity, it could be a source of additional growth. Creating appropriate employment opportunities for the fast-growing labour force with skill development that matches emerging demand patterns of a growing economy is a major challenge for deriving demographic dividents. Two points may be made in this connection. First, a faster and more stable expansion of labour-intensive industrial sectors, such as agro-processing, could be vital in absorbing the growing labour force since the labour absorption capacity of the services sector has been modest. Second, the working age population also happens to be the major saving class in an economy and the demographic dividend could potentially have a positive feedback effect on household saving rates.

While reforms in the product market have been extensive, the factor markets have remained virtually untouched. Factor market reforms would be essential to fully realise the gains from economic reforms. Labour laws applicable to organised industry in India are too restrictive for the exit of non-viable industries and stand in the way of reallocating factors to take advantage of new technology and changing market conditions. Some of the labour laws meant to protect the interests of the working class in effect protect only a small segment of labourers already employed in the organised sector and go against the interests of the working class as a whole. It is necessary to develop a regulatory framework that permits closure of non-viable units within a reasonable timeframe so that unemployed resources can be re-employed in other productive uses. As Krishna (2015)[15] points out, "restrictive labour laws

---

15. Krishna, K.L. (2012). "National Income", in Kaushik Basu and Annemie Maertens (eds.) (2012), *The Concise Oxford Companion to Economics in India*. New Delhi: Oxford University Press.

have not only reduced employment prospects in organised manufacturing but also constrained its growth by adversely affecting investment and productivity".

Similarly, the land market is another area that needs immediate attention. Problems with the century-old Land Acquisition Act have recently attracted attention due to constraints faced by industry and a new land acquisition act is under consideration by the Parliament. A thin land market within agriculture has also been a constraint for the sector's growth. Developing a proper lease market will require a regulatory framework that protects a land-owner's property rights but incentivises the introduction of technology and investment by ensuring tenancy certainty in the medium run. A proper tenancy registration system will also help tenants to claim benefits in the event of crop failures. Encouraging a contract farming system could help in developing linkages with agro-processing units. Similarly, opening up of the retail market to foreign players could help in developing supply chain and market linkages. The regulatory mechanism must ensure that both small and big players have access to the market on fair terms.

Regional backwardness/disparities is another issue of concern. The differences across states have long been a cause of concern, but increasingly, there is recognition of the problem of severe imbalances within states. Backward districts of otherwise well-performing states, present a dismal picture of intra-state imbalance and neglect. The centre and the states together must deal with this problem on a priority basis. We cannot let large parts of the country be trapped in a prison of discontent, injustice and frustration that will only breed extremism. Therefore, special efforts must be made to remove the discontent, dispense justice, instill a sense of fairness among the people and give them dignity and hope.

The growth process must be broad-based so that benefits of growth are widespread. When the benefits accrue to a small group and large sections are left behind, social stability becomes the casualty and the growth process itself comes to a halt. Admittedly, some rise in inequality cannot be avoided in the early stages of development as is evident from the global experience. But unchecked inequality could cause social problems such as those currently noticed in large parts of the tribal belt in the country. The fact that the ST and SC groups have the highest incidence of absolute poverty means that there is a need to reorient welfare programmes towards the STs and SCs. But, ironically, many states are not utilising even the mandated budgetary provisions under ST and SC sub-plans. The state must be an active agent in providing certain basic needs to all its citizens, particularly to those away from the mainstream. Without a new social contract towards this end, the growth process itself might be jeopardised. Developing a broad consensus for balancing the distributional objective with the growth objective requires innovative state craft.

Sustainable Development and Climate Change

Sustainable development is an imperative for achieving intergenerational equity. The business-as-usual approach to development has entailed unsustainable consumption patterns, which is essentially attributable to the developed countries. Anthropogenic activities are the dominant cause for climate change. Greenhouse gas (GHG) emissions grew on an average by 2.2 per cent per year between 2000 and 2010, as compared to 1.3 per cent per year between 1970 and 2000. India's per capita carbon emissions were 1.7 metric tonnes in 2010, well below the world average of 4.9 metric tonnes.

The year 2015 witnessed two landmark international events. The historic climate change agreement under the United Nations Framework Convention on Climate Change (UNFCCC) was adopted by 195 nations in Paris in December 2015, with the aim of keeping the rise in global temperature well below 2°C, which will set the world towards a low carbon, resilient and sustainable future. The world also witnessed the adoption of the Sustainable Development Goals (SDGs) in September 2015 which replace the Millennium Development Goals (MDGs) and set the development agenda for the next 15 years with the aim of guiding the international community and national governments on a path of sustainable development.

The Agreement provides binding obligation for developed countries to provide financial resources to developing countries for both mitigation and adaptation while encouraging other countries to provide support on voluntary basis. It reaffirms that developed countries will take the lead in mobilizing climate finance from a wide variety of sources, instruments and channels, noting the significant role of public funds. The decision also sets a new collective quantified goal from a floor of US$100 billion per year prior to 2025 , taking into account the needs and priorities of developing countries. Pre-2020 actions are also part of the decisions. The Agreement also called upon developed countries to scale up their level of financial support with a complete road map for achieving the goal of jointly providing US$100 billion by 2020 for mitigation and adaptation, by significantly increasing adaptation finance from current levels and to further provide appropriate technology and capacity building support.

The United Nations General Assembly (UNGA) in its 17th session in September 2015 announced a set of 17 SDGs and 169 targets which will stimulate action over the next 15 years. This set of goals replaces the MDGs which were coming to an end in 2015 and aims to work on the areas which could not be completed earlier. The agenda highlights poverty eradication, combating inequalities, promoting gender equality and the empowerment of women and girls as the ambient goal and has at its core the integration of the economic, social and environmental dimensions of sustainable development. This also calls for an invigorated global partnership for sustainable development, including multi-stakeholder partnerships, in addition to enhancing capacities of stakeholders in better quality measurement and compilation of data or information on sustainable development.

Domestically, many initiatives have been taken by India on climate change and sustainable development. India has submitted ambitious targets in its Intended Nationally Determined Contribution (INDC) in the renewable energy sector, mainly from solar and wind energy. With a potential of more than 100 GW, the aim is to achieve a target of 60 GW of wind power as well as 100 GW of solar power installed capacity by 2022. India's INDC is comprehensive and covers all elements, i.e. adaptation, mitigation, finance, technology and capacity building. The country's goal is to reduce overall emission intensity and improve energy efficiency of its economy over time, at the same time protecting the vulnerable sectors and segments of the economy and society. The principle of equity and Common but Differentiated Responsibilities (CBDR), historical responsibilities and India's development imperatives, enhanced adaptation requirements, etc. have been a recurring theme in the INDC document. India's INDC has been welcomed as fair and ambitious specifically on renewable energy and forestry sector.

India has also taken the initiative of setting up an International Solar Alliance (ISA), an alliance of 121 solar-resource-rich countries, lying fully or partially between the Tropic of Cancer and Tropic of Capricorn. This alliance was jointly launched by the Prime Minister of India and President of France on 30 November 2015 at Paris, on the sidelines of the 21st Conference of Parties to the UNFCCC. The Paris declaration on the ISA states that the countries share the collective ambition to undertake innovative and concerted efforts for reducing the cost of finance and technology for immediate deployment of competitive solar generation and to pave the way for future solar generation, storage and good technologies for countries' individual needs.

Successful implementation of the Paris Agreement, SDGs and the ambitious targets set out in the INDCs would require huge financing which cannot be met through budgetary sources alone. In this context it is important that the issue of mobilization and tracking of finance, with increased importance to adaptation and clean technology is adequately addressed.

The challenge for India is manifold. India is at the threshold of an urban flare-up. As population increases, demand for every key service will increase five-to sevenfold. These trends combined with the current challenges of poverty eradication, food and energy security, urban waste management, and water scarcity will put further pressure on our limited resources which will add to greater energy needs and cause a parallel increase in emission if decoupling does not take place. At the same time, hidden in this challenge are great opportunities. Unlike many countries, India has a young population and therefore can reap the fruits of demographic dividend. With more than half of the India of 2030 yet to be built, we have an opportunity to avoid excessive dependence on fossil fuel-based energy systems and carbon lock-ins that many industrialized countries face today. A conscious policy framework which takes into account both developmental needs and environmental considerations could help turn the challenges into opportunities.[16]

To quote Rajat Kathuria (2018) "India already has a version of carbon pricing in place and over time could expand the depth and breadth of the price signal. Moreover, the climate change problem has reached a level where it is no longer only a global commons issue. There are localised benefits linked to unilateral action. As the Kerala floods demonstrate, climate change will bring about extreme weather events and the impact will disproportionately be concentrated in the global south. The whole world has a role to play and no one, not least the developed world, can shirk responsibility. But for now, India cannot wait and there are immediate gains from pursuing low-carbon options that include job-creation and lower air pollution amongst several others."[17]

---

16. Govt. of India (2015). *Economic Survey 2014-15.*
17. Kathuria, Rajat (2018). "Sustainable Development: Harnessing Climate Change for Economic Growth", Financial Express, 22 October 2018.

9

Poverty in India

THE problem of poverty and unemployment is considered as the biggest challenge to development planning in India. High poverty levels are synonymous with poor quality of life, deprivation, malnutrition, illiteracy and low human resource development. The slogan of poverty eradication has been adopted by all political parties in one form or another, and there is a national agreement for the goal of poverty alleviation. The national consensus on poverty alleviation provided the necessary condition for launching various schemes and programmes aimed at achieving this objective. But the persistence of poverty during all these years suggests that the national consensus on objectives did not and could not provide sufficient conditions for poverty alleviation.

India accounts for about 20 per cent of the global count of those living on less than $1 a person per day, so that what happens in India is not only a reflection of worldwide trends, but one of their major determinants (Deaton and Kozel, 2005).

Poverty Estimates

Historically, the Indian statistical system has led the world in the measurement of poverty. The sample surveys that were pioneered by Mahalanobis at the Indian Statistical Institute in Kolkata in the 1940s and 1950s were moved into the government statistical system as the National Sample Survey Organisation (NSSO), whose household surveys are the basis for the regular publications on poverty by the Planning Commission (Ibid.).

National statistical systems collect more than survey data, and much non-survey information is relevant for the monitoring of living standards. Most important are the National Accounts Statistics (NAS), which provide widely used measures of aggregate performance, particularly GDP (gross domestic product) and its components, particularly consumption. Although these consumption estimates rely on surveys for several of their components, much also comes from other sources. And although there are important differences in definition between the survey and national accounts concepts of consumption, a well-functioning statistical system uses multiple estimates to cross-check and validate one another. And in India, there is a long and distinguished tradition of empirical work on such cross-checking and validation of the consumption estimates.

The Selection of Poverty Lines

The calculation of poverty measures requires two components, a distribution of household expenditure, and a poverty line or cut-off that separates poor from non-poor households. Although poverty lines are often linked to the amount of money that households need, to be able to buy a minimally satisfactory diet, the use and long-term survival of poverty lines depends on policy makers and others accepting them as useful (Ibid.).

The starting point for estimating the number of households below the poverty line is a normative nutritional requirement per person per day at some base point. There is a debate on the minimum calorie requirement, and whether it should be the same for all parts of the country. Most acceptable figures are 2,400 calories per person per day in rural areas, and 2,200 calories per person per day in urban areas. The next step is to translate the nutrient requirement into monetary terms. The expenditure level of households which are able to spend the requisite amount to obtain the desired calories serves as the cut-off point, or the poverty line. To adjust the poverty line over a period of time, price variations have to be considered and an appropriate price deflator has to be selected. The problem arises in deciding upon such a deflator.

Thus, the following elements mainly affect the magnitude of the poverty ratio: (i) the nutrition norm (translated into monetary terms) in the base year; (ii) price deflator used to update the poverty line; and (iii) pro rata adjustment in the number of households in different expenditure classes to determine the number of households below and above the poverty line. Different assumptions and methods are used for these three purposes, which accounts for the different estimates provided by scholars.

For some time, the magic number of ₹ 20 per head at 1960-61 prices was used. From late 1970s into the mid-1990s, the Planning Commission used two poverty lines for per capita household expenditure in India, ₹ 49 for rural households and ₹ 57 for urban households, so that prices were taken to be about 16 per cent higher for urban households. The poverty lines were held constant in real terms, and were converted to current rupees using the implicit price deflator of consumption in the National Accounts. This process had the disadvantage of ignoring interstate differences in price levels, as well as variations from state to state in urban to rural price differential. Furthermore, it might be doubted whether the national accounts consumption deflator was an ideal measure of inflation for households near the poverty line. These problems (and several others) were dealt with by an Expert Group in 1993, whose recommendations for new poverty lines were adopted (in a somewhat modified form) by the Planning Commission, and these 'Expert Group' poverty lines have been used in the official calculations of poverty in India from 1983 to the present day. According to these procedures, poverty lines are defined at the state level, separately for urban and rural households. Each line is updated by a state-specific price index, the state consumer price index for agricultural labourers (CPIAL) for rural lines, and the state consumer price index for industrial workers (CPIIW) for urban lines. (Separate procedures are followed for the small states and territories, sometimes assuming the poverty line of a nearby state, and sometimes its poverty rate.) There is no countrywide poverty line as such; instead, once the all-India rural and urban headcount ratios have been calculated, the all-India lines are defined implicitly as the lines which, when applied to all households, give the all-India poverty rates.

The Planning Commission, the nodal agency for estimating the number and proportion of people living below the poverty line at national and state levels, separately for rural and urban areas, makes poverty estimates based on a large sample survey of household consumption expenditure carried out by the NSSO approximately every five years. The methodology for estimation of poverty has been reviewed from time to time. The Planning Commission constituted an Expert Group under the Chairmanship of Professor Suresh D. Tendulkar in December 2005, which submitted its report in December 2009. The recomputed poverty estimates for the years 1993-94 and 2004-05 as recommended by the Tendulkar Committee have been accepted by the Planning Commission. As per the Tendulkar Committee Report, the national poverty line at 2004-05 prices was a monthly per capita consumption expenditure of ₹ 446.68 in rural and ₹ 578.80 in urban areas in 2004-05. The above poverty lines which refer to the national average vary from state to state because of price differentials. The Tendulkar Committee has mentioned in its report that the proposed poverty lines have been validated by checking the adequacy of actual private expenditure per capita near the poverty lines on food, education and health by comparing them with normative expenditures consistent with nutritional, educational and health outcomes. In order to have a two-point comparison of changes in head count ratio, the Expert Group has re-estimated poverty for 1993-94. The head-count ratios for 1993-94 and 2004-05 as released earlier by the Planning Commission and using the Tendulkar methodology, are given in Table 9.1. Even though the Tendulkar methodology gives higher estimates of headcount ratios for both 1993-94 and 2004-05, the extent of poverty reduction is 8.1 percentage points which is not very different from the reduction of 8.5 percentage points during the same period as per Lakdawala Methodology (*Economic Survey 2011-12*).

TABLE – 9.1

Poverty Ratios

(%)

	Earlier Estimates(URP) based on the Lakdawala Methodology		*Estimates (MRP)based on the Tendulkar Methodology*	
	1993-94	*2004-05*	*1993-94*	*2004-05*
Rural	37.3	28.3	50.1	41.8
Urban	32.4	25.7	31.8	25.7
Total	36.0	27.5	45.3	37.2

Note: URP: uniform reference period; MRP: mixed reference period.
Source: Planning Commission.

The Planning Commission has updated the poverty lines and poverty ratios for 2011-12 based on the recommendations of the Tendulkar Committee using Household Consumer Expenditure Survey 2011-12 data of the National Sample Survey (NSS) 68th round. Accordingly, with the poverty line at all India level at monthly per capita expenditure (MPCE) of ₹ 816 for rural areas and ₹ 1000 for urban areas in 2011-12, the poverty ratio in the country has declined from 37.2 per cent in 2004-05 to 21.9 per cent in 2011-12. In absolute terms, the number of poor declined from 407.1 million in 2004-05 to 269.3

million in 2011-12 with an average annual decline of 2.2 percentage points during 2004-05 to 2011-12 (Table 9.2). The Planning Commission constituted an Expert Group under the Chairmanship of Dr C. Rangarajan in June 2012 to 'Review the Methodology for Measurement of Poverty'.

TABLE – 9.2

Number and Percentage of Poor*

Year	*Poverty Line (in ₹)*		*Number of Poor (million)*			*Poverty Ratio (%)*		
	Rural	*Urban*	*Rural*	*Urban*	*Total*	*Rural*	*Urban*	*Total*
1993-94	-	-	328.6	74.5	403.7	50.1	31.8	45.3
2004-05	446.68	578.80	326.3	80.8	407.1	41.8	25.7	37.2
2011-12	816.00	1000.00	216.5	52.8	269.3	25.7	13.7	21.9
Annual Average Decline: 1993-94 to 2004-05 (percentage points per annum)						0.75	0.55	0.74
Annual Average Decline: 2004-05 to 2011-12 (percentage points per annum)						2.32	1.69	2.18

Note: * Estimated by Tendulkar Method.
Source: Planning Commission.
Economic Survey 2012-13, 2013-14, 2014-15.

With Rangarajan Committee Report (June 2014), we now have yet another methodology for measurement of poverty. The main criticism of the Tendulkar methodology was that its poverty lines had no explicit normative context and were based on the level of urban poverty as obtained from the earlier Lakdawala methodology. Rangarajan's brief was to arrive at normative poverty lines more widely acceptable than Tendulkar's. Rangarajan has attempted to extend the normative concerns beyond food to some basic non-food essential like clothing, education, home rent and conveyance and what was actually spent on these by those at the relevant fractiles class. This takes Rangarajan's final 2011-12 poverty lines from ₹ 933 to 972 per capita per month in rural areas and from ₹ 1,181 to ₹ 1,407 per capita per month in urban areas. The corresponding final Rangarajan poverty estimates are 30.9 per cent rural and 26.4 per cent urban which although only modestly more than Tendulkar in rural areas nearly doubles for urban poverty.

Poverty estimates based on the Tendulkar Committee methodology using household consumption expenditure survey data collected by the NSSO in its 68th round (2011-12) shows that the incidence of poverty declined from 37.2 per cent in 2004-05 to 21.9 per cent in 2011-12 for the country as a whole, with a sharper decline in the number of rural poor. While the rural poverty ratio declined from 41.8 per cent in 2004-05 to 25.7 per cent in 2011-12, the urban poverty ratio declined from 25.7 per cent in 2004-05 to 13.7 per cent in 2011-12. The rural poverty ratio still remains much higher than the urban. The high rural poverty can be attributed to lower farm incomes due to subsistence agriculture, lack of sustainable livelihoods in rural areas, impact of rise in prices of food products on rural incomes, lack of skills, underemployment and unemployment. Table 9.3 gives a picture of state-level rural and urban poverty (*Economic Survey 2015-16*, Vol.II).

Economic Growth and Poverty

It should be obvious enough that economic growth can be extremely helpful in removing poverty. This is both because the poor can directly share in the increased wealth and income generated by economic growth, and also because the overall increase in national prosperity can help in the financing of public services (including health care and education), which in turn can be particularly useful for the poor and the deprived. This does not, however, make economic growth the only means—not necessarily even the principal means—of poverty removal. There are so for at least three reasons.

First, poverty need not take the form only of low income; there are other kinds of deprivation reflecting various 'unfreedoms,' varying from prevalence of preventable or curable illness to social exclusion and the denial of political liberty.

Second, in particular the enabling roles of basic education, good health, microcredit facilities, land reforms, social security arrangements, environmental sustainability, legal provision and related factors.

Third, the fruits of economic growth may not be automatically utilised to expand basic social services. For example, South Korea did much better in channelling resources to education and health care than, say, Brazil did, which too had fast economic growth, and this greatly helped South Korea to better pursue growth with equity, compared with the-then Brazil. However, South Korea too continued to neglect arrangements for social security, thereby remaining vulnerable to

TABLE – 9.3

State-wise Poverty Situation in 2011-12

(in %)

Population poverty below line	*Rural poverty*	*Urban poverty*	*Total poverty*
Less than 10	Goa, Punjab, Himachal Pradesh, Kerala, Sikkim	Goa, Sikkim, Himachal Pradesh, J&K, Mizoram, Kerala, Andhra Pradesh, Tamil Nadu, Meghalaya, Maharashtra, Punjab, Tripura	Goa, Kerala, Himachal Pradesh, Sikkim, Punjab, Andhra Pradesh
10 to 20	Andhra Pradesh, Haryana, Meghalaya, Rajasthan, J&K, Nagaland, Tripura, Tamil Nadu, Uttarakhand	Gujarat, Haryana, Uttarakhand, Rajasthan, West Bengal, Karnataka, Nagaland, Odisha	J&K,Haryana, Uttarakhand, Tamil Nadu, Meghalaya, Tripura, Rajasthan, Gujarat, Maharashtra, Nagaland, West Bengal
20 to 30	Gujarat, West Bengal, Maharashtra, Karnataka	Arunachal Pradesh, Assam, Madhya Pradesh, Chhattisgarh, Jharkhand, Uttar Pradesh	Mizoram, Karnataka, Uttar Pradesh
30 to 40	Arunachal Pradesh, Manipur, Madhya Pradesh, Assam,Uttar Pradesh, Bihar,Odisha,	Bihar, Manipur	Madhya Pradesh, Assam, Odisha, Bihar, Arunachal Pradesh Manipur, Mizoram Jharkhand, Chhattisgarh
Above 40	Jharkhand, Chhattisgarh		

Source: Based on NITI Aayog estimates, 2011-12. *Economic Survey 2015-16*, Vol.II, p.209-210.

downside risks, and in fact paid a heavy price for this when the economic crisis of 1997 came. Removal of poverty and deprivation requires a great deal more than relying on one simple associative connection between economic growth and the incomes of the poor.

This broader picture of social progress also contains a useful reminder that eliminating deprivation is as much a matter of public action as one merely of economic growth.

Growth and Poverty Nexus

The strength of the relationship between growth and poverty is usually measured by the poverty elasticity with respect to per capita GDP. Poverty elasticity has been estimated in the range of -0.86 to -0.77 (Radhakrishna, 2008). The trickle-down effect of growth is rather weak. Moreover, preliminary analysis suggests further weakening of the relationship in the post-reform period. This is supported by the fact that there has been no significant acceleration in the process of poverty reduction during 1980-2005 despite an acceleration in the growth of per capita GDP. Empirical studies reveal that lack of assets such as land, human capital and skills constrain the poor from participating in, and benefiting from, growth. There is now a growing consensus that the poverty reduction strategy must also rely on direct measures since the present high growth, given its sectoral composition and degree of inclusiveness, may not eradicate poverty completely even by 2015. The National Rural Employment Guarantee Act (NREGA) which came into force in 2006, and is being implemented in 330 districts across the country can make a difference to the lives of those who have thus far been excluded from the growth process. Also, relevant for poverty reduction are the programmes such as the self-employment programmes (Swarnajayanti Gram Swarozgar Yojana), rural housing for the houseless, and social assistance to the aged and disadvantaged.

Comparison of India and China in terms of Poverty Reduction

India's record in poverty reduction pales before the achievements of China, which has been far more effective in reducing poverty. The incidence of poverty in China declined by a staggering 45 percentage points in two decades: from 53 per cent in 1981 to 8 per cent in 2001 (Ravallion and Chen, 2004). In contrast, India could reduce poverty by a mere 17 percentage points in two decades. India fares badly even on non-income dimensions of poverty. For instance, in the recent period, the incidence of malnutrition in India was four times more than that in China, the infant as well as under-five mortality rate in 2002 was double that in China and maternal mortality rate was 10-fold higher in India (UNDP, 2003). Although China managed to reduce poverty rapidly, the progress has been uneven across its regions (Ravallion and Chen, 2004).

In China too, there are concerns about whether all sections of society have benefited equally from the growth process. Whether the poor benefit from economic growth or not depends on the country's geographic spread and the sectoral composition of growth. In India, a similar concern emerges with apprehensions over its lopsided growth marked by its lagging agricultural sector, worsening rural urban disparity and growing regional imbalances. However, it is noteworthy that India fared better than China in achieving lower inequality. This is reflected in the higher income shares of the bottom groups. For instance, the share of the poorest 20 per cent in income (expenditure) was 8.1 per cent in India whereas it was only 5.9 per cent in China (UNDP, 2003).

It is interesting to note that the performance in reducing poverty between 2004-05 and 2009-10 varies considerably across states. The four southern states (Andhra Pradesh, Tamil Nadu, Kerala and to lesser extent Karnataka) all report impressive reduction in poverty, as do Maharashtra, Odisha, Madhya Pradesh (MP) and Himachal Pradesh. There is no improvement in Uttar Pradesh (UP) and Bihar, very little improvement in West Bengal and an actual deterioration in Assam. Punjab and Haryana had relatively lower poverty rates to begin with, but do not seem to have improved their position (see Ahluwalia, Ch. 11). How far these differences reflect differences in the pace and nature of growth in each state, and how far they reflect differences in the implementation of anti-poverty schemes, is a subject that needs further investigation based on the final official estimates of poverty obtained from unit level data.

Poverty and Inclusive Growth

The National Commission on Enterprises in the Unorganised Sector (NCEUS), in its report, suggested that 77 per cent of the total population of the country in 2004-05, had per capita consumption expenditure of less than ₹ 20 per day. However, it has been observed, based upon calculations on data for 1999-2000 (NSS 55th Round) and 2004-05 (NSS 61st Round) that per capita consumption expenditure of 78.3 per cent of the rural population and 42.5 per cent of the urban population was less than ₹ 20 per day in 1999-2000.

There is a direct relationship between aggregate poverty and average consumption. Growth of aggregate income/consumption is, therefore, a sufficient condition for reduction of overall or aggregate poverty.

Non-income Poverty Dimensions

Malnutrition

Data from the National Family Health Survey (NFHS-3) carried out in 2005-06 and District Level Household Survey on Reproductive Health (RCH) carried out during 2002-2004 show the worst forms of deprivation in India. As high as 46 per cent of children under 3 years of age (NFHS-3) and 49 per cent children under 6 years (RCH) suffered from malnutrition, and 79 per cent of children from anaemia (NFHS-3). These unfavourable child health outcomes could be, inter alia, attributable to failures in health care.

The national averages mask the huge variations in the incidence of child malnutrition across the states of India. In 2005-06, the incidence of child malnutrition varied among the major states from 27 per cent in Punjab and 29 per cent in Kerala and Jammu & Kashmir (J&K) to 60 per cent in MP (NFHS-3). It is to be noted that the nutritional status of children and adults in some of the middle-income states such as Kerala and Tamil Nadu was better than that in higher income states such as Maharashtra and Gujarat. This could be attributed to public interventions in the nutrition and health sectors. Factors such as public provision of safe drinking water and health care are also important determinants of nutritional well-being. Analysis of inter-household variations in child nutrition shows that the risk of malnutrition decreases with an improvement in household income, mother's nutritional status, her education and access to health care during child delivery. The mother's present nutritional status, in turn, depends on her childhood nutritional status.

Malnutrition is seriously retarding human development and is hampering further reduction in child mortality. The economic costs of the current scale of malnutrition are enormous. Improvements in incomes of the poor and supply of environmental and health services are the long-term solutions for the eradication of malnutrition. However, in the short run, direct nutrition intervention should be the priority.

A Stronger Welfare System and Improved Social Service Provision are Needed

While broad poverty rates have declined, international evidence suggests that this improvement could have been greater given sustained high economic growth. The comparison with another large emerging economy, Brazil, over the 1990s and 2000s is particularly striking. Measured in terms of the absolute reduction in poverty rates, the average pace of reduction there was similar to India, despite considerably slower economic growth. Measured in proportionate terms the rate of poverty reduction in Brazil was faster (Ravallion, 2011). This reflected falling inequality in Brazil underpinned by a comprehensive social security system with sizeable direct cash transfers to the poor (OECD, 2005). The relative under-performance in poverty reduction in India therefore calls into question the effectiveness of existing welfare safety nets and the provision of essential social services.

While the NREGA represents a major step in providing more systematic support to the needy, there is no national equivalent for urban residents. Although poverty rates are lower in urban areas, they remain high and urbanisation will continue to draw poor unskilled workers into the cities. Moreover, workfare schemes are ineffective as an instrument for aiding the elderly and incapacitated. The use of conditional cash transfers (CCTs) in India is generally limited, despite their growing popularity in other emerging economies and mounting evidence concerning their effectiveness (Box 9.1). Some CCT schemes operate at the state level, including the Apni Beti Apna Dhan initiative, which aims to encourage girls to stay in school longer. At the national level, the Janani Suraksha Yojana aims to reduce the number of maternal and neonatal deaths by encouraging women to give birth in a health facility. Since its introduction in 2005, the number of women benefiting from this initiative has expanded rapidly, reaching around 10 million by 2009 compared with 275 million live births (Ministry of Health and Family Welfare, 2010). An evaluation of the scheme by Lim *et al.* (2010) found that it increased the proportion of births in health facilities considerably, highlighting the potential benefit of expanding CCTs in India. There is also evidence from some Indian states that the old-age pension, an unconditional cash transfer, has been effective in supporting intended recipients (Dutta *et al.*, 2010). In addition to a renewed effort to reform subsidies, greater experimentation with new CCT schemes would be advisable. As with schemes operating in other emerging economies, these should focus on helping to achieve key health and education objectives and focus on BPL households (Mehrotra, 2010). Administering such schemes will become easier with the introduction of a new identification system, the Unique Identity Number, which is currently being rolled out on a voluntary basis.

BOX – 9.1

Conditional Cash Transfers

Conditional cash transfer (CCT) schemes, under which welfare payments are made directly to households provided they undertake specific activities, have expanded over the past two decades. Large-scale CCT schemes now operate in most Latin American countries, as well as an increasing number of countries in Asia, Africa and elsewhere. While providing the usual benefits associated with welfare programmes that involve cash payments, including redistributing wealth and supplementing the incomes of the poor, CCT schemes aim to reduce longer-term poverty by addressing under-investment in health and education. Such under-investment may occur, for example, if parents believe that the prospective earnings of their children are less sensitive to the level of education they receive than is actually the case.

Typically, CCT scheme conditions for payment focus on school enrolment and attendance for school-aged children, as well as regular health checks for younger children and pregnant women.

The empirical evidence on the impact of CCTs continues to mount, with many initiatives having been evaluated using a variety of methods. As many schemes have been in place for a number of years, evidence is also beginning to emerge on their longer-term impact. A common finding is that CCTs are effective in raising incomes of poor households and reducing the incidence of immediate poverty. The weight of evidence also indicates that CCTs have a positive impact on school enrolment and lower the incidence of child labour. Further, visits to health clinics have been found to rise with the introduction of CCTs. All of these findings point to beneficial longer-term effects. However, assessments of improvements in outcomes, measured in terms of health status or learning are sometimes less conclusive. One explanation for this possible divergence is that in some cases the quality of services may be so poor that greater use does not lead to material improvements in outcomes. In the case of health services this could include inadequate provision of information needed by households to bring about longer-term changes in lifestyle that are needed to promote good health. This underscores the importance of access to quality essential services for CCTs to be most effective in reducing longer-term poverty.

Excerpted from OECD (2011). *Economic Survey: India*, June.

Spending on social welfare is relatively high but the system is fragmented and coverage is often poor (Dutta *et al.*, 2010; OECD, 2010a). The lack of a comprehensive safety net leaves the poor vulnerable to economic shocks and reliant on family and other networks. It also limits the effectiveness of government interventions to assist the poor during severe economic downturns as scaling up existing programmes quickly can be difficult. Spending on social programmes is skewed towards food and other subsidies, and towards employment in public works schemes. The single largest initiative is the PDS which provides subsidised food and other items. The scheme is intended to help the neediest but there is considerable evidence of poor targeting and major delivery inefficiencies. A major recent initiative is the NREGA, a workfare scheme that provides a guarantee of a minimum 100 days of employment to rural inhabitants at a minimum wage.

A recent report (2018) on Global Multidimensional Poverty Index (MPI) released by UNDP and Oxford University covering 105 countries based on 10 indicators: health, child mortality, years of schooling, school attendance, cooking fuel, sanitation, drinking water, electricity, housing and assets has specifically discussed the case of India. Quoting the opening paragraph on India:

India has made momentous progress in reducing multidimensional poverty. The incidence of multidimensional poverty was almost halved between 2005/6 and 2015/16, climbing down to 27.5 per cent. The global Multidimensional Poverty Index (MPI) was cut by half due to deeper progress among the poorest. Thus within ten years, the number of poor people in India fell by more than 271 million—a truly massive gain.

"This is indeed high praise" remark Rangarajan and Dev (2018). The report also says that "the poorest groups had the biggest reduction in MPI during the period 2005/6 to 2015/16, indicating they have been catching up".

Poverty Alleviation Programmes

There is no doubt that growth is important for poverty reduction and pattern of growth has a specific role in this process. At the same time, it is also recognised that growth is necessary but not sufficient for removing poverty. Some poor are able to take up the opportunity offered by a growing economy, while some others are not, due to inadequacy of their capabilities in terms of resource endowment, skills and access to the system providing the opportunities. That is why programmes either to directly redistribute assets and incomes or to increase capabilities through public spending directed towards the poor have always been a part of public policy, not only with a view to alleviating poverty, but also for ensuring social justice and equity. Some of these, such as Integrated Rural Development Programme (IRDP) started in 1978, were designed to encourge self-employment among the poor by providing them assets often in the form of livestock. The IRDP along with other programmes that were subsequently introduced have came together under the banner of Swarnjayanti Gram Swarozgar Yojna (SGSY). A major focus of SGSY has been the promotion of small credit groups known as self-help groups (SHGs). Other programmes include subsidised house construction under the Indira Awas Yojana and Schemes that provide state funds for work on village infrastructure (the Jawahar Rojgar Yojana and more recently the National Rural Employment Programmes.[5]

Programme for Socially Disadvantaged

Some of the programmes are targeted at social groups recognised to have been disadvantaged due to historical discrimination and also happen to be among the poorest. Reservation for scheduled castes (SCs) and scheduled tribes (STs) in education and public jobs (and subsequently for the backward classes) and also, special dispensation for them in public programmes of financial and other kinds of support constitute very important parts of programmes in this category.

Land Reforms

Among the basic redistributive measures, land reforms can be considered as most important with high potential for poverty alleviation. Abolition of intermediaries and ceiling on landholding and allotment of surplus land to landless were among the early initiatives taken by the governments. These measures and tenancy reforms helped millions of farmers and landless labourers in gaining access to the most valuable asset in rural India, *viz.*, land; consolidation of landholdings, even though not a redistributive land reform measure, was also taken up in several states, leading in increase in private investment and productivity. Operation Barga in West Bengal is among the latest and relatively successful initiative. One would expect that all these measures did

5. Somanathan, Rohini (2012). "Poverty and Exclusion", in Kaushik Basu and Annemie Maertens (eds.), *The Oxford Companion to Economics in India* (Vol.II). New Delhi: Oxford University Press.

contribute to poverty reduction, though it is not possible to assess the precise impact they made. Land reforms were, however, not seriously pursued and effectively implemented in most of the states and they no longer seem to be on the policy makers' agenda in recent decades.

Public Distribution System (PDS)

Another major initiative in the area of redistributive policy consists of the provision of food at subsidised prices through the PDS. It aims at providing food security to the poor. Viewed initially as a price stabilisation measure, it has over the time been recognised as an important poverty alleviation programme and has been particularly oriented towards this end in the form of targeted PDS since 1997, with special entitlement and prices for the poor.

Programmes specifically designated as anti-poverty programmes have aimed to help the poor raise their incomes through provision of gainful employment. They have broadly been of two kinds: one, assisting the poor to acquire assets and/or start business enterprise to create self-employment, and two, providing wage employment mostly in public works to supplement incomes of the poor.

Public Investment in Human Capital and Public Goods

In order that the rapid and pro-poor growth is effective in alleviating poverty, it is important to ensure that enough efforts and investment are made in the areas of human and social development. A basic reason why the poor are not able to participate in and benefit from the rapid growth of the economy lies in their poor human capital endowment. With a relatively meagre public investment in education and health, the poor have very limited chance of augmenting their human capital endowments. Total social sector expenditure by centre and states together is only around 10 per cent of which share of education and health is only 2.5 and 2.1 per cent respectively. This needs to be increased considerably to make the link between high growth and poverty reduction more effective. Access of people to public goods, education, health, transport, communication services, water and electricity is the most certain means of ensuring 'trickle down' of growth for poverty reduction.[6]

---

6. Ibid

Concluding Remarks

Of late, a declining poverty-reducing impact of high growth has become a matter of concern. The argument that high growth may be necessary, but is not sufficient for poverty alleviation has, therefore, emerged strongly in the debate on poverty alleviation strategy. Major reliance for poverty reduction can be placed on economic growth, provided its pattern is made to be pro-poor. In the present context, it would imply greater emphasis on agricultural and rural development, on high employment growth through faster growth of labour-intensive manufacturing and accelerating growth in lagging states and areas. According to Rangarajan[7], policy makers must continue to focus on the twofold strategy of letting the economy grow fast and attacking poverty through poverty alleviation programmes.

---

7. Rangarajan, C. (2014). "The Need to Measure Poverty", *The Hindu*, August 7.

10

Unemployment and Employment Perspective

TO understand the concept of unemployment, it is necessary to understand the concept of labour force, for by definition, one who is not in the labour force cannot be unemployed. By the internationally accepted definitions, all persons who are working (have a job) and though not working, but are seeking and are available for work, are deemed to be in the labour force. Correspondingly, all those who are not working and are neither seeking nor available for work are considered outside the labour force and hence do not figure in employment or unemployment statistics.[1]

The growth rate of labour force is determined partly by the age structure of the population and the age- and sex-specific labour force participation rate that can be expected to obtain.

Concepts and Measurement

The labour force participation rate (LFPR), work participation rate (WPR) and unemployment rate (UR) are a few of the major indicators generally being used to assess labour market conditions. The LFPR is obtained by dividing the number of persons in the labour force with the total population. WPR, on the other hand, is obtained by dividing the number of persons in the workforce with total population. The unemployment rate is obtained by dividing the number of those unemployed with the total number of persons in the labour force.[2]

---

1. Dantwala, M.L. (1999). "Understanding Poverty and Unemployment", in Uma Kapila (ed.), *Indian Economy Since Independence*, 1999-2000 edition. New Delhi: Academic Foundation. p.865.
2. Government of India (2009). *The Challenge of Employment in India: An Informal Economy Perspective*, Report of the National Commission for Enterprises in the Unorganised Sector, Chairman: Arjun K. Sengupta, ch.3. New Delhi: Academic Foundation.

Unemployment is measured through labour force surveys that elicit the 'activity' status of the respondent for a given reference period. First, the respondent is identified as not working. Second, for those not working, the typical question in the form is: are you available for work, and have you made some effort to find work during the last x days. Those who answer in the affirmative are the unemployed while those who answer in the negative are the people who have opted out of the labour force. The labour force is the sum of the employed and the unemployed, and the rate of unemployment is the proportion of labour force that is unemployed. The reference period could vary from a week to four weeks to a year (Wadhwa and Ramaswami, 2007).[3]

In India, employment-unemployment surveys are conducted by the National Sample Survey Organisation (NSSO). Beginning with the 27th round in 1972-73, labour force surveys have been conducted every five years using standardised concepts and procedures based on the recommendations of the Committee of Experts.

The concepts/procedures presently being used in India for the classification are:

1. Usual Principal Status (UPS).
2. Usual Principal and Subsidiary Status (UPSS).
3. Current Weekly Status (CWS).
4. Current Daily Status (CDS).

Usual Principal Status: The labour force, in this context, is typically measured through the UPS which reflects the status of an individual during a reference period of one year. Thus, a person is classified as belonging to labour force, if he/she had been either working or looking for work during longer part of the 365 days preceding the survey. The UPS measure excludes from the labour force all those who are employed and/or unemployed for a total of less than six months. Therefore, persons who work intermittently, either because of the pattern of work in the household farm/enterprise or due to economic compulsions and other reasons, would not be included in the labour force unless their days at work and unemployment totalled half of the reference year (NCEUS, 2009).

---

3. Wadhwa, Wilima and Bharat Ramaswami (2007). "Unemployment, The Measurement of", in Kaushik Basu (ed.), *The Oxford Companion to Economics in India*. New Delhi: Oxford University Press.

Usual Principal and Subsidiary Status: The UPSS concept was introduced to widen the UPS concept to include even those who were outside the labour force on the basis of the majority time criterion but had been employed during some part of the year on an usual basis. In the NSS 61st Round Survey (NSSO, 2006a), all those who were either unemployed or out of labour force but had worked for at least 30 days over the reference year were treated as subsidiary status workers and hence, included in the labour force. UPSS is, thus, a hybrid concept incorporating both the major time criterion and priority to work status.

The UPSS measure was used on the ground that it was stable and inclusive. It is related to a picture emerging from a long reference period, and even those working for 30 days or more, but not working for the major part of the year, were included.

Current Weekly Status: The concept of CWS has been in use in the labour force surveys in India even before 1970, when the recommendations of the Dantwala Committee became available. It was primarily because the agencies like International Labour Organization (ILO) use estimates of employment and unemployment rates based on weekly reference period for international comparisons. In India, a person is classified to be in labour force as per CWS if she/he has either worked or is seeking and/or available for work at least for one hour during the reference period of one week preceding the date of survey.

Current Daily Status: The Dantwala Committee proposed the use of CDS rates for studying intensity of work. These are computed on the basis of the information on employment and unemployment recorded for the 14 half days of the reference week. The employment status during the 7 days is recorded in terms of half or full intensities. An hour or more but less than four hours is taken as half intensity and four hours or more is taken as full intensity. An advantage of this approach is that it is based on more complete information. A disadvantage is that it related to person-days, not persons. Hence, it had to be used with some caution.[4]

It has been observed that the estimates based on daily status are the most inclusive rate of 'unemployment' giving the average level of unemployment on a day during the survey year. It captures the unemployed days of the chronically unemployed, the unemployed days of usually employed who become intermittently unemployed during the reference week and unemployed days of those classified as employed

4. Government of India (2009). *op.cit.* no.2.

according to the criterion of CWS. The Eleventh Five Year Plan has largely used the CDS basis of estimation of employment and unemployment in the country.

Characteristics and Structure of the Indian Labour Market

India's labour market is characterised by a low female participation rate, visible in its poor labour sex ratio and also low worker-total population ratio. The overall LFPR stands at around 40 per cent which for women is 23 per cent. While the male LFPR has been stable at 55-56 per cent during three decades from 1983 to 2011-12, the female LFPR has shown a decline from around 30 per cent in 1983 to 23 per cent in 2011-12 (Table 10.1).

TABLE – 10.1

Labour Force Participation Rate and Workforce Participation Rate (UPSS) by Gender (All Ages): 1983 to 2011-12

Year	*LFPR*			*WFPR*		
	M	*F*	*P*	*M*	*F*	*P*
1983	55.1	30.0	42.9	53.9	29.6	42.0
1993-94	55.6	29.0	42.8	54.5	28.6	42.0
2004-05	55.9	29.4	43.0	54.7	28.7	42.0
2011-12	55.6	22.5	39.5	54.4	21.9	38.6

Note: M: Male; F: Female; P: Persons and WFPR: Workforce Participation Rate.

Source: Computed from unit level data of various NSSO rounds.

Institute for Human Development (2014). *India Labour and Employment Report 2014*. New Delhi: Academic Foundation.

The broad features of the labour market and employment prevailing in India are provided in Table 10.2. As can be seen from the table, regular wage employment constitutes about 18 per cent of the total employment. There was a somewhat significant rise in the percentage of regular workers after 2004-05 which was stagnant for two decades prior to that. However, over 60 per cent of the regular workers are informal workers with no social security and only around 40 per cent are formal workers. In other words, only 6.8 per cent of the total workers have regular formal jobs which can be categorised as good or decent jobs. It is also important to note that since 2004-05, there has been a one percentage point increase in regular formal jobs. A little less than one-third of the total workers are casual workers and this has been more or less stable (ranging between 30 and 33%) during the three decades from 1983 to 2011-12. Over half of the workers were self-employed in 2011-12 and the figure has declined by five percentage points since the middle of 2004-05 (Table 10.2 and Figure 10.1).

TABLE – 10.2

Status of Employment (UPSS), 1983 to 2011-12

Share (%) in Total Employment of :	*1983*	*1993-94*	*1999-2000*	*2004-05*	*2009-10*	*2011-12*
Regular wage employment	13.5	13.2	14.0	14.3	15.6	17.9
Formal	-	-	5.4	5.6	6.4	6.8
Informal	-	-	8.6	8.6	9.2	11.0
Casual wage employment	29.0	32.0	33.2	28.9	33.5	29.9
Self-employment	57.5	54.7	52.8	56.9	51.0	52.2
Casual and self employment	86.5	86.7	86.0	85.8	84.5	82.1
Organized sector	-	-	9.3	11.1	14.0	16.4
Unorganized sector	-	-	90.7	88.9	86.0	83.6

Note: Formal employment includes the regular workers with social security in organised sector.

Source: Computed from unit level data of various NSSO rounds.

IHD (2014). *India Labour and Employment Report 2014*.

About one-sixth of the total workers are in the organised sector and the rest (about 84%) are in the unorganised sector. It is also seen that since the early 1990s, there has been slow but steady growth of workers in the organised sector. While there has been some increase in regular formal wage employment, the bulk of the increase in regular wage employment has been in the informal component. This is a fact of considerable significance and is illustrative of the limitations of the employment impact of the Indian growth experience.

FIGURE – 10.1

Percentage Share of Employed by Work Status: 1983 to 2011/12

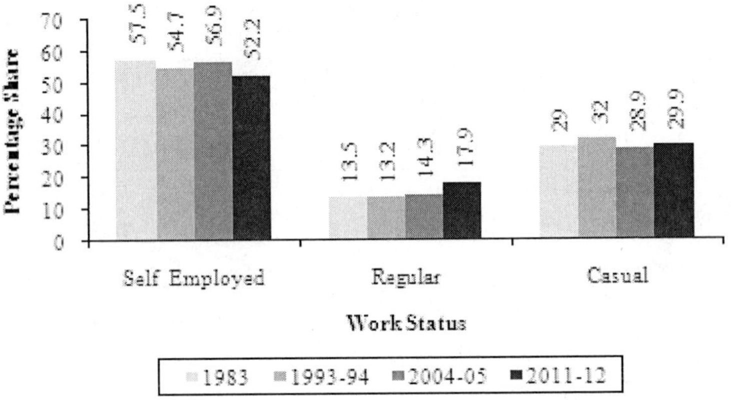

Source: IHD (2014). *India Labour and Employment Report 2014.*

The employment performance vis-à-vis growth has obviously not been satisfactory and suggests distorted and exclusionary growth. Thus, the Indian labour market is highly dualistic in nature and this dualism has sharpened over time, more so during the high-growth period. However, since 2004-05, it seems that there has been a small but noticeable change in the trend. The shares of regular employment, regular formal employment and organised sector employment have shown some increase, which is indeed healthy. This significant development needs to be studied carefully.

Trends and Patterns of Employment Growth

Aggregate employment has grown at an average annual rate of 2 per cent in India during the past four decades since 1972-73, although during the last few years the growth of employment has been substantially reduced. This pattern of employment growth has not been experienced by many countries historically. However, a large part of this growth of employment simply indicates growth in labour force. The growth of organised sector employment and particularly, formal employment has been slow. Of course, the rise in productivity and earnings of workers in the unorganised sector indicate some improvement in the employment conditions of informal workers.

Notwithstanding the quantitative expansion in employment growth, some disconcerting features of employment growth have emerged in recent years:

- Employment growth has decelerated.
- The employment content of growth has shown a decline.
- Sectors with higher employment potential have registered relatively slower growth.
- Agriculture, despite a sharp decline in its importance in GDP, continues to be the largest employer because the non-agricultural sectors have not generated enough employment to effect a shift of workforce.
- Most of the employment growth has been contributed by the unorganised sector, which is characterised by low incomes and poor conditions of work.
- Though employment growth in the organised sector has picked up in recent years, it has largely been led by an increase in employment of casual and contract labour.

Growth in Employment, GDP and Employment Elasticity

Although long-term employment growth over the period of about four decades, has been around 2.0 per cent per annum (which was only a little less than labour force growth), it has seen a declining trend from one decade to another: it was 2.4 per cent during 1972-73/1983, 2.0 per cent in the following 10 year period and 1.8 per cent during 1993-94/2004-05 (Table 10.3). There has been a sharp deceleration in employment growth between 2004-05 and 2011-12, as revealed by the latest round of NSSO. This has been largely due to a sharp fall in the WFPR of women, particularly in rural areas.[5]

The long-term trend of decline in the rate of employment growth is a fact that cannot be ignored. What is particularly intriguing is that this decline has been accompanied by acceleration in the rate of economic growth. Thus, when GDP grew at 4.7 per cent per annum during 1972-73 to 1983, employment growth was 2.4 per cent; GDP growth increased to 5.0 per cent, but employment growth declined to 2.0 per cent during 1983/1993-94; during 1993-94/2004-05, GDP

---

5. Institute of Human Development (2014). *India Labour and Employment Report 2014*. New Delhi: Academic Foundation.

TABLE – 10.3

Sector-wise Growth of Employment (UPSS) and Employment Elasticity

Sectors	*Employment Growth*				*Employment Elasticity*			
	1972-73/ 83	*1983/ 93-94*	*1993-94/ 2004-05*	*2004-05/ 2011-12*	*1972-73/ 83*	*1983/ 93-94*	*1993-94/ 2004-05*	*2004-05/ 2011-12*
Primary	1.70	1.35	0.67	–1.98	0.46	0.49	0.26	–0.42
Secondary (including Mining & Quarrying)	4.43	2.82	3.97	4.46	0.87	0.53	0.59	0.48
Tertiary	4.21	3.77	3.41	2.09	0.77	0.57	0.43	0.17
Non-Agricultural	4.30	3.36	3.64	3.15	0.81	0.55	0.48	0.28
Total	2.44	2.02	1.84	0.45	0.52	0.41	0.29	0.04

Source: Estimates based on various rounds of NSS data on employment and unemployment, adjusted by census population.

IHD (2014). *India Labour and Employment Report 2014*.

growth accelerated to 6.3 per cent, but employment growth further declined to 1.8 per cent; and during the period 2004-05/2011-12, when GDP growth was as high as 8.5 per cent, employment grew at an insignificant rate of 0.5 per cent. The declining trend in the employment component of growth is quite clearly seen in terms of the values of employment elasticity (ratio of employment growth to growth in value added) in Table 10.3. It was 0.52 during 1972-73/1983, which declined to 0.41 in the next 10-year period and further to 0.29 during 1993-94/ 2004-05. During 2004-05/2011-12, it declined to almost zero.

Patterns of Employment Growth at a Disaggregated Level

The employment growth rates have of course varied across sectors and activities. In the secondary sector (consisting of mining, manufacturing, electricity, water and gas, and construction), growth has been relatively high—in fact the highest among the three sectors, during 1972-73 to 2011-12. It has declined, over this period, with some fluctuations over the shorter periods, but has shown a significant increase during 1994 to 2012. Even during 2004-05 to 2011-12, when overall employment had virtually stagnated, it grew by around 4.5 per cent in the secondary sector. Employment growth in the tertiary or services sector has also been relatively high but has consistently declined over the three periods of 10 years each since 1972-73. The growth of employment in the primary sector, as expected, has been the lowest and has sharply declined between 2004-05 and 2011-12.

Primary Sector

The slow and declining growth of employment in agriculture is a result of the slow and declining rate of GDP growth of this sector and a decline in employment elasticity that turned negative in 2011-12. The negative growth in employment in agriculture also indicates that the sector is not able to absorb the existing workers and they are moving to non-agriculture. In the secondary sector, a high employment growth despite moderate rates of GDP growth has been possible due to relatively high and stable employment elasticity. But in the tertiary sector, a high GDP growth has not been accompanied by high growth in employment and this is reflected in a steep decline in employment elasticity (Table 10.3, Figures 10.2 and 10.3).

FIGURE – 10.2

Sector-wise Employment Growth 1972-73/1983 to 2004-05/2011-12 (UPSS)

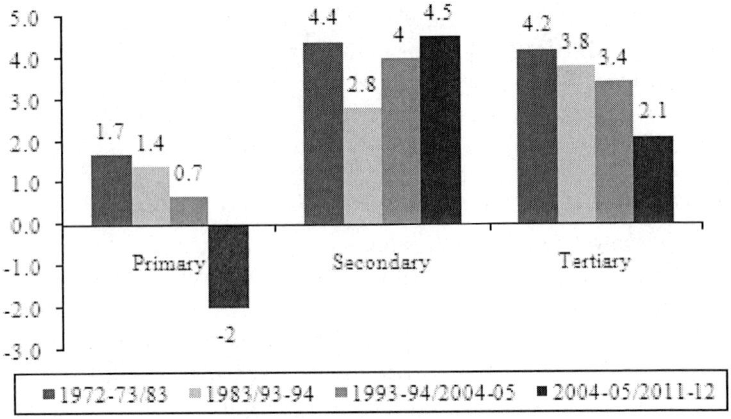

Source: Computed from unit level data of various NSSO rounds.
IHD (2014). *India Labour and Employment Report 2014.*

FIGURE – 10.3

Sector-wise GDP Growth 1972-73/1983 to 2004-05/2011-12 (UPSS)

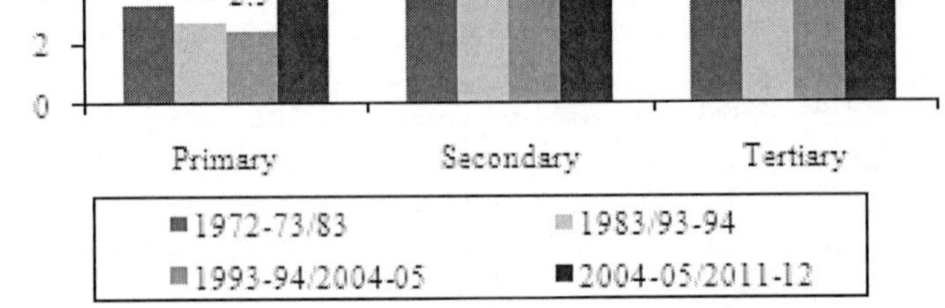

Source: Computed from unit level data of various NSSO rounds.
IHD (2014). *India Labour and Employment Report 2014*

Secondary Sector

Within the secondary sector, the construction sector experienced a relatively high and increasing rate of employment growth; it was over 7 per cent during 1994-2005, almost similar to its GDP growth. It recorded almost double digit employment growth between 2004-05 and 2011-12, when the total employment virtually stagnated.[6] Most of the employment generated in construction was of low quality, casual and irregular with low wages.

Employment growth in manufacturing has also been moderately high, and after declining during 1983/1993-94, it registered an increase in the next period, 1994-2005. But it experienced a decline in employment growth during 2004-05/2011-12. The employment elasticity in manufacturing has been relatively high except during 2005-2012.[7] There have been rather significant changes in the pattern of employment in manufacturing industries between 2004-05 and 2009-10, with some industries showing decline and others showing reasonably good growth.[8] The quality of employment, as expected, has been better than the construction sector.

Services Sector

In the services sector, trade and transport have shown the best employment performance, with both registering a growth of over 5 per cent during 1994-2005, after having seen a decline in growth rate, sharper in transport than in trade, during 1983-94, over 1973-83. Financial services, however, have recorded the highest increase in employment over the period 1993-94/2004-05. Even during 2004-05/2011-12, this sub-sector of services has registered an employment growth of about 8 per cent, while the trade and transport sub-sectors experienced about 2 per cent growth in employment. Thus, it appears that all sub-sectors of the tertiary sector with the possible exception of community, social and personal services have shown reasonably high potential for employment generation.[9]

There are a few emerging sectors like ‘computer hardware consultancy’, ‘software publishing’, ‘data processing’ and ‘maintenance

---

6. Appendix Table 7.1 (*India Labour and Employment Report 2014*) provides some details about the quantum and quality of employment generated in the construction sector during 2004-05/2009-10 at disaggregated level of 4-digits.
7. Appendix Tables 3.6 and 3.10a *(India Labour and Employment Report 2014)*.
8. Table 7.3 (*India Labour and Employment Report 2014*) which provides employment growth at 4 digit level.
9. Appendix Table 3.6 and Appendix Table 7.1 *(India Labour and Employment Report 2014)*.

and repair of office accounting and computing machinery', where although the share of total employment is not very large, their growth rate varies from 17 per cent to 54 per cent annually and the share of regular employment varies from 60 to 95 per cent with relatively high earnings.[10] It must, however, be noted that in most sub-sectors of services, while the GDP has seen high and increasing growth, employment growth has been on the decline. Employment elasticity has, therefore, declined sharply during the periods 1972-73/1983 to 2004-05/2011-12 from 0.81 to 0.16 in trade, from 0.91 to 0.13 in transport and from 0.71 to 0.12 in community, social and personal services. In financial services, it has declined from 1.25 to 0.39 during 1972-73/83 to 1983/1993-94, but again increased during 1983/1993-94 to 2004-05/ 2011-12 from 0.39 to 0.59.[11]

Overall Sectoral Pattern

Thus, it may be inferred that the employment content of growth has declined over time; Although it has varied across the sectors, the primary sector, consisting of mainly agriculture, has witnessed least employment growth, which in itself is not worrisome as this sector is home to the bulk of surplus labour. The sub-sectors of the tertiary sector such as financial services which are linked to globalisation have witnessed faster growth of employment. However, the manufacturing sector, which has significant multiplier effects with other sectors, has not registered high growth of employment during the recent period due to primarily low growth of output. The quality of employment generated in manufacturing sector, although better than agriculture and construction, was generally not good. Construction has witnessed high growth rate of employment but quality of employment is poor. But for the first time, there is an indication of a structural shift in employment, albeit small, from agriculture to other sectors which is a positive trend.

Gender Differentials in Employment Growth

Female employment, which accounts for around one-third of all employment, grew less than male employment during the past three decades (Table 10.5). During the period 2005-2012, the available estimates indicate a steep decline in the growth of employment. But the pattern of employment growth has an important gender dimension; there was an absolute decline in employment for rural females. In this

10. See Appendix Table 7.2, *India Labour and Employment Report 2014*.
11. See Appendix Tables 3.6 and 3.10a, *India Labour and Employment Report 2014*.

TABLE – 10.4

Percentage Shares of Employment (UPSS) and GDP in India

Sectors	*Sectoral Share in Employment*					*Sectoral Share in GDP*				
	1972-73	*1983*	*1993-94*	*2004-05*	*2011-12*	*1972-73*	*1983*	*1993-94*	*2004-05*	*2011-12*
Primary	73.92	68.6	63.98	56.3	48.90	41.1	35.5	28.4	19.0	14.1
Secondary (including Mining and Quarrying)	11.3	13.8	14.96	18.78	24.37	24.4	25.8	26.8	27.9	27.5
Tertiary	14.78	17.6	21.07	24.92	26.73	34.5	38.7	44.8	53.0	58.4
Non-agricultural	26.08	31.4	36.02	43.7	51.10	58.9	64.5	71.6	81.0	85.9
Total	100.0	100.0	100.0	100.0	100.0	100.0	100.0	100.0	100.0	100.0

Source: Estimates based on various rounds of NSS data on employment and unemployment.

period, for males, in both rural and urban areas, a slowdown in employment growth has occurred, but the sharp absolute decline for rural female warrants further investigation. India has the lowest participation rate for women in the workforce when compared to all its South Asian neighbours except Pakistan. A number of experts and commentators have attributed it to the marginalisation of women in the labour market because of the absence of suitable jobs for them. Others have termed it as a healthy development indicating rising enrolment of women in schools and colleges as well as withdrawal of a large number of women from work due to rising income (called income effect in economic discourse).

TABLE – 10.5

Growth of Employment (UPSS)

Years	*Rural*			*Urban*			*Total*		
	Male	*Female*	*Total*	*Male*	*Female*	*Total*	*Male*	*Female*	*Total*
1983-94	1.92	1.39	1.72	3.14	3.38	3.19	2.21	1.64	2.02
1994-2005	1.40	1.54	1.45	3.10	3.30	3.14	1.86	1.81	1.84
1983-2005	1.65	1.47	1.58	3.12	3.34	3.17	2.03	1.73	1.93
2005-2012	1.06	–2.76	–0.22	2.54	1.07	2.23	1.51	–2.04	0.44

Source: Computed from unit level data of various NSSO rounds and various decadal census reports.

Long Term Perspectives

In the long run, if India's high growth path is sustained the employment pattern will eventually move towards larger shares of the organised sector, non-agricultural activities and wage/salaried jobs; but it will take time. In 2011-12, agriculture employed about 49 per cent of workers but accounted for only 14 per cent of GDP; so the output per worker in agriculture is only one-sixth of that in non-agricultural activities. Differentials in productivity and the quality of work are likewise large between organised and unorganised enterprises, more so in urban areas. This asymmetry is a source of both macroeconomic imbalance and income inequality, and points to the need for rapid growth of modern employment. Although private organised sector employment is now growing, but it is doing so from a low base, and therefore even higher rate of employment growth translates only into a rather small absolute number of additional jobs, compared to the size of the labour market. Moreover, the decline in public employment shows no signs of abating.

Rapid growth of the manufacturing industry and modern services is needed to bring about a quicker shift of the workforce from agriculture to non-agriculture, reduce the disparity between the two and lead to an improvement in the quality of employment. But it is clearly not sufficient. There is no plausible rate of growth of employment in the private organised sector which would make this the main driver of employment growth in the Indian economy in the coming decades. So it is important to identify the patterns of growth of organised sector or of specific sectors of industries that have stronger links with the unorganised sector, and whose growth is more likely to have a positive impact on the growth of unorganised sector, so that the labour productivity and earnings in the sector becomes high. In fact, such a trend has been witnessed in India recently between 2004-05 and 2009-10, when growth of productivity and wages in the unorganised sector was higher than those in the organised sector. This has very important implications for the transfer of labour from the unorganised sector to the organised sector and consequent gradual transformation of the labour market (Ghose, 2012).[12]

It is important that the organised sector, particularly organized manufacturing, grows. Among other reasons, improvements in productivity, wages and the quality of work in the organised sector may indirectly filter through to the economy as a whole through its linkage with the unorganised sector. But unorganised employment is continuing to grow, and will continue to be the main source of employment for many years. Moreover, even in the organised sector, informal employment at least till recently has been increasing. It follows that the route towards a formal high productivity economy does not lie merely in organised sector growth. It is necessary to enhance the productivity of unorganised sector enterprises and ensure that the employment created in these enterprises meets minimum quality standards. In other words, a strategy for the formalisation of informal work is needed. In reality, for the vast majority of Indian workers, the main issue is not so much more work as better paid work. If the recent growth in labour productivity and wages in the unorganised sector is accelerated in future, it will make a significant dent on poverty and will also facilitate and accelerate the transfer of labour from subsistence agriculture sector to a more productive modern sector.

---

12. Ghose, Ajit K. (2012). "The Growth Employment Interaction in a Developing Economy", *The Indian Journal of Labour Economics*.

It is essential to rely on manufacturing-led growth for facilitating this process. This has been the path of growth in East and South-east Asia coupled with effective policy of human resource development (HRD) and India has to learn a lot from the experiences of these countries. In fact, China has also adopted this path and consequently wages and labour productivity in China are almost two and half times to three times the Indian levels, and the country is now widely believed to have passed the Lewis-turning point, thereby increasing the pressure of rising wages.[13]

Labour Market Reforms Would Help Boost Employment Creation

Firms confront a number of challenges when starting up and expanding, including gaining access to land and reliable electricity supply. They also face a range of labour market regulations administered by the state and central governments. More restrictive state level employment regulations have been shown to reduce labour market dynamism and reforms to ease regulations tend to increase the creation of regular jobs (OECD, 2007; Goldar and Aggarwal, 2010). At the central level, an important regulation that likely restricts job creation in large manufacturing firms, especially compared to smaller firms in the informal sector, is dismissal laws under the Industrial Disputes Act. Manufacturing firms with more than 100 employees must gain permission from the Ministry of Labour and Employment to dismiss just one worker, regardless of whether there are sound economic grounds for dismissal. While there is no additional requirement for collective dismissal, the need to gain permission to dismiss any worker means that India has amongst the strictest rules for dismissal of any OECD or emerging economy, as measured by the OECD employment protection legislation indicator. In 2009-10, under the Industrial Disputes Act, only 12 firms were officially granted permission to dismiss workers, with 2,146 workers dismissed in total (Ministry of Labour and Employment, 2010). Given the size of India's labour force, it is clear that many firms are avoiding their legal obligations (OECD, 2011).

The fact that employment protection rules, and the Industrial Disputes Act more generally apply only to firms with more than 100 employees, provides incentives for firms to stay small or to hide the

13. Institute of Human Development (2014). *India Labour and Employment Report 2014*. New Delhi: Academic Foundation.

full extent of their employment. As a result, compared with other large emerging economies, India's employment is dominated by small firms; Hasan and Jandoc (2010) report that 84 per cent of manufacturing employment in India is in firms with less than 50 employees, compared with 25 per cent in China. As well as providing less protection and training to workers, smaller firms often have greater difficulties gaining access to credit and tend to be less productive, which ultimately reduces the scope for higher wages. To promote job creation and poverty reduction, the government should reduce the administrative burden for dismissal faced by larger firms.

Restrictive labour market policies also encourage informal employment, which can impose significant costs on both firms and workers. Informal firms are less productive, smaller and so less likely to be able to take advantage of economies of scale and tend to have limited access to credit (Perry et al., 2007). Informal workers tend to be paid less than their formal counterparts, are less likely to receive training and more likely to lose their jobs in the event of an economic downturn (OECD, 2008). Few are covered by social protection schemes, such as unemployment insurance and pension schemes. Over a lifetime, this disadvantage can dramatically increase the risk of poverty, particularly in retirement. India's very high rate of informality also creates additional problems when trying to implement a comprehensive social insurance scheme.

In India, the scope to reform labour market laws at the level of the central government is limited due to the absence of consensus amongst the social partners. Nevertheless, a number of states have made reforms to the extent allowed by federal laws and the Constitution. These reforms have varied considerably across states (OECD, 2007). There is evidence that those states with the greatest reforms, have seen the fastest growth of manufacturing employment (Goldar, 2011).

Public Employment Programme for the Unorganised Workers: The Case of NREGA

Programmes to create direct employment opportunities for wage workers through public works have in the past focused on generation of supplementary employment opportunities, especially during lean periods. They have been considered as an important component of the anti-poverty strategy. These programmes are expected to create durable assets for the community and thus, enhance further economic activities. Wage employment programmes also push up demand for labour and thus, exert an upward pressure on the market wage rates by attracting people to public works programmes, thereby reducing supply of cheap labour, often at wages that would not even meet their bare basic needs.

Consistent with the approach for an employment-centred development strategy that would level up the informal economy, public employment programmes should be an integral part of planning and policy. Apart from the advantages that would accrue to the unemployed, underemployed and the poorly employed, such programmes will also have a positive macroeconomic impact via the increase in effective demand from the hitherto poor and vulnerable segments of the population. Viewed in this perspective, the enactment of the NREGA (National Rural Employment Guarantee Act) is a historic step in the Indian context.

Past experiences show that India's poverty alleviation strategy, including the National Rural Employment Programme (NREP), Rural Labour Employment Guarantee Programme (RLEGP), Jawahar Rozgar Yojana (JRY), Employment Assurance Scheme (EAS), Sampoorna Gramin Rozgar Yojana (SGRY), etc., leaned towards wage employment programmes. With specific reference to NREGA, the argument has been to treat it as a component of a full employment strategy for India (Bhaduri, 2005; IHD, 2009). By ensuring employment for a minimum number of days at minimum wages, the thrust was on 'employment first, with growth as an outcome', rather than the vice-versa (Bhaduri, 2005). It is also argued that this path towards full employment alone can ensure the 'economic content of participatory democracy', and allow for "development with dignity" (Ibid).

The path towards full employment lies in strengthening the sectors where the poor are located and stabilising their incomes, improving their asset base, constructing basic socioeconomic infrastructure at the local level, enabling access to paid work opportunities and exerting an upward pressure on market wages (IHD, 2009). NREGA as a programme is expected to create conditions for realisation of the above outcomes.

An Overview of the Scheme

NREGA has been envisaged from the perspective of 'right to employment' and guarantees 100 days employment at a minimum fixed wage rate, but more importantly it bestows an entitlement. The Act has also identified roles and responsibilities for the central and state governments, district and block administrations and the panchayats. The onus of guaranteeing 100 days of employment rests with the Government and the applicant can demand for unemployment allowance in case he/she does not get work. Apart from creation of work opportunities, the Act also provides for basic facilities at the worksite *viz.*, crèche, safe drinking water and medical aid.

The salient features revolve around recognition of the right to work and dignity to work. These include:

1. A right-based framework, with employment on demand.
2. At least 100 days of guaranteed wage employment in a financial year to every household whose adult members volunteer to do unskilled manual work.
3. Wage payment within 15 days.
4. Payment of unemployment allowance in case of non-provision of employment within 15 days (unemployment allowance to be at least one fourth of the minimum wage for the first 30 days, and at least one-half of the minimum wages thereafter).
5. Work within 5 kilometres of residence (if provided outside 5 km, 10% extra wage to meet additional transportation and living expenses).
6. Minimum wages to be paid by the state governments.
7. Priority for ensuring one-third of workers are women.
8. Mandatory basic worksite facilities—drinking water, shade, medical aid and crèche (if more than five children below age 6 are present).
9. Ban on the use of contractors and machinery, and allocation of funds in the ratio of 60:40 for unskilled and skilled/ material components of the work ensure the primacy of labour-intensive nature of work.
10. Equal wages for men and women.
11. Devolution of powers to the Panchayati Raj Institutions (PRI).
12. Mechanisms of accountability and transparency.
13. Creation of durable assets to strengthen the livelihood resource base of the rural poor.

The Performance

The NREGA, was launched in February 2006 in 200 most backward districts in the first phase and was expanded to 330 districts during 2007-08. The coverage was extended to all rural districts of the country in 2008-09. At present, 619 districts are covered under the NREGS.

The performance of the NREGA varies significantly across the states. There are some states where NREGA has managed to achieve its key outcomes very well and which have indeed innovated in many respects. In others, performance has been unimpressive and lacklustre. Given that the overall framework for the NREGA is similar across the states, clearly, the variations in performance depend on factors such as the political and administrative will of the governments, historical background of the state as well as the nature of civil society and public actions around the NREGA. But this also suggests that the state governments which have the responsibility of framing the rules as well as overseeing the actual implementation of the scheme on the ground can 'own' the scheme and give it a fillip. There is a lot of scope for state governments to innovate and adapt the scheme according to the local requirements. State-specific experiences are important sources for innovations which in turn provide valuable lessons for replication. The relative success of the scheme in some regions, and failure in others highlights the need to properly understand the reasons for inter- and intra-state variations and to replicate and adopt features of implementation of the better performing states.

Success Stories

The performance of the scheme in the state of Andhra Pradesh has been laudable because of strong political will and also because the state has had a rural worker and community mobilisation movement. In addition, Andhra Pradesh has successfully employed computerisation and e-governance mechanisms for monitoring the scheme. For example, funds are being transferred electronically; every job seeker has got a bank account and wages are paid through bank or post office account; the whole process from job application to registration is computerised.

In Rajasthan, which has the history of drought relief based public employment and active civil society, the success of NREGA is more impressive compared to other north Indian states. Dungarpur District was able to make NREGA more of a success because of the presence of effective grass-roots non-governmental organisation (NGOs) and their ability to mobilise the poor. Further, in Rajasthan, the innovative arrangement of having a 'mate' supporting worksite management has led to greater productivity of workers, easier worksite supervision and greater transparency in maintaining of work-related records. Facilitation of the scheme by the local civil society organisation, the Jagrut Adivasi Dalit Sangathan (JADS), in Pati block of Madhya Pradesh bears testimony to public action from below to inculcate the practice of work on demand through application, receipts at the time of submission of applications and ensuring the payment of unemployment allowance, if necessary.

In Kerala, the NREGA implementation pivots around the Kutumbashree [self-help groups (SHGs) of poor women]. These women are not only involved in identifying the public work projects, but also overseeing the implementation. Besides, Kerala has also used banks and post offices for wage payment. All these have resulted in high participation rate of women and an overall efficient system. Manifold increase in the number of work days, reduction in distress out-migration, enrolment in schools were observed in a study of eight states by Indian School of Women's Studies and Development, New Delhi.

Remaining Gaps

Poor awareness levels of workers regarding the scheme and the entitlements can be cited as a reason for its inability to take off in some regions. In the GBPSSI Study (2009) of six states, Rajasthan emerges favourably in this regard, with 90 per cent of workers knowing about the provision of 100 days of work. More than half of the respondents were aware of the minimum wages and the 15 days period within which wage payment should take place. This can be attributed, as already mentioned, to the state's active tradition of public mobilisation, state-initiated awareness drives and presence of workers' organisations such as the MKSS (Mazdoor Kishan Shakti Sangathan). In comparison, in the remaining five states where the survey was conducted, less that 50 per cent of the workers exhibited knowledge of the most basic provision of the scheme of employment for 100 days. Further, the demand based nature through which employment is offered under NREGA has still got a long way to go in terms of being operationalised, with 71 per cent of the respondents in the study being unaware that an application had to be submitted in order to gain work.

However, within the existing framework and limitations, many of the problems can be substantially overcome if the political and administrative leadership at the state and local levels plays a more proactive role in implementing the objectives of the NREGA.

Policy Agenda

A medium- to long-term employment strategy should be envisaged to deal with the challenges highlighted above. It should ensure that the organised sector, particularly manufacturing, grows much more rapidly than in the past and leads to a process of economy-wide productivity growth, along with employment expansion and rising wages. Even in the organised sector, informal employment should not grow at the cost of formal jobs.

Regulatory interventions in informal enterprises should ensure that a minimum quality of employment is maintained and the basic rights of workers are respected. The recent growth in the productivity and wages of workers in the unorganised sector is an important and welcome development. Although small, it has important implications for employment and development policies of the country. The need is to sustain and accelerate this process.

Appropriate policies and measures to address the issue of education and skills acquisition, and of skills mismatches need to be urgently put in place. The rising aspirations of the youth have to be met and the ongoing 'youth bulge' is likely to exacerbate this challenge. The challenge pertains not only to the achievement of a major quantitative expansion of the facilities for education and skill-training, but also to the equally important task of raising their quality. If it is to compete globally, India has to invest heavily in its National Skill Development Mission.

There are significant differences in access to quality employment across different social groups and regions. While economic growth in India has led to an increase in the quantity of employment, the access to quality jobs is still very low. Policy also needs to take into account the social and regional dimensions of access to employment. Affirmative action policies have played a role, but some states and regions, and certain deprived sections among the social groups need special attention. There is also a need to examine whether only sub-groups within the reserved groups, the poorest amongst the upper groups, and certain sections of minorities need to be included in the gamut of affirmative action policies.

Employment Scenario and Perspective

The Periodic Labour Force Survey (PLFS) has been designed to yield annual estimates of the labour force on employment and unemployment along with quarterly estimates for the urban areas. The first annual PLFS (2017-18) provides quarterly employment statistics for urban areas on Current Weekly Status (CWS) basis and annual estimates of employment indicators both in rural and urban areas on CWS and Usual Status Basis.[14] However, labour market estimates by PLFS is not strictly comparable with NSSO-EUS. For comparability, the result of the PLFS with earlier rounds of NSSO surveys need to be understood in the context with which the survey methodology and sample solution has been designed (*Economic Survey 2018-19*, Vol.2).

As per PLFS estimates, Labour Force Participation Rate (LFPR) in India has declined to 36.9 per cent in 2017-18 from 39.5 per cent in 2011-12 (NSSO) as per usual status. In rural areas, it has declined by 3.6 percentage points while it has declined by 0.1 percentage points in urban areas. The Worker Population Ratio (WPR) has also shown similar trend. As per usual status, WPR in India has declined to 34.7 per cent in 2017-18 from 38.6 per cent in 2011-12 (NSSO). The WPR has declined by 4.9 percentage points in rural areas while it has declined by 1.6 percentage points in urban areas (Table 10.6).

TABLE – 10.6

Key Labour Market Indicators for All Age Group in 2017-18

(in per cent)

Indicators	*Rural*	*Urban*	*Total*
		Usual Status	
LFPR	37.0	36.8	36.9
WPR	35.0	33.9	34.7
UR	5.3	7.8	6.1
		CWS	
LFPR	35.7	36.4	35.9
WPR	32.6	32.9	32.7
UR	8.5	9.6	8.9

Source: Annual Report, PLFS (2017-18)

14. A person who is unable to get work for even for an hour in the last seven days of reference week despite available and seeking for work is considered as unemployed under CWS while under usual status activity of a person is determined on the basis of reference period of 365 days preceding the date of survey.

The unemployment rate (UR) in India stood at 6.1 per cent with 5.3 per cent in rural areas and 7.8 per cent in urban areas as per usual status. As per CWS, the UR was 8.9 per cent with 8.5 per cent in rural areas and 9.6 per cent in urban areas (Table 10.6).

Keeping in view India's demographic advantage and with almost 93 per cent of the informal workforce, it is important to improve measures of employment through administrative statistics, which should be complemented by periodic surveys. In this direction, the Ministry of Statistics and Programme Implementation has started bringing out estimates of new subscribers/members enrolling in large social security schemes like the Employees' Provident Fund (EPF), Employees' State Insurance (ESI) Scheme and the National Pension Scheme (NPS). The next section examines the indicator for employment in formal sector based on the payroll data of EPFO.

What are the prospects for growth and quality of employment in India in the near future? It is a known fact that a high rate of economic growth has not been able to generate high employment growth, rather the employment growth has slowed down in recent years which has led many economists and others concerned to describe the recent experience as one of 'jobless growth.' Employment elasticities have declined in most sectors, though in some sectors like construction, trade and transport, they continue to be relatively high. A faster growth of these sectors will lead to an increase in overall employment growth. However, their share in employment is still small as compared to manufacturing which has shown a relatively low employment growth, and low and declining employment elasticity. Although manufacturing still has an employment elasticity of around 0.3 per cent, there are indications to suggest that it may improve. The export-oriented sub-sectors of manufacturing have recently experienced higher employment growth and employment elasticity. During the 1990s, employment in export-oriented industries grew at 3.36 per cent per annum and showed an employment elasticity of 0.48 (Goldar, 2003). A faster growth of manufactured exports, which now constitute over 75 per cent of total exports, as compared to 58 per cent in 1980, therefore, promises to be an important factor in reversing the declining trend in employment growth.[15]

15. Papola, T.S. (2012). "Employment Prospects", in Kaushik Basu and Annemie Maertens (eds.), *The New Oxford Companion to Economics in India* (Vol.I). New Delhi: OUP. pp.427-8.

According to Papola and Sharma,[16] new jobs that are required to be created are not likely to be in agriculture, they have to come from the non-agricultural sectors. In a 25-30 years perspective, employment structure must be envisioned as consisting of about 30-35 per cent in agricultural and 70-75 per cent in non-agricultural activities as against 51 per cent in agricultural and 49 per cent in non-agriculture in 2004-05. It would imply that all the new employment opportunities will be located in non-agricultural activities in the coming years. We need such reforms,

> That can substantially grow the more employment-intensive sectors which, outside agriculture, are: manufacturing; mining & quarrying; construction; transport, storage and communications; education; health; and real estate. For instance, the kind of restrictions that have hampered the growth of mining need to be reviwed and removed. It is perfectly possible today to conduct environmentally sensible mining. To ban or severely restrict mining altogether, as has been done by court decisions, will harm not only the sector but also employment growth. Similarly, additional telecommunications spectrum space must be allotted, and the mobile network needs to expand (Goswami, 2014).[17]

It is argued, industries—be these in manufacturing, utilities or infrastructure—have to get access to land to build factories, power plants and highways. While proponents will argue that the Right to Fair Compensation and Transparency in Land Acquisition, Rehabilitation and Resettlement Act, which was passed in August 2013, rectifies serious imbalances against those who were compelled to give up land, the fact is that it will significantly increase the cost of securing land for non-agricultural use. The cost—both price and procedural delays concomitant to the new law—can seriously alter project economics to a point where infrastructure work may be abandoned. What is needed is to look at the law and make amendments that, at the very least, reduce procedural delays.

Skill Development: The Challenge

Skill development is critical for achieving faster, sustainable and inclusive growth on the one hand and for providing decent employment

---

16. Papola and Sharma (2015). *Indian Economy Since Independence* (26th edition). New Delhi: Academic Foundation.
17. Goswami, Omkar (2014). "Generating Employment", in Bibek Debroy, Ashley J. Tellis and Reece Trevor (eds.). 2014. *Getting India Back on Track: An Action Agenda for Reform.* Random House, India.

opportunities to the growing young population on the other. The demographic window of opportunity available to India would make India the skill capital of world. India would be in position to meet the requirement of technically trained manpower not only for its growing economy but also of the aging advanced economies of the world. Boston Consultancy Group's study in 2007 had clearly indicated that by 2020 while India will have surplus of 56 million working people, the rest of the world will encounter a shortage of 47 million working people. However, skilling this large and growing young population from an exceedingly small base would be a big challenge for India. The skill strategy would have to accordingly model for these skill challenges in terms of outreach, quality, systemic/institutional set-ups, current status of skill development efforts and various economic policies.

Structural shifts in the economy in terms of increase in contribution of secondary and territory sectors to GDP and demographic dividend have implications for skills development strategy. India will have about 63 per cent of its population in the working age group by 2022. China's demographic dividend would start tapering off by 2015, but India would continue to enjoy it till 2040. India needs to provide skills and training to its young workforce if this window of opportunity is not to be lost. However, the availability of demographic dividend varies across the country with wide variation in Northern and Southern states. While the Northern states would have young population, the southern states have already started aging.

The rise in the share of the working-age population would lead to increase in demand for decent employment opportunities. However, the realisation of full potential of the demographic dividend depends on generation of adequate decent non-farm employment opportunities and upgradation of skills of existing as well as new entrants to the workforce

11

Economic Inequality in India

INDIAN economy has experienced high growth rates in GDP during the past two and a half decades, particularly during the period 2003-04 to 2010-11 when growth rates was hovering around 9 per cent except in two years 2004-05 when it was 7.1 per cent and 2008-09 when it declined to 6.7 per cent after three year of continuous above 9 per cent between 2005-06 to 2007-08. This has meant the creation of very substantial wealth. For example while, there were no billionaire in dollar terms in India as recently as 2000, the 2016 list by Forbes reports as many as 84 of them.[1] The 2018 list by Forbes ranks India as the third largest country of billionaires. The addition of this new wealth has in turn led to claims that economic reforms have generated massive income inequality (Bhagwati and Panagariya, 2012). Inequality has been a key theme in the research agenda of economists because of: (i) the intrinsic ethical attractiveness of equality and (ii) the significant implications of the inequality for many macroeconomic variables like growth and poverty.

Inequality

Before undertaking a study of inequality one is always confronted with the issue of how to measure inequality. Since it is impossible to describe and compare the distributions of income of the whole population, it is necessary to have summary measures. One can get an idea of inequality by using rough measures like the share of the, say, bottom 10 or top 10 per cent of the population. There is now a large body of literature dealing with the measurement of inequality (Sen, 1997).[2]

---

1. As per the data in the 30th Annual Forbes Billionaires list, 2016, in 2016, the World's billionaire population currently stands at 1,810 in 67 countries.
2. Sen, Amartya (1997). *On Economic Inequality*, Oxford University Press, expanded edition.

One of the most commonly used measures of income or consumption inequality is the Gini coefficient. It measures the extent to which the distribution of income or consumption among individuals deviates from equal distribution. A high value of the coefficient signifies a more unequal distribution.

HDR measures inequality in terms of two indicators. The first indicator is the income Gini coefficient which measures the deviation of distribution of income (or consumption) among the individuals within a country from a perfectly equal distribution. For India, the income Gini coefficient was 36.8 in 2010-11. In this respect, inequality in India is lower than many other developing countries e.g. South Africa (57.8), Brazil (53.9), Thailand (53.6), Turkey (40.8), China (41.5), Sri Lanka (40.3), Malaysia (46.2), Vietnam (37.6), as well as countries like USA (40.8), Hong Kong (43.4), Argentina (45.8), Israel (39.2), Bulgaria (45.3) etc., which are otherwise ranked very high in terms of human development index. The second indicator is the quintile income ratio, which is a measure of average income of the richest 20 per cent of the population to that of poorest 20 per cent. The quintile income ratio for

TABLE – 11.1

Inequality in India Computed Using Various Measures 1951-1988

Year	*Gini****	*Consumption** shares of bottom 20%*	*Consumption** shares of top 20%*	*Income*** shares of top 1%*
1951	35.56	7.0	43.0	13.42
1960	32.59	8.4	41.4	12.31
1965	31.14	8.8	40.0	10.92
1970	30.38	8.8	39.5	10.02
1973	29.17	9.0	38.1	7.02
1977	32.14	8.5	40.9	6.18
1983	31.49	8.6	40.5	6.46
1986	32.22	8.5	41.1	8.64
1988	31.15	9.0	40.5	8.52

Notes: * In percentages (Gini Index for consumption);

** Deininger-Squire (K. Deininger and L. Squire (1996). "A New Data Set Measuring Income Inequality", The World Bank Economic Review, 10: 565-91);

*** Banerjee-Piketty (A. Banerjee and T. Piketty (2005). "Top Indian Incomes, 1999-2000", The World Bank Economic Review, 19: 1-20).

Source: Mishra, Ajit (2012). "Inequality", in Kaushik Basu and Annemie Maetrey (eds.), *The Concise Oxford Companion to Economics in India*. New Delhi: Oxford University Press.

India was 5.6 in 2010-11. Countries like Australia (7.0), the USA (8.5), New Zealand (6.8), Singapore (9.8), the UK (7.8), Argentina (12.3), Mexico (14.4), Malaysia (11.4), Philippines (9.0), Vietnam (6.2) had higher ratios. This implies that the inequality between the top and bottom quintiles in India was lower than a large number of countries.

In the Indian context, the consumption expenditure surveys (National Sample Survey, NSS) constitute the most basic source of inequality measurement. These surveys are conducted on a regular basis and cover a fairly large sample of households. Recently, individual tax return data have been used to analyse the income shares of individuals in the top earnings bracket. Since most of the population is exempt from income taxation, it is possible to look at only the top 1 per cent of the population. The various measures in Table 11.1 provide a snapshot of inequality in India through the 1960s to the 1980s (Mishra, 2012).

Historically, inequality levels (wealth as well as income or consumption) in India during the 1950s were quite high. The average Gini index for consumption in the 1950s would be in excess of 35, the Gini index for land distribution for this period would also be in excess of 40. However, through the 1950s and 1960s, there has been a steady (though not substantial) decline in all these measures. The Gini index falls from 35 to a lower level of 30. The consumption share of the bottom 20 per cent of the population goes up and the corresponding share of the top 20 per cent declines. The income share of the top 1 per cent also shows significant decline. Many scholars attribute this trend to the slower growth and socialist policies of this period (Mishra, 2012).

Turning to the rural urban gap, we begin with the Monthly per capita expenditure (MPCE) defined first at household level to assign a value that indicates level of living to each individual or household. Based on the 68th round (2011-12) of the National Sample Survey (NSS), average MPCE [Modified Mixed Reference Period (MMRP) based] is ₹ 1281.45 and ₹ 2401.68 respectively for rural and urban India indicating rural-urban income disparities. However, monthly per capita rural consumption rose by 18 per cent in real terms in 2011-12 over 2009-10, while monthly per capita urban consumption rose by only 13.3 per cent. Thus the rate of increase in the MPCE of rural areas is higher than that of urban areas, indicating a bridging of the rural-urban gap (Table 11.2). Out of the MPCE, the share of food as per 66th round NSS data (2009-10) is ₹ 600 (57 per cent) and ₹ 881(44 per cent) for rural and urban India respectively, showing a higher share for food in rural compared to urban India.

Deaton and Dreze (2002), However point out that inequality seems to have risen on several fronts. There is evidence of greater regional inequalities. Compared to the 50th round, the adjusted data of the 55th round, shows increasing inequality across states. States with higher average per capita expenditure in 1993-94 are also the states recording higher growth in these per capita expenditures. The wage gap across various occupations has also widened. While the real wages for agricultural labourers have grown at the rate of 2.5 per cent per year, the corresponding growth rate for public-sector employees is almost double.

TABLE – 11.2

Average MPCE (Uniform Reference Period)

(in ₹)

NSS Round	*Year*	*Constant prices (2004-5)*		*Current prices (2011-12)*	
		Rural	*Urban*	*Rural*	*Urban*
68th Round	July 2011-June 2012	707.24	1359.75	1281.45	2401.68
66th Round	July 2009-June 2010	599.06	1200.01	927.70	1785.81
61st Round	July 2004-June 2005	558.78	1052.36	558.78	1052.36

Source: NSSO Press release 1 August 2012 (The results of 68th round of NSS data are provisional).

A similar pattern is observed for the income share of the top earners. As mentioned earlier, the income share of the top 1 per cent has been rising since the mid-1980s. Apart from a brief decline in the early 1990s, it shows considerable increase from 1993 onwards. In fact the rise in the share of the ultra rich (the top 1 per cent of this 1 per cent) is much more striking. Within the richer section, the ultra rich have experienced a much larger growth in income over the 1990s. This suggests that inequality amongst the rich is also increasing. Though it is not possible to make sweeping generalisations, there is enough indication to worry about the growth process becoming increasingly pro-rich in its orientation.

As yet there is no clear causal explanation for this apparent rise in inequalities in the 1990s. One can argue that this is an inevitable consequence of the high-growth phase in a development process. The famous Kuznets hypothesis postulates that inequality should follow an inverse U-shape along the development process. The early phase of development is associated with greater urbanisation and industrialisation resulting in greater income inequality. However, after a stage, as a large proportion of the labour force is absorbed in the industrial sector, inequality starts falling. Until recently, some of the developed economies of the West were believed to have exhibited such a pattern. For example, in the US, the share of the top 10 per cent rose from 50 per cent around 1770 to about 75 per cent around 1870 and then fell to 50 per cent in 1970. Such a view could be comforting in the sense that the rising inequality need not be a matter of concern (though the time scale is still a matter of concern). However, this hypothesis has not been significantly supported by empirical research. Moreover, the sectoral shift in the Indian context took place in the 1980s, and the rise in inequality cannot perhaps be attributed to it (Mishra, 2012).

It is important to recognise the rising inequality independently and seek proper causal explanation and not simply view it as by-product. If the growth process is highly uneven so that only a smaller section can benefit from it, it can have serious consequences for poverty reduction and further growth in the economy. For example, as Deaton and Dreze (2002) point out, the reduction in poverty over the 1990s has been significantly moderated by the rise in inequality. For the same level of inequality (same distribution of consumption), the growth in the 1990s would have implied a much larger reduction in poverty (Mishra, 2012).

One can also draw several lessons from the recent research on inequality and growth. A traditional view suggests that rising income and wealth inequality fosters higher growth by generating greater incentives to save and invest. However, this view has come under scrutiny recently and a large body of empirical as well theoretical research shows that inequality can be harmful for growth. From a political economy perspective, higher inequality leads to social conflict and greater demands for redistribution. The effects of these outweigh the positive incentive effects of inequality and the end result could be lower growth. Inequality affects growth negatively through various other channels as well. In the presence of imperfect (credit) markets and limited financial development, higher (wealth) inequality leads to under investment in physical and human capital and hence lower growth. According to Mishra, given the imperfect nature of markets in India there is danger of full growth potential not being realised in the future if inequality levels continue to rise.

According to Motiram and Vakulabharanam (2012), overall, the growth process has been associated with increasing inequality, both at the rural and urban levels, states that have seen higher growth rates have also seen bigger increases (or smaller reductions) in inequality.

TABLE – 11.3

Inequality (Gini) for Major States

State	1993-94			2004-05			2009-10		
	Rural	Urban	Total	Rural	Urban	Total	Rural	Urban	Total
Andhra Pradesh	0.290	0.323	0.312	0.294	0.375	0.345	0.286	0.395	0.364
Assam	0.179	0.290	0.216	0.199	0.320	0.240	0.251	0.330	0.283
Bihar	0.225	0.309	0.253	0.213	0.355	0.259	0.234	0.358	0.273
Gujarat	0.240	0.291	0.279	0.271	0.310	0.334	0.261	0.338	0.343
Haryana	0.314	0.284	0.311	0.339	0.366	0.355	0.310	0.368	0.339
Himachal Pradesh	0.284	0.462	0.325	0.310	0.326	0.328	0.314	0.415	0.336
Jammu & Kashmir	0.240	0.287	0.270	0.247	0.249	0.260	0.240	0.315	0.266
Karnataka	0.270	0.319	0.309	0.266	0.369	0.361	0.240	0.341	0.350
Kerala	0.301	0.343	0.316	0.381	0.410	0.393	0.439	0.527	0.473
Madhya Pradesh	0.280	0.331	0.315	0.277	0.407	0.357	0.297	0.367	0.351
Maharashtra	0.307	0.357	0.376	0.312	0.378	0.393	0.276	0.423	0.409
Odisha	0.246	0.307	0.282	0.285	0.353	0.324	0.268	0.401	0.326
Punjab	0.281	0.281	0.285	0.294	0.402	0.351	0.297	0.382	0.339
Rajasthan	0.265	0.293	0.280	0.250	0.371	0.303	0.230	0.396	0.300
Tamil Nadu	0.312	0.348	0.344	0.323	0.361	0.379	0.271	0.340	0.342
Uttar Pradesh	0.282	0.326	0.302	0.291	0.367	0.327	0.281	0.367	0.322
West Bengal	0.254	0.339	0.308	0.274	0.383	0.353	0.245	0.393	0.338
All-India	0.286	0.344	0.326	0.305	0.376	0.363	0.300	0.393	0.370

Note: (i) All-India includes all the states, and not just the major states.

(ii) Bihar includes Jharkhand, Madhya Pradesh includes Chhattisgarh, and Uttar Pradesh includes Uttarakhand.

Source: Authors' computations from NSS unit-level data. Motiram and Vakulabharanam (2012).

An interesting issue to examine is the link between growth and inequality. Are the states that are growing faster experiencing lower or higher increases in inequality? To address this question, we consider the period 2004-05 to 2009-10 and analyse the relationship between the rate of growth of real average consumption expenditure and the rate of change of inequality, separately for rural and urban areas, and for major states.

Again, we can discern a positive relationship, implying that states that grew faster have also experienced higher increases in inequality. It is worth noting a few cases—Jammu & Kashmir showed a high increase in urban inequality despite low growth, Andhra Pradesh showed a modest increase in inequality despite moderate growth, and Kerala showed both high growth and a high increase in inequality.

The overall picture that emerges is that states that have been experiencing faster growth have also been experiencing higher increases (lower reductions) in inequality. Essentially, growth is associated with increasing inequality. We think that this is a powerful and interesting result. However, given the presence of some outliers, we would like to be cautious about this assertion, in particular about a casual linkage.

Inequality after Economic Reforms

Motiram and Vakulabharanam (2012) present an overview of the relevant literature and changes in both vertical and horizontal inequality in nominal consumption expenditure since the 1990s, based upon the 50th (1993-94), 61st (2004-05) and 66th (2009-10) rounds of the NSS consumption expenditure survey. They show that interpersonal inequality has displayed a steadily rising trend in urban areas—the urban Gini index has increased from 34.4 per cent in 1993-94 to 37.6 per cent in 2004-05, and then to 39.3 per cent in 2009-10. This is also true for most of the states—they have witnessed an increase in urban inequality (as measured by the Gini index) during the period 1993-94 to 2009-10.

The critics of reforms have also raised a different concern; that growth has been uneven across states and that this has resulted in increased inequality among them. This is correct since richer states have grown faster them the poorer states on average. Panagariya (2010a) and Chakraborty *et al.* (2011) show the years 2003-04 to 2010-11 have seen nearly all states growing significantly faster than did in earlier period. Therefore, the rise in interstate inequality does not reflect the poorer states remaining poor or been further impoverished. Instead, it represents the richest states growing faster than the poorer states in an environment in which all states are growing faster.

It may be noted, two of the poorer states—Bihar and Odisha—are among the fastest growing states today. Their success shows that when the national policies are conducive to the growth and some of the states grow rapidly, the door to poorer states achieving similar success is also opened wider. When the rest of the economy is growing rapidly, the electorate in the poorer states will demand more from its leaders, prompting policy changes that increased prosperity.

Also, faster growth of some states opens the scope for larger-scale redistribution programme in favour of poorer states. A programme such as the National Rural Employment Guarantee Scheme (NREGS), which benefits the poorer states proportionately more, would not be feasible without certain states having large incomes to make the necessary revenue available.

Finally, labour is not immobile across states. It is well known that labour from Bihar has traditionally moved to Mumbai and Kolkata for jobs, as have people from the Punjab and the Hills. This means that faster growth will attract migrants from the slower growth states and regions, so that prosperity (as distinct from growth) will diffuse to the slower-growth areas through the usual channels such as remittances.

Yet another dimension of inequality relate to the socially disadvantage groups. Here again, critics often assert that the income differences between the Scheduled Castes and Scheduled Tribes on the one hand and non-Scheduled from the other have gone up during the year of rapid growth but such claims are not supported by empirical evidence. Using employment-unemployment survey data from NSS rounds conducted in 1983, 1987-88, 1993-94, 1999-2000 and 2004-05, Nahiri and Paul (2012) demonstrated that the wages of Scheduled Castes and Scheduled Tribes have been converging with those of non-Scheduled Castes since 1983. The Scheduled Castes and Scheduled Tribes have been able to take advantage of the rapid growth and structural changes in India during the post-reforms period and have rapidly narrowed their huge historical economic disparities with non-Scheduled Caste and Scheduled Tribes.

Section - III

Current Perspectives in Agriculture

Section - IV

Current Perspectives in Industry and Services

12

Agriculture: Role and Growth Performance

Importance of Agriculture in National Economy

Agriculture is the mainstay of Indian economy because of its high share in employment and livelihood creation, notwithstanding, its reduced contribution to the nation's GDP (gross domestic product). It is the most important sector of the Indian economy from the perspective of poverty alleviation and employment generation. The share of agriculture in national income has been declining from 56.5 per cent in 1950-51 to 39.6 per cent in 1980-81 and 26.3 per cent in 2001-02. As per the 2013-14 advance estimates released by CSO, the agriculture & allied sector accounted for 13.9 per cent of the GDP at 2004-05 prices in 2013-14 as compared to 16.8 per cent in 2007-08. According to the new series of national income released by the CSO, at 2011-12 prices the share of agriculture in total GDP is 18 per cent in 2013-14.

Agriculture's share in GDP has thus declined rapidly in the recent past. This is explained by the fact that whereas overall GDP has grown by an average of 8.62 per cent during 2004-05 to 2010-11, agricultural sector GDP has increased by only 3.46 per cent during the same period. The role of the agriculture sector, however, remains critical as it accounts for about 55 per cent of employment in the country. Moreover, this sector is a supplier of food, fodder and raw materials for a vast segment of industry. Hence the growth of Indian agriculture can be considered a necessary condition for 'inclusive growth.' More recently, the rural sector (including agriculture) is being seen as a potential source of domestic demand, a recognition that is even shaping the marketing strategies of entrepreneurs wishing to widen the demand for goods and services.

One of the paradoxes of the Indian economy is that the decline in the share of agricultural workers in total workers has been slower than

TABLE – 12.1

Changes in Structural Distribution of Economy and Employment

Sl. No.	*Year*	*Percentage Share in GDP*				*Percentage Share in Total Workers*		
		Agriculture & Allied	*Agriculture*	*Industry*	*Services*	*Agriculture & Allied*	*Industry*	*Services*
1	1950-51	51.9	41.8	16.2	29.5	72.1	10.7	17.2
2	1960-61	47.6	39.4	20.1	30.2	71.8	12.2	16.0
3	1970-71	41.7	34.2	23.6	33.3	72.1	11.2	16.7
4	1980-81	35.3	29.6	26.2	37.5	68.5	13.5	17.7
5	1990-91	29.5	24.9	27.6	42.5	66.9	11.9	19.2
6	2000-01	22.3	18.8	27.3	50.4	56.9	16.9	25.8
7	2010-11	14.6	12.4	27.9	57.5	54.6	45.4*	
8	2016-17	11.6	9.9	25.8	62.7	-	-	-

Note: * Combined share of industry and services sector.

Source: Deshpande and Shaha (2017).

Various issues of National Account Statistics, CSO: New Delhi and Population Census of India: NSS 68th Round, Report No. 554, pp.173, *Economic Survey*, various issues.

the decline in the share of agriculture in the GDP. Compared to other countries, India faces a greater challenge, since with only 2.3 per cent share in the world's total land area, it has to ensure food security for a population that accounts for 17.5 per cent of world population. This leads to excessive pressure on land, and area under food grain cultivation has not increased. Increasing agricultural production with limited natural resources in a sustainable manner for ensuring food and nutritional security and providing income security to farmers are major challenges before the government.

The share of GDP has been declining continuously over the period of six and half decades, so also the share of workforce. This has been observed in many studies and noted that the share of agriculture & allied activities in the GDP has come down from about 52 per cent to end at 12 per cent in 2016-17. Interestingly, this share declined sharply during 2000-01 and 2010-11 by about 8 per cent. Similar decline is seen in the share of workforce for the period 1990-91 to 2000-01. It is quite clear that this was the phase of liberalisation and possibly large rural population shifting to urban locations. It can be inferred that liberalisation has drawn out workforce from agriculture and rural India, but it has failed to increase the GDP generated in the sector proportionately. This is actually the residual of earlier policies and therefore, one can expect larger percolation of growth to the rural area if liberalisation has to be a successful policy.[1]

There are a few important pickups from the foregoing analysis that we should not miss for reading the changing agrarian structure of India. First, the share of GDP originating from agriculture & allied sector has been declining and this decline is quite sharp during the phase of liberalisation. This could be both due to the sharp increase in growth of GDP originating from non-agriculture sector or owing to the deceleration of growth in agriculture & allied sectors. On the safer side, we can assume that this decline in the share is mainly attributable to high incremental growth in the non-agricultural sector. But when we look at the relative shares of GVO (gross value of output) from agriculture, it is problematic that the share of crop sector is almost stagnant in real terms almost for the two decades. Second, it was observed that the share of rural population as well as cultivators in the total workforce is declining. It is well-known that the farmers do not

1. Deshpande, R.S. and Khalil Musa Shaha (2017). "Stranded at Jagged Crossroads: Agricultural Sector of India", in Uma Kapila (ed.) (2017), *India's Economy: Pre-Liberalisation to GST—Essays in Honour of Raj Kapila*. New Delhi: Academic Foundation.

TABLE – 12.2

Distribution of Household Owning Land and Area Owned by Size of Holdings in Rural Areas of India

	Size of Holdings	*1953-54*	*1961-62*	*1971-72*	*1982*	*1992*	*2003*	*2013*
I	Landless Households (%)	23.09	11.69	9.60	11.30	11.30	10.00	7.41
II	Percentage to All Rural Households							
1	Marginal (1.0 ha)	61.24	66.06	62.62	66.64	71.88	79.60	81.45
2	Small (1.01 – 2.0 ha)	13.49	9.16	15.49	14.70	13.42	10.80	10.80
	Sub-Total	74.73	75.22	78.11	81.34	85.30	90.40	92.25
3	Semi-Medium (2.01 – 4.0 ha)	12.50	12.86	11.94	10.78	9.28	6.00	5.41
4	Medium (4.01- 10.0 ha)	9.17	9.07	7.83	6.45	4.54	3.00	2.08
5	Large (10.01 ha & above)	3.60	2.85	2.12	1.42	0.88	0.60	0.26
III	Percentage to Total Area Owned							
1	Marginal (1.0 ha)	6.23	7.59	9.76	12.22	16.93	23.02	29.76
2	Small (1.01 – 2.0 ha)	10.09	12.40	14.68	16.49	18.59	20.38	23.53
	Sub-Total	16.32	19.99	24.44	28.71	35.52	43.40	53.29
3	Semi-Medium (2.01 – 4.0 ha)	18.40	20.54	21.92	23.38	24.58	21.97	22.07
4	Medium (4.01- 10.0 ha)	29.11	31.23	30.73	29.83	26.07	23.08	18.83
5	Large (10.01 ha & above)	36.17	28.24	22.91	18.08	13.83	11.55	5.81

Source: 1) Government of India (1968), Tables with Notes on Some Aspects of Landholdings in Rural Areas(States and All India Estimates), Report No. 144, New Delhi: NSSO, 2) Government of India (2006 & 2016), Household Ownership Holdings in India, 2003 & 2013, Report No. 491 & 571, NSS 59th Round and 71st Round respectively, New Delhi: NSSO.

Deshpande and Shaha (2017).

prefer farming as their main vocation both due to lower dignity assigned to the profession by the society as well as low income generation and dependence on state or financial institutions (formal or informal) even for bare survival. The Population Census data from 1991 and 2011 indicates that about 50 lakh cultivators have changed their profession from cultivation. As a result the number of cultivators indicated in the Population Census has declined by 50 lakh and the operational land has gone down by more than 31 lakh hectares. This would clearly mean that either they have changed their profession to agricultural labour, or migrated to urban areas in search of work in any of the available vocations in cities and abandoned cultivation of 31 lakh hectares. At the same time, we also observed that the share of agricultural labour has increased substantially during that period. Third, the marginalisation of the farmers both in terms of size of landholding as well as on the economic front could be clearly observed in rural India and that is manifested in the agitations we see in most of the states. This process of marginalisation and loss of dignity to the profession has sparked the agitations among farmers. This change has intensified quite significantly during the last three decades.[2]

Linkage between Agriculture and Other Sectors

The linkages between agriculture and industrial sectors, widely recognised in the literature,[3] focus on the role of agriculture as: (i) supplier of wage goods to the industrial sector, (ii) provider of raw materials to agro-based industries which have a weight of 21.2 per cent in the Index of Industrial Production (base: 1980-81=100) and weight of 17.6 per cent in the index with base 1993-94=100, and (iii) generator of agricultural income that enables rural demand for industrial products to take place. Empirical tests show that a unit increase in agricultural output would have a positive effect on both industrial production and national income. Rangarajan (1982) estimated that a 1 per cent increase in agricultural output tends to raise industrial production by 0.5 per cent and augment national income by 0.7 per cent. The experience in the 1980s and 1990s also lends support to this. During the 1980s, the trend growth rate of 3.2 per cent in agricultural production appeared to have contributed to accelerated industrial production. The decelerated growth rate in agricultural production seems to have impacted on growth of industrial production in the 1990s.

2. Ibid
3. Rudra, 1967; Chakravarthy, 1974; 1979; Raj, 1976; Mellor, 1976; Mitra, 1977; Krishna, 1982; Rangarajan, 1982.

TABLE – 12.3

Agriculture Sector: Key Indicators (At 2004-05 Prices) and New Series Data of 2011-12 Prices

(%)

	Item	*2007-08*	*2008-09*	*2009-10*	*2010-11*	*2011-12*	*2012-13*	*2013-14*	*2014-15*
1	Growth in GDP in agriculture & allied sector	5.8	0.1	0.8	8.6	5 (-)	1.4 (1.2)	4.7* (3.7)	(1.1)
	Share of agriculture & allied sectors in total GDP	16.8	15.8	14.6	14.6	14.4 (18.4)	13.9 (18.0)	13.9* (18.0)	(NA)
	Agriculture	14.3	13.4	12.3	12.4	12.3 (12.0)	11.8 (11.7)	NA (11.8)	(NA)
2	Share of agriculture & allied sectors in total gross capital formation (GCF)	6.4	7.8	7.3	6.3	7.0 (8.6)	7.1 (7.7)	NA (7.9)	(NA)
	Agriculture	5.9	7.2	6.7	5.8	6.5 (7.4)	6.5 (6.5)	NA (6.6)	(NA)
3	GCF in agriculture and allied sectors as per cent to GDP of the sector	16.1	19.4	20.1	18.5	20.8 (18.3)	21.2 (15.5)	NA (14.8)	(NA)
4	Employment in the agriculture sector as share of total workers (Census 2001)			58.2		54.6			(NA)
5	Agri exports (incl. marine products) as per cent of total exports			8.2	8.0	10.1	11.8	11.9(P)	(NA)

Note: Figures in bracket show the new series data at 2011-12 prices.

Source: Central Statistical Organisation (CSO) and Department of Agriculture and Cooperation. *Economic Survey 2012-13, 2013-14, 2014-15*

Importance of agriculture in the national economy is indicated by many facts. For example, agriculture is the main support for India's transport system, since railways and roadways secure bulk of their business from the movement of agricultural goods. Internal trade is mostly in agricultural products. Agricultural growth has direct impact on poverty eradication, containing inflation, raising agricultural wages and employment generation.

Any policy maker trying to alleviate India's poverty cannot neglect the fact that the *World Development Report 2008* clearly says that "GDP growth originating in agriculture is at least twice as effective in reducing poverty as GDP growth originating outside agriculture."

The power of agriculture in reducing poverty is observable in the Chinese case, especially during 1978-1984, the initial years of reform. China began its reform process with agriculture: by moving from the commune-based system to the household responsibility system, and by revising agricultural prices upwards by more than 20 per cent. The results were spectacular. The agricultural growth rate jumped to 7.1 per cent per annum during 1978-1984, up from 2.5 per cent during the pre-reform period of 1966-1977. This was followed by a dramatic reduction of poverty: from 33 per cent to 15 per cent in the early reform period between 1978 and 1984 (Gulati and Fan, 2008: 6). Much of this can be ascribed to the bottom-up approach of reforms adopted by China, that is, starting from the agricultural sector. This is unlike India, which chose a top-down approach, that is, initiating reforms in the non-agricultural sector. As a result, the process of poverty reduction has been held hostage to the 'trickle down' effect.

With 54 per cent of the workforce still dependent on agriculture for their livelihood, agriculture in India has a far-reaching impact on poverty reduction as well as on rural development. Agriculture forms the resource base for a number of agro-based industries. Thus, it would be more meaningful to view agriculture not as farming alone but as a holistic value chain, which includes farming, wholesaling, warehousing (including logistics), processing and retailing. Also, the fact that an average Indian spends more than 50 per cent of his monthly expenditure on food establishes the centrality of agriculture in the context of food security concerns [Government of India (GoI), 2006a].

An important aspect of 'inclusive growth' in the Eleventh Five Year Plan (2007-2012) and Twelfth Five Year Plan has been its target of 4 per cent per annum growth in GDP from agriculture & allied sectors. This target is not only necessary to achieve the overall GDP growth target of 8 per cent per annum without undue inflation, it is an important element of 'inclusiveness' since the global experience of growth and poverty reduction shows that GDP growth originating in agriculture is at least twice as effective in reducing poverty as GDP growth originating outside agriculture.

Agricultural Growth

Role of Institutional and Technological Factors in Agricultural Growth

It is important, at the very outset, to understand the institutional, demographic and sociopolitical context within which agricultural growth has been taking place. The prevailing framework had a profound impact on the pattern of agricultural development. This, in turn, has necessitated special strategies and policies for employment generation and poverty removal in rural areas. The thrust of policies, in the first decade of planning (1951-1961) was on institutional and agrarian reforms. In an agrarian economy like India with great scarcity and unequal distribution of land, coupled with a large mass of below poverty line (BPL) rural population, there are compelling economic and political arguments for land reform. Not surprisingly, it received top priority on the policy agenda at the time of Independence. In the decades following Independence, India passed a significant body of land reform legislation. The Constitution of 1949 left the adoption and implementation of land and tenancy reforms to state governments (Ghatak, 2007). The two basic objectives of land reforms were: (i) to remove such impediments on agricultural production as arise from the character of agrarian structure in rural areas and (ii) to reduce or eliminate exploitation of landless and small cultivators through measures of land redistribution.

Land reform legislation in India consisted of four main categories: abolition of intermediaries who were rent collectors under the pre-Independence land revenue system; tenancy regulation that attempted to improve the contractual terms for tenants, including crop shares and security of tenure; a ceiling on landholdings with a view to redistributing surplus land to the landless; and finally, attempts to consolidate disparate landholdings.

The New Technology

It was becoming clear by the mid-1960s that there was no alternative to technological change in agriculture for achieving self-sufficiency in food grains. Even those countries in Asia which could carry out radical land reforms and build up an adequate infrastructure for agriculture had taken to the path of modernising agriculture. Japan took the lead in this direction and China followed suit even after successfully experimenting with structural changes and mobilisation of a growing labour force for capital construction in agriculture.

Characteristics of New Technology

The distinguishing characteristic of the new technology lies in the substitution of traditional robust but low-yielding varieties of seed by the so-called high-yielding varieties (HYVs). These seeds have the physiological attribute of being able to turn large amounts of soil nutrients into grain rather than leaf growth. This enables the plant to produce higher yields, especially so if the supply of nutrients in the soil can be increased. This in turn creates the demand for chemical fertilisers to supplement the natural fertility of the soil. Because these contain nutrients in concentrated form, they have to be applied with adequate supplies of water to enable the plant to absorb them without damaging itself. A lack of adequate water supply not only reduces the yield but may do so substantially.

Thus, the basic technological characteristic of the new technology is the application of a number of inputs which are complementary to each other. The application of these joint inputs yields much larger volumes of output of food grains as a result, largely by increasing yield per acre. However, in order to assess the impact of the technology on Indian agriculture, we have to also take into account some of the economic characteristics of that technology. In an economy where labour is relatively plentiful, it has low opportunity cost.

Economic Aspects of New Technology

The new practices, therefore, are much more expensive to the farmer. This has three implications. Firstly, the extent to which the various inputs are applied in practice depends not on some technologically efficient dosage but on an economically optimum one. This depends in turn on the relative prices of inputs and outputs facing the producer. Minhas and Srinivasan have shown that fertiliser application is subject to diminishing returns, the economically optimum dose being smaller than the technical optimum. As technologically some of the inputs are complementary, the extent to which the application of a particular input can be profitably pushed depends also on the availability of, and the ability to purchase, other inputs. For example, the degree of fertiliser application that is profitable will depend on the availability of water and on the ability of a farmer to purchase the use of both inputs.

Secondly, the new technology is only worthwhile in terms of private benefits, e.g., if the farmer receives yields which are not only larger than traditional varieties but are substantially so, to make up for the additional variable costs of cultivation. This in turn requires, thirdly, a more intensive use of the fixed factor, e.g., land. The new technology opens up the possibility of multiple cropping; the economic imperative drives the farmer to it. This is compounded by the fact that while the new technology yields larger outputs, it is also more subject to risks. We have noted that the HYV seeds are prone to damage from flooding, water scarcity and pests. Moreover, because the farmer is a newcomer to these practices, he is also ignorant of how to respond if something goes wrong. Additionally, where he is involved in substantial cash outlays in order to utilise the new technology, he bears a liquidity risk. This is reinforced by the fact that very often, the farmer may have to resort to borrowing in order to meet the additional costs of cultivation. A crop failure saddles him with the burden of debt.

These economic aspects of the new technology are as important as its technological characteristics to our understanding of the impact of the 'Green Revolution' upon the agrarian economy, especially in relation to the problems of mechanisation and of unequal incidence of acceptance and use between large and small farmers. That impact can best be studied in terms of the effects of the new technology on output, employment and the regional and interpersonal distribution of gain arising from the adoption of that technology.

Green Revolution

Three Phases of Green Revolution

Gulati and Fan (2008)[4] identify three phases of the Green Revolution.

The First Phase, 1966-1972

To end its dependence on P.L. 480, India, prompted by the minister of agriculture at that time, C. Subramaniam adopted a new agricultural strategy to boost grain production accompanied by remunerative support price for farmers. In January 1965, the Agricultural Prices Commission was set up to recommend a minimum support price (MSP), followed by the Food Corporation of India (FCI) to take charge of the logistics of procuring major agricultural commodities (Gulati, 2003). In the same year, India took a bold step by allowing the introduction of new high-yielding seed varieties of wheat from Mexico. In 1966, India ordered the import of 18,000 tonnes of HYV wheat seeds that were distributed in the highly irrigated areas of Punjab, Haryana and

4. Gulati, A. and Shenggen Fan (eds.) (2008). *The Dragon and the Elephant—Agricultural and Rural Reforms in China and India*, ch.2. New Delhi: Oxford University Press.

western Uttar Pradesh where the past investments in irrigation had paid rich dividends.

The new seeds could yield more than double the existing levels and thus had the potential to dramatically increase wheat production and food grain supply. Under the new agricultural policy, the spread of HYVs was supported by public investments in fertilisers, power, irrigation and credit.

The total amount of food grains harvested increased from 74 million tonnes (mt) in 1966-67 to 105 mt in 1971-72, and that year India became self-sufficient, with grain imports declining to nearly zero.

These outcomes would not have been possible without the favourable pricing policy that provided farmers with adequate incentives, the dynamism of the national research system that proceeded to indigenise the new seeds to tackle their shortcomings (Gulati, 2003), and the availability of inputs including canal water, fertilisers, power and credit. In view of the strategic importance of these critical inputs, it was the responsibility of the government to ensure that farmers had affordable access to them. Subsidies, thus, became an instrument of agricultural policy in the late 1960s and acquired greater importance in the 1970s (Gulati and Narayanan, 2002a). The role of credit began to be important after 1969 following the nationalisation of banks.

Improved agricultural production resulting from modern input and technologies 'trickled down' to the poor and led to a rise in farmer income, while output growth and increased grain supplies caused a decline in real food grain prices, benefiting the poor. Thus, rural poverty declined significantly in this phase, from 64 per cent in 1967 to 56 per cent in 1973 (Datanet India Pvt. Ltd., 2006). Several government anti-poverty programmes were also introduced during the Fourth Five Year Plan in the early 1970s.[5]

Debacle and the Second Phase, 1973-1980

After the nationalisation of the banks, Prime Minister Indira Gandhi took other steps to extend the role of the state in key areas of economic management. In agriculture, private wholesale traders came under attack because, due to their speculative motives, they were regarded as responsible for fluctuations in food grain prices and supplies. Thus, in 1973-74, the government took over the wholesale trade in wheat, which proved a disaster (Chopra, 1981) and therefore, it was soon abandened.

5. Ibid

Wheat procurement was hindered by limited supply resulting from droughts in several states in 1972-73.

Following two consecutive droughts in 1972-73, food grain production decreased by 7.7 per cent (India, Ministry of Agriculture, 2003), and India slid back into the trap of food grain imports of an average of about 4 mt a year from the USA between 1973 and 1976.

After the oil shock, the government increased fertiliser subsidies to prevent a drop in consumption following the rise in fertiliser prices. In 1977, the retention price scheme was introduced for urea, the predominant fertiliser in Indian agriculture. During the 1970s, other input subsidies grew in importance within the state budget (Fan, Thorat and Rao, 2004), and the subsidy bill excluding fertilisers grew from ₹ 10 billion at constant prices to ₹ 33.2 billion, or from 0.5 per cent to 4.0 per cent of agricultural GDP between 1973 and 1980 (Gulati and Narayanan, 2002a).

Also during this period, groundwater irrigation increased in importance, with its share rising from 0.55 per cent to 19.5 per cent between 1960 and 1975 (Datanet India Pvt. Ltd., 2006) on account of private investment in tube wells by farmers who reinvested the income from the earlier burst in food grain production. As a result, power subsidies for water pumping grew dramatically, reaching 44 per cent of the total input subsidy at the start of the 1980s (Gulati and Narayanan, 2002a).

The extension of HYV technology from wheat to rice, favoured by the growth of tube wells, spread the Green Revolution to new areas, marking a new phase in the expansion of domestic production. From 1972-73 to 1979-80, production as well as yields of food grains showed remarkable growth, at 3.1 per cent and 2.5 per cent, respectively, and rural poverty declined from roughly 56 per cent to 50 per cent (Ministry of Agriculture, 2004).

The Third Phase, 1981-1990

In the 1980s, India consolidated its status as a food self-sufficient country. Rice production soared to 63.8 mt in 1986, up from 37.0 mt in 1964. Wheat output grew, too, from 12 to 47 mt in 1986, a year in which India had her first 25.4 mt of grain buffer stocks (Ministry of Agriculture, 2004). When in 1987 the 'worst drought of the century' struck the country, food needs could be easily met without any loss of lives (Gulati, 2003).

During this phase, the HYV technology spread eastward to states like West Bengal and Bihar, which experienced surpluses in rice, with output over the 1980s growing at 5.0 and 3.7 per cent, respectively (Datanet India Pvt. Ltd., 2006). However, in the rest of the country, the Green Revolution ran out of steam by 1985 once the new seed varieties had been widely adopted in the main producing regions. Yields for rice and wheat that had grown, respectively, by 3.5 per cent and 4.5 per cent per annum between 1967-68 and 1984-85 slowed down to 2.3 and 2.4 per cent per year between 1985-86 and 1999-2000 (IFPRI, 2004). With the HYV technology exhausting its impact in the mid-1980s, input subsidies were steadily increased to continue sustaining food grain production growth. By 1991, input subsidies had grown to 7.2 per cent of agricultural GDP as compared to 4.4 per cent in 1980 and 2.0 per cent of total GDP from 1.5 per cent in 1980 (Gulati and Narayanan, 2002a).

Throughout the Green Revolution, Indian agriculture laboured under a strictly regulated policy regime characterised by wide restrictions on production through licensing requirements and barriers to entry, as well as controls on pricing, movement and private trading of agricultural produce. On the external front, too, the sector was burdened with various tariff and non-tariff barriers to agricultural trade flows (Gulati and Fan, 2008).

The high level of protection accorded to industry produced high industrial prices and adverse terms of trade (ToT) for agriculture, reducing the relative profitability of the primary sector. Agriculture was overall net taxed (disprotected) on account of the overvalued rupee, which produced an anti-export environment for agriculture. The objectives of this framework were broadly dictated by the dominant strategy of the pre-reform era, that is, food self-sufficiency resulting from domestic supplies, aiming to: (i) ensure inexpensive food for consumers, (ii) protect farmers' incomes from price fluctuations and (iii) keep the balance of payments (BoP) in check (Gulati and Fan, 2008).

Reform Period, 1991 to the Present

Although the reforms were implemented in off-farm activities, they affected agriculture in at least two important ways (Landes and Gulati, 2003). First, the higher rate of economic growth and the consequent rise in per capita incomes resulting from the 1991-1993 reforms had a significant impact on food demand. Higher per capita incomes, growing at 4.5 per cent per annum in this phase as opposed to 3.6 per cent in the 1980s (WDI, 2004), led to the diversification of food demand into non-food grain crops such as fruits and vegetables, as well as meat—mainly poultry—and dairy products. Second, the lowering of industrial protection significantly improved the incentive framework for the sector through improvement in the domestic ToT between agricultural and industrial prices, which rose from 0.9 to 1.2 between 1991 and 2000 (Gulati and Fan, 2008).

Improved ToT for agriculture in turn resulted in an increase in the profitability of the primary sector relative to industry and led to an increase in private investments, which are now double the public investment in agriculture. These were increasingly directed to the production of horticultural produce, poultry, fish, milk and eggs in response to booming consumer demand for these high-value agricultural products, leading to a remarkable growth in output of these commodities during the 1990s relative to the previous decade.

As a result of these developments, growth rate of agricultural GDP went up from 3.0 per cent in the 1980s to 4.1 per cent in the aftermath of reforms between 1991 and 1996.

Deceleration in Agriculture Growth

There was a notable deceleration in the rate of growth of agricultural production during the 1990s, a fact highlighted by a number of studies in recent times (Mallik, 1997; Rao, 1998; Thamarajakshi, 1999; George, 1999; Pulapare, 2000).

Growth of agricultural GDP decelerated from over 3.5 per cent per year during 1981-82 and 1996-97 to only around 2 per cent during 1997-1998 and 2004-05 (Table 12.4). This deceleration, although most marked in rainfed areas, occurred in almost all the states and covered almost all the major sub-sectors, including those such as horticulture, livestock and fisheries where growth was expected to be high. Consequently, growth of agricultural GDP has been well below the target of 4 per cent in Ninth, Tenth and Eleventh Plans.

The Twelfth Five Year Plan (2012-13 to 2016-17) had envisaged a growth target of 4 per cent for agriculture and allied sectors, necessary for the Indian economy to grow at over 8 per cent. During the last three years, the growth rates in agriculture have been fluctuating at 1.5 per cent in 2012-13, 4.2 per cent in 2013-14, and (-) 0.2 per cent in 2014-15. According to the CSO estimates released on 8 February 2016, the growth in the 'agriculture, forestry and fishing' sector is estimated at

TABLE – 12.4

Average GDP Growth Rates—Overall and in Agriculture

(Per cent Per Year at 1999-2000 Prices)

	Period	*Agriculture & Allied Sectors*	*Total Economy*
1.	Pre-Green Revolution 1951-52 to 1967-68	2.54	3.69
2.	Green Revolution Period 1968-69 to 1980-81	2.44	3.52
3.	Wider Technology Dissemination Period 1981-82 to 1990-91	3.52	5.40
4.	Early Reforms Period 1991-92 to 1996-97	3.66	5.69
5.	Ninth Plan 1997-98 to 2001-02	2.50	5.52
6.	Tenth Plan Period 2002-03 to 2006-07	2.47	7.77
	Eleventh Plan Average (2007-2012)	3.3	7.7

Source: Eleventh Five Year Plan 2007-2012, Vol. III, 2008.
Mid-term Appraisal Eleventh Five Year Plan, 2010.

1.1 per cent in 2015-16. The estimates of GDP for the second quarter (July-September) of 2015-16, 'agriculture, forestry and fishing' sector also reported a growth well below the 4 per cent target, at 2.2 per cent. The shortfall in growth in agriculture is explained by the fact that 60 per cent of agriculture in India is rainfall dependent and there have been two consecutive drought years in 2013-14 and 2014-15. Moreover, there are issues of expansion in irrigation and its efficiency, growth of capital formation in the sector has been declining and there is volatility in the markets, especially of prices, altering and distorting cropping patterns of some crops. This suggests that for the agriculture sector to achieve a target of 4 per cent, a significantly different approach has to be followed.

Instability in Output

The reduction in variability is important since claims of acceleration or deceleration make sense only when variability is low. Also, it is a measure of how well the system is able to cope with inevitable bouts of aberrant weather and yet maintain the growth momentum. It should be noted that agricultural growth was positive in 2009-10 despite the worst drought in nearly 40 years. More generally, whereas earlier periods saw at least one and normally two years of negative growth in every five year, there has not been a single year of negative growth of agriculture & allied sectors after 2002-03.

The magnitude of secular decline in growth variability over the last 30 years is also important. This is now less than a third of its peak. A major role must have been played by the increase in irrigation from about 20 per cent of arable area in 1981 to 35 per cent today, based mainly on groundwater. However, since water tables have fallen and temperatures risen, the extent of variability decline is surprisingly large. Even assuming zero variability on irrigated land, this implies that variability on rain-fed land must have reduced very substantially. Clearly factors such as a more diversified agriculture, extended information reach and investments both on-farm and in watershed development appear to have enabled better responses to depleting natural resources and weather risk. Although there is considerable scope to improve each of these factors further, it is a matter of satisfaction that developments in these areas are having a positive effect (Twelfth Five Year Plan, Vol. II).

However, compared to other countries, India faces a greater challenge, since with only 2.3 per cent share in the world's total land area, it has to ensure food security for a population that accounts for 17.5 per cent of world population. This leads to excessive pressure on land, and area under food grain cultivation has not increased. Increasing agricultural production with limited natural resources in a sustainable manner for ensuring food and nutritional security and providing income security to farmers are major challenges before the government.

Regional Disparities and Intra-Personal Disparities

Perhaps the most widely debated issue about the Green Revolution is the growing disparities in income between different regions and classes of farmers. The experience after the mid-1970s covering nearly a decade and half reveals trends which are typical of a diffusion process. These trends are: the spread of the Green Revolution to new areas, the increasing adoption of new technology by the small farmers, the decline in the relative prices of food grains and the rise in real wages in agriculture in the less developed regions where new technology is spreading.

New Technology and Environmental Degradation

Pollution of environment due to the intensive use of chemical fertilisers and pesticides has become a major problem in the developed countries. In India, environmental degradation in the rural areas has arisen not so much from the high level of chemical inputs used as from deforestation and extension of cultivation to ecologically fragile areas. Land-saving technological changes by reducing pressure for extension of cultivation and by augmenting biomass contribute to the conservation of fragile areas and regeneration of forests.

Across different states in India, the extension of area under cultivation and the denudation of forests seem to be high where the progress of yield-increasing technology is slow. In such regions, the levels of agricultural income and wages are low and poverty levels are high. Similarly, the pressure from animals such as goats and sheep on forests and common lands has been increasing in regions where growth in crop production is slow. This is because the rural poor supplement their incomes by rearing these animals.

Major Factors Affecting the Growth Potential

A number of factors are constraining the growth potential of the sector.[6]

Lack of Long-term Policy Perspective

On the policy front, there was lack of long-term strategy for agricultural development. One will be surprised to find that only recently the government has come out with a national agricultural policy. From the very beginning of the planning process in India, especially from the Second Five Year Plan with the sectoral priorities of Mahalanobis model favouring industry, the emphasis has been placed on industry relative to agriculture (Bhide *et al.*, 1998). The policies followed for agricultural development suffers from a number of weaknesses. First, though there was no significant direct taxation of the sector, agricultural sector has suffered from a typical anti-agricultural bias due to the nature of policies followed in other sectors like industry, trade, exchange rate, etc. (Gulati, 1998). Agricultural policies provided little incentives for the farmers, as the agricultural prices were depressed (Indian farmers received lower price than international prices). As there were numerous controls and restrictions, the sector was disprotected *vis-à-vis* other sectors of the economy. The restrictions on agricultural exports were believed to be one of the prime reasons for the disprotection of the sector as compared to the industrial sector. Second, agricultural policies gave little emphasis on agricultural exports as a means

6. Jeromi, P.D. (2002). "Is Indian Agriculture Approaching the Limits to Growth", in Raj Kapila and Uma Kapila (eds.), *Economic Developments in India*. Vol. 58.

of stimulating domestic production (Jeromi, 1997). Third, it has excessive price-based focus than non-price factors like water, infrastructure, research and development (R&D), extension services, etc., which are important determinants of agricultural production in India, a fact highlighted more than three decades back by Dantwala (1967) and recently by Pulapare (2000) and Vaidyanathan (2000). These weaknesses of agricultural policies, *inter alia*, affected the faster growth of the sector and in creating a sound infrastructure base for future growth.

Investment in Agriculture and Subsidies

Elementary growth theory tells us that the growth of a sector depends upon the investments made in that sector, its capital-output ratio, and the efficiency of capital in that sector (Gulati, 2012).

For the Indian economy, the Five Year Plan documents often presume a capital-output ratio of 4:1, that is, by investing four units of capital, one can get one unit of output. Thus, if the overall investments in the economy hover around, say, 30 per cent of GDP, then GDP should be growing at around 7.5 per cent, presuming all other factors remain largely neutral. Yet GDP growth fluctuates above and below 7.5 per cent depending upon factors other than investments. Similarly in agriculture, agri-GDP is influenced by at least three factors: trends in both public and private capital formation in agriculture over multiple years; relative price incentives for agriculture, which are often measured as a ratio of prices of agri-products to prices of manufactured products (loosely referred to as terms of trade between the agriculture and manufacturing sectors); and rainfall.

Looking at agriculture from the point of view of investments in agriculture, it is true that during the 1980s and 1990s, the investments in agriculture hovered largely between 8 and 12 per cent of agri-GDP. Given that the capital-output ratio in agriculture also hovers around 4:1, it was futile to expect agriculture to perform wonders on the growth front. The average rate of growth in agri-GDP could not be expected to be more than 2.5 to 3 per cent, assuming other factors were neutral. During the same period, public investment in agriculture declined from over 4 per cent of agriculture GDP to 2 per cent.

The public investment in agriculture in real terms has witnessed steady decline from the Sixth Five Year Plan to the Tenth Plan. However, this trend was reversed in the Tenth Plan (2002-2007) and the Eleventh Plan.

As a proportion of the value added by agriculture to GDP, gross capital formation (GCF) in agriculture & allied sectors rose to 20.1 per cent in 2010-11 from 13.4 per cent in 2004-05 at 2004-05 prices.

More than 85 per cent of investment in the agricultural sector is by the private sector, the largest increase in private GCF was in labour-saving machines such as irrigation and water-saving equipment (Twelfth Five Year Plan, Vol. II: 8), evidently a result of the declining rural workforce and rising real wages (*Economic Survey*, 2013-14).

Further, a considerable amount of plan expenditure on agriculture is not on investment but on subsidies. Simplistic fiscal rules such as protecting plan expenditures more than non-plan expenditures add to the problem. For example, although the plan share in states' total expenditure on agricultural & allied sectors has improved considerably, much of this represents increase in plan subsidies at the cost of essential staff, particularly in the extension system and the cooperative sector. Even a relatively small percentage reduction in subsidies can finance relatively large increase in public investment in crucial areas such as soil amelioration, watershed development, groundwater recharge, surface irrigation and other infrastructure, and can also allow substantial expansion in the reach of critical farm support systems.

It is imperative to reduce these subsidies for stepping up public investment in agriculture. However, there is considerable political resistance, and in a democratic polity like India, the process of change towards rational pricing of inputs is bound to be slow. In these days of globalisation and easy flow of information, it is becoming difficult to convince the Indian farmers about the need to reduce such subsidies when their counterparts in the 'market economies' like the USA, European Community and Japan enjoy much higher levels of subsidies. It is not easy to convince the farmers in India that our resources are scarcer and their alternative uses in agriculture are more productive.

There is a lively debate in the literature on complementarity between public and private sector capital formation in agricultural sector. Public sector investment has a crucial role to play in creating infrastructure in terms of irrigation, roads, markets, storage facilities, rural electrification and technology development. Private sector capital formation is hard to come in these areas. Private sector capital formation is essentially taking place for short-term asset building and it is mainly in the areas of mechanisation, ground levelling, private irrigation, etc. Therefore, public sector capital formation needed to be augmented with a definite content and targeted focus, especially in the case of rain-fed areas, which lack not only in irrigation facilities, but also in other infrastructural facilities. It may also be mentioned here that public spending in agriculture is a common feature in both the developed and developing countries.

There is a view among the agricultural economists that the lagged effect of decline of capital formation during the 1980s has been one of the major reasons for the decelerated growth of the sector during the 1990s (Dev, 1998). Therefore, the subdued level of capital formation during the 1990s could have an impact on agriculture production in the coming years.

The experience of China shows that high rate of investment in agriculture can ensure big spurt in agricultural output (Rao and Gulati, 1994). Many of the problems of agriculture sector *viz.,* low productivity, low employment opportunities, high intensity of poverty, and inadequate infrastructure are attributed to inadequate and progressive decline in public investment in physical capital (irrigation, rural electrification, roads, markets, etc.), human capital (health, education and training) and development of non-farm sector. These arguments are reinforced by a recent report by UN World Food Programme (UNWFP) and M.S. Swaminathan Research Foundation (MSSRF) (2009) which recommends more public investment in agriculture, among others, to prevent further fall in agricultural productivity and to ensure a food-secured India (Mahendra Dev, 2013)

In formulating future policy toward public investment in agriculture and rural development, three areas should get priority: rural roads, electricity (including rural electrification), and major and medium irrigation projects (Panagariya, 2008). Rural roads that feed into major highways connect farmers to the market place, and electricity is the critical input in both agricultural and non-agricultural economic activities. The provision of these two critical amenities can go a long way toward allowing farmers to exploit their private entrepreneurial talents. Major and medium irrigation projects provide a key public input into agriculture.

Lagging Research and Development Efforts

Another important factor limiting the growth potential of the sector is the lack of breakthrough in research and development after the Green Revolution. Perhaps, it may be one of the reasons for the decline of productivity in the 1990s. India compares poorly with the productivity levels in major producing countries.

Since there is hardly any scope for further expansion of area under cultivation, the future production prospects depends largely on the improvements in the yield levels. Here what we need is to break the yield barrier and bridge the gap between the potential and actual yield through research and development (R&D) efforts. Indian Council of Agricultural Research (ICAR) studies reveal that there is vast unexplored technological potential for improvement in the yield of crops. In this context, Swaminathan (1999) noted that the 'low yield phenomena' in India should be considered as a 'yield reservoir' and it should be treated as an asset for future development of the sector. Exploiting the 'yield reservoir,' *inter alia*, requires substantial investment and development and deployment of high yielding seed varieties.

Technology Generation and Dissemination

With availability of land and water fixed, the goal of 4 per cent growth in agriculture can be achieved only by increasing productivity per unit of these scarce natural resources through effective use of improved technology. The research system has so far focused mainly on breeding varieties that increase the yield potential of individual crops by enabling more intensive use of inputs. But although such research did increase potential yields substantially in the past, it puts less emphasis on the efficient and sustainable use of soil nutrients and water and is no longer leading to adequate outcomes.

Unlike the Green Revolution technology that began with large farmers in resource-rich areas, community-managed sustainable agriculture focusing on marginal and small farmers in resource-poor, dry and drought-prone areas needs to be promoted.[7]

Rising Soil Degradation and Over-exploitation of Groundwater

Large-scale soil degradation and over-exploitation of groundwater are other important factors putting limits on growth of the sector. Around 40 per cent of India's total geographical area are officially estimated as degraded (some other estimates put the figure at 50%).

The emergence of rice-wheat crops system in states like Punjab and Haryana, on account of continuous increase in procurement prices, has resulted in over-exploitation of natural resource base. An ICAR study

7. Mishra, S. and D.N. Reddy (2011). "Persistence of Crisis in Indian Agriculture", in D.M. Nachane (ed.), *India Development Report 2011*. New Delhi: Oxford and Indira Gandhi Institute of Development Research.

found that soil health is deteriorating in Punjab and Haryana, and this is a major cause of decline or stagnation in productivity of cereals, particularly of rice and wheat. The study revealed that the organic carbon content in the soils in Punjab and Haryana has declined to 0.2 per cent in 1995 from 0.5 per cent in the 1960s. Soils with low phosphorus content have also increased to 73.0 per cent from only 3.5 per cent in 1975 in Haryana. Similarly, soils with high potash category have scaled down from 91.0 per cent in 1975 to 62.0 per cent in 1995. Further, consequent to the decontrol of prices of phosphorus and potash, there was decline in the application of these fertilisers. This caused nutrient imbalance in the soils. Now farmers have to apply more fertilisers to get the same yield as they were getting with less fertiliser 20-30 years ago. In case of groundwater, the study found that the rapid increase in the number of tube wells during the last three decades in the region has resulted in over-exploitation of groundwater. This decline forces the farmers to lower the pumps further deeper in the wells, which results in the use of irrigation with saline water.

As the present agricultural development strategy in India is centred mainly on the irrigated areas and the yield levels of crops in many irrigated areas are plateauing, there is a growing realisation that agricultural production cannot be increased beyond a point.

The irrigation potential in the country has been estimated at 85 million hectares. Even after full utilisation of the irrigation potential, nearly 45 per cent of the net cultivated area will have to depend on rainfall. As the present agricultural development strategy in India is centred mainly on the irrigated areas and the yield levels of crops in many irrigated areas are plateauing, there is a growing realisation that agricultural production cannot be increased beyond a point.

Degradation of Natural Resources

The pressing need to accelerate agriculture growth should not be at the cost of sustainability of our natural resource base, which is starkly limited. This is compounded by degradation of soil and over-exploitation of groundwater. Deforestation has affected both soils and water. Action on these environmental fronts cannot wait, especially in the face of a possibly looming adverse climate change due to global warming.

Subsidies vis-à-vis Investments and Farm Support Systems

An unfortunate trend over the past two decades has been that budgetary subsidies to agriculture have increased from around 3 per cent of agriculture GDP in 1976-1980 to about 7 per cent in 2001-2003.

During the same period, public investment in agriculture declined from 3.4 per cent of agriculture GDP to 1.9 per cent. Most of the subsidies are on fertiliser, power and irrigation water and have actually contributed to the degradation of natural resources noted earlier. The pricing of subsidised fertilisers is also probably responsible for higher usage of straight fertilisers and skewed usage of nutrients (Report of Working Group on Fertiliser Industry for the Twelfth Plan: 8). Indiscriminate use of NPK (nitrogen, phosphorus and potassium) has led to imbalanced use of soil nutrients, especially in Haryana and Punjab, leading to deterioration in soil quality and declining growth in land productivity in these states (*Economic Survey 2013-14*). Current trends in agricultural output reveal that the marginal productivity of soil in relation to the applications of fertilisers is declining. Even a relatively small percentage reduction in subsidies can finance relatively large increase in public investment in crucial areas such as soil amelioration, watershed development, groundwater recharge, surface irrigation and other infrastructure and also allow substantial expansion in the reach of critical farm support systems.

Agriculture's Terms of Trade and Farm Price Volatility

An important reason for recent farm distress was that farm prices fell even as farm production decelerated. After improving steadily from 1980 to 1997, the terms of trade turned against agriculture between 1999 and 2004 and reduced profitability of farming quite sharply. This occurred partly because domestic food demand slowed down and partly because Indian farm prices became more aligned with corresponding international prices at a time when world commodity prices were on the decline. Moreover, farmers are now subject to greater price risk since variability of world prices is much higher.

Farm Distress

While India was marching ahead in attaining and improving food security and leaving behind the era of food shortage, another crisis started building gradually in the form of agrarian distress. The distress turned serious during the early 1990s, though it started developing a few years earlier. Initially severe distress was confined to some pockets with poor resource endowments but gradually spread to many parts of the country. Incidents of farmers distress are reported even from agriculturally developed states like Punjab, Haryana and Kerala. The situation has become particularly bad during the last two years because of two successive failures of monsoon and abnormal rainfall in Rabi

2014-15 and highly deficit precipitation in Rabi 2015-16. These types of sufferings do not bode well for the country whose economy is growing at more than 7 per cent a year and which plans to be counted as globally powerful nation.

The distress is said to be the cause for some farmers to take the extreme step to end their lives by committing suicides. This kind of incidents further worsens the suffering of such families. The distress paints a very dismal picture of Indian agriculture. It threatens the future of agriculture sector and also reflects poor state of large population of farming community in the country. This paper is an attempt to understand the genesis, causes, nature and severity of agrarian distress and to propose measure and strategy to mitigate and banish agrarian distress in the country.

Genesis and Symptoms

It is ironical that despite so much concern about the agrarian distress in the country, there is no clear description of what is agrarian distress. Thus, before proceeding further, it is important to discuss what is agrarian distress. According to us agrarian distress is manifest at two levels: (i) sectoral or macro level, and (ii) household or farm level. Further, the distress could be absolute or it could be relative. The absolute agrarian distress characterises a situation of agriculture production becoming economically unviable or highly vulnerable. The relative agrarian distress implies rise in gap in performance of agriculture relative to rest of the economy. Agrarian distress at household level refer to a situation when the income of a agricultural household is not adequate to meet family and business obligations. The symptoms of agrarian distress are:

- Rising debt, loan default.
- Networth turning negative.
- Forced migration.
- Rise in hunger.
- Sale of productive assets like land, bullock, tractor, machinery to meet family expenditure.
- Sale of family assets to meet family expenditure.
- Adoption of untested and risky ventures.
- Dissatisfaction with the profession.
- Rise in tragedies like suicides.

The genesis of agrarian distress, at aggregate level, is rooted in structural imbalance in Indian economy which is reflected in two important indicators. The first one is the mismatch in the share of agriculture in national income vis-à-vis its share in workforce and the second one is ratio of per worker income in agriculture vis-à-vis non-agriculture. At the time of onset of green revolution (1970-1971), agriculture employed 69 per cent of workforce and shared about 42 per cent of national income (Table 12.5). As the green revolution progressed and spread, a sizeable proportion of labour force shifted from agriculture to non-agriculture sectors. Agriculture growth created backward and forward linkages leading to growth in employment in non-farm rural as well as urban sectors (Mellor and Lele 1973, Chadha 1986). However, the shift in labour force almost stopped somewhere between 1980-81 and 1990-1991. During 1980-81 to 2000-01, there was negligible shift in labour force from agriculture to non-agriculture whereas share of agriculture in national income reduced by one third.

TABLE – 12.5

Share of Agriculture and Non-agriculture Sectors in National Income and Workforce (%)

Year	*Share in National Income*		*Share in Workforce*	
	Agriculture	*Non-Agriculture*	*Agriculture*	*Non-Agriculture*
1950-51	51.81	48.19	68.85	31.15
1960-61	42.56	57.44	69.41	30.59
1970-71	41.95	58.05	69.36	30.64
1980-81	35.39	64.61	59.02	40.98
1990-91	29.02	70.98	58.38	41.62
2000-01	23.02	76.98	58.20	41.80
2010-11	18.21	81.79	54.59	45.41

Sources of basic data:

1. National Accounts Statistics, CSO, GoI. 2. Agricultural Statistics at a Glance 2016, Ministry of Agriculture and Farmers Welfare, GoI.

The decline in share of agriculture in national income resulted from a faster rate of growth in non-agriculture, which is considered natural in the development process, but it did not translate into creation of jobs in non-agriculture sector to pull workforce from agriculture sector after 1980-81. The situation started worsening with the beginning of economic reforms in 1991. The economic reforms resulted in acceleration in growth rate of non-agriculture sector but growth rate in agriculture sector did not follow a secular trend. Only for some brief spell, the growth rate went high which was soon followed by a spell of low growth.

Agrarian distress cannot be removed by doubling farm subsidies, raising MSP, and expanding MGNREGA, or food subsidies. The sustainable way to address this is to undertake development measures and policy reforms which can lead to fast growth in income per farmer.

National Policy for Farmers, 2007

Based on the recommendations of the National Commission on Farmers and in consultation with the concerned central ministries/ departments and the states, the GoI has adopted the National Policy for Farmers, 2007. Major policy provisions include provisions for asset reforms, water use efficiency, use of technology, inputs and services like soil health, good quality seeds, disease-free planting material, support services for women, credit, insurance, etc. Provisions have also been made for National Agricultural Bio-security System, setting up of farm schools in the fields of outstanding farmers to promote farmer- to-farmer learning and to strengthen extension services and expanding food security basket to include nutritious crops like *bajra*, *jowar*, *ragi* and millets mostly grown in dry land areas. A comprehensive National Social Security Scheme for the farmers for ensuring livelihood security by taking care of insurance needs on account of illness and old age is included.

Emerging Imbalances

Subsidies versus Public Investment

The Eleventh Plan document had highlighted that public investment in agriculture as per cent of agricultural GDP had halved between the 1980s and in the end of the Ninth Plan, while, simultaneously, budgetary subsidies to agriculture had doubled as proportion of agricultural GDP. The tendency for subsidies to increase much faster than public investment was checked to some extent during the Tenth Plan, but it reappeared again during the Eleventh Plan. Budgetary subsidies to agriculture (excluding food subsidy, which should be treated as a consumer subsidy) increased from an average of 4.1 per cent of agricultural GDP during the Tenth Plan to average 8.2 per cent in the first four years of the Eleventh Plan. Actual subsidies to agriculture were higher in both periods since Central Statistical Office (CSO) books budgeted subsidy on domestic urea manufacture entirely to industry and because part of the power subsidy received by agriculture is not budgeted but borne by utilities. Compared to these numbers, public investment in agriculture averaged only about 3 per cent of agricultural GDP during both plan periods.

The imbalance between subsidy expenditure and expenditure on public investment raises the issue whether a shift away from subsidies and towards greater public investment would not be beneficial. The usual argument for reducing subsidies is that it will improve the fiscal deficit, but that is not the relevant point in this context. There is a need to shift from subsidies to public investment aimed at increasing land productivity on the grounds that this would produce better agricultural outcomes and would also be more inclusive. This is particularly important in the context of strategies for combating the effect of climate change where public investment in conservation and management of water resources will be crucial.

There are also other uses of resources in agriculture which could be promoted if agricultural subsidies are restrained like trade-offs that subsidies might have with other non-plan revenue expenditures, particularly staffing of essential farm support systems such as extension. Moreover, capacity and skill shortages have made upgrading agricultural universities an urgent need.

Cereals Production and Build-up of Stocks

Another major imbalance is between production and consumption of cereals, particularly rice and wheat on the one hand which led to rising stocks and rising consumption of edible oils and pulses on the other hand which led to increase in imports.

An important and related issue is the likely future demand for food. The Twelfth Plan Working Group on Crop Husbandry, Demand and Supply Projections, Agricultural Inputs and Agricultural Statistics has made projections for food grains and other food items by the terminal year of the Twelfth Plan, that is, 2016-17 which would suggest that present levels of cereals production already exceed likely demand at the end of the Twelfth Plan. These projections are based on actual past patterns of observed demand and the fact that cereals consumption per capita has declined since at least mid-1990s. However, it is also the case that India has very high levels of malnutrition and, although there are many reasons for this, deficiencies in calorie intake remain one of the most important. With cereals supplying over 50 per cent of total calorie intake even now, falling cereals consumption is the main reason why per capita calorie intake has not increased despite rising incomes. It is not just that the share of cereals in total food expenditure is falling, even poor people are reducing the share of income spent on all foods in order to meet other non-food needs. In such a situation where there is a disjunction between such a basic element of human development as nutrition and other demands in an increasingly consumerist society, there is need to ensure that minimum nutrition requirements are actually met.

This means that agricultural production must diversify so as to satisfy both tastes and nutrition. In particular, MSP policy should be more restrained for rice and wheat and made more effective in case of pulses and oilseeds where India is a net importer. Although MSP for pulses and oilseeds have been increased substantially in recent years, farmers are still not encouraged enough to put in the effort and resources required to substitute for current imports of these commodities. This is primarily because procurement efforts in these commodities, which are currently not part of public distribution, simply do not offer farmers the certainty that they have from procurement effort in rice and wheat.

High Value Commodities: The Future Sources of Growth in Agriculture[8]

The agricultural production basket comprises of (i) food grains (wheat, rice, coarse cereals and pulses) and commercial or cash crops (cotton, sugar cane, oilseeds and other crops); and (ii) high value commodities such as fruits and vegetables, livestock (milk, meat, poultry and eggs) and marine products. As compared with food grains, commercial crops—particularly cotton and sugar cane (more than 355 mt of sugar cane as per the final estimates for 2006-07—have performed well over time. For cotton in particular, the technology breakthrough with Bt has worked wonders. In 2007-08, cotton exports reached an unprecedented level of 8.3 million bales (Cotton Corporation of India, 2007).

The production of cotton has been growing at the rate of 13.2 per cent during 2002-03 to 2007-08, and production more than doubled from 13.6 million bales in 2002-03 to 31.5 million bales in 2007-08 (Cotton Corporation of India, 2007). As a result of this blistering growth, India has emerged as the second largest producer of cotton in 2006-2007—next only to China and having overtaken the USA. India

8. This section is drawn from Gulati, Ashok (2010). "Accelerating Agricultural Growth: Moving from Farming to Value Chains", in Shankar Acharya and Rakesh Mohan (eds.) (2010), *India's Economy: Performance and Challenges*. New Delhi: OUP.

has also emerged as the second largest exporter of cotton (worth nearly $2 billion of cotton exports in 2007-08)—the highest ever in the 60-year history of independent India. The area under Bt cotton reached 7.6 million hectares in 2008, covering almost 65 per cent of the area under cotton and also accounting for more than 80 per cent of the hike in yields (James, 2008). A similar technology breakthrough in other crops can help overcome stagnation and invigorate the growth potential of the agricultural sector.

Thus, the high value segment holds the key to future sources of growth. This is primarily due to their higher expenditure elasticity compared to food grains. The share of high value agriculture in total agriculture (crops, livestock and fisheries) has increased from 37.2 per cent in TE 1982-93 to 46.8 per cent in TE 2007-08, indicating a distinct shift in production pattern.

Although the share of food grains in value of output of total agriculture is 24.9 per cent (TE 2007-08), it comprises of nearly 64 per cent of the gross cropped area (TE 2004-05). This is in contrast to fruit and vegetables that comprise less than 6 per cent of the gross cropped area but constitute 16 per cent of the total agriculture during the same periods. Dairy in India is a classic example that has steered India to the number one position in milk production (more than 100 mt), and is still based primarily on small holders. With the amendment of Milk and Milk Products Order (MMPO) in March 2002, private sector participation has increased in a significant way.

Changing tastes and preferences towards high-value food commodities are the rationale for diversification towards this segment. The westernisation of diets is a phenomenon that is being experienced by almost all South and Southeast Asian countries (Pingali, 2006). The average per capita consumption of food grains has exhibited a negative growth during 1991-2005, and there is a clear indication that the plate is skewed in favour of high value commodities.

Given the fact that the markets for these products are by and large free, and the demand is income elastic, changing demographics and socioeconomic indicators will ensure higher returns. In India, cereals are being increasingly overtaken by fruits, vegetables, milk, eggs and poultry. While the percentage of food to total expenditure has declined over time, the share of high value products within food expenditure is increasing.

An examination of food consumption expenditure in the country during the period 1987-88 to 2009-10 clearly reveals that there has been a shift in expenditure towards milk and milk products, egg, fish, meat, and vegetables both in rural and urban areas, whereas the share of consumption of cereals in the total food basket has gone down (Table 12.6).

TABLE – 12.6

Item-wise Share of Expenditure to Total Food Expenditure

	Rural		*Urban*	
	1987-88	*2009-10*	*1987-88*	*2009-10*
Cereals	41.1	29.1	26.6	22.4
Pulses and products	6.3	6.9	6.0	6.6
Milk and products	13.4	16.0	16.8	19.2
Egg, fish and meat	5.2	6.5	6.4	6.6
Vegetables	8.1	11.6	9.4	10.6
Sugar	4.5	4.5	4.3	3.7
Food total	100	100	100	100

Source: Key Indicators of Household Consumer Expenditure in India 2009-10, National Sample Survey (NSS) 66th Round

Per capita per month consumption of cereals has come down from 14.9 kg. in 1983 to 12.1 kg in 2004-05 in rural areas, while urban areas saw a decline from 11.6 kg to 9.9 kg during the same time period. In other words, the weighted share of cereal consumption has declined from 14.1 kg to 11.5 kg during the same time period.

Rapid economic growth, rising income levels and changing demographics have triggered a significant change. The rising number of nuclear families and the increasing number of women professionals are fuelling the change in consumption habits and preferences in favour of semi-processed and processed foods, as well as setting trends in eating out. It is being projected that, in the years to come, nearly 80 per cent of the consumption boom is likely to come from rising income levels (McKinsey and Company, 2007).

The most important aspect pertaining to our agriculture is high human resource relying on the primary sector. About 55 per cent of the population employed in agriculture depend on 14 per cent of the national income generated in agriculture. On the one hand, there is fluctuating agricultural growth and on the other distress in farm sector. The farmers most often complain that they are not properly rewarded for their production efforts. The supply chain for most agricultural commodities is highly fragmented with multiple intermediaries contributing to the inefficient handling and high transaction costs. The supply chain is characterised by lack of sufficient and efficient facilities like processing, product-specific transport models, grading, certification and packing.

The food processing sector in India is still in a nascent stage with only 8 per cent of the produce being processed as against 80-98 per cent in case of high income countries (GoI, 2008). The food processing sector is now receiving the boost with the annual growth of 13.2 per cent in registered food processing units during 2004-2010 (GoI, 2011a). In the above backdrop, there is a great need to strategically handle the situation in order to facilitate a self-sustainable and long-run growth of the agriculture sector, which is possible by focussing on what is termed as secondary agriculture. Though not a panacea for all ailments of the primary sector, it can definitely drive the growth.[9]

Secondary Agriculture: A Driver for Growth of Primary Agriculture

Secondary Agriculture includes "all practices and process which add value to primary agricultural commodities by using efficient technologies, market information and consumer preference." It should be noted that the term value addition in agriculture is a process of increasing the economic value and consumer appeal of an agricultural commodity. It is basically an alternative production and marketing strategy.[10]

Secondary agriculture, driving the growth of primary agriculture, is visualised as under:

1. Planned withdrawal of working force from primary sector by establishing appropriate linkages with secondary agricultural sector.
2. Encash the changing demand towards value added products by promoting diversification of primary agriculture so that farmers improve their production base.
3. Building strong demand through value addition and promotion for underutilised crops such as minor millets, medicinal and aromatic plants, and crop by-products so that farmers realise higher returns.

---

9. Ibid.
10. Ibid.

4. Encouraging rural industrialisation so that the demand for primary produce is increased as they are used as raw material by the industry and the required quality inputs are made available to improve primary agriculture.

5. Improve the supply chain management so that the transaction cost is reduced and market is expanded for primary agricultural commodities.

6. Develop human resource to undertake research and extension relating to secondary agriculture so that its expansion and increased efficiency will benefit the primary sector.

The secondary agriculture is regarded as a sunrise sector for the Indian economy, owing to its immense untapped potential. The impetus for development of secondary agriculture has been due to increasing consumers demand for value added goods like ready-to-eat, ready-to-serve, convenience food. This is again favoured by the growth of organised retail which makes the processed food easily available to the consumers. Secondly, the fast depletion of natural resources used for industries has created a demand for utilisation of non-conventional renewable agro-bioresources. Thus, demand-side factors are key drivers for creating market opportunities for end products of primary agriculture through the growth of secondary sector.[11]

Reforming the Three 'I's: Investments, Incentives and Institutions

Investments

Thus, in response to new demand patterns, developed markets and infrastructure, and a change in approach from farming towards a new agri-system will be needed. New investments will be needed to become the driving force in today's agriculture. While India has a large production base, the lack of infrastructure and organised market structure stand in the way of successful diversification. A World Bank (2007b) study shows that for horticulture produce, farmers typically receive about 12-15 per cent of the price paid by the retail consumer in the export market. Further studies conducted by the World Bank (2007c) on value chains of mango and *litchi* in Bihar show that a significant amount of the consumer price is lost in transport and wastage, and farmers receive 34 and 42 per cent of that price, respectively. This can

11. Ibid.

be further increased if the supply chain can be compressed and the wastage minimised (Gulati, 2010).

If one looks at the overall public resources being spent on agriculture, one is amazed to observe that three-fourth of the resources go primarily as subsidies on inputs like fertilisers, irrigation and power. Only one-fourth of the resources go as public investment in agriculture, and roughly 90 per cent of this is on major and medium irrigation. Moreover, over time, input subsidies in real terms have gone up much faster than investments in agriculture. This has severe implications for policy regarding the allocation of public resources (Gulati, 2010).

The International Food Policy Research Institute (IFPRI) research on marginal returns in terms of agricultural GDP from a unit of public expenditure across various categories within agriculture reveals that the returns are the highest on public expenditures devoted to agriculture R&D, followed by rural roads, education and irrigation, and lowest from fertiliser subsidies. Yet, the fertiliser subsidy in 2008-09 is more than ₹99,000 crore, indicating a huge inefficiency in the allocation of public expenditure. In fact, the fertiliser subsidy has remained a hard nut to crack for policy makers since the beginning of the reforms in 1991 (Gulati, 2010).

TABLE – 12.7

Returns in Growth to Investments and Subsidies

	1960s-1970s	*1980s*	*1990s*
Returns in agricultural GDP (₹ per Re. Spending)			
Roads	19.99	8.89	7.66
Education	14.66	7.58	5.46
Irrigation Investment	8	4.71	4.37
Irrigation subsidies	5.22	2.25	2.47
Fertiliser subsidies	1.79	1.94	0.85
Power subsidies	12.06	2.25	1.19
Credit subsidies	18.77	3	4.26
Agricultural R&D	8.65	7.93	9.5

Source: Fan *et al.* (2008).

The culture of proliferating subsidies is not only crowding out public investment in agriculture but also distorting cropping patterns, leading to environmental stress. For example, in Punjab, more than 75 per cent of blocks are overexploited in terms of groundwater. One of the key reasons for this overexploitation is the spread of paddy cultivation encouraged by free power (GoI, 2007a). Gujarat's Jyotigram experiment—wherein they have separated the feeder lines for agriculture—has shown that the situation can be improved (Shah and Verma, 2008). There are also technical solutions to distributing power subsidies directly to farmers through 'smart cards' that enable electronic meters to work. A whole literature regarding how many other countries have managed reforms in power subsidies is freely available (Gulati and Narayanan, 2003).

It is interesting to note that while public investment in agriculture is critical and important, in reality it forms only less than 25 per cent of the total investment in agriculture; 75 per cent comes from the private sector (GoI, 2008d). Moreover, the private sector responds much better to the incentive structures in agriculture. Thus, reforming the incentives in agriculture is as, if not more, important as public investments in agriculture. Thus, private investments should be encouraged to be the spur that can transform agriculture (Gulati, 2010).

Reforming Incentives

Price and Marketing Policy

Gulati maintains to reform incentives in agriculture, the first policy action has to be getting the 'prices right.' While the reduction of tariffs on manufactured products, the correction of exchange rate of the rupee, and the relaxation of export controls on several agricultural products since 1991 have helped reduce 'implicit taxation' on agriculture (Pursell *et al.,* 2009), there are still occasional interventions by the government (like export bans on wheat and rice, or limits on the stocking of grains by private trade in 2008) that dissuade the private sector to invest in agri-system. However, the main government intervention in agricultural markets currently comes through its policy of MSP for some 24 odd crops, although in practice this mainly works for rice, wheat, sugar cane and cotton, wherein there is some significant degree of procurement. Over time, this MSP has become *de facto* a procurement price, and discourages farmers to diversify into high-value crops that do not have such a support/ procurement price. To make the system more market oriented, it is critical to de-link the support price from procurement price, where the latter can be changed (up or down) depending upon market conditions, and in full competition with private trade within the same marketing year. This call for the abolition of all levies (on rice or sugar); the free movement of goods across the country; and the abolition of stocking limits, export bans, bans on future markets, etc., on private trade.

Reforming Institutions

While rationalising subsidies and incentives can pave the way towards greater investments, both public and private, it is important to bring about certain institutional reforms that create an enabling environment for private sector participation with a view to promoting efficiency.

Marketing and Warehouse Facilities

Improving marketing conditions and encouraging private sector participation require reforming the Agricultural Produce Marketing Committee (APMC) Act and abolishing the Essential Commodities Act (ECA). What started as a protective regime to restrict the exploitation of farmers in marketing their produce and ensuring a fair price has resulted in excessive government control. Cleaning up these archaic provisions can trigger private sector investment in developing regularised markets, logistics and warehouse receipt systems, futures markets, and in infrastructure (such as cold storage facilities, quality certification, etc.) for imports and exports. This is particularly relevant for the high-value segment that is currently hostage to high post-harvest losses and weak farm-firm linkages.

Reforming Land and Credit Markets

The linking of small and fragmented farms with large-scale processors and retailers remains a challenge in the high-value sector, and restricted land (lease) markets tend to compound the problem (Gulati, 2010). Allaying the fears of a farmer regarding possible alienation from his own land because of leasing it out to the retailer/processor requires the freeing up of land lease markets and rethinking the utility of ceiling laws. Legalising lease markets also protects the interests of the retailer/processor, and enables him to undertake larger investments. In this context, it may be helpful to ensure the registration of land deeds and the computerising of land records for bringing about greater transparency and reliability (GoI, 2006c).

The land and credit markets are intricately linked, and improving the marketability of land will enhance access of farmers to institutional credit. According to the 2003 estimates of NSSO, farmer households with less than 2 hectares of land accounted for 80 per cent of the indebted farmer households, and availed nearly 50 per cent of their loan requirements from non-institutional sources. What aggravates their plight is that nearly 38 per cent of it is acquired at a staggering interest rate of 30 per cent (GoI, 2007b). One could think of bringing the traditional moneylenders into the organised network as non-banking financial intermediaries (NBFIs), wherein National Bank for Agriculture and Rural Development (NABARD) can take the responsibility of refinancing them—suppose at an interest rate of 7 per cent, while they can still charge farmers up to 12 per cent rate of interest.

High-value agriculture is more income augmenting and has the potential to create both farm and off-farm employment opportunities.

Thus agriculture can no longer be confined to farming and needs to be integrated with other segments of the agri-food system such as input supply, logistics and warehousing, processing, and retailing/ wholesaling. This shifts the focus towards backward linkages that deliver inputs, extension services, market information and the like. Herein, the role of institutional arrangements such as rural or agri-business hubs coordinated by public-private-*panchayat* partnerships and contract farming led by cooperatives, corporates or producers' organisations needs to be explored.

To sum up 25 years of economic reforms have at least corrected two things that are critical to agriculture: (i) that the so-called 'anti-agriculture bias' emanating from overvalued exchange rates and high rates of protection to industry has been largely removed, and this was done very early in the reform process and (ii) the GCF in agriculture, which had dipped to its lowest levels to 6.99 per cent of agri-GDP in 1994-95, was revived and it touched a high of 21.1 per cent in 2012-13 at 2014-15 prices. These are commendable achievements of the reform process and will go a long way to strengthen the base of Indian agriculture.

Another noteworthy feature of Indian agriculture in an open economy environment is its gradual integration with the global economy. The exports plus imports of agricultural commodities as a percentage to agri-GDP increased steadily from about 5 per cent in 1991-92 to roughly 13 per cent in 2010-11. Indian agriculture today is almost three times more integrated with the global economy than it was 20 years back.

Trade Policies of Agri Products[12]

In 1990-91, much of Indian agriculture global trade (about 94 per cent of AGDP) was subject to many types of non-tariff barriers. These trade-restricting barriers included compulsory export and import

12. Gulati, Ashok and Shweta Saini (2018). "Twenty-Five Years of Policy Tinkering in Agriculture", in Uma Kapila (ed.) (2018), *Indian Economy Since Independence* (29th edition). New Delhi: Academic Foundation.

licensing, canalization (restriction of trade through generally one parastatal body), and use of MEPs (Pursell and Gulati 1993).

India's agri-trade policies have been ad hoc and unpredictable. These policies have been observed to be subservient to the overall objective of food security and price stabilization for the consumer, much to the detriment of the farmers who have borne the brunt of such ad hocism due to export restrictions. A case in point is the 2007-08 global food crisis, which triggered a ban of wheat and rice exports.

In 2004, the new government came with Dr Manmohan Singh as the prime minister. The import duties started easing as global prices of edible oils started rising. By 2008, these duties came down to zero! Even in FY 2016, with a moderate duty, India is importing more than 50 per cent of its consumption requirement, and self-sufficiency in edible oils now seems a distant dream. Cereal exports and imports were highly restricted, primarily through the 'canalization' route.

Gradually, over time, India opened exports of several other agri commodities. In commodities such as cotton and beef (buffalo meat), India has become the largest or second-largest exporter in FY 2014.

Despite the reforms and the impressive performance on the trade front, policy governing some of agri exports is still highly restrictive, especially in the case of pulses, sugar, oilseeds and edible oils. Not-so-essential commodities such as onions and potatoes are subject to sporadic bans or high MEPs, let alone basic cereals whose trade oscillates inter- and intra-year between trade regimes. These are elements of anti-agriculture bias that still exist, though not to the degree as it did before the 1991 reforms of exchange-rate correction and slashing of industrial tariffs.

For a High-yield Agri-trade

For the first time in the history of independent India, Indian agriculture has given a net trade surplus of more than $25 billion, in FY14. Its agri-exports crossed $42 billion *vis-à-vis* imports of about $17 billion indicating that Indian agriculture is quite export competitive. The Balassa index measuring export competitiveness for agriculture is 1.6 *vis-à-vis* only 1.0 for manufacturing products, implying that our agriculture is more competitive globally than our manufacturing sector.[13]

---

13. Gulati, Ashok (2014). "For a High Yield Agri-trade", *Financial Express,* June 6.

India's agri-export basket is quite diversified. But a few need special mention. India has emerged as the largest exporter of rice with exports touching \$7.7 billion, second-largest exporter of meat with exports of \$4.5 billion and cotton (\$3.6 billion), and a large exporter of number of other products ranging from marine products (\$5 billion) to oil meals (\$2.8 billion), spices (\$2.6 billion) and guar gum (\$2 billion). The most impressive growth in FY14 over FY13, in terms of size and growth rate, has been dairy & poultry registering a growth of 72 per cent, marine products of 45 per cent, meat and preparations of 36 per cent. Even rice has witnessed a growth of about 25 per cent growth in value terms though the quantity exported in FY14 may be similar at 10 million tonnes as in FY13. This is largely credited to the better price that Indian basmati has fetched this year. Even fresh fruits and vegetables, with a total of \$1.6 billion exports, registered a 29 per cent growth. This is commendable especially in the face of tough SPS laws in importing countries and somewhat weak value-chains that India has.[14]

The challenge for agriculture tomorrow comes not as much from opening it up to global markets, as from policies that still use severe export controls (be it rice, wheat, sugar or even cotton) and do not permit a single unified national market for agri-produce. Other concerns are the high and distorted structure of taxes and fees on agri-goods in certain states, levies that are still distorting the evolution of markets, the failure to give a clear signal on market reforms that can connect the farmers' organisations to organised processors and retailers without going through the anarchic *mandi* system, and failure to give the right signals to agri-scientists and entrepreneurs on new technologies related to GM crops for commercialisation. These reforms imply institutional reforms, and require strong political will at the centre. Only then can one hope that Indian agriculture will cross the barrier of 4 per cent growth on a sustainable basis and being much-needed prosperity in rural areas.

Domestic Agri Marketing and Production-Policy Reforms

Although agri commodities have national markets, the laws and practices under Essential Commodities Act (ECA, 1955) and Agriculture Produce Market Committee (APMC) Act make marketing of agri commodities less efficient and riskier. Under ECA, for example,

14. Ibid.

movement of commodities can be restricted between states, or even between districts within a state; limits on private sector stocks of 'essential commodities' can be imposed, strangulating the role of private players. Similarly, limited licensing of commission agents under APMC creates a 'rent-seeking' class of commission agents, who have oligopolistic powers and take away undue share in the value chains of most agri commodities. Future and forward markets in most agri commodities (except turmeric, pepper, potato, gur and castor seed) were banned in the pre-reforms era. Existence of a dualistic marketing system, particularly for rice and wheat, under which part of the marketed surplus of certain commodities is procured by the government (or its nodal agency called the Food Corporation of India (FCI)) to be distributed to an identified vulnerable section of the society at highly subsidized prices, complicates the already strangulated agri markets. Combining this with the government's levy system for rice and sugar, wherein the rice millers had to deposit a certain percentage of milled rice to FCI at fixed prices, further limits the efficiency of market systems. In some states, this levy ratio was as high as 70 per cent. After moderation in this ratio over the years, the government finally abolished it. In the case of sugar, the levy rate after peaking at 65 per cent in the pre-reforms era underwent moderation and was later abolished. Cotton too had a monopoly procurement scheme in Maharashtra but that too was eventually dismantled.

All such restrictive policies increased the gap between the farm-gate prices and the retail prices, thus accentuating the anti-agriculture bias in the system and the policymaking. Most of them have been relaxed and some (like levy system) have been phased-out during the twenty-five years of the piecemeal reforms. However, the draconian ECA and APMC policies are still in place inducing the markets with uncertainty and high risk. Quantifying the impact of all these on farmers' incentives is a challenging task, but Gulati and Sharma (1991) calculated this for the pre-1991 reform period and the results reinforced the presence of the anti-agriculture bias in Indian agri policies.

On the agri-production front, two promising missions were launched during the UPA-I period, which are noteworthy. One was the National Horticulture Mission (NHM) launched in 2005-06 and the other, as already mentioned, was NFSM, launched in 2007 in response to the 6 MMT wheat imports by India in FY 2007.

Farm profitability is central to achieving rapid and inclusive agricultural growth. The reports of the Commission on Agricultural

Costs and Prices show low net farm revenue for many crops, particularly rainfed. Diversification towards higher value crops and livestock remains the best way not only to improve farm incomes and accelerate growth, but also to reduce stress on natural resources which form farmers' production base. This needs better infrastructure and emphasis on integrated farming systems, combining crops and livestock, including small ruminants, for different location-specific endowments. This also requires innovative institutional and contractual arrangements so that small holders have the requisite technology and market access (*Twelfth Five Year Plan*, Vol. II).

Agricultural Policy Review (2018)*

OECD (Organisation for Economic Cooperation and Development) and ICRIER (Indian Council for Research on International Economic Relations) just released report (July 2018) highlights both the notable progress made by the country's agricultural sector over the past two decades and the important challenges now confronting the sector. As per the report, India's agriculture production has been increasing on average at about 3.6 per cent annually since 2011, sustained by improved access to inputs such as fertilisers and seeds, as well as better irrigation and credit coverage. The sector has also been diversifying from grains towards pulses, fruit, vegetables and livestock products, largely driven by evolving demographics, urbanisation and changing demand patterns. India has achieved a significant fall in the proportion of the population that is undernourished, from around 24 per cent in 1990-1992 to 15 per cent in 2014-16. It has also emerged as a major agricultural exporter of several key commodities, currently being the largest exporter of rice globally and the second largest of cotton. But for these past successes to continue into the future, India will need to accelerate existing reform efforts and to launch bold new policy initiatives.

The report also highlights the challenges now confronting the sector: declining but still persistent food insecurity and nutrition deficiencies, large numbers of small and resource poor farms, increasing water scarcity, low productivity growth, and the uncertain impacts of climate change.

According to the report agricultural policies in India are designed and implemented by a complex system of institutions. States have constitutional responsibility for many aspects of agriculture, but the

---

*. This section is drawn from OECD-ICRIER "Agricultural Policy Review of India" (July 2018). *http://icrier.org/pdf/Agriculture-India-OECD-ICRIER.pdf.*

central government plays an important role by developing national approaches to policy and providing the necessary funds for implementation at the state level. Nevertheless, no sufficiently strong mechanism exists to bring state and central level policy makers together to discuss problems, design solutions, and monitor performance.

Over the past several decades, agricultural policies have sought to achieve food security, often interpreted in India as self-sufficiency: seeking to ensure that farmers receive remunerative prices, while at the same time safeguarding the interest of consumers by making food available at affordable prices.

According to the study, farmers in India are impacted by a combination of complex domestic market regulations and by import and export trade restrictions, which together often lead to producer prices that are below comparable international market levels. Despite large subsidies to fertilisers, power, and irrigation, which offset somewhat the price-depressing effect of market interventions, the overall effect is that policy intervention actually reduces gross farm revenues by over 6 per cent per year (2014-16). As per the calculations of this report, the present policies generate a negative producer support estimate overall.

India contrasts with most other countries studied by the OECD because of the prevalence of negative market price support and its size. In the 2000 to 2016 period, producer prices have remained, for many years and for many commodities examined, below comparable reference prices in international markets.

This is partly policy-induced and partly related to other inefficiencies in the marketing chain. Policy-induced inefficiencies are due to minimum support prices being set below international prices for several commodities at different periods between 2000 and 2016, to domestic regulations, and to trade policy measures. Policies that govern the marketing of agricultural commodities in India include the Essential Commodities Act (ECA) and the Agricultural Produce Market Committee Acts (APMCs). Through these Acts, producer prices are affected by regulations influencing pricing, procuring, stocking, and trading commodities. Restrictions stemming from both the ECA and APMC Acts also deter private sector investment in marketing infrastructure. Differences among the states in the status of their respective APMC Acts and in how these Acts are implemented add to the uncertainties in supply chains and drive up transaction costs. Overall, the combination of market regulations and infrastructure deficiencies has had a price depressing effect.

In addition, a variety of trade policy measures applied in 2000-16 – such as export prohibitions, export quotas, export duties, or minimum export prices – have impeded the export of several key commodities and further contributed to depressing producer prices. For example, export restrictions or export bans were applied to wheat, non-basmati rice, chickpeas, sugar and milk at different times over the course of the period studied.

Virtually all of the budgetary transfers to agricultural producers in India are subsidies for variable input use, with overwhelmingly subsidised fertilisers, electricity, and irrigation water. On the other hand, public expenditures financing general services to the sector have declined over the last decades. Most of this expenditure is in development and maintenance of infrastructure (particularly hydrological infrastructure), followed by the cost of public stockholding and expenditure on the agricultural knowledge and innovation system.

On the other hand, the report finds that consumers pay on average 25 per cent less on all commodities as the result of policy interventions. However, in spite of the government's efforts to keep prices low, food insecurity and malnutrition persist, in part because the public food distribution system is poorly targeted, too costly, and subject to large inefficiencies and waste.

The sum of all agriculture and food-related spending (budgetary transfers to producers, to agriculture as a whole, and transfers to consumers from taxpayers), without accounting for the negative market price support, amounts to 1.9 per cent of India's GDP in 2014-16. This shows the high cost to the Indian economy and contrasts with the sector's poor performance in productivity growth, highlighting the need for resources to be applied more effectively.

India's agro-food sector is at a critical juncture, facing multiple challenges and multiple opportunities. The OECD-ICRIER report (2018) suggests a series of reforms which according to the report, if implemented, would help India improve food security for its vast population, advance the quality of life of its millions of smallholders, overcome severe resource and climate pressures, while generating sustainable productivity growth and creating a modern, efficient and resilient agro-food system that can contribute to inclusive growth and jobs throughout the economy. Infact Indian agriculture calls for big bang reforms, remarks Joshi (2019). "We have to modernise the sector, develop agricultural markets, promote exports of agricultural and processed commodities, consolidate small and marginal farmers, and expand the scope and amount of PM-KISAN. It is also an opportune time that a new agricultural policy may be drafted to prepare a medium and long-term roadmap for various reforms in the agriculture sector", (Joshi 2019).

Long-term Policies for Transforming the Agriculture Sector

"The NDA government with its massive mandate should concentrate on long-term policies for transforming the agriculture sector. It should focus on the following five long-term measures to revive agriculture", Mahendra Dev (2019)[15]:

> First, agricultural marketing reforms should be a priority. We should move away from consumer to producer-centric price policy. Agricultural markets have witnessed only limited reforms. They are characterized by inefficient physical operations, excessive crowding of intermediaries and, fragmented market chains. Due to this, farmers are deprived of a fair share of the price paid by the final consumers. We have been talking about APMC reforms for the last two decades. States have not shown any urgency in reforming agricultural markets. The central government including NITI Aayog should work with states in undertaking marketing reforms. There is little progress on e-NAM which is supposed to create a national market. For better price discovery, agriculture has to go beyond farming and develop value chains comprising farming, wholesaling, warehousing, logistics, processing and retailing.
>
> Second, agricultural exports should be promoted with various policies. Banning exports hurt farmers the most. This is one of the reasons for the glut in farm production and low prices. The National Export Policy is formulated in line with the goal of doubling the farmers' incomes and increase agricultural exports from the present $30 billion to over $60 billion by 2022. There is a need for a long-term consistent policy on exports and futures markets. India processes very limited quantities of fruits and vegetables. It should promote food processing in a big way.
>
> The third issue is of low productivity in Indian agriculture. Basics like seeds, fertilizers, credit, land and water management and technology are important. Similarly, investment in infrastructure,

15. Dev, Mahendra (2019). *Budget 2019: Five Long Term Measures to Revive Agriculture* June 14, 2019. *Source*: *Moneycentral.com*

including rural roads is needed. Water management should be given the highest priority. More than 60 percent of irrigation water is consumed by two crops rice and sugarcane. Basically, it is not investment alone but efficiency in water management, both canal and groundwater, that is important. India uses 2-3 times the water used to produce one tonne of grain in countries like Brazil, China and the US. This implies that water use efficiency can be improved significantly with better use of technologies including drip irrigation. Yields of several crops are lower in India as compared to several other countries. Technology can help to reduce the yield gaps and thus improve productivity. Government policies are biased towards cereals and we need to shift from rice, wheat-centric policies to promote millets, pulses, fruits, vegetables, livestock and fish.

Fourth, another major issue relates to the shrinking size of farms which is also responsible for farmers' distress. The average size of farm holdings declined from 2.3 hectares in 1970-71 to 1.08 hectares in 2015-16. The share of small and marginal farmers increased from 70 percent in 1980-81 to 86 percent in 2015-16. In this context, consolidation of land holdings becomes important for raising the incomes of farmers. The late Prof. B.S. Minhas had argued in the 1970s itself that compulsory consolidation of land holdings along with land development activities could enhance incomes in rural areas. Unfortunately, there is little discussion now on land fragmentation and consolidation of farm holdings. The other land policy needed relates to the legalization of land tenure. Organising small farmers in the form of producer organisations is also important.

Fifth, the linkages between agriculture and non-agriculture should be increased. The late Prof. T.N. Srinivasan argued that agricultural policies may be important but the fundamental factor for low productivity lies in non-agriculture. Recent data from NABARD shows that only 23 percent of rural income is from cultivation and livestock. Income from agriculture is not enough for farmers. Thus, we have to walk on both legs i.e. agriculture and non-agriculture for raising farmers' incomes.

To conclude, we need policies for sustainable and climate-smart agriculture, including conservation and zero budget natural farming. Programmes like PM-KISAN may be useful for farmers but long-term measures are required focusing both on supply and demand factors. Agriculture is a state subject and the Centre has to work closely with states in reviving this sector

ANNEXURE TABLE – 12.1

Action Plan for Doubling the Income of Farmers

The Government has set a target of doubling of farmers' income by the year 2022. For the said purpose, the Government had constituted an Inter-Ministerial Committee to examine issues relating to Doubling of Farmers' Income (DFI) and recommend strategies. The Committee has identified seven sources of income growth viz, improvement in crop productivity; improvement in livestock productivity; resource use efficiency or savings in the cost of production; increase in the cropping intensity; diversification towards high value crops; improvement in real prices received by farmers; and shift from farm to non-farm occupations. Several initiatives have already been rolled out on the recommendations of DFI Committee which inter-alia include advocating progressive market reforms through the State Governments, Encouraging contract farming through the State Governments by promulgating of Model Contract Farming Act, Up-gradation of Gramin Haats to work as centers of aggregation and for direct purchase of agricultural commodities from the farmers, e-NAM to provide farmers an electronic online trading platform, Distribution of Soil health Cards to farmers so that the use of fertilizers can be rationalized, Increase water efficiency through Pradhan Mantri Krishi Sinchayee Yojana (PMKSY)-" Per drop more crop", Better insurance coverage to crops for risk mitigation under Pradhan Mantri Fasal Bima Yojana (PMFBY), providing total interest subvention up to 5 per cent (inclusive of 3 per cent prompt repayment incentive) on short-term crop loans up to R3 lakh, thus making loan available to farmers at a reduced rate of 4 per cent per annum and extended the facility of Kisan Credit Card (KCC) for animal husbandry and fisheries related activities as well as Interest Subvention facilities to such categories of farmers.

Giving a major boost for the farmers' income, the Government has approved the increase in the Minimum Support Price (MSPs) for all Kharif & Rabi crops for 2018-19 season at a level of at least one and half times of the cost of production.

Further, with a view to provide social security net for small and marginal farmers as they have minimal or no savings to provide for old age and to support them in the event of consequent loss of livelihood, the Government has decided to implement a new Central Sector Scheme for providing old age pension of R3000/- to the eligible small and marginal farmers, subject to certain exclusion clauses, on attaining the age of 60 years. The scheme aims to cover around 5 crore beneficiaries in the first three years. It would be a voluntary and contributory pension scheme, with entry age of 18 to 40 years. The Government has approved a budgetary provision of R10774.50 crore for the scheme till March 2022. The Government has constituted an Empowered Body on 23.01.2019 for monitoring the implementation of the recommendations of the DFI Strategy.

Source: Ministry of Agriculture & Farmers Welfare.
Govt. of India (2019). *Economic Survey 2018-19, Vol. 2*, chapter 7.

13

Agriculture Price Policy, Food Management and Food Security

Agricultural Price Policy[1]

The government's price policy for agricultural commodities seeks to ensure remunerative prices to the growers for their produce with a view to encouraging higher investment and production, and to safeguard the interests of consumers by making supplies available at reasonable prices. The price policy also seeks to evolve a balanced and integrated price structure in the perspective of the overall needs of the economy. Towards this end, the government announces minimum support prices (MSPs) each season for major agricultural commodities and organises purchase operations through public and cooperative agencies. The designated central nodal agencies intervene in the market to undertake procurement operations with the objective of ensuring that market prices do not fall below the MSPs fixed by the government.

The government decides the support prices for various agricultural commodities after taking into account the recommendations of the Commission for Agricultural Costs and Prices (CACP), the views of state governments and central ministries as well as such other relevant factors as considered important for fixation of support prices.

The objectives of price policy as propounded from time to time are multiple and often conflicting. The price policy was evolved in the context of relative shortage of agricultural products, particularly of food

---

1. Kapila, Uma (2019). "Indian Agriculture: Developments, Issues, Policies and Agenda for Reforms", in Uma Kapila (ed.), *Indian Economy since Independence* (30th edition). New Delhi: Academic Foundation, ch. 18.

grains. Thus, we had the overriding objectives of the price policy as achieving self-sufficiency in food grains (understood as the availability of adequate food grains from domestic production) and protection of consumer from scarcity-induced speculative price rise. As V.S. Vyas points out, "The main function of prices, i.e., to act as signals for allocation of resources has been made subservient to income parity and food security objectives."

Apart from the consideration of income transfers, the policy is also directed to increase agricultural production by offering higher 'incentive' prices. A discriminatory price policy can be used to encourage inter-crop shifts in resource use. However, when it comes to aggregate agricultural output, greater reliance has to be placed on 'non-price' factors, e.g., generating and extending more efficient technologies. The available studies clearly bring out that aggregate supply response of agriculture is very weak. Thus, any attempt to use high prices to encourage agricultural production can bring in its wake irreparable distortions in the price structure.

These limitations of price policy are not very often recognised as also, the strength of price policy in affecting desirable shift in cropping pattern fully exploited. As Vyas remarks,

> In a mixed economy like ours an important objective of the price policy could be to give directions to the cropping pattern not only on the basis of the existing demand supply situation but also to take into account a qualitatively superior crop mix, e.g., to provide a price advantage to nutritionally superior crops or to the crops where the country may have comparative advantage. In fact, in this respect we seem to be regressing. In the 1970s price policy was used as an effective tool to encourage production of crops where superior technology was available (Vyas, 1989).

In recent years, we have largely neglected this aspect of price policy.

Further, there has been no clarity on the priority to be assigned among these numerous objectives, or the trade-off involved in pursuing these objectives simultaneously. If we are to go by the public pronouncements, the objectives sought to be achieved by the price policy include ensuring: (i) reasonable prices for the growers, (ii) reasonable prices for the grains released from public distribution system (PDS) and (iii) reasonable prices in the open market. A moment's reflection will show that in most of the circumstances, these aims conflict with each other. The price policy cannot resolve all conflicts in the society.

It must be recognised that price policy taken by itself is a weak instrument in giving directions to agricultural economy, more so as an instrument of income transfer. While the objective of providing an insurance cover in terms of guaranteed minimum prices to a large section of agricultural producers could be a worthy objective, but until and unless required resources are available and administrative machinery is in place, mere announcement of minimum prices for a large number of commodities may not serve any purpose. It may, in fact, do more harm with an erosion of the credibility of the government. In view of this, it is suggested that the support prices should be applicable only for a limited number of crops. Crops which can be considered as price leaders or the crops for which technological breakthrough is imminent ought to be covered under the price guarantees. The other crops to be considered for support are the crops grown under high-risk environment and there also it should be a transient measure i.e., till a viable crop insurance programme is evolved.

Along with limiting the scope for price policy is the need for a discriminatory and flexible approach to price interventions. By covering a large number of commodities on the one hand and by ensuring minimum prices in the guise of procurement prices on the other, not only government's commitment has enhanced to an unmanageable extent, it has also led to serious distortions in agricultural economy.

V.S. Vyas remarks,

> The time has come to take a serious look at the scope, instruments and institutions of agricultural price policy. There is a need to recognise that the price policy is a weak instrument for income transfers; our capacity to offer minimum support prices for a large number of commodities is limited; need for dovetailing agriculture and trade policies is urgent. Instrument of minimum support prices has to be used sparingly; procurement operations need to be made more business like; CACP should retain its expert character rather than trying to be representative of various interests, FCI should be decentralised and debureaucratised and the states should be made major stakeholders.

MSPs for food grains and other major commodities are recommended by the CACP, but are actually set by a committee chaired by the Prime Minister. CACP recommendations are based on several factors, but key factors are assessments of costs of production (CoP) and domestic and global market conditions. Historically, the MSPs for wheat and rice were generally increased at rates below inflation, and remained well under import parity prices. Although intended to be a national programme covering all major crops, the MSPs are generally defended by Government of India (GoI) purchases only for wheat and rice in the major surplus areas of Punjab, Haryana, western Uttar Pradesh and Andhra Pradesh (rice only) (Landes and Gulati, 2004).[2]

Beginning in the late-1990s, the MSPs set for wheat and rice became increasingly out of step with domestic market conditions. One key factor was (and still is) that the CoP concept used in setting the price became a 'full cost' measure that, in addition to variable input costs, included the rental value of land, the imputed value of family labour and a return to management. Another was pressure to compensate farmers for the price swings associated with changes in India's rice and wheat export policy during 1995 and 1996. For rice, higher market prices resulting from the initial removal of export restraints later created pressure for higher MSPs when world prices fell. Similarly for wheat, lower market prices following the re-imposition export restraints led the government to compensate farmers with higher MSPs. With these developments, the MSPs became disconnected from domestic market conditions and—when world prices fell from a temporary spike in 1996-1997—from competitive world market prices. The tendency for MSPs to be increased has likely been compounded as MSP benefits boost land rental, labour and management costs, thus leading to higher CoP.

An important factor affecting MSP policy in the 1990s concerns the changing political dimensions of the policy when India entered an era of coalition governments and the farm lobby became more influential. During 1995-96 to 2001-02, just before and during the accumulation of surpluses, the government set MSPs above the CACP recommendation in four out of seven years for rice and five out of seven years for wheat (Parikh *et al.,* 2002). Another key dimension is that the MSP mechanism is one of the few levers available to Indian policy makers and there is a tendency to try to use it to achieve multiple policy goals, including both price stabilisation and income support.

The failure of price policy to successfully adapt to the new environment has had a number of impacts. First, breaking with the historical pattern, domestic wheat and rice prices have tended to strengthen relative to both world and domestic prices, and to move above domestic market clearing levels. While benefiting the relatively few producers receiving wheat and rice MSPs, higher consumer prices have undoubtedly had negative impacts. Per capita wheat and rice

2. Landes, Rip and Ashok Gulati (2008). "Farm Sector Performance and the Reform Agenda", in K.L. Krishna and Uma Kapila (eds.) (2008), *Readings in Indian Agriculture and Industry*. New Delhi: Academic Foundation.

consumption has actually declined in recent years, as higher procurement and prices contributed to decline in consumption of open market supplies that have not been offset by subsidised distribution. A recent study of the economy-wide impacts of increasing the wheat and rice MSPs when they are above market clearing levels found that reduced consumption and investment associated with higher prices actually reduced incomes, both in aggregate and for most rural and urban income groups (Parikh *et al.*, 2002).

Second, by maintaining high prices, the government has become responsible for the storage and transport of most of the marketed surplus of fair-to-average quality (FAQ)-grade wheat and rice in the country—what some observers have termed a '*de facto* nationalisation' of grain trade. In addition to raising budgetary costs, the policy provides little incentive for private investment in grain storage, handling or distribution, with the exception of the fees traders can earn in the export of subsidised grain allocated by the government.

Third, by focusing on supporting relatively high prices only for wheat and rice in a few regions, MSP policy has not been made an effective tool for stabilising producer prices for other crops and supporting the diversification of agriculture.

Fourth, the budgetary cost of FCI operations under current policies has now reached about $5.5 billion. When policies support domestic prices above market clearing, much of this subsidy accrues to producers rather than consumers. Combined with the cost of subsidies on fertiliser and other inputs, the subsidy bill has burgeoned to about ₹ 43,668 crore annually, far exceeding both public and private capital formation in agriculture. Subsidy outlays are crowding out new investment needed to boost productivity and marketing efficiency.

Finally, the policy of maintaining high wheat and rice prices has contributed to emergent environmental problems, particularly associated with the intensive wheat-rice cropping system in northern India. When combined with the low cost of irrigation water—much of which is either free, stolen or subsidised—the strong price incentives for wheat and rice are contributing to the rapid deterioration of groundwater resources, and rising concern with deteriorating soil fertility in some areas.

In more recent period since 2008, two issues have been the subject of much debate: the unprecedented increase in global prices of agri-commodities and how Indian policy makers can make sure that their people do not suffer. Several factors—ranging from energy prices, diversion of grains and oils for bio-fuels, supply shocks from Australia and the European Union (EU), growing demand from Asia and Africa, export controls by certain countries (including India), and speculative funds in commodity markets—are supposed to be pushing global agricultural prices (Abbott *et al.,* 2008; ADB, 2008; Chand, 2008; FAO, 2007; OECD-FAO, 2008; Rosegrant, 2008; Von Braun *et al.,* 2008). Most of these studies paint a gloomy picture with respect to global prices. They suggest that the era of low agricultural prices is over, and that they are likely to remain high in the next 5-10 years. However, all these studies, despite their sincere efforts, remain weak on diagnostics, especially in terms of nailing down the relative importance of various factors that have driven the prices so high in 2008. Policy makers need to avoid knee jerk reactions as India's buffer stocks are comfortable and Indian food price inflation, though high, is way below the global food price inflation. However, in the long run, investments in agricultural research and development (R&D), infrastructure, and markets have to be increased in order to augment food supplies as also to accelerate the rates of growth in Indian agriculture (Gulati, 2010).

It must be recognised that price policy taken by itself is a weak instrument in giving directions to agricultural economy, more so as an instrument of income transfer. While the objective of providing an insurance cover in terms of guaranteed minimum prices to a large section of agricultural producers could be a worthy objective but until and unless required resources are available and administrative machinery is in place, mere announcement of minimum prices for a large number of commodities may not serve any purpose. It may, in fact, do more harm with an erosion of the credibility of the government. In view of this, it is suggested that the support prices should be applicable only for a limited number of crops. Crops which can be considered as price leaders or the crops, for which technological break through is imminent ought to be covered under the price guaranties. The other crops to be considered for support are the crops grown under high-risk environment and there also it should be a transient measure i.e., till a viable crop insurance programme is evolved.

Food Security and Food Management in India

Food security exists when all people, at all times, have physical and economic access to sufficient, safe and nutritious food that meets their dietary needs and food preferences to ensure an active and healthy life (FAO, 2018). The timely availability and affordability of food are critical for a developing country like India.

TABLE – 13.1

India's Food Security Score, 2018

Category	*India (Score)*	*Score of All Countries (average)*	*India's Rank out of 113 Countries*
OVERALL	**50.1**	**58.4**	**76**
1) Affordability	46.4	56.3	73
2) Availability	54.1	60.3	70
3) Quality and Safety	48.2	58.2	79
1) AFFORDABILITY			
1.1) Food consumption as a share of household expenditure	53.5	55.6	61
1.2) Proportion of population under global poverty line	66.0	80.9	87
1.3) Gross domestic product per capita (US$ PPP)	5.0	16.7	73
1.4) Agricultural import tariffs	46.4	75.4	108
1.5) Presence of food safety net programmes	50.0	65.5	66
1.6) Access to financing for farmers	75.0	62.6	43
2) AVAILABILITY			
2.1) Sufficiency of supply	27.4	56.8	100
2.2) Public expenditure on agricultural R&D*	0.0	15.6	62
2.3) Agricultural infrastructure	41.7	58.7	78
2.4) Volatility of agricultural production	93.5	86.4	39
2.5) Political stability risk	70.6	46.8	18
2.6) Corruption	25.0	37.6	49
2.7) Urban absorption capacity	94.8	76.9	3
2.8) Food loss	86.4	84.9	70
3) QUALITY AND SAFETY			
3.1) Diet diversification	39.7	56.0	81
3.2) Nutritional standards	100.0	80.1	1
3.3) Micronutrient availability	26.5	43.9	98
3.4) Protein quality**	18.5	47.2	98
3.5) Food safety	91.3	80.3	70

Note: * It is a measure of govt spending on R&D taken as a per cent of GDP. Taken from OECD and Agricultural Science & Technology Indicators.

** measures the amount of high-quality protein in the average national diet.

Source: Global Food Security Index, 2018, Economic Intelligence Unit, The Economist. *Economic Survey 2018-19, Vol. 2.*

The Global Food Security Index (GFSI), 2018 considered four core issues of food security across 113 countries: (i) affordability, (ii) availability, (iii) quality & safety and (iv) natural resources and resilience. The GFSI ranks countries on a score of 0-100 based on the first three categories while natural resources and resilience is used as an adjustment factor. A rank of 100 is considered most favourable. GFSI's major goal is to assess in a timely manner which countries are most and least vulnerable to food insecurity (Table 13.1).

India's food security challenges lie in the areas of low GDP per capita, sufficiency of supply, public expenditure on R&D and protein quality (Table 13.1). India ranks No.1 in Nutritional standards. India's overall Food Security Score is 50.1 out of 100 which ranks India 76 out of 113 countries. This reflects the need for India to further improve the management of food supply in various aspects.

MSP and Foodgrains Procurement

The main objectives of food management are procurement of food grains from farmers at remunerative prices, distribution of food grains to consumers, particularly the vulnerable sections of society, at affordable prices, and maintenance of food buffers for food security and price stability. The instruments used are MSP and CIP. The nodal agency for procurement, distribution, and storage of food grains is the FCI. Procurement at MSP is open-ended, while distribution is governed by the scale of allocation and its offtake by beneficiaries. The offtake of food grains is primarily under the targeted public distribution system (TPDS) and other welfare schemes of the GoI.

The principal policy objective of food management is to ensure food security, particularly for the vulnerable, through timely and efficient procurement and distribution of foodgrains. This involves procurement of foodgrains from farmers at remunerative prices, building up and maintenance of buffer stocks, storage, movement, and distribution of foodgrains to consumers at affordable prices and stability of foodgrain prices. The price instruments used are MSP and CIP (central issue price).

Thus, food management in India has three basic objectives: procurement of food grains from farmers at remunerative prices, distribution of food grains to the consumers particularly the vulnerable sections of the society at affordable prices, and maintenance of food buffers for food security and price stability. The instruments for food management are the minimum support price (MSP) and central issue price (CIP). The focus is on incentivising farmers by ensuring fair value for their produce through the MSP mechanism, distribution of food grains at subsidised rates to 6.52 crore BPL families, covering all households at the risk of hunger under Antyodaya Anna Yojana (AAY), establishing grain banks in chronically food-scarce areas and strengthening the PDS. The nodal agency which undertakes the procurement and distribution and storage of food grains is the Food Corporation of India (FCI). The procurement under the current system is open-ended at MSP, while the distribution is governed by the scale of allocation and its offtake by the beneficiaries. Rice and wheat are predominant cereals in procurement of food grains.

The Central Government takes several steps to prudently manage foodgrain stock, to ensure adequate availability of wheat and rice in the Central pool, to keep a check on the open market prices, to augment the domestic availability of wheat and rice, and to ensure food security. The Government specifically undertakes the following measures[3]:

(i) Announcing Minimum Support Prices and Central Issue Price

(ii) Undertake procurement of food grains through FCI and decentralised procurement by State Agencies

(iii) Maintain buffer stocks; and

(iv) Open market sale of wheat and rice to check inflation.

The Minimum Support Price (MSP) is announced for 22 crops before the sowing season. The objective is to give guaranteed prices and assured market to the farmers and protect them from price fluctuations. In 2018-19, the government raised the MSP of both kharif and rabi crops to ensure a return of at least 50 per cent above the cost of production to enhance farmers' income. An increase in MSP leads to increase in production, but only about one-third of the total production of foodgrains are procured. The rest of the foodgrains are sold in the open market (Table 13.2).

In States like Punjab, Haryana, Chhattisgarh, Uttar Pradesh, Madhya Pradesh etc. where MSP procurement is well established, there arise problems in storage of foodgrains. The procurement from these States exceeds the buffer stock norms fixed by the Government in 2015 (Table 13.2). While the offtake of food grains from the Central Pool for TPDS and other welfare schemes varies between 53-58 million tonnes, the stock of food grains in the Central Pool continues to be in excess of the prescribed buffer stock norms. As on 1st July, 2018, the Central stock was 65 million tonnes against the norm of 41 million

3. Government of India (2019). *Economic Survey 2018-19*, vol.2, ch. 7.

tonnes. The government tries to liquidate excess stocks through open market sale to bulk buyers above the reserve price, which equals the MSP plus the procurement cost. Bulk buyers prefer wheat over rice and in 2018-19 about nine million tonnes was sold in the open market of which 8.2 million tonnes was wheat. Exports of food grains by FCI at prices lower than the reserve price would effectively imply an export subsidy. Moreover, this would expose India to disputes in the multilateral trade framework. Exports of food grains by FCI either as aid or commercial sale has been less than 1 million tonnes.

TABLE – 13.2

Foodgrains Production, Procurement & Offtake (In million tonnes)

Years	*Foodgrains Production minus pulses*	*Foodgrains Procurement*	*Procurement (% share in Production)*	*Offtake (TPDS + Welfare schemes*	*Balance stock as of 1st July*
2015-16	235.22	64.91	27.6	53.73	54.72
2016-17	251.98	61.14	24.3	56.45	49.85
2017-18	259.60	69.10	26.6	57.85	53.48
2018-19	257.36	75.28	29.3	56.40	65.14

Source: Foodgrain Bulletin, DFPD.
Economic Survey 2018-19, vol.2.

TABLE – 13.3

Foodgrains Stocking Norms for Central Pool from January, 2015 (in million tonnes)

Date	Rice			Wheat			
	Operational stocks	*Strategic Reserve*	*Total*	*Operational stocks*	*Strategic Reserve*	*Total*	*Total Food grains*
1st April	11.58	2.00	13.58	4.46	3.00	7.46	21.04
1st July	11.54	2.00	13.54	24.58	3.00	27.58	41.12
1st October	8.25	2.00	10.25	17.52	3.00	20.52	30.77
1st January	5.61	2.00	7.61	10.8	3.00	13.80	21.41

Source: Department of Food and Public Distribution.
Economic Survey 2018-19, vol.2.

According to an Evaluation Study on Minimum Support Price conducted by Development Monitoring & Evaluation Office (DMEO), NITI Aayog (January 2016), in majority of the sample states, farmers are unaware of the MSP announcement before the sowing season. In Eastern India, in States such as Assam, West Bengal, the poor impact of the scheme could be judged from the fact that none of the selected farmers were even aware of the existence of such a scheme. In certain cases, though aware of the MSP, the absence of procurement centres in the villages, transportation costs, reluctance of mill owners to buy small quantities from the farmers remain stumbling blocks.

Public Distribution System (PDS)

The PDS has attracted considerable debate in recent years on the ground that the benefits of PDS are not reaching the poor on account of, *inter alia*, poor targeting and leakages in the system, despite its restructuring in 1997. It has also been argued that despite the huge food subsidy and the large-scale intervention, the food security of many households is still marginal or insufficient. In recent years, there has been a substantial rise in procurement of food grains (Table 13.4) by the public sector agencies on account of consistent increases in MSP, despite the recommendations of the CACP to freeze the same. It is argued that consistent increases in the MSP have distorted relative prices between alternate agricultural activities, land use patterns as well as the consumption of inputs.

Procurement higher than the offtake had resulted in a build-up of excessive stocks of food grains.

The percentage distribution of the economic cost of wheat and rice is given in Table 13.5. The pooled cost of grain (MSP and bonus) accounts for two-thirds of the economic cost of wheat and rice. The economic cost of foodgrains to the Food Corporation of India (FCI) has been increasing over the years. As the cost of production of crops is rising on account of labour costs, costs of inputs like fertilizers and commensurately the MSPs are also increasing. The increase in the food subsidy bill is determined by the rate at which the MSPs for wheat and rice increase and the economic cost of handling grains (their procurement, stocking and distribution to the targeted households).

TABLE – 13.4

Procurement, Offtake, Stocks and Food Subsidy

Year	*Procurement (million tonnes)*	*Offtake (million tonnes)*	*Stocks (million tonnes)*	*Food Subsidy (₹ crore)*
1	*2*	*3*	*4*	*5*
1993-94	26.40	18.61	20.54	5537
1994-95	24.99	19.44	26.80	5100
1995-96	22.24	24.35	20.82	5377
1996-97	20.03	25.63	16.41	6066
1997-98	23.82	18.96	18.12	7500
1998-99	24.22	20.73	21.82	8700
1999-2000	31.43	23.05	28.91	9200
2000-01	35.43	17.95	44.98	12010
2001-02	41.91	16.15	59.14	17494
2002-03	35.46	45.60	—	24176
2003-04	38.7	49.3	20.7	25160
2004-05	41.5	41.5	18.0 (Jan.)	25800
2005-06	42.4	42.3 (Jan.)	16.6	23071.00
2006-07	34.3	36.8	17.9	23827.59 (Jan. 2007)
2007-08	39.9	37.4	19.8	31259.68 (Jan. 2008)
2008-09	56.8	39.5	35.6	43668.08 (Jan. 2009)
2009-10	57.4	49.7	43.3	58242.45
2010-11	56.7	53.0	44.3	62929.56
2011-12	63.4	56.3	53.4	72370.90 (Jan. 2012)
2012-13	72.2	65.8	59.8	84554.00
2013-14	56.9	59.8	48.4	89740.02
2014-15	60.2	55.9	41.0	113171.16
2015-16	50.0*	43.6#	49.8@	105509.41^
2017-18**				134988.83

Note: * Procurement as on 18 January 2016; # Offtake up to November, 2015; @ Stock as on 1 January 2016 and stock for the previous years are as on 1 April; ^ Figures as on 6 January 2016; ** as on 28.11.2017.

Source: Various *Economic Survey 2003-04, 2013-14, 2014-15, 2015-16, 2017-18.*

TABLE – 13.5

Percentage Distribution of Economic Cost of Rice and Wheat

Year	*2010-11*	*2011-12*	*2012-13*	*2013-14*	*2014-15 (UA)*	*2015-16 (RE)*	*2015-16 (BE)*
Rice							
Pooled cost of grain	72.9	71.2	70.9	66.6	64.2	63.5	62.7
Procurement incidentals	15.8	16.5	16.6	15.0	16.9	16.4	16.3
Distribution cost	11.3	12.3	12.5	18.4	18.9	20.1	21.0
Economic cost (Total Cost)	100.0	100.0	100.0	100.0	100.0	100.0	100.0
Wheat							
Pooled cost of grain	71.2	7.5	69.6	67.4	62.9	66.8	65.5
Procurement incidentals	14.2	14.8	15.0	17.7	20.2	15.9	16.6
Distribution cost	14.6	15.1	15.4	14.9	16.9	17.2	17.9
Economic cost (Total Cost)	100.0	100.0	100.0	100.0	100.0	100.0	100.0

Note: UA: Unaudited; RE: Revised Estimates; BE: Budget Estimates.

Source: *Economic Survey 2015-16.*

Food Subsidy

Food subsidy comprises two main components. The first component includes subsidy provided to the Food Corporation of India (FCI) for procurement and distribution of wheat and rice under the National Food Security Act (NFSA), 2013 and other welfare schemes and for maintaining the buffer stock of food grains as a measure of food security. The second component comprises subsidy provided to States undertaking decentralized procurement. The acquisition and distribution costs of procuring food grains for the central pool constitute the economic cost. The difference between the per quintal economic cost and the per quintal Central Issue Price (CIP) gives the quantum of per quintal consumer subsidy.

The economic cost of wheat for FCI operations has increased from ₹1908.32 per quintal in 2013-14 to ₹2435.23 per quintal in 2018-19. Similarly, the economic cost of rice has increased from ₹2615.51 per quintal in 2013-14 to ₹3472.94 per quintal in 2018-19. However, the CIP of wheat and rice for NFSA beneficiaries has not been revised from

₹200 per quintal in case of wheat and ₹300 per quintal in case of rice. These rates were fixed under the National Food Security Act, 2013 initially for a period of three years from the date of commencement of the Act (July 13, 2013). Thereafter, they were to be fixed by the Central Government from time to time, while not exceeding the minimum support price (*Economic Survey 2018-19, vol.2*).

In order to ensure food security to the vulnerable sections, Government continues with the subsidized pricing under NFSA. This has resulted in widening of the gap between the economic cost and CIP and the per quintal food subsidy incurred by the Government has risen substantially over the years. The subsidized CIPs of ₹3/2/1 per kg for rice, wheat and coarse grains respectively under NFSA were earlier applicable only to the Antyodaya Anna Yojana Families (which constitute about 2.5 crore poorest of the poor households) under the Targeted Public Distribution System (TPDS). The BPL/APL categories were required to pay higher CIPs.

The NFSA provides a wider coverage than the erstwhile TPDS. It also made the Antyodaya CIPs uniformly applicable to all NFSA beneficiaries. APL/BPL categorization was done away with under NFSA. The wider coverage provided under the Act together with lower CIPs have obvious implications for the food subsidy bill.

TABLE – 13.6

Growth of Food Subsidy in India (other than sugar)

Year	*Food Subsidy (₹ crore)*	*Annual Growth (%)*	*Year*	*Food Subsidy (₹ crore)*	*Annual Growth (%)*
2000-01	12,010.00	30.54	2008-09	43,668.08	39.69
2001-02	17,494.00	45.66	2009-10	58,242.45	33.38
2002-03	24,176.45	38.20	2010-11	63,844.00	9.20
2003-04	25,160.00	4.07	2011-12	72,822.00	14.10
2004-05	25,746.45	2.33	2012-13	84554.00	16.83
2005-06	23,071.00	-10.39	2013-14	89740.02	6.13
2006-07	23,827.59	3.28	2014-15	113171.16	20.15
2007-08	31,259.68	31.19	2015-16	105509.41*	–

Note: * Figures as on January 2016.

Source : *Economic Survery 2009-10, 2012-13, 2014-15*, 2015-16.
Economic & Political Weekly (EPW), 8 June 2013, p.127.

PDS costs are high and increasing with leakages, high administrative costs, corruption and mismanagement. The costs including opportunity costs of resources diverted for subsidy are high in terms of the public investments in agriculture which are foregone and which can improve productivity. Additionally, subsidies bring distortions in the market and also pose a heavy burden on the government budget, especially during times when domestic or international prices are on the rise, when the Government has to resort to raising the MSPs of crops on a regular basis.

TABLE – 13.7

MSP and Issue Price for Wheat and Rice under TPDS

Marketing Season	*Minimum Support Price (MSP)*		*Central Issue Price (CIP)*					
			Wheat			*Rice*		
	Wheat	*Paddy*	*APL*	*BPL*	*AAY*	*APL*	*BPL*	*AAY*
2002-03	620[a]	530[a]	610	415	200	830	565	300
2003-04	630	550	610	415	200	830	565	300
2004-05	640	560	610	415	200	830	565	300
2005-06	650[b]	570	610	415	200	830	565	300
2006-07	750[d]	580[c]	610	415	200	830	565	300
2007-08	1,000	645[e]	610	415	200	830	565	300
2008-09	1,080	850[f]	610	415	200	830	565	300
2009-10	1,100	1000[g]	610	415	200	830	565	300
2010-11	1,170	1000[g]	610	415	200	830	565	300
2011-12	1285	1080	610	415	200	830	565	300
2012-13	1350	1250	610	415	200	830	565	300
2013-14	1400	1310	610	415	200	830	565	300
2014-15	1450	1360	610	415	200	830	565	300
2015-16	1525	1410	610	415	200	830	565	300

Notes:
a One-time special drought relief of ₹ 20 per quintal was given in the case of paddy over and above the existing MSP and ₹10 per quintal for wheat.
b An incentive bonus of ₹ 50 per quintal over the MSP given for wheat procured in RMS 2006-07 during the period 20 March 2006 to 30 June 2006.
c An incentive bonus of ₹ 40 per quintal over the MSP allowed for paddy procured in KMS 2006-07 till 31 March 2007. Applicability of bonus was extended up to 30 September 2007 for the states of Andhra Pradesh, Tamil Nadu, Orissa, West Bengal and Chhattisgarh. For Bihar and Kerala, it was extended up to 31 May 2007.
d An incentive bonus of ₹ 100 per quintal over the MSP given for wheat procured in RMS 2007-08.
e An incentive bonus of ₹ 100 per quintal over the MSP allowed for paddy/rice procured in the entire KMS 2007-08.
f An incentive bonus of ₹ 50 per quintal allowed over the MSP of paddy for KMS 2008-09.
g An incentive bonus of ₹ 50 per quintal allowed over the MSP of paddy for KMS 2009-10.
APL: above poverty line; BPL: below poverty line; AAY: Antyodaya Anna Yojana.

Source: *Economic Survey,* various issues including 2012-13, 2013-14, 2015-16.
EPW Vol XLVII(23). 8 June 2013.

Food subsidy being the difference between the economic cost of wheat and rice and their issue prices for different groups of beneficiaries is linked to the increase in the economic cost and the issue prices. While the economic cost of wheat and rice has gone up due to an increase in MSP, the issue price has been kept unchanged since 1 July 2002 (Table 13.7).

The government also spends around 35 per cent more beyond the MSP in the form of incidental and distribution costs. These incremental costs are direct cost. There may be indirect cost also. So for these obvious reasons, total food subsidy (for all crops) has gone up from ₹ 25,746 crore in 2004-05 to around ₹ 85,000 in 2012-13 and ₹ 1,13,171 crore in 2014-15.

Buffer Stock

The buffer norms for foodgrains in the central pool which were in existence since April 2005 have been revised in the backdrop of increased off-take of foodgrains under the TPDS in the last few years and with the coming into force of the NFSA with effect from 5 July 2013.The revised buffer norms are shown in Table 13.8.

TABLE – 13.8

Revision in Buffer Stock Norms

(in million tonnes)

As on	*Existing since April 2005*	*Revised*
1 April	21.2	21.04
1 July	31.9	41.12
1 October	21.2	30.77
1 January	25.0	21.41

Source: *Economic Survey 2014-15*.

As against the buffer stock norm of 21.41 million tonnes of rice and wheat (as on 1January of each year), total central pool stocks were 49.8 million tonnes as on 1 January 2016. Considering that the economic cost to the FCI for acquiring, storing, and distributing foodgrains is about 40-50 per cent more than the procurement price, the locked in extra stocks, particularly for the last five years in a row, reflect flaws in the food policy. This has also resulted in high cereal inflation despite bumper produce and overflowing stocks.

High economic cost necessitated a detailed review of the open-ended procurement policy, especially in states that offer high bonus on top of MSP and those that impose high taxes and statutory levies, as well as stocking and distribution policies. In this regard, the government set up a High Level Committee (HLC) in August 2014 under the chairmanship of Shri Shanta Kumar to suggest inter-alia restructuring or unbundling of the FCI with a view to improving its operational efficiency and financial management. The gist of its main recommendations is given in Box 13.1.

BOX – 13.1

Recommendations of High Level Committee on restructuring FCI

On procurement related issues:

- The FCI should hand over all procurement operations of wheat, paddy, and rice to states that have gained sufficient experience in this regard and have created reasonable infrastructure for procurement. The FCI will accept only the surplus (after deducting the needs of the states under the NFSA) from these state governments (not millers) to be moved to deficit states. The FCI should move on helping those states where farmers suffer from distress sales at prices much below MSP, and which are dominated by small holdings.
- Centre should make it clear to states that in case of any bonus being given by them on top of MSP, it will not accept grains under the central pool beyond the quantity needed by the state for its own PDS and OWS.
- The statutory levies including commissions need to be brought down uniformly to 3 per cent, or at most 4 per cent of MSP, and this should be included in the MSP itself (states losing revenue due to this rationalization of levies can be compensated through a diversification package for the next three-five years);
- The Government of India must provide better price support operations for pulses and oilseeds and dovetail their MSP policy with trade policy so that their landed costs are not below their MSP.
- Cash transfers in PDS should be gradually introduced, starting with large cities with more than 1 million population; extending it to grain surplus states; and then giving deficit states for the option of cash or physical grain distribution.

contd. ...

...contd. ...

On PDS- and NFSA-related issues:

- Given that leakages in the PDS range from 40 to 50 per cent, the GoI should defer implementation of the NFSA in states that have not done end to end computerization; have not put the list of beneficiaries online for anyone to verify; and have not set up vigilance committees to check pilferage from PDS.
- Coverage of population should be brought down to around 40 percent.
- BPL families and some even above that they be given 7kg/person.
- On central issue prices, while Antyodya households can be given grains at ₹ 3/2/1/kg for the time being, but pricing for priority households must be linked to MSP.

On stocking and movement related issues:

- FCI should outsource its stocking operations to various agencies.
- Covered and plinth (CAP) storage should be gradually phased out with no grain stocks remaining in CAP for more than 3 months.
- Silo bag technology and conventional storages wherever possible should replace CAP.

On Buffer Stocking Operations and Liquidation Policy:

- DFPD/FCI have to work in tandem to liquidate stocks in OMSS or in export markets, whenever stocks go beyond the buffer stock norms. A transparent liquidation policy is the need of hour, which should automatically kick-in when FCI is faced with surplus stocks than buffer norms.
- Greater flexibility to FCI with business orientation to operate in OMSS and export markets is needed.

  On direct subsidy to farmers: Farmers be given direct cash subsidy (of about ₹ 7000/ha) and fertilizer sector can then be deregulated.

On end to end computerization:

- The HLC recommends total end-to-end computerization of the entire food management system, starting from procurement from farmers, to stocking, movement, and finally distribution through the TPDS.

contd. ...

...contd. ...

On the new face of the FCI:

- The new face of the FCI will be akin to an agency for innovations in the food management system with the primary focus of creating competition in every segment of the foodgrain supply chain, from procurement to stocking to movement and finally distribution under the TPDS, so that overall costs of the system are substantially reduced and leakages plugged and it serves a larger number of farmers and consumers.

India's food security system is one of the largest in the world but is confined almost entirely to provisioning cereals. This system comprises the FCI which implements the MSP for cereals, holds buffer stocks, and delivers grain to a PDS with a network of about 400,000 FPS. Since its inception after the food shortages of the mid-1960s, this system has managed to help the country avoid famine, contain food price variability to much less than in world markets and offered enough price support for farmers to nearly triple cereals production. Quite apart from PDS entitlement, this delivered an almost steady decline in real market prices of cereals and rising per capita availability.

BOX – 13.2

National Food Security Act, 2013

The NFSA was notified on 10 September 2013, with the objective of providing food and nutritional security, by ensuring access to adequate quantity of quality food at affordable prices. It provides for coverage of up to 75 per cent of the rural population and up to 50 per cent of the urban population. It stipulates an entitlement of 5 kg of food grains per person per month for priority households and 35 kg per household per month for Antyodaya Anna Yojana (AAY) households at subsidized prices of ₹ 3 per kg of rice, ₹ 2 per kg of wheat, and ₹ 1 per kg of coarse grains. The states/UTs are to complete identification of eligible households under the NFSA by July 2014. So far 11 states, Rajasthan, Haryana, Himachal Pradesh, Bihar, Chhattisgarh, Karnataka, Madhya Pradesh, Maharashtra, Punjab, Chandigarh, and the NCT of Delhi, have implemented the NFSA and revised monthly TPDS allocations of food grains have been made to these states/UTs. The remaining states/UTs have been given allocation under the TPDS as per earlier norms.

The Act also has special focus on nutritional support to women and children. Pregnant women and lactating mothers during pregnancy and

contd. ...

...contd. ...

six months after the childbirth will also be entitled to maternity benefit of not less than ₹ 6000. Children up to 14 years of age will be entitled to nutritious meals or take-home rations as per prescribed nutritional standards. In case of non-supply of entitled food grains or meals, the beneficiaries will receive a food security allowance. The Act also contains provisions for setting up of grievance redressal mechanisms at district and state levels. Separate provisions have been made in the Act for ensuring transparency and accountability. The Act also contains measures for reforms in the TPDS, to be undertaken progressively by central and state governments. These reforms, inter alia, include doorstep delivery of food grains to TPDS outlets, application of information and communication technology tools, and diversification of commodities distributed under the PDS over a period of time. Based on the provisions of the Act, the foodgrain requirement for the TPDS and other schemes is estimated at 614.3 lakh tonnes. The average annual procurement of wheat and rice has been 617.8 lakh tonnes during 2008-09 to 2012-13, i.e. 33.2 per cent of average annual production. The estimated annual food subsidy for implementation of the Act at 2014-15 costs is about ₹ 1,31,066 crore.

Source: DFPD and *Economic Survey 2013-14*.

Conclusion

Currently, India is in an anomalous situation of being largely self-sufficient with large stocks of food grains on the one hand and registering high food inflation on the other, which is largely due to the government becoming the single largest buyer. In this scenario of bumper production and stocks, a paradigm shift in the role of the government in all aspects of foodgrain production and distribution is necessary.

With the FCI suffering from diseconomies of scale, adoption of the Direct Cash Programme (DCP) needs to be expanded to all states. This would save transport costs, transit losses and other leakages, and simultaneously increase food availability, reduce food prices in the open market, and ultimately reduce the food subsidy. The continued emphasis on procurement and distribution of rice and wheat is contrary to the ground reality that shows changing preference functions of consumers. A shift to a direct cash transfer system or food stamps would anchor our food policy to the requirements of the people and would additionally reduce the fiscal deficit.

Another critical issue is supply chain management in agricultural marketing in India. Farmers' access to markets is hampered by poor roads, rudimentary market infrastructure and excessive regulation. Many agricultural crops are perishable in nature, and post-harvest handling issues and marketing problems affect the farm incomes. It is necessary that we evolve mechanisms for linking wholesale processing, logistics and retailing with farm-production activities so as to generate enhanced efficiency, better farm prices, etc. The private sector should be allowed to operate in developing these market linkages for which suitable reforms will help. Recently the government allowed foreign direct investment (FDI) in retail, which has been supported by many farmer organisations as well, and it can pave the way for investment in new technology and marketing of agricultural produce in India.

There has been substantial increase in the MSPs of various crops over the last few years. Although considered necessary for incentivising farmers, the MSP signals the floor price for the produce. There is a huge cost involved in the process, in the form of food subsidy. Further, this policy of stocking food grains well above the buffer norms comes under criticism on the grounds of hoarding and creating artificial shortages in the market, thereby jacking up the prices of essential commodities. Urgent attention needs to be accorded to efficient food stocks management, timely offloading of stocks, and a stable and predictable trade policy.

14

Industrial Policy

The Industrial Scene at Independence

The main features of the industrial scene in India on the eve of planning (1950) were as under:

1. There was the preponderance of consumer goods industries *vis-à-vis* producer goods industries resulting in lopsided industrial development. In 1953, the ratio of consumer goods to producer goods worked out to be 62:38.
2. The industrial sector was extremely underdeveloped with a very weak infrastructure.
3. The lack of government intervention in favour of the industrial sector was considered as an important cause of underdevelopment.
4. Export orientation had been against the country's interests.
5. The structure of ownership was highly concentrated.
6. Technical and managerial skills were in short supply.

As a result, the national consensus was that economic sovereignty and economic independence lay in rapid industrialisation including particularly the promotion of industrial infrastructure.

Organised thinking concerning the direction of industrial development in India may be traced to the Statement of Industrial Policy, 1945; the Industrial Policy Resolution of 1948; the enactment of the Industries (Development and Regulation) Act (IDRA), 1951; the First and Second Five Year Plan documents; and the Industrial Policy Resolution of 1956.

The First Five Year Plan stated that the objective of industrial planning was to make good the deficiencies in production of key industrial items and to initiate development which would enable the cumulative expansion of such basic production. The scope and need for the development of India's industries was felt to be so great that it was necessary for the public sector to develop those industries 'in which private enterprise is unable or unwilling to put up the resources required and to run the risk involved.' The idea was that the rest of the field could be left free for private enterprise.

The Industrial Policy Resolution of 1948 had identified a small number of industries to be reserved for production by the public sector. The production of arms and ammunition, production and control of atomic energy, and ownership and management of railways were to be the sole preserve of the central government. However, coal, iron and steel, aircraft manufacturing, ship-building, manufacture of telegraph and wireless equipment (except radios), and minerals were reserved for production by central or state government undertakings.

The thinking concerning the public sector had changed during the course of the 1950s. As far as can be ascertained, the original thinking was concerned with the use of the public sector investment in industries which the private sector would find difficult to invest in. By 1956, this had changed towards an explicit preference for state ownership of industries that were termed as capturing the 'commanding heights of the economy.'

Industrial Control Regime 1950s to 1970s

The system of Indian industrial licensing, therefore, has its origins in a combination of thinking resulting from the exigencies and requirements of a war situation, Indian nationalistic aspirations and the socialistic leanings of some of the founding fathers of the country. The leaders of the private sector of the time were also in favour of strong governmental assertion. The industrial licensing system has operated in the country with the simultaneous operation of other schemes of governmental allocations and controls such as:

1. Five Year Plan documents.
2. Import and export controls.
3. Control of capital issues.
4. Control of foreign exchange.

5. Transport controls including allocation of raw materials.
6. Price controls.
7. Allocations of credit.

This suggests that the planners and policy makers in India understood the need for using a wide variety of instruments and controls to steer Indian industrial development in a desired direction. However, there has always been a mismatch between the intentions expressed and the licensing instruments available for realising these planning intentions. It should also be noted that whereas the original intention of licensing was to use this power selectively for the promotion of selected important industries, it was later used to control almost all industries with the result that *regulation rather than development became the more important feature of the system.*

Performance of the Industrial Licensing System

Until the recent industrial and trade policy reforms, the establishment and operation of an industrial enterprise in India required approvals from the central government at almost every step.

In addition to these approvals, since the enactment of the Monopolies and Restrictive Trade Practices (MRTP) Act in 1969, the firms covered under this needed to obtain separate MRTP clearances from the Department of Company Affairs. Further, resulting from the desire to promote small-scale industries, 836 items have been reserved for production in small-scale enterprises. Since 1956, there has also been a list of industries reserved for exclusive production in the public sector. Since 1977, there has also been a ban on the location of industries in the largest 20-30 cities. In 1988, this ban was extended to include municipal areas of all towns and cities and to specified areas of influence around the largest 21 cities.

That system was unsuited for directing investments has been well understood since the early 1960s. The most comprehensive description, evaluation and indictment of this system is that by Bhagwati and Desai (1970). The government appointed one committee after another in the 1960s to examine the industrial licensing system (The Swaminathan Committee, 1964; the Mahalanobis Committee, 1964; the Hazari Report, 1967; the Dutt Committee Report, 1969; and the Administrative Reform Commission, 1969). Despite the findings of most of these early committees, that the licensing mechanism was not serving its purpose of channelising investments into desired directions, there seems to have been a continuing inability of the government, until recently, to bring any substantative changes to the industrial licensing system.

India's import tariffs were among the highest in world with duty rates of above 200 per cent being fairly common. Imports of manufactured goods were completely banned. Policies towards foreign investment were quite restrictive reflecting the general protectionist thrust of industrial policy (Ahluwalia, 2012).[1]

It seems the promotion of a sheltered home market had a common appeal to the bureaucratic authoritarian state, urban manufacturers and multinationals that supplied technology and capital. Protection also met the state's objectives pursuing revenue and expenditure maximising activities through maximum revenue tariffs and export tariffs.

Thus, the interests of politicians, bureaucrats, multinationals as well as domestic industrial houses all coincided to keep Indian industry sheltered through the operation of the industrial control system.

Industrial Policy Reforms 1980s

Industrial policy changes of the 1980s represented a response to the heavily felt need for domestic deregulation. Experiments with industrial delicensing, weakening of MRTP provisions to provide larger scope for large industrial houses, incentives for modernisation of capital stock, policies for major industries such as textiles and sugar, gradual introduction of price decontrol for cement and aluminum, etc., were some of the major steps taken in the direction of domestic deregulation. A move away from physical controls to a system of financial incentives and disincentives and from discretionary to more market-oriented regulation formed the underlying thrust of the industrial policy changes of the 1980s.

A major exception to this thrust was the continuation of the policy of reservation of production for the small-scale sector particularly since it constituted an important hurdle in the way of developing export capability in sectors such as garments, leather products, sports goods, etc., where India has a comparative advantage. Industrial policy in the 1980s also paid little attention to facilitating the restructuring of the industrial sector by removing the numerous barriers to exit. The labour

---

1. Ahluwalia, Isher Judge (2012). "Industry", in Kaushik Basu and Annemie Maertens (eds.), *The New Oxford Companion to Economics in India* (Vol.I). New Delhi: OUP.

laws, the bankruptcy laws, the laws relating to rent control and urban land ceiling were some of the major legislative barriers which came in the way of moving resources away from the unproductive and economically non-viable sectors to the more vibrant sectors.

The Policy Regime in the 1990s

A process of reflection and debate on the need for a change in policies had been set in motion in India in the second half of the 1970s, i.e., about the same time that China was preparing for a major change in policy. It is worth noting that China went ahead with full force towards market orientation and doubled its GDP between 1978 and 1991. By contrast, India used the decade of the 1980s for hesitant experimentation in domestic deregulation, while retaining its highly protectionist trade policy regime and keeping its loss-making public sector intact. The reform on the industrial policy front, however, coincided with a sharp deterioration in the fiscal accounts of the government. As the Government of India's (GoI) policies became increasingly expansionary to support growing levels of current government expenditures on sharply rising interest payments, defence and subsidies, the gross fiscal deficit of the government increased from 6.2 per cent of GDP (gross domestic product) in 1980-81 to 8.3 per cent by 1990-91.

While the reorientation of industrial and trade policies evoked a better productivity response and led to substantially higher industrial growth in the 1980s, the deteriorating fiscal position and growing macroeconomic imbalances posed a serious challenge to the sustainability of the higher growth of the 1980s. The Gulf War of 1990 provided the trigger, which brought the underlying economic crisis to the force.

New Economic Policy (1991)

As Rangarajan has rightly stated, the year 1991 is an important landmark in the economic history of post-Independent India. The country went through a severe economic crisis triggered by a serious balance of payments (BoP) situation. The crisis was converted into an opportunity to introduce some fundamental changes in the content and approach to economic policy. The response to the crisis was to put in place a set of policies aimed at stabilisation and structural reform. While the stabilisation policies were aimed at correcting the weaknesses that had developed on the fiscal and the BoP fronts, the structural reforms sought to remove the rigidities that had entered into the various segments of the Indian economy. The structural reforms introduced in the early 1990s broadly covered the areas of industrial licensing, foreign trade, foreign investment, exchange rate management and the financial sector. From the point of view of industrialisation, changes in the areas of licensing and foreign trade and investment had important implications. Even before the onset of reforms, the problems associated with industrial licensing were well recognised. The approach document of the Eighth Plan (1991-1996) submitted in May 1990 had remarked:

> A return to the regime of direct, indiscriminate and detailed controls in industry is clearly out of question. Past experience has shown that such control system is not effective in achieving the desired objective. Also the system is widely abused and leads to corruption, delays and inefficiency (GoI, 1990).

Without going into details, the common thread running through the various policy measures introduced since 1991 has been the improvement of the efficiency of the system. The thrust of the New Economic Policy has been towards creating a more competitive environment in the economy as a means to improving the productivity and efficiency of the system. This was to be achieved by removing the barriers to entry and the restrictions on the growth of firms. The private sector was to be given a larger space to operate in as some of the areas reserved exclusively earlier for the public sector were now to be opened to the private sector. In these areas, the public sector would have to compete with the private sector, even though the public sector might continue to play the dominant role in the foreseeable future. What was sought to be achieved was the improvement in the functioning of the various entities, whether they were in the private or in the public sector.

The 10 years from 1991 to 2001, therefore, marked a significant transition for the Indian economy from a policy regime with very high rates of protection and all-pervasive quantitative restrictions to moderate rates of protection and removal of quantitative restrictions. The degree of tariff protection, however, was still higher than in most developing economies.

Opening up to Foreign Investment

The reforms of the 1990s marked a significant break with the past in respect of the policy towards foreign investment. From a policy which was restrictive and selective and supported mainly technology transfers, foreign investment policy in the 1990s became more open and more proactive as the rules were liberalised over time with a view not only to gain better access to technology, but also to build strategic alliances to penetrate world markets. Besides enlarging the scope for automatic approval over the years, the Foreign Investment Promotion Board was set up to expedite other applications for foreign investment. Specifically, liberal conditions were set up for attracting foreign investment in infrastructure sectors and export-oriented sectors.

Public Sector Reforms and Privatisation

Public sector reform remained an area of darkness in the 1990s. A significant practical approach was adopted in which the better performing public sector undertakings (PSUs) were given the freedom to access capital markets on the strength of their own performance. They were also given more autonomy in shaping their future. The non-performing PSUs, on the other hand, languished for want of budgetary support or reform.

Privatisation was not pursued as an option in the early phase of reforms. Instead, government policy concentrated on selective disinvestments of public sector equity with a view to finance fiscal deficits rather than address the issue of improving the returns on the capital invested. In 1997, the GoI set up the Disinvestment Commission. The commission gave a series of reports analysing the 50 or so cases of PSUs, which were referred to it and made detailed recommendations. Subsequently, the commission was wound up and a Department of Privatisation was created. While there have been some major privatisations, e.g., BALCO, VSNL, Maruti and IPCL, it remains a highly contentions issue.

There is no getting away from the need for reforming the public sector as the case of power sector makes it amply clear. For example, the pricing policy, which does not cover the cost of producing the infrastructure services, is eroding the economic viability of public sector infrastructure and stands in the way of attracting private investment into infrastructure. Since infrastructure services such as electric power, roads, ports, railways and telecommunications are crucial for industrialisation and these services cannot be imported, adequate investments (public or private) and efficient use of existing and new investments in these sectors are essential prerequisites for any strategy which seeks to accelerate the pace of economic growth. Unless public sector reforms are undertaken and economic viability of infrastructure operations ensured, private sector investment will not be attracted to these sectors.

Industrial Policy Objectives for the Twelfth Plan and Beyond[2]

Quoting the Twelfth Five Year Plan,

> Industrial policies, where they have succeeded, have generally not been an outcome of Centrally planned economies but of economies that have had the active involvement of private enterprises and other non-governmental stakeholders. Successful strategies evolve from ongoing productive interactions between government and producers. Therefore, the government must improve the process of interaction, collaboration and learning amongst producers and itself. This is very different from the paradigm of Indian industrial policy prior to India's economic reforms commencing in the 1980s. In that era, industrial planning was a topdown control activity with Government determining who should produce what, where and how much and also what technology they should use. The roadmap for the Twelfth Plan and beyond can definitely not be a return to this type of planning.

According to the Twelfth Plan document, in order to create a paradigm shift in the manufacturing sector, it is essential to consider the objectives over a longer time frame, such as 15 years. The National Manufacturing Policy, which was introduced in 2011, states these objectives and these are the underlying objectives that the plan aims to achieve as well. These objectives are:

1. Increase manufacturing sector growth to 12-14 per cent over the medium term to make it the engine of growth for the economy. The 2-4 per cent differential over the medium term growth rate of the overall economy will enable manufacturing to contribute at least 25 per cent of the national GDP by 2025.
2. Increase the rate of job creation in manufacturing to create 100 million additional jobs by 2025. Emphasis should be given to creation of appropriate skill sets among the rural migrant and urban poor to make growth inclusive.
3. Increase 'depth' in manufacturing, with focus on the level of domestic value addition, to address the national strategic requirements.
4. Enhance global competitiveness of Indian manufacturing through appropriate policy support.
5. Ensure sustainability of growth, particularly with regard to the environment.

---

2. This section is drawn from the Twelfth Five Year Plan 2012-2017, Vol. II, Ch. 13.

The contribution of the manufacturing sector to Gross Value Added (GVA) has been hovering around 17 per cent for the last four years. The government has taken several measures to accelerate the growth of the industrial sector so as to strengthen and sustain the momentum of economic growth. These are primarily focused on simplification and rationalization of procedures and processes for boosting investment, adopting a more open Foreign Direct Investment (FDI) policy and measures for creating a conducive business environment.

Some of the recent reforms are: reducing the list of industries that can be considered defence industries requiring industrial licence; and amendments in FDI policy which include allowing FDI in defence up to 49 per cent, in railway infrastructure up to 100 per cent and in the insurance and pension sector up to 49 per cent. The investment limit requiring prior permission from the Foreign Investment Promotion Board (FIPB)/Cabinet Committee on Economic Affairs has been increased from R1200 crore to R3000 crore. The definition of investment by Non Resident Indians (NRI), Persons of Indian Origin (PIO) and Overseas Citizens of India (OCI) in the FDI policy has been revised.

The government has launched several programmes/initiatives such as ease of doing business, Make in India, Invest India, and e-biz Mission Mode Project under the National e-Governance Plan. Further, the GoI is also building a pentagon of corridors across the country to boost manufacturing and to project India as a global manufacturing destination. Other bold measures include implementation of the Goods and Services Tax, Insolvency and Bankruptcy Code, introduction of inflation targeting regime and announcement of bank recapitalization, measures to facilitate ease of doing business including initiation and simplification of online application for Industrial License and Industrial Entrepreneur Memorandum, integration of twenty services with the eBiz portal which functions as a single window portal for obtaining clearances from various Government agencies, limiting the number of documents required for export and import to three by DGFT (*Economic Survey 2017-18,* Vol. II).

The challenges to developing and implementing a cohesive manufacturing strategy in democratic India are many. Cohesion can be brought about through more effective coordination amongst agencies, and more effective consultation amongst stakeholders.

15

Industrial Growth and Structure since 1951

Industrial Growth

Having looked into the industrial control regime and the performance of the industrial licensing system under different policy regimes and the trade liberalisation and industrialisation policy reforms of the 1990s in the previous chapter, let us now look at the industrial growth since Independence—the rate and pattern of growth and the structural changes.

Policy Regimes and Pattern of Growth[1]

According to Krishna (2013) the period since 1951 may be divided into five phases as in Table 15.1, according to policy regime:[2]

- 1951-52 to 1966-67: Evolution of Industrial Development Strategy.
- 1967-68 to 1980-81: Inward orientation and Industrial Stagnation.
- 1981-82 to 1990-91: Deregulation, and Acceleration of Growth.
- 1991-92 to 2000-01: Economic Reforms and Service-led Growth.
- 2002-03 to 2008-09: Recovery in Industrial Growth since 2002-03 and Recent Industrial Growth 2008-09 to 2013-14 and 2014-15 to 2015-16.

---

1. This section draws upon Acharya *et al.* (2006).
2. Krishna, K.L. (2015). "Industrial Development and Policies since Independence: Growth without Employment", in Uma Kapila (ed), *Indian Economy since Independence* (26th edition). New Delhi: Academic Foundation.

TABLE – 15.1

Annual Average Growth Rates of GDP and Major Sectors

	1900-01 to 1929-30	*1930-31 to 1946-47*	*1951-52 to 1966-67*	*1967-68 to 1980-81*	*1981-82 to 1990-91*	*1991-92 to 2000-01*	*2001-02 to 2010-11*
Agriculture & Allied	0.5	0.2	1.8	3.3	3.5	2.7	2.9
Industry	0.9	1.2	6.3	4.1	7.1	5.7	7.8
Services	1.6	1.7	4.8	4.3	6.8	7.6	9.4
GDP	0.8	0.8	3.4	3.8	5.6	5.6	7.9
GDP per Capita	0.4	-0.5	1.4	1.5	3.4	3.7	6.2

Source: Acharya *et al.* (2006: Table 6) and Krishna (2012: Table 1).
Data Sources: Sivasubramonian (2000) and CSO (2001) and EPW (2011).

Table 15.1 presents growth rates of GDP and major sectors for two phases in the pre-Independence period and five phases in the post-independence period. In the first phase after independence, 1951-1966, the industrialisation strategy was evolved as part of the development planning process. The First Five Year Plan, 1951-1956, however, accorded primacy to agriculture, irrigation and infrastructure. Compared to the pre-independence era, growth performance, overall and in industry sector, was indeed impressive. The strategy in the Second Plan (1956-1961) based on the celebrated Mahalanobis model emphasised heavy industry and public sector dominance. Against a background of 'export pessimism,' import substitution industrialisation (1SI) strategy was pursued. The foreign exchange crisis in 1957 prompted re-imposition of exchange controls. As a consequence of border wars with China in 1962, with Pakistan in 1965 and 1966, development planning received a setback. Average annual growth rate during the Third Plan (1961-1966) was 2.8 per cent compared to 4.3 per cent in the Second Plan. However, the industry sector maintained the growth rate of over 6.5 per cent (Acharya *et al.*, 2006, table 3.16). The 1966 devaluation-cum-liberalisation episode proved unsuccessful and at the end of this first period, the anti-foreign trade pro-import substitution bias got entrenched. Rather than shift to outward oriented policies and exploit the export potential of labour-intensive products, as South Korea did in the early 1960s, India extended import substitution to a diverse set of goods including machinery. Entry barriers in the form of industrial investment licensing policy came in the way of domestic competition, and as a result, efficiency gains from competition could not be reaped. According to careful analysts (e.g., Panagariya, 2008), this was a colossal policy mistake responsible for the lack luster performance of Indian manufacturing in the second phase 1967-1980.

In the second phase, 1967-1980, with the strengthening of import substitution strategy and imposition of various government controls, namely, nationalisation of major banks and insurance in 1969-70, Foreign Exchange Regulation Act (FERA), small-scale industries reservations, Monopoly and Restrictive Trade Practices (MRTP) Act, the policy environment became increasingly statist. Industrial growth during this phase decelerated to around 4.1 per cent per annum from 6.3 per cent attained in the earlier phase, leading to doubts about the efficacy of the system of detailed controls on industry, foreign trade and payments (Acharya *et al.*, 2006).

The third phase, 1981-1990, witnessed a substantial acceleration of overall GDP growth from 3.8 per cent per annum to 5.6 per cent, industry GDP growth increased by 3 percentage points from 4.1 to 7.1 per cent. Efforts at industrial liberalisation during 1980s, and better agricultural performance as a result of Green Revolution, and increasingly expansionist fiscal policy seemed to be the factors behind the vastly improved growth performance in this phase. However, the end of the period witnessed a severe balance of payments (BoP) crisis in the wake of the 1990 Gulf War and oil price hike.

As a policy response to the crisis at the beginning of the 1990s, wide ranging reforms in industrial deregulation, foreign trade policy, exchange rate and payments regime, capital markets and the banking sector, fiscal consolidation were introduced. These major reforms of 1991-94 resulted in acceleration of GDP growth to above 7 per cent per annum and industry sector growth to above 9 per cent. However, the pace of reforms slackened in mid-1990s and fiscal balances worsened thereafter, investment and exports lost momentum and growth slowed after 1997. Agriculture experienced significant slowdown and year-to-year fluctuations. Industry growth too decelerated and displayed milder fluctuations (Ahluwalia, 2012).

In the final and most recent phase, 2001-02 to 2010-11, in Table 15.1, industrial growth accelerated to 7.8 per cent per annum, services growth to about 9.4 per cent and GDP growth to 7.9 per cent per annum.

Per capita GDP growth accelerated appreciably by 2.5 percentage points to 6.2 per cent. The five-year period 2003-04 to 2007-08 was remarkable for witnessing an average annual growth rate of 8.7 per cent in GDP and 10.3 per cent in industry. The growth rate in 2006-07 was 9.6 per cent in GDP and 12.7 per cent in industry, a very impressive performance. However, as a consequence of the economic crisis in developed countries, GDP growth rate in 2008-09 dropped to 6.7 per cent, but recovered in the following two years. The first decade of the New Millennium as a whole witnessed most impressive growth performance, especially in the services sector.

The GoI Economic Survey for the year 2011-12 comments on the growth trends in the Indian economy during the past six decades, since 1950-51. It divides the period into two sub-periods 1950-51 to 1990-1991 and 1991-92 to 2011-12. The second sub-period corresponds to the period of major economic policy reforms. In the latter (reform) sub-period the GDP growth rate was 6.9 per cent per year, compared to 4.1 per cent in the first sub-period. In the 20-year period, 1991-92 to 2011-2012, GDP growth rate exceeded 6.0 per cent in as many as 14 years. The growth rate has accelerated significantly since 2003-04, registering an average growth rate of 8.2 per cent. The variation in the GDP growth rate appears to be largely due to variation in the growth rate of the industry sector, according to the Economic Survey 2011-12.

The growth rate of the agriculture sector has accelerated from 2.3 per cent during the 30-year period 1950-51 to 1980-81 to 3.1 per cent during 1980-81 to 2011-12. Growth in the industry sector has increased from 5.2 per cent to 6.4 per cent; growth in the service sector has accelerated very substantially from 4.4 per cent to 7.8 per cent. Service sector has become the 'engine of growth.' This pattern of growth has been termed 'Services Led Industrialisation.'[3]

Balakrishnan (2010) econometrically estimates the years of structural breaks in the annual time series of GDP and sectoral GDP for the Indian economy for the post-1950-51 period. The growth phases thus delineated, and the annual growth rates for overall GDP, GDP in manufacturing, GDP in registered manufacturing and GDP in unregistered manufacturing in 1999-2000 prices are presented in Table 15.2.

It may be seen from Table 15.2 that the years 1978-79 and 1990-1991 are the structural break years for the GDP series. GDP growth rate has accelerated from 3.5 per cent per year in Phase I to 4.4 per

3. See Rakshit (2007) and Singh (2008) for detailed analyses of the relevant issues.

cent in Phase II, the period of deregulation and partial liberalisation, and to 5.9 per cent in Phase III, the period of major and wide-ranging liberalisation. Growth acceleration is higher from Phase II to Phase III, than from Phase I to Phase II.

TABLE – 15.2

GDP Growth Rates in the Different Growth Phases: Economy and Manufacturing

		Overall GDP		
Phase	1950/51 to 1978/79	1979/80 to 1991/92	1990/91 to 2005/06	-
Growth rate (% p.a.)	3.48	4.38	5.89	
		Manufacturing GDP		
Phase	1950/51 to 1965/66	1966/67 to 1994/95	1995/96 to 2005/06	-
Growth rate (% p.a.)	5.93	4.75	6.59	
		Registered Manufacturing GDP		
Phase	1950/51 to 1965/66	1966/67 to 1982/83	1983/84 to 2005/06	-
Growth rate (% p.a.)	7.77	4.66	6.89	
		Unregistered Manufacturing GDP		
Phase	1950/51 to 1964/65	1965/66 to 1977/78	1978/79 to 1994/95	1995/96 to 2005/06
Growth rate (% p.a.)	4.79	3.83	3.46	5.18

Note: Growth phases have been econometrically delineated by Balakrishnan (2010).
Source: Balakrishnan (2010), appendix.

In the case of total manufacturing, the years of structural break were estimated to be 1965-66 and 1994-95. The growth rates in the three phases are 5.9 per cent, 4.8 per cent and 6.6 per cent. Growth rate decelerated by 1.1 percentage points from Phase I to Phase II. This phenomenon of deceleration in the mid-1960s has received considerable attention of researchers. It is gratifying to note that growth rate in the manufacturing sector has accelerated significantly to 6.6 per cent in the post-reform era from 4.7 per cent during the pre-reform phase 1966-67 to 1994-95.

As far as registered manufacturing sector is concerned, the second structural break occurred in 1982-83, during the period of deregulation. There has been no structural break in the post-reform period, however.

Unregistered manufacturing sector has witnessed three, rather than two, structural breaks, in 1964-65, 1977-78 and 1994-95. The growth rates are much smaller at 4.8 per cent, 3.8 per cent, 3.5 per cent and 5.2 per cent in the four phases compared to registered manufacturing. The extent of deceleration from Phase I to Phases II and III and the extent of acceleration from Phase III to Phase IV are also milder. Thus the growth patterns of the two segments of the manufacturing sector are rather dissimilar, and the registered segment has gained further in terms of output share.

In the most recent three-year period, 2011-12 to 2013-14, the industry sector witnessed steep deceleration in growth to an average of 3.4 per cent, compared to 7.8 per cent during the period 2001-02 to 2010-11. This is attributed to 'policy paralysis'.

Comparative Growth Rates in the 1980s and the 1990s

The average growth rate of the industrial sector (measured by the IIP) during the period 1992-93 to 1999-2000 was lower than that observed during the period 1980-81 to 1991-92. The growth rate was lower in all the three sectors i.e., manufacturing, mining and electricity. In terms of use-based classification also, there was a lower growth rate in basic and capital goods. However, the GDP (gross domestic product) from manufacturing sector at constant prices showed higher growth rates during the period 1992-93 to 1999-2000 when compared to the period 1980-81 to 1991-92 at the aggregate (total) level and amongst both registered and unregistered segments (Table 15.3).

Relative Contribution of Sectors to Total Production

Changes in the relative contribution of different sectors to the general IIP reflect another dimension of the structural changes in industrial production. Data presented in Table 15.4 reveal that the relative contribution of the manufacturing sector rose from 70.0 per cent during the 1980s to 81.6 per cent during the 1990s. However, in case of mining and quarrying, there was a noticeable decline. This was reflected in the changes in the weights assigned to different sector in the construction of IIP series. The weight for the manufacturing sector rose from 77.1 per cent in the earlier series of IIP with base 1980-81=100, to 79.36 per cent in the current series with base 1993-94=100. Correspondingly, the relative weights of mining and quarrying and electricity sectors declined from 11.46 per cent and 11.43 per cent in the old series to 10.47 per cent and 10.17 per cent, respectively, in the new series (Table 15.4).

TABLE – 15.3

Comparative Growth Rates in the Industrial Sector 1980-2000

Parameter	*Avg. Annual Growth Rate (1980-81 to 1991-92)**	*Avg. Annual Growth Rate (1992-93 to 1999-2000)**
Index of Industrial Production		
General	7.8	6.0
Manufacturing	7.6	6.3
Mining	8.4	3.3
Electricity	9.0	6.6
Use-based classification		
Basic goods	7.4	6.1
Capital goods	9.4	5.9
Intermediate goods	4.9	9.1
Consumer goods	6.0	6.3
of which:		
(i) Consumer durables	10.8	11.2
(ii) Consumer non-durables	5.3	5.1
GDP-Manufacturing at 1993-94 Prices		
Total	6.1	7.4
Registered	6.8	8.1
Unregistered	5.0	6.2

Note: * Simple average of the annual growth rates.
Source: *Economic Survey, 2000-01.*

TABLE – 15.4

Relative Contribution of Sectors to the Industrial Production

(%)

	Sector	1981-82 to 1990-91 (Average)	1992-93 to 1998-99* (Average)
	1	2	3
i)	Manufacturing	70.0	81.6
ii)	Electricity	14.4	14.4
iii)	Mining and quarrying	15.6	4.0
	General Index	**100.0**	**100.0**

Note: * The data relating to 1991-92 were excluded in this period because production was almost stagnant.

During the 1990s, while the relative contributions of basic and capital goods sectors declined, there was a rise in those of intermediate and consumer goods sectors (Table 15.5). In the new series (Base: 1993-1994=100), the weights of basic and capital goods sectors were reduced and those of intermediate goods and consumer goods sectors were raised.

TABLE – 15.5

Relative Contribution of Sectors to Industrial Production (Use-based Classification)

(%)

	Sector	1981-82 to 1990-91 (Average)	1992-93 to 1998-99* (Average)
	1	2	3
1.	Basic goods	43.6	35.8
2.	Capital goods	25.0	7.1
3.	Intermediate goods	14.6	35.2
4.	Consumer goods	16.8	21.9
	General Index	**100.0**	**100.0**

Note: * The data relating to 1991-92 were excluded in this period because production was almost stagnant.

The relatively low contributions of the basic and capital goods sectors to overall industrial output in the 1990s reflect, among others, the impact of trade liberalisation, particularly imports, and of financial liberalisation that enabled the corporate sector to make financial gains through 'other income,' as also the lack of competitiveness requiring industrial restructuring and modernisation of technologies in a number of industries.

The Manufacturing Slowdown (1996-2002)

The loss of momentum in manufacturing growth, which occured in the latter part of 1996, has since continued during the second phase of the reform period. At the disaggregated two-digit level, the manufacturing sector witnessed substantial deceleration in 11 industry groups with a combined weight of 64 per cent in the manufacturing production. Six industry groups with a combined weight of 36 per cent withstood the slowdown and posted an accelerated growth during 1996-2002. However, in view of their relatively low weight, the manufacturing sector, as a whole, registered a slowdown.

Factors Causing the Slowdown: Some Hypotheses

A number of hypotheses in terms of cyclical and structural factors have been put forward to explain the slowdown in the manufacturing activity during this period.[4] The explanations provided, however, fall short of giving a satisfactory answer to what has led to the manufacturing slowdown and its persistence. The onset of slowdown is often attributed to the saturation of the pent-up domestic demand of 'once-for-all' nature for a host of import-intensive goods, which could be domestically assembled or produced following trade liberalisation (Chandrasekhar and Ghosh, 2002). The short-run increase in domestic demand was seemingly facilitated by easy access to credit, including consumer credit in the wake of financial liberalisation. Once that pent-up demand of transitory nature was satisfied, industry entered the phase of slowdown in the absence of demand support—domestic or exports.

Another hypothesis on the onset of slowdown relates to the 'credit crunch' which, it is argued, triggered off the manufacturing slowdown (Sen *et al.,* 1997; Desai, 2001). The unexpected and temporary tightening of liquidity in money markets during 1995-96, resulting from large dollar sales by the RBI to contain volatility in the forex market, was mistaken to be an expression of deflationary credit policy (Acharya, 2002).

Given below is an account of these cyclical and structural factors which have impacted upon industrial growth in recent years.

4. This section is drawn from RBI *Report on Currency and Finance 2001-02.*

Cyclical Factors in Industrial Slowdown

Cyclical factors have generally been recognised as an important source of industrial slowdown. In this context, the significant fall in government capital investment especially since 1995 has been recognised as the key contributor to the slowdown (Nayyar, 1996). It is, however, important to underscore that while the contraction in government expenditure does have adverse implications for the manufacturing growth, it declined even during the manufacturing boom (1992-93 to 1995-96). Thus, decline in government expenditure *per se* does not provide a satisfactory explanation of the slowdown.

The manufacturing slowdown can also be seen in terms of decline in fixed investment in industry in the context of over-expansion of capacities during the manufacturing boom, slump in the capital market for new issues and rise in real interest rates in 1995-96 (Acharya, 2002). The increase in real fixed investment in manufacturing from 6.8 per cent of GDP in 1990-91 to 13.0 per cent in 1995-96 and the subsequent decline to 7.9 per cent by 2000-01 seems to have mirrored the pattern of manufacturing growth.

Among the other cyclical sources of demand, the lagged effect of the negative agricultural growth in 1995-96 seems to have worked towards slowing down the growth of rural demand for consumer durables and non-durables subsequently [Government of India (GoI), 2000]. As the demand for industrial products, particularly the consumer durables, is significantly influenced by the rural demand, fluctuations in the agricultural production seem to have adversely impacted the industrial growth.

The cyclical downswing was not confined to the domestic sources of demand but was also clearly visible in manufacturing exports. In anticipation of high potential demand in the wake of reforms, the manufacturing sector built up huge capacity through imports of capital goods during 1994-1997 (Table 15.5). Such capacity build-up was not sustainable on the basis of normal growth in domestic demand, and the only feasible outlet was the exports market. However, signs of exports slowdown were visible in 1995-96 when manufacturing exports decelerated. Subsequently, with slowdown in the world trade, sluggishness in the global manufacturing prices and variations in the cross-currency exchange rates, manufacturing exports growth declined to a meagre 3.6 per cent by 1996-97. The real appreciation of rupee between 1993 and 1995 and the Asia-wide slowdown in exports following the loss of market share to China also contributed to the slowdown in exports.

As is evident from the foregoing analysis, the growth momentum in manufacturing slackened towards the end of 1996, largely under the influence of factors outside the realm of public policy in the short-run. The movement in major indicators of aggregate demand, *viz.*, domestic capital formation, government capital expenditure, capital goods production, import of capital goods, manufacturing exports and private final consumption expenditure, all witnessed deceleration during the latter phase of the reforms.

Structural Factors

To the extent the slowdown is prolonged and protracted, it seems to have its origin in structural factors, including inadequate industrial restructuring undertaken in the face of growing openness of the economy and the associated external competitive pressure. The inadequacy of institutional and structural reforms, which held back the industrial restructuring, has, thus, emerged as a binding constraint on manufacturing growth in the liberalised trade regime.

Infrastructure Constraints in the Industrial Sector

The industrial performance continues to be hampered by physical infrastructure bottlenecks with the demand-supply imbalances persisting and growing during the reform period.

The deteriorating infrastructure services represent a direct fall out of shrinkage in infrastructure investment in the context of grossly inadequate internal resources of public infrastructure entities and dwindling plan outlay for infrastructure. The real capital formation in electricity, gas and water supply declined to 2.6 per cent of GDP during the 1990s from 2.9 per cent during the preceding decade. A similar trend was observed for railways. Within the 1990s also, there was a decline in the real gross capital formation in sectors like electricity, gas and water supply, and the railways between the first and the second half. The investment in infrastructure sector as a whole has shown clear decline of one percentage point of GDP between the first and the second halves of the 1990s. This decline can be attributed to declining government investment on infrastructure—a fall out of the prevailing fiscal situation—which was a major contributing factor for the economic slowdown in the latter part of the 1990s.

The pace of public investment in infrastructure slowed down substantially during this period on account of rising fiscal imbalances of the government, both at the centre and the states. As a result, public investment in major infrastructure sectors declined in real terms during the reform period. The rates of return from infrastructure services extended by the government continue to be abysmally low, constraining the ability to generate internal resources for investment. For instance, the rate of return on investment for the state power sector deteriorated from (-)12.7 per cent in 1991-92 to (-)32.8 per cent in 2001-02.

Recovery in Industrial Growth since 2002-03

The industrial recovery in 2002-03 (5.7%), which consolidated during 2003-04 (7.0%), has gathered momentum since then reaching 8.4 per cent in 2004-05, 8.2 per cent in 2005-06 and 11 per cent in 2006-07.

The double-digit growth since 2003-04 in capital goods sector indicates the capital formation taking place in the industrial sector, which can help in strengthening the upswing. The ongoing growth process, which is investment-led and fairly evenly spread within manufacturing sector, reflects the medium and long-term optimism on the part of investors.

TABLE – 15.6

Growth Rates

	CAGR in Ninth Plan	*2002-03*	*2003-04*	*2004-05*	*2005-06 (QE)*	*2006-07 (RE)*	*CAGR in Tenth Plan*
GDP	5.5	3.8	8.5	7.5	9.0	9.4	7.6
Agriculture, forestry and fishing	2.0	–7.2	10.0	0.0	6.0	2.7	2.1
Industry (manufacturing)	4.5 (3.8)	6.8 (6.8)	6.0 (6.6)	8.4 (8.7)	8.0 (9.1)	11.0 (12.3)	8.0 (8.7)
Services#	8.1	7.4	8.9	10.0	10.3	11.0	9.5

Note: # Construction is included in services;
QE = Quarterly Estimates. Figures in parentheses relate to manufacturing.

Source: CSO.
Government of India (2008). *Eleventh Five Year Plan 2007-2012*, Planning Commission.

Measured by investment, the manufacturing sector's share in total fixed investment (gross fixed capital formation) has gone up from around 27 per cent in 1980s to about 40 per cent in the current decade. (Nagaraj, 2011)[5]

The rising demand in both domestic and external markets was a major contributory factor but the impressive performance of manufacturing was due in no small measure to the cumulative effect of industrial and fiscal policy changes carried out since the economic reforms of 1991-92. The competitive environment created by the reduction of external barriers to trade finally started to bear fruit. Against a compound annual growth rate (CAGR) of 6.3 per cent in the Ninth Five Year Plan, exports of manufactures registered a CAGR of more than 19 per cent during the Tenth Five Year Plan.[6]

A major feature of the performance of industry was the remarkable increase in the export share of manufacturing sustained during the entire plan period. Against a CAGR of 6.3 per cent achieved during the Ninth Plan, exports of manufactured products had a CAGR of 19.9 per cent during the Tenth Five Year Plan.

Recent Industrial Growth 2008-09 to 2013-14 and 2014-15 to 2015-16

Recent industrial growth, measured in terms of IIP, shows fluctuating trends. Growth had reached 15.5 per cent in 2007-08 and then started decelerating. Initial deceleration in industrial growth was largely on account of the global economic meltdown. As per the IIP, industrial production which had slowed down to 2.5 per cent in 2008-09, improved in the next two years to reach 8.2 per cent in 2010-11, declined for the next three years successively, to reverse the trend in 2014-15. The main reasons for the declining industrial growth are high interest rates to tackle persistent inflation, slowdown in investment, and loss of business confidence.

Thus post 2008-09, industrial sector, consisting of manufacturing, mining, electricity and construction, showed remarkable recovery and steady growth for three years but lost momentum thereafter owing to a combination of supply-side and demand-side constraints. Industrial performance in 2013-14 remained lackluster for the second successive year. The latest GDP estimates show that industry grew by just 1.0 per cent in 2012-13 and slowed further in 2013-14, posting a modest

5. Nagaraj, R. (2011). "Industrial Performance, 1991-2008: A Review", in D.M. Nachane (ed.), *India Development Report 2011*. Indira Gandhi Institute of Development Research, New Delhi.
6. Government of India (2008). *Eleventh Five Year Plan 2007-2012*. Planning Commission.

increase of 0.4 per cent. While these figures may see upward revision once Annual Survey of Industries (ASI) data is available, there is no denying that industrial revival may take longer and needs stronger initiatives to emulate the peak growth achieved in the recent past (*Economic Survey 2013-14*).

The drop in industrial growth had been mainly owing to deceleration in manufacturing as it constitutes about 60 per cent of industry GDP. In addition to a slowdown in fixed investment, several domestic and external factors such as higher interest, infrastructure bottlenecks, inflationary pressure leading to rising input costs, drop in domestic and external demand for some sectors have together contributed to low growth in the manufacturing sector. In contrast, world manufacturing gained strength in 2013-14. One possible reason for the contrasting performance of Indian and global manufacturing production is the upsurge in demand for consumer durables such as motor vehicles in the industrialised economies. The consumer durables segment index contracted by 12.2 per cent in 2013-14 as against a growth of 2.0 per cent during the previous year. The consumer durables segment, in particular the automotive sector, in India is constrained by a limited domestic market owing to low per capita income. Major items in the consumer durables basket of the IIP that declined during 2013-2014 are gems and jewellery, passenger cars, colour TV sets, and telephone instruments. The gems and jewellery segment suffered partly due to restrictive gold imports.

The consumer non-durables segment index increased by 5.0 per cent in 2013-14 in comparison with a 2.8 per cent rise registered in the previous year. The food products sub-group index, consisting mainly of consumer non-durables, declined by 1.1 per cent on account of an 8.2 per cent decline in sugar production in 2013-14. The intermediate goods index has shown a 3.1 per cent increase in 2013-14 as compared to 1.6 per cent in the previous financial year. The performance of basic goods remained more or less the same as in the previous year.

The use-based industrial classification of IIP estimates identifies the capital goods segment as the weak performer in the manufacturing sector. The index of capital goods declined by 6.0 per cent in 2012-13 and further by 3.6 per cent in 2013-14 (Table 15.7). This segment has been hit by the steady deceleration in fixed investment in the past three years. The slow pace of mega projects implementation and a decline in the number of new projects has adversely impacted the capital goods segment. The fabricated metal products, machinery and equipment, and commercial vehicles segments are reeling under recession. During

2013-14, there was a decline of 16 per cent in commercial vehicles production. Only electrical machinery within the capital goods segment has registered 14.5 per cent growth in 2013-14 as compared to 0.6 per cent in 2012-13. As against the poor performance of the Indian capital goods sector, the global performance has been robust. Globally the five fastest growing manufacturing sectors in recent years have been (i) basic metal, (ii) radio, TV and communications equipment, (iii) office accounting and computing machinery, (iv) electrical machinery and apparatus, and (v) transport.

TABLE – 15.7

Growth in the IIP and Its Major Components

(%)

Broad Sectors	*Weight*	*2008-09*	*2009-10*	*2010-11*	*2012-13*	*2013-14*
Overall IIP	100.0	2.5	5.3	8.2	1.1	-0.1
In terms of structured national industrial classification						
Mining	14.16	2.6	7.9	5.2	-2.3	-0.6
Manufacturing	75.53	2.5	4.8	9.0	1.3	-0.8
Electricity	10.32	2.7	6.1	5.5	4.0	6.1
In terms of use-based classification						
Basic goods	45.68	1.7	4.7	6.0	2.4	2.1
Capital goods	8.83	11.3	1.0	14.8	-6.0	-3.6
Intermediates	15.69	0.0	6.0	7.4	1.6	3.1
Durables	8.46	11.1	17.0	14.2	2.0	-12.2
Non-durables	21.35	-5.0	1.4	4.3	2.8	5.0

Source: Ministry of Statistics and Programme Implementation (MOSPI).
Economic Survey 2011-12, 2013-14.

Another area of concern is the sudden dip in imports of capital goods during 2012-13 and 2013-14 due to economic slowdown and rupee depreciation. The imports of machinery, electrical machinery, transport goods and electronic goods have declined in the last two financial years. Capital goods imports declined by 3.4 per cent in 2012-13 and 14.7 per cent in 2013-14.

During April-December 2014-15, industrial production attained a growth of 2.1 per cent owing mainly to recovery in the mining sector and impressive growth in the electricity sector (Table 15.7). The manufacturing sector continues to remain tepid, registering growth of 1.2 per cent in April-December 2014-15.The low growth in manufacturing is mainly due to high rate of interest, infrastructure bottlenecks, and low domestic and external demand.

In terms of use based classification, basic goods and capital goods have witnessed marked improvement in performance registering growth rates of 6.9 per cent and 4.8 per cent , intermediate goods have grown by 1.7 per cent, while consumer goods have declined by 4.9 per cent during April- December 2014-15 as compared to the same period in 2013-14. The decline in growth of consumer goods is accentuated by the (-)15.2 per cent growth in consumer durables (*Economic Survey 2014-15*).

Industrial Growth 2015-16 to 2017-18

As per the latest Quarterly Estimates of Gross Domestic Product, overall industrial sector growth was significantly higher at 5.8 per cent in Q2 as compared to 1.6 per cent in Q1 of 2017-18. This was mainly due to the robust growth of 7.0 per cent in manufacturing sector in Q2 of 2017-18, as seen in Table 15.9. As per the first advance estimate of national income 2017-18, overall industrial sector growth is at 4.4 per cent with manufacturing growth at 4.6 per cent (*Economic Survey 2017-18*).

TABLE – 15.8

Growth of Sectoral Gross Value Added

(%)

	*Share in GVA**	*2015-16*	*2016-17*	*2017-18*	
				Q1	*Q2*
Mining & quarrying	3.0	10.5	1.8	-0.7	5.5
Manufacturing	18.1	10.8	7.9	1.2	7.0
Electricity, gas, water supply & other utility services	2.2	5.0	7.2	7.0	7.6
Construction	8.0	5.0	1.7	2.0	2.6
Industry	31.2	8.8	5.6	1.6	5.8

Note: * Share in GVA as in 2016-17 (at constant prices)
Source: Central Statistics Office
Economic Survey 2017-18, Vol. II

The Index of Industrial Production (IIP) is another measure of industrial performance, released by Central Statistics Office (CSO). CSO revised the base year of IIP in May, 2017 from 2004-05 to 2011-12. The latest series with base year 2011-12 is more representative of the current structure of the industrial sector. Table 15.9 indicates the Sectoral and Use-based growth rates for the last two years and the current fiscal year.

TABLE – 15.9

Index of Industrial Production (IIP) Growth Rates

(%)

	Weight	*2015-16*	*2016-17*	*2017-18 (April-November)*
General Index	100	3.3	4.6	3.2
Sectoral Classification				
Mining	14.4	4.3	5.3	3.0
Manufacturing	77.6	2.8	4.4	3.1
Electricity	8.0	5.7	5.8	5.2
Use Based Classification				
Primary goods	34.0	5	4.9	3.4
Capital goods	8.2	3	3.2	2.1
Intermediate goods	17.2	1.5	3.3	0.9
Infrastructure/construction goods	12.3	2.8	3.9	3.8
Consumer durables	12.8	3.4	2.9	-1.4
Consumer non-durables	15.3	2.6	7.9	9.4

Source: Central Statistics Office

IIP registered a 25 month high growth of 8.4 per cent with manufacturing growing at 10.2 per cent in November 2017. Higher growth in capital goods, infrastructure/construction and consumer non-durable have had a significant impact. During April-November 2017, the growth was 3.2 per cent. The major industry groups that have contributed positively to growth during this period are coke and refined petroleum products; pharmaceuticals, medicinal chemicals and botanical products; basic metals; computer, electronic and optical products; and motor vehicles, traillers & semi-trailers. The industry groups that have contributed negatively are tobacco products; wearing apparel; rubber and plastic products; other non-metalic mineral products and electrical equipment.

As per the Use-based classification of IIP, in 2017-18 (April-November), Consumer nondurables have shown consistency and have registered a growth of 9.4 per cent. Growth of the Index of Primary Goods has witnessed a comparatively lower rate at 3.4 per cent during this period mainly due to suboptimal performance of Mining Sector and Petrol/Motor spirit industry. Infrastructure/Construction goods in 2017-18 (April-November) recorded a growth of 3.8 per cent as compared to

5.0 per cent in same period last year on account of sub-par performance of the cement sector. The performance of Capital goods has not been upto expectations mainly due to the impact of destocking after announcement of GST in the first quarter of 2017-18.

TABLE – 15.10

Growth in the production of Eight Core Industries (per cent)

Sector	*Weight*	*2015-16*	*2016-17*	*April-November 2017-18*
Coal	10.3	4.8	3.2	1.5
Crude Oil	9.0	-1.4	-2.5	-0.2
Natural Gas	6.9	-4.7	-1.0	4.4
Refinery Products	28.0	4.9	4.9	3.6
Fertilizers	2.6	7	0.2	-1.1
Steel	17.9	-1.3	10.7	7.2
Cement	5.4	4.6	-1.2	0.6
Electricity	19.9	5.7	5.8	4.9
Overall Index	100	3.0	4.8	3.9

Source: Department of Industrial Policy and Promotion

Competing Explanations for the Trends[7]

Many would agree that industry underperformed, but the reasons proffered for it could vary considerably.[8] By no stretch of imagination could state policy constrain industrial decision-making any longer. With India's tariff getting reduced, and with numerous bilateral trade and investment treaties, India's openness became comparable to its Asian peers. Crucially, if the much derided permit–licence raj had held up industrial growth during the planning era, then why did industrial output and exports not zoom after the reforms?

Protagonists of reforms, however, would contend that the reforms have not gone far enough or the agenda remains incomplete—with restrictions remaining on foreign direct investment (FDI) (especially in retail trade), labour market regulation (in the ability to hire and fire at will), full convertibility of capital, etc. These arguments seem

7. This section is drawn from Nagaraj, R. (2018). "Economic Reforms and Manufacturing Sector Growth", in Uma Kapila (ed.) (2018), *Indian Economy Since Independence* (29th edition), ch. 23. New Delhi: Academic Foundation.

8. For the details of the arguments reported in this section, see Nagaraj (2011) for a critical review of industrial performance until the boom of 2008.

questionable. There is no clear theoretically valid and empirically sound association between pro-market reforms and growth (Rodrik 2011). There is perhaps room for critically examining what has been the outcome of the liberalisation carried out thus far.

What has India's open-door policy for FDI led to? In the last decade, the most significant variety of FDI inflow has been private equity (PE), venture capital (VC), and hedge funds (HF), which are, by definition, loosely regulated alternative investment funds that are part of shadow banking. They are not even considered as FDI by the United Nations Conference on Trade and Development definition since they are not for the long-term. Quantitatively, the most important of these sources is PE funds, which, by definition, acquire existing assets and sell these after three–five years in the stock market after restructuring. These are hardly the kind of foreign capital that India needs for getting technology and acquiring industrial capability. Table 23.2 provides information on PE and VC inflows into India since 2005 and an illustrative list of projects in which they have invested during 2015. Economic implications of PE investment are that it is financing of domestic consumption using foreign debt, not productive investment.

The labour market rigidity hypothesis is seriously contested; careful reviews of the literature find little support for the widely held proposition (Kannan and Raveendran 2009; Teitelbaum 2013; Sood et al. 2014). That the labour market rigidity argument holds little water now can be gauged by the recent news report that Larsen & Toubro, India's largest machinery and construction firm (turnover $16 billion) reportedly laid off 14,000 workers (11.2% of its workforce of 1.22 lakh workers) during July–September 2016 (Prasad 2016). It amply demonstrates that the "hire and fire" policy effectively rules the organised labour market today.

Arguably, the retrenched workers are temporary or contract workers who are not protected by labour laws, which are the bone of contention. But, the fact that such a large enterprise employs non-permanent workers in such large numbers only goes to show how the seemingly rigid laws do not apply to a growing segment of organised workers and that the laws really have no teeth. Hence, the contention that labour laws are holding up flexible and efficient use of labour simply does not hold water.

Currently, policymakers are using the World Bank's "Ease of Doing Business" (EDB) as a measure of hurdles faced by entrepreneurs, and are busy trying to improve India's global ranking to attract more foreign investment. This dubious measure, both conceptually and empirically, hardly explains the foreign investment inflows in developing countries, as evident from a World Bank research paper quoted below:

> The World Bank's Ease of Doing Business reports have been ranking countries since 2006. However, do improvements in rankings generate greater foreign direct investment inflows? ... The paper shows this relationship is significant for the average country. However, when the sample is restricted to developing countries, the results suggest an improved ranking has, on average, an insignificant (albeit positive) influence on foreign direct investment inflows. ... Finally, the paper demonstrates that, on average, countries that undertake large-scale reforms relative to other countries do not necessarily attract greater foreign direct investment inflows. This analysis may have important ramifications for developing country governments wanting to improve their Doing Business Rankings in the hope of attracting foreign direct investment inflows. (Jayasuriya 2011).

If the foregoing arguments are reasonable and evidence credible, then we should look elsewhere for the reasons of the industrial stagnation. The answer perhaps lies with the structuralist economic arguments and the long-term constraints, such as less than satisfactory or poor agriculture performance after the reforms. Moreover, despite gradual improvements, land productivity in agriculture continues to be a modest fraction of the global average.

Further, lack of adequate public infrastructure investment (as capacity creation for power generation by proxy) seems to be holding back industrial growth.

At the moment, in the aftermath of the global financial crisis, Indian industry is suffering from excess capacity in major industries like steel, coal and machinery, as investment rates and exports have fallen. Fixed capital formation ratio, for instance, has fallen by almost 10 percentage points, from close to 40 per cent of GDP in 2008. As the private corporate sector is mired in debt, and the banking sector is left holding non- performing assets, there is little option but to revive public investment to boost investment and domestic output (Nagaraj 2014).

Need for Reconfiguring Development State

While the foregoing arguments for removing the structural constraints on industrial growth still hold, it is perhaps an opportune moment to revisit the role of state support for industrialisation. Admittedly, state intervention during the planning era (1950–1980) had many shortcomings (too widely acknowledged to bear repetition), and many aspects of it may have outlived their utility. Yet, perhaps, the rush to open up markets after 1991 (under stressed macroeconomic conditions) seems to have hurt long-term industrial and trade prospects. So, there seems to be a need to rebalance the equation between the state and the market keeping in view the strategic considerations.

The basic arguments for industrial policy come from Nicholas Kaldor's stylised fact that faster manufacturing sector growth propels the rest of the economy following Verdoon's law of positive externalities. In a somewhat similar vein is Paul Krugman's (1995) hypothesis of economies of locational agglomeration giving rise to positive externalities. Finally, the arguments of market failures due to information imperfections, and state intervention solving the coordination problem offer credible reasons for having an industrial policy Suzumura (1997). More over, the comparative Asian experience (starting with Japan to a contemporary account of China and Vietnam) offers powerful empirical arguments for industrial policy.

Three aspects of industrial and investment policies that seem to need careful attention are: (i) long-term finance, (ii) domestic research and development (R&D) efforts, and (iii) bilateral investment and trade treaties. India seems to have a disadvantage vis-à-vis its trading partners, especially with respect to China in all these policies. As part of financial liberalisation, India turned its development financial institutions (DFIs)—such as IDBI (the Industrial Development Bank of India) and ICICI (Industrial Credit and Investment Corporation of India)—into commercial banks, resulting in shortening of loan maturity, thus constraining capital-intensive manufacturing and infrastructure financing. The domestic debt market was expected to fill the vacuum, and that has not happened (as in most industrialising countries). In response, large firms were allowed to borrow internationally even for investments in the non-traded goods sector, leading to currency and maturity mismatches, thus raising potential financial instability.

China, which is still not officially granted the status of a market economy, is known to use cheap credit (including trade credit) as an instrument for penetrating international markets, especially in project exports. Commercial sources often suggest that Indian firms are perhaps unable to match the Chinese firms' commercial terms, despite producing goods of comparable quality and variety. This is not new. Historically, finance is widely used as an instrument of trade policy.

If the above speculation is correct, then there is a case for revisiting national development or investment banks for supply of long-term, low-cost credit for industrial capital formation. Such a case has acquired greater urgency in the context of the continuation of the global financial crisis, and the need for public investment to pull the depressed economies out of the present crisis (Skidelsky and Martin 2011; Turner 2015).

Another setback after the industrial reforms has been the decline in domestic industrial R&D. The licences to import technology and capital in the pre-reform era were conditional upon setting up domestic R&D centres (sweetened with fiscal concessions) to promote indigenous know how. After the reforms, firms no longer needed to make such efforts, and foreign firms had no reason to invest in R&D in India that could potentially compete with their parent firms' global interests. The net result: stagnation in R&D efforts, best illustrated again with a Chinese comparison. In 1996, both China and India spent the same share of their GDP on R&D, at 0.6 per cent. However, by 2011, the ratio for China had tripled to 1.8 per cent of GDP, whereas for India the ratio had marginally moved up to 0.8 per cent. Interestingly, despite its liberal FDI policy, China did not take its eyes off the strategic significance of R&D, whereas India perhaps lost its focus in the free market rhetoric (Mani and Nabar 2016; Mani 2016).

At the height of the financial opening-up in the last decade, India signed a large number of bilateral free trade and investment agreements, whose outcome for industry appears to be questionable (Dhar et al. 2012). In particular, the treaty with Thailand, a large base of the Japanese automotive industry, seems to have hurt Indian automotive firms', enabling the duty-free entry of goods. If the observation is correct, then there is perhaps merit in reviewing such agreements. This is not to argue for unconditional protectionism or unalloyed faith in the state's capacity to promote industrialisation, but to seek for a more reasoned, rule-based support for industry. This should not be seen as a plea for putting the clock back; such a view would be a historical. What is needed, perhaps, is the redefining and reconfiguring of the boundaries of state and market in view of the changed ground realities, comparative experiences, and the renewed analytical arguments for suitable state intervention.

Why did Manufacturing Sector's Share in Total Employment Stagnate?[9]

Despite a respectable trend growth of over 6.5 per cent per year, manufacturing sectors' share in total employment has been stagnating

---

9. Nagaraj (2011) *op.cit.*

(Table 15.11). *Prima facie*, it represents the failure of the reforms to promote labour-intensive manufacturing in spite of doing away with the import substitution bias in the industrial policy. Partly, growing capital intensity of production in general perhaps explains the employment stagnation, as it has become much easier to import the latest labour-saving equipment in an open trade regime with modest tariffs (if any).

TABLE – 15.11

Employment in the Industrial Sector

	Persons Employed (million)			*Share in Employment (%)*			*Share in GDP (%)*		
	1999-2000	*2004-05*	*2009-10*	*1999-2000*	*2004-05*	*2009-10*	*1999-2000*	*2004-05*	*2009-10*
Mining	2.3	2.6	2.9	0.6	0.6	0.6	3.0	2.9	2.3
Manufacturing	43.8	56.1	52.4	11.0	12.2	11.4	15.1	15.3	16.0
Electricity	1.0	1.2	1.3	0.3	0.3	0.3	2.3	2.1	2.0
Construction	17.5	26.1	44.2	4.4	5.7	9.6	6.5	7.7	7.9
Industry	64.6	85.9	100.7	16.2	18.7	21.9	26.9	27.9	28.1

Note: Employment as per usual principal and subsidiary status (UPSS) basis.
Source: *Economic Survey 2011-12.*

With economic reforms, it had been expected that the industrial sector would emerge as the key to additional employment opportunities for the labour force. There has been significant increase in employment opportunities in the industrial sector, though most of these additional opportunities have been created in the construction sector. In 2009-10, the construction sector employed 9.6 per cent of the workforce as against a 7.9 per cent share in GDP. There has also been an increase in employment opportunities in the mining sector. However, in the manufacturing sector, overall employment opportunities have declined in 2009-10 compared to 2004-05 (Table 15.11).

There could, however, be some deeper structural reasons as well, with increasing sub-contracting (outsourcing) of manufacture of parts and auxiliary services to the unorganised sector, and forging of close supply-chain networks. Such an organisation of production is quite the opposite of the vertically integrated production structures that were common in the early years of industrialisation. After the reforms, with increased competitive pressure, under the liberalised rules of resource use, and with lax enforcement of labour laws, firms have apparently restructured their production processes by shedding labour. Conceivably, some of the employment lost in the organised sector would have reappeared in the unorganised sector, though no direct evidence for it is available. Therefore, while the stagnation of the industrial employment share is a cause for concern, it perhaps represents an outcome of the changing market conditions, organisation of production and technology in an open labour-surplus economy.

Table 15.12 presents growth rates of GDP and employment in manufacturing and the total economy for four sub-periods of the long period 1972-73 to 2009-10.

TABLE – 15.12

Growth of GDP and Employment (UPSS) in Manufacturing: 1972-73 to 2009-10

(Per cent per annum)

	1972-73 to 1983	*1983 to 1993-94*	*1993-94 to 1999-2000*	*1999-2000 to 2009-10*
(1)	*(2)*	*(3)*	*(4)*	*(5)*
		GDP		
Manufacturing	5.5	4.9	6.9	8.0
Total economy	4.7	5.0	6.5	7.5
		Employment		
Manufacturing	4.3 (0.61)	2.0 (0.41)	1.6 (0.24)	1.9 (0.25)
Total economy	2.4 (0.56)	2.0 (0.41)	1.0 (0.16)	1.5 (0.20)

Note: Figures in parantheses are employment elasticities (EE).

Source: Papola and Sahu (2012: tables 1, 2 and 3).

As may be seen in Table 15.12, manufacturing GDP growth has accelerated from 4.9 per cent per annum during 1983 to 1993-94 to 6.9 per cent during 1993-94 to 1999-2000 and further to 8.0 per cent during 1999-2000 to 2009-10. But employment growth in the manufacturing sector has decelerated from 2.0 per cent during 1983 to 1993-94 to 1.6 per cent 1993-94 to 1999-2000. Although it has accelerated to 1.9 per cent in the first decade of the 21st century, it is much lower than the GDP growth in manufacturing and much lower than the employment growth rate during 1972-73 to 1983. The employment elasticity declined from 0.61 to 0.41. It has been around 0.25 in the post-reform period.

Much of the growth in employment in manufacturing during the past two decades seems to have occurred in the unorganised segment of the sector (see Goldar, 2009). Basu and Maertens (2010) deal with the issue of job creation for the large labour force in South Asia. Drawing on the experience of growth in manufacturing and services sectors in South Asian countries, they note the disappointing outcome in terms of creation of good jobs which has limited the poverty reduction impact of rapid growth. They trace the disappointing outcome in India to the restrictive labour laws. Those laws have not only reduced employment prospects in organised manufacturing but also constrained its growth by adversely affecting investment and productivity. In all South Asian countries including India, inadequate and weak infrastructure has also constrained the expansion of the manufacturing sector and job creation. The policy conclusions are quite obvious.

At the present juncture of India's economic development, an accelerated, fast growth of the manufacturing sector and large scale creation of jobs in Indian manufacturing is quite essential for attaining and sustaining a rapid and inclusive economic growth in India, which would greatly help in alleviating poverty in the country. Large increases in employment in Indian manufacturing are critical for providing job opportunities to the youth (especially the uneducated or less educated youth) who will be entering the labour force in large numbers in the coming decades. The need for stepping up the rate of growth in manufacturing output and creating manufacturing jobs on a large scale in India is widely recognised, both in academia and in government policy circles.

The emphasis placed by the government on manufacturing sector growth and creation of manufacturing sector jobs is clearly reflected in the National Manufacturing Policy (NMP) of 2011 and the Make-in-India initiative launched in 2014. The NMP had, in 2011, set a target of raising the share of manufacturing in aggregate GDP (gross domestic product) from about 15 per cent (as prevailing at that time) to about 25 per cent in a period of about 10 years (by 2022 or so) and creating 100 million new jobs in that process. Attainment of this target of NMP requires a marked acceleration in the growth rate of manufacturing. Goldar (2015a) has observed that if the average growth rate of aggregate GDP is taken to be about 8 per cent per annum till 2022, then the manufacturing sector needs to grow at the rate of about 13 per cent per annum for reaching the target manufacturing share in GDP of 25 per cent by 2022. It may be added here that if a slightly longer period is considered for the attainment of the goals of the NMP, and it is assumed that the average growth rate in aggregate GDP would be about 8 per cent per annum during the period 2016-17 to 2025-2026, then for reaching the target share of 25 per cent by 2025-26, the required growth rate in manufacturing is around 12 per cent per annum. Indeed, as one of its key objectives, the NMP sought to enhance the growth rate of manufacturing to 12-14 per cent per annum in the medium term. By contrast, in the recent past, 2011-12 to 2015-16, the average annual growth rate in manufacturing real GVA (gross value added) was about 7 per cent per annum. Evidently, a significant step up in the growth rate in manufacturing real GVA is required for attaining the targets of the NMP (Goldar, 2017).[10]

Why did the Reforms Fail to Deliver the Expected Results?

Still, the principal question remains unanswered: why did the speeding up of the reforms after 1991 not yield faster output, employment and labour-intensive growth? The protagonists would contend that the reforms have remained incomplete, with the persistence of the labour market rigidities (lack of entrepreneurial freedom to hire and fire workers at will), infrastructure bottlenecks, and incomplete financial integration, including full convertibility of the currency (Kocchar *et al.*, 2006; Panagariya, 2008; Krueger, 2009, among others).

Based on cross-country analysis, Kocchar *et al.* argue that India has followed idiosyncratic policies in promoting skill-intensive industries, discouraging labour-intensive manufactures—a pattern that has not changed after the reforms because of the labour market rigidities. These scholars also contend that on average Indian firms tend to be small because workers cannot be fired, preventing them from reaping the advantages of economies of scale in production. But, since skilled workers and professionals are outside the purview of trade unions, India has specialised in skill-intensive industries.

What then are the facts of the matter? The average factory size in registered manufacturing in 2004-05 was 35 workers per factory, declining steadily over the last half century from over 140 workers (Nagaraj, 1985). At the other end of the scale, household manufacturing

---

10. Goldar, Bishwanath (2017). "Growth, Productivity and Job Creation in Indian Manufacturing", in Uma Kapila (ed.) 2017, *India's Economy: Pre-Liberalisation to GST–Essays in Honour of Raj Kapila.* New Delhi: Academic Foundation.

has become marginal with the expansion of smaller-sized workshops and factories. These are long-term trends of industrial change, unaffected by the reforms.

India's Unique Pattern of Development

We now take up the unique aspect of Indian industrial development. In a very insightful analysis of Indian industrialisation since Independence, Kochhar *et al.* (2006) argue that India pursued an 'idiosyncratic' pattern of development which resulted in direct shift of labour from agriculture sector to the service sector, bypassing the intermediate stage (industrial sector) to a considerable extent. Within manufacturing, India has emphasised skill-intensive rather than labour-intensive industries and industries with typically higher average scale. Analysing the pattern of growth of fast-moving Indian states in the reform era, they come to the conclusion that it is unlikely that India will adopt the pattern of development followed by other countries. This prediction has serious implication for the employment potential of the manufacturing sector in the years to come.[11]

The Organisation for Economic Co-operation and Development (OECD), 2007) notes that India has followed a unique development path with the share of manufacturing in total GDP not increasing with economic growth, and attributes this feature to 'deeply rooted problems' in the manufacturing sector constraining its growth, although some of these have been eased with reforms. Manufacturing firms were not able to fully exploit their comparative advantages of low-labour costs and have remained very small in scale—yet capital-intensive—limiting productivity gains as well as job creation. In recent years, there has been some employment expansion due to some liberalisation of labour laws, but many of the new jobs are of low quality. Large firms still face obstacles to restructuring employment, constraining their ability to compete effectively.

Conclusions

Ending the strategic role of the state-led import-substituting industrialisation, the two decades of industry and trade policy reforms have dismantled the output and investments controls. Quality and variety of goods produced have improved; relative price of capital goods has declined (enhancing the productivity of fixed investment),

11. Krishna (2014) *op.cit.* no.1

although the import content in domestic production has risen. The unintended boom in the export of information technology (IT) and related services can be clearly seen as a consequence of early investments in heavy industry and scientific and technical education. A growing number of Indian firms have gained technical expertise to run factories and firms across the globe, leveraging their domestic competence and, in turn, to acquire technology to enhance their domestic cababilities. (Nagaraj, 2011)

Yet, these achievements have not translated into faster and labour-intensive industrial growth or growth in industrial exports, as compared to the 1980s. As a result, the services sector has replaced manufacturing as the economy's leading sector. Although India did not witness de-industrialisation, as the critics of the reforms apprehended, industry's share of domestic output and employment has stagnated; its share in merchandise export has declined, with rising exports of primary exports (mainly of iron ore). Why did the reforms fail to deliver a faster and equitable industrial growth? In other words, why did the reforms fail to promote labour-intensive growth and manufactured exports, as in East Asia and China?

Liberal economic reforms or the market-friendly policy framework constructed over the last quarter century has not served the manufacturing sector well, despite faster economic growth, and output diversification. The goal of rapid industrialising to catch up with Asian peers, in an open trade and capital regime employing abundant labour for labour-intensive exports, did not materialise. There has been undeniable improvement in domestic competition with the rise in the quality and variety of goods produced and exported. Yet, the share of manufacturing in GDP has stagnated, and its share in merchandise exports declined, and import content in domestic consumption shot up.

An eroding industrial base has found political expression in the current political dispensation's slogan, "Make in India," or in the previous regime's National Manufacturing Policy, 2011, albeit these ideas are yet to get translated into workable policies and suitable instruments for implementation. The easy starting point of it would be to try producing domestically what is being imported. The sharp rise in imports during the recent years clearly shows the potential to indigenes production quickly.

Ruling dispensations, regardless of their political colour and candour, have argued for "finishing" or "completing" the liberal economic reforms agenda, including institutional reforms, to reap their virtuous outcomes. However, after a quarter century of persuasion, such an advocacy rings hollow as it does not have support either in theory or in comparative experience. Worldwide rethinking on the virtues of unbridled globalisation of trade and investment after the global financial crisis is a testament to limits of such arguments, in the current stage of political democracy.

The policymakers' single-minded focus on improving India's ranking in the World Bank's Ease of Doing Business index (mainly by whittling down protective measures for the working poor) seems seriously misplaced as the index has no analytical basis or empirical support. Further, easing of entry of foreign capital even into defence production is completely misplaced when most of the FDI inflow is from private equity firms, which specialise in flipping assets for quick returns, not digging their heels for long-term growth of shared gains.

Unalloyed faith in liberal reforms seems passé (Ostry et al. 2016). As Dani Rodrik (2016) said recently,

> The new model of globalisation stood priorities on their head, effectively putting democracy to work for the global economy, instead of the other way around. The elimination of barriers to trade and finance became an end in itself, rather than a means toward more fundamental economic and social goals. Societies were asked to subject domestic economies to the whims of global financial markets; sign investment treaties that created special rights for foreign companies; and reduce corporate and top income taxes to attract footloose corporations.

With global economic recession continuing after eight years of the financial crisis, and its political fallout in terms of Brexit, or ultra nationalism in the US, and the proposed scrapping of the Trans-Pacific Partnership by the US seem clear signals of the current limits to globalism. Considering the current global political and economic uncertainties, it would be prudent to pause and reflect on the liberal model. There is perhaps a need to revitalise the idea of the development state for retaking the initiatives for industrialisation.

According to Nagaraj, the principal drawback of the reforms is its exclusive focus on removing supply constraints at the neglect of demand. There is a growing consensus on the need to raise agriculture productivity to find markets for industrial goods (Nagaraj, 2011).

Such a vision should not be misconstrued as a plea for a reversal to uncritical infant industry protection or complete delinking from international trade and capital flows. Surely, with rising agriculture productivity and structural transformation, industrial growth will have to turn increasingly to exports for sustaining domestic growth. Yet, for a large economy like India—to paraphrase Arthur Lewis—exports will have to be the efficient lubricant for the large domestic economy, especially to meet energy import needs. It calls for strategic integration with the global economy and reinventing industrial policy keeping in view the long-term national goals.

The structuralist economic view of India's long-term constraints, as low agriculture productivity (compared to the global average), poor public infrastructure and extreme energy import dependence, seem to hold considerable value to this date. So, at a macroeconomic level, such a view would call for state intervention to step up domestic savings and public investment, and insulate the domestic economy from shortterm volatility emanating from the global economy.

We probably need to identify industries and products in which imports are succeeding on account of easy credit, and those which require productivity improvement. There is apparently a need for reconfiguring a strategy for capital goods development (in items like information and communications technology hardware or in solar energy), in which India has become seriously import- dependent, undermining the strategic national interests. This is not, however, a plea for blanket import substitution, and export pessimism, but for infusing technological dynamism to recapture the domestic market and the dynamic comparative advantage in trade. Capital and technology import should be accompanied with commitments for R&D investment.

There is a need to reimagine the role of domestic financial institutions to provide long-term credit for capital intensive industries, infrastructure and exports; along the lines advocated (separately) by Robert Skidelsky and Adair Turner in the current global context. These measures necessarily have fiscal counterparts, which need to be addressed by revisiting fiscal rules.

Similarly, domestic R&D, expenditure which has barely inched up during the reforms as a share of the GDP—compared to China, which tripled the ratio—needs to be seriously viewed and corrected if our present political dispensation is serious of realising its dream of techno-nationalism.

16

Micro, Small and Medium Enterprises (MSMEs)

THE micro, small and medium enterprises (MSME) sector has emerged as a highly vibrant and dynamic sector of the Indian economy over the last few decades. It is estimated that this sector contributes about 45 per cent of manufacturing output and 40 per cent of total exports of the country and employs about 69 million persons in over 29 million units throughout the country. Within the MSME sector, there is a significant concentration of micro enterprises, both in terms of working enterprises and employment. There are over 6,000 products ranging from traditional to high-tech items manufactured by the MSMEs. The sector also covers the enterprises established in *khadi* and village industries and coir sector (Planning Commission, 2012).[1]

With 3.6 crore units spread across the country, that employ 8.05 crore people, Micro, Small and Medium Enterprises (MSME) have a contribution of 37.5 per cent to the country's GDP. The sector has huge potential for helping address structural problems like unemployment, regional imbalances, unequal distribution of national income and wealth across the country. Due to comparatively low capital costs and their forward-backward linkages with other sectors, MSMEs will play a crucial role in the success of the Make in India initiative (*Economic Survey 2015-16*, Vol.II).

The MSEs are, however, more than just GDP (gross domestic product) earners; they are instruments of inclusive growth which touch upon the lives of the most vulnerable, the most marginalised—women, Muslims, scheduled castes (SCs) and scheduled tribes (STs)—and the most unskilled. Being the largest source of employment after

1. Planning Commission (2012). *Twelfth Five Year Plan (2012-2017)*, Vol. II, Ch. 13.

agriculture, the MSE sector in India enables 850 lakh men, women and children living in urban slums, upcoming towns, remote villages and isolated hamlets to use indigenous knowledge, cultural wisdom and entrepreneurial skills for the sustenance of their lives and livelihoods (Planning Commission, 2008).[2]

Role of SMEs in Global Economy: International Scenario

Worldwide, MSMEs have been recognised as engines of economic growth.

The overall contribution of small firms—formal and informal—to the GDP and employment remains about the same across low-, middle- and high-income group countries. As income increases, the share of the informal sector decreases and that of the formal SME sector increases. In Brazil, MSEs represent 20 per cent of the total GDP. Of the country's 4.7 million registered businesses, 96.8 per cent are MSEs and—along with the other 9.5 million informal enterprises—they employ 59 per cent of the economically active population. Similarly, informal and micro enterprises account for 39 per cent of labour force and contribute to 24 per cent of the GDP in South Africa; SMEs employ 27 per cent of the labour force and contribute 32 per cent to the GDP; while large enterprises employ 34 per cent people and account for 44 per cent of GDP. SMEs comprise over 90 per cent of all industrial units in Bangladesh contributing between 80 per cent and 85 per cent of the industrial employment and 23 per cent of the total civilian employment. They contribute three-quarters of the household income in both the urban and the rural areas. In Japan, SMEs employ more than 70 per cent of the wage earners, contributing over 55 per cent of value added in the manufacturing sector. In Thailand in 2003, there were 2,006,528 enterprises of which 99.5 per cent were SMEs. These SMEs generated products worth 38.1 per cent of GDP and in 2003 they employed 60.7 per cent of Thailand's working population.

The real importance of the SMEs, however, can be seen in China where over 68 per cent of the exports come from the SMEs. China has created more SMEs in the last 20 years than the total number of SMEs in Europe and the US combined. Their numbers have increased from about 1 million private sector SMEs in the 1990s to 40 million in 2004. In China, an

2. Planning Commission (2008). *Eleventh Five Year Plan 2007-2012*, Vol. III.

industrial SME is defined as having up to 2,000 employees, while a small business has less than 300 employees and a medium-size business has employees between 301 and 2,000 (Planning Commission, 2008).

Defining MSMEs: MSMED Act, 2006

There is no globally accepted definition of MSMEs. Different countries use different criterion; most of the definitions are based on investment ceiling and number of people employed. In India, the Micro, Small and Medium Enterprises Development (MSMED) Act, 2006, defines MSMEs. It introduces the concept of 'enterprise' as opposed to the earlier concept of industry. According to the act, MSMEs are classified into the following: (i) enterprises engaged in the manufacture or production of goods pertaining to any industry specified in the first schedule to the Industries (Development and Regulation) Act (IDRA), 1951, and (ii) enterprises engaged in providing or rendering services. Table 16.1 defines the MSMEs in both these sectors.

TABLE – 16.1

Definition of MSMEs

	Manufacturing Sector
Enterprises	Investment in plant and machinery (original cost excluding land and building and the items specified by the then ministry of small scale industries, vide its notification No. S.O.1722(E) dated 5 October 2006)
Micro enterprises	Does not exceed ₹ 25 lakh
Small enterprises	More than ₹ 25 lakh and less than ₹ 5 crore
Medium enterprises	More than ₹ 5 crore and less than ₹ 10 crore
	Service Sector
Enterprises	Investment in equipments
Micro enterprises	Does not exceed ₹ 10 lakh
Small enterprises	More than ₹ 10 lakh and less than ₹ 2 crore
Medium enterprises	More than ₹ 2 crore and less than ₹ 5 crore

Source: MSMED Act, 2006.
Planning Commission (2008).

The Act also provides for a statutory consultative mechanism at the national level with a balanced representation of all the sections of stakeholders and with a wide range of advisory functions. Establishment of specific funds for promotion, development and enhancement of the competitiveness of these enterprises; notification of schemes/ programmes, progressive credit policies and practices; preference to products and services of MSEs in the government procurement; more effective mechanisms for mitigating the problems of delayed payments; and a scheme for easing the closure of business by these enterprises are some features of the act.

Role of MSMEs in Indian Economy

To Generate Large-scale Employment

As countries develop, the share of agriculture in providing employment and in GDP decreases. According to the Australian economist Chris Hall, the SMEs contribute about 70 per cent of net new jobs across the globe, while larger firms tend to be job destroyers.

The MSE sector in India has grown significantly since 1960, when there were only 12,376 MSEs providing employment to 10 lakh people—of which, direct employment was 1.85 lakh; annual production level was ₹ 875 crore. At the beginning of the Tenth Plan, 249 lakh people in the rural and urban areas were employed in 105.21 lakh MSEs. This has increased to 295 lakh people in 128 lakh units now; an average annual growth rate of 4.4 per cent in the number of these units and 4.62 per cent in employment. If the units in the *khadi* industries, village industries and coir industries are taken into account, the employment is estimated to be over 332 lakh. With the inclusion of handlooms, handicrafts, wool and sericulture, the total job in the MSE sector in India goes up to 650 lakh. The employment intensity of the registered units indicates that an investment of ₹ 0.72 lakh is required for creating one employment in MSME sector as against ₹ 5.56 lakh in the large organised sector.

Not only do MSEs generate the highest employment per capita investment, they also go a long way in checking rural-urban migration by providing villagers and people living in isolated areas with a sustainable source of employment. Among the MSEs in India, the dispersed food products sector generates maximum employment (13.7% of total employment in the MSE sector), followed by non-metallic mineral products (10.9%) and metal products (10.2%). In chemicals and chemical products, machinery parts except electrical parts, wood products, basic metal industries, paper products and printing, hosiery and garments, repair services, and rubber and plastic products, the contribution ranges from 9 per cent to 5 per cent. In all other industries, the contribution is less than 5 per cent.

Per unit employment is highest (20) in units engaged in beverages, tobacco and tobacco products. Next come cotton textile products (17), non-metallic mineral products (14.1), basic metal industries (13.6), and electrical machinery and parts (11.2). Per unit employment is highest (10) in the metropolitan areas and lowest (5) in the rural areas. Non-metallic products contribute 22.7 per cent to the employment generated in the rural areas, followed by food products (21.1%), wood products, and chemicals and chemical products. As for the urban areas, food products and metal products almost equally share 22.8 per cent employment. Machinery parts except electrical, non-metallic mineral products, and chemicals and chemical products between them account for another 26.2 per cent employment. Metal products, machinery and parts except electrical, and paper products and printing (total share being 33.6 per cent) are the leading industries in metropolitan areas (Planning Commission, 2008).

To Sustain Economic Growth and Increase Exports

Non-traditional products account for more than 95 per cent of the small-scale industry (SSI) exports. The performance of garments, leather, and gems and jewellery units has been remarkable in the last decade. The SSI sector dominates in export of sports goods, readymade garments, woollen garments and knitwear, plastic products, processed food, and leather products. The US, Europe and West Asia are the major export destinations.

There is tremendous potential to expand the quantum of exports from traditional MSEs because they are handcrafted and hence eco-friendly and exclusive. Further, while MSEs are unable to take advantage of economies of scale, they are ideal for meeting small order quantities—a bonus in industries such as readymade garments, home furnishings, etc.

MSEs often act as ancillary industries for LSIs providing them with raw materials, vital components and backward linkages. For instance, large cycle manufacturers of Ludhiana rely heavily on the small MSEs of Malerkotla which produce cycle parts. MSEs also promote eco-friendly growth, especially in difficult terrains and the ecologically sensitive areas. In large tracts of barren desert land in Barmer and Kutch, in the scattered *dhani*s of Udaipur, in the hilly hamlets of Jammu & Kashmir (J&K), Ladakh, Himachal and the Northeast, in the tribal hinterlands of central India, they are the only source of livelihood.

Making Growth Inclusive

The MSE sector is a microcosm of all vulnerabilities—it touches upon the lives of women, children, minorities, SCs and STs in the villages, in the urban slums and in the deprived pockets of flourishing towns and cities. For many families, it is the only source of livelihood. For others, it supplements the family income. Thus, instead of taking a welfare approach, this sector seeks to empower people to break the cycle of poverty and deprivation. It focuses on people's skills and agency.

Different segments of the MSE sector are dominated by different social groups. Women are mostly found in the unregistered sector—food processing enterprises, manufacturing enterprises and weaving—and often work part time in the family enterprises. Women and small children roll *bidis*, make *agarbattis*, do *zari* and sequin work for meagre wages. Large number of Muslims are found in the unorganised weaving sector and in powerlooms. In the Northeast, most women weave. In states like Tripura, 50 per cent of rural men and 35 per cent rural women are engaged in MSEs. In Nagaland and Mizoram, over 68 per cent of urban men are with MSEs (Planning Commission, 2008).

The Twelfth Plan has listed the following as the objectives for the MSME sector:

1. Promoting competitiveness and productivity in the MSME space.
2. Making the MSME sector innovative, improving technology and depth.
3. Enabling environment for promotion and development of MSMEs.
4. Strong presence in exports.
5. Improved managerial processes in MSMEs.

Status and Key Challenges

There are some inherent challenges faced by the sector which have a strong impact on its growth. These relate to (i) availability of credit and institutional finance, (ii) outdated technology and innovation, (iii) need for skill development and training, (iv) inadequate industrial infrastructure, and (v) marketing and procurement.

State governments are formulating and implementing heterogeneous sets of regulations. Apart from inspections and compliances, insolvency provisions make it difficult to restructure and rehabilitate sick and dying businesses in the SMEs sector. Procedures to buy and acquire land are costly. Registration of land sale and purchase deeds, transfer of title, and acquiring of construction permits are complicated and time-consuming procedures. While some states have taken steps to promote ease of doing business in recent years, the majority of states are still far from having a friendly eco system for small businesses.

Globalisation and Small Industry Performance[3]

The remarkable shift in India's SSI policy since 1991, in tune with the overall trend of economic liberalisation, represents the sector-specific dimension of the change in the macroeconomic policy environment for SSI. The most visible plank of SSI protection policy prior to 1991 was the reservation of product lines for exclusive manufacturing in the SSI sector. The policy was introduced in 1947 with a list of 47 items which was expanded steadily to comprise 504 items in 1977, and after the recast of the list based on National Industrial Classification (NIC) codes, the list of items increased to 807 in 1978. By 1991, the list included 836 items (Bala Subrahmanya, 1995). Since then, however, the list of reserved items for exclusive manufacturing has been curtailed steadily. Today, the list of items reserved for the SSI sector comprises only 20 items (DCMSME, 2014). To the extent of 816 de-reserved items from the list, the SSI sector would have been exposed to intense competition vis-à-vis large firms, in the era of globalisation. On the positive front, to enhance the competitiveness of SSI, the government has introduced several policy measures backed by institutions to provide better access to finance, technology and marketing, among others (Ministry of MSMEs, 2010).

The above discussion brings out that policy changes that have taken place since 1991 at the global, national and sectoral levels and their implications for SSI present a mixed bag of challenges and opportunities. The limited, location-specific, empirical research findings reveal that SSI has gained on different fronts whereas lost on some other fronts. Overall, it would be appropriate to conclude that globalisation and domestic economic liberalisation together would have considerably contributed to the intensification of competitive environment for Indian SSI locally as well as globally.

In the process, less competitive ones would have suffered whereas more competitive ones would have gained. Further, a considerable number of SSI enterprises would have responded to the emerging

3. This section is drawn extensivily from Bala Subrahmanya, M.H. (2014) "Small-scale Industrialisation under Globalisation: Is the Tide Turning Around?" in Uma Kapila (ed.), *Indian Economy since Independence* (25th ed.). New Delhi: Academic Foundation.

competitive environment by enhancing their competitiveness, by taking advantage of the market forces on the one hand, and policy intervention, on the other, wherever appropriate. The overall growth performance and contribution of SSI to the national economy in the era of globalisation have to be analysed against this backdrop.

SSI Performance in the Globalisation Era

The SSI sector in India comprises two sub-sectors: registered and unregistered. The registered SSI sector comprises factories registered under Indian Factories Act, 1948, and those registered with the District Industries Centres (DICs) in the states and union territories of India, among others. The unregistered SSI, on the other hand, includes non-factory enterprises and those which are not registered with the DICs, among others (Ministry of MSMEs, 2012).

The registered SSI sector represents a more developed/modern segment of the SSI, as it primarily includes factories and those registered with the DICs. Therefore, examining its growth performance and contribution to the national economy (based on census data) might be more meaningful. Therefore, registered SSI performance has been examined in terms of (i) growth of units, exporting units, employment, values of output and exports (both at 2004/05 prices), (ii) relative contribution of registered SSI to national income, organised sector employment and total exports, (iii) degree of internationalisation, (iv) growth of ancillarisation, and (v) growth of sickness, from 1987/88 to 2001/02 and from 2001/02 to 2006/07.

Performance of the SSI Sector: Pre-liberalisation Period versus Liberalisation Period

The growth performance of SSI units, employment, output and exports for the pre-liberalisation period and for the liberalisation period (Figure 16.1) as well as for the decades from the 1970s to 2000s is presented in Table 16.2. The growth rate of SSI, on an average, has declined considerably in terms of units and even employment, but has improved marginally in terms of output and exports, in the liberalisation period compared to the pre-liberalisation period. The decade-wise performance provides more insights. The growth of SSI units declined in the 1980s compared to that of the 1970s, and it declined further in the 1990s but remained steady in the 2000s compared to that of the 1990s.

FIGURE – 16.1

SSI Growth Performance in the Pre-Liberalisation and Liberalisation Periods

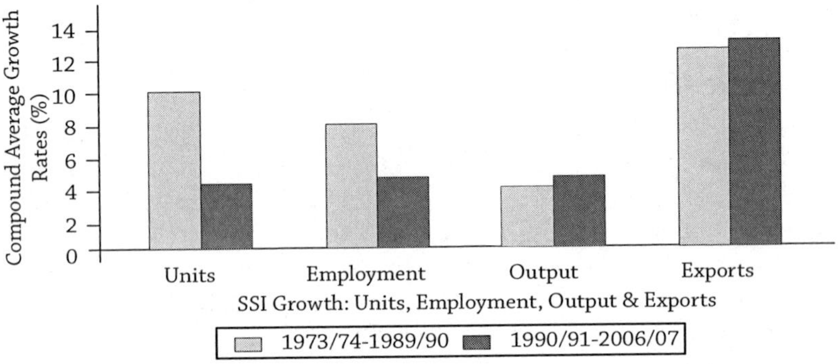

TABLE – 16.2

Growth Performance of SSI: Pre-Liberalisation *versus* Liberalisation

	Period	*Units*	*Employment*	*Output*	*Exports*
Pre-liberalisation	1973/74-1989/90	9.67	7.14	3.66	12.09
Liberalisation	1990/91-2006/07	4.06	4.34	4.34	12.62
1970s	1973/74-1980/81	11.19	8.66	3.36	13.95
1980s	1980/81-1989/90	8.51	5.97	3.89	10.66
1990s	1990/91-2000/01	4.06	4.21	0.11	12.87
2000s	2000/01-2006/07	4.06	4.56	11.78	12.20

Source: Ministry of MSMEs.

The growth of SSI employment, similar to that of SSI units, declined in the 1980s compared to that of the 1970s, and it declined further in the 1990s but improved marginally in the 2000s compared to that of the 1990s. The growth of output, unlike units and employment, improved marginally in the 1980s compared to that of the 1970s, but declined sharply in the 1990s and improved remarkably in the 2000s compared to the earlier decades. The growth of exports, unlike units, employment and output, has remained, more or less, steady all through the pre-liberalisation and liberalisation periods. Although the growth of exports declined in the 1980s compared to that of the 1970s, it improved modestly in the 1990s but declined marginally in the 2000s compared to that of the 1990s. On the whole, it may be appropriate to conclude that while

SSI growth suffered in terms of units and employment, in terms of output, SSI has improved, and in terms of exports it could hold on to its ground to a large extent, in the liberalisation period relative to the pre-liberalisation period. The question is why this has happened. The possible reasons could be the following:[4]

1. New SSI units might not have come up as significantly in the liberalisation period as compared to the pre-liberalisation period due to the threat of competition. This would have affected directly SSI employment generation as well.
2. Those new SSI units that have come up in the liberalisation period might be much more capital-intensive than those that have come up in the past. Even some proportions of the existing SSI units might have modernised themselves, to rely less on labour. This was one of the objectives of technology upgradation and modernisation achieved by some of the machinery SMEs in Bangalore.
3. Those SSI units which lacked access to basic infrastructural facilities and which could not strengthen their competitiveness would have exited from the market, thereby affecting SSI employment and output initially.
4. A significant proportion of existing SSI units might have strengthened their competitiveness through technology up-gradation and modernisation, among others, particularly to take advantage of the developments in the global market.

Performance of the Registered SSI in the Liberalisation Period: 1987/88-2006/07

The growth performance of registered SSI sector in terms of units, exporting units, employment, values of output and exports (both at 2004/05 prices) for the liberalisation period is presented in Table 16.3. The growth of registered SSI units has suffered in the 2000s compared to that of the 1990s, but employment has grown considerably in the 2000s, and output growth was much more impressive, whereas export orientation of the registered SSI sector (in terms of exporting units and value of exports) has improved remarkably in the 2000s. Broadly, this would corroborate the overall SSI growth performance that we have observed earlier. It appears that SSI growth performance (in terms of

4. Ibid.

employment, output and exports) might have suffered initially but it has been able to recover impressively subsequently.

TABLE – 16.3

Registered SSI Performance: Census Data: 1987/88-2006/07

Period	*Units*	*Employment*	*Output*	*Exporting Units*	*Exports*
1987/88-2001/02	6.33	3.78	3.57	3.47	3.87
2001/02-2006/07	3.22	9.55	27.20	58.21	46.82

Source: Subrahmanya (2014).

How did the registered SSI contribution to the national economy change in the liberalisation period? This is the other pertinent issue essential to examine. The relative contribution of registered SSI to gross domestic product (GDP) in terms of gross value added (GVA), organised sector employment and total exports is given in Table 16.4. The share of registered SSI in India's GDP has more than doubled from 3.35 per cent to 6.73 per cent between 1987/88 and 2006/07, and its share in total organised sector employment increased marginally from 20 per cent to about 23 per cent between 1987/88 and 2001/02 but increased considerably to more than 34 per cent between 2001/02 and 2006/07. Although the share of registered SSI exports declined sharply from about 16 per cent in 1987/88 to about 6 per cent in 2000/01, it bounced back and doubled to reach almost 12 per cent in 2006/07. These statistics imply that though the registered SSI growth performance and contribution might have suffered in the initial decade of economic liberalisation, the sector appeared to have turned the corner in the decade of 2000s.

TABLE – 16.4

Registered SSI Contribution to GDP, Employment and Total Exports

Year	*GDP*	*Organised Sector Employment*	*Total Exports*
1987/88	3.35	20.00	15.94
2001/02	NA	22.65	5.90
2006/07	6.73	34.13	11.88

The improved economic health of registered SSI sector is reflected in another parameter, i.e., industrial sickness. While the second SSI Census did not provide figures relating to SSI sickness, the subsequent two census provided these figures. Sickness in the registered SSI sector has declined both absolutely and relatively (Table 16.5). The number of sick SSI units reduced to almost one-half in 2006/07 compared to 2001/02, and even as a percentage of total registered SSI units, sick SSI units declined to less than half of the figure of 2001/02 in 2006/07. This reduction in sickness could be attributed to two factors: (i) sickness has been cured and (ii) fresh sickness has not emerged as intensively as in the past. This might be the outcome of improvements in SSI internal strength and favourable external environment, since the identified causal factors for SSI sickness comprised both internal and external factors (such as management deficiencies, insufficient financial control, inadequate attention to research & development (R&D), obsolete technology, inadequate demand, shortage of raw materials, inadequate working capital, infrastructural bottlenecks, etc.) which often operated in combination (DCSSI, 2002). Therefore, sickness reduction may be considered another indicator of an improvement in the SSI performance.

TABLE – 16.5

Sickness in SSI: 2001/02-2006/07

Year	*Total SSI Units*	*Sick SSI Units*	*% of Sick SSI Units*
2001/02	1374974	192328	13.98
2006/07	1561000	101270	6.49

There are two more issues concerning SSI performance, namely, (i) ancillarisation and (ii) degree of internationalisation. The promotion of inter-firm linkages between large firms and SSI through subcontracting and ancillarisation in both public and private sectors has been an important dimension of India's SSI Policy. Accordingly, Small Industries Development Organisation (SIDO) resorted to proactive promotion of ancillarisation through vendor development programmes and subcontracting exchanges as early as in the 1980s (DCSSI, 1989). In 1995, government introduced a scheme to encourage subcontracting exchanges by SSI associations (Bala Subrahmanya, 1998). The merits of subcontracting relationship, in addition to assured marketing, though to a lesser degree, covered technical assistance, finance, supply of raw materials and training (Sahu, 2007). Therefore, any growth of ancillarisation and subcontracting relationship between SSI and large firms would be advantageous to the performance of the former.

The second and third Censuses of SSI provide data on ancillary units but not the fourth Census. There was a considerable increase in the number of ancillary units between 1987/88 and 2001/02, and as a result, the percentage of ancillary units increased from <1 per cent to >5 per cent (Table 16.6). Since then, the number of ancillary units might have gone up further. But this figure takes into account only formal sub-contracting relationships, whereas a significant proportion of SSI in states like Karnataka (particularly, in cities like Bangalore) has informal sub-contracting relationships with large firms including MNCs (Bala Subrahmanya et al., 2001; Kumar and Bala Subrahmanya, 2010). The growing inter-firm linkages, formal as well as informal, would have benefited the economic performance of SSI. Empirical evidence in the context of Bangalore has revealed that SMEs, which have internal technical competence and obtain external support from their large enterprise customers, among others, are able to enhance their innovation performance and thereby their economic performance (Bala Subrahmanya, 2013a).

TABLE – 16.6

SSI and Ancillarisation: 1987/88-2001/02

Year	*Ancillary Units*	*Total SSI Units*	*% of Ancillary Units*
1987-88	3028	582368	0.52
2001-02	69848	1374974	5.08
2006-07	NA	1561000	NA

How does SSI respond to the growing global opportunities is another important issue having implication for its performance. With increasing global competition, falling barriers to international trade and improved international information and communication technology (ICT) networks, globally active SMEs are emerging in considerably large numbers across the world and it is expected to gain further momentum in the future (Ruzzier *et al.*, 2006). An export strategy has been the primary foreign-market entry mode adopted by SMEs in their internationalisation efforts (Wolff and Pett, 2000). This is because exporting fits the capabilities of SMEs by offering them a greater degree of flexibility and minimum resource commitments combined with minimum risk exposure (Young *et al.,* 1989). The growing trend of SSI entering the international markets through exports can be observed in the Indian context as well (Table 16.7).

Both exporting SSI units and value of SSI exports have increased considerably between 1987/88 and 2006/07, absolutely as well as relative to the total SSI units and total SSI output. The degree of internationalisation in terms of units (exporting SSI units as a percentage of total SSI units) though declined to 0.53 per cent in 2001/02 from 0.78 per cent in 1987/88, increased to 2.95 per cent in 2006/07. The degree of internationalisation in terms of export value (value of SSI exports as a percentage of total SSI output) marginally went up from 5.82 per cent in 1987/88 to 6.06 per cent in 2001/02 and further to 9.60 per cent in 2006/07 (Table 16.7). At the national level, several factors would have contributed to this increasing trend of SSI internationalisation. Of them, the most notable one is the structural shift in the composition of SSI exports from traditional to non-traditional items (Bala Subrahmanya, 2011). Among the factors which facilitated the growth of SSI internationalisation, MNCs and E-Commerce as the modes of entry stood out significantly, in the context of Bangalore (Bala Subrahmanya, 2013b).

TABLE – 16.7

Degree of Internationalisation

Year	*Exporting Units*	*Total Units*	*DOI**	*Value of Exports (at 2004/05 prices)*	*Total Output (at 2004/05 prices)*	*DOI***
1987/88	4554	582368	0.78	249902	14180777	5.82
2001/02	7344	1374974	0.53	1230826	23171027	6.06
2006/07	46012	1561000	2.95	NA	60649632	--
2006/07#	46675	1563974	2.98	6791400	67925307	9.60

Notes: DOI* = Percentage of exporting units in total SSI units.
DOI** = Percentage of value of SSI exports in the value of total output.
Includes medium enterprises.

In brief, the overall SSI growth performance indicators revealed that the growth pattern in the liberalisation period is not significantly different from that of the pre-liberalisation period, with the exception of the growth rates of units and employment. Although the growth rates of SSI units and employment, more or less, steadily declined in the pre-liberalisation period, on an average, the growth rates of units and employment were much higher in the pre-liberalisation period compared to that of the liberalisation period, which did not exhibit any definite pattern of growth. Although the average growth rates of output and exports are higher in the liberalisation period relative to the pre-liberalisation period, the differences in the annual growth rates between the two periods of time are not statistically significant.

However, the performance indicators of the registered SSI sector are more pronounced. Although its growth rates (in absolute terms) were lower in the 1990s, it recorded a substantial recovery thereafter. Its contribution to national income and organised sector employment increased significantly. Further, there are indicators of its improved performance in terms of reduced sickness, improved linkages with large firms, and better penetration of the international market. Given the 'encouraging' performance of registered SSI, the key policy initiatives were introduced by the GoI subsequent to the Micro, Small and Medium Enterprises Development (MSMED) Act, 2006, to strengthen the SSI/SME sector further, and its implications need to be examined.

Inferences and Conclusions (In the Context of Recent Policy Initiatives)

The analysis of SSI performance indicates that SSI sector is undergoing transformation with an initial suffering and a subsequent recovery, and the recovery is more pronounced in the case of registered SSI. Its performance in terms of employment generation, output growth as well as export growth, its relative contribution to national GDP, organised sector employment and total exports are considerable and significant, particularly in the early 2000s. There are further indicators of improved economic health of SSI in the form of: (i) reduced industrial sickness, (ii) improved linkages with large firms, and (iii) increasing degree of internationalisation, with its resultant benefits. This lends credence to the observation made earlier that,

> Irrespective of the degree of support extended by the government and irrespective of the amount of efforts put in by SSI and their associations, India is going to experience the emergence of SSI sector, which is qualitatively superior, technologically vibrant and internationally competitive, in the next five to ten years because the 'inefficient ones' are likely to vanish gradually (Bala Subrahmanya, 2004).

However this could be largely true with respect to the registered SSI, which accounted for just about 6 per cent of the total MSMEs in 2006/07, whereas the remaining 94 per cent of the enterprises belonged to the unregistered sector (GoI, 2010).

The unregistered SSI would predominantly comprise micro enterprises, particularly confined to rural India, operating with obsolete technology, limited access to institutional finance, and limited marketing/management expertise. Given this, how to transform the huge unregistered SSI into the registered SSI and how to enhance the competitiveness of the overall SSI are the two foremost challenges confronted by the policy makers.

The shift in the SSI policy emphasis from protection to promotion of competitiveness began with the introduction of an exclusive policy for SSI in 1991 (Ministry of Industry, 1991). Since then, the policy support in the 1990s and early 2000s has been largely to enable the SSI to overcome the key challenges to their performance and growth, namely, finance, technology and marketing, among others (Bala Subrahmanya, 2004). Since 2005/06, several major policy initiatives have been taken by the GoI to promote SSI competitiveness, which are as follows (Ministry of MSMEs, 2010):

- The promulgation of MSMED Act 2006, which clubbed micro and small enterprises with medium enterprises and provided a common legal framework, for their integrated development and enhancing competitiveness.
- As part of the National Manufacturing Competitiveness Programme (NMCP), 10 specific initiatives were taken in 2007/08 to enhance the competitiveness of the entire value chain of the MSME sector.
- Limited Liability Partnership (LLP) Act, 2008, was introduced to enable early corporatisation of MSMEs and tap the capital market for fund raising. Accordingly, SME platforms are created in Bombay Stock Exchange (BSE) and National Stock Exchange (NSE) in 2012 (Ministry of MSMEs, 2013).
- To develop a road map for the development and promotion of MSMEs, a Task Force was created by the Prime Minister of India in 2009 (GoI, 2010). The Task Force, which comprised, among others, six specific theme-based sub-groups (on credit, marketing, infrastructure/technology/skill development, exit policy, labour and taxation) submitted its report in 2010 suggesting (i) immediate policy measures, (ii) medium-term institutional measures, and (iii) legal and regulatory structures to create a conducive environment for entrepreneurship and growth of MSMEs.

- The Working Group on MSMEs Growth for 12th Five Year Plan (2012-2017) made recommendations on six thematic verticals: (i) finance, including credit, (ii) infrastructure, (iii) technology, (iv) marketing and procurement, (v) skill development and training, and (vi) institutional structure. The Working Group reinforced the recommendations made by the Task Force earlier (Ministry of MSMEs, 2012).
- The Inter-Ministerial Committee for Accelerating Manufacturing in Micro, Small and Medium Enterprises made recommendations on (i) the promotion of start-ups, (ii) facilitating operation and growth (covering credit, technology and marketing), (iii) closure and exit, and (iv) labour laws and regulations (Ministry of MSMEs, 2013).

These policy initiatives are clear and consistent, aimed at transforming the ecosystem for the MSME sector by influencing their (i) birth (encouraging start-ups), (ii) operations and growth (by simplifying laws and regulations, and facilitating their access to credit, better technology and dynamic markets, apart from skilled labour and reliable infrastructure), and (iii) orderly and easy exit. Thus, the emerging focus of India's MSME policy aims at covering the entire life cycle of MSMEs to ensure a healthy, vibrant and competitive MSME sector. To conclude, the 'appropriate policy information diffusion and effective penetration of policy support' amongst the MSMEs can have a desirable impact on the competitiveness, particularly, of registered SSI, slowly and steadily in the years to come.[5]

5. Ibid.

17

Public Sector in the Indian Economy

THE declared social objective of the Indian development strategy since Independence has been growth with social justice which was sought to be achieved within the democratic political framework and for which India adopted the concept of mixed economy. The expansion of the public sector was considered to be a major instrument with which the state in a mixed economy can influence the pace as well as the composition of economic activity with a view to pursuing the social objective.

The Rationale

In India, the rationale for the public sector has been explicit or implicit in all plan documents as well as policy statements, although the emphasis has changed in degrees depending upon the constraints faced and the emerging major issues of the time.

Tracing the chronological developments in this connection, we find that as far back as 1948, the Industrial Policy Resolution declared, "A dynamic national policy must... be directed to a continuous increase in production by all possible means, side by side with measures to secure its equitable distribution." For this purpose, while recognising that the "State must play a progressively active role in the development of industries," it was conceded that in the conditions then prevailing "the mechanism and the resources of the State may not permit it to function as widely as may be desirable." The First Five Year Plan that followed did not have a clear-cut strategy of development and hence, it did not contain any operational statements on the public sector.

It was in the context of the Mahalanobis strategy that the approach to the public sector got further crystalised. The long-term growth orientation in an import-substitution dominated strategy required that the domestic capacity creation be biased in the direction of producing capital goods to produce more capital goods. According to Tendulkar,[1] the distinct preference for the public sector in this strategy can be traced to the following reasons.

First, the concentration of economic power that would result from the uncontrolled operation of the market forces can be reduced through the extension in the public ownership of means of production.

Secondly, private investors may demand a higher risk premium for investment in certain industries than would be socially justified. Off-shore drilling of oil is one example in this connection.

Thirdly, the scale of investment efforts in certain heavy industries may be beyond the capital-raising capacity of the private sector e.g., steel mills, heavy electrical machinery.

Fourthly, the public sector, through the appropriate price policy for its output will generate investible surpluses for further investment in the economy.

Fifthly, by production as well as distribution of certain universal intermediate inputs like coal, steel, electricity etc., the state will be able to control the composition of private economic activity in a socially desirable direction.

Finally, the public sector would assume the role of a model employer and its employment and wage policies would have a moderating influence on the corresponding policies in the private sector.

Analysing these reasons, one finds that public sector was expected to fulfil varied and sometimes conflicting objectives. The generation of investible surplus was bound to conflict with subsidies involved in keeping the prices of certain universal intermediates at low levels as well as the public sector's role as a model employer.

In the 1960s and 1970s, the public sector policy has been largely guided by the Industrial Policy Resolution of 1956 which gave the public sector a strategic role in the economy. Massive investments have been made over the past four decades to build a public sector which

---

1. Tendulkar, S.D. "Approach to the Public Sector in the Context of an Overall Development Strategy", in Uma Kapila (ed.), *Indian Economy Since Independence* 2000-01 edition. New Delhi: Academic Foundation.

had a commanding role in the economy. Many key sectors of the economy are today dominated by mature public enterprises that have successfully expanded production, opened up new areas of technology and built up a reserve of technical competence in a number of areas.

As a result, the country's ranking in terms of industrialisation with other developing countries is quite high. India's comparative advantages such as a large pool of well-trained workforce, technical skills in manufacturing and chemical industries primarily stem from the public sector.

Over the years, the size of the public sector has increased and currently, there are 473 central public sector undertakings (PSUs) including banks and insurance companies. Out of these, 104 are listed and 369 unlisted, while at the state level there are 1,160 state PSUs. It is estimated by informed financial analysts that the valuation of the central PSUs on P/E basis for the listed companies and on P/B basis for the unlisted companies is now placed at $450-$500 billion or 40-45 per cent of the country's GDP (gross domestic product).[2]

Performance of Central Public Sector Enterprises

The CPSEs play a significant role in Indian economy. According to Department of Public Enterprises, there are 339 CPSEs as on 31 March, 2018. Out of these 339 CPSEs, 257 are in operation and 82 are non-operational during 2017-18. Out of the operating 257 CPSEs, 184 CPSEs were profit making, 71 loss making and 2 CPSEs at no profit no loss. The profit of profit making CPSEs (184) stood at ₹1,59,635 crore, while the loss of loss-making CPSEs (71) stood at ₹31,261 crore during 2017-18. The overall net profit of the 257 operating CPSEs went up by 2.29 per cent to ₹1,28,374 crore during 2017-18. Further, the CPSEs contribution to the total Central Exchequer decreased by 2.98 per cent in 2017-18 as against the previous year. A comparative analysis of the performance of a few CPSEs vis-a-vis private sector using 5 year average net profit margin (in per cent) in selected sectors show that there is a great scope for improvement for CPSEs in some sectors as the private sector firms have performed relatively better than the public sector firms.[3]

---

2. Kelkar, Vijay (2010). "On Strategies of Disinvestment and Privatisation", (26th Sir Purshotamdas Thakurdas Memorial Lecture, January 29, Mumbai) in Uma Kapila (ed.), *Indian Economy since Independence* (24th edition). New Delhi: Academic Foundation.
3. Government of India (2019). *Economic Survey 2018-19, Vol.2.*

Central PSEs' Profitability

What is the correct measure of profitability? It depends upon the purpose. From the view point of a private individual, the ratio of net profits to equity capital (or net worth) may be appropriate, but it may be unsuitable to measure a PSE's contribution to the economy, for many reasons. First, PSEs usually have a high depreciation cost since they have to invest not only in plant and machinery, but also on social overhead capital, for which budgetary provisions are made. Second, a PSE's capital structure is not aimed to maximise return on shareholders' investment, but provision of goods and services that the market has not (or inadequately) succeeded in supplying—the argument of 'missing market.' Third, very often PSEs start with a high proportion of debt as government expects a certain interest on its loans. When the enterprise commences production it is often saddled with a high debt-equity ratio, which is usually renegotiated to make the enterprise commercially viable. Finally, for the economy, what matters is not the capital structure but return on total capital employed. Thus, gross profit to total capital employed is a better measure of public sector profitability, which we have used below (Nagaraj, 2008).

Thus measured, according to Nagaraj, profitability of the central PSEs has increased from around 8 per cent in the mid-1970s to 21 per cent in 2003-04—a respectable figure by any reasonable reckoning. Such rosy estimates may conceal the effect of high mark-up, cost-based administered pricing in the performance of petroleum companies. Surely, net of the petroleum sector, the profitability is lower, but with an unmistakable rising trend, at 18 per cent return on gross capital employed in 2003-04.

Thus, the central PSEs as a source of NDNFEs' (Non Departmental and Non Financial Enterprises) poor financial position is ruled out, leaving us mainly with the utilities and infrastructure services at the state level—that is, state electricity boards (SEBs) and road transport corporations (RTCs). In principle, public irrigation would belong to this category, as it accounts for a sizeable share of plan expenditure in most states.

According to Nagaraj, the real culprit of poor public sector saving is not the central PSEs (that have been the subject of much of reforms) but inadequate pricing of the utilities and infrastructure services, and lack of recovery of user charges for the services rendered. Perhaps a telling evidence of the problem, in the aggregate, is the movement of the public sector price deflator, relative to the GDP deflator since 1960-61. Over the last 40 years, public sector prices never exceeded the overall price level, and in 2003-04 the relative price stood just 83 per cent of what it was in 1960-61. In other words, public sector prices have risen since 1951 at a slower rate than the overall prices in the economy over the long-run, adversely affecting its financial position. However, as these are decreasing cost industries, their prices can be expected to rise relatively slowly. But they are also capital-intensive industries, where the principle of access to these services on social considerations raises the cost of provision. Moreover, the public sector, being an instrument of public policy, is often made to shoulder many social responsibilities, increasing its expenditure, which needs to be recovered from reasonably pricing the output or from the budget. With a growing fiscal imbalance, reasonable pricing is the only avenue to compensate for the services rendered.

The main findings according to Nagaraj are:

1. There is a distinct improvement in the efficiency of resource use in the public sector in the aggregate since the second half of the 1980s, and a corresponding fall in the average capital-output ratio.
2. Improvement in physical efficiency, in part, may reflect a fall in public sector employment growth (however, measured).
3. Thermal power plants in India that account for the bulk of electricity generation (and a sizeable share of public investment) show an uninterrupted rise in efficiency.
4. These trends are, however, inadequately reflected in public sector financial performance, despite a sustained improvement in profitability of the central PSEs (even excluding the petroleum enterprises).
5. Thus, the source of financial distress is the utilities and infrastructure services, like the SEBs, RTCs and the railways.
6. The SEBs' revenue-cost ratio deteriorated since the 1990s; the same is true of the railways and the RTCs.
7. That inadequate pricing of the output public sector utilities is the main reason for their deteriorating financial position is illustrated by a 17 percentage point fall in the public sector price deflator output relative to the GDP deflator over the last 40 years since 1960-61.

Reasons and Implications

What accounts for the changes in the performance of the public sector? Arguably, the market-oriented reforms since the 1980s could have induced the desired effect. But, such an explanation would seem too facile to be taken seriously, in the absence of a casual explanation between the reforms and the observed improvement (Nagaraj, 2008).

But probably what has perhaps been happening is: (i) a hardening of the budget constraint, accompanied by a greater managerial autonomy, and (ii) a growing competition in the product market. In NDNFEs, between 1960-61 and 2002-03, government's budgetary support (sum of equity capital and loans) declined, and the share of internal resources (depreciation and net saving) rose, both as a proportion of gross fixed capital formation. In 1963-64, budgetary support was 97.6 per cent of fixed capital formation, which came down to as little as 16.9 per cent in 1996-97; the share of internal resource went up from 11.2 per cent in 1960-61 to 73 per cent in 2002-03. Changes in market conditions and financial governance could have ensured greater accountability and cost consciousness. But these advantages could not get translated into improved financial results, as pricing and recovery of user charges continued to remain a matter of public policy. The problems of inadequate electricity pricing, incomplete metering of power usage and recovery of user charges are too well known to be recounted here.

According to Nagaraj, the real problem is not the lack of efficiency in production, but one of pricing and collection of user charges. Hence, unless these problems are squarely addressed, public sector finances are unlikely to shape up.

Public Sector and 1991 Industrial Policy

To improve the performance of the public sector, the Government of India (GoI) announced in July 1991 the new Industrial Policy which contained the following decisions pertaining to the public sector.

1. Portfolio of public sector investments will be reviewed with a view to focus the public sector on strategic, hi-tech and essential infrastructure. Whereas some reservation for the public sector is being retained, there would be no bar for area of exclusivity to be opened up to the private sector selectively. Similarly, the public sector will be allowed entry in areas not reserved for it.

2. Public enterprises which are chronically sick and which are unlikely to be turned around will, for the formulation of revival/rehabilitation schemes, be referred to the Board for Industrial and Financial Reconstruction (BIFR), or other similar high level institutions created for the purpose. A social security mechanism will be created to protect the interests of workers likely to be affected by such rehabilitation packages.
3. In order to raise resources and encourage wider public participation, a part of the government's share-holding in the public sector would be offered to mutual funds, financial institutions, general public and workers.
4. Boards of public sector companies would be made more professional and given greater powers.
5. There will be a greater thrust on performance improvement through the memorandum of understanding (MoU) system through which managements would be granted greater autonomy and will be held accountable. Technical expertise on the part of the government would be upgraded to make MoU negotiations and implementation more effective.

The Industrial Policy 1991 provides a new approach to public enterprises. The new policy emphasises that measures must be taken to make these enterprises more growth oriented and technically dynamic. According to the New Industrial Policy, the priority areas for growth of public enterprises in the future will be the following: Essential infrastructure goods and services; exploration and exploitation of oil and mineral resources; technology development and building of manufacturing capabilities in areas which are crucial in the long-term development of the economy and where private sector investment is inadequate; manufacture of products where strategic considerations predominate such as defence equipment.

Government will strengthen those public enterprises which fall in the reserved areas of operation or are in high priority areas or are generating good or reasonable profits. Such enterprises will be provided a much greater degree of management autonomy through the system of MoU.

Policies toward CPSEs and their Implementation

In accordance with the mandate in the National Common Minimum Programme (NCMP), the two main elements of the GoI policy have been devolution of full managerial and commercial autonomy to successful, profit-making companies, and modernisation and restructuring of sick PSUs (as well as sell-off or closure of chronically sick CPSEs).

Policy developments for CPSEs mainly relate to increased delegation of financial and operational powers and revival of CPSEs. With a view to delegating enhanced financial and operational powers to CPSEs, the government introduced the Navratna Scheme in July 1997. In December 2010, the government introduced the Maharatna Scheme enhancing financial delegation to CPSEs. Coal India Limited and Neyveli Lignite Corporation Limited were conferred Maharatna and Navratna status respectively in 2011 and the number of CPSEs under these categories increased to 5 and 16 respectively. In December 2004, the government established a Board for Reconstruction of Public Sector Enterprises (BRPSE) to advise on revival/restructuring of sick and loss-making CPSEs. The BRPSE has made recommendations in respect of 62 CPSEs until 31 October 2011. The government, in turn, has approved proposals for revival of 43 CPSEs and closure of two. Soon the BRPSE may be on its way out and a new panel will be set up to bring the ailing PSU's on track. The PMO has given its in principle approval to the proposal for winding up the panel. The move is expected to clear way for the government to sell stakes in most of the 65 sick central public sector companies or close down non viable ones, once the proposal comes in to being. A loss making PSU will be considered for revival only if it is operational in a strategic area or if banks are willing to lend it money without government guarantee. In case a PSU has a market share of 10 per cent, then at least govt. may continue its efforts to revive it. If a company's return is lower than the rate its pays to lenders, it may be considered only a case for strategic sale.[4]

Privatisation

There has been a significant move towards privatisation in economies across the globe. Several industrial countries have embraced it as have most of the transition economies for East Europe and large parts of the developing world. In India, privatisation or disinvestment of the public sector emerged as a major public policy option after the country embarked on a process of economic reforms in 1991.

Privatisation may be broadly defined as the transfer of various activities from the public to the private sphere. Specifically, it could

---

4. *Economic Survey 2014-15.*

mean the sale by government or state-owned enterprises (SOEs) to private economic agents. It could refer to a sale that is effected in full or in part. It can also mean a partnership between the public and private sectors through a transfer of responsibilities from the public to private sector. In terms of broad political economy, it could also simply mean a shrinking of the welfare state (Nayak, 2012).[5]

Privatisation: Indian Experience since 1991

In 1991, when the government embarked on a comprehensive process of economic reform and liberalisation, the public sector in India accounted for more than one-fifth of the country's GDP. Since a large number of public sector enterprises (PSEs) regularly showed negative profit margins, the government was keen on a programme of privatisation, calling it disinvestment instead.

In the interim budget of 1991-92, the government took a policy decision to disinvest up to 20 per cent of the equity in selected PSUs in favour of mutual funds and financial or investment institutions in the public sector. The disinvestment, which was to broad base the equity, was to improve management and enhance the availability of resources for these enterprises. The Rangarajan Committee report on the Disinvestment of Shares in PSEs in April 1993 emphasised the need for substantial disinvestment, and recommended that the percentage of equity to be divested could go up to 49 per cent for industries especially reserved for the public sector. It recommended that in exceptional cases, such as enterprises that had a dominant market share or where separate identity had to be maintained for strategic reasons, the target public ownership level could be kept at 26 per cent, that is disinvestment could take place to the tune of 74 per cent. In all other cases, it recommended 100 per cent disinvestment of the government stake. Holding of 51 per cent or more equity by the government was recommended only for six scheduled industries, namely: (i) coal and lignite, (ii) mineral oils, (iii) arms, ammunitions and defence equipment, (iv) atomic energy, (v) radioactive minerals, and (vi) railway transport.

In 1996, the government set up the Disinvestment Commission with a view to formulate procedures so that any decision to disinvest would be taken and implemented in a transparent manner. The revenues generated from such disinvestment were to be allocated for education and health and for creating a fund to strengthen PSEs. By August 1999,

---

5. Nayak, Pulin (2012). "Privatisation", in Kaushik Basu and Annemie Maertens (ed.), *The Oxford Companion to Economics in India*. Vol. II.

the Disinvestment Commission made recommendations on 58 PSEs. The recommendations indicated a shift from public offerings to strategic/trade sales, with transfer of management. The Commission also observed that the essence of a long-term disinvestment strategy should be not only to enhance budgetary receipts, but also to minimise budgetary support to unprofitable units while ensuring their long-term viability. By 1998, government was of the view that 'in the generality of cases its shareholding in PSEs will be brought down to 26 per cent.' In PSEs involving strategic considerations, namely arms and ammunitions, atomic energy and railway transport, government was to retain majority voting.

By 2000-01, the government's policy regarding privatisation and public sector restructuring comprises the following considerations: restructure and revive potentially viable PSEs, close down PSEs that cannot be revived, bring down government equity in all strategic PSEs to 20 per cent or lower, if necessary, and fully protect the interests of workers. The entire receipt from disinvestments and privatisation was to be used for meeting expenditure in social sectors, restructuring of PSEs and meeting public debt.

The Ministry of Disinvestment was converted into a Department under the Ministry of Finance with effect from 27 May 2004 after the UPA (United Progressive Alliance) government headed by Dr Manmohan Singh as Prime Minister assumed office. From this point on, the disinvestment programme had to be in conformity with the NCMP. All privatisations were from now on to be considered on a transparent and consultative case-by-case basis. It was made explicit that the UPA would retain the existing Navaratna companies, which include the BHEL (Bharat Heavy Electricals Limited), in the public sector and that these will be permitted to raise resources from the capital market. The government constituted a 'National Investment Fund' in January 2005 into which the realisation from sale of minority shareholding of the government in profitable PSEs would be channelised. This fund would be maintained outside the Consolidated Fund of India, and the income from this fund would be used for the following purposes: (i) invest in social sector projects that promote education, health care and employment and (ii) capital investment in selected profitable and revivable PSEs that yield adequate returns, in order to enlarge their capital base to finance expansion or diversification.[6]

6. Ibid.

According to Kelkar[7] disinvestment is an area of economic policy with multiple objectives. The most important objective should be that of increasing the efficiency with which the labour and capital, that is in existing PSUs, are converted into GDP. In addition, other auxiliary goals include enhancing investment in the country, creating new traditions of corporate governance catering to consumer interests by maximising competition in product markets, and reducing the stock of public debt. An important positive impact of disinvestment upon our fiscal problems would flow through a higher GDP growth.

Policies on disinvestment must be particularly mindful of its ramifications to the political economy. The disinvestment process can lead to dispersed share ownership amongst millions of households. This would disperse wealth in the country. It would help create a middle-class constituency which has a stake in the profits of PSUs and (more generally) in the economic well-being of the country. This could have larger ramifications for the reforms programme. The design of disinvestment policy needs to cater to these multiple goals. In particular, a narrow focus upon maximising proceeds is unlikely to yield sound policies on disinvestment.

Regarding the policy for deployment of resources generated through disinvestment/privatisation which is currently channelised from the National Investment Fund, Kelkar argues that this is a restrictive policy and we should liberalise this fully by allowing the government to use these resources as a part of the budgetary resources to create new public capital assets—whether in the form of better urban infrastructure by providing capital grants to our cities or for revamping the country's energy base through an ambitious solar energy programme or the expansion of rural road network or for recharging the country's depleting water bodies and cleaning of rivers. This would require the union government sharing the proceeds from disinvestment or privatisation with the state governments on a systematic basis on the lines of the Finance Commission's devolution formula for the sharing of union taxes with the states.

For coming decades, water, environment and urban infrastructure are going to be the key binding constraints on India's growth ambition. To remove these binding constraints, we will require large investments to accelerate the country's march towards high quality growth. Disinvestment and privatisation policy has now assumed strategic importance in our country.

---

7. Kelkar (2010). *op.cit.*

According to Kelkar (2010),[8] India's future lies in building a new institutional architecture with government as regulator and with the private sector doing investment. If we think of the next 25 years, a very substantial portion of the investment in all regulated industries in India is going to come from the private sector. It makes more sense for the government to reorganise itself, shifting into the role of the umpire and away from the role of the player.

We need a bold and imaginative programme for disinvestment and privatisation calling for restructuring of the portfolio of the country's 'public capital assets.' It does not mean a retreat of the state but essentially a re-engineering of its portfolio of public capital assets. This will help our country meet the challenges of the first half of the 21st century just like our PSUs helped the country in the second half of the 20th century to overcome our industrial backwardness.

In conclusion, we may quote Minhas (2007) which is very relevant even today.[9]

> The choice between the public sector enterprises and private firms is not a simple either/or question. While there may be eminently good reasons for promoting public sector production under certain circumstances, nevertheless there is no basis whatever for the doctrine of the so-called commanding heights. The Indian economy is struggling in the deep swamps of inefficiency. Its deliverance from this inefficiency trap can be vastly facilitated if both the public sector and private firms are exposed more and more to global competition and the arbitrary bureaucratic controls for the regulation of entry and freedom of exit of firms are substantially rolled back.

There is certainly no clear superiority of private *vis-à-vis* public ownership from the standpoint of economic theory. More than ownership, it would seem that the degree of competition and the regulatory environment are more relevant to productive efficiency. The empirical evidence presents a mixed picture. As the world environment gets more competitive, it would be necessary to put the sizeable assets of the PSEs in countries like India to more productive use. Ultimately, it is this consideration that should be of relevance rather than the simplistic presumption that the public sector is necessarily inefficient or that privatisation is an all-purpose panacea.[10]

---

8. Minhas, B.S. (2007). "Public *versus* Private Sector: Neglect of Lessons of Economics in Indian Policy Formulation", in Uma Kapila (ed.), *Indian Economy since Independence*, 19th edition, 2008-09 (Ch. 18), New Delhi: Academic Foundation.
9. Ibid.
10. Nayak (2012). *op.cit.* no. 6

18

Services in the Indian Growth Process

Introduction

THE services sector covers a wide range of activities from the most sophisticated information technology (IT) to simple services provided by the unorganised sector, such as the services of the barber and plumber. National Accounts Classification (NAC) of the services sector incorporates trade, hotels and restaurants; transport, storage and communication; financing, insurance, real estate and business services; and community, social, and personal services. In World Trade Organization (WTO) and Reserve Bank of India (RBI) classifications, construction is also included.The phenomenal expansion of services worldwide led to services being regarded as an engine of growth and even as a necessary concomitant of economic growth. Development economics suggests that development is a three-stage process. The dominance of the services sector in the growth process is usually associated with the third stage of growth. During the 1980s and 1990s, services accounted for a share of about 70 per cent of GDP in industrialised countries and about 50 per cent in developing countries.

In India growth of services picked up in the 1980s, and accelerated in the 1990s, when it averaged 7.5 per cent per annum, thus providing an impetus to industry and agriculture, which grew on average by 5.8 per cent and 3.1 per cent respectively. Growth in the services sector has also been less cyclical and more stable than the growth of industry and agriculture (in the sense of having the smallest coefficient of variation).

A notable feature of the structural transformation of the services sector has been the growth of skill-intensive and high value added sectors, i.e., software, communication and financial services. The rapid growth of services can be attributed, *inter alia*, to the advent of IT and the knowledge economy. This has enhanced the growth of the high productivity segment of the services sector as well as a variety of service activities involving low productivity activities catering to a large mass of people. The phenomenal growth of low skilled service activities has occurred due to reduced opportunities in the manufacturing sector, particularly in the unorganised sectors.

Some of the activities in the services sector are multidimensional, being part of industry as well as services, such as IT and construction. Service statistics in most countries including India provide information on value addition of various activities of business services, hotels, trade, financial services, etc. For an empirical analysis, sub-sectors including trade, transport and communication, financing, insurance, real estate and business services can be categorised as producer services with hotels and restaurants and other services as consumer services. Government services comprise public administration and defence services. During 1999-2000, producer services accounted for about 70 per cent of the total services followed by consumer services (17%) and government services (13%). The high share of producer services reflects the strong inter-linkages between services and goods producing sectors of the economy.

Rapid growth of the service sector is not unique to India. The existing literature shows that as an economy matures, the share of services in output increases consistently. To begin with, the increase occurs along with an increase in the share of industry. Thereafter, the service share grows more rapidly, accompanied by a stagnant or declining share of the industrial sector. Cross-country experience suggests that the first stage occurs until the country reaches lower middle income status, while the second stage commences once it becomes an upper middle income country.

Consistent with the trend observed in other countries, India's growth experience has been characterised by a decline in the share of agriculture in GDP and an increase in the shares of industry and services. Between 1950 and 1990, agriculture's share in the GDP declined by around 25 per cent with the corresponding increase in the share of services and industry being distributed roughly evenly. However, since the 1990s, the share of industry in overall GDP has remained at around 27 per cent, while the entire decline in the share of agriculture from 32 per cent to 22 per cent of GDP has been matched by a corresponding rise in the share of services in the economy. This is in contrast to other developing economies, where the decline in the share of agriculture in GDP has been followed by a corresponding rise in the share of industry, in particular manufacturing, and later in services. Thus, India seems to be an aberration in terms of the service sector having a much greater role in its economy than in other countries at similar or even higher levels of income. It appears to have leapfrogged from the primary to the tertiary sector.

TABLE – 18.1

Sectoral Growth Rates

	Average Growth (in per cent per annum)		
	1951-1980	*1981-1990*	*1991-2000*
Agriculture	2.1	4.4	3.1
Industry	5.3	6.8	5.8
Services	4.5	6.6	7.5
GDP	3.5	5.8	5.8

Source: Gordon and Gupta, 2003.

The service sector has played an important role in enabling this improved economic performance during the post-reform period. Services have been the fastest growing sector of the Indian economy in recent years and have helped accelerate the overall growth rate of the economy (Table 18.1). Services have also facilitated India's integration with the world economy through trade and capital flows. The phenomenal growth and export performance witnessed in services like information technology (IT) and business process outsourcing (BPO) has placed India on the global map. Services have also helped improve productivity in other sectors of the economy, thus contributing to an improvement in the economy's overall competitiveness (Chanda, 2019).[1]

This trend contrasts with what is observed in many other developing economies, where the decline in the share of agriculture has been followed by a corresponding rise in the share of industry, in particular manufacturing, and later in services. The industrial sector has increased its share only marginally over this period in India. Thus, there has been a leapfrogging of the economy from dependence on the

1. Chanda, Rupa (2019). "India's Services Sector: Trend, Opportunities and Challenges", in Uma Kapila (2019) (ed.), *Indian Economy Since Independence (30th edition)*. New Delhi: Academic Foundation.

TABLE – 18.2

Growth in Sectoral and Overall Output at factor cost and constant prices, 2005-16 (%)

	Annual and average annual growth rate in overall and sectoral output, %												*Average*			*CAGR*	
	2005	*2006*	*2007*	*2008*	*2009*	*2010*	*2011*	*2012*	*2013*	*2014*	*2015*	*2016*	*2000-2004*	*2005-2009*	*2010-2016*	*1990-2000*	*2000-2016*
Gross domestic product (GDP)	9.2	9.2	9.0	6.1	8.0	8.7	6.8	5.4	6.1	7.2	7.9	6.6	5.4	8.3	7.0	4.7	6.7
Agriculture, hunting, forestry, fishing	5.2	4.2	5.8	0.0	0.9	8.7	5.0	1.5	5.6	-0.2	0.7	4.9	1.7	3.2	3.7	2.2	2.7
Industry	8.7	12.3	9.1	4.0	9.7	8.5	6.3	4.5	4.2	8.6	10.2	7.0	5.6	8.8	7.0	5.0	7.0
Services	11.1	10.0	10.3	9.5	9.9	8.7	7.7	7.0	6.9	8.9	9.0	6.9	7.3	10.1	7.9	6.4	8.1

Note: Services include construction

Source: http://unctadstat.unctad.org/wds/ReportFolders/reportFolders.aspx?sCS_ChosenLang=en(accessed October 1, 2018) primary sector to the tertiary sector. Within the services sector, trade and distribution services account for the largest share followed by community, personal and social services and transport services (various issues of Economic Survey and UN National Accounts Statistics). Figure 18.1 shows the relative contributions of the primary, secondary, and tertiary sectors in India's GDP and the steady shift in this composition between 1980 and 2016 towards services.

FIGURE – 18.1

Composition of GDP Across Sectors (%)

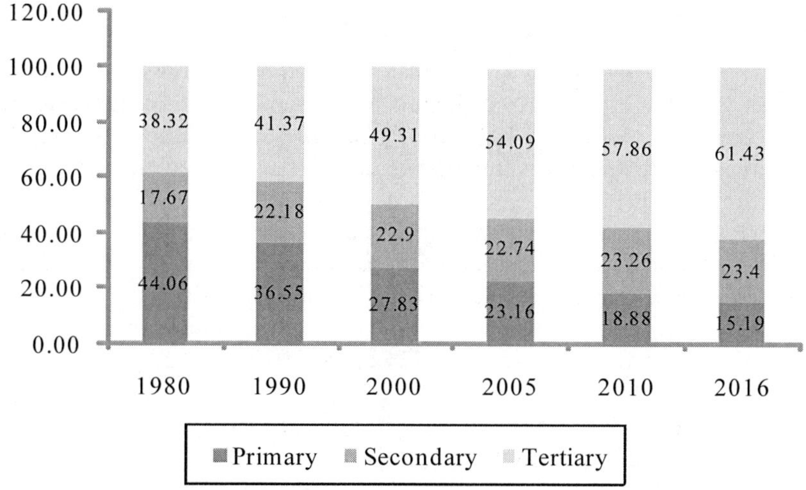

Note: Primary: Agriculture, hunting, forestry, fishing
Secondary: Mining, manufacturing, utilities
Tertiary: Services, construction

Source: *http://unctadstat.unctad.org/wds/ReportFolders/reportFolders.aspx?sCS_ChosenLang=en* (accessed: November 20, 2018)

The service sector's contribution to overall employment has risen, though this has not been commensurate to the growth in services output. According to ILO estimates, services share in employment rose only slightly from 21.6 per cent to 23.8 per cent between 1991 and 2001. According to the 2010-11 Economic Survey, the tertiary sector's share of employment increased only modestly by 4.2 per cent between 1993-94 and 2007-08 while during the same period, its share in GDP increased by over 10 per cent, implying a low employment elasticity. Although India features among the leading services producer countries, the share of services in its employment was the lowest at 28.7 per cent in 2014 whereas the share of this sector in other leading service producer countries was around two-thirds. This share increased by a mere 4.7 per cent between 2001 and 2014 and in 2017 accounted for 33.5 per cent of employment (World Bank Database; Economic Survey 2010-11, Table 10.1; Economic Survey 2015-16 (Vol. 2),Table 7.1 and Figure 7.1). Most of this employment has been concentrated in trade and distribution, construction, hotel and restaurants, and community and personal services segments. The employment trends further reveal that very rapidly growing service segments such as communication and financial services have had relatively lower employment elasticity, indicating that their growth has mainly been based on productivity gains and technological improvements.

It is worth noting that Indian data on services output and employment are subject to problems of data collection, disaggregation, and coverage. India's Wholesale Price Index (WPI)does not capture services while the Consumer Price Index fails to cover it fully. An experimental price index has been developed by the DIPP for selected services such as air, telecom, banking and port services. The aim is to initially use this service price index as a complement to the WPI and later to merge it with the WPI. There are efforts underway to improve statistical measurement and coverage of services under the aegis of a National Statistical Commission (Chanda, 2019).

Growth and Sectoral Shares, Cross-country Evidence and Indian Experience

The evolution of sectoral shares in output, consumption and employment as economies grow has been studied by economists for well over 50 years. During the 1950s and 1960s, research by Kuznets and Chenery suggested that development would be associated with a sharp decline in the proportion of GDP generated by the primary sector, counterbalanced by a significant increase in industry, and by a more modest increase in the service sector. Sectoral shares in employment were predicted to follow a similar pattern.

With the benefit of more data on development than was available to Kuznets and Chenery, recent literature has tended to emphasise the growing importance of service sector activity (Inman, 1985; Kongsamut *et al.*, 2001). For example, Kongsamut *et al.* (2001) analyse a sample of 123 countries for 1970-1989 and show that rising per-capita GDP is associated with an increase in services and a decline in agriculture both in terms of share in GDP and employment. In other words, the sectoral share given up by agriculture as the economy matures goes more to the services sector and less to industry than the Kuznets-Chenery work had suggested. The modern view is that as an economy matures, the share of services (in output, consumption and employment) grows along with a decline in agriculture. By contrast, the share of industry first increases modestly, and then stabilises or declines (Gordon and Gupta, 2003).

Such a pattern of growth is visible in the cross-country data on shares in GDP (Table 18.2). These data suggest two stages of development. In the first, both industry and services shares increase as countries move from low income to lower middle income status, while in the second, the share of industry declines and that of services increases as the economy moves to upper middle and higher income levels.

How does the Indian experience fit in with this pattern? In the four decade period, 1950-1990, agriculture's share in GDP declined by about 25 percentage points, while industry and services gained equally. The share of industry has stabilised since 1990, and the entire subsequent decline in the share of agriculture has been picked up by the services sector. Thus, while over the four decades, 1950-1990, the services sector gained a 13 per cent share, the gain in the 1990s alone was 8 percentage points. Consequently, at current levels, India's services share of GDP is higher than the average for other low-income countries.

TABLE – 18.3

Sectoral Shares in GDP in 2001, Global Averages
(Per cent of GDP)

	Agriculture	*Industry*	*Services*	
Low income	24	32	45	Stage I
Lower middle income	12	40	48	
Upper middle income	7	33	60	Stage II
High income	2	29	70	

Source: World Bank's WDI, 2003, table 4.2. Definition: Low income: per capita GDP<$745; Lower middle: $746-2975; Upper middle: $2976-9205; and high: >$9206.

Services GDP: International Comparison

In the US$ 74.0 trillion world gross value added (GVA) in 2014, the share of services (at current prices), and growth rate (at constant prices), improved marginally to 66.0 per cent and 2.5 per cent respectively over 2013. But in the last thirteen years, the share of services in world GVA has declined by 2.7 percentage points (pp). Among the world's top 15 countries in terms of gross domestic product (GDP), the US ranks first in both services GVA and overall GDP, followed by China in second and Japan in third position. India ranked ninth in terms of overall GDP and tenth in terms of services GVA in 2014, climbing one rung in both rankings. However, among these top 15 nations, in the period 2001-13, the maximum increase in services share to GVA was recorded by Spain (9.7 pp), followed by India (7.8 pp) and China (6.8 pp).

As in the case of overall GDP, services GVA also did not fully recover from the impact of the 2008 global financial crisis with a general slowdown trend in the growth rate of services for the world and across nations (except Brazil) in the post crisis period (2010-14) compared to the pre-crisis period (2001-8). Brazil was an exception, showing good growth in services in 2012 and 2013, which in turn was due to very high growth in the wholesale, retail trade, restaurants and hotels category. The compound annual growth rate (CAGR) of world services in the post crisis period (2010-14) at 2.5 per cent was lower than the 3.0 per cent in the precrisis period (2001-8). Despite the slowdown in the post crisis period, India showed the fastest service sector growth with a CAGR of 8.6 per cent, followed by China at 8.4 per cent. In 2014 India's service sector growth at 10.3 per cent was noticeably higher than that of China at 8.0 per cent (Table 18.4) (*Economic Survey 2015-16*).

As per the UN National Accounts Statistics data, India ranked 7th in terms of GDP size and 9th in terms of services sector size in 2017. Note that India's rank has since risen to 6th in terms of GDP but the 2017 numbers have been used here for purposes of comparison (Table 18.4). Notably, among these 15 countries, India has the second fastest growing services sector after China, registering a growth of 7.9 per cent both in 2017 and during 2007-17 in CAGR terms. India also ranks second after the UK in terms of services share in exports, with the shares as high as seen in developed countries, such as U.S.A, France and Spain.

In contrast, among top 15 economies in terms of GDP and Services GVA in 2017, India ranks the second lowest after China in terms of services share in Gross Value Added (GVA) and ranks the lowest in terms of services share in employment. In addition, compared to the experience of other countries, services share in India's employment at 34 per cent is significantly lower than services share in GVA at 54 per cent (*Economic Survey 2018-19, Vol.2*).

TABLE – 18.4

Services Sector Performance among Top 15 Countries

Country	*Rank in*	*GDP (US$*	*Services GVA*	*Services Sector Growth (Per cent)*			*Share of GVA*		*Services Sector Employment*		*(Per cent) Exports*	
	2017	*2017*	*2017*	*2016*	*2017*	*CAGR (2007-17)*	*2007*	*2017*	*2007*	*2017*	*2007*	*2017*
World		80.5	51.7	2.4	2.9	2.3	67	68	44	51	20	23
USA	1	19.5	15.7	2.0	2.2	1.6	77	81	78	79	29	33
China	2	12.2	6.1	7.7	8.3	8.7	42	50	39	56	9	9
Japan	3	4.9	3.4	0.4	0.9	0.3	69	71	68	71	14	21
Germany	4	3.7	2.3	1.3	2.1	1.0	69	68	68	72	14	17
UK	5	2.6	1.9	1.9	1.7	1.4	78	79	76	81	42	44
France	6	2.6	1.8	1.6	2.1	1.2	77	79	73	77	26	32
India	7	2.6	1.3	7.5	7.9	7.9	48	54	26	34	37	38
Brazil	8	2.1	1.3	-2.6	-1.4	1.5	68	72	60	69	12	13
Italy	9	1.9	1.3	1.0	1.1	-0.1	71	74	66	70	19	18
Canada	10	1.6	1.1	2.2	2.9	2.1	67	71	76	78	14	17
Russia	11	1.6	0.9	-0.6	2.2	1.6	59	62	62	66	11	14
S. Korea	12	1.5	0.8	2.5	2.2	2.9	60	58	67	70	16	13
Australia	13	1.4	1.0	2.9	3.1	2.7	70	73	75	78	23	22
Spain	14	1.3	0.9	2.2	2.5	1.0	68	73	66	76	32	30
Mexico	15	1.2	0.7	3.9	3.1	2.8	62	64	61	61	6	6

Source: UN National Accounts Statistics database for GDP and GVA, World Bank database for employment, and WTO database for exports. *Economic Survey 2018-19, Vol. 2.*

TABLE – 18.5

Performance in Services: International Comparision

Country	Rank in		Services Growth Rate (%) Y-o-Y				CAGR 2001-2008	CAGR 2010-2014	Share of Services in GVA		Employment		Total Exports		Services Export Growth (%) Y-o-Y				CAGR 2001-2008	CAGR 2010-2014
	Overall GDP	Services GVA	2001	2009	20013	2014	2008	2014	2001	2014	2001*	2014*	2001	2014	2001	2009	2013	2014	2008	2014
US	1	1	2.0	-2.0	0.9	2.3	2.2	1.8	77.4	78.4	75.0	81.2	27.2	29.8	-3.6	-4.2	5.1	3.7	9.5	6.1
China	2	2	10.2	11.1	8.2	8.0	11.7	8.4	40.9	47.7	12.7	47.0	11.0	9.0	9.1	-13.4	-3.9	12.4	25.9	7.9
Japan	3	3	1.3	-3.1	1.3	0.1	0.9	0.9	69.0	72.0	63.9	69.1	13.6	18.8	-6.9	-14.6	1.2	19.2	11.8	5.2
Germany	4	4	3.1	-3.0	0.4	1.3	1.4	1.3	68.7	69.0	64.6	70.4	12.8	15.0	5.6	-8.5	8.4	4.3	15.8	4.9
UK	5	5	3.5	-2.6	2.8	2.8	2.9	2.6	73.6	78.4	73.7	79.1	30.1	40.0	-0.8	-13.8	2.3	7.9	14.5	5.8
France	6	6	1.9	-2.0	0.8	0.7	1.8	1.2	74.7	78.9	69.9	75.8	19.8	31.4	-0.5	-13.6	7.4	5.3	15.8	7.4
Brazil	7	8	2.3	2.1	11.9	1.1	3.9	6.9	68.2	71.0	59.4	76.6	13.0	14.8	-2.7	-8.9	-1.7	4.7	18.6	6.8
Italy	8	7	2.3	-2.7	-1.1	0.0	0.8	-0.6	70.5	74.3	63.1	69.5	18.9	18.0	2.1	-16.3	4.8	3.6	10.5	3.8
India	9	10	7.2	10.7	8.9	10.3	9.3	8.6	45.2	53.0	24.0	28.7	27.9	32.6	4.8	-12.5	2.2	5.0	30.1	7.5
Russia	10	12	3.3	-5.1	2.2	1.0	7.6	2.6	55.9	60.0	58.6	65.8	9.9	11.5	17.3	-19.8	12.4	-6.1	26.0	7.5
Canada	11	9	3.5	1.2	1.9	2.4	2.9	2.3	65.9	69.9	74.8	78.2	12.7	15.2	-3.6	-8.7	-0.1	-4.0	9.9	3.0
Australia	12	11	3.8	1.8	2.8	2.6	3.4	2.8	69.9	70.1	67.9	69.5	21.8	18.1	-8.9	-7.6	-0.8	1.5	13.3	3.9
S. Korea	13	14	4.9	1.4	2.9	3.1	4.2	3.0	59.0	59.4	62.6	69.5	16.3	15.6	-4.9	-20.5	0.2	3.1	17.4	6.6
Spain	14	13	4.0	-0.9	-0.8	1.1	3.9	0.4	65.3	75.1	62.0	76.3	32.2	29.2	6.0	-14.8	5.0	4.3	13.2	4.6
Mexico	15	15	1.1	-3.7	2.3	2.0	3.6	3.4	57.6	59.0	56.1	62.4	7.2	5.0	-7.5	-16.1	24.6	4.6	5.3	8.4
World			2.6	-0.8	2.2	2.5	3.0	2.5	68.7	66.0	35.9	50.9	19.4	20.6	19.9	-10.9	5.4	4.9	15.0	6.4

Notes: Rank and share are based on current prices (2014); growth rates are based on constant prices (US$); construction sector is excluded in services GDP.

* For employment data in 2001 and 2014, the available data of nearest preceding years is used.

Source: Computed from UN National Accounts Statistics for GDP/GVA, World Bank database for employment and World Trade Organization (WTO) database for services trade. *Economic Survey 2015-16*.

India's Services Employment

The pattern of the sectoral share of employment has changed with the share of agriculture falling and of industry and services rising steadily. Services share in employment at 28.5 per cent in 2011-12 is higher than in industry at 24.4 per cent. Among the different services sectors, from 1993-94 to 2011-12, there was continuous increase in employment share in trade, hotels, and restaurants; transport, storage, and communication; and financial, insurance, real estate and business services. Employment share in community, social, and personal services has fallen continuously except in 2011-12 when there was an increase compared to 2009-10 and 2004-05. Employment elasticity has increased for both services and industry in 2009-10 to 2011-12 compared to 2004-05 to 2009-10, though industry had relatively higher employment elasticity. Among services, employment elasticity was the highest in 'financial, insurance, real estate, and business services' and 'transport, storage, and communication' (Table 18.6).

World Services Trade

After growing robustly in the last 12 years from 2001 to 2013 with a CAGR of 9.9 per cent, world services export growth has been seeing a see-saw movement. It was at 0.1 per cent in 2001, reached a high of 21.5 per cent in 2004, fell steeply to a negative 9.4 per cent in 2009, rebounded quickly to 9.8 per cent in 2010 and 12.2 per cent in 2011, but decelerated to 2.2 per cent in 2012. It has again picked up to 5.5 per cent in 2013.

The impact of the global financial crisis was more pronounced in services trade than services GVA, with the CAGR of world commercial services exports during the postcrisis period decelerating to 6.4 per cent compared to the 15.0 per cent during the precrisis period. In the pre-crisis period, among the top 15 services producer countries, the services exports CAGR of India was the fastest at 30.1 per cent, followed by China at 25.9 per cent. However, during the post crisis period, it decelerated in both India and China, with Mexico registering the highest growth at 8.4 per cent, followed by China at 7.9 per cent and India at 7.5 per cent.

The growth story overall and services of world and India in the 2000s began from almost the same level of around 4-5 per cent in 2000. But over the years, India's overall and services growth rates have outpaced those of the world. Interestingly, unlike world services growth, which has been moving in tandem with its overall growth with

TABLE – 18.6

Sector-wise Employment Trends (UPS)

	Absolute number (million) (Share in percent given in parentheses)					*Employment Elasticity*			
	1993-94	*1999-00*	*2004-05*	*2009-10*	*2011-12*	*1993-94 to 1999-00*	*1999-00 to 2004-05*	*2004-05 to 2009-10*	*2009-10 to 2011-12*
Agriculture	204.3	214.7 (61.1)	226.8 (58.5)	220.5 (54.5)	204.4 (51.6)	0.3 (47.1)	0.7	-0.2	-0.5
Industry	53.5	61.7 (16.0)	81.0 (16.8)	93.1 (19.5)	106.1 (21.8)	0.4 (24.4)	0.9	0.3	0.9
Services	76.6	90.6 (22.9)	108.0 (24.7)	113.7 (26.0)	123.9 (26.6)	0.3 (28.5)	0.5	0.1	0.5
Trade, hotels, and restaurants	26.8 (8.0)	34.1 (9.3)	46.5 (11.2)	48.4 (11.3)	50.5 (11.6)	0.4	0.8	0.1	0.3
Transport, storage, and communication	11.0 (3.3)	15.0 (4.1)	18.7 (4.5)	19.9 (4.6)	22.8 (5.2)	0.5	0.4	0.1	0.6
Financial, insurance, real estate and business services	3.7 (1.1)	4.8 (1.3)	7.5 (1.8)	9.4 (2.2)	10.7 (2.5)	0.5	1.6	0.4	0.6
Community, social, and personal services	35.1 (10.5)	36.7 (10.0)	35.3 (8.5)	36.1 (8.4)	39.9 (9.2)	0.1	-0.2	0.1	1.1
Total	334.4	367.0 (100.0)	415.7 (100.0)	427.4 (100.0)	434.4 (100.0)	0.2 (100.0)	0.4	0.1	0.1

Note : Employment elasticity is calculated by CAGR method, Employment elasticity = (CAGR employment)/(CAGR GDP at FC constant 2004-05 prices) for the respective period. UPS- usual principal status

Source : Based on data from National Sample Survey Office (NSSO) different round reports and CSO.

mild see-saw movements over the years, India's services growth has been consistently above its overall growth in the last decade except for 2003 (when the former was marginally lower than the latter). Thus, for more than a decade, this sector has been pulling up the growth of the Indian economy with a great amount of stability.

India's Services Trade

The contribution of services to India's trade and FDI flows has also been growing over the past decade, facilitating India's integration with the world economy. India's services exports have steadily grown from a mere $2.9 billion in 1980 to $6.7 bn in 1995, rising to $16.7 billion in 2000 and growing more than tenfold to $183.9 billion in 2017. Services imports have also risen significantly, from $2.9 billion in 1980 to $10.2 billion in 1995, rising to $19.2 billion in 2000 and further to $154 billion in 2017. India has moved to a slight services trade surplus over the years, which has in part helped offset its otherwise persistent and growing trade deficit in goods.

India's services exports grew at an average annual growth rate of 23.5 per cent during the 1996-2005 period second only to Ireland and compared to 15.3 per cent for China. However, there has been a deceleration over the 2005-17 period, with the average annual growth rate of India's services exports declining to 9.9 per cent, reflecting the overall slowdown in the world economy post the 2008 financial crisis and mirroring growth trends in other countries such as Ireland and Singapore. It is worth noting, however, that China's services exports registered similar growth during this latter period at 9.6 per cent, reflecting a narrowing of the gap between the two countries in growth performance. In CAGR terms, India's services exports grew the most rapidly among all countries at 11.1 per cent over the 2005-17 period and exceeded the sector's CAGR for output and overall exports during this same period. As a result, the share of services in India's total exports has risen from 18.1 per cent in 1995 to over 37.7 per cent in 2017. These trends highlight the export-oriented nature of services growth in the Indian economy as well as India's growing competitiveness in the world services market and its liberalization of services imports, especially in the post 2000 period.

Rapid growth in services trade has led to India's increased penetration of the world services market over the past two decades, reflecting India's growing competitiveness in global services, especially in the post 2000 period. India's share in world services exports has risen from less than 1 per cent in the 1980s and 1990s to 1.9 per cent in 2005, 2.9 per cent in 2010 and was 3.44 per cent in 2017. Its share in world services imports has similarly increased from 0.7 per cent in 1990 to 2.3 per cent in 2005 and further to nearly 3 per cent in 2017.

India remained the eighth largest exporter of commercial services in the world in 2016 (WTO, 2017) with a share of 3.4 per cent, which is double the share of India's merchandise exports in the world at 1.7 percent. Moreover, the ratio of services exports to merchandise exports increased from 35.8 per cent in 2000-01 to 58.2 per cent in 2016-17 indicating the growing importance of the services sector in India's exports. While, India's services exports registered a CAGR of 8.3 per cent during 2006-07 to 2016-17, in 2015-16 it registered negative growth of (-) 2.4 per cent. Services sector export growth returned to positive territory with 5.7 per cent growth rate in 2016-17.

India's services imports exhibited growth of 17.4 per cent in April-September 2017-18 as payments on transport sector increased by 15.0 per cent. Among the other major services imports, travel grew by 12.0 per cent and business services by 11.3 per cent (Table 18.7). The rise in business services payments was primarily led by higher payments for import of research and development services, professional & management consulting services and technical, trade related and other business services. Though the software services imports had a share of only 4.3 per cent, its growth was 47.6 per cent.

Lower growth in services exports than in imports led to a decline in net services receipts in 2015-16 and 2016-17. Net services receipts rose by 14.6 per cent during April-September of 2017-18. Net surplus in services financed about 49 per cent of India's merchandise deficit in 2017-18 H1 and cushioned the current account deficit. (Table 18.7). (*Economic Survey 2017-18*).

The growing role of software and business services in India's services-sector exports reflects India's comparative advantage in skill and knowledge-intensive labour-based services.

India's growing presence in global BPO services is based on its huge labour endowment, varied skill sets and low-cost but quality manpower coupled with a rapidly growing domestic IT industry. According to the Financial Times, half of the world's largest 500 companies and many government agencies contract out IT and business process work to India across a wide range of services, including medical and legal transcriptions, customer support, human-resource management and administration, financial and accounting processes, technical suport, logistics, sales, and R&D (research and development), to name a few (Chanda, 2012).

TABLE – 18.7

Export Performance of Major Services

	Value (US$ bn)	*Share (%)*	*Growth Rate (%)*			
	2016-17	*2016-17*	*2015-16*	*2016-17*	*2016-17 H1*	*2017-18 H1*
Services Exports	163.1	100.0	-2.4	5.7	4.2	16.2
Travel	23.2	14.2	4.6	9.3	7.6	27.7
Transportation	15.9	9.7	-19.9	13.2	9.6	6.9
Miscellaneous	121.2	74.3	-0.9	4.1	3.1	15.6
Software Services	73.7	45.2	1.4	-0.7	0.0	2.3
Business Services	32.9	20.2	2.0	13.6	8.4	7.6
Financial Services	5.1	3.1	-12.7	3.1	-4.1	-13.4
Services Imports	95.7	100.0	3.7	13.0	16.5	17.4
Travel	16.4	17.2	-3.4	11.1	15.7	12.0
Transportation	14.1	14.8	-6.8	-6.3	-10.0	15.0
Miscellaneous	63.0	65.9	9.8	19.5	26.5	19.3
Software Services	3.6	3.7	-0.3	32.9	25.9	47.6
Business Services	32.3	33.7	12.5	3.7	8.3	11.3
Financial Services	5.9	6.1	-12.4	86.7	69.3	-0.2
Net Services Exports	67.5	100.0	-9.0	-3.2	-10.0	14.6

Source: RBI's Balance of Payments (BoP) data (BPM-6).
Economic Survey 2017-18, Vol. II.

Apart from software and BPO services, there are emerging export opportunities in various other services, such as health, education, and tourism. There are concerted effors underway to establish India as a hub for medical tourism services. Similarly, there is growing interest among Indian higher-education institutions in exporting education services through establishment of offshore campuses as well as twining and partnership arrangements. It is again worth noting that trade data on services are subject to problems of coverage and classification.

To boost services exports, the Government in its mid-term Review of Foreign Trade Policy 2015-2020, has increased incentives under Services Exports from India Scheme (SEIS) by 2 per cent, leading to an additional annual incentive of ₹1,140 crore which could help services exports including Hotel & Restaurant, Hospital, Educational services, etc. Although world trade volume of goods and services is projected to accelerate in 2018, enhanced global uncertainty, protectionism and stricter migration rules would be key factors in shaping India's services exports.

India's services exports have in general grown much more rapidly than its merchandise exports. Further, India's penetration of the world services markets not only exceeds that for goods but has also risen more rapidly, particularly in the latest decade (Chanda, 2019).

IT-BPO Services

The computer and information services segment has played a critical role in India's integration with the world economy and in placing India on the global services map. It has also been the growth driver in India's service sector. Turnover in the IT-BPO services industry has increased from $70bn or 6 per cent of GDP in 2009 to $152.6 bn in 2016-17 or close to 8 per cent of GDP. The industry association, NASSCOM, has targeted revenue of $350 bn by 2025. In line with the growth in IT-BPO revenues, there has also been considerable employment growth in the IT-BPO sector. Today, it is the largest private sector employer providing 3.7 million jobs and a larger number of indirect jobs. The BPO segment alone accounted for 1.15 million jobs in 2017. Between 2001 and 2017, the IT-BPO industry has created 3.7 million jobs and in the 2014-16 period, it has created an additional 600,000 jobs (NASSCOM, 2017).

The industry is highly export-oriented. Export earnings account for three fourths of the industry's revenue. Figure 29.10 highlights the importance of this segment in India's services exports and stronger export orientation compared to other countries.

IT and BPO services exports have risen from a mere $754 million in 1995/96 to $9.6 billion in 2002-03, to $47.5 billion in 2009, and reached $117 billion in 2016-17, of which IT services accounted for $66 bn, business process services for $22 bn and software products and engineering services for $25 bn. Growth has been driven by a mix of companies in this sector, involving a variety of delivery models, including captive subsidiaries and offshore development centres of foreign companies as well as large, small, and medium-sized Indian companies. Overall, India's share in the global IT services market was 52 per cent and its share in the global BPO sourcing market was 38 per cent in 2016-17.

The US has been the most important market for India's IT-BPO exports, with a projected share of 62 per cent in 2016-17 followed by the UK and Continental Europe with shares of 17 and 11 per cent, respectively. Other regions such as Asia-Pacific and the Middle East are growing as markets for Indian IT-BPO exports.

India's IT-BPO exports are in a variety of verticals, including the banking and financial services industry (BFSI), telecom, manufacturing, retail, healthcare, and travel and tourism. Despite the financial crisis of 2008, BFSI remains the most important vertical. However, segments such as healthcare and retail have shown rapid growth in recent years. There has also been a gradual movement up the value chain and end-to-end solutions being provided by Indian IT firms, with the growing number of offshore R&D centres being established in India and a shift towards higher-end services such as business analytics, equity research, and market research. Some Indian companies are also adopting the global delivery model by setting up development centres in other regions to take advantage of low costs, cater to the local market and to overcome immigration and data protection related challenges. Such trends are being forced by growing competition, increased commoditization of lower-end-services, and pressures on margins and business opportunities due to protectionist policies in the developed world, as highlighted earlier.

According to the AT Kearney Offshore Location Attractiveness Index, India has consistently ranked highest among offshoring destinations, due to the combination of its skill availability, favourable business environment, and low cost. The 2017 Index places India as the leading offshoring destination, much ahead of China which is placed second. Today, India accounts for 55 per cent of the offshore IT-BPO market (A.T. Kearney, 2017).Twenty four per cent of the 271 new global delivery centres that were set up worldwide by US based firms in 2017 were in India (NASSCOM, 2018).The country is expected to remain an important part of the global outsourcing market in future, notwithstanding emerging competition from other developing countries and regions and challenges posed by automation (Chanda, 2019).

Factors Underlying the Services Growth

What are the factors behind the dynamism of the services sector in India, one explanation suggested in the literature for fast growth in services is that the income elasticity of demand for services is greater than one. Hence, the final demand for services grows faster than the demand for goods and commodities as income rises.

TABLE – 18.8

Share and Growth of India's Services Sector (GVA at Basic Price)

(%)

	Share and Growth			Growth	
	2013-14	*2014-15**	*2015-16*	*2016-17@*	*2017-18#*
Total Services	50.9(7.8)	52.6(10.3)	52.9 (9.7)	7.7	8.3
Trade, Repair, Hotels and Restaurants	11.5(7.2)	11.8(10.7)	11.4 (11.2)**	7.8**	8.7**
Trade & Repair Services	10.5(7.7)	10.7(10.8)	10.4 (10.9)	–	–
Hotels & Restaurants	1.0(2.4)	1.1(9.5)	1.0 (14.4)	–	–
Transport, Storage, Communication & Services Related to Broadcasting	6.7(8.7)	6.9(8.4)	7.0 (9.3)	–	–
Railways	0.8(6.0)	0.8(7.7)	0.8 (7.0)	–	–
Road Transport	3.2(6.2)	3.2(6.3)	3.2 (6.7)	–	–
Air Transport	0.1(8.7)	0.2(12.8)	0.2 (16.8)	–	–
Financial Services	5.8(4.8)	5.7(7.9)	5.8(6.8)	5.7^	7.3^
Real Estate, Ownership of Dwelling & Professional Services	14.3(12.5)	14.9(11.8)	15.3 (12.5)	–	–
Public Administration and Defence & Others	5.9(3.2)	6.2(9.8)	13.4 (6.9)	11.3	9.4
Construction	9.0(4.6)	8.8(4.4)	8.1 (5.0)	1.7	3.6
Total Services (+construction)	59.8(7.3)	61.4(9.4)	61.0 (9.1)	6.9	7.7
Total (All Sectors)	100.0(6.3)	100.0(7.1)	100.0 (7.9)	6.6	6.1
GDP (Market Price Constant 2011-12)	(6.6)	(7.2)	(8.0)	7.1	6.5

Notes: Shares are in current prices and growth in constant 2011-12 prices; Figures in parentheses indicate growth rate; * First RE; @ Provisional Estimates for 2016-17; # First Advance estimates, ** Also includes transport, storage, communication & services related to broadcasting; ^ Also includes Real estate, ownership of dwelling & professional services..

Source : Central Statistics Office (CSO).. Economic Survey 2015-16, 2017-18.

A rising share of services in GDP is regarded as an outcome of higher income elasticity of demand for services. The empirical studies have shown that the income elasticity of demand for services could be greater than or equal to unity (Gemmell, 1982; Summers, 1985; Bergstand, 1991; Falvey and Gemmell, 1991). Income elasticity of demand for services increases with rising income which favours the fulfilment of more sophisticated desires. During the development process, distribution of GDP and employment registers sectoral shifts. Such shifts may occur on account of the hierarchy of needs, distinguished into basic needs for food and shelter and needs for other material and non-material goods including services (Maslow, 1970). According to this view, income elasticity of demand depends on per capita income and differs across various sectors.

The empirical estimates of price and income elasticity for various categories of services in India are summarised in Table 18.9. It is important to mention that the actual behaviour of the services sector in real GDP depends on the relative strength of the coefficients of income and price elasticity.

TABLE – 18.9

Income and Price Elasticities for the Services Sector

Sector	*Income Elasticity*	*Price Elasticity*
1	*2*	*3*
Services	1.20 *	-0.68 *
1. Producer services	1.22 *	-0.78 *
2. Consumer services	1.00 *	-0.10
3. Government services	1.41 *	-1.05 *

Note:* : Statistically significant at 1 per cent.

The income elasticity of demand is greater than unity and price elasticity is negative and significant for the total services, producer services and government services. In other words, demand for overall services rises with increase in per capita GDP and decreases with increase in prices of services. The higher income elasticity of demand in the case of producer services underscores its forward linkages. This is corroborated by the emergence of producer services comprising advertising, publicity, marketing and other IT-related activities in the recent period as important service industries in India. Therefore, producer services can be regarded as a major source of economic growth.

Another explanation is that technical and structural changes in an economy make it more efficient to contract out services that were once produced in the industry. This type of outsourcing has been called the 'splintering' of industrial activity. Splintering results in an increase in net input demand for services from the industrial sector, as well as the services sector growing proportionately faster than other sectors.

The empirical evidence (Gordon and Gupta, 2003) shows that while splintering and high income elasticity of demand for services have served to stimulate services growth in India, it is necessary to look beyond these factors to fully explain the growth acceleration since the 1990s. In particular, important roles also seem to have been played by economic reforms, the advent of the IT era, and growing external demand for services exports. Industrial sector reforms have also been carried out in India and the question arises why the industrial sector has not experienced the same sustained high level of growth that the service sector has experienced. This could be because industrial growth is more dependent on infrastructure development (such as roads and ports), which have acted as a bottleneck to growth. Labour restrictions and small-scale reservations may also have disadvantaged industry more than services. In addition, the faster growing services activities seem to be more intensive in skilled labour, with which India is well endowed.

A number of studies have attempted to explain the fast growth in the share of service activity observed in cross-country data. The literature draws a distinction between demand and supply factors.

On the supply side, the share of services can be boosted by a switch to a more service-input intensive method of organising production. Such a change in production methods can arise as a result of increasing specialisation as the economy matures. For example, over time, industrial firms may make greater use of specialist sub-contractors to provide services that were previously provided by the firms themselves. Legal, accounting and security services are obvious candidates to be contracted out. Bhagwati (1994) calls this process of specialisation splintering. Kravis (1982) points out that splintering will lead to growth in the share of services in GDP, even when GDP itself is not growing.

On the demand side, an increase in the output share of services can arise from rapid growth in the final demand for services. This could be from domestic consumers with a high income elasticity of demand for services, or from foreign consumers with a growing demand for the country's service exports. Demand-led growth of this type is likely to result, at least initially, in higher prices of services, as well as a shift of resources into the production of services.

Both demand-side and supply-side factors have been shown to have played important roles in this 'services revolution' (Rakshit, 2007). Two types of demand for services are the final demand from consumers (both domestic and exports) and the intermediate demand for services from the other two sectors of the economy of industry and agriculture. Faster growth of the final demand for service sector output is indicated by growth in private household consumption expenditure and a rapid growth of export of services. During the time period 1995-2005, private consumption of services grew at an average of 8.6 per cent and export of services grew at 19.1 per cent that are much higher than the growth rate of services GDP (8.0%). Household income elasticity demand for services averaged 1.5 per cent for the 10-year period (Rakshit, 2007). A key supply-side factor widely mentioned has been the 'splintering' of production activity. This refers to 'outsourcing' of activities previously carried out 'in house' by industrial firms like marketing, legal services, transport, security, repair and maintenance. This outcome of the splintering process gets reflected in the greater service input per unit of output (intensity of use of services) in industry. Available evidence suggests that the intensity with which services are used in industry and agriculture has not changed much over time (Eichengreen and Gupta, 2011). Therefore, the growth in the intermediate demand for services is largely attributed to increasing output and not to outsourcing by manufacturing firms. A supply factor of importance has been technological change or total factor productivity growth (TFPG) in the service sector. Indirect evidence in support of this factor is the declining incremental capital-output ratio and increasing labour productivity growth in the service sector since 1995. Real GDP estimates by sector are not available separately for rural and urban segments in India. However, as most of the manufacturing and services activities are dominated by the urban sector, it can be safely assumed that similar high output growth rates were achieved in the urban sector as a whole.

Service activity can also be stimulated by technological advances, whereby new activities or products emerge as a result of technological breakthrough—such advances are likely to be particularly relevant in the case of the IT sector (e.g., the Internet), telecommunication (cellular phone services) and to some extent in financial services (credit cards, ATMs, etc.).

Economic reform measures initiated since 1991 also impacted on the performance of the services sector. First, reforms in the domestic industrial environment which resulted in rising manufacturing growth provided synergies to the services sector in the form of increased demand for producer services. Second, the liberalisation of the financial sector provided an environment for faster growth of the financial services. Third, reforms in certain segments of infrastructure services also contributed to the growth of services. Consequently, the services sector posted a much higher growth during the reform period as compared with the pre-reform period with its share touching the 50 per cent mark.

Services GVA

As reported in the Economic Survey 2018-19 (vol.2) services sector's, share (total services excluding construction) in India's GVA is 54.3 per cent in 2018-19 (P) with a growth rate of 7.5 per cent lower than the growth rate of 8.1 per cent in 2017-18 and 8.4 per cent in 2016-17.

TABLE – 18.10

Services Sector Performance in India's GVA

Sector	*Share in GVA (%) 2018-19 (P)*	*Growth (% YoY)*						
		2016-17	*2017-18*	*2018-19 (P)*	*2018- 19 (P)*			
					Q1	*Q2*	*Q3*	*Q4*
Total Services (Excluding Construction)	54.3	8.4	8.1	7.5	7.1	7.3	7.2	8.4
Trade, hotels, transport, communication and services related to broadcasting	18.3	7.7	7.8	6.9	7.8	6.9	6.9	6
Financial, real estate & professional services	21.3	8.7	6.2	7.4	6.5	7	7.2	9.5
Public administration, defence & other services	14.7	9.2	11.9	8.6	7.5	8.6	7.5	10.7

Note: Shares are in current prices and growth in constant 2011-12 prices; P= Provisional Estimates

Source: Central Statistics Office (CSO), Ministry of Statistics and Programme Implementation.
Economic Survey 2018-19 (vol. 2), p.229.

State-wise Comparison of Services

Out of the 33 States and Union Territories(UTs) for which data are released for new base 2011-12 series by CSO, the services sector is the dominant sector, contributing to more than half of the gross state value added (GSVA) in 14 states and UTs. The major services in most of the states are trade, hotels and restaurants, followed by real estate, ownership of dwellings and business services. However, there is wide variation in terms of share and growth of services GSVA. Out of the 32 states and UTs for which data are available for 2016-17 (or latest year for which data are available), in terms of services GSVA share, Delhi and Chandigarh are at the top with over 80 per cent share (Chandigarh 88.9 and Delhi 84.3), while Sikkim is at the bottom with 30.2 per cent share (*Economic Survey 2018-19*).

Foreign Direct Investment in India's Service Sector

There has been a significant growth in FDI inflows in 2014-15 and 2015-16. (Apr-Oct) in general and to the services sector in particular. Though there is ambiguity in the classification of FDI in services, the combined FDI share of the top 10 service sectors such as financial and non-financial services under services sector, telecommunications, trading, computer hardware and software, construction, hotels and tourism, hospital and diagnostic centres, consultancy services, sea transport, information and broadcasting can be taken as the best estimate of services FDI, though it could include some non-service elements. This share is 53.3 per cent of the cumulative FDI equity inflows during the period April 2000-October 2015 and 53 per cent during 2014-15. If the shares of some other services or service-related sectors like retail trading, ports, agriculture services, education, and air transport are included, then the total share of cumulative FDI inflows to the services sector would increase to 55.6 per cent and 54.5 per cent respectively for the above two periods (Table 18.11).

In 2014-15, while total FDI equity inflows grew by 27.3 per cent to US$ 30.9 billion, FDI equity inflows to the services sector (top 10 services including construction) grew by a whopping 70.4 per cent to US$16.4 billion (*Economic Survey 2015-16*).

Liberalisation of Services in India

Services have been a critical part of the overall economic reform and liberalisation process in India. Much of the recent structural and institutional reforms as well as the liberalisation/deregulation strategies

TABLE – 18.11

FDI Equity Inflows in the Services Sector

Sr	Sub-Sectors	Value (in US$ million)			Percentage to total		Growth rate (%)	
		2014-15	2015-16 (Apr. to Oct.)	April 2000 to Oct. 2015	2014-15	April 2000 to Oct. 2015	2014-15	2015-16 (Apr. to Oct.)
1	Services sector*	4443.3	3874.1	46586.8	14.4	17.2	99.7	134.5
2	Telecommunications	2894.9	949.6	18007.7	9.4	6.7	121.5	-61.6
3	Trading	2728.0	2372.1	10432.5	8.8	3.9	103.1	52.5
4	Computer software & hardware	2296.0	4122.5	19139.8	7.4	7.1	103.9	530.9
5	Construction #	1639.4	1151.0	28649.5	5.3	10.6	-4.2	33.6
6	Hotel & tourism	777.0	714.6	8631.0	2.5	3.2	59.8	46.0
7	Hospital & diagnostic centres	567.9	377.2	3322.4	1.8	1.2	-17.1	67.2
8	Consultancy services	458.1	384.8	3194.1	1.5	1.2	60.3	11.2
9	Sea transport	333.2	295.7	1841.6	1.1	0.7	1526.3	119.9
10	Information & broadcasting	255.0	515.1	4484.5	0.8	1.7	-40.5	813.7
	Top 10 service categories (1-10)	16392.8	14756.9	144289.9	53.0	53.3	70.4	74.7
	Total FDI equity	30930.5	21873.7	270506.8	100.0	100.0	27.3	26.1

Note: * Financial, banking, insurance, non-financial business, outsourcing, R&D, courier, technology testing and analysis, other; #Combined with infrastructure activities and townships, housing, built-up infrastructure and construction-development projects.

Source: Based on Department of Industrial Policy and Promotion (DIPP) data. *Economic Survey 2015-16.*

have involved the opening up of key services such as telecommunications, banking, and insurance to attract much-needed foreign capital and technology, and to encourage competition and efficiency in these areas to induce positive externalities for the rest of the economy. Many services, including construction, tourism, health, and computer-related services, for instance, have been put on automatic approval route for FDI. Government monopoly in many critical services has been eliminated, with further liberalisation planned or already announced.

Evidence suggests that services that have been liberalised most have typically experienced higher growth rates. Areas such as business services (mainly IT and IT-enabled services), communication, banking, and insurance, which have been liberalised, have exhibited higher growth rates, with wider efficiency and growth benefits to the rest of the economy. On the other hand, services with limited opening, like air-transport, legal, and real-estate services, have grown much more slowly, with likely adverse effects on economy-wide competitiveness and growth performance.

Productivity estimates also corroborate the role played by competition and integration with global markets in improving efficiency in the services sector. Estimates by McKinsey indicate that telecommunications and software services have much higher productivity levels than other services sectors in India, owing to factors such as global and domestic competition and changes in ownership structure, which have in turn enabled technological externalities, knowledge spillovers, improved management practices, and technology diffusion. In addition, liberalisation in certain services has also impacted positively on export opportunities.

For instance, the opening up of areas like telecommunications to FDI has had a positive impact on export opportunities in IT and BPO services. Evidence also indicates increased usage of services in manufacturing and resulting productivity gains in India's manufacturing sector. Further liberalisation of the services sector is likely to yield sector-specific and economy-wide gains in terms of growth, export, efficiency, and competitiveness.

India and Trade Negotiations in Services

India has been actively involved in the WTO services negotiations. It has taken a pro-active position in the services negotiations on temporary cross border movement of service providers (mode 4) and cross border supply of services (mode 1) under the General Agreement on Trade in Services (GATS). In 2004, India made a joint submission along with several other developing countries for a Service Provider Visa under the GATS, with the aim of expanding and ensuring more predictable and transparent market access for intra-company transferees, contractual service suppliers, and independent professionals. India also submitted a joint proposal on mode 1 in 2004 to secure market access in outsourcing across a wide range of services, to pre-empt potential protectionism in this area.

In the Doha Round request-offer process, there was pressure on India from key WTO member countries to make binding and more liberal commitments on commercial presence (GATS mode 3) across a wide range of services. India received requests from several developed countries to multilaterally bind in the liberalization it has undertaken autonomously in sectors such as banking, insurance, and telecommunications, where India's commitments fall short of the existing levels of liberalization. India also received requests to open other services such as retail, higher education, legal and accountancy services to foreign commercial presence. India has largely taken a quid pro quo approach to the services negotiations, i.e., offering to exchange commitments on foreign commercial presence in return for market access in modes 1 and 4. In its August 2005 revised services offer, it significantly improved upon the earlier commitments on commercial presence, aligning its offer more closely with autonomous liberalization initiatives in services. However, with the stalling of the Doha Round negotiations these offers have not been converted into legally binding commitments. Other important multilateral developments involving services include the Trade in Services Agreement (TISA), a plurilateral agreement among 23 like-minded countries, which account for more than 70 per cent of global services trade, in which India did not agree to participate (European Commission portal). More recently, in 2017, India reinvigorated the services discussions by submitting a draft text on Trade Facilitation in Services(TFS) which aimed at addressing behind-the-border administrative and procedural barriers to services trade and to make existing market access commitments under the GATS meaningful. Following comments and suggestions from WTO members, India revised its proposal and moderated its level of ambition by limiting the application of this agreement only to existing commitments scheduled under the GATS. While the TFS text has given a direction to the services negotiations in the WTO, the outcome remains unclear given recent protectionist measures on mobility and data flows in key markets.

Although India has always been a supporter of multilateralism, with the slowdown in multilateral negotiations, India, like other countries, has increasingly turned towards signing bilateral and regional trade agreements. In recent years, it has entered into broad-ranging trade negotiations which go beyond goods to cover services, investment, labour mobility, and other issues which have a bearing on services trade. This trend commenced in 2005 with the entry into force of the India-Singapore CECA followed by several comprehensive bilateral agreements in succession with Korea in 2010, with Japan and Malaysia in 2011, and the expansion of the existing ASEAN-India FTA to include services and investment in 2015. Several agreements are at different stages of negotiation, including with the EU and Australia. India is also currently engaged in the Regional Comprehensive Economic Partnership (RCEP) negotiations which involve ASEAN, Japan, Korea, Australia, New Zealand and China. In all these agreements, India's aim is to facilitate investments in various services from its partner countries in return for securing its interests in sectors such as IT-BPO and various other professional services, mainly through easier access for Indian service suppliers to these markets. The prevailing view is that India's main interest and competitive advantage lies in services and that concessions it makes on goods can be traded off against concessions it can secure from partner countries in services and for key modes such as mode 4 and mode 1. Increasingly, however, this view is being countered due to the difficulties in obtaining effective market access in services from India's FTA partners.

An examination of the sectoral coverage of commitments shows that both India and its partners have either bound the status quo or have taken GATS plus commitments in terms of the number of services sectors and subsectors scheduled. Some schedules go beyond the offers made in the Doha round request-offer process. Available evidence suggests, however, that these commitments have not translated into effective market access. This is because the commitments remain subject to limitations due to behind-the-border regulatory barriers and the introduction of discriminatory national policies. Mobility of professionals remains undermined by recognition and qualification barriers, the absence of MRAs with partner countries in selected professional services, employment laws and discriminatory practices. Although occupation lists have been included in these FTAs, discussions among regulatory authorities have not taken off. It is increasingly being felt that the RCEP agreement may not yield major market access gains in services for India unless India can negotiate for greater transparency and easing of regulatory barriers while continuing with steps to boost its own competitiveness.

The preceding discussion clearly highlights that the service sector has not only outperformed other sectors of the Indian economy, but has also played an important role in India's integration with world trade and capital markets. There is, however, growing debate within the country about the sustainability of a services-led growth process. No country in history has been able to grow rapidly in a sustained manner based on services alone. The manufacturing sector has always been part of the growth success. Hence it remains to be seen whether this model of growth also holds for India or not. The prevailing view today is that India needs broad-based growth as its services sector is largely driven by external demand. If high growth is to be sustained within services, then creation of internal demand is necessary and this is only possible with a vibrant manufacturing sector.; Moreover, employment concerns cannot be addressed without concomitant growth in manufacturing since, as highlighted earlier, the faster-growing services are those that are not generating sufficient growth in employment opportunities for the masses. More broad-based growth within the services sector is required. Services such as trade and distribution, tourism, and construction, which have high employment intensities and large backward and forward linkages with other sectors need to grow more rapidly. In this regard, further infrastructural and regulatory reforms and FDI liberalisation in services can help diversify the sources of growth within India's services sector and provide the required momentum (Chanda, 2010).

The government has taken a number of policy initiatives to promote services exports which include the Service Exports from India Scheme (SEIS) for increasing exports of notified services from India; organizing Global Exhibitions on Services (GES) and services conclaves to augment exports of various services and position India as a key player in world services trade; besides some initiatives in sectors like tourism and shipping. Given the potential of India's services exports, services-sector negotiations both at multilateral and bilateral/regional levels are of vital importance to India (Box 18.1).

BOX – 18.1

WTO Services Negotiations and Bilateral Negotiations including Services Trade

WTO negotiations

- The 10th session of the WTO Ministerial Conference was held in Nairobi, Kenya, from 15 to 18 December 2015. In the area of services trade, the conference took decisions such as implementation of preferential treatment in favour of services and service suppliers of least developed countries (LDC) and increasing LDC participation in services trade; and moratorium on payment of customs duties on electronic transmissions until 2017.
- Preferential treatment for LDCs: So far, 21 members, including India, have notified preferential treatment to LDCs in services trade. India has offered this in respect of: (i) article XVI of the General Agreement on Trade in Services (GATS) (Market Access); (ii) technical assistance and capacity building; and (iii) waiver of visa fees for LDC applicants applying for Indian business and employment visas. The fee waiver will be valid until 31 December 2030. India is the only member which has offered waiver of visa fees. This is a unique and almost path-breaking offer by India. So far, visa issues have remained untouched in the WTO/free trade agreements (FTA). India's offer should give significant advantage to service suppliers from LDCs vis-à-vis service suppliers from any other country.
- E-commerce: The WTO Members agreed to maintain the current practice of not imposing customs duties on electronic transmissions until the next Ministerial Conference which will be held in 2017.

Bilateral agreements:

- India has signed comprehensive bilateral trade agreements, including trade in services, with the governments of Singapore, South Korea, Japan and Malaysia. An FTA in services and investment was signed with the Association of South East Asian Nations (ASEAN) in September 2014, which came into effect from 1 July 2015.
- India has joined the Regional Comprehensive Economic Partnership (RCEP) plurilateral negotiations. The RCEP is a proposed FTA which includes the 10 ASEAN countries and its six

contd...

...contd...

FTA partners, viz. Australia, China, India, Japan, South Korea and New Zealand. The RCEP is the only mega-regional FTA of which India is a part.

- India is also engaged in bilateral FTA negotiations including trade in services with Canada, Israel, Thailand, the EU, the European Free Trade Association (EFTA), Australia and New Zealand. Dialogue is under way with the US under the India-US Trade Policy Forum (TPF), with Australia under the India-Australia Joint Ministerial Commission (JMC), with China under the India-China Working-Group on Services, and with Brazil under the India-Brazil Trade Monitoring Mechanism (TMM).

Source: Based on inputs from the Department of Commerce, Government of India.

Looking Ahead

The services sector is like an uncharted sea with plenty of opportunities that have not been fully tapped. A targeted policy of removing bottlenecks in major and potential services can result in large dividends in the form of higher services growth and services exports, which in turn can help in pulling up the economy to higher growth levels.

India's services sector, which showed resilient growth after the recovery of the global economy following the global financial crisis, has been showing subdued performance in recent times. Despite the slowdown, the prospects continue to be bright for many segments of the sector. Looking ahead, the government's focus on infrastructure development, favourable regulatory policies like liberalization of FDI norms, increasing number of multimodal logistics service providers, growing trend of outsourcing logistics to third party service providers and entry of global players are expected to provide impetus to logistics services. Though shipping services are at a low key at present, with increased imports of POL (petroleum, oil and lubricants) for stocks build up to take advantage of low crude oil prices, containerization of export and import cargo and modernization of ports with private sector participation, recovery of the shipping and port services sector can be expected.

Quoting Rupa Chanda (2019), "Looking ahead, more broad-based growth within the service sector and greater linkages between services and manufacturing are required to ensure balanced, equitable, and employment-oriented growth, with spillovers for productivity and competitiveness to the rest of the economy. India will need to leverage its growing service sector and particularly its more competitive segments within services more effectively for the benefit of the rest of the economy. This will require a focus on increasing efficiency in India's services sector as an input to the manufacturing sector. If India is to move into higher value added manufacturing for the global market, the government must pay attention to developing capacity across two broad clusters of services; first, those services such as transport and logistics which directly enhance connectivity and efficiency in trade and second, those services such as R&D and business support services which add value to manufacturing and enable product differentiation and internationalization. Such a focus would require investment in transport and digital infrastructure, reducing regulatory restrictions that affect services both at the border and behind- the-border, and steps to strengthen and sustain India's advantage in knowledge and skill-intensive business and professional services by liberalizing these segments and encouraging competition, by harmonizing and internationalizing domestic standards and by emphasizing innovation".

19

Foreign Direct Investment

Introduction

Foreign direct investment (FDI), being a non-debt capital flow, is a leading source of external financing, especially for the developing economies. It not only brings in capital and technical know-how, but also increases the competitiveness of the economy. Overall it supplements domestic investment, much required for sustaining the high growth rate of the country. Since 2000, significant changes have been made in the FDI policy regime by the government to ensure that India becomes an increasingly attractive and investor friendly destination.

Role of FDI

Growth impulses originating from FDI are primarily ascribed to superior technology and greater competition that generally accompany FDI. Local firms of many developing host countries also do not invest enough on research & development (R&D) to offer and sustain competition with transnational corporations (TNCs). Investment on R&D by TNCs in foreign affiliates is, however, found to be low, accounting for as little as 1 per cent of the total R&D investment even though TNCs are generally viewed as R&D intensive [United Nations Conference on Trade and Development (UNCTAD), 1999]. Despite the usual concerns that inappropriate technology is generally transferred to the foreign affiliates, empirical assessments suggest that technology—both public and private—that accompanies FDI is complementary and inter-firm collaboration helps in augmenting

---

This chapter is drawn extensively from Kumar, Nagesh (2015). "Foreign Direct and Portfolio Investments Flows and Development: A Perspective on Indian Experience", ch. 35 in Uma Kapila (ed., 2017), *Indian Economy since Independence* (28th edition). New Delhi: Academic Foundation.

growth. In such cases also, FDI may augment growth in a country if its initial technology gap is higher and openness to FDI is significant.

Whether FDI promotes competition or facilitates development of oligopolistic structures depends upon whether FDI crowds-out or crowds-in domestic investment. FDI can potentially displace domestic producers by preempting their investment opportunities. It is possible, however, that the adverse growth effect emanating from crowding-out could be more than offset by the increase in productivity resulting from advanced technology that often accompanies FDI.

Since trade is an important vehicle for growth, FDI could also contribute to growth by promoting exports. For sustaining an export-led growth strategy, it becomes important to attain dynamic shifts in comparative advantage and FDI can play a major role in imparting the desired dynamism on account of its global marketing network.

In India FDI directly impacts on output growth by augmenting the available investible capital. However, a far more important impact of FDI is through externalities leading to higher efficiency and productivity. FDI typically serves to increase competition in markets, bring new technology into India, and foster skill acquisition amongst domestic labour. FDI by international corporations is also central to the process of India being utilised as a platform for global production chains, which would pave the way for strong exports growth.

FDI Policy: A Historical Perspective

Over the last five decades, there have been significant changes in approaches and policies relating to FDI in India in tune with the developments in the industrial policies and also foreign exchange situation, from time to time. There is a view in the literature that the attitude and approach to FDI reflected the under current of balance of payments (BoP) crisis in the respective periods. Depending upon the thrust and direction of the policies at different time period, one can identify four distinct phases in the evolution of the policies:

1. first phase from 1950 to 1967—characterised by receptive attitude or cautious welcome;
2. second phase from 1967 to 1980—marked by restrictive and selective policies;
3. third phase from 1980 to 1990—gradual liberalisation; and
4. fourth phase from 1991 till date—paradigm shift to open door policy (Jain, 1994; Subrahmanian *et al.*, 1996; Kumar, 1998).

Major features of FDI policies during the above four phases are reviewed below. Table 19.1 provides the major features of FDI policies during the four phases.

TABLE – 19.1

Major Features of FDI Policies during the Four Phases

Phase I 1950-1967	*Phase II 1967-1980*	*Phase III 1980-1990*	*Phase IV 1991 Onwards*
Receptive Attitude or Cautious Welcome	*Restrictive Attitude*	*Gradual Liberalisation*	*Open Door Policy*
• Non-discriminatory treatment to FDI.	• Restriction on FDI without technology.	• Higher foreign equity in export-oriented units allowed.	• Liberal policies relating to technology collaboration, foreign trade and foreign exchange.
• No restrictions on remittance of profits and dividends.	• Above 40 per cent stake not allowed.	• Procedure for remittance of royalty and technical fees liberalised.	• Encouraging FDI in core and infrastructure industries.
	• Allowed only in priority area.		• FERA replaced with FEMA.
• Ownership and control with Indians.	• FDI controlled by FERA.	• Fast channel for FDI clearance.	• Procedures transparent.
			• Liberal approach for NRI investments.
	• Discretionary power in sanctioning the projects.		• FDI need not be accompanied by technology.
			• FDI through mergers and acquistions.
			• FDI in services and financial sector banks, NBFCs, insurance.

After pursuing a restrictive policy towards FDI for over four decades with a varying degree of selectivity, India changed tracks in 1990s and embarked on a broader process of reforms designed to increase her integration with the global economy. Among the reform measures implemented included a departure from the restrictive policy towards FDI, a much more liberal trade policy besides reforms of capital market and exchange controls. The New Industrial Policy (NIP) announced on 24 July 1991 marked a major departure with respect to FDI policy with the abolition of industrial licensing system except where it is required for strategic or environmental grounds, creation of a system of automatic clearance of FDI proposals fulfilling the conditions laid down, such as the ownership levels of 50 per cent, 51 per cent, 74 per cent and 100 per cent foreign equity and opening of new sectors such as mining, banking, insurance, telecommunications, construction and management of ports, harbours, roads and highways, airlines, and defence equipment, to foreign owned companies subject to sectoral caps. Foreign ownership up to 100 per cent is permitted in most manufacturing sectors—in some sectors even on automatic basis—except for defence equipment where it is limited to 26 per cent and for items reserved for production by small-scale industries where it is limited to 24 per cent. The dividend balancing and the related export obligation conditions on foreign investors, which applied to 22 consumer goods industries, were withdrawn in 2000 (Kumar, 2005a). In September 2012, India allowed FDI in multibrand retail and in civil aviation. Sectoral caps were revised upwards in July 2013 in some sectors like telecom to 100 per cent, in insurance to 49 per cent, and in defence equipment beyond 26 per cent on a case-by-case basis (Kumar, 2014).

In September 1992, the Indian government announced guidelines for investments by foreign institutional investors (FIIs) in the Indian capital market. FIIs were now welcome to invest in all types of securities traded on the primary and secondary market with full repatriation benefits and without restrictions on either volume of trading or lock-in period. This liberalisation has led to considerable inflows of portfolio inflows making the country most exposed to portfolio inflows. In June 2013, FII investments were reclassified as foreign portfolio investor (FPI) which is subject to their holding in a company within 10 per cent of its equity. Any holdings beyond 10 per cent will qualify as FDI.

Recognising the importance of outward investment for competitiveness of enterprises, the policy governing outward FDI has also been liberalised since 1991. With the build up of foreign exchange reserves, the limits for outward investments have been gradually relaxed and Indian enterprises are now permitted to invest abroad up to 100 per cent of their net worth on automatic basis (Ibid.).

India has also entered into 65 Double Taxation Avoidance Treaties, and Bilateral Investment Promotion and Protection Agreement (BIPAs) with 58 countries (Ibid.).

The current phase of FDI policy is characterised by negative listing, permitting FDI freely except in a few sectors indicated through a negative list. Under the current policy regime, there are three broad entry options for foreign direct investors. In a few sectors, FDI is not permitted (negative list); in another small category of sectors, foreign investment is permitted only till a specified level of foreign equity participation; and the third category, comprising all the other sectors, is where foreign investment up to 100 per cent of equity participation is allowed. The third category has two subsets: one consisting of sectors where automatic approval is granted for FDI (often foreign equity participation less than 100 per cent) and the other consisting of sectors where prior approval from the Foreign Investment Promotion Board (FIPB) is required. FDI policy changes increasingly reflect the requirements of industry and are based on stakeholders' consultation. Upfront listing of negative sectors has helped focus on reform areas, which are reflected in buoyant FDI inflows.

With a view to liberalizing and simplifying the FDI policy to provide ease of doing business climate in the country that will also lead to larger FDI inflows, the government has undertaken various reforms. A number of sectors have been liberalized, including defence, construction, broadcasting, civil aviation, plantation, trading, private sector banking, satellite establishment and operation and credit information companies. During 2015-16, FDI policy in the pension sector has been revised to permit foreign investment up to 49 per cent, with 26 per cent under automatic route. Manufacturing of medical devices and white label ATM operations have been opened up to 100 per cent FDI under automatic route (*Economic Survey 2015-16*, Vol.II).

The various reforms in the FDI sector have led to a significant increase in FDI inflows into India. During April-November 2015, total FDI inflows were US$34.8 billion as compared to US$27.7 billion during April-November 2014, showing a 26 per cent surge. FDI equity inflows also increased from US$18.9 billion during April-November 2014 to US$24.8 billion during April-November 2015, showing 31 per cent growth. There were FDI inflows into sectors like computer software and hardware, services, trading, automobile industry, construction (infrastructure) activities, chemicals (other than fertilizers) and telecommunications. FDI statistics of the last fifteen years reveal that the services sector has accounted for the highest inflows (17.6% of total FDI inflows into India), followed by construction development (8.8%), computer hardware and software (7.2%), telecommunications (6.6%) and the automobile industry (5.2%).

There are wide variations in the FDI inflows into India from different countries. However, Singapore, Mauritius, Netherlands and the USA account for the major share. Out of FDI equity inflows of US$24.8 billion during 2015-16 (April- November), more than 60 per cent have come from two geographically small countries named Singapore and Mauritius. These inflows need perhaps to be examined more closely to determine whether they constitute actual investment or are diversions from other sources to avail of tax benefits under the Double Tax Avoidance Agreement that these countries have with India (*Economic Survey 2015-16*).

A country-wise analysis of the FDI inflows in major sectors from 2011 to 2015 (till November) from top five countries are given in Table 19.2.

TABLE – 19.2

FDI Inflows to Major Sectors from Top Five Host Countries (in %) from 2011-12 to 2015-16 (November)

Sectors	*Singapore*	*Mauritius*	*Netherlands*	*US*	*Japan*
Services sector	18.6	18.9	15.4	19	20
Computer software and hardware	13.8	6.2	3.2	9.8	1
Trading	11.8	2.4	10	3.2	4.6
Telecommunications	8.6	11.5	0.3	2	0.1
Drugs & pharmaceuticals	6.6	1.0	0.6	2	3
Power	5.0	6.1	2.7	4	0.3
Construction (infrastructure)	3.5	3.9	0.2	3.5	0.5
Hotel tourism	2.3	10.6	0.6	0.8	0.1
Automobiles	1.9	1.5	8.7	17.8	21
Chemicals	NA	1.6	8.9	1.8	2.7
Petroleum and natural gas	0.7	1.1	8.4	0.1	1.2

Source: *Economic Survey 2015-16*.

The Government of India has taken a series of measures to improve 'Ease of Doing Business' in the country. Existing rules have been simplified and information technology introduced to make governance more efficient and effective. Large improvements in World Economic Forum and World Bank rankings testify to the reforms implemented in this regard. Reflecting the better economic performance and the commitment of the government to reforms, the global perception about India's competitiveness has improved as per the Global Competitiveness Index of the World Economic Forum. Significantly, at position 55, India went up 16 rungs in 2015-16, which is the largest gain among the major economies (*Economic Survey 2015-16,* Vol.II).

FPI Inflows and their Impact

The rapid rise in inflows of portfolio investments in India since 2003-04 is summarised in Table 19.3. Large magnitudes of portfolio investments in the form of short-term equity investments by FII have flowed in as the Indian economy gathered momentum and capital markets started giving attractive returns. The annual net inflows, however, are highly volatile.

TABLE – 19.3

FDI and Foreign Portfolio Investment Flows to India

	Gross Inflows/ Gross Investments	*Direct Investments to India*	*FDI by India*	*Net Foreign Direct Investment*	*Net Portfolio Investment*	*Total (in million USD)*
2000-01	4029	4029	759	3270	2590	5860
2001-02	6130	6125	1391	4734	1952	6686
2002-03	5035	4976	1819	3157	944	4101
2003-04	4322	4322	1934	2388	11377	13765
2004-05	6051	5986	2274	3712	9291	13003
2005-06	8961	8900	5867	3033	12492	15525
2006-07	22826	22739	15046	7693	6947	14640
2007-08	34843	34727	18836	15891	27434	43325
2008-09	41873	41707	19364	22343	-14032	8311
2009-10	37745	33108	15143	17965	32396	50361
2010-11	34847	27829	16524	11305	30292	41597
2011-12	46556	32957	11097	22860	17171	39031
2012-13	34298	26953	7134	19819	26891	46710

Source: Extracted from RBI's Handbook of Statistics on Indian Economy, 2013, and *www.rbi.org.in.*

FII inflows rose to a sizeable $27 billion in 2007-08 that led to not only stock prices booming, with BSE Sensex more than doubling from under 10,000 to 20,000, but also the rupee exchange rate appreciating sharply from ₹ 47 in 2006 to ₹ 38 to a US dollar in 2008. In 2008-09, in the wake of global financial crisis, there was a net outflow of FII to the tune of $14 billion that brought down the BSE Sensex from nearly 20,000 points to less than 9,000 points in the early part of 2009. Much more importantly it led to a sharp depreciation of rupee by nearly 25 per cent in early 2009. The depreciation would have been greater had the Reserve Bank of India (RBI) not intervened in the market by selling dollars. This depleted the RBI's foreign exchange reserves by $58 billion to about $252 billion from $310 billion from 2007-08 to 2008-2009. However, as FIIs returned quickly to the market in the wake of recovery, the FII inflows to the country in 2010 were of the order of $32 billion bringing the Sensex back above 20,000 points in October 2010. Despite the RBI's market intervention to offset the subsequent exchange rate pressure, the rupee appreciated by nearly 8 per cent, although foreign exchange reserves were augmented to about $284 billion. FII inflows have become primary determinants of the movements in the stock exchange indices and the exchange rate of the rupee (see Kumar, 2011). As there are sharp movements in these inflows linked to global developments, they become channels of transmission of instability to the country's financial system. As a result, the rupee has been on a roller coaster ride: from ₹ 44 per dollar in January 2007 to ₹ 39 in January 2008 to increase again to ₹ 49 per dollar in January 2009 to ₹ 44 in October 2010. The rupee fluctuated around ₹ 54 in 2012 and early 2013 and after May 2013 depreciated sharply to cross ₹ 60 to a dollar, as there was outflow of FIIs in anticipation of roll back of quantitative easing policy by Federal Reserve in the US and as concerns about India's rising current account deficit (CAD) mounted.

Besides the volatility, FII inflows have a very high servicing burden. Among foreign resources such as FDI, foreign borrowings, non-resident Indian (NRI) deposits, American Depositary Receipts (ADRs), global depositary receipts (GDRs), FII investments are most expensive in terms of servicing burden (Kumar, 2011). This is because they come to chase primarily good returns at the stock markets and exchange rate speculation. In 2007-08, Indian stock markets were giving around 44 per cent return. That means for every dollar India received in FII flows, it became liable to pay $1.44 in one year. As they are stock price makers rather than takers, they manage to exit safely before major crashes of markets thereby precipitating the declines.

One may argue that FII inflows help a country to build foreign exchange reserves. What is not appreciated very well is the fact that exposure to these inflows also enhances the need to have large foreign exchange reserves due to their highly volatile nature. Therefore, developing countries such as India should rely for their foreign resource needs more on FDI inflows and where possible raise ADRs/GDRs and deposits from NRIs rather than relying on the FIIs. In view of their high cost and their other deleterious effects such as volatility, a number of emerging economies such as Brazil, South Korea and Indonesia have recently imposed capital controls to moderate their volatility. The unprecedented injection of liquidity by the governments in developed countries in the wake of global financial crisis is likely to find its way to emerging economies of Asia like India to take advantage of higher returns. There is now a growing consensus on the relevance of capital controls as aspects of the policy tool kit for the governments in emerging economies (UN-ESCAP, 2010; Ostry et al., 2010). The benefits of maintaining open capital accounts, if any, are ambiguous.

India as an Emerging Source of FDI Outflows

Another important emerging trend with respect to FDI in India is its emergence as a significant source of FDI outflows. Like FDI inflows, the major turnaround in their outflows came in 2006 when outflows more than quadrupled in one year to $14 billion and peaked to nearly $20 billion in 2007 before declining to around $15 billion in subsequent years in the wake of global financial crisis (Table 19.4). The big break came with Indian enterprises using their outward investments to acquire larger companies in the advanced economies as a part of their effort to augment their bundles of strategic assets including known brand names, proprietary knowledge and global marketing networks in order to jump start their global orientation. The past few years have seen several multibillion-dollar acquisitions of western firms by Indian companies including Tata Steel-Corrus, Tata Motors-Jaguar/Land Rover, Handalco-Novelis, among others.

Impact of FDI on Growth and Domestic Investment

FDI inflows could contribute to growth rate of the host economy by augmenting the capital stock as well as with infusion of new technology. However, high growth rates may also attract more FDI inflows by enhancing the investment climate in the country.

TABLE – 19.4

Foreign Direct Investment (FDI) Outflows Originating in India

(million USD)

	World	*Developing Economies*	*Developing Economies: Asia*	*India*
2001	747657	83087	49155	1397
2002	528496	47484	34987	1678
2003	570679	46668	23961	1876
2004	925716	122792	91404	2175
2005	888561	132507	86425	2985
2006	1415094	239336	151400	14285
2007	2198025	316863	228154	19594
2008	1969336	328121	223116	19257
2009	1175108	268476	210925	15927
2010	1451365	400144	273033	13151
2011	1711652	422582	304293	12456
2012	1346671	440164	302130	8486
2013	1410810	454067	3261013	1679

Source: Extracted from UNCTAD database 2014.

The empirical studies on the nature of the relationship between FDI and domestic investments suggest that the effect of FDI on domestic investment depends on host government policies. Governments have extensively employed selective policies and imposed various performance requirements such as local content requirements (LCRs) to deepen the commitment of multinational enterprises (MNEs) to the host economy. The Indian government has imposed a condition of phased manufacturing programmes (or local content requirements) in the auto industry to promote vertical inter-firm linkages and encourage development of the auto component industry (and crowding-in of domestic investments). A case study of the auto industry where such a policy was followed shows that these policies (in combination with other performance requirements *viz*., foreign exchange neutrality) have succeeded in building an internationally competitive vertically integrated auto sector in the country (Kumar, 2005).

FDI and Export-Platform Production

A number of developing countries have used FDI to exploit the resources of MNEs such as globally recognised brand names, best practice technology or by increasing integration with their global production networks, among others, for expanding their manufactured exports. In this respect, China has had a considerable success in exploiting the potential of FDI for export-oriented production. A very substantial (55%) proportion of manufactured exports of China are undertaken by foreign invested enterprises, which account for as much as 80 per cent of all technology-intensive exports (UNCTAD, 2005). Foreign enterprises while setting up export-oriented production bases created 23 million jobs by 2003 making China a global factory. Export-oriented FDI also helps in bringing world's best practice technology as the affiliate has to compete globally right from the beginning. It also enhances the chances of FDI inflows crowding-in domestic investments and reducing the chances of crowd-out as the foreign affiliate would be mainly catering to the outside markets rather than eating into domestic firms' markets. It would also create fresh possibilities of market information spillovers for domestic firms on export possibilities.

Unlike the East Asian countries, India has not been able to exploit the potential of FDI for export-oriented production. The bulk of FDI inflows in India are market-seeking coming for tapping the domestic market with the share of foreign affiliates in exports around 10 per cent. Therefore, the quality of FDI in respect of export-orientation is poorer compared to FDI received by East Asian countries. In this respect, two observations can be made. The first is that recent studies of export-performance are beginning to indicate a relatively superior performance of foreign enterprises in terms of export orientation compared to early studies suggesting a poorer performance of foreign companies (see Kumar and Joseph, 2007). Therefore, MNEs are beginning to exploit the potential of India as base for export-oriented production (Kumar, 2013).

Export-obligations have also been employed fruitfully by many countries to prompt MNE affiliates to exploit the host country's potential for export platform production. For instance, in China which has succeeded in expanding manufactured exports with help of MNE affiliates, regulations stipulate that wholly owned foreign enterprises must undertake to export more than 50 per cent of their output (Rosen, 1999: 63-71). As a result of these policies, the proportion of foreign enterprises in manufactured exports has steadily increased to over 55 per cent as observed above (Ibid.).

Concluding Remarks and Policy Lessons

Although starting from a low base, India has also been able to increase its share in FDI inflows received by developing countries especially in the past few years and is catching up with Southeast Asian countries in terms of share of these inflows in capital formation. India is also attracting large magnitudes of portfolio equity flows from FIIs which are highly volatile.

The above discussion also shows that even though India may be attracting increasing magnitudes of FDI inflows, they are yet to harness their development potential fully. The empirical studies suggest that the country has received FDI inflows of mixed quality and the developmental impact has been uneven. India can learn a great deal from the experiences of China and other Southeast Asian countries in this regard. China has had a much greater success in harnessing the potential of FDI for building high technology export-oriented industrial base using a variety of policy instruments and performance requirements. On the other hand, India is getting exposed in a significant manner to the FPI flows that are not only highly volatile but also expensive in terms of servicing burden.

Policy Lessons

In general, the above analysis brings out the role of government policy in attracting and benefiting from FDI inflows for development. In light of this discussion, we may now draw a few policy lessons for the region and other similarly placed developing countries.

First of all, liberalisation of FDI policy may be necessary but not sufficient for expanding FDI inflows. The overall macroeconomic performance continues to exercise a major influence on the magnitude of FDI inflows by acting as a signalling device for foreign investors about the growth prospects for the potential host economy. Hence, paying attention to macroeconomic performance indicators such as growth rates of industry through public investments in socioeconomic infrastructure and other supportive policies and creating a stable and enabling environment would crowd-in FDI inflows. Studies have shown that policies that facilitate domestic investments also pull in FDI inflows. While investment incentives may not be efficient, active promotion of FDI by developing certain viable projects and getting key MNEs interested in them could be useful in attracting investments in desirable directions.

The evidence suggests that the government policies play an important role in determining the quality or developmental impact of

FDI and in facilitating the exploitation of its potential benefits by host country's development. The various performance requirements such as phased manufacturing programmes, export performance requirements and domestic ownership requirements have also been employed by the governments to achieve their developmental policy objectives. Even with liberalised policy, some policy direction to FDI is desirable as has been demonstrated by the case of East Asian countries.

Another sphere where governmental intervention may be required to maximise gains from globalisation is in diffusion of knowledge brought in by foreign enterprises. An important channel of diffusion of knowledge brought in by MNEs in the host economy is vertical inter-firm linkages with domestic enterprises. Many governments—in developed as well as developing countries alike—have imposed local content requirements on MNEs to intensify generation of local linkages and transfer of technology (see Kumar, 2005b, for evidence). The host governments could also consider employing proactive measures that encourage foreign and local firms to deepen their local content as a number of countries, e.g., Singapore, Taiwan, Korea and Ireland, have done so successfully.

FDI Outlook

Liberalisation of FDI policy may be necessary but not sufficient for expanding FDI inflows. The overall macroeconomic performance continues to exercise a major influence on the magnitude of FDI inflows by acting as a signalling device for foreign investors about the growth prospects for the potential host economy. Hence, paying attention to macroeconomic performance indicators, creating a stable and enabling environment would crowd-in FDI inflows.[1] Studies have shown that policies that facilitate domestic investments also pull in FDI inflows. While investment incentives may not be efficient, active promotion of FDI by developing certain viable projects and getting key MNEs interested in them could be useful in attracting investments in desirable directions.

1. Kumar, Nagesh (2012). "FDI", in Kaushik Basu and Annemie Maertens (eds.), *The New Oxford Companion to Economics in India* (Vol.I). New Delhi: Oxford University Press.

SECTION - V

Financial Sector and External Sector

Financial Sector:

20. The Financial Sector: Structure, Performance and Reforms

External Sector:

21. Foreign Trade and Trade Policy

22. Balance of Payments

23. India and the WTO

20

The Financial Sector

Structure, Performance and Reforms*

THE financial sector in the Indian economy has had a checkered history. The story of the post-independent (i.e., post-1947) Indian financial sector can perhaps be portrayed in terms of three distinct phases—the first phase spanning over the 1950s and 1960s exhibited some elements of instability associated with laissez faire but underdeveloped banking; the second phase covering the 1970s and 1980s began the process of financial development across the country under government auspices but which was accompanied by a degree of financial repression; and the third phase since the 1990s has been characterized by gradual and calibrated financial deepening and liberalization (Mohan and Ray, 2017).

Indian Financial Sector: 1950–1990—From Laissez Faire to Government Control

The Reserve Bank of India (RBI) was founded in 1935 under the Reserve Bank of India Act "...to regulate the issue of Bank Notes and keeping the reserves with a view to securing monetary stability in India and generally to operate the credit and currency system of the country to its advantage." Apart from being the central bank and monetary policy authority, the RBI is the regulator of all banking activity, including non-banking financial companies, manager of statutory reserves, debt manager of the government, and banker to the government.

---

*. This chapter is drawn extensively from Mohan, Rakesh and Partha Ray (2017). "Indian Financial Sector: Structure, Trends and Turns", *IMF Working Papers* WP/17/7. Reprinted in Uma Kapila (2018), *Indian Economy Since Independence* (29th edition, ch. 31). New Delhi: Academic Foundation.

At the time of independence in 1947, India had 97 scheduled[1] private banks, 557 "nonscheduled" (small) private banks organized as joint stock companies, and 395 cooperative banks. Thus, at the time of India's independence, the organized banking sector comprised three major types of players, viz., the Imperial Bank of India, joint-stock banks (which included both joint stock English and Indian banks) and the foreign owned exchange banks. The decade of 1950s and 1960s was characterized by limited access to finance of the productive sector and a large number of banking failures.[2] Such dissatisfaction led the government of left-leaning Prime Minister (and then Finance Minister) Mrs Indira Gandhi to nationalize fourteen private sector banks on 20 July 1969; and later six more commercial banks in 1980. Thus, by the early 1980's the Indian banking sector was substantially nationalized, and exhibited classical symptoms of financial repression, viz., high pre-emption of banks' investible resources (with associated effects of crowding out of credit to the private sector), subject to an intricate cobweb of administered interest rates, and accompanied by quantitative ceilings on sectoral credit, as governed by the Reserve Bank of India.

Besides the commercial banks, there were four other types of financial institutions in the Indian financial sector: development finance institutions (DFIs), co-operative banks, regional rural banks and post-offices.

Over the 1950s and 1960, in the absence of effective capital markets, a network of DFIs was established over much of the developing world, usually encouraged by external aid agencies.[3] The sources of funds of these DFIs were diverse but raised primarily from the domestic bond market, from multilateral institutions like the World Bank, refinance window of the RBI, and government budgetary provisions. But by the 1990s, with stoppage of refinance from the RBI and government budgetary provisions, and accumulation of nonperforming assets, it became clear that the DFIs would not be viable in the long run. Consequently, the IDBI and ICICI have been converted

1. The 'scheduled' banks were banks "which were included in the Second Schedule to the RBI Act and those banks in British India that subsequently became eligible for inclusion in this Schedule by virtue of their paid-up capital and reserves being more than Rs 500,000 in the aggregate...the power to include or exclude banks in or from the Schedule was vested with the Governor General in Council" (RBI, 2008)
2. As against 566 commercial banks operating in 1951, only 89 survived by 1969, the rest went into liquidation or amalgamation during 1951–1969; see RBI (2008) for details.
3. World Bank (1989) noted, "Development finance institutions have been perhaps the most common means of directing credit. They were actively encouraged and supported by bilateral and multilateral creditors. Virtually all developing and high-income countries have at least one, and many have a special institution for each priority sector" (p. 57).

into commercial banks, and the IFCI is effectively non-functional. NABARD, the NHB and SIDBI are continuing largely as refinance institutions with support from the government.[4]

As of 2015, there are 1,579 urban co-operative and 94,178 rural cooperative banks. A majority of these banks tend to operate in a single state, and they are regulated and supervised by state-specific Registrars of Cooperative Societies (RCS), along with overall oversight by the Reserve Bank of India. Thus there has been dual control of regulation and supervision of co-operative banks between the state-specific RCSs and the RBI, which has often been problematical. They have also suffered from governance problems along with the incidence of frequent local political interference which has hampered the effectiveness of these banks. There have also been slow to modernize.

Regional Rural Banks (RRBs) were established in 1975 as local level banks in different states of India. They are co-owned by the Central and State Governments, and by sponsoring public sector banks. Unlike the cooperative banks, RRBs are structured as commercial banks and were established with a view to developing the rural economy.

The Post Office Savings Bank (POSB) has a customer base of about 330 million account holders as on March 2015 (Government of India, 2016). thereby contributing significantly to financial inclusion on the deposit side.[5] However, the POSB offers only deposit and remittance facilities but not any credit to account holders.

The Bombay Stock Exchange, the first stock exchange in India, was founded in 1875. However, by modern standards, the Indian equity market was still quite underdeveloped till about the late 1980s. It was governed by an archaic regulatory structure whereby the Controller of Capital Issues (CCI) in the finance ministry was the effective equity market regulator. Government bonds were available on tap at a fixed coupon and primarily catered to deficit financing of the government. Draconian foreign exchange controls resulted in a virtually non-existent market for foreign exchange.

Insurance in India has had a long history. The life insurance business was nationalised in 1956 giving birth to the Life Insurance Corporation of India (LIC), which then had had a monopoly in the

4. IDBI: Industrial Development Bank of India; ICICI: Industrial Credit and Investment Corporation of India; IFCI: Industrial Finance Corporation if India; NABARD: National Bank fir Agriculture and Rural Development; NHB: National Housing Bank; SIDBI: Small Industries Development Bank of India.

5. Recently the Indian postal department has been given license to open a payments bank.

insurance business till the late 1990s when the Insurance sector was opened to the private sector.[6] The general insurance business was nationalized later in 1972 when 107 insurers were amalgamated and grouped into just four government owned companies.

Thus, by the end of the 1980s, the financial sector in India was virtually owned by the government with nationalized banks and insurance companies and a single public sector mutual fund. Consequently, reforming the financial sector was a very important part of Indian economic reforms initiated in the early 1990s. Thus, over the years, the Indian financial sector has emerged as a substantial segment of the economy comprising diverse financial institutions and various markets.

Banking in India since the 1990s: Towards Modern Competitive Banking

The initial foundation of the banking sector reforms in India came from two official reports, viz., the Report of the Committee on Financial System (Reserve Bank of India, 1991) and the Report of the Committee on Banking Sector Reforms (Government of India, 1998), both chaired by former Governor of the RBI, M Narasimham. The Narasimham Committee 1991 was primarily devoted to enhancing operational freedom in the commercial banking sector and recommended measures like reduction of pre-emption of banks' investible resources (via a reduction of cash reserve ratio (CRR) and statutory liquidity ratio (SLR)) and gradual elimination of the administered interest rate structure. Narasimham Committee 1998 recommended further measures for modernising the banking sector through better regulation and supervision, and introduction of prudential norms. It also suggested a review of the bank ownership structure in India.

Other elements of financial sector reforms in India include significant reduction of financial repression (including removal of automatic monetisation); dismantling of the complex administered interest rate structure to enable the process of price discovery; providing operational and functional autonomy to public sector institutions; preparing the financial system for increasing international competition; opening the external sector in a calibrated manner; and promoting financial stability in the wake of domestic and external shocks (Mohan,

6. The LIC absorbed 154 Indian, 16 non-Indian insurers as also 75 provident societies—245 Indian and foreign insurers in all; see IRDA (2007) for details.

2006). All these measures were designed to create an efficient, productive and profitable financial sector. Illustratively, gradual reduction of CRR from 15 per cent to about 4 per cent, and reduction in the SLR[7] from nearly 40 per cent to 21.5 per cent between the early 1990s and the mid-2010s have made a huge improvement to the availability of lendable resources to the banking sector.[8]

With the initiation of reforms and the transition to indirect, market-based instruments of monetary policy in the 1990s, the RBI made conscious efforts to develop an efficient, stable and liquid money market by creating a favourable policy environment through appropriate institutional changes, instruments, technologies and market practices.

A bunch of new private sector commercial banks were licensed in the mid-1990s, the first time since bank nationalisation, in order to introduce competition, enhance efficiency and induce innovation in the banking sector.

Information technology has played a key role in this transformative journey of Indian banking. Technology has enabled more effective, lower cost and real-time delivery of financial services, through the establishment of a modern payments system. Setting up of the Indian Financial Network (INFINET) as the communication backbone for the financial sector, introduction of a Real Time Gross Settlement System (RTGS) and core banking solutions across banks encompassing most of their branches across India, are some of the major technological initiatives implemented. Establishment of the Institute for Development and Research in Banking Technology (IDRBT) by the Reserve Bank in 1996 has helped greatly in promoting connectivity among all the banks through development of and propagation of common IT standards throughout the system. The new private sector banks, with no legacy issues to constrain them, enthusiastically adopted the new information technology from their inception, thereby also acting as a competitive spur to induce similar adoption by public sector banks.

Select Outcomes

Over the years there has been a huge increase in the extent of financialization of the Indian economy. This is reflected in upward trend in aggregate deposit and credit as a percentage of GDP. Post 1990s, all

---

7. The proportion of aggregate deposits that a bank has to keep in government and other approved securities.
8. All percentages are with respect to net demand and time liabilities of commercial banks.

the reform measures led to the emergence of a modern banking sector in India and resulted in improvement in many of the profitability, efficiency and stability indicators of commercial banking in India (Table 20.1). The new private sector banks, along with the housing finance company HDFC, ushered in the era of retail lending and housing finance in India, starting in the late 1990s (Ahluwalia, 1999). Public sector banks followed suit with a lag. This change helped greatly in increasing the demand for automobiles, two wheelers and other consumer durables, and promoted overall economic growth in the country, while also helping in diversifying the asset base of banks.

TABLE – 20.1

Select Indicators of Scheduled Commercial Banks (excluding Regional Rural Banks)

Year	*March 1980*	*March 1990*	*March 2000*	*March 2010*	*March 2015*
No. of Banks	75	75	101	85	91
Credit - Deposit Ratio (%)	63.32	61.64	49.26	73.66	78.31
Investment-Deposit Ratio (%)	31.50	33.58	45.97	36.42	33.59
(Credit + Investment) - Deposit Ratio (%)	94.82	95.22	95.23	110.09	111.90
Ratio of Deposits to Total Liabilities (%)	73.78	70.60	81.08	78.76	78.40
Ratio of Net Interest Margin to Total Assets (%)	NA	3.48	5.24	2.54	2.64
Ratio of Intermediation Cost to Total Assets (%)	NA	4.61	4.79	1.78	1.77
Ratio of Wage Bills to Intermediation Cost (%)	NA	65.68	66.96	55.23	54.26
Ratio of Wage Bills to Total Expense (%)	NA	19.77	19.06	14.85	13.13
Ratio of Operating Profits to Total Assets (%)	NA	0.39	3.21	2.17	2.02
Return on Assets (%)	NA	0.39	1.28	1.05	0.81
Return on Equity (%)	NA	23.37	22.58	14.31	10.42

Source: Statistical Tables Relating to Banks in India, RBI, various issues.
IMF Working Paper WP/17/7.

Money Markets

The short-term money market which has links with the entire spectrum of the financial system comprises five segments:

1. the call money market,
2. the inter-bank term deposit market,
3. the bills re-discount market,
4. the Treasury bill market, and
5. the inter-corporate funds market.

In recent years, new money market instruments such as certificates of deposits (CDs), commercial paper (CP) and 182 days treasury bills have been introduced so as to impart liquidity and depth to the money market. Moreover, a specialised money market institution, named the Discount and Finance House of India (DFHI), has been established with the objective of providing liquidity to money market instruments, thereby helping to develop an active secondary market.

Major reforms in the money market were introduced from 1991 onwards, though some measures had been initiated in 1987. The reforms included the introduction of new participants, instruments (CP, CD and inter-bank participation certificates), and maturities of treasury bills. To regulate short-term liquidity in the system, the RBI introduced repurchase transactions (repo) on 10 December 1992 and a liquidity adjustment facility (LAF) on 5 June 2000 under which it absorbs (repo) or injects liquidity (reverse repo) in the system each day. The repo rate has become an important signalling instrument for the financial markets, and the LAF has succeeded in reducing volatility in the call rate.

The RBI is the most important constituent of the money market. Money market falls under the direct purview of regulation of the RBI owing to its implications for conducting monetary policy. The primary objective of the RBI operations into the money market has been to ensure that short-term interest rates and liquidity are maintained at levels consistent with overall monetary policy objective.

> Monetary policy (understood broadly, to include financial regulatory policy) is of such importance in part because the financial sector is so important: the financial sector has been likened to the brain of an economy, and if the financial sector does not work well, the economy does not work well. In many countries around the world—including the US and the EU—the financial sector has not done what it should

have done and done what it should not have done; the costs of their failures in the US alone amount to trillions of dollars (Stiglitz, 2013).[9]

Emerging Issues

Notwithstanding such trends, the Indian banking sector continued to remain predominantly public in nature, with the public sector banks still accounting for more than 70 per cent of total banking sector assets. A recent official report argued for reduction in government shareholding to below 50 per cent to allow more autonomy to banks as well as to create distance between the government and governance of banks (RBI, 2014). However, during 2014–15, despite their substantive share in total assets, public sector banks accounted for only 42 per cent in total profits (RBI, 2015), down from 74 per cent in 2003–04. Are the public sector banks inherently less efficient than the private banks? Or, is their less impressive performance an outcome of an inefficient governance structure subject to bureaucratic interference? Do Indian banks continue to suffer from the imperatives of societal concerns and thus, torn between the dilemmas of efficiency and equity? The fact that the performance of public sector banks had converged to that of the new private sector banks by 2008–09, before deteriorating subsequently poses a further puzzle, raises further questions about the determinants of their performance.

The issue of recent deterioration of asset quality in public sector banks has emerged as the key concern surrounding the banking sector today. Earlier, gross non-performing assets (GNPAs) of the Indian banking sector, as a percentage of gross advances, had come down from 15 per cent in 1998 to 3.3 per cent in 2009: since then GNPAs have increased steadily to 5.1 per cent by the end of 2015. Taking a wider definition, the stressed assets (i.e., gross NPA plus restructured standard assets plus written off accounts) for the banking system as a whole increased from 9.8 per cent in 2012 to 14.5 per cent in 2015; stressed assets in public sector banks increased from 11.0 per cent to 17.7 per cent during the same period (Mundra, 2016a, 2016b).

Interestingly, in recent years, small industries as well as agricultural loans do not seem to have contributed the lion's share of this formation of NPAs, as they used too in the past. It is the industrial sector—primarily the infrastructure and steel sectors that have experienced greater deterioration in asset quality. Thus, questions are being asked

9. Kapila, Uma (ed.) (2013). "Introduction", *Indian Financial Reforms: Priorities and Policy Thrust Post Global Financial Crisis*. New Delhi: Academic Foundation.

as to how such NPAs got accumulated in recent years. First, in the aftermath of the North Atlantic Financial Crisis[10] the RBI relaxed credit norms in order to encourage bank lending—a phenomenon that is called "regulatory forbearance" in Central Bank Speak.[11]

Second, in the period following the NAFC, an array of structural factors and the sharp fall in commodity prices has led to sharp declines in the profitability of sectors such as steel; this could have caused the problem of unpaid debt to banks from these and associated sectors.

Third, the government thrust on infrastructure investment through public-private-partnerships (PPP) led to huge new debt being contracted by highly leveraged Indian corporate entities investing in infrastructure. Government pressure combined with private sector enthusiasm for PPP infrastructure projects may have led banks to deviate from the rigorous discipline of credit appraisal and due diligence.

Fourth, there are allegations of governance issues with the management of select public sector banks and cases of political interference. Thus, in select cases lending decisions could have got divorced from discipline of standard credit evaluation process and due diligence (Credit Suisse, 2015).

Financial inclusion

Financial inclusion has been a concern in India since at least the early part of the last century. The setting up of a postal savings bank, rural and urban co-operative banks, regional rural banks, and the nationalisation of banks, were all done at different points in time to promote financial inclusion. Despite all the decades of social sector banking and success in spreading the banking network, there has been

---

10. We use the term "North Atlantic" Financial Crisis (NAFC), rather than "Global" Financial Crisis advisedly. No financial institutions had to be rescued by governments or central banks outside North America and Europe. So NAFC is a better label for this crisis, just as the Asian Financial Crisis was not seen as a Global Financial Crisis. Both financial crises did have global economic impacts.

11. Three major measures were taken: (a) provisioning requirements for most of the types of standard assets was reduced to a uniform level of 0.40 per cent; (b) risk weights on banks' exposures to certain sectors were revised downward; and (c) as one-time measures and for a limited period, prudential regulations for restructured account were modified for applications received up to 31 March 2009—the modifications permitted restructured accounts to be treated as standard assets, provided they were standard on the eve of the crisis, i.e., 1 September 2008, even if they turned non-performing at the time of restructuring. In fact, RBI (2014a) noted, "While it may be somewhat legitimate to justify regulatory forbearance in times of major crises, forbearance for extended periods and as a cover to compensate for lenders/borrowers' inadequacies engenders moral hazard. ... Hence, an early end to regulatory forbearance may be the right step" (p. 45).

evidence that poorer sections of the society have not been able to access financial services adequately from the organized financial system (NABARD, 2008).[12]

India's approach to financial inclusion has been multi-pronged. One of its major corner-stones is the presence of stipulations on "priority sector lending" by the commercial banks. For this purpose, priority sector includes the following categories, viz., agriculture; micro, small and medium enterprises; export credit; education; housing; social infrastructure; renewable energy; and others (like weaker section of the community). Indian commercial banks are required to lend 40 per cent of their credit to the priority sector.[13] Now Foreign banks with 20 branches and above also have to achieve the 40 per cent total within a maximum period of five years over April 2013—March 2018 as per the action plans submitted by them and approved by RBI. Besides, there are sub-targets within this overall 40 per cent target; illustratively, 18 per cent has to be disbursed to agriculture while 7.5 per cent has to be disbursed to the small and medium enterprises. In recent times, introduction of Priority Sector Lending Certificates (PSLCs) have enabled banks to achieve the priority sector lending target and sub-targets by purchase of these instruments in the event of shortfall. Further, commercial banks can also invest the amount of their shortfalls in the Rural Infrastructure Development Fund (RIDF) run by NABARD. There are several diverse dimensions of financial inclusion such as, income, region/province, caste, gender, economic size of the firm/household, and type of economic activity. The incidence of farmers' suicides has also cast doubt about the efficacy of the formal credit delivery mechanism as well as the limitations of credit disbursals from micro-finance institutions and self-help groups. The All India Debt and Investment Survey of December 2013 indicated that during 2012–13, non-institutional sources (i.e., sources of credit other than government, banks, insurance companies, pension funds, financial companies, and so on) continued to play a major role in providing credit to the rural

12. Similar sentiments were echoed in the report of the Committee on Financial Sector Reforms (Chairman: Raghuram Rajan; Government of India, 2009), which noted: "Financial sector policies in India have long been driven by the objective of increasing financial inclusion, but the goal of universal inclusion is still a distant dream (p. 49).

13. Technically, the ambit of the target of priority sector credit is with respect to "adjusted net bank credit (ANBC) or credit equivalent amount of off-balance sheet exposure, whichever is higher". ANBC denotes the outstanding Bank Credit in India minus bills rediscounted with RBI and other approved Financial Institutions plus permitted non SLR bonds/debentures under Held to Maturity (HTM) category plus other investments eligible to be treatedas part of priority sector lending (e.g. investments in securitized assets); see RBI's "Master Circular - Priority Sector Lending- Targets and Classification", available at https://rbi.org.in/Scripts/BS_ViewMasCirculardetails.aspx?id=9857#C8

TABLE – 20.2

Outstanding Debt of Rural Household: Institutional versus Non-Institutional Sources (%)

Sources of Credit	*1951*	*1961*	*1971*	*1981*	*1991*	*2002*	*2012**
Non-institutional	92.8	85.2	70.8	38.7	36.0	42.9	40.2
Landlords	3.5	0.9	8.6	4.0	4.0	1.0	
Agricultural moneylenders	25.2	45.9	23.1	8.6	7.1	10.0	
Professional moneylenders	46.4	14.9	13.8	8.3	10.5	19.6	
Institutional	7.2	14.8	29.2	61.3	64.0	57.1	59.8
of which:							
Government	3.7	5.3	6.7	4.0	6.1	2.3	
Co-operative societies	3.5	9.1	20.1	28.6	21.6	27.3	
Commercial banks n.a.	0.4	2.2	28.0	33.7	24.5		
Total	100.0	100.0	100.0	100.0	100.0	100.0	100.0

Note: * There are issues relating to comparability of the constituent groups of data collected under 59th round of NSS (for 2002) and 70th round of NSS (2012).

Source: Mohan (2011b) and NSS (2012).

households—about 19 per cent of all rural households have acquired credit from noninstitutional sources while for urban households about 10 per cent by non-institutional agencies (Table 20.2).

There are, of course, two ways of interpreting such trends and it is difficult to decide whether the glass is half empty or three quarters full (Mohan, 2011b). In fact, the improvement in financial inclusion in the recent past can be associated with an activist stance of the authorities in ensuring financial inclusion. Some the key measures in this regard include opening of No-Frills accounts in commercial banks; introduction of a credit card specifically for the farmers' community (Kisan Credit Card); and engaging Business Correspondents (BC) as intermediaries for providing financial and banking services. A recent major initiative is the Pradhan Mantri Jan-Dhan Yojana (Prime Minister's People Money Scheme). Introduced in August 2014, this scheme has now become synonymous with a National Mission on Financial Inclusion and has envisaged universal access to banking facilities with at least one basic banking account for every household.

Apart from accessing basic banking services like credit, insurance and pension facility, the beneficiaries get a Debit card having inbuilt accident insurance cover of ₹100,000. By July 2016, over 230 million new bank accounts were opened and ₹400 billion was deposited under the scheme.[14]

There are three recent developments with regard to entry of new private sector banks. First, after nearly 10 years of no new banking licenses, licenses were granted in 2015 to two existing financial institutions to become universal commercial banks: IDFC Ltd (an integrated infrastructure finance company) and Bandhan Financial Services (a large micro finance organisation).[15] Two new major types of small and differentiated banks—payments banks and small finance banks—have also emerged as the newest entrants in the Indian financial sector. While payments banks are essentially narrow banks (i.e., without any lending activity) which can raise deposits of up to ₹100,000 and pay interest on these balances just like a savings bank account does, their basic business model is geared towards utilising newer mobile technology and payment gateways whereby they can enable transfers and remittances through a mobile phone and can issue debit cards and ATM cards usable on ATM networks of all banks. Ever since August 2015 when the RBI issued licenses to 11 entities[16] to establish payments banks, there is speculation whether this would usher in a new era of Indian banking. At the same time, small finance banks are being licensed to further financial inclusion primarily through mobilization of savings as well as supply of credit to small business units (such as, small and marginal farmers; micro and small industries; and other unorganised sector entities) through high technology-low cost operations. Small finance banks are similar to regular commercial banks except that their scale of services will be much smaller: 50 per cent of their loans should be of ticket sizes under ₹2.5 million. Small banking licenses have been issued to 10 entities, most of which are successful micro-finance institutions. The use of new information technology is expected to propel these new banks in their efforts to enhance financial inclusion.

---

14. *http://www.pmjdy.gov.in/* (accessed in August 2016)
15. More recently (on 5 May 2016), deviating from past practice of stop and go licenses, the RBI released Draft Guidelines for 'on tap' Licensing of Universal Banks in the Private Sector.
16. Three of these entities have already surrendered their licenses as of July 2016.

Many of these developments mark a departure from the past. Illustratively, unlike the past when only universal banking licences were issued, now differentiated banking licenses are also being issued. Similarly, although there has been a general policy of not issuing bank licenses to non financial big industry houses, payments banks licenses were issued to some big industry houses as well. The justification is that since payments banks are essentially narrow banks not permitted to do any lending, the possibility of conflict of interest arising from intra group lending is not an issue. Thus, going forward these small but differentiated banks could constitute competitive challenges to the existing commercial banks in terms of access to financial savings for on lending. Will there be flight of retail deposits from bigger commercial banks to these banks from the same pool of depositors, or will they be effective in enhancing overall financial savings in the system? The business model of payments banks may face some challenges since their earning opportunities will be restricted to investments in government securities.

To summarize the story of the Indian banking sector in recent times: At the risk of oversimplification, the following trends can be highlighted. First, while commercial banks have seen an all-round improvement in key financial indicators, particularly in areas of capital adequacy, asset quality and earnings, their recent trends raise some disquieting developments. Second, "the financial results of the co-operative banking structure however, show some degree of vulnerability, though they may not be systemically very large" (RBI, 2009). Third, the new entrants in the financial sector, viz., payments banks and small savings banks are at this juncture where they are really unknown unknowns. Finally, while various efforts towards financial inclusion seemed to have borne fruit, there is much to achieve.

The Insurance Sector Since the 1990s: Opening up the Doors

A high-powered committee, set up in 1993 by the Government of India and headed by former RBI Governor, R. N. Malhotra, initiated the reforms process in the Indian insurance sector. Apart from opening up the insurance sector to private players—both to domestic and foreign players (preferably through joint ventures with Indian partners), the Committee recommended establishment of the Insurance Regulatory and Development Authority (IRDA) as an autonomous body to regulate, develop and promote competition in the insurance sector. The IRDA was finally constituted as an autonomous body in 1999 and incorporated as a statutory body in April 2000. The mission of IRDA is "to protect the interests of the policyholders, to regulate, promote and ensure orderly growth of the insurance industry and for matters connected therewith or incidental thereto."

With the enactment of the IRDA Act, 1999, the monopoly conferred to the Life Insurance Corporation in 1956 and to the General Insurance Corporation in 1972 was repealed, allowing private sector players to enter the insurance sector. A recent development in the insurance sector has been enhancement of the limit of foreign investment in insurance sector from 26 to 49 per cent under the automatic route.

As of March 2015, this sector comprised 24 life insurance companies and 28 general insurance companies, and one national reinsurer. Among the life insurers, the Life Insurance Corporation (LIC) as the sole public sector company accounts for the lion's share in insurance business. Among the non-life insurers there are six public sector insurers. In addition to these, there is the sole national re-insurer, namely, General Insurance Corporation of India (GIC). Out of 28 non-life insurance companies, there are five private sector players dealing exclusively in health, personal accident and travel insurance segments.

With about 360 million policies, India's life insurance sector is perhaps the biggest in the world in terms of number—reflecting India's population size. The general insurance business in India is currently at ₹847 billion in 2014–15 or about 0.7 per cent of GDP. In 2014, with a share of 2.1 per cent in the global life insurance business, India has been ranked 11th among the 88 countries in life insurance business (Swiss Re, 2015). In non-life insurance while vehicle insurance accounted for nearly 40 per cent of the gross direct premiums earned in 2015–16, penetration of health insurance is rather poor. In fact, despite the absolute size of the insurance sector, penetration in this sector leaves much to be desired.

The current issues facing Indian insurance are diverse. The key issue is the need for much greater expansion of insurance services, particularly that of life insurance and health insurance. Apart from the need for better spread of social protection, the expansion of insurance funds is also essential for the development of capital markets, particularly the corporate debt market which is typically dependent in institutional investors. Other issues include the efficiency and spread of distributional channels, the level of government control, regulatory constraints, and consumer education and protection (IMF, 2013).

Continuance of an archaic agent-based distribution channels has led to allegations of mis-selling of insurance products as well as low persistency of insurance policies in India (Government of India, 2015). Besides, there is a huge untapped potential in sectors like health insurance.

Capital Market: Uneven Progress in Different Segments

Is the Indian financial system bank-based or market based? Significant change is happening in this sphere. Table 31.6 in this context reports the resource mobilization by the commercial sector. Interestingly, Indian corporates' recourse to non-bank sources tended to hover between 40–50 per cent during the period 2009–10 through 2015–16. Both domestic as well as foreign sources are significant in the case of non-bank funding sources. However, in terms of resource mobilization, the Indian capital market has depended heavily on private placement whose costs are found to be much lower.

Bond/Debt Market

Traditionally the bond market is differentiated on the basis of ownership viz., government bonds and corporate bonds. The story of Government bond market is intimately interlinked with the evolution of fiscal policy in India. A system of unbridled deficit financing via fixed coupon ad-hoc Treasury bill market has been transformed into a market driven auction process in electronic platform by late 1990s. Institutionally, creation of primary dealers (PDs) to function as market makers (both in primary and secondary markets) in government bond market since 1995 is a major development in this sector (Mohan and Ray, 2011). With increased volume of transactions liquidity in this market have increased as well.

In contrast, the corporate debt market in India has been far less developed. Much of the transactions in this market are concentrated in the bonds of blue-chip corporates and the market is predominantly a private placement market with limited liquidity. In terms of outturn, the market size at around 15 per cent of GDP is much smaller than bank assets (89% of GDP) and equity markets (80% of GDP).

Equity Market

The Indian equity market has undergone a radical transformation since the initiation of financial sector reforms since the early 1990s. The reform measures were aimed at, "(i) creating growth-enabling institutions; (ii) boosting competitive conditions in the equity market through improved price discovery mechanism; (iii) putting in place an appropriate regulatory framework; (iv) reducing the transaction costs; and (v) reducing information asymmetry, thereby boosting the investor confidence" (RBI, 2007).

A key reform in this respects repealing of the Capital Issues (Control) Act, 1947 in 1992 whereby the process of raising capital from the market has been liberalised.

The success story of the Indian equity market has been driven by two major institutions, both established under government auspicious, viz., Securities and Exchange Board of India (SEBI) and the National Stock Exchange (NSE). While SEBI, the securities market regulator, was established in 1988, it was given statutory powers in April 1992 through the SEBI Act, 1992, which set out its basic functions as, "...to protect the interests of investors in securities and to promote the development of, and to regulate the securities market and for matters connected therewith or incidental thereto." Thus, SEBI is the overall capital market regulator charged with the orderly functioning of the securities market.

Though the more traditional stock market, the BSE (formerly known as Bombay Stock Exchange) was established as early as 1875, it was essentially a mutualised exchange and was not modernized. The NSE was established in 1992 as the first demutualized electronic exchange in India. Over time, the NSE emerged as a modern electronic trading platform and took new initiatives to introduce derivative trading in India. Though subsequently, BSE too has modernised, at the current juncture the NSE (and in particular its derivative segment) has the lion's share of the equity market turnover.

The Indian equity market has witnessed significant improvement, since the early 1990s—this is reflected in metrics such as, size of the market, liquidity, transparency, stability and efficiency. Illustratively, despite its volatility, India's market capitalization to GDP ratio stood nearly 70 per cent at the end of 2016 but its share of global market capitalisation was only 2.3 per cent at the end of 2015. Changes in the regulatory and governance framework have brought about significant improvement in investor confidence over time (RBI, 2007).

Mutual Funds (MFs): The Early Reformer

A mutual fund is a mechanism for pooling resources by issuing units to investors and then investing funds in securities, in both equity and debt. The MFs as a group have played a very important role in the Indian capital market. During 1963–1988, the Unit Trust of India (UTI) had a monopoly in the MF industry and its assets under management grew to about ₹67 billion by 1988. The reform process of the MF industry started in 1988 when non-UTI, public sector mutual funds set up by public sector banks, the LIC and the GIC entered the market. Subsequently, private sector funds were allowed to enter the MF industry in 1993. The issuance of the SEBI (Mutual Fund) Regulations in 1996 paved the way for further operational freedom for the players in the MF industry. By January 2003, there were 33 mutual fund companies with total assets of ₹1.2 trillion—of which the UTI's share was little more than one-third.

The US-64 scheme of the UTI ran into difficulty in 2001, which resulted in the next rounds of reforms. The UTI was bifurcated into two separate entities—one broadly representing the assets of the then US-64 scheme, assured return and certain other schemes, and the other called the UTI Mutual Fund (sponsored by select public sector banks and the LIC) which operates like any other MF. As of March 2016, there were 44 asset management companies in the country with assets under management (AUM) of around ₹13.5 trillion (or 10 per cent of GDP), which though high, is far below the deposits of the commercial banks (at about ₹99 trillion or 73 per cent of GDP) (ICRA, 2016).

In a country where direct investments by households in equity and debt market are meager, MFs have a huge potential to grow. The recent growth in 'assets under management' of the MF industry from 16 non-metro towns /cities bears testimony to this.

Pension Funds: A Late Entrant

India, like most of the developing economics, does not have a universal social security system and the pension system has largely catered to the organized segment of the labor force. While, till recently, public sector/government employees typically had a three-fold structure comprising provident fund, gratuity[17] and pension schemes, the bulk of the private sector (with the sole exception of the major corporates) had access only to provident funds, a defined-contribution, fully funded benefit program providing lump sum benefits at the time of retirement. The Employees' Provident Fund (EPF) is the largest benefit program

---

17. Gratuity refers to the lump-sum amount payable to the retiring Government servant; a minimum of 5 years qualifying service and eligibility to receive service gratuity/pension is essential to get this one time lump sum benefit.

operating in India. Reflecting this state of affairs, the significance of pension funds in the Indian financial sector has been rather limited. In terms of size, India's pension funds stood at 0.3 per cent of its GDP, as against China's 1 per cent or Brazil's 13 per cent (OECD, 2015).

The pension funds sector has undergone significant reforms. In recognition of the possibility of an unsustainable fiscal burden in the future, the Government of India moved from a defined-benefit pension system to a defined-contribution pension system, called the "New Pension System" (NPS) in January 2004. While the Government constituted an interim regulator, the Interim Pension Fund Regulatory and Development Authority (PFRDA) to regulate the pension sector in 2003, it finally started functioning as a statutory regulator for the NPS in 2014. As of March 2016, there were 8.7 million subscribers with assets under management (AUM) amounting to Rs. 1.18 trillion. Under the present scheme, a subscriber has the option to select any one of the 8 pension funds, which are primarily floated by public sector banks and/or insurance companies. Considering the fact that India's population is around 1.25 billion in which the share of the old (i.e., 60 years and above) is around 10 per cent, pension funds in India have, in principle, a large potential—both as a social security measure as well as means to providing a depth to the financial markets, in both debt and equity market segments. Going forward, pension funds will emerge as sources of funds in infrastructure and other projects with long gestation period, as well as for providing depth to the equity market (perhaps looking for absorbing stocks arising out of disinvestment program of the government).

Non-Banking Finance Companies (NBFCs): Checkered Trend

Apart from the banks, India has a number of non-banking financial companies (NBFCs). The fundamental difference between banks and NBFCs in India are three: (a) NBFCs cannot accept demand deposits; (b) NBFCs do not form part of the payment and settlement system and cannot issue checks drawn on itself; and (c) deposit insurance facility is not available to depositors of NBFCs, unlike in case of banks. The NBFCs is far from being a homogenous entity and include many diverse types of financial institutions from a housing finance company to an equipment leasing company.[18] The diversity among the entities of the NBFC sector is also reflected in attributes like sizes and the extent of regulatory oversight. As of March 2016, there were 11,682 NBFCs registered with the RBI, of which 202 were deposit-accepting and 11,480 were non-deposit accepting NBFCs, of which 220 were declared as systemically important (i.e., those with an asset size of Rs one billion or more).[19] In the popular discourse the role of NBFCs are seen from two distinct angles: (a) they have been very useful for sectors/activities that are generally excluded from formal banking activities; and (b) at some regularity some of the deposit raking NBFCs have been source of financial irregularity in some localized pockets and raised the issue of consumer protection.

Concluding Observations

Where does the Indian financial sector stand? At the risk of broad generalization, thc following broad trends could be highlighted as key features of the Indian financial sector. As a consequence of successive reforms over the past 25 years, there has been significant progress in making interest and exchange rates largely market determined, though the exchange rate regime remains one of managed float, and some interest rates remain administered. Considerable competition has been introduced in the banking sector through new private sector banks, but public sector banks continue have a dominant share in the market. Contractual savings systems have been improved, but provident and pension funds in India are still in their infancy. Similarly, despite the introduction of new private sector insurance companies coverage of insurance can expand much further, which would also provide greater depth to the financial markets. The extent of development along all the segments of the financial market has not been uniform. While the equity market is quite developed, activities in the private debt market are predominantly confined to private placement form and continued to be limited to the blue-chip companies. Going forward, the future areas for

18. These include: (i) Asset Finance Companies (AFCs); (ii) Loan Companies (LCs); (iii) Investment Companies (ICs); (iv) Infrastructure Finance Companies (IFCs); (v) Core Investment Companies (CICs); (vi) Infrastructure Debt Funds (IDF-NBFCs); (vii) NBFC-Microfinance Institutions (NBFC-MFIs); (viii) Factoring companies (FCs); (ix) Mortgage Guarantee Companies (MGCs); (x) Residuary Non-Banking Companies (RNBCs); (xi) Housing Finance Companies; (xii) Mutual Benefit Companies; and (xiii) Chit Fund companies.

19. See the RBI "Master Circulars- Miscellaneous Instructions to NBFC- ND-SI" of July 01, 2015; available at https://rbi.org.in/scripts/BS_ViewMasCirculardetails.aspx?id=9835

development in the Indian financial sector would include further reduction of public ownership in banks and insurance companies, expansion of the contractual savings system through more rapid expansion of the insurance and pension systems, greater spread of mutual funds, and development of institutional investors. It is only then that both the equity and debt markets will display greater breadth as well as depth, along with greater domestic liquidity.

While India continues its journey towards a financially inclusive regime through innovative policies involving a multi-pronged approach, it has come a long way from a financially repressive regime to a modern financial sector where public sector financial institutions tend to compete with the private sector financial institutions. The Indian authorities while reforming the financial sector had to constantly keep the issues of equity and efficiency in mind.

In India, growth with equity has been the central objective right from the inception of the planning process. The objective of financial inclusion is to provide financial services at affordable cost to those who are excluded from the formal financial system. This is vital for sustaining long-term equitable development, since a large proportion of the households/areas do not have access to basic banking facilities, notwithstanding the existence of vast institutional framework in the country. An important challenge is to channelise more savings to the financial system, particularly in rural areas and from the urban informal sector. This would need further penetration of the banking system. The RBI's emphasis on financial inclusion is important in attaining this objective over time. There is also enormous potential for extending finance in semi-urban and rural areas for productive activities, which may require strengthening the banking correspondent (BC) relationship, simultaneously enhancing the risk assessment and risk management capacities in order to maintain credit quality and sustain the credit growth in these sectors. Besides benefiting the unbanked masses, this will also ensure viability and scalability of banks' financial inclusion initiatives (Ibid.).

In a fast changing world, financial policy has to catch up with the needs of future India that people are aspiring to build. The next wave of reforms will be through strengthening the institutional foundation—both laws and organisations, improving and polishing the financial processes, and by taking well-designed policy decisions that will enhance clarity, consistency and transparency for a globalised India.

21

Foreign Trade and Trade Policy*

Trade Policy

India adopted an 'inward looking' strategy of industrialisation. This strategy relied on encouraging domestic production for the domestic market behind high tariffs and high degree of effective protection to the domestic industry. This resulted in an uncompetitive domestic industrial structure.

Far from viewing foreign trade as an engine of growth, Indian planners sought to minimise import demand and viewed exports more or less as a necessary evil mainly to generate the foreign exchange earnings to meet that part of the import bill not covered by external assistance.

India's participation in world markets declined steadily during the second half of the 20th century, with only a marginal improvement following the reforms of the 1990s. Its share of world merchandise exports was 2.2 per cent in 1948, higher than China's 0.9 per cent or Japan's 0.4 per cent. It fell to one-fifth its initial level, 0.5 per cent, in 1983 and recovered only marginally to 0.7 per cent in 2000. Japan, in contrast, progressively increased its share from 0.4 per cent in 1948 to a peak of 10.0 per cent in 1993. China's share first increased to a high of 1.3 per cent in 1963, then fell to a low of 1.0 per cent in 1973, later recovering dramatically after its opening to the world economy in 1978 to 4.0 per cent in 2000.

---

*: This chapter is drawn extensively from Kapila, Uma (ed.) (2019). "India's External Sector: Policies Developments and Issues" (Editorial notes) in *Indian Economy since Independence* (30th edition). New Delhi: Academic Foundation.

There is no widely accepted single quantitative indicator that captures the depths and degree of integration of a given country with the world economy, but the ratio of exports plus imports to GDP (gross domestic product) is a commonly used measure. India's ratio was a mere 16.6 per cent in 1980. India has become more integrated with the world economy since then. There has been marked improvement as trade-GDP ratio increased from 21.8 per cent in 2000-01 to 44.1 per cent in 2013-2014 (*Economic Survey 2013-14*).

India's inward orientation has had significant economic costs in lowering overall growth and stagnating living standards.

The origins of economic nationalism in India can be traced to the beliefs held by those fighting for independence from British rule. They perceived the British colonial policy of laissez-faire and free trade to be the major causes of India's economic underdevelopment. Their thoughts about economic development strategies and vision of a state-guided closed economy were heavily influenced by Soviet planning. They viewed international trade as a 'whirlpool of economic imperialism'.

India's international trade policy had the direct effect of limiting its participation in world trade. It sought to minimise imports by supporting indigenous production and by according priority to domestic use in the disposition of production. Import tariffs, based on the recommendations of the Tariff Commission, were initially used to provide infant-industry protection to selected industries. The ambitious investment in heavy industries at the start of the Second Five Year Plan (1956-1961) led to a significant spurt in import demand and a rapid depletion of foreign exchange reserves, and it precipitated a BoP (balance of payments) crisis in 1957.

QRs (quantitative restrictions) on imports were initially imposed to meet the crisis but continued until early 2001 in varying intensities. Graded import tariffs (highest on 'least essential' consumer goods, lower on industrial intermediate inputs, and the lowest on capital goods deemed 'essential' for development) were also introduced in the 1960s in an effort to contain BoP deficits.

Persistent deficits in the BoP were mitigated by increases in tariff levels and in the severity of QRs rather than by devaluation of the rupee.

Reflecting the change in the perception towards the external sector and its role in the overall strategy of development, the policies relating to India's foreign trade, over the years have, undergone significant changes.

The policy changes have been influenced, inter alia, by the recommendations of a number of committees, which were set up during the 1970s and the 1980s. In this context, mention may be made about two prominent committee reports—the Report of the Committee on Import Export Policies and Procedures (Chairman: P.C. Alexander, 1978) and the Report of the Committee on Trade Policies (Chairman: Abid Hussain, 1984). The Alexander Committee recommended simplification of the import licensing procedure and provided a framework involving a shift in the emphasis from 'controls' to 'development'. Following the recommendations of the Alexander Committee, selective import liberalisation measures were initiated in the late 1970s primarily aiming at making the import of capital goods easier. Imports of certain raw materials that were not available indigenously were also placed under the OGL (open general licence) List. The emphasis of the policy efforts was also to simplify the procedures governing India's foreign trade. During this period, special measures were initiated to boost the export of project goods.

The Abid Hussain Committee envisaged 'growth-led exports' rather than 'export-led growth' and stressed upon the need for harmonisation of foreign trade policies with other economic policies arguing for a phased reduction of effective protection. The Committee also favoured announcement of trade policies for longer periods in order to impart a degree of continuity and facilitate long-term planning of export business. In line with these recommendations, long-term trade policy was introduced with the announcement of an import-export policy covering the period 1985-1988. The policy was formulated with the aim of boosting exports and encouraging efficient import substitution. Following the announcement of two more such three-year Import Export Policies, these policies are being announced for a longer period of five years beginning with the Export-Import (EXIM) Policy for 1992-1997.

The Crisis of 1991: A Turning Point

The CAD rose to a record 3.2 per cent of GDP in 1990, and debt-service payments amounted to as much as 35.3 per cent of current foreign exchange receipts. Foreign exchange reserves were down to a level barely enough to finance imports for two and a half months. Short-term debts amounted to a dangerously high level of 146.5 per cent of foreign exchange reserves by the end of March 1991. The rate of inflation soared, exceeding 10 per cent in 1990. Expectations of an imminent devaluation of the rupee led to the withdrawal of deposits by

NRI (non-resident Indians). A spectre of default on short-term loans and a downgrading of India's credit rating loomed.

Although the external payments crisis provided the immediate impetus for change, other political factors had been pushing India toward radical policy reforms. First, the country's cautious and limited deregulation of the 1980s had delivered more rapid growth. Although this growth turned out not to be sustainable, it made further liberalisation of the policy regime politically acceptable. Second, the collapse of the Soviet Union not only eroded crucial external support for India's position on matters of its security and national interest, but also reduced the country's access to defence supplies on concessional terms.

More important, the collapse of the world's leading centrally planned economy undermined India's faith in central planning. Several perceptive observers—some in government (see Jha, 1980 and Dhar, 1990), others independent academics (the earliest being Bhagwati and Desai, 1970 and Bhagwati and Srinivasan, 1975)—had drawn attention to the fact that state controls on economic activity and inward orientation had cost India dearly in slow growth. Their voices would have continued to be ignored had it not been for the collapse of the Soviet Union and, equally important, China's spectacular growth after the 1978 reforms that opened its planned economy to the rest of the world and allowed a greater role for markets. The fear of being left behind by China led policymakers to realise that this crisis, unlike the earlier ones, could not be handled without bringing about radical changes in the economic policy regime.

The severity of the economic crisis of 1991 provided an opportunity for the government to undertake major microeconomic policy reforms.The reforms indeed heralded a major change in the country's development strategy. India gradually abandoned the use of quantitiative controls in economic management in favour of market-based instruments. There was a decisive move away from inward orientation and toward greater integration with the global economy.

The trade policy changes in the post-1991 period sought to minimise the role of quantitative restrictions and substantially reduce the tariff rates on the lines suggested by the Tax Reforms Committee (Chairman: Raja J. Chelliah). The developments in India's trade policy during this period need to be viewed in conjunction with policy reforms initiated in other spheres of the economy. The devaluation of the rupee in July 1991 and the transition to the market-based exchange rate regime deserve mention in this regard. These measures were aimed, inter alia, at enhancing the price competitiveness of exports. The policies governing foreign investment and foreign collaboration also have undergone significant change, which have a bearing on trade performance. Apart from unilateral measures, the liberalisation of India's trade policies also reflects the multilateral commitments of the country to the WTO.

The focus of these reforms has been on liberalisation, openness, transparency and globalisation with a basic thrust on outward orientation focusing on export promotion activity and improving competitiveness of Indian industry to meet global market requirements. In early 2002, the government presented a MTES (medium term export strategy) for 2002-2007 providing a vision for creating a stable policy environment with indicative sector-wise targets, with a mission to achieve one per cent of global trade by 2007 which luckily had been achieved.

The foregoing discussion on India's foreign trade policy brings out certain distinctive features of the policy changes introduced since early-1990s. In the first place, there has been a clear shift in emphasis from import-substitution to export-promotion.

Secondly, the reach of the export incentives has been broadened to cover a large number of non-traditional and non-manufactured export items.

Thirdly, the policy stance marks a move away from the provision of direct export subsidy to indirect promotional measures. Apart from the discernible change in trade policy, the 1990s was also characterised by the introduction of market-based exchange rate regime.

All these developments put together contributed to a distinct change in the structure of India's trade, at the disaggregated levels between the 1980s and the 1990s.

Structural Changes in India's Foreign Trade during 1980s and 1990s

The impact of trade reforms is evident from the changing structure of India's foreign trade in terms of diversity of markets and products and also in the form of higher degree of trade openness (resulting from higher export growth and the associated increase in the capacity to import). Following the various policy initiatives taken by the government, there was a perceptible improvement in India's export performance in the initial phase of the reform period—both at the overall level and across commodities. The commodity composition of India's export basket has changed in favour of technology intensive and industrial products such as, engineering goods, besides high-value agricultural products. The destination profile of India's exports shows that the developing countries have gained considerable prominence over the years. The commodity composition of imports is affected by various factors such as impact of trade policy, domestic demand and international prices. The sourcing pattern of imports has also changed, mostly in favour of the developing countries.

Diversification of exports constitutes an important element of India's export promotion strategy. Reflecting the policy thrust as also the evolving pattern of industrial development, India has gradually transformed from a predominantly primary products exporting country into an exporter of manufactured goods. However, it may be noted that this was more prominent in the 1970s. The progress has, however, stalled thereafter. Aided by various export promotion measures, the share of 'manufactured goods' in India's total exports increased from 70.7 per cent during 1987-1990 to 75.3 per cent during 1992-1997 and further to 77.4 per cent during 1997-2002. Exports of petroleum products have also increased in the recent years. The commodity composition within the major groups has also undergone a considerable transformation. Within the 'primary products' group, the share of 'ores and minerals' in total exports has declined, while the share of 'agricultural and allied products' remained almost unchanged at around 18 per cent between 1990-91 and 1998-99 but declined thereafter to 13.4 per cent in 2000-01. The falling share of 'ores and minerals' has been offset by the increase in share of 'engineering goods' within the manufactured products group—an indication of upward movement of India's exports in the value-addition chain. Similarly, exports of processed agricultural products also showed marked improvement in the post-reform years, whereas the shares of traditional export items such as tea, coffee, cereals, handicrafts and carpets declined. Among other major manufactured products, the share of 'chemicals and allied products' has improved while that of 'leather and manufactures' has declined between the years 1990-91 and 2001-02 (Table 32.1).

TABLE – 21.1

Average Share of Exports of Selected Commodities

(%)

Category	*1987-1990*	*1990-91*	*1992-1997*	*1997-2002*
	1	*2*	*3*	*4*
Primary Products	24.2	23.8	21.9	18.5
Manufactured Goods	70.7	71.6	75.3	77.4
of which:				
Leather and Manufactures	7.5	8.0	5.8	4.6
Chemicals and Allied Products	5.9	7.2	7.2	9.1
Engineering Goods	11.0	12.4	13.8	14.7
Readymade Garments	11.2	12.3	12.0	12.2
Textile Yarn, Fabrics, Made-ups	8.0	8.5	10.9	11.2
Handicrafts Including Gems and Jewellery	22.6	18.9	19.7	20.1
Petroleum Products	3.1	2.9	1.8	2.1

Source : Directorate General of Commercial Intelligence and Statistics (DGCI&S).

Destination-wise analysis of the Indian exports indicates an unchanged position in respect of the Organisation for Economic Cooperation and Development (OECD) group being the largest market, increasing prominence of the Organisation of Petroleum Exporting Countries (OPEC) and the developing countries (Asia, Africa and Latin America), and a steep erosion in the relative position of the Eastern Europe. With the break-up of the Soviet Union, the share of the East European countries fell dramatically from 17.9 per cent in 1990-91 to just 2.9 per cent in 2001-02, primarily on account of the termination of rupee trade and its adverse impact on exports of agricultural products such as tea, tobacco and spices to this region. The loss of this market share was, however, made up by increasing the shares in developing countries and the OPEC region, both of which doubled between the years 1987-88 and 2001-02 (Table 32.2).

TABLE – 21.2

Direction of India's Foreign Trade—Share in Total Exports

(%)

Group/Country	*1987-88*	*1990-91*	*1995-96*	*1999-2000*	*2000-01*	*2001-02*
	1	*2*	*3*	*4*	*5*	*6*
I. OECD Countries	58.9	56.5	55.7	57.3	52.7	49.3
of which:						
a. EU	25.1	27.5	27.4	25.5	23.4	22.5
b. North America	19.7	15.6	18.3	24.4	22.4	20.8
of which: USA	18.6	14.7	17.4	22.8	20.9	19.4
c. Asia and Oceania	11.6	10.4	8.3	5.8	5.1	4.5
d. Other OECD Countries	2.5	3.0	1.6	1.6	1.9	1.6
II. OPEC	6.1	5.6	9.7	10.6	10.9	11.9
III. Eastern Europe	16.5	17.9	4.2	3.5	3.0	2.9
IV. Developing Countries	14.2	17.1	28.9	28.4	29.2	30.9
a. Asia	11.9	14.4	23.0	22.3	22.5	23.6
b. Africa	2.0	2.2	4.8	4.2	4.4	5.2
c. Latin American Countries	0.3	0.5	1.2	1.9	2.3	2.1

Source: DGCI&S.

India's export share in world trade increased perceptibly during the 1990s. India's exports as a percentage of world exports improved to 0.56 per cent during 1991-1996 and further to 0.65 per cent during 1996-2002 from 0.48 per cent in the 1980s. The ratio was 0.71 per cent in 2000-01. Nonetheless, India's share in world exports was still very low and appears unimpressive when compared with the other major trading Asian countries, such as, China and other East Asian economies like Malaysia, Thailand, Singapore, Korea and Indonesia. China demonstrated the most dramatic change as its share in world exports more than doubled in a decade from 2.0 per cent in 1991 to 4.4 per cent in 2001 (Table 32.3).

TABLE – 21.3

India's Share in World Imports and in Imports of Major Trading Partners

(%)

Group/Country	Annual 1981	Annual 1986	Annual 1990	Average 1991-1995	Average 1996-2000
	1	*2*	*3*	*4*	*5*
World	**0.5**	**0.7**	**0.6**	**0.6**	**0.7**
Industrial Countries	**0.4**	**0.6**	**0.5**	**0.5**	**0.5**
of which:					
United States	0.5	0.6	0.7	0.8	0.9
Japan	0.7	1.0	0.9	0.9	0.8
Belgium	0.3	0.4	0.6	0.6	0.8
Italy	0.2	0.2	0.4	0.5	0.6
Germany	0.3	0.3	0.5	0.5	0.5
United Kingdom	0.6	0.5	0.6	0.8	0.8
Developing Countries	**1.1**	**0.5**	**0.9**	**0.8**	**1.1**
of which:					
Malaysia	0.7	0.8	0.7	0.8	0.9
Singapore	0.5	0.6	0.6	0.7	0.7
Thailand	4.0	0.6	1.6	1.3	1.0
Bangladesh	0.3	2.2	4.6	9.6	12.9

Source : Direction of Trade Statistics, International Monetary Fund (IMF), various issues.

India's Merchandise Trade: 2001 to 2016-17

The rapid and over threefold rise in India's merchandise exports from less than US$100 billion prior to 2005-06 to over US$300 billion in 2011-12 was composed of a rather high growth in exports of POL (petroleum, oil and lubricants) as well as non-POL exports. Imports grew in the same period at a faster rate and the levels of merchandise trade deficit went up particularly in 2011-12 and 2012-13. A large part of the widening owed to global commodity price rise even in a milieu of tepid global economic growth. India's greater integration with the world economy was reflected by the trade openness indicator, merchandise trade to GDP, which increased from 13.9 per cent in 1991-92, to 27.0 per cent in 2004-05 and further to 41.0 per cent in 2013-14. However, it moderated to 37.1 per cent in 2014-15 as a result of subdued exports and imports.

Since late 2014-15 (December 2014), India's merchandise exports have been declining continuously. Both developed and developing countries are also witnessing a fall in exports as a result of subdued economic conditions and a downward spiral in crude oil prices. Since the latter half of 2014, there has been a southward movement in the growth of exports from India and major countries of the world and export growth of different countries have moved in tandem with the world economic situation.

In line with subdued global growth and trade, India's exports declined by 1.3 per cent and 15.5 per cent in 2014-15 and 2015-16 respectively. The trend of negative growth was reversed somewhat during 2016-17 (April-December), with exports registering a growth of 0.7 per cent to US$198.8 billion from US$197.3 billion in 2015-16 (April-December). During 2016-17 (April-December) POL exports constituting 11.1 per cent of total exports declined by 9.8 per cent to US$22.0 billion over corresponding previous period, while non-POL exports grew by 2.2 per cent to US $176.8 billion. A large number of export sectors have moved to positive growth territory in April-November 2016-17 as compared to 2015-16.

The Critical Role of Exports

Pointing out the critical role of exports, NITI Aayog's Three Year Action Agenda 2017-2018 to 2019-20 states the following:

There are only four developing countries that have successfully transformed themselves within three decades: South Korea, Taiwan, Singapore and China. In every one of these cases, exports have played a key role. China, with its population comparable to that of India, offers the most relevant example. In 2015, the world merchandise exports amounted to USD 16.6 trillion. China accounted for 13.72 per cent of these exports and India only 1.67 per cent. Even accounting for the fact that China's GDP was 5.2 times of that of India in 2015, India's share in world exports was low.

Despite its much lower wages, India exported only USD 18.2 billion worth of apparel in 2015 compared to USD 175 billion by China. Vietnam, which is less than one-tenth of India in terms of population as well as GDP, exported more apparel in value terms than India. The gap between India and China was even starker in electrical and electronic products with the two countries exporting about USD 8 billion and USD 782 billion, respectively. The story is no different in footwear with India exporting USD 2.5 billion and China USD 51.2 billion in 2015.

Why do exports matter? On the demand side, Indian firms often complain that there is inadequate demand for their products. Yet, the world market in merchandise exports at USD 16.6 trillion in 2015 is extremely large. Why are Indian firms not able to take advantage of this massive demand? The likely explanation is that their products are not competitive in the global economy. The flip side of this point is that the discipline of the global economy is what leads to fast productivity growth. Exports must compete against the best in the world and must therefore constantly upgrade technology, management and product quality to remain competitive.

Imports

The commodity-structure of India's imports has also shown marked changes, reflecting, inter alia, the impact of trade policy, the movements in international prices and the pattern of domestic demand. The share of oil imports in India's total imports increased from 17.1 per cent during 1987-1990 to 23.9 per cent during 1992-1997 and further to 27.2 per cent in 2001-02. While the share and absolute value of these imports showed sharp fluctuations over the years mainly on account of the large movements in international crude prices, the volume of such imports has grown significantly on account of increase in domestic consumption and the stagnation in domestic crude oil production. Given the large swings in international crude prices, as also a trend rise in the oil import bill, there is a need for a comprehensive review of energy policy of the country covering the demand-supply aspects, as well as the price policy. Renewed efforts to improve energy supply from domestic sources by encouraging explorations, and stepping up of production and refining capacities are necessary to bring about a structural change in this area.

Reflecting the impact of a series of policy measures undertaken in the post-reform years starting with the repeal of the Gold Control Order in 1991 for liberalising the imports of gold and silver, these imports showed a sharp pick-up from 1992-93. The imports of gold and silver (including passenger baggage) rose from a meagre US$ 6 million in 1991-92 to US$ 1.3 billion in 1992-93 and further to US$ 5.9 billion in 1997-98. A large part of the increase in these imports could be due to a switchover from the unofficial channel to the official channel, initially through the NRI baggage route and subsequently through the OGL route. In the subsequent years, however, these imports have stabilised and in fact, declined to US$ 4.6 billion in 2001-02.

Imports of capital goods registered sharp increases in the initial reform years from US$ 4.5 billion in 1992-93 to US$ 10.3 billion in 1995-96, but exhibited a declining trend thereafter. The share of these imports, which had declined from 29.5 per cent in 1987-88 to 24.2 per cent in 1990-91, rose in the post-reform period to 28.2 per cent in 1995-96 but dropped to 18.1 per cent in 2001-02, reflecting the lack of investment demand associated with the sluggish pace of domestic industrial activity. Among other import items, the relative shares of fertilisers, non-ferrous metals, 'metalliferrous ores and metal scrap' and 'iron and steel' generally showed a declining trend.

There are noticeable changes in the sources of India's imports and in country shares. The share of the OECD countries and the Eastern Europe in India's imports declined between the years 1987-88 and 1999-2000 while that of the developing countries and the OPEC group increased during the same period. The share of India's imports from the OPEC region rose significantly to 25.9 per cent in 1999-2000 from 16.3 per cent in 1990-91, mainly on account of the increase in the oil imports.

Composition of Trade

Factor endowments, trade policies, technology, and movements in global commodity prices have had a strong bearing on the composition of India's trade over time. The global financial crisis of 2008 in conjunction with commodity price shocks significantly affected the composition. There was a rebound in 2010-11 in terms of robust global growth, relatively stable global commodity prices and a pick-up in trade. A comparison of the current composition with respect to 2010-11 may, therefore, be apposite. The top eight export sectors—petroleum products, gems and jewellery, textiles, chemicals and related products, agriculture and allied sector, transport equipment, base metals and machinery—continue to dominate India's export basket, accounting for nearly 86.4 per cent of total exports in 2014-15 (as compared to 78.1% in 2010-11). Petroleum, crude and products occupy top position among the top eight export sectors with an 18.3 per cent share of total exports in 2014-15 (as against 14.6% in 2010-11). The share of gems and jewellery exports declined from 17 per cent in 2010-11 to 13.3 per cent in 2014-15. The shares of agriculture and allied exports, chemicals and related products and transport equipment in total exports have increased from 7.1 per cent, 8.3 per cent and 6.6 per cent respectively in 2010-11 to 9.7 per cent, 10.2 per cent and 8.6 per cent in 2014-15.

Overall export growth declined by 1.3 per cent in 2014-15, but this was a mixed bag of a decline in exports of petroleum products, gems and jewellery and agriculture and allied products, which constituted 41.3 per cent of India's total exports in 2014-15, as against growth in exports of transport equipment, base metals and machinery which exhibited growth rates of 20.2 per cent, 10.6 per cent and 12.2 per cent respectively in 2014-15. Low growth rates of 0.5 per cent and 3.0 per cent were exhibited by exports of textiles and chemical and related products. Although the share of marine products and leather and leather manufactures is low in India's total exports, they registered high growth rates of 9.8 per cent and 8.3 per cent respectively in 2014-15. Data available on commodity wise performance (April-December 2015) indicates that the decline in export was broad-based.

However, export growth in 2016-17 was fairly broad based with positive growth in major categories except textiles and allied products, and leather and leather manufactures. In 2017-18 (April- November) among the major sectors, there was good export growth in engineering goods and Petroleum crude and products; moderate growth in chemicals and related products, and textiles & allied products; but negative growth in gems and jewellery (Table 32.5) (*Economic Suvey 2017-18*, Vol.II).

Similarly imports into India declined by 0.5 per cent to US$448.0 billion in 2014-15 as compared to US$450.2 billion in 2013-14, on account of a fall in POL imports by 16.0 per cent. The decline in POL imports owed to a fall in international crude oil prices (Indian basket) from US$105.5 per barrel in 2013-14 to US$ 84.2 per barrel in 2014-15. Petroleum, crude and products, chemicals and related products, gold, electronic goods and machinery accounted for 62.5 per cent of India's total imports in 2014-15. Major items of imports like chemicals and related products, electronic goods and gold registered growth rates of 8.2 per cent, 13.8 per cent and 19.9 per cent respectively in 2014-15. Imports of petroleum crude and products, transport equipment and pearls, precious and semi-precious stones witnessed a decline in growth rates by 16.0 per cent, 5.4 per cent and 5.8 per cent respectively.

TABLE – 21.4

Sector-wise Share and Growth Rate of Exports 2015-16 to 2017-18

(%)

Rank		*Share (%)* 2015-16	2016-17	2017-18 (Apr-Nov) (P)	*Growth rate (%)* 2015-16	2016-17	2017-18 (Apr-Nov) (P)
1	Engineering goods	23.1	24.4	25.9	-17.0	11.1	22.4
2	Gems and Jewellery	15.0	15.7	14.4	-4.8	10.5	-3.8
3	Chemicals and related products**	14.7	14.2	14.5	0.6	1.6	11.9
	of which						
	Drug & pharmaceutical	6.2	5.8	5.4	9.9	-1.2	-0.7
4	Textiles &allied products	13.7	13.0	11.8	-3.2	-0.5	3.8
	of which						
	Textiles	5.6	5.2	4.9	-8.5	-2.3	5.9
	Clothing	8.1	7.8	6.9	0.8	0.7	2.4
5	Petroleum crude &products	11.7	11.4	11.8	-46.2	3.1	17.6
6	Agriculture and allied products*	9.9	9.5	9.7	-17.6	0.3	15.0
7	Electronic goods	2.2	2.1	2.0	-5.3	0.0	4.5
8	Marine products	1.8	2.1	2.7	-13.5	23.8	29.5
9	Ores and minerals	0.8	1.2	1.0	-16.4	61.6	12.9
10	Leather & leather products	2.1	1.9	1.9	-10.3	-4.4	0.9
	Total exports including others	100.0	100.0	100.0	-15.5	5.2	11.2

Notes: *: including plantation **: including plastic and rubber products. P : Provisional

Source: Computed from D/o Commerce database.

Economic Survey 2017-18, Vol. II.

During 2015-16 (April-December), total imports declined by 15.9 per cent to US$295.8 billion as against US$351.6 billion in 2014-15 (April-December). Detailed commodity breakup shows that imports of electronic goods, agriculture and allied products and fertilisers registered growth rates of 11.5 per cent, 6.9 per cent, and 19.4 per cent respectively. Machinery, an important item of capital goods import, registered low growth of 0.8 per cent while transport equipment imports witnessed negative growth of 12.6 per cent in 2015-16 (April-December).

Sector-wise, import of Petroleum, Oil and Lubricants (POL) increased by 4.8 per cent in 2016-17 and 24.2 per cent in 2017-18 (Apr-December), mainly due to an increase in international crude oil price (Indian Basket) from US$ 46.2 /bbl in 2015-16 to US$ 47.6 /bbl in 2016-17 and to US$ 53.6 /bbl in 2017-18 (April-December). Among the other important import items, low or negative growth was registered in most of them in 2016-17, except electronic goods; ores & minerals and agriculture and allied products. Capital goods imports grew marginally, though the transport equipments subcategory registered high growth. In 2017-18 (April- November) all major sectors registered positive growth with the capital goods imports, which are needed for industrial activity, registering a 11.3 per cent growth (*Economic Suvey 2017-18*, Vol.II).

Direction of Trade

The slowdown in terms of global economic growth and trade volumes was also manifested in the direction of trade statistics. The share of advanced economies that were adversely affected by the global slowdown in total Indian exports fell significantly. The shares of Europe (consisting of the EU, the European Free Trade Association [EFTA] and other European countries) and America (consisting of North America and Latin America) declined from 23.6 per cent and 20.1 per cent respectively in 2004-05 to 18.1 per cent and 19.0 per cent respectively in 2014-15. The share of the CIS & Baltics, which was 1.3 per cent in 2004-05, declined marginally to 1.1 per cent in 2014-15 while there was marginal increase in the share of Asia from 47.9 per cent in 2004-05 to 49.6 per cent in 2014-15. The export share of Africa in India's total exports increased from 6.7 per cent in 2004-05 to 10.6 per cent in 2014-2015.

Exports to America grew by 8.9 per cent and Africa by 5.2 per cent in 2014-15 over the previous year while exports to some other destinations declined, for example Europe (by 3.5%), Asia (by 1.0%) and the CIS & Baltics (by 2.7%). During 2015-16 (April-December), on the other hand, there was a broad-based decline in exports to all the five regions. In terms of major countries, India's exports to the USA, the UAE and Hong Kong (with shares of 13.7%, 10.6% and 4.4% in India's total exports) increased by 8.4 per cent, 8.2 per cent and 6.8 per cent respectively in 2014-15. On the contrary, India's exports to China (3.8% share), Saudi Arabia (3.6% share), Singapore (3.2% share) and the UK (3.0% share) witnessed negative growth of 19.6 per cent, 8.7 per cent, 21.6 per cent and 4.8 per cent respectively in 2014-15. These seven countries together account for 42.3 per cent of India's total exports in 2014-15. During 2015-16 (April-December), all seven major destinations witnessed negative growth.

Similarly, India's import sources have also undergone change over time. India's imports from Europe (share) declined from 23.0 per cent in 2004-05 to 16.5 per cent of total imports in 2014-15. On the other hand, the import shares of Africa, America and Asia in India's total imports increased during the same period. India's imports from Europe and Africa increased by 4.1 per cent and 5.5 per cent respectively in 2014-15 over the previous year, while imports from America and Asia declined by 2.7 per cent and 3.4 per cent respectively. Among the top countries for India's imports, China with a share of 13.5 per cent in total imports, registered a positive growth rate of 18.4 per cent in 2014-2015. Imports from Switzerland, Indonesia and Korea, with shares of 4.9 per cent, 3.4 per cent and 3.0 per cent also registered positive growth rates of 14.6 per cent, 1.7 per cent and 8.5 per cent respectively in 2014-15. However, India's imports from Saudi Arabia (6.3% share), the UAE (5.8% share) and the USA (4.9% share) declined by 22.8 per cent, 9.9 per cent and 3.1 per cent respectively in 2014-15. Imports from all five major regions (including CIS & Baltics) declined in 2015-16, with imports from America registering the highest decline (April-December). India's imports from China registered positive growth of 2.5 per cent in 2015-16 (April-December), while imports from other major countries registered negative growth rates.

Trade Deficit

India's trade deficit increased almost steadily from US$28.0 billion in 2004-05 to US$118.6 billion in 2010-11. It grew exponentially to reach unsustainable levels of US$183.4 billion and US$190.3 billion respectively in the next two years. However, it moderated to US$135.8 billion in 2013-14 as a result of measures taken by the government to contain trade and CADs. In 2014-15, the trade deficit was marginally higher at US$137.7 billion. Trade deficit continued to be at a lower level due to the decline in the value of POL imports by 16.0 per cent, caused by a fall in international oil prices by 20.2 per cent. Trade deficit can be decomposed into POL deficit and non-POL deficit. POL deficit (POL exports minus POL imports), the major component of trade deficit, which was hovering at around US$100 billion from 2011-12 to 2013-14, declined to US$81.5 billion in 2014-15 and to US$44.2 billion in 2015-16 (April-December). Within non-POL deficit, gems and jewellery deficit (net exports of pearls, precious and semi-precious stones, gold, silver and other gold jewellery) declined sharply from US$40.9 billion in 2012-13 to US$17.0 billion in 2013-14, reflecting restrictions placed on these imports, but subsequently increased to US$21.1 billion in 2014-15.

India's trade deficit (on custom basis) which had registered continuous decline since 2014-15, widened to US$ 74.5 billion in H1 of 2017-18 from US$ 43.4 billion in H1 of 2016-17. India's trade deficit was US$ 108.5 billion in 2016-17, with the reduction in both POL deficit and non POL deficit. In 2017-18 (April-December) trade deficit (on customs basis) shot up by 46.4 per cent to US$ 114.9 billion with POL deficit growing by 27.4 per cent and non-POL deficit by 65.0 per cent (*Economic Survey 2017-18*, Vol.II).

Among India's trading partners, the top five countries with which India has negative bilateral trade balance are China, Switzerland, Saudi Arabia, Iraq and South Korea while the top five countries with which it has surplus trade balance are USA, UAE, Bangladesh, Nepal and UK. India has the highest trade deficit with China. Its share in India's total trade deficit increased from 20.3 per cent in 2012-13 to 47.1 per cent in 2016-17 and 43.2 per cent in 2017-18 (April-September) (*Economic Survey 2017-18*, Vol.II).

Foreign Trade Policy: 2015-2020

Trade Policy Measures

In the wake of declining exports, the government took various measures to boost exports in the Union Budget 2015-16 and a new Foreign Trade Policy (FTP) for the period 2015-2020 was announced on 1 April 2015, with a focus on supporting both manufacturing and services exports and improving the 'ease of doing business'. The new FTP aims to increase India's exports to US$900 billion by 2019-20. Its salient features are given in Box 21.1. It also provides the roadmap adopted by the government to align it with the 'Make in India' and 'Digital India' programmes and to ease trade. Box 21.2 lists some important trade facilitation measures undertaken by the government to improve ease of doing business.

BOX – 21.1

Salient Features of the FTP 2015-2020

Merchandise Export from India Scheme: The six different schemes of the earlier FTP (Focus Product Scheme, Market Linked Focus Product Scheme, Focus Market Scheme, Agriculture Infrastructure Incentive Scrip, Vishesh Krishi and Gram Udyog Yojana and Incremental Export Incentive Scheme) which had varying sector-specific or actual user only conditions attached to their use have been merged into a single scheme, namely the Merchandise Export from India Scheme (MEIS). Notified goods exported to notified markets will be incentivised on realised FOB value of exports. Countries have been grouped into three categories—namely Category A: traditional markets, Category B: emerging & focus markets and Category C: other markets for grant of incentives. The government has expanded the coverage of the MEIS on 29 October 2015 by adding 110 new items. The incentive rate/country coverage of 2228 items has been enhanced.

Service Export from India Scheme: The Served from India Scheme (SFIS) has been replaced with the Service Export from India Scheme (SEIS). The SEIS applies to 'service providers located in India' instead of 'Indian service providers'. Thus it provides for incentives to all service providers of notified services who are providing services from India, regardless of the constitution or profile of the service provider. The rates of incentivisation under the SEIS are based on net foreign exchange earned. The incentive issued as duty credit scrip, will no longer carry an actual user condition and will no longer be restricted to usage for specified types of goods but be freely transferable and usable for all types of goods and service tax debits on procurement of services/goods.

Incentives (MEIS & SEIS) to be available for SEZs: FTP 2015-20 extends the benefits of the MEIS and SEIS to SEZ (special economic zones) as well, which will give a new impetus to the development and growth of SEZs.

Duty credit scrips are freely transferable and usable for payment of custom duty, excise duty and service tax: All scrips issued under the

contd. ...

...contd. ...

MEIS and SEIS and the goods imported against these scrips are fully transferable. Scrips issued under these schemes can be used for the following:

(a) Payment of customs duty on import of inputs / goods including capital goods, except items listed in Appendix 3A.

(b) Payment of excise duty on domestic procurement of inputs or goods, including capital goods as per notification of DoR (Department of Revenue).

(c) Payment of service tax on procurement of services as per DoR notification. Basic customs duty paid in cash or through debit under duty credit scrip can be taken back as duty drawback as per DoR rules, if inputs so imported are used for exports.

Other measures

(a) Under the Export Promotion Capital Goods (EPCG) scheme, in case capital goods are procured from indigenous manufacturers, specific export obligation has been reduced to 75 per cent. This is designed to help the indigenous capital goods manufacturing industry.

(b) Under the MEIS, export items with high domestic content and value addition have generally been provided higher levels of incentives.

(c) Hard copies of applications and specified documents which were required to be submitted earlier for incentive schemes and duty exemption schemes have now been dispensed with.

(d) Landing documents of export consignments as proof for notified market can now be digitally uploaded as specified.

(e) There will be no need to submit copies of permanent records/ documents repeatedly with each application, once the same are uploaded in the exporter/importer profile.

(f) Dedicated e-mail addresses have been provided for faster and paperless communication with various committees of the Directorate General of Foreign Trade (DGFT), e.g. Norms Committee and Exim Facilitation Committee.

Source: *Economic Survey 2015-16*, Vol. II.

BOX – 21.2

Recent Measures for Trade Facilitation

(a) The government has reduced the number of mandatory documents required for exports and imports to three each, which is comparable with international benchmarks. The trade community can file applications online for various trade-related schemes. Online payment of application fees through credit/debit cards and electronic funds transfer from 53 banks has been put in place.

(b) Customs single window initiative: The Union Budget 2014-15 announced an Indian Customs Single Window Project to facilitate trade. This project envisages that importers and exporters will electronically submit their customs clearance documents at a single point with customs. Any permissions required from other regulatory agencies (such as animal quarantine, plant quarantine, drug controller and textile committee) could be obtained online without the importer/exporter having to separately approach these agencies. The single window will thus provide importers/exporters a single point interface for customs clearance of import and export goods, thereby reducing personal interface with governmental agencies, dwell time and cost of doing business. With effect from 1 April 2015, an electronic exchange facility has been established between customs and the Food Safety and Standards Authority of India (FSSAI), the Department of Plant Protection, Quarantine and Storage (PQIS) at the Jawaharlal Nehru Port Trust (JNPT) (Nhava Sheva), inland container depot (ICD), Tughlakabad and ICD, Patparganj, for online message exchange, including no objection certificates (NOC) with/from these agencies. Other regulatory agencies such as animal quarantine, the textile committee, the drug controller of India and wildlife authorities are also being brought within the ambit of single window customs clearance.

(c) 24x7 customs clearance: With effect from 31 December 2014, the facility of 24x7 customs clearance for specified imports, namely goods covered under 'facilitated' bills of entry, and specified exports, namely factory stuffed containers and goods exported under free shipping bills, have been made available at 18 seaports. Similarly, the facility of 24x7 customs clearance for specified imports, namely goods covered by facilitated bills of entry and all exports, namely goods covered by all shipping bills has been extended at 17 air cargo complexes. This will help in faster

contd. ...

...contd. ...

clearance of such import and export goods, reduce dwell time and lower the transaction cost.

(d) One of the major objectives of the new FTP is to move towards a paperless 24x7 working environment. A new facility has been created to upload documents in exporter/importer profile so that exporters are not required to submit documents repeatedly.

(e) Attention has also been paid to simplifying various 'aayat niryat' forms, bringing in clarity in different provisions, removing ambiguities and enhancing electronic governance.

(f) The DGFT has launched a new-look website, making it more user-friendly and easy to navigate. The DGFT website has a large dynamic component whereby the trade community can file applications online for IEC (importer exporter code) and various other schemes of the DGFT. Exporters can also see the status of their electronic bank realisation certificates almost in real time. The website is rich in content with all documents related to FTP along with a responsive online grievance redressal system.

(g) The DGFT launched a 'DGFT' mobile application in June 2015. The application allows exporters/importers to access foreign trade policy and other related documents in an easy-to-use searchable format and check status of transmission of various authorizations and shipping bills, etc.

(h) Training/outreach programmes for exporters:

- The Niryat Bandhu Scheme has been galvanized to achieve the objectives of Skill India. Outreach activities are being organized at MSME (micro, small and medium enterprises) clusters with the help of export promotion councils (EPCs) and other willing 'industry partners' and 'knowledge partners'. More than 20,000 entrepreneurs have been given exposure by DGFT regional offices under the Niryat Bandhu Scheme. In September 2015, the DGFT in collaboration with the Indian Institute of Foreign Trade (IIFT) has launched 'Niryat Bandhu at Your Desktop', an online certificate programme in export import business. The programme has elicited very good response. Four programmes have been completed.
- An ambitious outreach programme has been launched by the Department of Commerce (DoC) for exporters located in the major export clusters/cities. The programme focuses on:

contd. ...

...contd. ...

- Training exporters to utilize free trade agreements (FTA).
- Taking inputs from exporters on FTAs under negotiation, for example the Regional Comprehensive Economic Policy (RCEP).
- Promoting awareness about the contents of the www: indiantradeportal.in launched by the DoC.

(i) Other important measures:

- A Council for Trade Development and Promotion has been constituted in July 2015 to ensure continuous dialogue with the governments of states/union territories (UT) on measures for providing an international trade-enabling environment and for making the states active partners in boosting India's exports. The first meeting of the council was held on 8 January 2016.
- The state/UT governments have been requested to develop their export strategy, appoint export commissioners, address infrastructure constraints restricting movement of goods, facilitate refund of VAT (value-added tax)/octroi/state-level cess, address other issues relating to various clearances and build capacity of new exporters in order to promote exports. States and UTs have also been issued user-ids and passwords to facilitate access to the foreign trade database maintained by the Directorate General of Commercial Intelligence & Statistics (DGCI&S) to extract the export data relating to their states.

Source: *Economic Survey 2015-16*, Vol. II.

Two important developments on the trade policy front during the year relate to the mid-term review of Foreign Trade Policy(FTP) and the recent multilateral negotiations of WTO in December 2017. Besides these, there were some developments on the trade logistics front and anti-dumping measures.

FTP: Mid Term Review and Subsequent Trade Related Policies

In the mid-term review of FTP released on 5th December 2017, some additional measures have been taken to help India's trade sector. Besides, on 15th December 2017, a special package for employment generation in leather and footwear sector was approved by the Government which is also likely to help exports from this sector (Box 21.3).

BOX – 21.3

Highlights of the Mid Term Review of Foreign Trade Policy and Subsequent Trade Related Policies

- MEIS (Merchandise Exports from India Scheme) incentives for two sub-sectors of Textiles i.e. Ready Made Garments and Made Ups increased from 2 per cent to 4 per cent involving additional annual incentives of `2743 crore.
- Across the board increase of 2 per cent in existing MEIS incentive for exports by MSMEs/labour intensive industries amounting to `4576 crore.
- To provide an impetus to the services trade, the SEIS (Service Export from India Scheme) incentives have been increased by 2 per cent for notified services such as Business, Legal, Accounting, Architectural, Engineering, Educational, Hospital, Hotels and Restaurants amounting to `1140 crore.
- The validity period of the Duty Credit Scrips has been increased from 18 months to 24 months to enhance their utility in the GST framework. GST rate for transfer/sale of scrips has been reduced to zero from the earlier rate of 12 per cent.
- New trust based Self Ratification Scheme introduced to allow duty free inputs for export production under duty exemption scheme with a self-declaration. Under this scheme, instead of getting a ratification of the Norms Committee for inputs to be used in the manufacture of export products, exporters will self-certify the requirement of duty free raw materials/ inputs and take an authorization from DGFT. The scheme would initially be available to the Authorized Economic Operators (AEOs).
- Contact@DGFT service for Complaint Resolution has been activated on the DGFT website (www.dgft.gov.in) as a single

contd. ...

contd

window contact point for exporters and importers for resolving all foreign trade related issues.

- To focus on improving Ease of Trading across Borders for exporters and importers, a professional team envisaged to handhold, assist and support exporters with their export related problems, accessing export markets and meeting regulatory requirements.
- New Logistics Division created in the Commerce Department to develop and coordinate implementation of an Action Plan for the integrated development of the logistics sector, by way of policy changes, improvement in existing procedures, identification of bottlenecks and gaps and introduction of technology in this sector.
- For clarity, a negative list of capital goods which are not permitted under the EPCG (Export Promotion on Capital Goods) scheme has been notified.
- The concept of Domestic Tariff Area (DTA) sale from Export Oriented Units (EoUs) on concessional and full duty has been removed and hence, the limit on entitlement of DTA sale has also been removed. Consequently, restriction on DTA sale of motor cars, alcoholic liquors, books and tea has been removed.
- Second Hand Goods imported for the purpose of repair/refurbishing/re-conditioning or re-engineering have been made free, thereby facilitating generation of employment in the repair services sector.
- Issue of working capital blockage of the exporters due to upfront payment of GST on inputs has been addressed. Under advance authorization Export Promotion for Capital Goods (EPCG) Scheme, 100 per cent EoU's, exporters have been extended the benefit of sourcing inputs/capital goods from abroad as well as domestic suppliers for exports without upfront payment of GST. Further an e wallet will be launched from 1st April 2018 to make these schemes operational from 1st April, 2018.
- The Union Cabinet Committee on 15th December 2017, approved the special package for employment generation in leather and footwear sector. The package involves implementation of Central Sector Scheme "Indian Footwear, Leather & Accessories Development Programme" with an approved expenditure of `2600 crore over the three years from 2017-18 to 2019-20. The scheme

contd. ...

...contd. ...

would lead to development of infrastructure for the leather sector, address environment concerns specific to the leather sector, facilitate additional investments, employment generation and increase in production. The Special Package has the potential to generate 3.24 lakhs new jobs in 3 years and assist in formalization of 2 lakh jobs as cumulative impact in Footwear, Leather & Accessories Sector.

Source : Based on inputs from Department of Commerce.
Economic Survey 2017-18, Vol. II.

Multilateral Negotiations

During the Ministerial Conference (MC11), India stood firm on its stand on the fundamental principles of the WTO, including multilateralism, rule-based consensual decision making, an independent and credible dispute resolution and appellate process, the centrality of development, which underlies the Doha Development Agenda (DDA), and special and differential treatment for all developing countries (*Economic Survey 2017-18*, Vol.II).

Appendix Table – A-21.1...(next page)

APPENDIX TABLE – A-21.1

Value of Exports and Imports—1950-51 to 2018-19

(US$ million)

Year	*Exports*	*Imports*	*Trade Balance*	*Rate of Change (%)*	
				Exports	*Imports*
1950-51	1269	1273	-4	24.9	-1.5
1960-61	1346	2353	-1007	0.3	16.7
1970-71	2031	2162	-131	8.8	3.5
1980-81	8486	15869	-7383	6.8	40.2
1990-91	18143	24075	-5932	9.2	13.5
2000-01	44560	50536	-5976	21.0	1.7
2005-06	103092	149167	-46076	23.4	33.8
2006-07	126360	185747	-59387	22.6	24.5
2007-08	163132	251654	-88522	29.0	35.5
2008-09	185295	303696	-118401	13.6	20.7
2009-10	178751	268373	-109622	-3.5	-5.0
2010-11	251136	369769	-118633	40.5	28.2
2011-12	305964	489319	-183356	21.8	32.3
2012-13	300401	490739	-190336	-1.8	0.3
2013-14	314405	450200	-135795	4.7	-8.3
2014-15	310338	448033	-137695	-1.3	-0.5
2015-16	262291	381008	-118717	-15.5	-15.0
2016-17	275852	384357	-108505	5.2	0.9
2017-18	303526	465581	-162055	10.0	21.1
2018-19 (P)	329536	514034	-184498	8.8	10.4

Note: a: growth rate on provisional over revised basis.

Source: Government of India (GoI), *Economic Survey, 2011-12, A-81, 2014-15, A-87.*
Economic Survey 2017-18, Vol. II (Table 4, p. 88).
Economic Survey 2018-19, Vol.2, Statistical Appendix Table (A 105).

22

Balance of Payments

Balance of Payments

BoP comprises current account, capital account, errors and omissions, and changes in foreign exchange reserves. Under current account of the BoP, transactions are classified into merchandise (exports and imports) and invisibles. Invisible transactions are further classified into three categories, namely: (i) services–travel, transportation, insurance, GNIE (government not included elsewhere) and miscellaneous (such as communication, construction, financial, software, news agency, royalties, management and business services), (ii) income, and (iii) transfers (grants, gifts, remittances, etc.) which do not have any quid pro quo.

Under capital account, capital inflows can be classified by instrument (debt or equity) and maturity (short or long-term). The main components of capital account include foreign investment, loans and banking capital. Foreign investment comprising FDI and portfolio investment consisting of FIIs (foreign institutional investors) investment, ADRs/GDRs (American depository receipts/global depository receipts) represents non-debt liabilities, while loans (external assistance, ECBs (external commercial borrowings) and trade credit) and banking capital including NRI deposits are debt liabilities.

India's Balance of Payment Trends: 1950-51 to 2015-16

According to Deepak Mohanty, India's BoP evolved reflecting both the changes in our development paradigm and exogenous shocks from time to time. In the 60-year span, 1951-52 to 2011-12, six events had a lasting impact on our BoP: (i) the devaluation in 1966; (ii) first and second oil shocks of 1973 and 1980; (iii) external payments crisis of 1991; (iv) the East Asian crisis of 1997; (v) the Y2K event of 2000; and (vi) the global financial crisis of 2008.

The first phase can be considered from the 1950s through mid-1960s. In the early 1950s, India was reasonably open. For example, in 1951-52, merchandise trade, exports plus imports, accounted for 16 per cent of GDP. Overall current receipts plus payments were nearly 19 per cent of GDP. Subsequently, the share of external sector in India's GDP gradually declined with the inward looking policy of import substitution. Moreover, Indian export basket comprised mainly traditional items like tea, cotton textile and jute manufactures. Not only the scope of world trade expansion in these commodities was less, but additionally India had to face competition from new emerging suppliers, such as Pakistan in jute manufactures and Ceylon and East Africa in tea.

During this period, policy emphasis was on import saving rather than export promotion, and priority was given to basic goods and capital goods sector. It was argued that investment in heavy industries would bring in saving in foreign exchange, as output from such industries would replace their imports in the long-run. Import-substituting strategies were expected to gradually increase export competitiveness through efficiency-gains achieved in the domestic economy. But this did not happen. Hence, exports remained modest. In fact our external sector contracted in relation to GDP from the level observed in the early 1950s. By 1965-66, merchandise trade was under 8 per cent of GDP and overall current receipts and payments were below 10 per cent of GDP.

Notwithstanding the contracting size of the external sector, as imports growth outstripped exports growth, there was persistent CAD. Emphasis on heavy industrialisation in the Second Five Year Plan led to a sharp increase in imports. On top of this, the strains of Indo-China conflict of 1962, Indo-Pakistan war of 1965 and severe drought of 1965-1966 triggered a major BoP crisis. India's international economic relations with advanced countries came under stress during the Indo-Pak conflict. Withdrawal of foreign aid by countries like the US and conditional resumption of aid by the Aid India Consortium led to contraction in capital inflows. Given the low level of foreign exchange reserves and burgeoning trade deficit, India had no option other than to devalue. Rupee was devalued by 36.5 per cent in June 1966.

TABLE – 22.1

Balance of Payments : Summary

(US$ million)

Sl. No.	Items	1990-91	2000-01	2012-13	2013-14	2014-15	2015-16	2016-17	2017-18	2017-18 Apr-Dec	2018-19 Apr-Dec (P)
I	**Current Account**										
	1. Exports	18,477	45,452	3,06,581	318607	3,16,545	2,66,365	2,80,138	3,08,970	2,26,753	2,49,869
	2. Imports	27,915	57,912	5,02,237	466216	4,61,484	3,96,444	3,92,580	4,69,006	3,45,166	3,95,142
	3. Trade Balance	-9,438	-12,460	-1,95,656	-147609	-1,44,940	-1,30,079	-1,12,442	-1,60,036	-1,18,413	-1,45,272
	4. Invisibles (net)	-242	9,794	1,07,493	115212	1,18,081	1,07,928	97,147	1,11,319	82,762	93,407
	a. Services	980	1,692	64,915	72965	76,529	69,676	67,455	77,562	57,398	60,254
	b. Income	2,069	12,854	-21,455	-23028	-24,140	-24,375	-26,291	-28,681	-20,861	-20,452
	c. Transfers	-3,752	-5,004	64,034	65276	65,692	62,627	55,983	62,438	46,225	53,605
	5. Current Account Balance	-9,680	-2,666	-88,163	-32397	-26,859	-22,151	-15,296	-48,717	-35,651	-51,865
II	**Capital Account**										
	6. External Assistance	2,204	410	982	1032	1,725	1,505	2,013	2,944	1,514	2,160
	7. External Commercial Borrowings	2,254	7,861	8,485	11777	1,570	-4,529	-6,102	-183	-1,175	2,785
	8. Non-Resident Deposits	1,537	2,316	14,842	38892	14,057	16,052	-12,367	9,676	5,040	6,977
	9. Foreign Investment	103	5,862	46,711	26386	73,456	31,891	43,224	52,401	43,718	14,766
	of which:										
	a. FDI	97	3,272	19,819	21564	31,251	36,021	35,612	30,286	23,879	24,820
	b. Portfolio Investment	—	—	26,891	4822	42,205	-4,130	7,612	22,115	19,839	-10,054
	10. Other Flows	2,283	-3,740	-5,105	-10813	1,028	3,242	7,495	6,138	1,393	-485
III	**Reserves Change [increase (-) / decrease (+)]**	**1,278**	**-5,842**	**-3,826**	**-15508**	**-61,406**	**-17,905**	**-21,550**	**-43,574**	**-30,338**	**17,502**

Note: PR: partially revised. P: Provisional

Source: *Economic Survey 2012-13, 2013-14, 2014-15.*

Economic Survey 2017-18, Vol. II., Economic Survey 2018-19, Vol. 2, Ch.6, Annexure II.

Although India's export basket was limited, the sharp devaluation clearly increased the competitiveness of India's exports. Concurrently, India had to undertake a number of trade liberalising measures. Even though the net impact of devaluation was a contentious issue among the leading economists, data show that exports growth, though modest, outpaced imports growth.

In fact, the current account turned into a surplus in 1973-74 as not only the exports growth was significant but invisible receipts also showed a sharp turnaround from deficit to surplus mainly on account of official transfers which largely represented grants under the agreement of February 1974 with the US Government on the disposition of PL 480 and other rupee funds. Since surplus in CAB (current account balance) was used for repaying rupee loans under the same agreement with the US, accretion to reserves was only marginal.

First and Second Oil Shocks of 1973 and 1980

India's BoP remained comfortable during the 1970s. The adjustment to the first oil shock of 1973-74 was rendered smooth by a happy combination of buoyant exports, spurt in private transfer receipts and increased inflow of aid. Exports, benefited by the expansion in global trade, rose at an annual rate of 6.8 per cent in volume terms and by 15.6 per cent in US dollar terms during the decade. An effective depreciation of the rupee occurred due to the link with Pound Sterling until 1973 and later, because of the lower growth in prices in India relative to other countries. Private transfers rose seven-fold from US$296 million in 1974-75 to US$2,175 million in 1979-80 and in fact, in the post first oil shock period, financed roughly 80 per cent of the trade deficit. Within two years of the shock, the CAB turned into surplus and it was only in 1978-79 that a deficit of about 0.2 per cent of GDP appeared. The utilisation of aid was significant and was substantially higher than the financing requirement for the decade, allowing for a build-up of reserves. At the close of the decade, the foreign exchange reserves stood at US$ 7361 million providing cover for over 7 months of imports.

During the 1980s, issues relating to the BoP came to occupy the centre stage in terms of India's macroeconomic management. The impact of the second oil shock of 1979, the full effects of which spilled over into the 1980s, was more severe than that of the 1973-74. Between 1978-1979 and 1981-82, imports almost doubled. The increase in POL imports accounted for a little over half the increase in the overall imports. This was followed by the second-round effects on non-POL imports. Export performance was depressed by the severe international recession of 1980-1983 and recorded a volume growth of just a little over 3 per cent. Net invisible receipts continued to provide support to the BoP, largely in the form of earnings from tourism and the sustained buoyancy of private transfers. However, the sharp widening in the merchandise trade deficit resulted in a turnaround in the CAB from a surplus in 1977-78 to a deficit in 1981-82 of the order of US$3,166 million or 1.8 per cent of GDP. Adjustment efforts consisted essentially of an EFF (extended fund facility) negotiated with the IMF, although there were also intensified efforts to improve domestic production of crude petroleum.

During the 1980s, BoP again came under stress. The second oil shock led to a rapid increase in imports in early 1980s. Oil imports increased to about two-fifth of India's imports during 1980-1983. At the same time, India's external sector policy was changing towards greater openness. Various measures were undertaken to promote exports and liberalise imports for exporters during this period. However, several factors weighed against external stability. First, despite a number of export promotion measures, the subdued growth conditions in the world economy constrained exports growth. Second, the surplus on account of invisibles also deteriorated due to moderation in private transfers. Third, the debt servicing had increased with greater recourse to debt creating flows such as external ECBs and NRI deposits. Fourth, deterioration is the fiscal position stemming from rising expenditures accentuated the twin deficit risks.

External Payment Crisis of 1991

The Crisis: 1990-1992

In 1991, India found itself in its worst BoP crisis since 1947. The fact that there was a crisis in the making during the second half of 1980s had been evident for a long time. The inflow of foreign borrowing had increased at a rapid rate during the late 1980s. This was due to the excess domestic expenditure over income—the fiscal deficit of the centre and the states soared to over 11 per cent in 1991. During this period, total public debt as a proportion of GNP (gross national product) doubled, reaching the level of 60 per cent and foreign currency reserves were depleted rapidly.

Matters were made worse by an accompanying double-digit inflation in 1990-91. The oil price increase resulting from Iraq's invasion of Kuwait in August 1990 reinforced the crisis-like situation in India.

India's credit rating got downgraded as, for the first time in its history, India was on the verge of defaulting on its international commitments and was denied access to external commercial credit markets. A net outflow of NRI deposits commenced in October 1990 and continued during 1991. The only way left for India was to borrow against the security of its gold reserves transported abroad.

But something good emerged out of the BoP crisis of 1991—the long overdue economic reforms. Apart from an immediate programme of macroeconomic stabilisation, structural reforms were also introduced in the industrial and trade policy regimes with a view to improving the efficiency, productivity and international competitiveness of India's economy.

The broad approach to reform in the external sector was laid out in the Report of the High Level Committee on Balance of Payments (Chairman: C. Rangarajan, 1993).

The impact of policy changes was reflected in lower CAD and its comfortable financing in subsequent years. India could manage the external shocks that emanated from the East Asian crisis in 1997 and subsequently, the rise in international oil prices and bursting of dotcom bubble in 1999-2000. Indeed, the Indian economy remained relatively insulated from the East Asian crisis owing to the reforms undertaken in previous years and proactive and timely policy measures initiated by the RBI to minimise the contagion effect. Monetary tightening coupled with flexible exchange rate and steps to bolster reserves through issuance of RIBs (resurgent India bonds) helped in stabilising the BoP.

The BoP came under some stress again in the first half of 2000-2001 due to a sharp rise in oil prices and increase in interest rates in advanced countries. At the same time, India's software exports got a boost following the demands to address the Y2K challenges. This also encouraged migration of Indian software engineers to the advanced countries. As a result, the surplus in the services exports and remittance account of the BoP increased sharply which more than offset the deficit in the trade account. Software exports rose from 0.9 per cent of GDP in 1999-2000 to a peak of 3.8 per cent of GDP by 2008-09. Private remittances also rose from 2.7 per cent of GDP to 3.8 per cent during this period. Thus, in the 2000s software exports and private remittances emerged as two main financing items for the current account mitigating to a large extent the merchandise trade deficit. Owing to a combination of factors, in fact, the current account recorded a surplus during 2001-

2004. Subsequently, as international oil prices started rising and domestic growth picked up, deficit in current account re-emerged during 2004-05 to 2007-08 albeit remained range bound.

After a period of stability, India's BoP came under stress in 2008-2009 reflecting the impact of global financial crisis. As capital inflows plummeted, India had to draw down its foreign currency assets by US$ 20 billion during 2008-09. Stress, since the collapse of Lehman Brothers largely, emanated from decline in India's merchandise exports and deceleration in growth in services exports. Although there was some improvement during 2010-11 on the back of a strong pick-up in exports mainly led by diversification of trade in terms of composition as well as direction, it proved to be short-lived. BoP again came under stress during 2011-12 as slowdown in advanced economies spilled over to EDEs, and there was sharp increase in oil and gold imports.

India's BoP during 2011-12 to 2018-19

Post the 2008 global financial crisis, EMDEs (emerging market and developing economics) had to face periodic shocks or stresses emanating from policies in advanced economies as well as through financial channels notwithstanding the efforts of the G-20 at coordination of policy responses to the crisis. The Indian economy had to weather the shocks which got amplified on account of confluence of weak external demand and relatively strong domestic demand with large dependence on crude oil imports whose price levels remained elevated until the second half of the current fiscal. These shocks led to widening of the CAD in 2011-12 which continued through the first quarter of 2013-14. With external financing sources remaining volatile, the less than adequate quantity and deteriorating quality of financing resulted in a sharp depreciation of the rupee. The policy responses that were put in place in 2013-14 helped overcome the stress through reduction in the levels of CAD and this, along with ample financing, led to reserve accretion that helped build resilience—a process that continues through the current fiscal.

India has consistently run a current account deficit (CAD), driven by a deficit on merchandise trade. In contrast, India maintains a surplus on service trade, and positive net transfers from abroad (collectively called invisible earnings). In the past five years, current account deficit has averaged about 1.9 percent of GDP a year, while merchandise trade deficit has averaged 7.4 percent of GDP a year. Both current account deficit and merchandise deficit have steadily declined over the past five years. Meanwhile invisible earnings have averaged 5.5 percent a year, but have declined too in the past few years, due to weaker earnings from services exports and private transfers from abroad.[1]

India's balance of payment situation showed some signs of stress during H1 of 2018-19 as sharp rise in crude oil prices caused current account deficit (CAD) to deteriorate. However, CAD moderated somewhat in Q3-2018-19 as international crude oil prices eased. Until end of Q3 for which data is available (April-December 2018-19), India's CAD stood at US$51.9 billion (2.6% of GDP) as compared to US$35.7 billion (1.8% of GDP) a year ago for the same period. The widening of the CAD was largely on account of a higher trade deficit driven by rise in international crude oil prices (Indian basket) making merchandise imports grow relatively faster than exports. The trade deficit increased to US$145.3 billion during the same period from US$118.4 billion in the corresponding period of previous year. India's CAD has been increasing for some years now after attaining a high of 0.6 per cent of GDP in 2016-17. It increased to 1.8 per cent of GDP in 2017-18 and has been projected at 2.4 per cent for the full year of 2018-2019. Expectedly the increase in CAD is driven by increasing merchandise trade deficit, which as proportion of GDP, increased from 4.9 per cent in 2016-17 to 6.0 per cent in 2017-18 and further enhanced to 6.7 per cent in 2018-19.[2]

Recent Trade Policy Developments

The Government of India announced a new export support policy and a hike in import duty for electronics in December 2017, as well as wide-spread custom rate increases as part of the budget announced in February 2018. As part of the export support policy, the government announced an annual package to the tune of INR 84.5 bn. to provide export incentives for the laborintensive manufacturing sectors. The government also announced an increase in import duties for electronics, raising duties from 10 to 15 percent on items such as mobile phones and video recording devices, and by 10 percentage points on household electronics such as lamps and microwaves.73 It also relaxed FDI norms in retail, airlines and construction sector.74 Finally, the budget presented for the year 2018-19 proposed increases on customs duties on a range of products.[3]

1. The World Bank (2018). *India Development Update*, March 2018, Part II, pp. 71-73.
2. *Economic Survey 2018-19, Vol. 2*, Ch. 6.
3. Ibid (1).

Managing Capital Flows

A major issue that most emerging market countries need to address is how to cope with a world of greater capital mobility. There is general agreement that the emergence of large pools of international capital, highly mobile across borders, provides an important opportunity for developing countries to access additional capital to finance their development in both the private and the public sectors. However, it is also true that free capital mobility brings with it the risk of volatility. This risk is particularly great for developing countries because investor perceptions of the prospects of individual developing countries are more vulnerable to contagion effects which could lead to volatility that is not justified by underlying fundamentals. Developing countries also face problems because they typically lack financial system strong enough to deal with inward and outward capital mobility.

The difficult choices facing developing countries are usually described in terms of a 'trilemma' or the 'impossible trinity' which asserts that in a world of internationally integrated capital market flows, a country cannot simultaneously achieve all three objectives of free capital mobility, a stable exchange rate and an independent monetary policy. It is possible to have an independent monetary policy (i.e., a target interest rate or money supply growth) and exchange rate stability, but in that case capital flows have to be controlled. Alternatively, if capital flows are completely free, it is necessary to give up either exchange rate stability or the ability to set monetary policy independently. In practice, few governments make firm choices for all times, and a mixed strategy is often adopted. The exchange rate is flexible but not fully flexible, capital flows are moderated in various ways or monetary policy is forced to adjust in various ways. All these choices involve costs. However, there is general agreement that it is undesirable to allow too large an appreciation in the exchange rate in response to capital inflows that may be temporary. Efforts to avoid appreciation by unsterilised intervention run the risk of increasing liquidity and money supply with a possible increase in inflationary pressure. On the other hand, resort to sterilised intervention imposes interest cost on the budget.

These problems illustrate the merit of the cautious approach adopted by the government in the matter of liberating capital inflows. The advantages of accessing pool of capital to finance development are recognised in the commitment to move gradually to fuller capital account convertibility. But the move is to be made gradually at a pace which enables the authorities to deal with unexpected volatility. In controlling capital flows, it is important to recognise the relative attractiveness of different types of flows. In this regard, FDI is the most preferred form of flow. Investments in Indian firms through the stock market and by venture capital funds in unlisted companies are also potentially beneficial. ECB and other short-term flows are areas where one can introduce an element of control to moderate sudden surges. However, even with capital calibration, it is not easy to manage a surge in capital inflows, if it occurs. In such situations, it is necessary to explore ways of limiting the fiscal cost of sterilising large growth of reserves, either by making these flows less attractive or by means that do not require costly sterilisation.

Rapid capital inflows have implications on the macroeconomic policy setting. Given the RBI's policy of intervening to dampen volatility and maintain orderly conditions in the foreign exchange market, the capital inflows have also reflected in the growth in NFA (net foreign exchange assets) of the RBI. As a part of its monetary management, RBI has been sterilising a part of the rupee funds consistent with its monetary policy stance. RBI's overall monetary policy stance factors in the objective of price stability, reducing inflationary expectations while remaining supportive of growth, ensuring regular flow of credit and maintaining orderly conditions in financial markets.

While India is a net importer of capital, capital inflows have been declining over the last few years. This is primarily driven by a decline in external borrowing and deposits by non-resident Indians. While loans and banking capital amounted to an average 1.05 and 1.02 percent of GDP between 2012-13 and 2014-15, net inflows from these sources declined to 0.02 and 0.11 percent of GDP a year in the last three fiscal years.[4]

Capital inflows, as percent of GDP, increased in the first half of 2017-18. Portfolio inflows and loans increased to an average of 1.2 and 0.3 percent of GDP in the first half of 2017-18, up from 0.3 and 0.08 percent in 2016-17, respectively. The share of FDI in GDP was comparable between 2016-17 and the first half of 2017-18, at approximately 1.6 percent of GDP. Banking capital recovered from previous year and averaged 0.5 percent of GDP in the first half of 2017-18.[5]

4. Ibid (1).
5. Ibid (1).

External Debt

Post 1991 BoP crisis, India's prudent external debt policies and management with a focus on sustainability, solvency, and liquidity have helped contain the increase in size of external debt to a moderate level and it is compositionally better with a longer term maturity profile.

Over the years, the composition of India's external debt stock has undergone structural transformation. The proportion of concessional debt in total external debt came down from an average of 42.9 per cent during 1991-2000 to 28.1 per cent in 2001-2010 and further to 12.4 per cent during 2011-2014. It stood at 8.7 per cent at end-September 2015 as compared to 8.8 per cent at end-March 2015. Non-government external debt has been predominant in total external debt and its proportion has been going up over the years. Non-government debt went up from 45.3 per cent of total external debt in the 1990s to 65.6 per cent in the decade of 2000s. In the last five years, it has been at an annual average of 79.0 per cent and at end-September 2015, it stood at 81.6 per cent. The main external debt indicators are given in Table 32.6.

India's total external debt stock at end-September 2017 was at US$ 495.7 billion, recording an increase of US$ 23.9 billion (5.1%) over its level at end-March 2017. Long-term external debt increased by 5.0 per cent to US$ 403.0 billion, while short-term debt registered a rise of 5.4 per cent to US$ 92.7 billion. The maturity profile of India's external debt continues to be dominated by long-term loans. Annex I and II present the disaggregated data on external debt outstanding in Indian rupee and US dollar terms respectively. The composition pattern of India's external debt at end-September 2017 compared to end-March 2017 shows slight increase in commercial borrowings (1.7 percentage points) with commensurate falls in other components mainly NRI deposits falling by 1.0 percentage point (Ministry of Finance, December 2017).

Currency Composition of External Debt

Regarding the currency composition of India's total external debt. US dollar denominated debt accounted for 50.0 per cent of India's total external debt at end-September 2017, followed by Indian rupee (35.7%), SDR (5.7%), Japanese Yen (4.4%), Euro (3.2%), Pound Sterling (0.6%) and others (0.4%)(ibid).

International Comparison

Cross-country comparison of external debt based on the World Bank's annual publication titled International Debt Statistics 2018, which contains the external debt data for the year 2016 indicates that India continues to be among the less vulnerable countries. India's key debt indicators compare well with other indebted developing countries. Among the top 20 developing debtor countries, India's external debt stock ratio to GNI (gross national income) at 20.4 per cent was the second lowest, just after China. In terms of the cover provided by foreign exchange reserves to external debt, India's position was fifth highest at 74.8 per cent and India's debt service ratio is eighth lowest.

TABLE – 22.2

India's Key External Debt Indicators

(%)

Year	*External Debt (US$ billion)*	*External Debt to GDP*	*Debt Service Ratio*	*Concessional Debt to Total Debt*	*Foreign Exchange Reserves to Total Debt*	*Short-term External Debt# to Foreign Exchange Reserves*	*Short-term External Debt# to Total Debt*
1	*2*	*3*	*4*	*5*	*6*	*7*	*8*
2007-08	224.4	18.0	4.8	19.7	138.0	14.8	20.4
2008-09	224.5	20.3	4.4	18.7	112.2	17.2	19.3
2009-10	260.9	18.2	5.8	16.8	106.9	18.8	20.1
2010-11	317.9	18.2	4.4	14.9	95.9	21.3	20.4
2011-12	360.8	21.1	6.0	13.3	81.6	26.6	21.7
2012-13	409.4	22.4	5.9	11.1	71.3	33.1	23.6
2013-14	446.2	23.9	5.9	10.4	68.2	30.1	20.5
2014-15	474.7	23.9	7.6	8.8	72.0	25.0	18.0
2015-16	485.1	23.5	8.8	9.0	74.3	23.1	17.2
2016-17PR	471.8	20.2	8.3	9.3	78.4	23.8	18.6
End-Sept 2017 QE	495.7	*	*	9.1	80.7	23.2	18.7

Note: PR: Partially Revised; QE: Quick Estimates. # Short Term External Debt is based on Original Maturity. Debt Service Ratio is the proportion of gross debt service payments to current account receipts (net of official transfers) *: Not worked out for part of the year

Source: *Economic Survey 2017-18.*

The Quarterly External Debt Statistics (QEDS) database, jointly developed by the World Bank and the IMF, brings together detailed external debt data of countries that are subscribing to IMF's Special Data Dissemination Standard/General Data Dissemination System. The position in respect of the highly indebted developing countries and subscribers to this arrangement for the first two quarters of the calendar year 2017, which has been published by the World Bank shows that though India is the third largest debtor country among developing countries, the share of short-term debt to total debt is only 18.6 per cent and 18.3 per cent in 2017-Q1 (end-March) and 2017-Q2 (end-June) respectively compared to China's 59.0 per cent and 60.1 per cent for these periods (Details in Annex VI). The top debtor nation in the world is the US. India is not among the top debtor countries of the world and is placed at 26th position at end-June 2017.

India's external debt has remained in safe limits as shown by the external debt to GDP ratio of 23.7 per cent and debt service ratio of 7.5 per cent in 2014-15. The prudent external debt policy of the Government of India has resulted in external debt remaining within safe and comfortable limits and in containing its rise. The external debt management policy followed by the Government of India continues to emphasise monitoring of long- and short-term debt, raising sovereign loans on concessional terms with long-term maturities, regulating ECBs through end-use and all-in-cost restrictions and rationalising interest rates on NRI deposits.

Foreign exchange cover to total external debt improved to 80.7 per cent at end-September 2017 as compared to 78.4 per cent at end-March 2017, with the ratio of short term debt by original maturity to foreign exchange reserves falling to 23.2 per cent at end-September 2017 from 23.8 per cent at end-March 2017.

International comparison of external debt situation based on World Bank data shows that among the top 20 developing debtor countries in 2016, India's external debt stock to Gross National Income (GNI) ratio at 20.4 percent was the second lowest after China's 12.8 per cent. In terms of the foreign exchange reserves cover to external debt, India's position is the fifth highest and India's debt service rate is the eight lowest. As per the World Bank data, though India is the third largest debtor country among developing countries (after China and Brazil), India's share of short term debt to total debt is only 18.6 percent and 18.3 per cent in 2017Q1 (end-March) and 2017 Q2(end-June) compared to China's 59.0 per cent and 60.1 per cent respectively. India is not among the top debtor countries in the world (including developed and developing) with 26th position at end-June 2017 (*Economic Survey 2017-18*, Vol. II).

TABLE – 22.3

International Comparison of Top 20 Developing Debtor Countries, 2016

Sl.	*Country*	*External Debt Stock to Gross National Income (%)*	*Debt Service Ratio (%)*	*Foreign Exchange Reserves to Total Debt (%)*	*Total External Debt Stock (US $ million)*
1	*2*	*3*	*4*	*5*	*6*
1	China	12.8	5.3	212.0	14,29,468
2	India	20.4	17.3	74.8	4,56,140
3	Philippines	21.1	12.6	95.0	77,319
4	Brazil	30.9	51.2	66.7	5,43,257
5	Thailand	31.4	5.0	136.8	1,21,497
6	Indonesia	35.1	39.6	35.9	3,16,431
7	Argentina	35.7	34.9	19.1	1,90,490
8	Peru	37.7	15.1	87.1	69,503
9	Mexico	40.7	19.4	41.1	4,22,657
10	Russian Federation	42.0	19.2	60.5	5,24,686
11	Colombia	43.3	28.9	38.2	1,20,282
12	Vietnam	45.6	3.9	42	86,953
13	Turkey	47.8	39.3	22.7	4,05,656
14	South Africa	50.9	13.2	29.1	1,46,040
15	Romania	52.9	23.3	37.7	95,888
16	Sri Lanka	59.0	17.9	11.1	46,608
17	Malaysia	69.6	4.9	46.5	2,00,364
18	Bulgaria	76.4	23.6	59.7	39,657
19	Ukraine	127.8	29.3	12.4	1,17,983
20	Kazakhstan	135.1	44.3	12.2	1,63,758

Note: *: Data pertains to 2016. Note: Countries are arranged based on ratio of external debt stock to GNI presented in column no.3 in the Table.

Source: World Bank, International Debt Statistics, 2018.

Foreign Exchange Reserves: Approach, Developments and Issues

The subject of foreign exchange reserves has received renewed interest in recent times in the context of increasing globalisation, acceleration of capital flows and integration of financial markets. The debt-banking-financial crises in several countries have also necessitated the need for an international financial architecture in which the management of foreign exchange reserves has emerged as one of the critical issues.

Contextually, the subject of foreign exchange reserves may be broadly classified into two interlinked areas, viz., the theory of reserves and the management of reserves. The theory of reserves encompasses issues relating to institutional and legal arrangements for holding reserve assets, conceptual and definitional aspects, objectives for holding reserve assets, exchange rate regimes and conceptualisation of the appropriate level of foreign reserves. In essence, a theoretical framework for reserves provides the rationale for holding foreign exchange reserves. Reserve management is mainly guided by the portfolio management consideration, i.e., how best to deploy foreign reserve assets subject to statutory stipulations? The portfolio considerations take into account, inter alia, safety, liquidity and yield on reserves as the principal objectives of reserve management. The institutional and legal arrangements are largely country specific and these differences should be recognised in approaching the critical issues relating to both reserve management practices and policymaking (Reddy, 2002).

The motives for holding reserves may be broadly classified under three categories, viz., transaction, speculative and precautionary. International trade gives rise to currency flows, which are assumed to be handled by banks driven by the transaction motive. Similarly, speculative motive is left to individuals or corporates. Central bank reserves, however, are characterised primarily as a last resort stock of foreign currency for unpredictable flows, which is consistent with precautionary motive for holding foreign assets. Precautionary motive for holding foreign currency, like the demand for money, can be positively related to wealth and the cost of covering unplanned deficit, and negatively related to the return from alternative assets. Furthermore, foreign exchange reserves are instruments to maintain or manage the exchange rate, while enabling orderly absorption of international capital flows. Official reserves are mainly held for precautionary and transaction motives keeping in view the aggregate of national interests, to achieve balance between demand for and supply of foreign currencies, for intervention, and to preserve confidence in the country's ability to carry out external transactions.

The objectives for maintaining reserves are:

1. maintaining confidence in monetary and exchange rate policies;
2. enhancing capacity to intervene in foreign exchange markets;
3. limiting external vulnerability by maintaining foreign currency liquidity to absorb shocks during times of crisis including national disasters or emergencies;
4. providing confidence to the markets, including credit rating agencies, that external obligations can always be met (thus reducing the overall costs at which foreign exchange resources are available to all the market participants); and
5. adding to the comfort of the market participants, by demonstrating the backing of domestic currency by external assets.

India's approach to reserve management, until the BoP crisis of 1991 was essentially based on the traditional approach, i.e., to maintain an appropriate level of import cover defined in terms of number of months of imports equivalent to reserves. For example, the import cover of reserves shrank to three weeks of imports by the end of December 1990, and the emphasis on import cover constituted the primary concern say, till 1993-94. The approach to reserve management, as part of exchange rate management, and indeed the overall external sector policy underwent a paradigm shift with the adoption of the recommendations of the High Level Committee on BoP, 1993 (Chairman: C. Rangarajan). The Committee had recommended that the foreign exchange reserve targets be fixed in such a way that they are generally in a position to accommodate imports of three months. In the view of the Committee, the factors that are to be taken into consideration in determining the desirable level of reserves are:

1. the need to ensure a reasonable level of confidence in the international financial and trading communities about the capacity of the country to honour its obligations and maintain trade and financial flows;

2. the need to take care of the seasonal factors in any BoP transaction with reference to the possible uncertainties in the monsoon conditions of India;
3. the amount of foreign currency reserves required to counter speculative tendencies or anticipatory actions amongst players in the foreign exchange market; and
4. the capacity to maintain the reserves so that the cost of carrying liquidity is minimal.

With the introduction of market determined exchange rate, a change in the approach to reserve management was warranted and the emphasis on import cover had to be supplemented with the objective of smoothening out the volatility in the exchange rate, which has been reflective of the underlying market condition. Against the backdrop of currency crises in East Asian countries and in the light of country experiences of volatile cross-border capital flows, there emerged a need to take into consideration a host of factors. The shift in the pattern of leads and lags in payments/receipts during exchange market uncertainties brought to the fore the fact that besides the size of reserves, the quality of reserves also assumes importance. Unencumbered reserve assets (defined as reserve assets net of encumbrances such as forward commitments, lines of credit to domestic entities, guarantees and other contingent liabilities) must be available at any point of time to the authorities for fulfilling various objectives assigned to reserves. As a part of prudent management of external liabilities, the policy is to keep forward liabilities at a relatively low level as a proportion of gross reserves.

With the changing profile of capital flows, the traditional approach to assessing reserve adequacy in terms of import cover has been broadened to include a number of parameters which take into account the size, composition and risk profiles of various types of capital flows as well as the types of external shocks to which the economy is vulnerable. A sufficiently high level of reserves is necessary to ensure that even if there is prolonged uncertainty, reserves can cover the liquidity at risk on all accounts over a fairly long period. Taking these considerations into account, India's foreign exchange reserves have reached a very comfortable level.

Developments

Beginning from a low level of US$5.8 billion at the end of March 1991, India's foreign exchange reserves gradually increased to US$38.0 billion by end March 2000, US$314.6 billion at end May 2008, before declining to US$252.0 billion at the end of March 2009. The decline in reserves in 2008-09 was inter alia a fallout of the global crisis and strengthening of the US dollar vis-à-vis other international currencies. During 2009-10, the level of foreign exchange reserves increased to US$279.1 billion at end March 2010, mainly on account of valuation gain as the US dollar depreciated against most of the major international currencies. In fiscal 2010-11, foreign exchange reserves have shown an increasing trend and reached US$ 304.2 billion. After falling to $294.4 in 2011-12 and $292.0 in 2012-13, the reserves again rose to 304.2 and end-September 2014 increased to 313.8 (Table 22.4).

TABLE – 22.4

Summary of Changes in Foreign Exchange Reserves

(US$ billion)

Sl. No.	*Year*	*Foreign Exchange Reserves at the End of Financial Year (end-March)*	*Total Increase(+)/ Decrease(-) in Reserves*	*Increase (+)/ Decrease (-) in Reserves on BoP Basis*	*Increase(+)/ decrease(-) in Reserves due to Valuation Effect*
1	*2*	*3*	*4*	*5*	*6*
1.	2006-07	199.2	47.6	36.6	11.0
2.	2007-08	309.7	110.5	92.2	18.3
3.	2008-09	252.0	-57.7	-20.1	-37.6
4.	2009-10	279.1	27.1	13.4	13.7
5.	2010-11	304.8	25.8	13.1	12.6
6.	2011-12	294.4	-10.4	-12.8	2.4
7.	2012-13	292.0	-2.4	3.8	-6.2
8.	2013-14	304.2	12.2	15.5	-3.3
9.	2014-15	341.6	37.4	61.4	-24.0
10.	2015-16	360.2	18.5	17.9	0.6
11.	2016-17	370.0	9.8	21.6	-11.8
12.	2017-18	424.5	54.6	43.6	11.0
a.	Apr.-Dec. 2017-18	409.1	39.1	30.3	8.8
b.	Apr.-Dec. 2018-19	395.6	-29.0	-17.5	-11.5

Source: *Economic Survey 2017-18*, Vol. II., *2018-19, Vol. 2.*

A summary of changes in the foreign exchange reserves since 2006-07, with a breakdown into increase/decrease on BoP basis and valuation effect, is presented in Table 22.4.

India continues to be one of the countries that have sizeable foreign exchange reserves particularly considering that some of the other major reserve holders are nations with large current account surpluses (Table 22.5). Intervention in the foreign exchange markets by the RBI so as to manage the exchange rate of the rupee and guard against volatility without targeting a specific rate is behind the accumulation of reserves generally; in the specific context of developments in 2013-14, the intervention was to provide a measure of comfort against the elevated levels of vulnerability indicators which are expressed as proportions of reserves.

TABLE – 22.5

Foreign Exchange Reserves of Some Major Countries

Sl. No.	*Country*	*Foreign Exchange Reserves at end Dec. 2014 (US$ billion)*
1.	China	3840.0#
2.	Japan	1312.1
3.	Switzerland*	526.6
4.	Russian Federation	388.5
5.	Brazil	363.6
6.	Korea, Republic of*	363.2
7.	China, P.R. Hong Kong*	344.6
8.	India	320.6
9.	Germany	192.7
10.	Thailand*	163.7
11.	France*	161.6
12.	Italy*	143.3

Note: * Latest data available for the month of November 2014 only. # www.pbc.gov.cn
Source: IMF Except China and India.
Economic Survey 2014-15.

Among the major economies with CAD, India is the second largest foreign exchange reserve holder after Brazil (Table 32.9). India's foreign exchange reserves at US$328.7 billion at end-January mainly comprised foreign currency assets amounting to US$303.3 billion, accounting for 92.3 per cent of the total.

India's foreign exchange reserves reached US$ 409.4 billion on end-December 2017. Foreign exchange reserves grew by 14.1 percent on a y-o-y basis from end-December 2016 (US$ 358.9 billion) to end-

December 2017 (US$ 409.4 billion) and it grew by 10.7 percent from end-March 2017 (US$ 370.0 billion) to end-December 2017. The import cover of India's foreign exchange reserves was 11.1 months at end-September 2017 as compared with 11.3 months at end-March 2017. Within the major economies running current account deficit, India is among the largest foreign exchange reserve holder and sixth largest among all countries of the world (*Economic Survey 2017-18*, Vol. II).

Foreign Exchange Rate Policy

The exchange rate policy is guided by the broad principle of careful monitoring and management of exchange rates with flexibility, while allowing the underlying demand and supply conditions to determine exchange rate movements over a period in an orderly manner. Subject to this predominant objective, RBI intervention in the foreign exchange market is guided by the objectives of reducing excess volatility, preventing the emergence of destabilising speculative activities, maintaining adequate level of reserves, and developing an orderly foreign exchange market.

There are two distinct phases in the exchange rate of the rupee. The rupee continued exhibiting a two-way movement with an appreciating trend till about July 2011, after which the trend reversed and it started declining sharply from September 2011 onwards, due to factors relating to the uncertain global economy.

The sharp fall in value of rupee can be explained by the supply-demand imbalance in the domestic foreign exchange market on account of slowdown in FII inflows, strengthening of US dollar in the international market due to the safe haven status of US Treasuries and heightened risk aversion and deleveraging due to the Euro area crisis that impacted financial markets across emerging market economies. Apart from the global factors, there were several domestic factors that have added to the weakening trend of the rupee, which include increasing CAD and high inflation. In order to reduce the volatility of exchange rate value of the rupee, the RBI intervened in the foreign exchange market through sale of US dollars amounting to US$20.1 billion in 2011-12. Further, in view of the sharp depreciation of the rupee in 2011-12, the RBI announced various policy measures that were aimed at curbing speculative behaviour of banks and corporate in the foreign exchange market.

The vulnerability of the rupee as well as the currencies of other emerging market and developing economies came to the fore in May

2013 as a result of the announcement by US Fed about tapering of its asset purchases. While capital flows on a net basis continued to be broadly adequate at that time, the rupee depreciated sharply on the vulnerability concerns affecting expectations on the rupee emanating from the confluence of factors of elevated CAD and large withdrawal from the FII debt segment. However, the rupee became resilient when the US Fed taper actually happened subsequently (*Economic Survey 2013-14*).

Exchange Rate

The average annual exchange rate of the rupee depreciated sharply from `54.4 per US dollar in 2012-13 to `60.5 in 2013- 14 and was broadly stable at `61.1 per US dollar in 2014-15. The rupee had depreciated to its lowest level of `68.4 per US dollar on 28 August 2013. In 2014-15, although the rupee declined in value against the dollar by 1.0 per cent, it became stronger against other currencies. It appreciated, for example, against the Japanese yen and the euro by 8.2 per cent and 4.7 per cent respectively.

During 2015-16 (April-January), the average exchange rate of the rupee depreciated to `65.04 per US dollar as compared to `60.92 per US dollar in 2014-15 (April-January). The Indian rupee depreciated against the dollar as the dollar strengthened against all the major currencies owing to stronger growth in the US and also because China's growth and currency developments this year deteriorated, impacting the outlook on other EMDE owing to risk aversion perceptions of global investors. The rupee witnessed bouts of volatility, taking cues from a combination of domestic and global developments which included contraction in exports; portfolio outflows on concerns about outlook and other concerns; and the gradual process of normalisation of monetary policy in the US and global bond market sell-off. The rupee remained in a narrow range of `62.16 to R64.17 per US dollar till early August 2015. However, it came under pressure, breaching the level of R65 per US dollar by mid-August to rise above R66 per US dollar by end-August, triggered by devaluation of the Chinese RMB on 11 August and the Chinese stock-market meltdown on 24 August. The rupee stabilized in September 2015 and traded in a narrow range but again depreciated in October to December 2015. In fact, the rupee slumped to as low as `68.44 per dollar on 12 February 2016, its lowest since end-August 2013. Thus, during 2015-16, the general tendency of appreciation of the US dollar against major currencies and uncertainty and volatility in the international financial market resulted in depreciation of the rupee-dollar exchange rate. However, the rupee appreciated against the euro and the pound sterling from September 2015 onwards. It is also instructive to note that in 2015-16 so far, the rupee has performed better than the currencies of most of the other emerging market economies (except the Chinese yuan) (*Economic Survey 2015-16*).

The REER (real effective exchange rate) is an important indicator of export competitiveness as it takes into account the level of inflation differences across countries apart from the basket of nominal exchange rates of partners.

During 2015-16 (April-January), NEER (Trade weighted—36 currencies) and REER (Trade weighted—36 currencies) appreciated by 1.7 per cent and 3.7 per cent respectively over 2014-15 (April-January). The rupee in real effective terms appreciated continuously from the early 2014 onwards and the movement in nominal effective terms does not exhibit any noticeable upward or downward pattern. REER is also a common measure of the alignment of a currency to its true value which is usually indicated by excess or shortfall by +/- 5 per cent of base year level of the index (Box 22.1).

BOX – 22.1

Impact of Exchange Rate Volatility on some Select Sectors

Empirical evidence on the effects of the exchange rate and exchange rate volatility on trade in India from some recent research studies is at best ambiguous. In fact, research results which find positive, negative or no effect of exchange rate volatility on the volume of international trade are based on varied underlying assumptions and only hold in certain cases.

However, there is some evidence that volatility in exchange rate has impact on different sectors and firms at different levels. Dhasmana (2013) used the industry-specific real exchange indices to study the impact of real exchange rate changes on the performance of Indian manufacturing firms from 2000 to 2012. The main findings of the study are that real exchange rate changes affect firm-level performance through the import cost channel but not the export competitiveness channel in the short run. The fact that the import cost channel is dominant in the short run indicates that episodes of real depreciation are likely to result in a contraction in real output growth at least in the

contd...

...contd...

short run. This study also calculated the elasticity of output growth with respect to real exchange rate for different industries. A positive sign of elasticity of output indicates a decrease in output growth in response to a real depreciation on account of increased cost of imported inputs. The study observed that the chemicals industry has the highest elasticity of output growth with respect to real exchange rate (a 1% real depreciation causing output growth to decline by 12.5 basis points for an average firm) while the footwear industry has the smallest elasticity (0.38). The elasticity of output of some other sectors as per the study were: rubber (9.8), textile (4.8), plastic (5.4), and metal and metal products (5.1).

Movement in exchange rate has different impact on different sectors. High-import-intensity sectors like petroleum products (86.2% imported raw materials consumed), and chemical and chemical products (77.4%) are more impacted by rupee depreciation as a weaker rupee increases the value of imported inputs. Low-importintensity sectors remain in an advantageous position especially in price-sensitive international markets.

An RBI working paper (2014) titled 'Impact of Real Exchange Rate Volatility on Use-Based Industrial Production in India' found that components of the IIP (index of industrial production) like the capital goods, basic goods, and intermediate goods sectors are adversely affected by significant movements in the 36 country REER. The impact of real exchange rate volatility on the basic goods sector is small. Moreover, the consumer goods sector, with items such as passenger cars, apparel, antibiotics and sugar having large weights in the group, is also not much affected by REER volatility due to low import content and production supported by sufficiency of domestic demand. On the other hand, capital goods are dependent on imports and therefore are more impacted by unexpected changes in both exchange rate and relative prices. Thus, periodic review of the 'neutral' (or equilibrium) REER is an imperative.

References

Dhasmana, Anubha (2013). "Transmission of Real Exchange Rate Changes to the Manufacturing Sector Performance", Working Paper No. 435, IIMB.

RBI Working Paper series no WPS (DEPR) 05/2014, "Impact of Real Exchange Rate Volatility on Use-Based Industrial Production in India".

Source: *Economic Survey 2015-16*, Vol. II.

During 2017-18 (up to December 2017), the rupee generally traded with an appreciating bias against the US dollar, barring intermittent depreciation in September and October 2017. The rupee strengthened by 2.5 per cent to a level of `64.24 per US dollar during December, 2017 from the level of `65.88 per US dollar during March 2017 on the back of significant capital flows, both foreign portfolio flows and FDI. Improved macroeconomic conditions coupled with reforms initiated by the Government were mainly responsible for the buoyant capital flows. The rupee was one of the least volatile EM currencies during April-December 2017 and traded in the range of 63.63 to 65.76 per US dollar.

On an average, the rupee has appreciated so far against most other major currencies besides the US dollar (April–December, 2017). The rupee appreciated by about 6.0 per cent against the pound sterling, 0.2 percent against the Euro and 9.2 per cent against the Japanese Yen during the period April-December, 2017 over the same period of the last fiscal year (*Economic Survey 2017-18*, Vol.II).

Global Economic Developments and their Implications for India[6]

India has been integrating with the rest of the world. India being a large emerging market, and in the same asset class as the other large emerging markets, its capital inflows, exchange rate, and asset prices co-move strongly with other emerging markets; and are impacted by economic developments and monetary policy of advanced economies and by global liquidity conditions.

This global integration presents both opportunities and challenges for India. Global growth is poised to accelerate. Global growth has recovered in 2017, against the backdrop of benign financing conditions and improving confidence. Growth is estimated to have reached 3.0 percent in 2017 from 2.4 percent last year; and is forecast to continue to grow at an average rate of 3.0 percent between 2018-20. Growth is estimated to have picked up in more than half of the world's economies, resulting in a broad-based global upturn and providing supportive external conditions for India. Advanced economies gained momentum in 2017, with growth estimated to have rebounded to 2.3 percent in 2017. Growth among emerging market and developing economies (EMDEs) has also accelerated in 2017. EMDE growth is projected to

6. This section draws on staff's own research as well as on the World Bank's Global Economic Prospect (January 2018 and previous issues), India Development Update, March 2018.

strengthen to 4.5 percent in 2018 and to an average of 4.7 percent in 2019-20, reflecting improved global manufacturing activity, robust global trade, broadly favorable financing conditions, and firming commodity prices.

The steady integration of the Indian economy with the global economy is reflected in the high and increasing correlation between Indian GDP growth and the world GDP growth. In view of this high correlation, the positive outlook for the global economy bodes well for India's own growth prospects in coming years (World Bank, 2018).

Concluding Remarks

The Indian economy is exposed to global developments by virtue of being a large emerging market. Improving global growth and trade outlook presents an opportunity that India should brace itself to leverage. Increasing oil prices could impact the current account deficit and inflation but the price is projected to stay range bound by the World Bank. Changing financial conditions currently presents the biggest external challenge. Financial integration impacts emerging markets on both sides of the cycle. When financial conditions are benign, easy flows of short term capital results in exchange rate appreciation and asset price inflation that the policy makers find difficult to cope with. When financial conditions tighten, it causes financial volatility and disruption. While international financial integration is considered a mixed blessing, these issues warrant a renewed debate in India, and possibly in other emerging market countries, on the optimal level of integration.

With the gradual external liberalisation of Indian economy, not only the size of BoP has increased manifold, but the pattern of current and capital account has changed. Even though the reform process has strengthened resilience of India's external sector, at the same time vulnerabilities arise with greater exposure of the economy to the rest of world through liberalised trade and investment environment.

Quoting Rangarajan (2018)[7], "the world is entering a new phase as far as trade is concerned. Seventy years ago, it was the developed countries that were preaching the virtues of globalisation and free trade. The developing countries were then expressing concerns about total free

7. Rangarajan, C. (2018). "Some Issues in External Sector Management", chapter 33 in Uma Kapila (2018), *Indian Economy Since Independence*, 29th edition, New Delhi: Academic Foundation.

trade. Now the tables have been turned. It is the developed countries that are turning against free trade and are moving towards protectionism. This has come certainly at a wrong time for India. It is only now that India is fully ready to be integrated with the rest of the world, even though India still has certain concerns".

23

India and the WTO

World Trade Organization

The World Trade Organization (WTO) is an international organisation that oversees the operation of the rules-based multilateral trading system. The WTO is based on a series of trade agreements negotiated during the Uruguay Round (UR) (1986-1994), the eighth and final trade round conducted under the General Agreement on Tariffs and Trade (GATT). The Treaty of Marrakesh established the WTO at the close of the Uruguay Round in 1994. The WTO began operations on 1 January 1995, it was comprised of 148 members. The WTO is one of the big three international organisations that oversee economic relations among nations, joining the International Monetary Fund (IMF) and the World Bank.

The WTO's main function is to monitor and enforce trade rules in the global economy. The WTO administers the complex trade agreements listed in the WTO agreement. Article 1 of the WTO agreement, the General Agreement on Tariffs and Trade, deals with rules of merchandise trade. The General Agreement on Tariffs and Trade in Article 1 is often called GATT 1994 to distinguish it from the original GATT agreement of 1947. Article 2, the General Agreement on Trade in Services (GATS), pertains to the trade of commercial services. Article 4, the Agreement on Trade-related Aspect of Intellectual Property (TRIPS), provides uniform legal protections for scientific, technological and artistic achievements. In addition, the WTO is a forum for trade negotiations, a dispute settlement mechanism, a source of technical expertise on trade and development for the world's poorer countries, and a sister organisation to the World Bank and IMF. Unlike the World Bank and IMF, the WTO does not make loans to countries.

The WTO inherited many of GATT's guiding principles. These fundamental principles are incorporated in the numerous agreements that comprise the Agreement Establishing the World Trade Organization. In its *Understanding the WTO* (2003), the WTO identified five core principles.

The first principle is 'trade without discrimination,' which involves most-favoured-nation (MFN) status and national treatment. MFN states that a trade concession granted to one WTO member automatically applies to all members. National treatment guarantees equal treatment of imported goods with domestically produced output in nations' markets.

The second principle is freer trade through the progressive liberalisation of trade regimes.

The third principle is the predictability of trade rules. Predictability, in this context, prevents governments from arbitrarily raising existing tariffs or non-tariff trade barriers.

The fourth principle is fair competition. Fair competition attempts to level the playing field in international trade and minimise the market distortions caused by export subsidy, dumping and other disruptive trade practices.

The fifth principle is economic development through trade. Economic development for the world's poorer countries should be enhanced by trade assistance and increased market access through preferential trade arrangements.

The WTO's dispute settlement process is the enforcement arm of the organisation. The WTO's apparatus for dispute settlement is stronger and more defined than GATT's dispute settlement procedures. The WTO's dispute settlement process is the essence of multilateralism. That is, a country or group of countries can air trade grievances in a global forum. A trade complaint is made to the WTO's Dispute Settlement Body (DSB), which consists of the entire WTO membership. The DSB, in turn, establishes a panel of three to five experts to hear the evidence and render a ruling. The panel's ruling can only be reversed by a unanimous vote of the DSB. Under normal conditions, the entire process takes one year or less to complete. One or both sides in the dispute can appeal the panel's decision. A seven-member Appellate Body considers an appeal and renders a decision. Again, only a unanimous vote of the DSB can reverse the Appellate Body's ruling. The appellate process could add as much as three months to the dispute settlement process. A member country found guilty breaking WTO trade rules is required to correct the violation with due speed. The DSB is empowered to initiate retaliatory tariffs or other trade sanctions for non-compliance with a WTO ruling.

Over the past 20 years, the world has experienced a significant economic and geopolitical shift. Developing countries' participation in international trade has risen considerably faster than world trade. WTO figures for 2011 show that their share of trade rose to 47 per cent on the export side and 42 per cent on the import side, the highest levels ever recorded since 1948. This growing share of trade is led by emerging countries such as India, China, Brazil, Malaysia or Mexico, all of which have become drivers of economic growth and are now asserting their role in global governance. These countries have made the most of their trade opening opportunities, and their vibrant economies make them increasingly attractive markets for trade and investment. They are also proving relatively resilient to external shocks.

Emerging economies' dynamism and the level of competitiveness they have achieved require the definition of a new equilibrium in international trade relations. According to Lamy (2013),[1] the gap between developed and emerging economies narrows, it requires a new balance of rights and obligations, of contributions between countries at different levels of development. Developed countries are growing more reluctant to make concessions to emerging economies that are in direct competition with them. On the other hand, developing countries are reluctant to accept much higher levels of commitments while they still face development challenges. This dichotomy is proving a hard challenge for the trading system and is stalling progress in multilateral negotiations, much as it is stalling progress in climate change or on the quota and voice within the International Monetary Fund (IMF).

Another challenge for the multilateral trading system in the 21st century is the rise of preferential trade arrangements (PTAs). The stalling of the Doha Development Round and the uncertainty it brings about has led countries to seek trade openings bilaterally or regionally. As of January 2012, over 500 regional trade agreements had been notified to the WTO, of which more than 300 are currently in force. The proliferation of PTAs demonstrates an appetite for trade opening and can be a blessing for the multilateral trading system as they can be the forerunners of further opening at the multilateral level. However, as their number increases, the risk also grows that members of different

1. Lamy, Pascal (2013). "WTO: Building a Global Trading System for the 21st Century", in Nitin Desai and Rajiv D. Mathur (eds.), Growth and Equity: Essays in Honour of Pradeep Mehta. New Delhi: Academic Foundation. pp.57-63..

trade agreements would implement increasingly divergent regulatory systems. As the global economy becomes more integrated, regulatory divergence poses further obstacles for businesses that seek more coherent and predictable rules that can only be achieved multilaterally.[2]

In addition to structural changes in trade dynamics, new emerging issues—often dubbed as '21st century issues'—are changing the perception of international trade. As the reality of trade is decoupling from the mere consideration of exchanges in goods and services, its linkages to other areas of international cooperation are becoming more evident. Some of the issues that the WTO is being called to look upon include the relationship between trade and climate change, exchange rate policies, food security, energy policies, competition and investment.[3]

Although some of these issues are not entirely new, their implications for the multilateral trading system are taking new forms as more challenging and complex links emerge. In this context, some observers are wondering whether the WTO should not step up its engagement in the debate about the future structure of global governance. Indeed, the organisation has achieved considerable progress since its establishment. The interest shown by acceding countries in joining the organisation speaks volumes about the value of its rules and agreements. With Russia becoming a WTO member, about 97 per cent of world trade will be under the aegis of the WTO, making it even more attractive to the present and prospective members. Even as the mere repository of trade rules, the WTO will continue to play a role in global governance, but its relevance would be greatly diminished if it fails to keep up with this changing trade environment.[4]

A successful conclusion of the Doha Development Round would certainly be the best overhaul for the multilateral trading system. The issues contained in the negotiating agenda, including disciplines for trade-distorting agriculture subsidies, elimination of export subsidies, reduction of industrial tariff peaks, efficient customs procedures, further opening in services and deeper integration of least-developed countries in the trading system, are as relevant today as they were 10 years ago. These issues need to be resolved. However, currently the Doha Round is at an impasse. At the Eighth WTO Ministerial Conference in

2. Debroy, Bibek and Debashis Chakraborty (2006). The Trade Game: Negotiation Trends at WTO and Concerns of Developing Countries. New Delhi: Academic Foundation.
3. Ibid.
4. Ibid.

December 2011, WTO members recognised the need to strengthen the WTO and to look at innovative ways of solving the negotiating impasse without striding away from the original Doha mandate. Amongst the suggested approaches, there have been calls for a pragmatic, step-by-step approach that would deliver small but steady results, thus reinstating confidence in the multilateral trading system.[5]

The WTO should also continue to press for building trade capacity in developing and least developed countries through ‘Aid for Trade,’ which in reality should be renamed ‘Investment for Trade.’ For many countries, the trade opportunities that the WTO offers can only be transformed into realities if an investment is made through development assistance, to build trade capacity at home.

Further, Lamy[6] remarks, inaction is not an option. For the WTO to remain relevant in the new century, it needs to keep advancing. The world of the 21st century needs a global trading system that is relevant, dynamic and comprehensive; a system that is responsive to the needs of its members and to the expectations of the world citizens that it serves; a system that contributes to development, poverty alleviation and growth through enhanced economic opportunities, a system for the 21st century that is able to lead the world out of the stalemate that it is in and reinject trust and confidence in international cooperation. Even in the 21st century, the WTO needs to be able to make a difference in the world economy for the benefit of all, especially for the poorest amongst us. “The difference between rich and poor is not wealth, but opportunity,” says Nobel Laureate Prof Muhammad Yunus. By equipping the WTO with a 21st century software, the organisation will continue to contribute to global prosperity by ensuring that the new opportunities created by a changing global context are available to all.

India and the WTO

India was one of the 23 founding Contracting Parties to the GATT that was concluded in October 1947. India has often led groups of less developed countries in subsequent rounds of multilateral trade negotiations (MTNs) under the auspices of the GATT.

Despite being a founder member of GATT, India was never very active in various negotiating rounds until late 1980s. Since the Indian economy followed the import-substitution led growth strategy during

5. Ibid.
6. op.cit.

1960s and 1970s, gaining from the import liberalisation at principal export markets (the EU and US) was never a prime objective. In addition, a considerable proportion of India's trade was directed to the Soviet bloc countries, and the presence of this assured market weakened the incentive to search for newer outlets. On the other hand, opening the domestic market to foreign competition through progressive tariff cuts was perceived harmful for the local industries. Instead, the country was more willing to discuss trade- and development-related issues at UNCTAD forums in collaboration with other developing countries like Brazil (primarily through the G-77 network). Despite adoption of a proactive approach at WTO, India still feels comfortable to discuss trade-related issues at UNCTAD forums for coalition building among developing countries on areas pertaining to mutual interest.

India's Participation in WTO Meetings

Table 23.1 illustrates India's participation in WTO meetings.[7]

During the Seattle-Doha period, India, for the first time, started communicating its dissatisfaction over several issues and sharing its position with other countries at various appropriate forums of WTO and other international bodies. Broadly speaking, a clearly distinguishable and proactive stand emerged before the Doha ministerial, and India became particularly concerned with: (i) non-realisation of anticipated benefits (e.g., Agreement on Textiles and Clothing and Agreement on Agriculture), (ii) inequities and imbalances in WTO [Trade-related Aspects of Intellectual Property Rights (TRIPSs), subsidies, anti-dumping, etc.], and (iii) non-binding nature of special and differential provisions (market access, DSB, etc.). In short, India strongly objected to the inclusion of any new issue in the negotiating agenda before realisation of UR promises, the non-implementation of which was costly to developing countries.

Buoyed by the success achieved at Doha, India tried to utilise the two-year period before Cancun in a much productive manner and coalition-formation experience with other developing countries were fruitful not only for general agreements that affected merchandise and services trade, but also in case of institutional arrangements like dispute settlement. The movement towards a proactive strategy at the WTO was

7. Sengupta, Dipankar, Debashis Chakraborty and Pritam Banerjee (eds.) (2006). "India at the WTO: The Story so Far", in Beyond the Transition Phase of WTO: An Indian Perspective on Emerging Issues. Academic Foundation in association with Centre de Sciences Humaines, New Delhi.

TABLE – 23.1

India at the WTO Meetings

No. of Ministerial	*Place of Occurrence*	*Year*	*Outcome*	*India's Role*
1.	Singapore	1996	Information Technology Agreement was signed. In addition, four new issues were discussed, Trade and Investment, Competition Policy, Transparency in Government Procurement, and Trade Facilitation.	Mere presence.
2.	Geneva	1998	Global E-commerce Agreement was signed. Also, the implementation issues were discussed.	Mere presence.
3.	Seattle	1999	The negotiations failed as several developed countries wanted to incorporate environmental and labour-standard related issues under the wings of WTO. The move was strongly opposed by developing countries.	Was vocal against introduction of environmental and labour-standard issue under WTO.
4.	Doha	2001	A new round was launched and the concerns for developing countries like India (e.g., TRIPS and Public Health) were attended. The market access and implementation issues were also given due notice.	Mostly singled out in its protest. However, made its presence and position felt for the first time.
5.	Cancun	2003	The members could not arrive at a common view point even on the last date of the conference. The ministerial decided to take stock of progress in negotiations and other work under the Doha Development Agenda. The developing country solidarity at the ministerial was formed for the first time.	Actively protested against EU-US draft on agriculture jointly with other developing countries.
6.	Geneva	2004	Five member countries came forward to create an atmosphere for initiating multilateral negotiations once again.	Played a constructive role in the process while protecting countries' interests

Source: Compiled from WTO Ministerial Declarations and other documents.

accompanied towards implementing an increasingly WTO compatible regime at home and frustration mounted at not obtaining the desired level of market access in principal export destinations. In Cancun, India principally negotiated over liberalisation of agricultural trade and trade in services.

In addition, the intensity of proactive approach was further noticed in the sharp increase in the number of joint submissions at WTO, ranging from agriculture to services. Interestingly, the Indian submissions to WTO, both joint and individual, stressed both export promotion (enhancement of market access) and domestic protection (e.g., provision of special products, special safeguard mechanism in agriculture) much vigorously. On the other hand, domestic reforms have been regularly undertaken in order to enhance compliance with WTO.

WTO Negotiations and India

The Doha Round of trade negotiations at the WTO has been under way since 2001. The negotiations cover several areas such as agriculture, market access for non-agricultural products, trade-related intellectual property (IP) rights, rules (covering anti-dumping and subsidies) and trade facilitation. The conduct, conclusion and entry into force of the outcome of the negotiations are parts of a single undertaking, that is 'nothing is agreed until everything is agreed.'

While the years 2007 and 2008 saw intensive discussions in the WTO and progress achieved on several complex subjects, the negotiations were slow to resume following the December 2008 break at the WTO.

The Doha Round of trade negotiations in the WTO effectively made very little progress after 2008. Throughout 2009 and 2010, discussions continued but no headway was made on any substantive issue in the negotiations. (A summary of India's stand on key negotiating issues is given in Box 23.1.) However, the subject featured on the agenda of almost every major international meeting and there were strong affirmations of political support for an early conclusion of the Doha Round. Discussions continued in Geneva during March and April 2011, in a variety of formats. Reports on each area of the negotiations were issued on 21 April 2011. These documents provided an overview of the status of negotiations in each area covered in the Doha Development Agenda. While they indicated significant progress in many areas, they also captured the wide gaps remaining on many issues.

In October-November 2011, concerted efforts were made by some of the developed country members of the WTO to use the G20 Leaders Summit in November 2011 to advance an agenda for the Eighth WTO Ministerial Conference scheduled to be held in Geneva in December 2011. Specifically, they wanted to set the stage for plurilateral agreements on selected issues in the WTO negotiations (rather than multilateral agreements); get WTO members to agree to a commitment abjuring the use of export restrictions; and introduce new issues for negotiation, namely climate change, energy security and food security. The weeks preceding the Eighth WTO Ministerial Conference saw hectic activity in the WTO as some members attempted to put various issues on the agenda for ministerial decision. These proposals, however, did not receive support amongst WTO members. At the Eighth Ministerial Conference from 15 to 17 December, ministers adopted a number of decisions on IP, electronic commerce, small economies, least developed countries' (LDCs') accession, a services waiver for LDCs, and trade policy reviews. A number of members expressed strong reservations about plurilateral approaches. Many members stressed that any different approaches in the work ahead should conform to the Doha mandate, respect the single undertaking, and be truly multilateral, transparent and inclusive. In looking at future work, a large number of ministers stressed the centrality of development. Many underlined the need to give priority to issues of interest to LDCs, including cotton. Many mentioned the importance of all three pillars in the agriculture negotiations. Many also mentioned trade facilitation, special and differential (S&D) treatment, S&D monitoring mechanism and NTMs. In an unprecedented display of unity, a coalition of more than a hundred developing countries, including India, Brazil, China and South Africa, met on the sidelines of the conference and issued a declaration emphasising the development agenda. They roundly criticised suggestions for plurilateral agreements to replace decision making by multilateral consensus.

In order to promote transparency and provide better understanding of the trade policies and practices of its members, the WTO has a mechanism for regular review of their trade policies. Depending upon its share in world trade, each member's trade policy is reviewed by the WTO at fixed periodic intervals. India's TPR is carried out every four years. The TPR offers an opportunity to other WTO members to ask questions and raise concerns on different aspects of policies and practices of the country under review. The Fifth TPR of India was held on 14 and 16 September 2011 in the WTO. Before the meeting, the

BOX – 23.1

India's Stand on Key Negotiating Issues: A Summary

Agriculture

- Substantial and effective reductions in overall trade-distorting domestic support (OTDS) of the US and EU;
- Self-designation of an appropriate number of special products (SPs);
- An operational and effective Special Safeguard Mechanism (SSM);
- Simplification and capping of developed country tariffs.

Non-Agricultural Market Access (NAMA)

- Adequate and appropriate flexibilities for protecting economically vulnerable industries;
- Participation in sectoral initiatives only on a non-mandatory and good faith basis without prejudgment of the final outcome, with substantial special and differential treatment provisions for developing countries;
- Serious consideration of non-tariff barrier (NTB) textual proposals with wide support such as the horizontal mechanism.

Services

- Need for qualitative improvement in the revised offers especially on Modes 1 (cross-border supply) and 4 (movement of natural persons);
- Appropriate disciplining of domestic regulations by developed countries.

Rules

- Tightening of disciplines on anti-dumping (deletion of zeroing clause and reiteration of the lesser duty rule)
- Effective special and differential treatment for developing countries on fisheries subsidies.

Trade-related Aspects of Intellectual Property Rights (TRIPS)

- Establishing a clear linkage between the TRIPS Agreement and the Convention on Bio-diversity (CBD) by incorporating specific disclosure norms for patent applications;
- Enhanced protection for geographical indications (GIs) other than wines and spirits.

Source: *Economic Survey 2011-12.*

WTO Secretariat circulated a compilation of India's written replies to 886 advance questions raised by 26 WTO members. During the review, most of the members commended the resilience of the Indian economy that smoothly withstood the adverse effects of global financial crisis without taking recourse to protectionist measures. Members appreciated India for using its trade policy to promote sustainable development and inclusive growth. Members also noted India's positive engagement in Doha Round negotiations. Some of the members, notably the US, raised concerns in certain areas, namely tariffs and duties, licensing and restrictions, trade defence measures (anti-dumping), SPS and technical barriers to trade (TBT), government procurement, incentive schemes to promote investments and exports and protect agriculture, tariff protection on agriculture, services and investments. Responses to the issues raised were provided in India's Closing Statement on 16 September 2011.

The Ninth Ministerial Conference of the WTO held in Bali, Indonesia, from 3 to 7 December 2013 strengthened the credibility of the WTO as an institution. The outcome ensured that the development dimension remains the central focus in the Doha Round. It reaffirmed India's leadership role amongst the developing countries and demonstrated its constructive approach in negotiations. India played a key role in arriving at a breakthrough and shaping the agreement. India ensured an outcome which secures its supreme national interests. It was made amply clear that while being fully prepared to engage, India will never compromise on fundamental issues pertaining to food security, livelihood security, and the welfare of its poor (Box 23.2).

The Tenth Ministerial Conference of the WTO was held in Nairobi, Kenya during 15-19 December 2015. This was the first such meeting to be hosted by an African nation. The outcomes of the Conference, referred to as the 'Nairobi Package' include Ministerial Decisions on agriculture, cotton and issues related to least developed countries (LDCs). These cover public stockholding for food security purposes, a Special Safeguard Mechanism (SSM) for developing countries, a commitment to abolish export subsidies for farm exports particularly from the developed countries and measures related to cotton. Decisions were also made regarding preferential treatment to LDCs in the area of services and the criteria for determining whether exports from LDCs may benefit from trade preferences.

The divergence in viewpoints as regards the fate of the Doha Round continued during the Conference. The Nairobi Ministerial Declaration reflects divergence amongst the WTO membership on the relevance of reaffirming the Doha Development Agenda (DDA) as the basis of future negotiations. This was despite the fact that India, along with many other developing countries, from groups such as the G-33, LDCs, and the Africa Group, wanted a reaffirmation of the mandate of the Doha Round. India pointed this out in a written submission to the Director General, WTO and the Chair of the Tenth Ministerial Conference, the Kenyan foreign minister as well as in a statement at the closing ceremony on 19 December 2015. While reflecting that there are divergences, the Ministerial Declaration also notes the "strong commitment of all Members to advance negotiations on the remaining Doha issues." It records that WTO work would maintain development at its centre. It also reaffirms that provisions for special and differential treatment shall remain integral (*Economic Survey 2015-16*).

As regards the introduction of other new issues for discussion, the Declaration acknowledges the differences in views and states that any decision to launch negotiations multilaterally on such issues would need to be agreed by all Members. As the future of the Doha Round appeared in doubt, India sought and succeeded in obtaining a reaffirmative Ministerial Decision on Public Stockholding for Food Security Purposes honouring both the Bali Ministerial and General Council Decisions. The decision commits members to engage constructively in finding a permanent solution to this issue. Similarly, a large group of developing countries has long been seeking a SSM for agricultural products. In order to ensure that this issue remains on the agenda of future discussion in the WTO, India negotiated a Ministerial Decision which recognizes that developing countries will have the right to have recourse to an SSM as envisaged in the mandate. Members will continue to negotiate the mechanism in dedicated sessions of the Committee on Agriculture in Special Session. The WTO General Council has been mandated to regularly review progress of these negotiations.

WTO Members also agreed to the elimination of agricultural export subsidies subject to the preservation of special and differential treatment for developing countries such as a longer phase-out period for transportation and marketing export subsidies for exporting agricultural products. Developed countries have committed to removing export subsidies immediately, except for a few agricultural products, and developing countries will do so by 2018. Developing countries will keep the flexibility to cover marketing and transport subsidies for agriculture exports until the end of 2023, and the LDCs and net food-importing developing countries would have additional time to cut such export subsidies. The Ministerial Decision contains disciplines to ensure that other export policies are not used as a disguised form of subsidies. These disciplines include terms to limit the benefits of financing support to agriculture exporters, rules on state enterprises engaging in agriculture trade, and disciplines to ensure that food aid does not negatively affect domestic production. Developing countries, such as India, will have a longer implementation period. One of the Decisions adopted extends the relevant provision to prevent 'evergreening' of patents in the pharmaceuticals sector. This decision would help in maintaining an affordable and accessible supply of generic medicines. India supported outcomes on issues of interest to LDCs including enhanced preferential rules of origin for LDCs and preferential treatment for LDC serviccs providers. India already offers duty-free, quota-free access scheme to all LDCs, which provides a comprehensive coverage with simple, transparent and liberal rules of origin. India has also recently made available substantial and commercially meaningful preferences in services to LDCs.

Another area under negotiation in Nairobi dealt with the rules on fisheries subsidies. Several countries, such as China, Egypt, South Africa, Korea and Saudi Arabia, were opposed to disciplining rules on fisheries subsidies due to the lack of clarity. The overwhelming opposition to this item on the agenda was in tune with India's position. There was no outcome in this area of the negotiations. On the issue of rules on Anti-dumping, India strongly opposed a proposal that would give greater power to the WTO's Anti-Dumping Committee to review Members' practices. There was no convergence in this area and, hence, no outcome was achieved. At the Ministerial Conference, a group of 53 WTO members, including both developed and developing countries, agreed on the timetable for implementing a deal to eliminate tariffs on 201 Information Technology products. Duty-free market access to the markets of the members eliminating tariffs on these products will be available to all WTO members. Though not a party to the Agreement, India can also avail of such duty-free market access.

As reported in the *Economic Survey 2017-18* (p. 92, vol. II), the Eleventh Ministerial Conference (MC11) of World Trade Organisation (WTO) ended without a Ministerial Declaration or any substantive outcome, though the unanimous view was that it was extremely well-conducted with complete openness and transparency and the process afforded everyone ample opportunity to express their views.

In the run-up to MC11, decisions were expected on a permanent solution on food security and other agriculture issues. Unfortunately, the strong position of one of the member against agricultural reforms based on current WTO mandates and rules, led to a deadlock without any outcome on agriculture or even a work programme for the next two years. However, the existing mandates and decisions ensure that work will go forward and members will continue to work on issues such as the permanent solution on public stockholding for food security purposes, agricultural Special Safeguard Mechanism and agricultural domestic support. Some of the other decisions that were taken included a Work Programme on disciplines on Fisheries Subsidies with a view to arriving at a decision by MC12. It was also decided to continue with the non-negotiating mandate of the existing Work Programme on E-commerce. Ministerial Decisions on new issues like Investment Facilitation, MSMEs, gender and trade, which lacked a mandate or consensus, were not taken forward.

Further during the Ministerial Conference (MC11), India stood firm on its stand on the fundamental principles of the WTO, including multilateralism, rule-based consensual decisionmaking, an independent and credible dispute resolution and appellate process, the centrality of development, which underlies the Doha Development Agenda (DDA), and special and differential treatment for all developing countries (*Economic Survey 2017-18*, Vol. II).

To conclude, while India, so far, may not have been able to gain a lot from the negotiations, it certainly came out of seclusion during the Doha Ministerial (2001) and is currently leading the developing country coalitions at WTO. Furthermore, expansion of the negotiating agenda (e.g., environmental services) in recent years depicts an evolving learning curve, which is no less important. A similar 'learning through trading' is observed in the case of several other developing countries as well. On the other hand, the aversion of several developed countries towards ensuring free trade is becoming quite obvious in recent years.

24

Indian Economy Today

An Overview and Comparative Perspective

JAWAHARLAL NEHRU'S famous speech at the 'stroke of the midnight hour', when India became independent, spoke of 'ending poverty and ignorance and disease and inequality of opportunity' and building a 'prosperous, democratic and progressive' nation. How has India performed? For the first three decades after independence, growth performance was poor (of course better than under colonial rule). The poverty ratio did not fall, and the number of people in poverty rose substantially. In those days, India was often compared to a slow-moving snail or tortoise. It was thought of as 'a country of the future that will always remain so'. However, things have changed, since around 1980, and especially after the economic reforms in 1991, India has been among a dozen or so of the fastest growing countries of the world. The poverty ratio has fallen sharply but India still has around a quarter of its billion plus population surviving in extreme poverty. To become a prosperous and high income contry in the next two decades. India will have to achieve economic growth that is, superfast and inclusive i.e., a growth rate of 8 per cent or above and growth that is widely shared. However, the current context is that far from speeding up, India's growth has shown signs of slowing down (Joshi 2016, 2018).

After achieving unprecedented growth of over 9 per cent for three successive years between 2005-06 and 2007-08 and recovering swiftly from the global financial crisis of 2008-09, the Indian economy has been going through challenging times that culminated in lower than 5 per cent growth of GDP at factor cost at constant prices for two consecutive years, i.e., 2012-13 and 2013-14. Sub-5 per cent GDP (gross domestic product) growth for two years in succession was last witnessed a quarter of a century ago in 1986-87 and 1987-88. Persistent uncertainty in the global outlook, caused by the crisis in the Euro area and general slowdown in the global economy, compounded by domestic structural constraints and inflationary pressures, resulted in a protracted slowdown. The slowdown is broadly in sync with trends in other emerging economies, but relatively deeper. India's growth declined from an average of 8.3 per cent per annum during 2004-05 to 2011-12 to an average of 4.6 per cent in 2012-13 and 2013-14. Average growth in the emerging markets and developing economies including China declined from 6.8 per cent to 4.9 per cent in this period (calendar-year basis). What is particularly worrisome is the slowdown in manufacturing growth that averaged 0.2 per cent per annum in 2012-13 and 2013-14 (*Economic Survey 2013-14*).

After two consecutive years of moderation, GDP growth improved marginally in 2013-14 due to a rebound in the growth of 'agriculture and allied activities' and electricity, besides buoyant activity in 'financing, insurance, real estate and business services'. While the value added in mining and manufacturing contracted, services sector growth remained unchanged. The low overall growth reflected contracting fixed investment and slowing consumption, though there was an improvement in export growth aided by rupee depreciation and contraction in imports due to subdued demand conditions and policies to dissuade gold imports.

According to RBI Annual Report 2014, the weak business sentiment, infrastructure bottlenecks, low public investment, domestic political uncertainty and an uneven global recovery led private fixed investment to contract. The uncertainty in the legal and regulatory framework in key areas such as environmental clearances, land acquisition and use of natural resources, especially mining activity, added to the low business confidence and affected investments in the economy. Private final consumption expenditure moderated on account of low income growth and high inflation. Macro instability, however, diminished considerably with the narrowing of the twin deficits of both current account and fiscal and the gradual reduction in inflation.

India's Increasing Importance to Global Growth

India has made striking progress in its contribution to the global growth of GDP in PPP (purchasing power parity) terms. PPP represents the number of units of a country's currency required to purchase the same amount of goods and services in the domestic market as the US dollar would purchase in the US, thus adjusting for purchasing power differentials between currencies in relevant markets. India's contribution to global growth in PPP terms increased from an average of 8.3 per cent during the period 2001 to 2007 to 14.4 per cent in 2014. During the 1990s, the US's contribution to the global GDP growth in PPP terms was, on an average, around 16 percentage points higher than India's. The picture changed dramatically in 2013 and 2014 when India's contribution was higher than that of the US by 2.2 and 2.7 percentage points respectively.

The global economy—in particular the global growth powerhouse, China—is rebalancing, leading to an increasing role for India. After the onset of the multiple crises in different parts of the world, India's contribution has become much more valuable to the global economy.India's share in world GDP has increased from an average of 4.8 per cent during 2001-2007 to 6.1 per cent during 2008-2013 and further to an average of 7.0 per cent during 2014 to 2015 in current PPP terms (IMF).

India is the seventh largest economy in terms of Gross Domestic Product (GDP) in current US$ and has emerged as the fastest growing major economy (Figure 24.1). The average growth rate of India was

FIGURE – 24.1

Global Comparison among Top Ten Economies

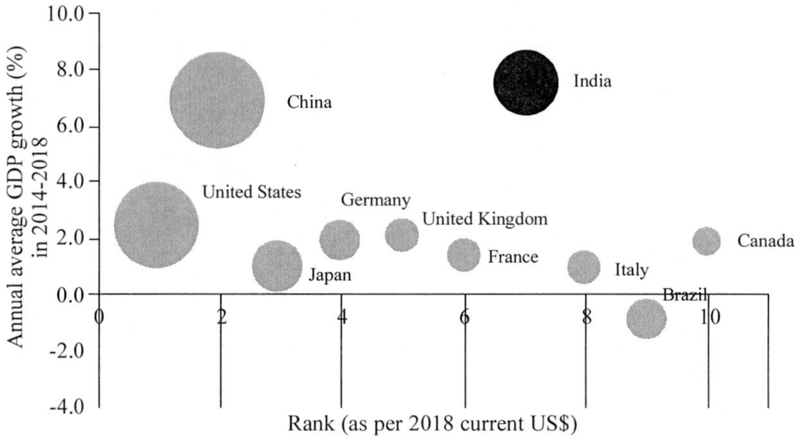

Note: For France and Italy GDP of the year 2018 is the estimated figure of International Monetary Fund. Size of circle represents GDP (PPP) at current international dollar terms.

Source: WEO, April 2019 database
Economic Survey 2018-19, Vol. II)

TABLE – 24.1

Growth in GDP and Other Key Indicators

Data Categories	*Unit*	*2012-13*	*2013-14*	*2014-15*	*2015-16*	*2016-17*	*2017-18*	*2018-19*
1	*2*	*3*	*4*	*5*	*6*	*7*	*8*	*9*
GDP and Related Indicators								
GDP (2011-12 prices)	₹ Crore	9226879[2R]	9839434[2R]	10536984	11369493	12298327	13179857	14077586[a]
Growth Rate	%	5.6	6.6	7.5	8.0	8.2	7.2	6.8[a]
GVA at Basic Prices (2011-12 prices)	₹ Crore	8546552[2R]	9084369[2R]	9719023	10491870	11318972	12104165	12906936[a]
Growth Rate	%	5.4	6.3	7.2	8.0	7.9	6.9	6.6[a]
Savings Rate	% of GDP	33.8	33.0	33.1	31.1	30.3	30.5	na
Capital Formation Rate	% of GDP	38.6	34.7	34.4	32.1	30.9	32.3	na
Per Capita Net National Income (At current market prices)	₹	71050	79412	86454	94797	104659	114958	126406[a]
Production								
Foodgrains	Million tonnes	257.1	265.0	252.0	251.5	275.1	285.0	283.4[b]
Index of Industrial Production[a] (Growth)	%	1.1	-0.1	4.0	3.3	4.6	4.4	3.6
Electricity Generation (Growth)	%	4.0	6.0	14.8	5.6	4.7	4.0	3.5
Prices								
Inflation (WPI) (average)	%	7.4	6.0	1.2	-3.7	1.7	3.0	4.3
Inflation CPI (Combined) (average)	%	10.2	9.5	5.9	4.9	4.5	3.6	3.4

Contd...

.contd...

Data Categories	Unit	2012-13	2013-14	2014-15	2015-16	2016-17	2017-18	2018-19
1	2	3	4	5	6	7	8	9
GDP and Related Indicators								
External Sector								
Export Growth (US$)	%	-1.8	4.7	-1.3	-15.5	5.2	10.0	8.8
Import Growth (US$)	%	0.3	-8.3	-0.5	-15.0	0.9	21.1	10.4
Current Account Balance (CAB)/GDP	%	-4.8	-1.7	-1.3	-1.1	-0.6	-1.9	-2.6[c]
Foreign Exchange Reserves	US$ billion	292.0	304.2	341.6	360.2	370.0	424.5	412.9
Average Exchange Rate	₹/US$	54.40	60.51	61.14	65.5	67.1	64.5	69.9
Money and Credit Broad								
Money (M3) (annual)	% change	13.6	13.4	10.9	10.1	10.1	9.2	10.5
Scheduled Commercial Bank Credit	% change	14.1	13.9	9.0	10.9	8.2	10.0	13.3
Fiscal Indicators (Centre)								
Gross Fiscal Deficit	% of GDP	4.9	4.5	4.1	3.9	3.5	3.5	3.4[d]
Revenue Deficit	% of GDP	3.7	3.2	2.9	2.5	2.1	2.6	2.3[d]
Primary Deficit	% of GDP	1.8	1.1	0.9	0.7	0.4	0.4	0.3[d]

Notes: na: Not available; a: Provisional estimates, b: Third advance estimate, c: (April-December) 2018, d: Provisional Actual.

Source: *Economic Survey 2017-18* (Vol. II)., *2018-19 (Vol. 2)*.

not only higher than China's during 2014-15 to 2017-18 but much higher than that of other top major economies (measured in terms of GDP at current US$ terms) as well. With Purchasing Power Parity (PPP) adjustments, India's GDP at current international dollar, ranks third in the world (as shown by the size of circles in Figure 24.1).

The contribution of the Indian economy to the GDP of EMDEs and world economy has increased consistently over the years. In a span of less than a decade, India's contribution to EMDEs GDP has increased by around 1.3 percentage points and to the world economy by around 0.7 percentage points. India's share in GDP of EMDEs stood at 8 per cent in 2018. As per the WEO, April 2019 of IMF, going forward, the growth of world economy will be bolstered mainly by growth in China and India and their increasing weights in world income. In EMDEs group, India and China are the major drivers of growth. The global economy—in particular the global growth powerhouse, China—is rebalancing, leading to an increasing role for India. Hence, India's contribution has become much more valuable to the global economy.

The Search for Prosperity

Though India's economic advance now attracts hyped-up predictions and exaggerated hopes, Joshi remarks in his recent book (2016) that the foundations of its success are fragile. At the same time it is also a fact that India is performing below its potential.

> That India will eventually become a prosperous country is all but certain. The question is how long this will take. This issue has become all the more pertinent because India's growth has slowed in the last few years. Though it is by some measures the third-largest economy in the world, it still has a quarter of its billion-plus people surviving in extreme poverty, and more than two-thirds of its people poor enough to have exceedingly circumscribed opportunities to lead a fulfilling life (Joshi, 2016).

An ambitious goal for India would be to become a prosperous country by, say, 2040. What does prosperity mean? According to Joshi, it could be defined as the level of per capita income enjoyed by the lower rung of high-income countries today, with the rider that national income should be widely shared and even the poorest people should have decent standards of living. To reach this goal,

> India would require high-quality per capita growth of income of around 7 per cent a year for a period of twenty-four years, from 2016.

> By 'high-quality' growth I mean, firstly, growth that is inclusive. If per capita growth were 7 per cent a year, then high-quality growth would require that the incomes of poor people also rise by at least 7 per cent a year (or preferably by quite a lot more). Secondly, by high-quality growth, I mean growth that is environmentally friendly (Joshi, 2016).

If India were to maintain seven per cent a year per capita growth until 2040, India's annual per capita income at PPP would rise from its current level of about \$5,600 to five times its current level, i.e. to about \$28,000 (all the income figures in this paragraph are in constant 2011 PPP dollars). This would make India firmly a high-income country by today's standards, with a per capita income comparable to countries such as Greece and Portugal that are in the lower rung of high-income countries today. If, in addition, growth was inclusive, the incomes of the poorest Indians would also increase by at least a multiple of five and probably a lot more; change that would obviously make a huge positive difference to their lives. With eight per cent a year per capita growth, India's per capita income in 2040 would be \$35,000, roughly equal to that of South Korea in 2016 (South Korea is approximately the median country today in a ranking of high-income countries by per capita income). With six per cent a year per capita growth, India's per capita income would quadruple and reach around \$22,000, a level at which it would just about slip into the category of high-income countries by today's standards, comparable to countries such as Chile and Hungary (Joshi, 2016).

What are the prospects for achieving the challenging goal of rapid, high-quality per capita growth of 6-8 per cent a year for the next two or three decades? According to Joshi, the reforms undertaken in India at the start of the 1990s, and thereafter, were effective, but are now running out of steam, and were in any case partial and incomplete. Moreover, India's fast growth during the first decade of the 21st century was propelled by a highly liquid and expanding world economy. Such a benign global environment looks very unlikely to return any time soon. In the domestic arena, progress remains to be made in many areas such as public sector ownership, banking sector reform, rules governing bankruptcy and exit, infrastructure provision, employment creation, and delivery of public services. These involve substantive matters in which 'reform by stealth', which has been the Indian way of doing things, will be unlikely to suffice. More liberalisation is necessary. But it is not sufficient because the state does not perform its core functions effectively.

As already discussed, each country has to work out for itself to achieve the right balance between the state and the market to suit its particular circumstances. India has failed to do that. The Indian state has systematically underestimated the prevalence and the cost of 'government failure'. It often intervenes, arbitrarily or to correct supposed market failures, without any clear evidence that the market is failing, and so ends up damaging resource allocation and stifling business drive. "That is why India is regarded as one of the worst places in the world to do business" (Joshi, 2016). Sometimes the government intervenes justifiably, but in a ham-fisted way, for example in its regulation of land, labour and capital markets. It quite properly intervenes for redistributive purposes but does so ineptly and ineffectively through price controls, which impair economic efficiency by distorting relative prices, and through administrative delivery mechanisms, which are costly and corrupt. It fails to harness private initiatives in public services such as healthcare and education because it ignores the distinction between paying for services and producing them. It does not understand the importance of putting the incentive structure right for getting government functionaries to perform. It does not fully appreciate that private sector competition with the public sector is necessary to improve the quality of provision of public services (Joshi, 2016).

At the same time, the Indian state does not deliver in the areas that fall squarely in its province, such as administering law and order, ensuring macroeconomic stability, delivering speedy justice, making sure that public services are provided, and creating an effective and adequate safety net for poor people. There is also plenty of evidence that the culture of public service has deteriorated.

It follows from the above that both the state and the state-market relationship need urgent reform, which is no easy task in the context of India's political economy, with its democratic turbulence and powerful vested interests.

Radical Reform: Rationale and Setting

Economic policy after 1980, and especially after 1991, followed what is called a 'partial reform model'. Its focus was mainly on deregulating goods markets and, to a lesser extent, financial markets. To this end, restrictions on foreign trade and investment were liberalised. Investment licensing was abolished and the reservation of hundreds of items for production by small-scale firms was progressively scrapped. A beginning was made in liberalising interest rates and reducing government capture of bank credit. Even so, the process of change did not go nearly far enough. In many crucial respects, the reforms remained incoherent and incomplete (Joshi, 2016).

The basic flaw of the partial reform model is a failure to put the role of the state, and the relation between the state, the market and the private sector, on the right footing—a failure that continues to this day. There is, in India, an overall lack of clarity about the economic borders of the state, i.e., what the government should own, finance, regulate, produce or leave well alone. The Indian state is still too much of a jack of all trades, remarks Joshi. Deeper liberalisation is necessary to release business energy and allow the market to perform its dynamic and allocative role, combined with 'smart regulation' to correct market failures. Smart regulation would recognise that 'government failure' can be as harmful as market failure. It would be accurate, transparent and independent of vested interests from outside and from within the state itself. This kind of regulation is an art that India has yet to learn. A key function of the state is to enable individuals and society to flourish by ensuring the provision of pure public goods and 'public services' for all citizens, and a robust safety net to protect them from extreme poverty. Pure public goods must certainly be paid for by the state because the market is incapable of doing so, and this is often also true of public services that the poor cannot afford to buy. But it does not follow that the state must necessarily produce and deliver public services or even pure public goods. This may sometimes be done more efficiently by private markets, although some contracting or regulation by the state would almost always be necessary. Nonetheless, there remain plenty of things that the state and only the state can do. Unfortunately, the Indian state has shown itself unequal to the challenge of discharging core tasks. This is partly because it has taken on too much that is outside its proper domain. But it is also in part because its implementation capacity is deficient and in addition, subject to corruption and crony capitalism on an extensive scale. These shortcomings are serious enough to hamper, perhaps even to wreck, India's prospects for rapid and inclusive growth. The implication is that the state urgently needs to reform itself. A radical reform agenda would have to address all these deficiencies (Joshi, 2016).

In a recent paper Rangarajan and Srivastava (2017) discussing the "Underlying Drivers of India's Potential Growth" have pointed out "given tepid global growth prospects in the medium term, India will have to depend largely on its domestic growth drivers." In their study the domestic saving rate was identified as the most potent growth augmenting driver. The phase of high growth that India achieved during three consecutive years—2005-06, 2006-07, and 2007-08—was characterised by: (i) high savings and investment rates, and (ii) low incremental capital-output ratio. In these three years, real growth rate for GDP at 2004-05 market prices were, respectively, 9.3 per cent, 9.3 per cent, and 9.8 per cent. In these three years, the saving rates relative to GDP, both measured at current prices, were 33.4 per cent, 34.6 per cent,and 36.8 per cent respectively. The investment rates, measured at 2004-05 prices, were 34.9 per cent, 36.2 per cent and 39 per cent. The ICORs at 2004-05 prices were respectively, 3.9 per cent, 3.6 per cent and 3.8 per cent.

Outlook for Growth

India's long-run potential GDP growth is substantial, about 8-10 per cent. But its actual growth in the short-run will also depend upon global growth and demand. After all, India's exports of manufactured goods and services now constitute about 18 per cent of GDP, up from about 11 per cent a decade ago. Reflecting India's growing globalisation, the correlation between India's growth rate and that of the world has risen sharply to reasonably high levels. For the period 1991-2002 this correlation was 0.2. Since then, the correlation has doubled to 0.42. In other words, a 1 percentage point decrease in the world growth rate is now associated with a 0.42 percentage point decrease in India's growth rates (*Economic Survey 2015-16*, Vol. I).

Accordingly, if the world economy remains weak, India's growth will face considerable headwinds. For example, if the world continues to grow at close to 3 per cent over the next few years rather than returning to the buoyant 4-4½ per cent recorded during 2003-2011, India's medium-term growth trajectory could well remain closer to 7-7½ per cent, notwithstanding the government's reform initiatives, rather than rise to the 8-10 per cent that its long-run potential suggests. In other words, in the current global environment, there needs to be a recalibration of growth expectations and consequently of the standards of assessment.

In contrast, in the current scenario, the saving and investment rates have fallen and the ICOR is higher. In 2015-16, it is estimated to be 4.4, which is the lowest in recent years but still higher than 2005-2008 levels. Although export growth is currently negative, imports have fallen even faster, leading to net exports contributing positively to GDP growth in 2013-14 and 2014-15, although by a very small margin. Yet in a scenario where exports are falling or show low growth, reliance has to be more on domestic consumption. In such a situation, it will be quite a challenge to uplift the savings rate significantly. This will require lowering of the government's revenue deficit from its current levels. The key to higher growth would therefore be lower ICOR. Policies that lead to higher productivity would support higher growth in the short term. However, over the medium term, high growth can be sustained only by raising the savings and investment rate.

We also need to improve the ICOR which would be possible only through improving productivity. This would require sustained effort by the government to improve ease of doing business, facilitate better supply chains (through GST), and overcome infrastructure deficiency. It will also require businesses to do better in innovations, supply chain management, and training (Rangarajan and Srivastava, 2017).

Accelerating economic growth must be on top of the agenda of the new government. It is only a fast growing economy that will generate the surpluses which are necessary to address many of our socio-economic problems and to privide social safety nets (Rangarajan 2019).

Going by the World Bank's index of Ease of Doing Business, India has made significant progress, with its rank improving from 130th among 189 economies in 2016 to 77th among 190 economies in 2018. According to Kaushik Basu (2019) this should have helped India create more jobs and boost exports. But it did not "In retrospect, it is clear what is happening. Instead of making a general effort to cut bureaucratic costs, there has been a disproportionate focus on the ten measures the World Bank tracks as a proxy measure of a nation's bureaucratic cost, which in reality has many more dimensions. This kind of pure gaming of the system earned India a pat on the back from the World Bank but did not do much else" (Basu, 2019).

Comparative Perspective

Comparisons with the Non-African Poor

According to Drèze and Sen (2013), leaving sub-Saharan Africa aside, India is not well placed at all in international comparisons of living standards. Contrary to the increasingly used rhetoric which suggests that India is well on its way to becoming an economic 'superpower', this is far from the real picture, even in terms of per capita income. In fact, despite rapid economic expansion in recent years, India remains one of the poorest countries among those outside sub-Saharan Africa. According to the World Bank, only 15 countries outside sub-Saharan Africa had a 'gross national income per capita' lower than India's in 2011: Afghanistan, Bangladesh, Burma, Cambodia, Haiti, Kyrgyzstan, Laos, Moldova, Nepal, Pakistan, Papua New Guinea, Tajikistan, Uzbekistan, Vietnam and Yemen. India does indeed have a large gap in world living standards to overcome. What is disturbing, given the past, is not India's comparatively low position in terms of income per head among the countries in the world outside sub-Saharan African, but how badly India does in terms of non-income features of living standards even within this group of poorest non-African countries (Table 24.2).

India has, by the choice of our cut-off point, the highest GDP per capita in this particular group, with the rank of being number 1 among these 16 countries. Aside from GDP per capita, as the last column indicates, India's rank among these 16 poor countries is 10th or worse in most cases. Not only are India's figures worse than the average for the other 15 countries for all social indicators presented here (except for the total fertility rate and male literacy rate), its rank in this group is an inglorious 10th for child mortality, 11th for female literacy and mean years of schooling, 13th for access to improved sanitation and DPT immunisation, and absolutely the worst (along with Yemen) in terms of the proportion of underweight children.

According to Drèze and Sen (2013), the common characterisation of India's current economic growth rate of around 6 per cent per year as 'dismal' is hard to justify because India's rate of economic growth, though reduced, is still among the fastest in the world (as it would still be, even if the prediction of a 5% growth rate by some agencies proved to be true). But 'dismal' would indeed be a very good adjective to describe the picture of comparative living standards, as Table 24.2 reveals.

Some of these comparisons are quite instructive. For instance, Vietnam fares enormously better than India in terms of all these indicators, in spite of being poorer than India. So, incidentally, does Nicaragua, with virtually the same per capita GDP as India. Uzbekistan, too, is far ahead of India in many respects, with, for instance, universal literacy in the younger age groups, universal access to improved sanitation, and (nearly) universal immunisation of children—all goals that are nowhere near being achieved in India. Another striking contrast

TABLE – 24.2

Comparisons with World's 16 Poorest Countries, Outside Sub-Saharan Africa: Selected Indicators

	India	*Average for other Poorest Countries*[a]	*India's Rank among 16 Poorest Countries*[b]
GDP Per Capita, 2011 (PPP, constant 2005 international $)	3,203	2,112	1
Life Expectancy at Birth, 2011 (years)	65	67	9
Infant Mortality Rate, 2011 (Per 1,000 live births)	47	45	10
Under-5 Mortality Rate, 2011 (Per 1,000 live births)	61	56	10
Total Fertility Rate, 2011 (children per woman)	2.6	2.9	7
Access to Improved Sanitation, 2010 (%)	34	57	13
Mean Years of Schooling, Age 25+, 2011	4.4	5.0	11
Literacy Rate, Age 15-24 years, 2010 (%)			
Female	74[c]	79	11
Male	88[c]	85	9
Proportion of children below Five Years who are undernourished, 2006-2010d (%)			
Underweight	43	30	15
Stunted	48	41	13
Child Immunisation Rates, 2011 (%)			
DPT	72	88	13
Measles	74	87	11

Notes: a: Population-weighted average of country-specific indicators. In two cases of missing data for a particular country (e.g., literacy rates for Afghanistan), the average was taken over the remaining countries; b: Based on ranking from 'best' to 'worst'. In case of 'ties', India was ranked first; c: 2006; d: Latest year for which data are available within 2006-2010.

Source: World Development Indicators (online, 1 January 2013). Mean years of schooling from Human Development Report 2013 and child undernutrition data from UNICEF (2012). This table focuses on 16 countries with per capita GDP lower than or equal to India's, outside sub-Saharan Africa. These are: Afghanistan, Bangladesh, Burma, Cambodia, Haiti, India, Kyrgyzstan, Laos, Moldva, Nepal, Pakistan, Papua New Guinea, Tajikistan, Uzbekistan, Vietnam and Yemen.

Drèze and Sen (2013: ch. 3, table 3.1).

is between India and Nepal, which has much the same social indicators as India, with barely one-third of India's per capita income (the last makes Nepal one of the very poorest countries outside Africa, along with Afghanistan and Haiti) (Drèze and Sen, 2013).

It could be argued that one would expect India not to fare as well, in many ways, as other countries at a similar level of per capita income, because India is growing quite fast and it takes time for higher per capita incomes to translate into better social indicators. In a country growing at 7 per cent per year in per capita terms, per capita income would double in 10 years, but it would quite possibly take longer, even with significant efforts, to bring social indicators level with those of countries that were once twice as rich. The basic concern remains that, for whatever reasons, India is not doing well at all in many respects even in comparison with some of the poorest countries in the world. This is not to disparage India's achievements, but to put them in perspective, and to focus on the deficiencies that plague India most and which have to be overcome (Drèze and Sen, 2013.).

India's Decline in South Asia

According to Drèze and Sen (2013), one indication that there is something defective in India's 'path to development' arises from the fact that India is falling behind every other South Asian country (with the exception of Pakistan) in terms of many social indicators, even as it is doing spectacularly better than these countries in terms of the growth of per capita income (the comparative picture presented as in Table 24.3).

Drèze and Sen have looked at the same issue from another angle. Table 24.4 displays India's 'rank' among South Asia's six major countries respectively around 1990 and today. As expected, in terms of the absolute level of per capita income, India's rank has improved—from fourth (after Bhutan, Pakistan and Sri Lanka) to third (after Bhutan and Sri Lanka). In terms of the rate of expansion of income per head, India is now at the top of this group (as it is of most groups of countries in the world). But in most other respects, India's rank has worsened, in fact quite sharply in many cases. Overall, only one country in South Asia (Sri Lanka) clearly had better social indicators than India in 1990, but now India looks second worst, ahead of only Pakistan.

TABLE – 24.3

South Asia: Selected Indicators (1990 and Latest)

		South Asia						*China*
		India	*Bangladesh*	*Bhutan*	*Nepal*	*Pakistan*	*Sri Lanka*	
GDP Per Capita, PPP:	1990*	1,193	741	1,678	716	1,624	2,017	1,121
(constant 2005 international $)	2011	3,203	1,569	5,162	1,106	2,424	4,929	7,418
Life Expectancy at Birth:	1990*	58	59	53	54	61	70	69
(years)	2011	65	69	67	69	65[f]	75[f]	73[f]
Infant Mortality Rate:	1990*	81	97	96	94	95	24	39
(per 1,000 live births)	2011	47	37	42	39	59	11	13
Under-5 Mortality Rate:	1990*	114	139	138	135	122	29	49
(per 1,000 live births)	2011	61	46	54	48	72	12	15
Maternal Mortality Ratio:	1990	600	800	1,000	770	490	85	120
(per 100,000 live births)	2010	200	240	180	170	260	35	37
Total Fertility Rate:	1990*	3.9	4.5	5.7	5.2	6.0	2.5	2.3
(children per woman)	2011	2.6	2.2	2.3	2.7	3.4[f]	2.3[f]	1.6[f]
Access to Improved Sanitation (%):	1990	18	39	n/a	10	27	70	24
	2010	34	56	44	31	48	92	64
Infant Immunisation (DPT) (%):	1990*	59	64	88	44	48	86	95
	2011	72	96	95	92	80	99	99

contd...

.contd...

		South Asia						China
		India	*Bangladesh*	*Bhutan*	*Nepal*	*Pakistan*	*Sri Lanka*	
Infant Immunisation (measles) (%):	1990*	47	62	87	57	50	78	95
	2011	74	96	95	88	80	99	99
Mean Years of Schooling, age 25+:	1990	3.0	2.9	-	2.0	2.3	6.9	4.9
	2011	4.4	4.8	2.3e	3.2	4.9	9.3	7.5
Female Literacy Rate, age 15-24 (%):	1991a	49	38	-	33	-	93	91
	2010b	74	78	68	78	61	99	99
Proportion (%) of Underweight Children:	1990c	59.5	61.5	34	-	39	29	13
	2006-10d	43	41	13	39	31	21	4

Notes: * Three-year average centred on the reference year (e.g. , 1989-1991 average when the reference year is 1990).
a 1990 for China; the Sri Lanka figure is an interpolation between 1981 and 2001 figures.
b 2006 for India, 2005 for Bhutan, 2009 for Pakistan.
c 1988 for Bhutan, 1991 for Pakistan, 1987 for Sri Lanka.
d Latest year for which data are available within this period.
e 2002-2012.
f 2010.

Source: Mean years of schooling from Human Development Report 2013, online; other indicators from World Development Indicators, online (1 January 2013); Some of the country-specific figures for 1990 are subject to a significant margin of error; the focus is best kept on broad patterns rather than exact numbers; Drèze and Sen, 2013.

TABLE – 24.4

India's Rank in South Asia

	Indicator	*India's Rank among Six South Asian Countries (Top=1, Bottom=6)*	
		In 1990	*Around 2011*
1.	GDP Per Capita	4	3
2.	Life Expectancy	4	5
3.	Infant Mortality Rate	2	5
4.	Under-5 Mortality Rate	2	5
5.	Maternal Mortality Ratio	3	4
6.	Total Fertility Rate	2	4
7.	Access to Improved Sanitation	4-5[a]	5
8.	Child Immunisation (DPT)	4	6
9.	Child Immunisation (measles)	6	6
10.	Mean Years of Schooling, Age 25+	2-3[a]	4
11.	Female Literacy Rate, Age 15-24	2-3[a]	4
12.	Proportion of Underweight Children	4-5[a]	6

Note: a: Ambiguous rank due to missing data for Bhutan (or Nepal, in the case of 'underweight children').

Source: See Table 38.3. The six countries considered here are Bangladesh, Bhutan, India, Nepal, Pakistan and Sri Lanka.

India among the BRIC

While the South Asian perspective has been much neglected in India, another group of countries is commonly seen as comprising its 'peer group': Brazil, Russia, India and China (also known as the BRIC countries). These nations do have some important features in common, starting with their gigantic populations.

India is actually an exception within this group, in important ways. For instance, while every country in the group has achieved universal or near-universal literacy in the younger age groups, India is still quite far from this elementary foundation of participatory development: one-fifth of all Indian men in the age group of 15-24 years, and one-fourth of all women in the same age group, were unable to read and write in 2006. Similarly, child immunisation is almost universal in every BRIC country except India. In fact India's immunisation rates are abysmally low even in comparison with those of other South Asian countries including Bangladesh and Nepal. India also stands out dramatically in

TABLE – 24.5

Selected Indicators for 'BRIC' Countries

	India	*China*	*Brazil*	*Russia*
GDP Per Capita (PPP, 2005 constant international $), 2011	3,203	7,418	10,279	14,821
Life Expectancy at Birth, 2010				
Female	67	75	77	75
Male	64	72	70	63
Infant Mortality Rate, 2011	47	13	14	10
Under-5 Mortality Rate, 2011	61	15	16	12
Total Fertility Rate, 2010	2.6	1.6	1.8	1.5
Access to Improved Sanitation, 2010 (%)	34	64	79	70
Mean Years of Schooling, Age 25+, 2011	4.4	7.5	7.2	11.7
Literacy Rate, Age 15-24, 2010 (%)				
Female	74[a]	99	99[c]	100
Male	88[a]	99	97[c]	100
Undernourishment among Children below 5, 2006-10b (%)				
Underweight	43	4	2	n/a
Stunted	48	10	7	n/a
Child Immunisation Rates, 2011 (%)				
DPT	72	99	96	97
Measles	74	99	97	98
Public Expenditure on Health, 2010:				
As a Proportion of Total Health Expenditure (%)	29	54	47	62
As a Proportion of GDP (%)	1.2	2.7	4.2	3.2
Per Capita (PPP, 2005 constant international $)	39	203	483	620
Public Expenditure on Education as a Proportion of GDP, 2010 (%)	3.3	n/a	5.6[c]	4.1[d]

Note: a 2006.
b Latest year for which data are available within this period.
c 2009.
d 2008.

Source: *World Development Indicators* (online, 1 January 2013).
Drèze and Sen (2013: Ch.3, table 3.7).

terms of the extent of undernourishment among children. While this terrible problem has largely disappeared in other BRIC countries, it is still rampant in India, where more than 40 per cent of all children below the age of five are underweight, and an even higher proportion (close to 50%) are stunted. Rapid economic growth has not achieved much on its own, during the last 20 years or so, to reduce India's horrendous levels of child undernourishment, or to enhance child immunisation rates. Similarly, making a swift and decisive transition to universal literacy in the younger age groups would take more than just waiting for the growth of per capita incomes to make it easier for parents to send their children to schools (Drèze and Sen, 2013).

In others words, as Drèze and Sen point out, the required 'catching up' pertains not only to per capita incomes but also—very importantly—to public services, social support and economic distribution. It is, in fact, worth noting that among these four countries, India is the only one that has not (at least not yet) gone through a phase of major expansion of public support or economic redistribution. China made enormous progress (especially in comparison with India) very early towards universal access to elementary education, healthcare and social security—much before embarking on market-oriented economic reforms in 1979. While there were some setbacks in some of these fields in the 1980s and 1990s, notably in the field of healthcare, China's growth-oriented policies during that period benefited a great deal from the solid foundations of human development that had been laid earlier, and also retained that commitment in many ways, for instance through guaranteed and equitable access to land in rural areas. Further, the undoing of socialised healthcare in the 1980s and 1990s, for which China paid a heavy price, was reversed again from around 2004. The principle of universal health coverage has reappeared in China's health planning, and rapid progress has been made in that direction: it appears that nearly 90 per cent of the people are now covered by the revamped, publicly funded health system.

Russia, too, had put in place a comprehensive system of social protection and public services during the Communist period. As in China, the system came under heavy stress after economic reforms—of a more extreme variety—were introduced in the early 1990s. In Russia, however, the breakdown was far more serious, and compounded by an economic catastrophe (possibly the worst economic recession in modern history, lasting for the best part of a decade), not unrelated to the lethal advice of Western experts who kept predicting an imminent 'economic miracle' in a newly marketised Russia even as the economy kept sinking. There was, eventually, an economic take-off of a limited sort (in the 2000s), but only after the economy and social infrastructure had been substantially ruined, or handed over to business magnates. This prolonged economic crisis was associated with an equally catastrophic deterioration of the health of the Russian population, particularly men, who now have the same sort of life expectancy as Indian men (see Table 24.5). Even then, some of the social achievements of the earlier period remained, including universal basic education, involving schooling well beyond literacy. And as in China, there have been major efforts to rebuild public services and the social security system in Russia in recent years, with help from sustained economic growth from the turn of the century.

In Brazil, progressive social policies are comparatively recent, and followed a period of rapid economic growth, instead of preceding it as in China; it is perhaps interesting that the social indicators of Brazil and China look quite similar today (Table 24.5), even though they reached a similar situation through very different routes. For a long time, Brazil combined rapid economic growth with repressive governance, massive inequality and endemic deprivation. However, this picture has radically changed during the last 20 years, at time of ambitious and wide-ranging initiatives in the fields of health, education and social security (largely driven by the democratic upsurge that followed the end of military dictatorships), and the results have been impressive.

Challenges and Prospects

There is a lot of discussion of the need to raise the rate of growth of the Indian economy, which has fallen from its peak of 9 per cent per year not long ago to around 6 per cent at the beginning of 2013 and below 5 per cent in 2013-14. Although Europe and the US would feel lucky to be assured of even half of the reduced rate of growth that India currently has. The deep concern about increasing economic growth is perfectly understandable. Growth does raise household incomes and helps to remove poverty, especially if health, education and other basic capabilities that enable people to participate in the growth process are widely shared. It also generates public revenue that can be used to expand the social and physical infrastructure as well as for other constructive purposes. However, enhancing overall economic growth is only one of many different concerns that need attention in reversing the deprivations of the vast majority of Indians, and in reducing the astounding inequalities that characterise India today.

These challenges, according to Drèze and Sen, call for wide-ranging changes in public policy and a reorientation of the democratic dialogue in India. There is a strong case for forceful public demand for much larger allocations to basic public services (such as school education, healthcare, nutritional support and environmental protection), and for much more comprehensive programmes of economic equity and social security, as well as the development of the physical and social infrastructure. There is also a need for radical reform of the organisation of public services to make them more accountable and efficient.

As rightly pointed out by Drèze and Sen (2013), there is a large part of the Indian population—a relatively small minority but still quite large in absolute numbers—for whom growth alone does just fine, since they are already comparatively privileged and need no special social assistance to benefit from economic growth. They are in a good position to obtain substantial benefits from GDP expansion, as indeed they have been doing—sometimes intensified by governmental intervention in their direction (through, for example, fuel subsidies, from which they disproportionately benefit). This adds to their already privileged economic and social opportunities.

Some improvements in the lives of even the disadvantaged do, of course, tend to occur with economic growth, as employment and entrepreneurial opportunities expand, particularly for those who are not prevented from seizing these opportunities by ill health, lack of schooling, social barriers, or other disadvantages. But public support to the underprivileged is extremely important, in general, in helping them to overcome these disadvantages and in ensuring that the fruits of economic growth are shared widely. Without it, a great many lives will continue to be tormented by hunger, poverty, illness and other deprivations, despite spurts in aggregate economic growth (as indeed has been happening over the recent past).

The constructive use of public resources generated by economic growth to enhance human capabilities contributes not only to the quality of life but also to higher productivity and further growth. In fact, the so-called 'Asian experience', beginning with Japan in the late 19th century, then South Korea, Taiwan, Singapore and eventually all of China, has been based on a skilful use of the complementarity of economic expansion and human advancement through education, health care, better nutrition and other determinants of human capability. This is a two-way relationship, of which relatively little use has been made by India, thereby not only making the country fall behind in terms of quality of life and social indicators of living standards, but also making its long-run growth process more fragile and less participatory than it would have been otherwise.

Drèze and Sen (2013) point out how India has missed out fairly comprehensively on a large part of the lessons of Asian economic development, which has rapidly enhanced human well-being and capability along with—indeed as a part of—pursuing fast economic growth. A critical part of the 'East Asian strategy' has been the use of public revenue, itself expanded by economic growth, to remove huge deficiencies in social, educational and health services, and to meet the growing demands of social and physical infrastructure, while making public services more accountable and efficiently organised. China's experience also shows that devoting much more public revenue than India does to the education, healthcare and nutrition of the people is compatible with—and can be very helpful for—high and sustained economic growth. Comparing India's miserable allocation of 1.2 per cent of GDP to public expenditure on health with China's much higher figure of 2.7 per cent, what is striking is not only the lack of understanding of the demands of public health in India but also how limited the understanding of many champions of economic growth are of the actual requirements for fast and sustained economic growth.

India with a large and young population has a great demographic advantage. The proportion of working-age population is likely to increase from approximately 58 per cent in 2001 to more than 64 per cent by 2021. While this provides opportunities, it also poses challenges. Policy makers have to design and execute development strategies that target this large young population.

The demographic advantage is unlikely to last indefinitely. Therefore timely action to make people healthy, educated and adequately skilled is of paramount importance.

India's demographic cycle is about 10-30 years behind that of the other countries, indicating that the next few decades present an opportunity for India to catch up to their per capita income levels (*Economic Survey 2016-17*, Vol.1).

This demographic pattern will have important growth consequences. It seems that the peak of the demographic dividend is approaching fast for India and this will be reached in the early 2020s for India as a whole i.e. within two years (Economic Survey 2016-17, Vol.1).

What the Economy Needs Now?

In October 2018, thirteen economists[1] got together in the hope that, as the country gears up for elections, they could start a conversation by identifying a set of policy ideas that might help in the policy vision.

They identified eight top challenges facing the economy and also provided proposals to deal with each[2]. These have been summarised below:

1. The massive aggregate fiscal deficit of the states and the Centre combined leaves fewer, costlier, resources for private investment. We should aim to hit the FRBM (Fiscal Responsibility and Budget Management[3]) suggested 5 per cent of GDP by 2023. This should be achieved through increased revenues resulting from better compliance and more progressive taxation, and better target spending. Any state's borrowing above agreed limits should be funded through special bonds free of any federal guarantee. For supervising fiscal federalism a Centre-state council modelled on the successful GST Council should be set up.
2. Dispite massive past government intervention, and often because of it, three sectors that are distressed today are agriculture, power and banking. Farmers do need assistance. However, the instruments used—loan waivers, inflated MSPs without adequate procurement and input price subsidies—often aggravate the problem. What is required is—enhancing investment in new technologies and irrigation and move towards lump-sums payment to farmers with holding below a certain limit, in the spirit of Telangana's Rythu Bandhu scheme. Similarly for distressed state-owned power distribution companies, we need to follow the well known solutions—better metering, less distorted pricing of both power and energy inputs, and the use of new, cleaner technologies for distributed production and decentralizing distribution. All these require rethinking the government's role, as will any sustainable solution to banking sector

---

1 Economists include: Pranjul Bhandari, Sajjid Chinoy, Maitreesh Ghatak, Amartya Lahiri, Neelkanth Mishra, Prachi Mishra, Karthik Muralidharan, Rohini Pande, Eswar Prasad, and E. Somanathan.

2 This analysis is drawn, and gratefully acknowledged, from 'Afterword' authored by Abhijit Banerjee and Raghuram Rajan in the book: "What the Economy Needs Now" (eds), Abhijit Banerjee, Gita Gopinath, Raghuram Rajan and Mihir S. Sharma (2019). New Delhi: Juggernaut.

3. FRBM Act, 2003 was enacted by the Parliament of India to institutionalise financial decipline and overall management of the public funds by moving towards a balanced budget.

distress.

3. We need a better business environment—whether to create the jobs for those leaving agriculture, urban schools or our universities, or to promote our miserably inadequate exports.
4. Sustainable growth requires more effective but less burdensome regulation. The choking cities and climate change are posing a great threat. Municipalities need the powers and funding to deal with these challenges, which means more decentralization.
5. As government has to provide for benefits, but is not always best suited to deliver them, to reduce the implementation burden, government should move towards cash transfers. As a first step, beneficiaries of all specific government subsidy programmes should have the choice between cash transfers and benefits in kind.
6. We need more skilled personnel in government—at higher levels in technical areas like digitisation, trade negotiation and environmental regulation, but also at lower levels outside the larger cities.
7. The Right to Education Act focuses on input requirements for schools that have little bearing on learning outcomes, which have deteriorated alarmingly. Learning must be the central focus, with all schools, public and private, responsible for delivering a minimum level of basic skills to every child.
8. We need to address the coming explosion of non communicable diseases which will require engagement with front line providers. The vast majority of these may have no formal qualifications, but the evidence suggests they can be trained and pushed towards practising better medicine.

Rakesh Mohan in a recent paper (June 2019) discusses the need to focus attention on the primacy of growth as a policy objective. As the achievement of annual economic growth of about 7 percent has almost become commonplace, the country is now in danger of suffering from a degree of complacency. If India is to eliminate poverty and achieve upper middle income status in the foreseeable future, by around 2035, it must elevate its growth trajectory to the next level. The paper analysises the key macroeconomic tasks ahead to take growth back to 8-9 percent: sustained increase in savings, particularly in financial savings, and investment, fiscal consolidation through enhanced tax revenues, along with a step up in infrastructure investment. It also highlights the need to revive animal spirits in the private sector to rekindle investment, particularly in an internationally competitive manufacturing sector. This would need the maintenance of a realistic competitive exchange rate, along with implementation of long overdue bold land and labour reforms, incentivising labour using manufactured exports, and a focus on industrial research and development. Efficient growth promoting private sector functioning requires the next generation of reforms to concentrate on the institutional and technical strengthening necessary to empower government at all levels, which enables it to ensure delivery of essential public goods and services, particularly in health and education.

"India's growth record since independence suggests that it is capable of recording sustained growth over a long period, even if it is punctuated by some periods of lower growth because of business cycles or other reasons. Its institutional system has also demonstrated that significant policy changes are made in response to changing circumstances. Sometimes this is done relatively quickly, whereas at other times there may be significant delays before the needed policy change is done. Within this sustained growth record there have been specific bursts when India has made a break and ascended to a higher growth trajectory. One such departure was made soon after independence with the initiation of growth-oriented planning in the 1950s, while the second departure was initiated with the 1991 economic policy reforms when India opened its economy to the world. In each case the departure resulted from an all-encompassing policy focus on attaining higher economic growth, with other policy objectives made secondary", remarks Mohan (2019).

Mohan further reiterates, "it is now more than 25 years since these policy reforms were initiated. As the achievement of annual economic growth of about 7 percent has almost become commonplace, the country is now in danger of suffering from a degree of complacency. The time is now right for India to aspire to further elevation of its growth trajectory to the next level. A sustained annual growth rate of around 8-9 percent is needed to ensure annual per capita growth of about 7 percent, which would then ensure doubling of per capita income in every decade. It is only then that India can expect to eliminate poverty completely. It will also enable it to be among the three largest economies in the world by about 2035".

This then must be the overarching objective of economic policy over the next couple of decades. Such growth cannot be achieved unless focus is brought back to placing economic growth as the primary objective of economic policy.

There has perhaps been some disenchantment with growth as a primary policy objective because:

- There has been inadequate generation of employment leading to "Jobless Growth".
- Growth impulses have not been transmitted adequately to agriculture on which at least half the population depends leading to widespread agricultural distress.
- There is inadequate access for the vast majority of the population to basic services such as water, sanitation, health and education.

Rakesh Mohan's paper has argued in favor of a growth policy focus that takes account of these issues. Progress on each of these three problems can only be made if there is a new thrust on growth-oriented economic policy in which the government recognises its own crucial role in providing essential public goods and services. The incentivising of labour augmenting investment in both agriculture and industry also needs a new policy focus along with more efficient public sector functioning and the provision of essential infrastructure, R&D and other services, all designed to enable the private sector to revive its animal spirits for enhanced investment and growth.

Such a reorientation of policy will need enhanced government expenditures in both public investment for public goods and services, and for the provision of universal basic services. This needs to be distinguished from "Universal Basic Income" (UBI) that has received considerable policy support in recent times from both economists and policymakers alike. If the vast majority of people do have access to basic services there would be little demand for UBI, remarks Mohan.

It goes without saying that the first condition for sustained growth is an enhancement of investment levels, both public and private, but which are to be achieved while maintaining macroeconomic stability centered on fiscal prudence. Much of the Indian growth record has been possible due to sustained growth in domestic savings and associated investments. The use of external savings has been relatively limited as a proportion of total investment. The immediate priority for taking the country to a higher growth trajectory is to improve its fiscal quality. Focused attention now needs to be given, to increasing efficiency and compliance in tax revenue collection so that the Indian overall tax/GDP ratio rises to levels that are consistent with comparable international experience. This would enable a shift of fiscal expenditure composition towards increases in public investment for the delivery of public goods and services, which in turn would crowd in private investment rather than crowding it out (Mohan 2019).

If such macro-economic stabilisation, in terms of both fiscal deficit and inflation, can indeed be achieved over the next couple of decades, along with a change in the composition of expenditures, the macro-economic projections presented in Rakesh Mohan's paper suggest that it is within the realms of feasibility that the Indian economy can return to an 8-9 percent growth path for a sustained period of a couple of decades in the future. This would then begin to replicate a kind of growth experience exhibited by East and South East Asian countries, including China, in the immediate past and Japan in earlier periods. Although the task ahead will be more difficult now in view of the protracted slow-down in global economic growth and in global trade, the silver lining in future expectations according to Rakesh Mohan is that the weight of the global economy is shifting to emerging market and developing economies (EMDEs) in Asia, Latin America and Africa. Thus, even if the North Atlantic economies of North America and Europe do suffer secular stagnation in growth, as some are predicting, it is possible that the impact of global growth may be mitigated by counter balancing growth in EMDEs.

Another significant point raised in Mohan's paper, "the current fiscal policy focus is much more on efficient distribution of government subsidies, as distinguished from government expenditures, being directed to growth enhancing investments in both physical and social infrastructure that would contribute to lasting productivity gains in the economy as a whole. The point of departure on this issue is to argue for the provision of basic services rather than expansion of subsidies".

Taking India to a higher growth trajectory is, therefore, quite feasible but it will need much more focused attention to the primacy of growth as a policy objective, and understanding of the important role of a competent government (Mohan 2019).

In closing to quote Basu (2019), "most economic policy mistakes cause short or medium term hardships. The greater, long-run worry for India is the divisiveness that some groups are propagating. India has been home to not just Hindus of various castes, but Christians, Jews, Muslims, Parsis, Sikhs and Buddhists. Driving a wedge between upper caste Hindus and the rest can damage the entire nation's morale and cause long-run damage to growth".

Also as very rightly remarked by Kelkar (2019), "the deep determinants of this remarkable growth experience of ours have been institutions, demographic transition, modern technology and accumulation of both human and physical capital. In my view, the most important of these factors has been our democratic framework, a key foundational institution. Our democracy has proved to be sine qua non for effectively formulating key economic policies and conducting policy reforms in a country that is so diverse. It is also of fundamental importance for maintaining social harmony. I cannot overemphasize the need for maintaining continuous vigilance to safeguard social harmony in our highly diverse society. In this endeavour, the 'majoritarianism' will need to be eschewed. As the proverb goes 'United we stand and divided we fall'."

References

Banerjee, Abhijit et al. (2019). *What the Economy Needs Now*. New Delhi: Juggernaut, India.

Basu, Kaushik (2019). "India's Current Economic Paradox: Growth Numbers aren't Reflected by other Indicators", *Times of India*, 19 April 2019.

Drèze, Jean and Amartya Sen (2013). *An Uncertain Glory: India and its Contradictions*. Allen Lane: Penguine Books.

Government of India, Ministry of Finance (2018). *Economic Survey 2017-18, Vol. I & Vol. II*. New Delhi.

————. (2019). *Economic Survey 2018-19, Vol. 2*. New Delhi.

Joshi, Vijay (2016). *India's Long Road: The Search for Prosperity*. London: Penguine Random House India.

————. (2019). "India's Economic Reforms: Reflections on the Unfinished Agenda", Ch. 4, in Uma Kapila (ed.), *Indian Economy Since Independence* (30th ed.). New Delhi: Academic Foundation.

Kelkar, Vijay (2019). "Towards India's New Fiscal Federalism", *Sukhamoy Chakravarty Memorial Lecture at the 55th Annual Conference*, June 8, 2019.

Krishnan, V.S. (2018). *GST: A Transformational Tax Reform*. New Delhi: Academic Foundation.

Mohan, Rakesh (2019). "Moving India to A New Growth Trajectory: Need for a Comprehensive Big Push", Brookings India Research Paper No. 072019. June 2019.

Rangarajan, C. (2019). "Government's Key Agenda must be to Accelerate Growth", *The Hindu*, May 5, 2019.

Rangarajan, C. and D.K. Srivastava (2017). "Underlying Drivers of India's Potential Growth", Economic and Political Weekly LII(25-26). June 24-July 1.

Rao, Govinda M. (2019). "Reformist Government? Walk the Talk", *Financial Express*, June 4, 2019.

Reserve Bank of India (2014). *The Annual Report 2013-14*. Mumbai. 21 August.

This chapter is extensively drawn from Kapila, Uma (2019) (ed.), *Indian Economy Since Independence* (30th edition, ch. 38). New Delhi: Academic Foundation.

Glossary of Selected Terms

Absolute advantage. Occurs when a nation or other economic region is able to produce a good or service more efficiently than a second nation or region.

Absorptive capacity. The ability of a country to absorb foreign private or public financial assistance (to use the funds in a productive manner).

Acquisition. Occurs when one firm buys controlling interest in a target firm; acquisitions of foreign firms by transnational corporations are an important form of foreign direct investment.

Advanced economies. The twenty-nine richer, more industrialised countries in the world; also called the developed countries.

Agenda 21. A landmark document that established guidelines for global sustainable economic development; *Agenda 21* was adopted at the Rio Earth Summit in 1992.

Age structure of the population. The age composition of a given population. For example, in LDCs, the age structure of the population is typified by a large portion of population under 15 years old, a slightly smaller proportion aged between 15 and 45 years, and a very small proportion above 45 years old.

Agricultural sector. An economic sector comprised of farms, dairies, poultry and livestock farms, forestry, and fishing and shellfish industries.

Asian Development Bank (ADB). A regional development bank that serves Asia and the Pacific region.

Balance of payments (BoP). A summary statement of a nation's financial transactions with the outside world.

Balance of trade. The difference between the value of a nation's total imports and total exports in a given period of time.

Bank for International Settlements (BIS). An international organisation designed to promote international monetary and financial cooperation among central banks, and serves as a bank for central banks and international organisations.

Basic economic questions. The universal questions that all economies, past and present, have answered, including what, how, and for whom to produce.

Big Three. The dominant multilateral organisations that oversee economic relations among countries—the International Monetary Fund, World Bank, and World Trade Organization.

Bottlenecks. Sectors in the economy where the development process leads to a more rapid expansion of demand than supply in the goods or factor markets.

Brain drain. The emigration of highly educated and skilled professional and technical manpower from the developing to the developed countries.

Buffer stocks. Stocks of commodities held by countries or international organisations to moderate the commodities' price fluctuations.

Bretton Woods System. The institutions and operation of the international monetary system from 1946 to 1973.

Business cycle. A recurring, but irregular pattern of upswings and downswings in economic activity on the national, or global levels.

Calorie requirement. The calories needed to sustain the population at normal levels of activity and health, taking account of its age and sex distributions, average body weights, and physical environment.

Capital account. The portion of a country's *balance of payments* that shows the volume of *private foreign investment* and public *grants* and *loans* that flow into and out of a country over a given period, usually one year.

Capital deepening. Occurs when the real capital per worker increases in a country over time.

Capital flight. The excessive cross-border transfers of financial capital, often an outflow of funds from developing countries to more stable advanced economies.

Capital formation. The process of increasing the amount of capital goods in a country; capital formation stems from savings and productive investments.

Capital goods. The items that are designed to produce other goods; a factor of production.

Capital-intensive production. A method of producing goods and services that relies on the use of sophisticated capital goods.

Capitalism. A type of economic system based on the private ownership and control of the factors of production—natural resources, human resources, and capital goods.

Capital markets. The institutions that channel surplus money into medium- and long-term productive investments, investments of at least one year in duration.

Capital-output ratio. A ratio that shows the units of capital required to produce a unit of output over a given period of time.

Capital stock. The total amount of capital goods in a country.

Cash crops. Agricultural output produced for sale in domestic or global markets rather than for the household's consumption; examples are cotton, rubber and coffee.

Civil society organisations (CSOs). A variety of non-governmental and non-profit groups, or citizen's associations, that work to improve society and the human condition.

Closed economy. An economy in which there are no foreign trade transactions or any other form of economic contacts with the rest of the world.

Collusion. An agreement among producers to limit the supply, market share, and price of a good; used by producer cartels.

Command economy. A highly centralised economic system in which the government owns or controls the factors of production—natural resources, human resources, and capital goods; viewed as an economic model.

Common market. A type of regional trade agreement that creates a free trade area, uniform external trade policy, and other types of regional economic integration.

Communism. An economic system based on government ownership and control of the factors of production—and on the theories of Karl Marx.

Comparative advantage. Occurs when a nation or economic region is able to produce a product at a lower opportunity cost compared to another nation or region.

Competition. The economic rivalry that exists among producers of a similar product.

Competitiveness. The factors that influence economic performance in a nation's macroeconomy and microeconomy.

Concessional terms. Favorable credit terms on loans, including a low interest rate and extended repayment period; offered by some multilateral development institutions to the poorest developing countries.

Conditionality. The requirement imposed by the *International Monetary Fund* that a borrowing country undertake fiscal, monetary, and international commercial reforms as a condition to receiving a *loan* for *balance of payments* difficulties.

Consumer price index (CPI). Measures the percentage change in the price of a uniform market basket of goods and services every month; the CPI is used to calculate the inflation rate.

Cooperative. A voluntary association of people who jointly own and control a productive enterprise to satisfy the economic, social, or cultural needs of members; also called a co-op.

Corporation. A type of business that is owned by stockholders, but typically run by professional managers.

Corruption. The abuse of the public trust for personal gain.

Crude birthrate. The number of children born alive each year per 1,000 population (a crude birthrate of 20 per 1,000 is the same as a 2 per cent increase).

Deathrate. The yearly number of deaths per 1,000 population—an annual crude deathrate of 15 per 1,000 would involve 1.5 per cent of the population.

Debt-service ratio. The ratio of interest and principal payments due in a year to export receipts for that year.

Decile. A 10 per cent portion of any numerical quantity; a population divided into deciles would be divided into 10 equal numeric groups.

Default. Occurs when a government refuses to make scheduled payments on its debts.

Deforestation. The clearing of forested land.

Democracy. A type of political system in which political authority is derived from the people, either directly or through freely elected representatives.

Democratic socialism. A type of economic system in which core socialist beliefs guide national economic policy, and democratic institutions govern the nation.

Demographic transition. The phasing-out process of population growth rates from a virtually stagnant growth stage characterised by high *birthrates* and *death rates*, through a rapid-growth stage with high birthrates and low death rates, to a stable, low-growth stage in which both birth and death rates are low.

Dependency burden. The proportion of the total population aged 0 to 15 and 65+, which is considered economically unproductive and therefore not counted in the labour force.

Devaluation. A government action that lowers the value of its currency relative to other countries' currencies.

Developing countries. The poorer, less industrialised countries in the global economy.

Developed World. The now economically advanced capitalist countries of Western Europe, North America, Australia, New Zealand, and Japan. These were the first countries to experience sustained long-term *economic growth*.

Developing countries. The present countries of Asia, Africa, the Middle East, Latin America and East Europe and the Former Soviet Union, mainly characterised by low *levels of living*, high rates of *population growth*, low *income per capita*, and general economic and technological *dependence* on developed economies.

Digital divide. The information and communications technologies (ICTs) gap between the "have" and "have not" countries.

Doha Development Agenda (DDA). A 2001 World Trade Organization statement pledging support for fair trade and sustainable economic development.

Dumping. An illegal trade practice that occurs when a company from one nation sells its output in a second country at a price lower than its production costs, or lower than the price charged in its own domestic market.

Economic freedom. The ability of individuals and businesses to freely choose how to use their private property in an economy.

Economic growth. The steady process by which the productive capacity of the economy is increased over time to bring about rising levels of national output and income.

Economic infrastructure. The physical capital that underpins economic growth and development; examples include transportation and communications systems, public utilities, and courts.

Economic integration. The merging to various degrees of the economies and economic policies of two or more countries in a given region.

Economic planning. A deliberate and conscious attempt by the state to formulate decisions on how the *factors of production* shall be allocated among different uses or industries, thereby determining how much of total *goods* and *services* shall be produced in one or more ensuing periods.

Economic policy. A statement of objectives and the methods of achieving these objectives (policy instruments) by government, political party, business concern, etc. Some examples of government economic objectives are maintaining *full employment,* achieving a high rate of *economic growth*, reducing *income inequalities* and regional development inequalities, and maintaining price stability. Policy instruments include fiscal policy, monetary and financial policy, and legislative controls (e.g., price and wage control and rent control).

Economic sanctions. Any restrictions on trade, investment, or foreign aid that are intended to pressurise a country to change a policy or action.

Economic system. Represents all economic activity in a country; different types of economic systems answer the basic economic questions in different ways.

Economies of scale. The decline in the average cost of producing a good as the rate of output rises; highlights the advantages of bigness.

Ecosystems. Systems consisting of organic and inorganic matter and natural forces that interact and change; basic ecosystems include grasslands, forests, agricultural areas, freshwater, and coastal.

Embargo. A type of economic sanction often designed to influence a domestic or international policy in a second country; embargoes can be comprehensive or selective.

Emerging market economies (EMEs). Refers to countries that have made significant strides toward capitalism and sustainable economic development.

Empowerment of women. The idea that giving women power over their economic, social, and *reproductive choices* will raise their status, promote development, and reduce population growth.

Entrepreneur. A person who starts a new business, develops a new product, or devises a new way to produce a product; a risk-taker and innovator.

Environmental degradation. A wide variety of human-induced and naturally occurring stresses on the natural environment.

Euro. The common currency of the European Union; the euro replaced the national currencies of 12 EU countries in 2002.

European Union (EU). A unique intergovernmental organisation that coordinates economic, foreign, security, and judicial policies among its 25 member nations.

Exchange rates. The value of one currency compared to a second currency.

Export processing zone (EPZ). An industrial area that offers special incentives to attract foreign direct investment, and in which export industries produce products.

Export promotion. Governmental efforts to expand the volume of a country's exports through *export incentives* and other means in order to generate more *foreign exchange* and improve the *current account* of its *balance of payments.*

Expropriation. The government's seizure of private physical assets or financial assets without compensation to the previous owner.

External Debt. The money owed by a nation to a foreign government or commercial bank, a multilateral organisation, or other creditor; also called foreign debt.

Factors of production. The resources used to produce goods or services, including natural resources, human resources, and capital goods; entrepreneurship is often considered a fourth factor of production; also called productive resources.

Fertility rate. The yearly number of children born alive per 1,000 women within the childbearing age bracket (normally between the ages of 15 and 49 years). The total *fertility rate* (TFR) is the number of children that would be born to a woman if she were to live to the end of her childbearing years and bear children at each age in accordance with the prevailing age-specific fertility rates.

Final goods. Commodities that are consumed to satisfy wants rather than passed on to further stages of production. Whenever a final good is not consumed but is used as an *input* instead, it becomes an *intermediate producer good.*

Fixed exchange rate system. A system of converting nations' currencies at a rate tied to gold or to the US dollar; the fixed exchange rate system was an important feature of the Bretton Woods System from 1946 to 1973.

Flexible exchange rate. The exchange value of a national currency that is free to move up and down in response to shifts in demand and supply arising from international trade and finance.

Foreign aid. A grant of money, technical assistance, food, capital equipment, or other assistance from one country to another.

Foreign direct investment (FDI). Overseas investments by private multinational corporations.

Foreign exchange gap. Exists when the planned merchandise *trade deficit* exceeds the value of capital inflows thus causing output growth to be limited by inadequate *foreign exchange.*

Foreign exchange market. A network of commercial banks, investment banks, brokerage houses, and other financial institutions that buy and sell currencies for profit; also called the forex market.

Foreign reserves. The value of a country's holdings of foreign currencies, gold, and IMF special drawing rights (SDRs); the reserve is sometimes tapped to make international payments.

Free trade. Refers to international trade that is not restricted by trade barriers—such as tariffs and import quotas—or other distortions such as subsidies.

Free trade area. A type of regional trade agreement that eliminates trade barriers among members.

General Agreement on Tariffs and Trade (GATT). A multilateral agreement that established rules for international trade from 1948 to 1994.

Global economy. The international network of individuals, businesses, governments, and multilateral organisations, which collectively make decisions about the production, consumption, and distribution of goods and services.

Globalisation. The freer cross-border movements of goods and services, labour, technology, real capital, and financial capital to create an integrated and interdependent global economy.

Global warming. The gradual warming of world surface temperatures over time, due mainly to the greenhouse effect.

Good governance. The honest, competent administration of governments, businesses, civil society organisations, multilateral organisations, and other decision-making bodies in the global community.

Government failure. Situation in which government intervention in an economy worsens outcomes.

Gradualism. A cautious approach to economic transition, based on experimentation and the gradual infusion of successful market reforms.

Green revolution. The boost in grain production associated with the scientific discovery of new *hybrid seed* varieties of wheat, rice, and corn that have resulted in high farm yields in many LDCs.

Green technologies. Environmentally friendly technologies that promote the efficient use of resources and reduce waste and pollution.

Gross domestic product (GDP). The total money value of all newly produced final goods and services in an economy in a given year.

Gross national income (GNI). The people's total income derived from domestic and foreign sources; the broadest measure of national income; previously called the gross national product (GNP).

Group of Eight (G8). An organisation of eight industrialised economies that discuss and form common policies on matters of global concern; comprised of the G7 plus Russia.

Group of Seven (G7). The seven leading industrialised developed nations (the United States, Canada, Great Britain, France, Germany, Japan, and Italy), who meet annually to discuss global economic issues.

Group of Seventy-seven (G77). A coalition of 133 developing countries; originally formed to promote economic justice in the global economy.

Group of Twenty (G20). A forum comprised of advanced economies, and emerging market and developing countries; designed to strengthen the global financial architecture and promote sustainable economic development.

Hard currency. The currency of a major advanced economy, such as the US dollar, Japanese yen, or EMU euro; used in many types of international transactions.

Human capital. Workers whose abilities and skills have been enhanced by education, training, apprenticeships, or other means.

Human development. Reflects the realistic range of choices that people have to live happy and productive lives.

Human Development Index (HDI). An index of people's well-being; an annual HDI is published by the United Nations Development Program.

Human resources. The people involved in production; human resources is a factor of production.

Import substitution. A trade strategy that challenges domestic businesses to produce substitute goods for items normally imported; designed to reduce the country's dependence on foreign goods.

Indicative planning. A collaborative, inclusive economic planning process employed by some democratic socialist economies.

Industrial Revolution. The economic transition from small-scale labour-intensive production to large-scale capital-intensive production in factories and mills; the Industrial Revolution began in Great Britain during the 1700s.

Infant industry. A newly formed industry in a country; the infant industry argument is used to defend protectionist trade policies, such as tariffs and import quotas.

Infant mortality rate. Deaths among children between birth and 1 year of age per 1,000 live births.

Inflation. An increase in the overall price level in an economy; two types of inflation are demand-pull and cost-push inflation.

Inflation rate. Measures the percentage increase in the overall price level over time.

Informal economy. Refers to business activity that is not reported to the government.

Innovation. The process of converting scientific discoveries and technological advances into profitable business ventures, products, or production processes.

Intellectual property rights. Refers to legal codes and structures to protect people's creative endeavours, including industrial property and copyrights.

International Bank for Reconstruction and Development (IBRD). A member-owned development institution that provides low-interest loans and technical assistance mainly to middle-income developing countries; part of the World Bank Group.

International Labor Organization (ILO). A specialised agency of the United Nations that promotes worker rights and decent work in the global economy.

International Monetary Fund (IMF). An international financial institution (IFI) designed to promote global financial and economic stability, growth and development; a specialised agency in the United Nations System.

International trade. The cross-border exchange of goods or services; occurs when an individual, business, government, or other entity imports or exports products.

Investment goods. Items not designed for present consumption, including capital goods, inventories, and residential housing.

Inward-looking development policies. Policies that stress economic *self-reliance* on the part of LDCs, including the development of indigenous *appropriate technology*, the imposition of substantial protective *tariffs* and *nontariff trade barriers* to promote *import substitution,* and the general discouragement of *private foreign investment*.

Joint venture. A business agreement between two or more companies to produce or sell a product; usually short-term in nature.

Labour force. Consists of individuals of employable age, who have a job or are actively seeking employment.

Labour-intensive production. A method of producing goods or services that relies on physical labour; often associated with production in the developing countries.

Land reform. A deliberate attempt to reorganise and transform existing *agrarian systems* with the intention of improving the distribution of agricultural incomes and thus fostering *rural development.*

Least developed countries (LDCs). Refers to 50 of the world's poorest developing countries; most low-income developing countries are LDCs.

Life expectancy at birth. The number of years newborn children would live subject to the *mortality* risks prevailing for the cross section of population at the time of their birth.

Literacy. The ability to read and write.

Literacy rate. The percentage of the population age 15 and over able to read and write. Literacy rates are often used as one of the many social and economic indicators of the state of development of a country.

Market economy. A type of economic system in which the private sector owns and controls the factors of production—natural resources, human resources, and capital goods; viewed as an economic model.

Market failure. A phenomenon that results from the existence of market imperfections (e.g., *monopoly* power, lack of *factor mobility*, significant *externalities,* lack of knowledge) that weaken the functioning of a free-market economy—it fails to realise its theoretical beneficial results. Market failure often provides the justification for government interference with the working of the *free market*.

Market mechanism. The interaction of supply and demand in free markets to determine prices and allocate resources without government intervention.

Merger. Occurs when two or more firms combine their assets, or equity, to form a single larger firm; mergers of firms headquartered in different countries is a type of foreign direct investment.

Mergers and acquisitions (M&As). Occur when two existing companies are legally joined under single ownership; M&As are a type of foreign direct investment.

Microeconomic theory of fertility. An extension of the theory of consumer behaviour of individual couples. The central proposition of this theory is that family formation has costs and benefits and hence the size of families formed will depend on these costs and benefits. If the costs of family formation are high relative to its benefits, the rates at which couples will decide to bring forth children will decline, and *vice versa*.

Millennium Development Goals (MDGs). The eight specific objectives for human and economic development in the global economy, established by the United Nations in 2000.

Mixed economy. An economy that combines features of the market economy and command economy models; in common usage, mixed economies refer to economic systems that lean toward the market model.

Most favored nations (MFN). Agreement that a trade concession granted by one World Trade Organization member to another member automatically applies to all members; a basic principle of the General Agreement on Tariffs and Trade and the WTO.

Multilateral environmental agreements (MEAs). The formal protocols, conventions, treaties, or declarations negotiated by countries to protect or restore the natural environment.

Nationalisation. The government's seizure of private productive assets with compensation to the previous owner.

Newly industrialising countries (NICs). A small group of countries at a relatively advanced level of economic *development* with a substantial and dynamic industrial sector and with close links to the international trade, finance, and investment system (Argentina, Brazil, Greece, Mexico, Portugal, Singapore, South Korea, Spain, and Taiwan).

New protectionism. Wide range of non-tariff trade barriers erected by developed countries against the manufactured exports of developing nations; typically as quotas or 'voluntary' export restrain by LDCs.

Non-Governmental organisation (NGO). A special interest group that conducts research, disseminates information, and advocates for change at the national and international levels.

Non-renewable resources. Resources that are consumed during production and cannot be replenished, such as oil and natural gas.

Offshoring. Occurs when a producer from one country outsources production to another country.

Organization for Economic Co-operation and Development (OECD). A thirty-member intergovernmental organisation that collects and analyses statistical data, discusses global trends and issues, and forms binding and non-binding economic and social policies.

Organization of the Petroleum Exporting Countries (OPEC). An eleven-member producer cartel comprised of major petroleum-producing countries.

Paradigm. Implicit assumptions from which theories evolve; a *model* or framework of analysis.

Political will. A determined effort by persons in political authority to achieve certain economic objectives, such as elimination of inequality, poverty, and unemployment through various reforms of social, economic and institutional structures. Lack of political will is often said to be one of the main obstacles to *development* and one of the main reasons for the failure of many *development plans.*

Private property rights. The legal codes and other protections that guarantee people's right to own, control, buy, sell, and profit from private property.

Private sector. The part of an economy whose activities are under the control and direction of non-governmental economic units such as households or firms. Each economic unit owns its own *resources* and uses them mainly to maximise its own well-being.

Privatisation. Selling public assets (corporations) to individuals or private business interests.

Protectionism. The government's use of import controls, such as tariffs and import quotas, and export subsidies to protect local industries and jobs.

Public consumption. All current expenditures for purchases of *goods* and *services* by all levels of government: includes capital expenditures on national defence and security.

Public good. An entity that provides benefits to all individuals simultaneously and whose enjoyment by one person is in no way diminished by that of another.

Public Sector. The portion of an economy whose activities (economic and noneconomic) are under the control and direction of the state.

Purchasing power parity (PPP). The purchasing power of a country's currency: the number of units of that currency required to purchase the same basket of goods and services that a US Dollar would buy in the United States.

Quality of life. The overall conditions under which people live.

Quota. A physical limitation on the quantity of any item that can be imported into a country, such as so many automobiles per year. Also a method for allocating limited school places by noncompetitive means—for example, by income or ethnicity.

Recession. A period of slack general economic activity as reflected in rising unemployment and excess productive capacity in a broad spectrum of industries.

Redistribution policies. Policies geared to reducing *income inequality* and expanding economic opportunities in order to promote *development*. Examples include *progressive income tax policies*, provision of services financed out of such taxation to benefit persons in the lower-income groups, *rural development* policies giving emphasis to raising *levels of living* for the rural poor through *land reform* and other forms of asset and wealth redistribution.

Regional trade agreement (RTA). An agreement that creates preferential trade concessions among member countries.

Remittances. Money earned by foreign-born or immigrant workers in one country but sent to family, friends, business associates, or others in the home country; sometimes viewed as a type of foreign aid.

Renewable resources. Resources that can be replenished, such as sunlight and forests.

Replacement fertility. The level of *fertility* at which childbearing women have just enough daughters to replace themselves in the population. This keeps the existing population size constant through an infinite number of succeeding generations.

Reproductive choice. Argument that women should be able to determine on an equal status with their husbands and for themselves how many children they want and what methods to use to achieve their desired family size.

Research and development (R&D). Scientific investigation with a view toward improving the existing quality of human life, products, *profits, factors of production*, or knowledge. There are two categories of R&D: basic R&D (without a specific commercial objective) and applied R&D (with a commercial objective).

Scale-neutral. Unaffected by size; applied to *technological progress* that can lead to the achievement of higher output levels irrespective of the size (scale) of a firm or farm, making it equally applicable to small- and large-scale production processes. An often-cited example is the *hybrid seeds* of the *green revolution*, which can theoretically increase yields on both small and large farms (if *complementary resources* such as fertiliser, irrigation, and pesticides are available).

Self-esteem. The feeling of worthiness that a society enjoys when its *social, political*, and *economic systems* and *institutions* promote human respect, dignity, integrity, self-determination, etc.

Social capital. A country's broad infrastructure; social capial is provided by the government for the collective welfare of the people.

Socialism. A type of economic system based on public ownership and control of key resources and industries; strands range from democratic socialism to communism.

Special Drawing Rights (SDR). The International Monetary Fund's unit of account, roughly comparable to the European Union's euro, the US dollar, or other national unit of account.

Statism. An economic philosophy that supports active government intervention in the economy, including the nationalisation of key industries.

Subsidy. A government payment to a business, mainly to support domestic producers; viewed as a type of protectionism in international markets.

Subsistence agriculture. An agricultural system designed to satisfy the personal consumption needs of households rather than to produce surpluses for export.

Supply chain. A network of businesses that are collectively responsible for the production and distribution of a product.

Subsistence economy. An economy in which production is mainly for personal consumption and the standard of living yields no more than the basic necessities of life—food, shelter, and clothing.

Subsistence farming. Farming in which crop production, stock rearing, and other activities are conducted mainly for personal consumption, characterised by low productivity, *risk*, and *uncertainty*.

Sustainable development. Pattern of *development* that permits future generations to live at least as well as the current generation.

Sustainable economic development. Occurs when an economy achieves sustained economic growth and substantive improvements in people's quality of life.

Sustenance. The basic *goods* and *services*, such as food, clothing, and shelter, that are necessary to sustain an average human being at the bare minimum *level of living*.

Tariff. A fixed percentage tax on the value of an imported commodity levied at the point of entry into the importing country.

Technological progress. Increased application of new scientific knowledge in form of inventions and *innovations* with regard to both *physical* and *human capital*. Such progress has been a major factor in stimulating the long-term *economic growth* of contemporary developed countries.

Technology transfer. The sharing of advanced technology between transnational corporations and their affiliates or other related firms.

Tenant farmer. One who farms on land held by a *landlord* and therefore lacks secure ownership rights and has to pay for the use of that land, for example, by surrendering part of his output to the owner. Examples are found in the Latin American and Asian *agrarian systems*.

Terms of trade. A measure of the relative prices of a country's exports and imports.

Trade barrier. Government policies designed to discourage or prohibit imports, such as import tariffs and import quotas.

Trade deficit. Occurs when the value of a country's imports is greater than its exports.

Trade liberalisation. Refers to government policies that result in freer trade; includes the removal of trade barriers and business subsidies.

Trade-off. The necessity of sacrificing (trading off) something in order to get more of something else—for example, sacrificing consumption now for consumption later by devoting some present *resources to investment*.

Trade-Related Aspects of Intellectual Property (TRIPS). An international agreement designed to protect intellectual properties in global markets; administered by the World Trade Organization.

Trade surplus. Occurs when the value of a country's exports is greater than its imports.

Traditional economy. An economic system that relies on custom or tradition to answer the basic economic questions.

Transition countries. The 28 countries of eastern and central Europe and central Asia that are in the process of transforming from communism to capitalism, and from totalitarianism to democracy; also called transition economies.

Transnational corporation (TNC). A company that is based in one country, but owns or controls other companies, called affiliates, in one or more additional countries.

Transparency. Refers to a free flow of information; transparency promotes accountability of governments, transnational corporations, multilateral organisations, and others; it also promotes inclusion of the marginalised in global decision making.

Trickle-down theory of development. The notion that *development* is purely an economic phenomenon in which rapid gains from the overall growth of *gross national product* and *income per capita* would automatically bring benefits (trickle down) to the masses in the form of jobs and other economic opportunities. The main preoccupation is therefore to get the growth job done while problems of *poverty*, unemployment, and *income distribution* are perceived to be of secondary importance.

Two-gap model. Theoretical *foreign aid* model comparing *savings* and *foreign exchange* gaps to determine which is the binding constraint on *economic growth*.

Underemployment. Occurs when workers are employed at jobs beneath their skill level, at jobs that do not fully utilise their skills, or at jobs that offer insufficient work hours.

Unorganised money market. The informal and often usurious credit system that exists in most developing countries (especially in rural areas) where low-income farms and firms with little collateral are forced to borrow from *moneylenders* and loan sharks at exorbitant rates of *interest*.

Unsustainable debt. A country's inability to service, or make payments on, its external debt without decimating its domestic economy.

Urbanisation. The process of becoming more urban; the shift of population and economic activity from rural areas to cities.

Venture capital. Money invested to create new businesses; also called risk capital.

Vicious cycle. A self-reinforcing situation in which factors tend to perpetuate a certain undesirable phenomenon—for example, low incomes in poor countries lead to low consumption, which then leads to poor health and low *labour productivity* and eventually to the persistence of *poverty*.

Wage-price spiral. *Vicious cycle* in which higher consumer prices (e.g., as a result of *devaluation*) cause workers to demand higher wages, which in turn cause producers to raise prices and worsen inflationary forces.

World Trade Organization (WTO). An international organisation that oversees the operation of the rules-based multilateral trading system.

Select Bibliography

Acharya, Shankar (2015). *Towards Economic Crisis (2012-2014) and Beyond.* New Delhi: Academic Foundation.

———. (2009). *India and Global Crisis*. New Delhi: Academic Foundation.

Acharya, Shankar and Rakesh Mohan (2010). *India's Economy: Performance and Challenges (Essays in honour of Montek Singh Ahluwalia).* New Delhi: OUP.

———. (2006). *Essays on Macroeconomic Policy and Growth in India*. New Delhi: Oxford University Press.

Ahluwalia, I.J. (2005). "Trade Liberalisation and Industrial Performance in India", in S.D. Tendulkar *et al.*, (eds.), *Industrialisation in a Reforming Economy*, Essays for K.L. Krishna. New Delhi: Academic Foundation.

Ahluwalia, Montek Singh (2015). "India's Growth Performance and Prospects: An Update", in Uma Kapila (ed.) (2014), *Indian Economy since Independence* (26th edition). New Delhi: Academic Foundation.

Bala Subrahmanya, M.H. (2014). "Small Scale Industrialisation under Globalisation: Is the Tide Turning Around ", in Uma Kapila (ed.) (2014), *Indian Economy since Independence* (25th edition). New Delhi: Academic Foundation.

———. (2008). "Small Industry and Globalisation: Implications, Performance and Prospects", in K.L. Krishna and Uma Kapila (eds.) *Readings in Indian Agriculture and Industry*. New Delhi: Academic Foundation.

Banerjee, Abhijit, Gita Gopinath, Raghuram Rajan and Mihir S. Sharma (eds.) (2019). *What the Economy Needs Now*. New Delhi: Juggernaut, India.

Basu, Kaushik and Annemie Maertens (ed.) (2012). *The Concise Oxford Companion to Economics in India*. New Delhi: Oxford University Press.

Basu, Kaushik (ed.) (2004). "The Indian Economy: Up to 1991 and Since", *India's Emerging Economy, Performance and Prospects in the 1990s and Beyond*, Ch.1, OUP.

Bhagwati, Jagdish and Arvind Panagariya (2012). *India's Tryst with Destiny: Debunking Myths that Undermine Progress and Addressing New Challenges.* New Delhi: Collins Business.

Bhagwati, Jagdish (1998). "The Design of Indian Development", in Ahluwalia I.J. and Little I.M.D (eds.), *India's Economic Reforms and Development*. Essays for Manmohan Singh. New Delhi: Oxford University Press.

Bhagwati, J. and P. Desai (1970). *India Planning for Industrialisation*. London: Oxford University Press.

Bhagwati, Jagdish and T.N. Srinivasan (1993). "India's Economic Reforms", Ministry of Finance, GoI, New Delhi. Reproduced in Uma Kapila (ed.), *Indian Economy Since Independence* (2001 edition). New Delhi: Academic Foundation.

Bisaliah, S., S. Mahendra Dev and Syed Saifullah (2013). *Investment in Indian Agriculture: Macro and Micro Evidences*. New Delhi: Academic Foundation.

Bloom, David E. (2017). "Population Dynamics in India and Implications for Economic Growth", in Uma Kapila (ed.) (2017), *Indian Economy Since Independence* (28th edition). New Delhi: Academic Foundation.

Byres, Terence J. (ed.) (1998). *The Indian Economy, Major Debates Since Independence*, Oxford University Press.

Cassen, R.H. (1978). *India: Population, Economy and Society*, Ch. 4.

Cassen, Robert and Joshi, Vijay (eds.) (1995). *India: The Future of Economic Reform*. New Delhi: Oxford University Press.

Chakravarthy, Sukhamoy (1987a). *Development Planning: The Indian Experience*, Oxford University Press.

Chakrabarty, K.C. (2013). "Indian Economy: Imperatives for Second Generation Reforms" (Ch. 2), in Uma Kapila (ed.) (2013), *Indian Financial Reforms: Priorities and Policy Thrust Post Global Financial Crisis*. New Delhi: Academic Foundation.

Chandra, K. Sumar *et al.* (eds.) (2013). *Agrarian Crisis in India: The Way Out*. New Delhi: Academic Foundation.

Charles, Bettleheim, *India Independent*..

Chaturvedi, B.K. and Shekhar Chandra (2015). *Corruption and Economic Growth*. New Delhi: Academic Foundation.

Chengappa, P.G. (2013). "Secondary Agriculture: A Driver for Growth of Primary Agriculture in India", *Indian Journal of Agricultural Economics* 68(1). January-March 2013.

Commission on Growth and Development (2008). *The Growth Report, Strategies for Sustained Growth and Inclusive Development*.

Dandekar, V.M. "Forty Years After Independence" in Bimal Jalan (ed.), *Indian Economy: Problems and Prospects*. New Delhi: Viking.

Dantwala, M.L. (1981). *Understanding Poverty and Unemployment*, Artha Jignasa, (April-June). Bombay: Indian Merchants Chamber.

Debroy, Bibek and Debashis Chakraborty (2006). *The Trade Game Negotiation Trends at WTO and Concerns of Developing Countries*. New Delhi: Academic Foundation..

Desai, A.V. (2001). "A Decade of Reforms", in *Economic Developments in India*, Vol. 47. New Delhi: Academic Foundation.

Desai, Nitin and Rajeev D. Mathur (2013). *Growth and Equity: Essays in Honour of Pradeep Mehta*. New Delhi: Academic Foundation.

Deshpande, R.S. and Khalil Musa Shaha (2017). "Stranded at Jagged Crossroads: Agricultural Sector of India", in Uma Kapila (ed.) (2017), *India's Economy: Pre-Liberalisation to GST—Essays in Honour of Raj Kapila*. New Delhi: Academic Foundation.

Deshpande, R.S., *et al.* (eds.) (2008). *Glimpses of Indian Agriculture: Macro and Micro Aspects* (A set of 2 vols.). New Delhi: Academic Foundation.

Dev, Mahendra S. (ed.) (2015). *India Development Report*. IGIDR. Mumbai: Oxford University Press..

———. (2013). *India Development Report*. IGIDR. Mumbai: Oxford University Press.

Dev, Mahendra S. and N. Chandrasekhara Rao (eds.) (2009). *India: Perspectives on Equitable Development*. New Delhi: Academic Foundation.

Drèze, Jean and Amartya Sen (2013). *An Uncertain Glory: India and Its Contradictions*. Allen Lane: Penguine Books.

———. (2002). *India: Development and Participation*, Oxford University Press.

Dyson, Tim (2008). "India's Demographic Transition and its Consequences for Development", in Uma Kapila (ed.), *Indian Economy Since Independence*, 2015 (26th edition). New Delhi: Academic Foundation..

EPW Research Foundation (2013). *India: A Pocket Book of Data Series 2013*, New Delhi: Academic Foundation.

Ghosh, Nilabja and C.S.C. Sekhar (eds.) (2013). *The Future of Indian Agriculture*. New Delhi: Academic Foundation.

Gordon, Jim and Poonam Gupta (2003). "Understanding India's Services Revolution", Paper prepared for the IMF-NCAER Conference, *A Tale of Two Giants: India's and China's Experience with Reform*, November 14-16.

Goswami, Omkar (2014). "Generating Employment", in Bibek Debroy, Ashley J. Tellis and Reece Trevor (eds.) (2014), *Getting India Back on Track: An Action Agenda for Reform*. Random House India.

Government of India. *Economic Survey*, various issues including 2018-19. New Delhi: Ministry of Finance.

———. (2001). "Report of the Task Force on Employment Opportunities", (Chairman: M.S. Ahluwalia), Reproduced in Planning Commission *Reports on Labour and Employment.* New Delhi: Academic Foundation.

Government of India, Niti Aayog (2017). Three Year Action Agenda 2017-18 to 2019-20 (April).

———. Planning Commission (2012). *Twelfth Five Year Plan.*

———. (2012). *Twelfth Five Year Plan* Approach Paper.

———. (2010). *Mid-term Appraisal of the Eleventh Five Year Plan.*

———. (2009). *Macro-Modelling for the Eleventh Five Year Plan of India*, edited by Kirit S. Parikh. New Delhi: Academic Foundation.

———. (2008). *Eleventh Five Year Plan* 2007-2012.

———. (2006). *Approach Paper to the 11th Plan.*

———. (2006). *Tenth Five Year Plan* 2002-07.

———. (2005). *Mid-term Appraisal of the Tenth Five Year Plan.*

Goyal, S.K. (2014). *India's Policy Milieu: Economic Development, Planning and Industry.* New Delhi: Academic Foundation.

Gulati, Ashok (2012). "Reforming Agriculture", in Uma Kapila (ed.), Two Decades of Economic Reforms. New Delhi: Academic Foundation.

Gulati, A. and Shenggen Fan (2008). *The Dragon and the Elephant—Agricultural and Rural Reforms in China and India.* New Delhi: Oxford University Press.

Hashim, S.R. *et al.*, (eds.) (2009). *Indian Industrial Development and Globalisation* (Essays in Honour of Professor S.K. Goyal). New Delhi: Academic Foundation.

Helpman, Elhanan (2005). *The Mystery of Economic Growth.* New Delhi: Academic Foundation.

Institute for Human Development (2014). *India Labour and Employment Report 2014: Workers in the Era of Globalisation.* New Delhi: Academic Foundation.

ILO (2013). *World of Work Report 2013: Repairing the Economic and Social Fabric.* New Delhi: Academic Foundation.

———. (2012). *World of Work Report 2012: Better Jobs for a Better Economy.* New Delhi: Academic Foundation.

Jalan, Bimal (ed.) (1992). *The Indian Economy: Problems and Prospects.* New Delhi: Viking Penguin, India.

———. (1996). *India's Economic Policy—Preparing for the 20th Century*, Viking Penguin, India.

James, K.S. (2008). "Glorifying Malthus: Current Debtate on 'Demographic Dividend' in India", *Economic and Political Weekly*, Vol. XLIII, No. 25, June 21-27.

Jha, Veena (2012). *India Emerging: The Reality Checks.* New Delhi: Academic Foundation.

Jayaram, N. and R.S. Deshpande (eds.) (2008). *Footprints of Development and Change*. New Delhi: Academic Foundation.

Joshi, Vijay (2017). "India's Economic Reforms: Reflections on the Unfinished Agenda", Eighteenth L.K. Jha Memorial Lecture, December 11, 2017 (RBI Bulletin February 2018) in Uma Kapila (ed.) (2018), *Indian Economy Since Independence*, 29th edition. New Delhi: Academic Foundation.

Joshi, Vijay (2016). India's Long Road: The Search for Prospects. Penguin: Random House, India.

Joshi, Vijay and I.M.D. Little (1997). *India's Economic Reforms: 1991-2001*, Oxford University Press.

Joshi, Seema (2008). *Growth and Structure of Tertiary Sector in Developing Economies.* New Delhi: Academic Foundation.

Kapila, Raj and Uma Kapila (eds.) (2017). *Economic Developments in India*, (various volumes); latest volume: Vol. 240 (monthly update). New Delhi: Academic Foundation.

———. (2015). *India's Development Story*. New Delhi: Academic Foundation.

———. (2006). *India's Economy: A Journey in Time and Space*. New Delhi: Academic Foundation.

———. (2002). *A Decade of Economic Reforms in India*. New Delhi: Academic Foundation.

Kapila, Uma (ed.) (2019). *Indian Economy since Independence* (30th edition). New Delhi: Academic Foundation.

———. (2019). *Indian Economy–II: Macroeconomic Policies Sectoral Developments and Performance* (2019 edition). New Delhi: Academic Foundation.

———. (2018). *Indian Economy–I: Economic Development and Policy* (2018-19 edition). New Delhi: Academic Foundation.

———. (2017). *India's Economy: Pre-Liberalisation to GST (Essays in Honour of Raj Kapila)*. New Delhi: Academic Foundation.

———. (2016). *Indian Economic Development Since 1947* (2016-17 edition). New Delhi: Academic Foundation.

———. (2016). *Indian Economy: Economic Development and Policy* (2016-17 edition). New Delhi: Academic Foundation.

———. (2014). *The Emerging Big Picture: Making Sense of India's Economy* (2 Vols.). New Delhi: Academic Foundation.

———. (2013). *Indian Financial Reforms: Priorities and Policy Thrust Post Global Financial Crisis*. New Delhi: Academic Foundation.

———. (2012). *Two Decades of Economic Reforms*, New Delhi: Academic Foundation.

———. (2010). *India's Economic Development Since 1947*, New Delhi: Academic Foundation, (5th edition).

Kelkar, Vijay (2010). "On Strategies for Disinvestment and Privatisation", (26th Sir Purshotam Das Thakur Das Memorial Lecture, Jan, 2010) in Uma Kapila (ed.) (2018), *Indian Economy Since Independence* (29th edition). New Delhi: Academic Foundation.

———. (2001). "Economic Reforms Agenda: Micro, Meso and Macro Economic Reforms", in *Economic Developments in India*, Vol. 44. New Delhi: Academic Foundation.

Kindleberger Charles P. and Bruce Herrik (1977). *Economic Development*, 3rd (ed.) International Students Edition.

Krishna, K.L. (2017). "Industrial Development and Policies since Independence: Growth without Employment", in Uma Kapila (ed.) (2017), *Indian Economy Since Independence (28th edition).* New Delhi: Academic Foundation.

———. (2008). "Industrial Growth and Diversification", in Uma Kapila (ed.), *Indian Economy Since Independence.* New Delhi: Academic Foundation.

Krishna, K.L and Uma Kapila (2009). *Readings in Indian Agriculture and Industry.* New Delhi: Academic Foundation.

Krishnaji, N. (1990). "Agricultural Price Policy: A Survey with Reference to Indian Foodgrains Economy", in Uma Kapila (ed.), *Indian Economy Since Independence* (2001-02 edition). New Delhi: Academic Foundation.

Kochhar, Sameer (ed.) (2013). *An Agenda for India's Growth: Essays in Honour of P. Chidambaram.* New Delhi: Academic Foundation.

———. (2012). *Policymaking for Indian Planning: Essays on Contemporary Issues in Honour of Montek S. Ahluwalia*. New Delhi: Academic Foundation.

Krueger, O. Anne (2002). *Economic Policy Reforms and the Indian Economy.* New Delhi: Oxford University Press.

Kumar, Nagesh (2009). "Liberalisation, Foreign Direct Investment Flows and Development: Indian Experience in the 1990s", in K.L. Krishna and Uma Kapila (eds.) *Readings in Indian Agriculture and Industry*. New Delhi: Academic Foundation.

Kumar, Rajiv (2014). *Exploding Aspirations: Unlocking India's Future*. New Delhi: Academic Foundation.

Kumar, Rajiv *et al.* (2015). *Resurgent India: Ideas and Priorities*. New Delhi: Academic Foundation.

Lamy, Pascal (2013). "WTO: Building a Global Trading System for the 21st Century", in Nitin Desai and Rajiv D. Mathur (eds.), *Growth and Equity: Essays in Honour of Pradeep Mehta*. New Delhi: Academic Foundation. pp.57-63.

Meier, G. (1995). *Leading Issues in Economic Development*, 6th Ed. Ch. I-A pp., 7-9.

Ministry of Commerce and Industry (2010). Annual Supplement 2010-11 and the Foreign Trade Policy 2009-2014.

Mishra, Prachi (2013). "Has India's Growth Story Withered?", *Economic and Political Weekly* XLVIII(15), April 13.

Mohan, Rakesh (ed.) (2017). *India Transformed: 25 Years of Economic Reforms*. Penguin Random House India.

Mohan, Rakesh (2008). "Growth Record of Indian Economy 1958-2008", *Economic and Political Weekly*, Feb. 14, 2008.

———. (2002). *Facets of the Indian Economy*. New Delhi: Oxford University Press.

———. (1992). "Industrial Policy and Controls", in Bimal Jalan (ed.), *The Indian Economy: Problems and Prospects*. (Viking Penguin), India.

Mohanty, Deepak (2012). "Indian Economy: Progress and Prospects", in Uma Kapila (ed.) (2012), *Two Decades of Economic Reforms: Towards Faster, Sustainable and More Inclusive Growth.* New Delhi: Academic Foundation.

———. (ed.) (2012). *Regional Economy of India: Growth and Finance*. New Delhi: Academic Foundation.

Mujumdar, N.A. (2014). *Reinventing Development Economics: Explorations from the Indian Experiment*. New Delhi: Academic Foundation.

———. (2011). *India's New Development Agenda: Building a Value-based Society*. New Delhi: Academic Foundation.

———. (2007). *Inclusive Growth: Development Perspectives in Indian Economy*. New Delhi: Academic Foundation.

———. (2004). *Economic Reforms Sans Development.* New Delhi: Academic Foundation.

Mujumdar, N.A. and Uma Kapila (eds.) (2006). *Indian Agriculture in the New Millennium* (two volumes set). New Delhi: Academic Foundation.

Nachane, D.M. (ed.), India Development Report 2011. Indira Gandhi Institute of Development Research, Mumbai, Oxford, New Delhi.

Nagaraj, R. (2014). "Public Sector Performance Since 1950—A Fresh Look: An Update", in Uma Kapila (eds.) *Indian Economy since Independence* (25th edition). New Delhi: Academic Foundation.

———. (2013). "India's Dream Run, 2003-2008: Understanding the Boom and its Aftermath", *Economic and Political Weekly* XLVIII(20), May 18

———. (2005). *Aspects of India's Economic Growth and Reforms.* New Delhi: Academic Foundation.

———. (2008). "India's Recent Economic Growth: A Closer Look", *Economic and Political Weekly,* Vol. XLIII, No. 15, April 12-18.

National Commission for Enterprises in the Unorganised Sector, Govt. of India (2009). Chairman: Arjun K. Sengupta. *The Challenge of Employment in India: An Informal Economy Perspective*, Vol. I and Vol. II. New Delhi: Academic Foundation.

Nayak, Pulin (2016). "Revisiting India's Growth", *Economic and Political Weekly*, August 20.

Nayyar, Deepak (2006). "Economic Growth in Independent India", *Economic and Political Weekly*, April 15-21.

———. (1996). *Economic Liberalisation in India: Analytics Experience and Lessons.* Orient Longman.

Nurul Islam (2005). *Exploration in Development Issues.* New Delhi: Academic Foundation.

OECD Insights (2010). *Sustainable Development: Linking Economy, Society, Environment* (Tracey Strange & Anne Bayley). New Delhi: Academic Foundation.

OECD Economic Surveys: India 2017. New Delhi: Academic Foundation. November.

OECD Economic Surveys: India 2014. New Delhi: Academic Foundation. November.

———. Economic Surveys: India 2011. New Delhi: Academic Foundation. June.

———. Economic Surveys: India 2007. New Delhi: Academic Foundation.

Panagariya, Arvind (2010). "India on the Growth Turnpike: No State Left Behind", in Sameer Kochhar (ed.), *India on the Growth Turnpike (Essays in honour of Vijay L. Kelkar).* New Delhi: Academic Foundation.

———. (2008). *India: The Emerging Giant.* New Delhi: Oxford University Press.

Pauli, Gunter (2015). *The Blue Economy* (200 Projects Implemented; US$ 4 Billion Invested; 3 Million Jobs Created). New Delhi: Academic Foundation.

Premchand, A. (2016). *Public Expenditure Management and Public Policy in India.* New Delhi: Academic Foundation.

Radhakrishna, R. (2019). *Essays on Indian Economy (5 vols.).* New Delhi: Academic Foundation.

Radhakrishna, R. (ed.) (2008). *India Development Report 2008*, Indira Gandhi Institute of Development Research. New Delhi: Oxford University Press.

Radhakrishna, R., S.K. Rao, S. Mahendra Dev and K. Subbarao (eds.) (2006). *India in a Globalising World: Some Aspects of Macroeconomy, Agriculture and Poverty* (Essays in Honour of C.H. Hanumantha Rao). New Delhi: Academic Foundation,

Raghavan Srinivasa, T.C.A (ed.) (2012). *On the Turnpike: Indian Economy since 1947 & Indian Economic Service at 50*. Ministry of Finance, Govt. of India. New Delhi: Academic Foundation.

Rajaraman, Indira (2016). *Economically Speaking*. New Delhi: Academic Foundation.

Rangarajan, C. (2015). "Counting the Poor: Measurement and Other Issues", Ch. 16, in Uma Kapila (ed.), *Indian Economy Since Independence* (26th edition).

———. (2014). "Growth and Investment: The Interlinks", Ch. 35, in Uma Kapila (ed.), *Indian Economy Since Independence* (25th edition).

———. (2013). "The Indian Banking System: Some Issues" (ch. 4), in Uma Kapila (ed.) (2013), *Indian Financial Reforms: Priorities and Policy Thrust Post Global Financial Crisis*. New Delhi: Academic Foundation.

———. (2009). *India: Monetary Policy Financial Stability and Other Essays*. New Delhi: Academic Foundation.

———. (2003). *Select Essays on Indian Economy*. New Delhi: Academic Foundation.

———. (2003). "India's Balance of Payments: The Emerging Dimensions", in Uma Kapila (ed.), *Indian Economy Since Independence* (2003 edition). New Delhi: Academic Foundation.

Rao, C.H.H (2014). *Essays on Inclusive Growth and Some Reminiscences*. New Delhi: Academic Foundation.

———. (2005). *Agriculture, Food Security, Poverty, and Environment: Essays on Post-reform India*. New Delhi: Academic Foundation.

———. (2005). *Essays on Agricultural Growth, Farm Size and Rural Poverty Alleviation in India*. New Delhi: Academic Foundation.

———. (2005). *Essays on Development Strategy, Regional Disparities and Centre-State Financial Relations in India*. New Delhi: Academic Foundation.

———. (2003), *Reform Agenda for Agriculture*, EPW, Feb 15.

Rao, C.H.H, B.B. Bhattacharya and N.S. Sidharathan (ed.) (2005). *Indian Economy and Society in the Era of Globalisation and Liberalisation*. New Delhi: Academic Foundation.

Rao, M. Govinda (2017). *Financial Express*, September 5.

———. (2015). "Role and Functions of NITI Aayog", *Economic and Political Weekly* (4), January 24.

Rao, V.M. and P.D. Jeromi (2000). "Modernising Indian Agriculture, Priority Tasks and Critical Policy", Study No. 21, DRG, DEAP, Reserve Bank of India, reproduced in Uma Kapila (ed.), *Indian Economy Since Independence* (14th edition). New Delhi: Academic Foundation.

Reserve Bank of India (2004). *Report on Currency and Finance 2003-04* and various issues.

Sen, Amartya (2000). *Development as Freedom*. New Delhi: Oxford University Press.

Sengupta, Dipankar, Debashis Chakraborty and Pritam Banerjee (2006). *Beyond the Transition Phase of WTO: An Indian Perspective on Emerging Issues*. New Delhi: Academic Foundation in association with Centre de Sciences Humaines.

Sengupta, Jaishree (2007). *A Nation in Transition: Understanding the Indian Economy*. New Delhi: Academic Foundation.

Sharma, Mihir S. (2015). Restart: The Last Chance for the Indian Economy. Random House India.

Sheel, Alok (2015). *Looking Back at Macroeconomics 101: A Ringside View of the Global Financial Crisis from Asia in Real Time*. New Delhi: Academic Foundation.

Srinivasan, R. (2015). *Development Perspectives: Malcolm Adiseshiah Memorial Lectures*. New Delhi: Academic Foundation.

Srinivasan, T.N. (2009). *Trade, Growth and Poverty Reduction*. New Delhi: Academic Foundation.

———. (2000). *Eight Lectures on India's Economic Reforms*. Oxford University Press.

———. (2003). "Foreign Trade Policies and India's Development", reproduced in Uma Kapila (ed.), *Indian Economy Since Independence* (2003 edition). New Delhi: Academic Foundation.

Srinivasan, T.N. and S.D. Tendulkar (2003). *Reintegrating India with the World Economy*. New Delhi: Oxford University Press.

Singh, Surjit and V. Ratna Reddy (eds.) (2009). *Changing Contours of Asian Agriculture: Policies, Performance and Challenges* (Essays in Honour of Professor V.S. Vyas). New Delhi: Academic Foundation.

Tarapore, S.S. (2012). *Financial Policies and Everyday Life: The Indian Context*. New Delhi: Academic Foundation.

Tellis, Ashley J. (2014). "Completing Unfinished Business: From the Long View to the Short", in Bibek Debroy, Ashley J. Tellis and Reece Trevor (eds.) (2014), *Getting India Back on Track: An Action Agenda for Reform*. Random House India.

Tendulkar, S.D. (1981). *Indian Development Strategy: Compulsions and Constraints*, Working Paper No. 23, (1 June), Delhi School of Economics, reproduced in Uma Kapila (ed.), *Indian Economy Since Independence* (2001 edition). New Delhi: Academic Foundation.

Todaro, M., *(2008). Economic Development, 8th edition. Delhi: Pearson Education (Singapore) Pvt. Ltd.*

UNDP (2018). *Human Development: Indices and Indicators, 2018*. Statistical Update.

UNDP (2016). *Human Development Report 2016*. UNDP/Academic Foundation.

———. (2014). *Human Development Report 2013: The Rise of the South: Human Progress in a Diverse World*. UNDP/Academic Foundation.

———. (2011). *Human Development Report 2011*.

———. (2010). *Human Development Report 2010*.

———. (2008). *Human Development Report 2007-08*.

United Nations (2008). *Trade and Development Report*. New Delhi: Academic Foundation.

Vaidyanathan, A. (2013). *India's Evolving Economy Puzzles and Perspectives*. New Delhi: Academic Foundation.

———. (2003). *Economic Reforms and Development*. New Delhi: Academic Foundation.

Virmani, Arvind (2006). *Propelling India from Socialist Stagnation to Global Power*, (Two volume set). New Delhi: Academic Foundation.

———. (2004). *Accelerating Growth and Poverty Reduction: A Policy Framework for India's Development*. New Delhi: Academic Foundation.

Vasudevan, A. (2014). *Central Banking for Emerging Market Economies: A Relook in the Context of the Global Financial Crisis*. New Delhi: Academic Foundation.

Vyas, V.S. (2005). *Food Security in Asian Countries in the Context of Millennium Goals*. New Delhi: Academic Foundation.

World Bank (2018), *India Development Update*, March 2018.

———. (2015), *World Development Report*. New Delhi: Oxford University Press.

———. (2012), *World Development Report*. New Delhi: Oxford University Press.